Conversion Tables

Conversion Tables
Volume 2
Dewey-LC

Second Edition

Mona L. Scott

1999
LIBRARIES UNLIMITED, INC.
Englewood, Colorado

Libraries Unlimited, Inc.
P.O. Box 6633
Englewood, CO 80155-6633
1-800-237-6124
www.lu.com

ISBN 1-56308-596-8 (set)
ISBN 1-56308-850-9 (Vol. 1 LC-Dewey)
ISBN 1-56308-848-7 (Vol. 2 Dewey-LC)
ISBN 1-56308-849-5 (Vol. 3 Subject Headings—LC and Dewey)
ISBN 1-56308-597-6 (Disk version)

Contents

Introduction

Analyzing and compiling the first edition of *Conversion Tables: LC-Dewey; Dewey-LC* proved to be an enormous undertaking and the exigencies of publication precluded inclusion of Library of Congress subject headings. For the second edition, however, LC subject headings are included as a separate section comprising Volume 3. Volumes 1 and 2 now consist of the LC-Dewey conversion table and the Dewey-LC conversion table, respectively. It is hoped the division of the book into three separate volumes will facilitate concurrent use of different volumes which, in turn, will facilitate libraries' conversion projects and daily cataloging activities.

Materials referenced in the *Conversion Tables* are the 21st edition of the *Dewey Decimal Classification*; the most current edition of the various volumes of the Library of Congress classification schedules available to me at the NASA/Goddard Space Flight Center Library and the library of the School of Library and Information Science at Catholic University of America in Washington, D.C.; the 1996 edition of *Library of Congress Subject Headings*; and the 1994 edition of *Library of Congress Free-Floating Subdivisions*. Library of Congress subject authority files were consulted regularly to maintain the currency of country or nation names.

Conversion Tables was conceived as a cataloging tool that could be a standard reference in any cataloging department for daily copy cataloging activities, as well as massive projects of converting from one classification system to the other. For the former, the conversion tables most frequently will be used to convert individual MARC records from bibliographic utilities that include only one classification number. With the addition of the LC subject heading table, *Conversion Tables* also can be used as a call number assigning tool.

The LC and Dewey Decimal classification schemes approach the organization of knowledge from different perspectives. This can been seen in how LC and Dewey view language and the literatures of each language. LC classes them together in the Ps while Dewey separates them, placing language in the 400s and literature in the 800s. Similarly, LC places military and naval sciences in stand-alone classes, U for military science and V for naval science; Dewey places both in the so-called megaclass 300s, which includes virtually all of the social sciences.

As the two schemes differ so greatly in basic concepts, it was necessary to analyze the concepts of each order to select the corresponding numbers or alphanumeric notations to construct the tables. Ultimately, it involved assigning more than 52,000 class notations.

Structure of Tables

This cataloging tool is arranged in three sections each in its own volume: LC to Dewey, Volume 1; Dewey to LC, Volume 2; and Subject Headings with corresponding classifications, Volume 3. Thus, each section contains the same lists of classifications in the two systems and corresponding subject headings but in different arrangements.

Example:

LC to Dewey tables

LC	Dewey	Subject Heading
DS109.93	956.9404	Palestine—History—Partition, 1947

Dewey to LC tables

Dewey	LC	Subject Heading
956.9404	DS109.93	Palestine—History—Partition, 1947

Subject Heading tables

Subject Heading	LC	Dewey
Palestine—History—Partition, 1947	DS109.93	956.9404

The notation for a general concept, such as Philosophy which is 100 in Dewey and B in the Library of Congress Classification, will have divisions and subdivisions broken down into smaller concepts and thus more detailed notations (Philosophy—Congresses is 105 in Dewey and B20 in LC).

The differences discussed above also result in more than one notation corresponding to the other, or even a whole range of numbers and alphanumeric notations corresponding to the other. For example, 951.041 in the Dewey schedule under the history of China corresponds to seven LC notations in these tables, in the range DS773.83 to DS777.45.

Dates in the LC and Dewey schemes have been a problem. The two schemes often do not agree on the date that an event occurred. For example, the LC classification indicates that the Time of Troubles in Russian history was from 1598-1613, but the Dewey scheme uses the dates 1605-1613. However, in other places the dates match perfectly, as in the history of Tunisia. To aid in the conversion, I have often used a range of dates from Table 1 in the Dewey Classification to indicate a century, rather than the single date.

The following conventions have been used:

- Diacritics have not been included in the subject headings.
- Within the class numbers and subject headings, "/" indicates a choice and is usually contained within parentheses or brackets.
- As in conventional cataloging rules, brackets [ ] contain words added by the author.

Instructions for Use of the Tables

To convert a classification from LC to Dewey or Dewey to LC, find the section containing the table from which you wish to convert. Locate the classification from which you wish to convert in the left column. As indicated above, it may be included in a range of "numbers" or alphanumeric notations that correspond to the other classification, or it may fall between two classifications. In these cases, locate the class nearest in concept by using the Subject Headings. The classification to which you wish to convert is in the middle column, with the subject heading on the right.

The Subject Heading section provides a shortcut to the call number assigning process. Using that section, you can search for the subject heading that reflects or approximates the subject matter of the item that is being cataloged and note the appropriate classification next to it. This notation may be the classification that is needed, or will lead you to the appropriate one in the schedules.

Dewey-LC Conversion Table

Dewey	LC	Subject Heading	Dewey	LC	Subject Heading
001.2	AZ	Learning and scholarship	004.1	QA76.6-.66	Electronic digital computers—Programming
001.201	AZ101-111	Learning and scholarship—Philosophy	004.11	QA76.88	Supercomputers
001.2090	AZ200-361	Learning and scholarship—History	004.16	QA76.89	Pen-based computers
			004.22	QA76.9.A73	Computer architecture
001.20902	AZ321	Learning and scholarship—History—Medieval, 500-1500	004.33	QA76.54-.545	Real-time data processing
			004.35	QA76.5	Multiprocessors
			004.35	QA76.5	Parallel computers
001.2092	CT	Scholars	004.36	QA76.9.D5	Electronic data processing—Distributed processing
001.2094	AZ600-765	Learning and scholarship—Europe	004.6	TK5105.5-.9	Computer networks
001.2095	AZ770-795	Learning and scholarship—Asia	004.67	TK5105.87-.888	Wide area networks (Computer networks)
001.2096	AZ800-821	Learning and scholarship—Africa	004.678	TK5105.875.I57	Internet (Computer network)
001.2097	AZ501-516	Learning and scholarship—North America	004.68	TK5105.7-.85	Local area networks (Computer networks)
001.20973	AZ503-513	Learning and scholarship—United States	005	QA76.76.C64	Software compatibility
001.2098	AZ517-588	Learning and scholarship—Latin America	005	QA76.9.T48	Text processing (Computer science)
001.2099	AZ850-881	Learning and scholarship—Australia	005.1	QA76.6-.66	Programming (Electronic computers)
			005.1	QA76.758	Software engineering
001.40681	Q180.55.G7	Endowment of research	005.1	QA76.9.A43	Computer algorithms
001.4226	HA31	Statistics—Graphic methods	005.112	QA76.6	Modular programming
001.94	CB156	Civilization—Extraterrestrial influences	005.115	QA76.63	Logic programming
			005.117	QA76.64	Object-oriented programming (Computer science)
001.94	GN750-751	Lost continents	005.13	QA76.7-.73	Programming languages (Electronic computers)
001.942	TL789-.6	Unidentified flying objects			
001.944	QL89.2.S2	Sasquatch	005.13	QA76.3.D	DIST (Computer program language)
001.96	AZ999	Errors, Popular			
001.96	BF1001-1999	Superstition	005.13	QA76.5	EGPS (Computer program language)
001.96	AZ999	Superstition			
002.09	Z4-8	Books—History	005.16	QA76.76.S64	Software maintenance
003	QA402-.37	System analysis	005.3	QA76.76.A65	Application software
003.01	Q295	System theory	005.3	QA76.75-.9	Computer software
003.2	CB158-161	Forecasting	005.3	TK5105.9	Communications software
003.20904	CB160-161	Twentieth century—Forecasts	005.3	QA76.76.D63	Software documentation
			005.3	QA76.76.S46	Shareware (Computer software)
003.3	QA76.9.C65	Computer simulation			
003.5	Q300-390	Cybernetics	005.43	QA76.6.U84	Utilities (Computer programs)
003.5	Q317-321	Bionics	005.43	QA76.76.O63	Operating systems (Computers)
003.503	Q304	Cybernetics—Dictionaries			
003.5071	Q316	Cybernetics—Study and teaching	005.43	QA76.76.S95	Systems software
			005.437	QA76.9.U83	User interfaces (Computer systems)
003.509	Q305	Cybernetics—History			
003.54	Q350-390	Information theory	005.4476	QA76.76.O63	Distributed operating systems (Computers)
003.7	Q325-390	Self-organizing systems			
003.83	QA402	Discrete-time systems	005.45	QA76.6	Macro processors
004	QA75.5-.95	Computers	005.452	QA76.6	Interpreters (Computer programs)
004	QA76.9.D6	Electronic data processing documentation			
			005.453	QA76.76.C65	Compilers (Computer programs)
004.019	QA76.9.H85	Human-computer interaction			
004.03	QA76.15	Computers—Dictionaries	005.7	QA76.55-.57	Online data processing—Downloading
004.09	QA76.17	Computers—History			
004.1	QA76.85	Fifth generation computers	005.72	QA76.9.D337	Electronic data processing—Data entry

Dewey	LC	Subject Heading	Dewey	LC	Subject Heading
005.72	QA76.9.D345	Electronic data processing—Data preparation	015.5694	Z3476-3480	Bibliography, National—Israel
005.74	QA76.9.D3	Database management	015.59	Z3221-3415	Bibliography, National—Asia, Southeastern
005.74	QA76.9.D32	Databases	015.6	Z3501-3975	Bibliography, National—Africa
005.74	QA76.9.D26	Database design			
005.74	QA76.9.F53	File processing (Computer science)	015.71	Z1365-1401	Bibliography, National—Canada
005.74	QA76.9.D3	Database management	015.72	Z1411-1431	Bibliography, National—Mexico
005.741	QA76.9.F5	File organization (Computer science)	015.729	Z1501-1595	Bibliography, National—West Indies
005.746	QA76.9.D33	Data compression (Computer science)	015.73	Z1215-1363	Bibliography, National—United States
005.758	QA76.9.D3	Distributed databases	015.8	Z1601-1939	Bibliography, National—South America
005.8	QA76.9.D314	Database security			
005.8	QA76.76.P76	Software protection	015.94	Z4001-4439	Bibliography, National—Australia
005.8	QA76.9.A25	Computer security			
005.84	QA76.76.C68	Computer viruses	016	AI	Indexes
005.86	QA76.9.D348	Data recovery (Computer science)	016.07	AI21	Newspapers—Indexes
			016.78	ML111-158	Music—Bibliography
005.86	QA76.9.B32	Electronic data processing—Backup processing alternatives	017.4	Z998-1000.5	Catalogs, Booksellers'
			020	Z665-720	Library science
006.3	BC137-138	Logic machines	020.92	Z720	Librarians
006.3	Q334-342	Artificial intelligence	021.65	Z674.7-.83	Library information networks
006.31	Q325.6	Reinforcement learning (Machine learning)	023.2	Z682-.4	Librarians
			023.2	Z682.4.C65	Library consultants
006.31	Q325.5-.78	Machine learning	023.4	Z682.4.A45	Library administrators
006.32	QA76.87	Neural computers	025.1	Z678-.88	Library administration
006.32	QA76.87	Neural networks (Computer science)	025.11	Z683-.2	Library finance
006.33	QA76.9.D32	Deductive databases	025.173409(1-9)	CD101-392	Government publications—[By region or country]
006.33	QA76.76.E95	Expert systems (Computer science)	025.1734094	CD101-215	Government publications—Europe
006.332	Q387-.5	Knowledge representation (Information theory)	025.1734094	CD271-272	Government publications—Australia
006.35	QA76.9.N38	Natural language processing (Computer science)	025.1734095	CD221-254	Government publications—Asia
			025.1734096	CD255-269	Government publications—Africa
006.4	Q327	Pattern perception			
006.6	T385	Computer graphics	025.17340971	CD331-332	Government publications—Canada
006.7	QA76.575	Multimedia systems			
006.7	TK6687	Interactive video	025.17340972	CD333-334	Government publications—Mexico
006.7	QA76.76.I59	Interactive multimedia			
010	Z1001-9000	Bibliography	025.173409728	CD335-350	Government publications—Central America
011.7	AY2001	Directories			
015	Z1201-4980	Bibliography, National	025.173409729	CD351-362	Government publications—Caribbean Area
015.4	Z2000-2959	Bibliography, National—Europe	025.17340973	CD309-311	Government publications—United States
015.47	Z3401-3409	Bibliography, National—Asiatic Russia	025.1734098	CD365-392	Government publications—South America
015.4756	Z3461-3465	Bibliography, National—Armenia	025.1734099(5-6)	CD291	Government publications—Oceania
015.5	Z3126-3415	Bibliography, National—Asia			
015.55	Z3366-3370	Bibliography, National—Iran	025.2	Z689-.8	Acquistions (Libraries)
015.56	Z3013-3028	Bibliography, National—Middle East	025.21	Z689-.5	Book selection
			025.26	Z675.D4	Depository libraries
015.5691	Z3481-3485	Bibliography, National—Syria	025.2761	Z688.M4	Acquisition of medical literature
015.5692	Z3466-3470	Bibliography, National—Lebanon	025.277	Z688.A7	Acquisition of art catalogs

Dewey	LC	Subject Heading	Dewey	LC	Subject Heading
025.28305	Z692.S5	Acquisition of serial publications	027.0496	CD1930-1989.5	Archives—Balkan Peninsula
			027.05	CD2001-2291	Archives—Asia
025.284	Z692.D38	Acquisition of databases	027.051	CD2030-2059.5	Archives—China
025.286	Z692.M3	Acquisition of maps	027.052	CD2160-2189.5	Archives—Japan
025.31	Z695.83	Catalogs, Union	027.054	CD2080-2099.5	Archives—India
025.31	Z710	Library catalogs	027.05694	CD2010-2919.5	Archives—Israel
025.3132	Z678.9-.93	Libraries—Automation	027.06	CD2300-2491	Archives—Africa
025.3132	Z699-.5	Machine-readable bibliographic data	027.07(4-9)	CD3070-3609	Archives—[United States, By state]
025.3132	Z678.93.D85	Dynix (Computer system)	027.071	CD3620-3649.6	Archives—Canada
025.32	Z693-695.83	Descriptive cataloging	027.072	CD3650-3679.5	Archives—Mexico
025.52	Z674.2-.5	Information services	027.0728	CD3690-3859.5	Archives—Central America
025.56	Z711.2	Library orientation	027.0729	CD3860-3985	Archives—Caribbean area
025.56	Z704	Library rules and regulations	027.073	CD3020-3615	Archives—United States
025.58	Z711.3	Library use studies	027.08	CD4000-4279.5	Archives—South America
025.7	Z700.9-701.5	Books—Conservation and restoration	027.09(3/4)	CD2500-2529.5	Archives—[New Zealand/ Australia]
025.82	Z702	Book thefts	027.09(5-6)	CD2795	Archives—Oceania
025.84	Z701.3.D4	Books—Deacidification	027.091734	Z675.V7	Rural libraries
026	Z675.A2	Special libraries	027.1	CD977	Personal archives
026.1	Z987-997.2	Book collecting	027.2	Z675.P85	Proprietary libraries
026.3046	Z675.D28	Demographic libraries	027.3	Z675.R4	Rental libraries
026.6	T11.9	Archives, Technical	027.5	Z675.G7	Government libraries
026.61	R119.8	Archives, Medical	027.5	Z675.C8	Public libraries
026.6176	Z675.D3	Dental libraires	027.5	Z675.G7	Libraries, Governmental, administrative, etc.
026.62913	Z675.A5	Aeronautical libraries			
027	Z662-664	Libraries	027.662	Z675.H7	Hospital libraries
027	CD921-4280	Archives	027.665	Z675.P8	Prison libraries
027.001	CD947	Archives—Philosophy	027.67	Z675.C5	Church libraries
027.0021	Z683	Library statistics	027.69	Z675.B8	Business libraries
027.0021	Z711.3	Library statistics	027.7	LB3044.7-.74	Instructional materials centers
027.0025	CD941	Archives—Directories			
027.0028	CD973	Archives—Methodology	027.7	Z675.U5	Academic libraries
027.003	CD945	Archives—Dictionaries	027.8	Z675.S3	School libraries
027.005	CD921	Archives—Periodicals	028	Z1003-.5	Books and reading
027.0071	CD987-988	Archives—Study and teaching	028.7	Z711	Reference books
			028.7	AG103-190	Handbooks, vade-mecums, etc.
027.009	CD995-4280	Archives—History			
027.009	Z721-871	Libraries—History	028.7	AG195-196	Questions and answers
027.0(4-9)	CD1000-4280	Archives—[By region or country]	030	AY	Almanacs
			030	AG240-243	Curiosities and wonders
027.04	CD1000-2000	Archives—Europe	030.9	AY30-39	Almanacs—History
027.041	CD1040-1199.5	Archives—Great Britain	031	AY51-381	Almanacs—America
027.043	CD1220-1378.195	Archives—Germany	031.0971	AY410-425	Almanacs—Canada
			032.0994	AY1600-1636	Almanacs—Australia
027.0436	CD1120-1149.5	Archives—Austria	033.1	AY850-860	Almanacs—Germany
027.0437	CD1150-1169.5	Archives—Czechloslovakia	034.1	AY830-839	Almanacs—Great Britain
027.0438	CD1740-1759.5	Archives—Poland	035.1	AY890-899	Almanacs—Italy
027.0439	CD1170-1189.5	Archives—Hungary	036.1	AY1000-1009	Almanacs—Spain
027.044	CD1190-1219.5	Archives—France	036.9	AY1010-1019	Almanacs—Portugal
027.045	CD1400-1658	Archives—Italy	050	AI	Periodicals—Indexes
027.046	CD1850-1879.5	Archives—Spain	050	AP	Periodicals
027.0469	CD1880-1899.5	Archives—Portugal	050	AY	Yearbooks
027.047	CD1710-1739.5	Archives—Russia	050	PN4700-5650	Periodicals
027.0481	CD1810-1829.5	Archives—Norway	050.835	AP200-230	Youths' periodicals
027.0485	CD1830-1849.5	Archives—Sweden	051	PN4840-4899	American newspapers
027.0489	CD1770-1789.5	Archives—Denmark	051	PN4901-4920	Canadian periodicals
027.04912	CD1790-1809.5	Archives—Iceland	051	AP2-9	English periodicals
027.0492	CD1690-1733.3	Archives—Netherlands	052	PN5111-5130	English periodicals
027.0493	CD1670-1689.5	Archives—Belgium	053.1	PN5201-5220	German periodicals
027.0494	CD1900-1929.5	Archives—Switzerland	053.1	AP30-36.7	German periodicals

Dewey	LC	Subject Heading	Dewey	LC	Subject Heading
053.931	AP14-17	[Dutch/Flemish] periodicals	069.50946	AM362	Collectors and collecting—Spain
054.1	AP20-28.7	French periodicals			
054.1	PN5171-5790	French periodicals	069.509469	AM363	Collectors and collecting—Portugal
055.1	AP37-39	Italian periodicals			
055.1	PN5241-5250	Italian periodicals	069.50947	AM356	Collectors and collecting—Russia
056.1	PN5317.P4	Spanish periodicals			
056.9	PN5321-5330	Portuguese periodicals	069.5095	AM372-385	Collectors and collecting—Asia
058	PN5280.5-5310	Scandinavian periodicals			
058.81	PN5281-5290	Danish periodicals	069.5096	AM387-389	Collectors and collecting—Africa
059.89	AP85	Greek periodicals			
059.9171	PN5271-5280	Russian periodicals	069.50971	AM313	Collectors and collecting—Canada
059.924	AP91-93	Jewish periodicals			
060	AS	Learned institutions and societies	069.509728	AM314	Collectors and collecting—Mexico
060	AS	Academies and learned societies	069.509728	AM315-322	Collectors and collecting—Central America
060	AS6	Congresses and conventions	069.509729	AM323-329	Collectors and collecting—West Indies
060.9	AS5	Learned institutions and societies—History	069.50973	AM303-311	Collectors and collecting—United States
069	AM	Museums			
069.01	AM111-157	Museums—Methodology	069.5098	AM330-341	Collectors and collecting—South America
069.0681	AM122	Museum finance			
069.083	AM8	Chidren's museums	069.50993	AM393	Collectors and collecting—New Zealand
069.09	AM10-101	Museums—[By region or country]	069.50994	AM390-391	Collectors and collecting—Australia
069.094	AM40-70	Museums—Europe			
069.0941	AM41-43	Museums—Great Britain	069.5099(5-6)	AM395-396	Collectors and collecting—Oceania
069.0943	AM49-51	Museums—Germany			
069.0944	AM46-48	Museums—France	069.53	AM141-145	Museum conservation methods
069.0945	AM54-55	Museums—Italy			
069.0946	AM65	Museums—Spain	070.172	AN	Newspapers
069.0947	AM66	Museums—Portugal	070.172	PN4700-5650	Press
069.0947	AM60-61	Museums—Russia	070.175	PN4784.N5	Newsletters
069.0948	AM61.5-64	Museums—Scandinavia	070.4	PN4700-5650	Journalism
069.09495	AM52-53	Museums—Greece	070.4	PN4749	Journalism—Social aspects
069.09496	AM69	Museums—Balkan Peninsula	070.4071	PN4785-4823	Journalism—Study and teaching
069.095	AM71-79	Museums—Asia			
069.0951	AM72	Museums—China	070.4074	PN4720	Journalism—Exhibitions
069.0952	AM77-78	Museums—Japan	070.41	PN4778	Journalism—Editing
069.096	AM80-91	Museums—Africa	070.43	PN4781	Reporters and reporting
069.0971	AM21-22	Museums—Canada	070.4333092	PN4823	War correspondents
069.0972	AM23-24	Museums—Mexico	070.435	PN4784.E53	Electronic news gathering
069.09728	AM25-27	Museums—Central America	070.444	PN6700-6790	Comic books, strips, etc.
069.0973	AM11-13	Museums—United States	070.44932	PN4751	Journalism—Political aspects
069.098	AM33-35	Museums—South America			
069.0993	AM96-98	Museums—New Zealand	070.449796	PN4784.S6	Sports journalism
069.0994	AM93-95	Museums—Australia	070.484	PN4882.5	Afro-American press
069.099(5-6)	AM99-100	Museums—Oceania	070.484	PN4882.5	Afro-American newspapers
069.5	AM200-401	Collectors and collecting	070.49	TR820	Photojournalism
069.509	AM221	Collectors and collecting—History	070.49796	TR821	Photography of sports
			070.5	Z1008	Book clubs
069.509(4-9)	AM301-396	Collectors and collecting—[By region or country]	070.5	Z278-550	Publishers and publishing
			070.5	Z549	Book clubs
069.5094	AM342-371	Collectors and collecting—Europe	070.509(4-9)	Z289-550	Publishers and publishing—[By region or country]
069.50941	AM343-347	Collectors and collecting—Great Britain	070.52	PN163	Literary agents
			070.520973	KF3084	Authors and publishers—United States
069.50943	AM350	Collectors and collecting—Germany	070.592	Z231.5.L5	Small presses
			070.594	Z286.S37	Scholarly publishing
069.50944	AM349	Collectors and collecting—France	071	PN4840-4900	American periodicals

Dewey	LC	Subject Heading	Dewey	LC	Subject Heading
072.(1-8)	PN5111-5129	English newspapers	111.850901	BH91-116	Aesthetics, Ancient
073-078	PN5110-5355	European periodicals	111.850902	BH131-137	Aesthetics, Medieval
078.489	PN5281-5289	Danish newspapers	111.850903	BH151-208	Aesthetics, Modern
079.5	PN5360-5449	Asian periodicals	111.8509031	BH161-168	Aesthetics, Modern—16th century
079.6	PN5450-5499	African periodicals	111.8509032	BH171-178	Aesthetics, Modern—17th century
079.72	PN4930.5-4959	Journalism—West Indies			
079.8	PN5000-5106	South American periodicals	111.8509033	BH181-188	Aesthetics, Modern—18th century
079.94	PN5510-5590	Australian periodicals			
080	LC6501-6560.4	Lectures and lecturing	111.8509034	BH191-198	Aesthetics, Modern—19th century
081	AC1-8	American essays			
083	AC16-19	Dutch essays	111.850904	BH201-208	Aesthetics, Modern—20th century
083.1	AC30-35	German essays			
083.91	AC103-104	Yiddish essays	111.8509495	BH221.B	Aesthetics, Byzantine
084.1	AC20-25	French essays	111.85095	BH101-102	Aesthetics, Oriental
085.1	AC40-45	Italian essays	111.850971	BH221.C	Aesthetics, Canadian
086.(1/9)	AC70-75	[Spanish/Portuguese] essays	113	BD645	Harmony of the spheres
089.91992	AC132-133	Armenian essays	113	BD581	Philosophy of nature
089.924	AC101-102	Hebrew essays	113	BD493-708	Cosmology
089.927	AC105-106	Arabic essays	113.09	BD494-497	Cosmology—History
089.945	AC80-85	Finno-Ugric essays	113.0901	BD495	Cosmology, Ancient
089.951	AC149-150	Chinese essays	113.0902	BD495.5	Cosmology, Medieval
089.956	AC145-146	Japanese essays	113.8	BD430-435	Life
089.96	AC177-189	African essays	114-115	BD620-655	Space and time
089.97	AC195	Indian essays	115	BD638	Time
089.99221	AC168-169	Indonesian essays	116	BD373	Change
09	PR9632.2-.6	New Zealand prose literature	117	BD331	Matter
091.09495	PA3301-3371	Manuscripts, Greek (Papyri)	117	B105.O7	Order (Philosophy)
092	Z240-241.5	Block books	117	BD493-708	Matter
096.2	Z1030	Vellum printed books	119	B105.Q34	Quantity (Philosophy)
098.3	PN171.F6-.F7	Literary forgeries and mystifications	121	BC171	Truth
100	B	Philosophy	121	B820.3	Epistemics
103	B49-50	Philosophy—Terminology	121	BD143-237	Knowledge, Theory of
103	B40-48	Philosophy—Dictionaries	121	BC181	Judgment (Logic)
105	B1-8	Philosophy—Periodicals	121.2	BD201	Skepticism
106	B11-18	Philosophy—Societies, etc.	121.35	BD214	Senses and sensation
106	B20	Philosophy—Congresses	121.4	B105.I54	Innate ideas (Philosophy)
107.1	B52-.65	Philosophy—Study and teaching	121.4	BD222	Subjectivity
			121.4	BD220	Objectivity
109	B69-4695	Philosophy—History	121.5	BD215	Belief and doubt
109.22	B104	Philosophers	121.6	BD215	Belief and doubt
110	BD95-131	Metaphysics	121.6	BD183	Inquiry (Theory of knowledge)
110	BD331	Spiritualism (Philosophy)	121.63	BD171	Certainty
111	BD300-450	Ontology	121.63	BC141	Probabilities
111	B836	Relationism	121.65	BC171-173	Evidence
111	BD331	Reality	121.68	B820	General semantics
111.1	BD331	Substance (Philosophy)	121.68	B105.M4	Meaning (Philosophy)
111.5	BD398	Nothing (Philosophy)	121.68	BD240-241	Hermeneutics
111.6	BD411	Finite, The	121.8	BD232	Values
111.6	BD411	Infinite	121.8	BD430-435	Values
111.6	BD416	Absolute, The	122	BD530-595	Causation
111.8	BD352	Attribute (Philosophy)	123	B105.D47	Determinism (Philosophy)
111.82	BD236	Identity	123.3	BC141	Chance
111.82	BD396	Whole and parts (Philosophy)	123.3	BD595	Chance
111.85	BH	Aesthetics	123.7	BD417	Necessity (Philosophy)
111.8503	BH56	Aesthetics—Dictionaries	124	BD530-595	Teleology
111.8505	BH1-8	Aesthetics—Periodicals	126	BD331	Personality
111.8506	BH19	Aesthetics—Congresses	127	BF1001-1389	Subconsciousness
111.85071	BH61-62	Aesthetics—Study and teaching	128	BD450	Philosophical anthropology
			128	B105.I56	Intentionality (Philosophy)
111.8509	BH81-208	Aesthetics—History	128	B105.B64	Body, Human (Philosophy)

5

Dewey	LC	Subject Heading	Dewey	LC	Subject Heading
128.1	BD419-428	Soul	133.5263	BF1727.2	Taurus (Astrology)
128.2	BD418-.5	Philosophy of mind	133.5264	BF1727.25	Gemini (Astrology)
128.3	BD181.7	Memory (Philosophy)	133.5265	BF1727.3	Cancer (Astrology)
128.37	B105.E3	Emotions (Philosophy)	133.5266	BF1727.35	Leo (Astrology)
128.37	B815	Emotions	133.5267	BF1727.4	Virgo (Astrology)
128.46	BD436	Love	133.5272	BF1727.45	Libra (Astrology)
133	BF1001-1389	Parapsychology	133.5273	BF1727.5	Scorpio (Astrology)
133	BF1001-1999	Supernatural	133.5274	BF1727.6	Sagittarius (Astrology)
133	BF1404-2050	Occultism	133.5275	BF1727.65	Capricorn (Astrology)
133.025	BF1409	Occultism—Directories	133.5276	BF1727.7	Aquarius (Astrology)
133.03	BF1025	Parapsychology—Dictionaries	133.5277	BF1727.75	Pisces (Astrology)
133.03	BF1407	Occultism—Dictionaries	133.5832	BF1729.P6	Astrology and politics
133.05	BF1001-1008	Parapsychology—Periodicals	133.585	BF1729.S34	Science and astrology
133.06	BF1404	Occultism—Congresses	133.5861	BF1718	Medical astrology
133.06	BF1021	Parapsychology—Congresses	133.593927	BF1714.A6	Astrology, Arab
			133.59443	BF1714.B7	Buddhist astrology
133.071	BF1040.5	Parapsychology—Study and teaching	133.59444	BF1714.J28	Jaina astrology
			133.59445	BF1714.H5	Hindu astrology
133.09	BF1028-.5	Parapsychology—History	133.6	BF910-940	Palmistry
133.09	BF1421-1429	Occultism—History	133.6	BF908-940	Hand
133.09(4-9)	BF1434	Occultism—[By region or country]	133.82	BF1161-1171	Telepathy
			133.88	BF1371-1389	Psychokinesis
133.092	BF1408-.2	Occultists	133.89	BF1111-1156	Hypnotism
133.092	BF1026-1027	Parapsychology—Biography	133.892	BF1389.A8	Aura
133.1	BF1444-1486	Apparitions	133.9	B841	Spiritualism (Philosophy)
133.1	BF1444-1486	Ghosts	133.9	BF1389.T7	Transfiguration (Spiritualism)
133.122	BF1475	Haunted houses	133.9	BF1275.G85	Guides (Spiritualism)
133.142	BF1483	Poltergeists	133.9	BF1228-1389	Spiritualism
133.3	BF1745-1779	Divination	133.9013	BF1045.N4	Near-death experiences
133.3	BF1845-1891	Fortune-telling	133.9013	BF1063.D4	Deathbed hallucinations
133.3	BF1045.D42	Decision-making—Psychic aspects	133.91	BF1281-1315	Channeling (Spiritualism)
			133.92	BF1378	Materialization
133.323	BF1628	Dowsers	133.92	BF1375	Table-moving (Spiritualism)
133.323	BF1628	Dowsing	133.92	BF1385	Levitation
133.32424	BF1879.T2	Tarot	133.95	BF1389.A7	Astral projection
133.3248	BF1745-1779	Sibyls	135.3	BF1074-1099	Dreams
133.3248	BF1745-1779	Oracles	135.47	BF1585-1623	Cabala
133.32480938	DF125	Oracles, Greek	137	BF889-905	Graphology
133.32480938	DF261.D35	Delphian oracle	138	BF839.8-861	Physiognomy
133.33	BF1623.S9	Symbolism	139	BF866-885	Phrenology
133.3337	BF1779.F4	Feng-shui	141	B823	Idealism
133.334	BF1777	Omens	141.3	B905	Transcendentalism (New England)
133.335	BF1623.P9	Numerology			
133.3359	BF1623.P9	Symbolism of numbers	141.3	B823	Transcendentalism
133.42	BF1501-1562	Demonology	141.4	B824	Individualism
133.422	BF1546-1561	Devil	141.5	B828.5	Personalism
133.422	BF1546-1550	Satanism	142.7	B829.5	Phenomenology
133.423	BF1556	Vampires	142.7	BD352	Phenomenalism
133.425	GN475.6	Evil eye	142.78	B819	Existentialism
133.425	BF1553	Evil eye	142.78	B818.5	Existential phenomenology
133.426	BF1555	Demoniac possession	144	B821	Humanism
133.427	BF1559	Exorcism	144	B778	Humanism
133.43	BF1562.5-1584	Witchcraft	144.3	B831.5	Pragmatics
133.43	BF1585-1623	Magic	144.3	B832	Pragmatism
133.43	GN475.3	Magic	144.6	B843	Utilitarianism
133.44	BF1558	Incantations	145	B823.3	Ideology
133.44	BF1561	Talismans	146	B828.2	Naturalism
133.5	BF1651-1729	Astrology	146.32	B809.8	Dialectical materialism
133.52	BF1716-.28	Houses (Astrology)	146.4	B831	Positivism
133.52	BF1716.28	Eighth house (Astrology)	146.42	B824.6	Logical positivism
133.5262	BF1727	Aries (Astrology)	146.44	B816	Empiricism

Dewey	LC	Subject Heading	Dewey	LC	Subject Heading
146.5	BD646	Atomism	152.33	BF378.I6	Habit
146.7	B818	Evolution	152.33	BF335-337	Inhibition
147.4	B812	Dualism	152.33	BF337.B74	Habit breaking
147.4	BD394	Pluralism	152.334	BF295-.5	Perceptual-motor learning
148	B814	Eclecticism	152.335	LB1123	Left- and right-handedness
149.2	B835	Realism	152.4	BF511-593	Emotions
149.3	B828	Mysticism	152.4	BF575.A45	Ambivalence
149.5	B829	Optimism	152.4	BF575.H3	Hate
149.6	B829	Pessimism	152.4	BF575.G8	Guilt
149.7	B833	Rationalism	152.4	BF575.D57	Disappointment
149.73	B837	Skepticism	152.4	BF327	Attitude (Psychology)
149.73	B779	Skepticism	152.4	BF575.E53	Embarrassment
149.8	HX914-917	Nihilism	152.41	BF575.L8	Love
149.91	BD125	Scholasticism	152.41	BF575.E55	Empathy
149.91	B839	Scholasticism	152.42	BF515	Pleasure
149.91	B839	Neo-Scholasticism	152.42	BF575.H27	Happiness
149.94	B828.36	Ordinary-language philosophy	152.46	BF575.A6	Anxiety
149.96	B841.4	Structuralism	152.46	BF575.F2	Fear
150	BF150-172	Mind and body	152.46	BF575.W8	Worry
150	BF	Psychology	152.47	BF575.H6	Hostility (Psychology)
150.1	BF38.5-39.8	Psychology—Methodology	152.47	BF575.A5	Temper
150.14	BF32	Psychology—Terminology	152.47	BF575.A5	Anger
150.192	BF204.5	Existential psychology	152.47	BF575.F7	Frustration
150.192	BF204.5	Phenomenological psychology	152.47	RC569.5.A53	Anger
			152.48	BF575.J4	Jealousy
150.1943	BF199	Behaviorism (Psychology)	153	BF444	Human information processing
150.195	BF173-175.5	Psychoanalysis			
150.195	BF175.4.C68	Psychoanalytic counseling	153	BF311	Cognitive styles
150.195	BF175.5.C37	Castration complex	153	BF309-499	Consciousness
150.1953	BF175.5.A33	Adlerian psychology	153	BF337.C62	Cognitive balance
150.198	BF204	Humanistic psychology	153	BF309-499	Cognition
150.198	BF204.7	Transpersonal psychology	153	BF201	Cognitive psychology
150.1982	BF203	Gestalt psychology	153.12	BF376	Memory disorders
150.287	BF176-.5	Psychological tests	153.12	BF370-387	Memory
150.3	BF31	Psychology—Dictionaries	153.12	BF378.S54	Short-term memory
150.5	BF1-8	Psychology—Periodicals	153.123	BF365-395	Reproduction (Psychology)
150.6	BF20	Psychology—Congresses	153.123	BF378.R44	Reminiscing
150.71	BF77-80.7	Psychology—Study and teaching	153.124	BF378.R4	Recognition (Psychology)
			153.14	BF380-387	Mnemonics
150.72	BF76.5-.6	Psychology—Research	153.15	BF318-319.5	Learning, Psychology of
150.724	BF76.6.E94	Experiential research	153.15	LB1060	Learning
150.8996073	BF109	Afro-American psychologists	153.15	LB1060-1091	Learning, Psychology of
150.9	BF81-105	Psychology—History	153.152	LB1067.5	Visual learning
150.92	BF109	Psychologists	153.1523	BF357	Imitation
152.1	BF231-299	Senses and sensation	153.1526	BF319.5.O6	Operant conditioning
152.14	BF241	Visual perception	153.1526	BF319.5.P34	Paired-association learning
152.1423	BF311	Pattern perception	153.1532	LB1065	Attention
152.1423	QP360	Pattern perception	153.1533	BF321.I5	Interest (Psychology)
152.15	BF251-.5	Hearing	153.1533	BF575.E6	Enthusiasm
152.15	BF353.5.N65	Noise—Psychological aspects	153.1533	LB1065	Interest (Psychology)
			153.154	LB1059	Transfer of training
152.15	BF205.N6	Noise	153.2	BF365-395	Association of ideas
152.166	BF271	Smell	153.3	BF410	Inspiration
152.166	BF271	Odors	153.3	BF408	Creative ability
152.167	BF261	Taste	153.3	BF408-426	Creative thinking
152.182	BF275	Touch	153.32	BF367	Eidetic imagery
152.182	BF285	Muscular sense	153.32	BF408-426	Imagination
152.1882	BF299.07	Orientation (Psychology)	153.32	BF367	Imagery (Psychology)
152.1886	BF482	Fatigue	153.35	BF408-426	Creation (Literary, artistic, etc.)
152.1886	LB1075	Mental fatigue			
152.3	BF295-.5	Movement, Psychology of			

Dewey	LC	Subject Heading	Dewey	LC	Subject Heading
153.35	BH301.C84	Creation (Literary, artistic, etc.)	154.63	BF1099.F34	Family in dreams
			154.63	BF1099.N53	Nightmares
153.42	BF441-449.5	Thought and thinking	154.63	RC499.D7	Dreams
153.42	LB1590.3-.5	Thought and thinking	154.64	BF1073.S58	Sleeptalking
153.43	BF442	Reasoning (Psychology)	154.7	BF1111-1156	Mesmerism
153.44	BF315.5	Intuition (Psychology)	154.7	BF1156.S8	Mental suggestion
153.45	BF778	Values	154.7	RC490-499	Hypnotism
153.6	BF455-463	Speech	154.72	QH504	Biomagnetism
153.6	LB1139.L3	Speech	155	BF712-724.85	Developmental psychology
153.68	B105.L54	Listening (Philosophy)	155	BF697.5.S44	Self-presentation
153.68	BF323.L5	Listening	155	BF720.P56	Symbolic play
153.69	BF637.N66	Nonverbal communication (Psychology)	155.2	BF697-.5	Self
			155.2	BF697-.5	Self psychology
153.73	BF321-323	Apperception	155.2	BF698.35.I55	Inner child
153.73	LB1067	Apperception	155.2	BF697-.5	Individuality
153.733	BF321-323	Attention	155.2	RC473.D43	Defense Mechanisms Inventory
153.733	BF323.L5	Listening			
153.736	BF323.S8	Subliminal perception	155.2	BF818-839	Character
153.736	RC499.S92	Subliminal perception	155.2076	BF818-839	Character tests
153.752	BF469	Space perception	155.232	BF698.35.D64	Dogmatism
153.752	BF469	Spatial behavior	155.232	BF698.35.P43	Pedantry
153.752	BF467-475	Space and time	155.232	BF575.A3	Aggressiveness (Psychology)
153.753	BF468	Time perception	155.232	BF575.S39	Self-confidence
153.753	BF475	Rhythm	155.232	BF698.35.P49	Pessimism
153.8	BF608-635	Will	155.232	BF698.35.P36	Passivity (Psychology)
153.8	BF501-505	Achievement motivation	155.232	BF698.35.O57	Optimism
153.8	BF199	Motivation (Psychology)	155.232	BF698.35.N44	Negativism
153.8	BF632	Self-control	155.232	BF575.B3	Bashfulness
153.8	LB1071	Will	155.232	BF575.D34	Dependency (Psychology)
153.83	BF448	Decision-making	155.232	BF698.35.A87	Authoritarianism (Personality trait)
153.85	BF210	Electronic behavior control			
153.85	BF637.B4	Behavior modification	155.232	BF698.35.P47	Perfectionism (Personality trait)
153.85	BF319.5.R4	Reinforcement (Psychology)			
153.85	BF505.R48	Reward (Psychology)	155.232	BF698.35.C45	Charisma (Personality trait)
153.853	BF633	Brainwashing	155.232	RC569.5.D47	Dependency (Psychology)
153.9	BF431-433	Intellect	155.234	BF698.35.D48	Determination (Personality trait)
153.9	LB1134	Learning ability			
153.93	BF431-433	Ability—Testing	155.24	BF335-337	Adjustment (Psychology)
153.93	BF431-432.5	Intelligence tests	155.24	RC455.4.S87	Adjustment disorders
153.9324	BF432.5.N64	Non-Verbal Ability Tests	155.25	BF723.M54	Moral development
153.9324	BF432.5.N65	Nonverbal intelligence tests	155.26	BF795-811	Temperament
153.94	BF432.5.D53	Differential Aptitude Tests	155.28	BF698.4-.8	Personality assessment
153.94	BF432.5.M85	Multidimensional Aptitude Battery	155.282	RC473.G7	Graphology
			155.283	BF698.8.D9	Dynamic personality inventory
153.98	BF412-426	Genius			
154.2	BF315	Subconsciousness	155.283	BF698.8.P48	Personality questionnaires
154.22	BF175.5.S93	Superego	155.283	BF698.8.M5	Minnesota Multiphasic Personality Inventory
154.22	RC473.E36	Ego Function Assessment			
154.24	BF175.5.S92	Sublimation	155.284	BF698.7	Projective techniques
154.24	RC569.5.C68	Complexes (Psychology)	155.2842	BF698.8.R5	Rorschach Test
154.24	RC489.T73	Transference (Psychology)	155.3	BF723.S4	Psychosexual development
154.3	P96.F36	Fantasy in mass media	155.3	BF723.S42	Sex role in children
154.4	BF491-493	Hallucinations and illusions	155.3	BF692-.5	Sex (Psychology)
154.4	BF209.L9	LSD (Drug)	155.3	BF692.15	Sexual animosity
154.4	BF209.M4	Mescaline	155.332	BF692.5	Masculinity (Psychology)
154.4	BF1045.A48	Altered states of consciousness	155.4	BF721-723	Child psychology
			155.4	LB1101-1139	Child development
154.4	BF1045.D76	Drugs—Psychic aspects	155.412	BF720.E45	Emotions in children
154.6	BF1073.S56	Sleep positions	155.412	BF723.E6	Emotions in children
154.6	BF1068-1073	Sleep	155.412	BF723.F4	Fear in children
154.63	BF1099.L82	Lucid dreams	155.41246	BF723.A5	Anxiety in children

Dewey	LC	Subject Heading	Dewey	LC	Subject Heading
155.41247	BF723.F7	Frustration in children	158.1	BF698-.9	Personality
155.41247	BF723.A4	Temper tantrums in children	158.1	BF637.S4	Self-actualization (Psychology)
155.413	BF723.C5	Cognition in children	158.1	BF697.5.S46	Self-esteem
155.4133	BF723.C7	Creative ability in children	158.125	BF637.T68	Transcendental Meditation
155.4133	BF723.D7	Drawing ability in children	158.2	BF637.C45	Interpersonal communication
155.41332	BF723.F28	Fantasy in children			
155.4138	BF723.S25	Self-control in children	158.2	RC489.A77	Assertiveness training
155.4139	BF723.A25	Ability in children	158.25	BF575.F66	Friendship
155.418	BF723.S75	Stress in children	158.3	BF637.C6	Counseling
155.4182	BF723.S24	Self in children	158.3	BF637.C56	Psychological consultation
155.41825	BF723.P4	Personality development	158.3	RC466-.3	Mental health counseling
155.422	BF719-720	Infant psychology	158.35	BF637.C6	Group counseling
155.42221	BF720.S45	Sensory stimulation in newborn infants	158.39	BF761-768	Interviewing
			158.4	BF637.L4	Leadership
155.42221532	BF720.A85	Attention in newborn infants	158.5	BF637.N4	Negotiation
155.42224	BF720.E45	Emotions in infants	158.7	BF481	Work
155.42239	BF720.A24	Ability in infants	158.7	BF481	Work—Psychological aspects
155.443	BF723.S43	Sibling rivalry			
155.444	BF723.T9	Twins—Psychology	158.7	HF5548.7-.85	Psychology, Industrial
155.455	BF723.G5	Gifted children	158.7	RC967.5	Industrial psychiatry
155.4567	GN372	Feral children	158.72	HF5548.85	Job stress
155.4567	RJ507.F47	Feral children	158.723	BF481	Burn out (Psychology)
155.5	BF724-.3	Adolescent psychology	160	BC34-35	Logic, Medieval
155.5	BF724-.3	Youthfulness	160	BC177	Reasoning
155.5	LB1135	Adolescence	160	BC181	Proposition (Logic)
155.51	BF710	Maturation (Psychology)	160	BC	Logic
155.512	BF724.3.E5	Emotions in adolescence	160	BC38-39	Logic, Modern
155.51247	BF724.3.A34	Agressiveness (Psychology) in youth	160	BC25-32	Logic, Ancient
			160.1	BC50-57	Logic—Methodology
155.51247	BF724.3.A34	Agressiveness (Psychology) in adolescence	160.5	BC1	Logic—Periodicals
			160.6	BC5	Logic—Congresses
155.533	HQ1229	Young women—Psychology	160.71	BC59	Logic—Study and teaching
155.633	HQ1206-1216	Women—Psychology	160.9	BC11-39	Logic—History
155.66	BF724.6-.65	Middle age—Psychological aspects	161	BC80-99	Induction (Logic)
			165	BC199.C6	Contradiction
155.67	BF724.8-.85	Aged—Psychology	165	BC175	Fallacies (Logic)
155.7	BF699-711	Genetic psychology	165	BC199.P2	Paradox
155.82	GN502-517	Ethnopsychology	165	BC199.F5	Fictions, Theory of
155.82	GN270-279	Ethnopsychology	167	BC183	Hypothesis
155.8496073	E185.625	Afro-Americans—Psychology	169	BD190	Analogy
155.8497	E98.P95	Indians of North America—Psychology	170	BJ1480-1486	Happiness
			170	BJ1471	Conscience
155.9	BF353-.5	Man—Influence of environment	170	BJ1410-1418	Right and wrong
			170	BJ1400-1408.5	Good and evil
155.9	BF353-.5	Environmental psychology	170	BJ991-1185	Ethics—Textbooks
155.9042	BF575.S75	Stress (Psychology)	170	BJ	Ethics
155.915	BF353.5.W4	Weather—Psychological aspects	170.1	BJ37-60	Ethics—Philosophy
			170.202	BJ1075-1077	Ethics—Outlines, syllabi, etc.
155.92	BF575.L7	Loneliness	170.3	BJ63	Ethics—Dictionaries
155.93	BF575.D35	Loss (Psychology)	170.44	BJ1545-1697	Conduct of life
155.93	RC455.4.L67	Loss (Psychology)	170.5	BJ1-8	Ethics—Periodicals
155.93083	BF723.L68	Loss (Psychology) in children	170.6	BJ10-11	Ethics—Societies, etc.
155.935	BF789.D5	Disasters—Psychological aspects	170.71	BJ66-68	Ethics—Study and teaching
			170.9	BJ71-982	Ethics—History
155.937	BF175.5.D4	Death instinct	170.901	BJ101-214	Ethics—History
155.937	BF789.D4	Death—Psychological aspects	170.902	BJ231-255	Ethics, Medieval
			170.90(23-31)	BJ271-285	Ethics, Renaissance
155.962	HV6089	Prison psychology	170.903	BJ301-982	Ethics, Modern
156	BF660-685	Psychology, Comparative	170.9033	BJ311	Ethics, Modern—18th century
158	BF636-637	Psychology, Applied			
158	BF637.S8	Success			

Dewey	LC	Subject Heading	Dewey	LC	Subject Heading
170.9034	BJ315	Ethics, Modern—19th century	177.3	BJ1420-1428.3	Truthfulness and falsehood
			177.3	BJ1500.P7	Promises
170.904	BJ319	Ethics, Modern—20th century	177.3	BJ1535.S6	Slander
			177.62	BJ1533.F8	Friendship
170.935	BJ136-138	Ethics, Assyro-Babylonian	177.7	BJ1476	Forgiveness
170.938	BJ160-224	Ethics, Greek	177.7	BJ1533.K5	Kindness
170.943	BJ751-759	Ethics, Germanic	178	BJ1535.A8	Avarice
170.9438	BJ847-850	Ethics, Polish	179	BJ1535.C7	Cruelty
170.944	BJ701-704	Ethics, French	179.3	HV4701-4890.7	Animal rights
170.9495	BJ801-804	Ethics, Greek	179.5	BJ1535.S9	Swearing
170.95	BJ961-977	Ethics, Oriental	179.6	BJ1533.C8	Courage
170.95	BJ116-118	Ethics, Chinese	179.7	R726	Assisted suicide
170.951	BJ965-968	Ethics, Chinese	179.7	R726	Euthanasia
170.9519	BJ973-976	Ethics, Korean	179.8	BJ1534-1535	Vices
170.952	BJ969-971	Ethics, Japanese	179.8	BJ1534-1535	Vice
170.954	BJ121-123	Ethics, Indic	179.8	BJ1535.A6	Anger
171	BJ10.E8	Ethical culture movement	179.8	BJ1535.P9	Pride and vanity
171.2	BJ1360	Humanistic ethics	179.9	BJ1533.S27	Self-reliance
171.2	BJ1475.3	Humanitarianism	179.9	BJ1533.P3	Patience
171.2	BJ1365-1385	Ethics, Positivist	179.9	BJ1533.P9	Prudence
171.2	BJ1340	Existential ethics	179.9	BJ1533.D49	Self-control
171.4	BJ1491	Hedonism	179.9	BJ1477-1486	Cheerfulness
171.7	BJ1298-1335	Ethics, Evolutionary	179.9	BJ1533.M73	Modesty
171.7	BJ1390-.5	Communist ethics	179.9	BJ1533.C5	Cheerfulness
171.7	BJ1388	Socialist ethics	179.9	BJ1518-1691	Virtue
171.8	BJ1474	Altruism	179.9	BJ1533.G8	Gratitude
171.9	BJ1474	Self-interest	179.9	BJ1533.H7	Honesty
171.9	BJ1474	Egoism	180	B108-708	Philosophy, Ancient
174	BJ1498	Work	181	B121-162.7	Philosophy, Oriental
174	BJ1725	Professional ethics	181	B5000-5295	Philosophy, Oriental
174.2	RK52.7	Dental ethics	181.043	B162	Philosophy, Buddhist
174.2	SF756.39	Veterinarians—Professional ethics	181.044	B162.5	Jaina philosophy
			181.06	B154-157	Philosophy, Jewish
174.2	RC455.2.E8	Psychiatric ethics	181.06	B157.C65	Jewish cosmology
174.2	RC455.2.E8	Psychotherapists—Professional ethics	181.07	B740-753	Philosophy, Islamic
			181.09561	B162.6	Philosophy, Shinto
174.2	R724-726	Medical ethics	181.11	B125-128	Philosophy, Chinese
174.2	RT85	Nursing ethics	181.11	B5230-5234	Philosophy, Chinese
174.2	RS100.5	Pharmaceutical ethics	181.112	B127.C65	Philosophy, Confucian
174.4	HF5387	Business ethics	181.112	B127.N4	Neo-Confucianism
174.915	BF76.4	Psychologists—Professional ethics	181.114	B163	Philosophy, Taoist
			181.119	B139.1-.4	Philosophy, Korean
174.9375	LB3609	Student ethics	181.12	B5243-5244	Philosophy, Japanese
174.957	QH332	Bioethics	181.12	B135-138	Philosophy, Japanese
174.962	TA157	Engineering ethics	181.2	B140-143	Philosophy, Egyptian
174.972	NA1995	Architects—Professional ethics	181.3	B5025-5099	Philosophy, Middle Eastern
			181.3	B755-759	Philosophy, Jewish
174.97914	PN2056	Actors—Professional ethics	181.3	B5055-5059	Philosophy, Israeli
174.98	PN154	Literary ethics	181.4	B130-133	Hinduism
175	BJ1498	Leisure	181.45	B132.Y6	Yoga
175	PN1995.5	Motion pictures—Moral and ethical aspects	181.482	B132.A3	Advaita
			181.5	B150-153	Philosophy, Iranian
176	BJ1533.C4	Chastity	181.(6-8)	B5025-5099	Philosophy, Middle Eastern
176	HQ31-64	Sexual ethics	181.6	B145-148	Philosophy, Babylonian
176.082	HQ46	Sexual ethics for women	181.92	B5295	Philosophy, Arab
176.0835	HQ35	Sexual ethics for teenagers	181.92	B740-753	Philosophy, Arab
			182	B193	Atomism
177.1	BJ1520-1688	Courtesy	183	B279	Hedonism
177.1	BJ1533.C9	Courtesy	183.1	B288	Sophists (Greek philosophy)
177.2	BJ1535.G6	Gossip	183.6	B285	Megarians (Greek philosophy)

Dewey	LC	Subject Heading	Dewey	LC	Subject Heading
184	B398.C34	Plato's cave (Allegory)	211.3	BL200	Theism
184	B398.G6	God (Greek religion)	211.3	BD555	Theism
184	B398.I3	Idea (Philosophy)	211.32	BL217	Polytheism
184	B398.L9	Platonic love	211.33	BL218	Dualism (Religion)
184	B491.R44	Refutation (Logic)	211.34	BL221	Monotheism
186	B525	Skeptics (Greek philosophy)	211.4	BL2700-2790	Skepticism
186.3	B271	Eclecticism	211.4	BL2700-2790	Rationalism
186.4	B645	Neoplatonism	211.6	BL2700-2790	Secularism
186.4	B517	Neoplatonism	211.8	BL2700-2790	Atheism
188	B528	Stoics	213	BL224-226	Creation
189	B720-785	Philosophy, Medieval	213	BL263	Evolution—Religious aspects
189	B630-708	Philosophy, Ancient	220	BS	Bible
189.4	B734	Scholasticism	220.046	BS646	Apocalyptic literature
189.5	B728	Mysticism	220.071	BS585-613	Bible—Study and teaching
190	B770-785	Philosophy, Renaissance	220.076	BS612	Bible—Examinatons, questions, etc.
190	B790-5739	Philosophy, Modern			
190	B802	Enlightenment	220.0846	BS680.A34	Aged in the Bible
191	B850-945	Philosophy, American	220.09	BS445-460	Bible—History
191	B981-995	Philosophy, Canadian	220.092	BS570-580	Bible—Biography
192	B1111-1674	Philosophy, English	220.1	BS480	Bible—Evidences, authority, etc.
193	B2521-3396	Philosophy, German			
194	B1801-2430	Philosophy, French	220.13	BS480	Bible—Inspiration
195	B3551-3656	Philosophy, Italian	220.15	BS647-649	Bible—Prophecies
196.1	B4561-4568	Philosophy, Spanish	220.(4-5)	BS537	Bible—Language, style
196.9	B4591-4598	Philosophy, Portuguese	220.(4-5)	BS420-429	Bible—Concordances
197	B4201-4279	Philosophy, Russian	220.4	BS450-460	Bible—Versions
198.1	B4411-4445	Philosophy, Norwegian	220.49	BS560	Hieroglyphic Bibles
198.5	B4455-4495	Philosophy, Swedish	220.5	BS450-460	Bible—Versions
198.8	B4711-4800	Philosophy, Finnish	220.49	BS560	Hieroglyphic Bibles
198.9	B4325-4395	Philosophy, Danish	220.5	BS405-408	Bible—Abridgments
199.437	B4801-4805	Philosophy, Czech	220.51	BS1-3	Bible. Polyglot
199.438	B4687-4691	Philosophy, Polish	220.52	BS135-198	Bible. English
199.439	B4811-4815	Philosophy, Hungarian	220.6	BS500-534.8	Bible—Criticism, interpretation, etc.
199.492	B4041-4095	Philosophy, Dutch			
199.493	B4151-4175	Philosophy, Belgian	220.6	BS1181.2	E document (Biblical criticism)
199.494	B4628-4651	Philosophy, Swiss			
199.495	B3500-3515	Philosophy, Greek (Modern)	220.6	BS1181.17	D document (Biblical criticism)
199.498	B4821-4825	Philosophy, Romanian			
199.561	B4871-4875	Philosophy, Turkish	220.64	BS477	Symbolism in the Bible
199.6	B5300-5320	Philosophy, African	220.64	BS478	Typology (Theology)
199.72	B1015-1019	Philosophy, Mexican	220.68	BS520.5	Myth in the Bible
199.728	B1025-1026	Philosophy, Central American	220.7	BS482-498	Bible—Commentaries
199.729	B1028-1029	Philosophy, West Indian	220.817	BS680.E84	Ethics in the Bible
199.8	B1030-1084	Philosophy, South American	220.8301	BS670	Sociology, Biblical
200	BL48-50	Religion	220.83058.	BS661	Ethnology in the Bible
200.25	BL35	Religion—Directories	220.83067	BS680.S5	Sex in the Bible
200.5	BL1-10	Religion—Periodicals	220.830685	BS680.F3	Family—Biblical teaching
200.6	BL11-21	Religion—[Societies/ Congresses]	220.8330	BS670	Economics in the Bible
			220.83638	BS680.F32	Famines in the Bible
200.71	BL41	Religion—Study and teaching	220.837	BS680.E3	Education in the Bible
			220.85	BS660-667	Nature in the Bible
200.94	BL690-980	Europe—Religion	220.852	BS655	Astronomy in the Bible
200.956	BL660-687	Middle East—Religion	220.9	BS637	Bible—Chronology
210	BL51	Religion—Philosophy	220.9	BS569	Genealogy in the Bible
210	BL51	Fictions, Theory of	220.9	BS635-636	Bible—History of Biblical events
210	BL51	Knowledge, Theory of (Religion)			
			220.9505	BS546-559	Bible stories
210	BL175-190	Natural theology	221.071	BS1193-1195	Bible. O.T.—Study and teaching
210	BL210	Analogy (Religion)			
211	BL215	Anthropomorphism	221.09	BS1130-1134	Bible. O.T.—History
211.2	BL220	Pantheism	221.092	BS580	Bible. O.T.—Biography

Dewey	LC	Subject Heading	Dewey	LC	Subject Heading
221.(4-5)	BS1121-1128	Bible. O.T.—Concordances	230	BT	Christian doctrinal theology
221.(4-5)	BS701-1013	Bible. O.T.—Versions	230	BR115.C5	Civilization, Christian
221.47	BS767-815	Bible. O.T. Latin	230	BR115.H5	History (Theology)
221.48	BS737-765	Bible. O.T. Greek	230	BR1-129	Christianity
221.6	BS1160-1191.5	Bible. O.T.—Criticism, interpetation, etc.	230	BS2397	Bible. N.T.—Theology
			230-299	BL74-98	Religions
221.65	BS1104	Bible. O.T.—Harmonies	230.01	BT40-55	Philosophical theology
221.68	BS1183	Myth in the Old Testament	230.041	BS543	Bible—Theology
221.7	BS1143-1158	Bible. O.T.—Commentaries	230.0411	BS1192.5	Bible. O.T.—Theology
221.837	BS1199.E38	Education in the Bible	230.046	BT82.25	Dominion theology
221.92	BS1199.P7	Priests, Jewish	230.046	BR1615-1617	Liberalism (Religion)
222.1	BS1221-1285.5	Bible. O.T. Pentateuch	230.0464	BT83.57	Liberation theology
222.106	BS1225	Documentary hypothesis (Pentateuchal criticism)	230.071	BV4019-4180	Theology—Study and teaching
222.11	BL325.D4	Noah's ark	230.071	BV4163	Pretheological education
222.11	BS1237	Forbidden fruit	230.0711	BV4019-4160	Theological seminaries
222.11	BS1237	Eden	230.0711	BV4164	Seminary extension
222.11	BS658	Deluge	230.082	BT83.55	Feminist theology
222.110922	BS573	Patriarchs (Bible)	230.08996	BT82.7	Black theology
222.1109505	BS658	Noah's ark	230.09	BT20-30	Theology, Doctrinal—History
222.12	BS1245	Manna	230.1	BT1115	Apologetics—Early church, ca. 30-600
222.16	BS1281-1285.5	Ten commandments			
223	BS1401-1405.5	Hebrew poetry, Biblical	230.2	BX1752	Catholic Church—Apologetic works
223.2	BS1445.M4	Royal Psalms			
223.2	BS1419-1450	Bible. O.T. Psalms	230.2	BX1746-1755	Catholic Church—Doctrines
223.9	BS1481-1490	Bible. O.T. Song of Solomon	230.342	BX5137-5140	Church of England—Doctrines
224	BS1501-1675.5	Prophets			
225-228	BS1901-2970	Bible. N.T.	230.373	BX5929-5930.2	Episcopal Church—Doctrines
225.071	BS2525-2544	Bible. N.T.—Study and teaching	230.42	BX9420-9422.2	Reformed Church—Doctrines
225.09	BS2315-2318	Bible. N.T.—History			
225.(4-5)	BS1901	Bible. N.T.—Versions	230.6(1-5)	BX6330-6331.2	Baptists—Doctrines
225.(4-5)	BS2301-2308	Bible. N.T.—Concordances	230.7	BX8330-8331.2	Methodist Church—Doctrines
225.6	BS2350-2393	Bible. N.T.—Criticism, interpretation, etc.			
			231	BT98-180	God
225.68	BS2378	Demythologizcation	231	BT99	God—Biblical teaching
225.7	BS2333-2348	Bible. N.T.—Commentaries	231	BT124	Immanence of God
225.92	BS580.A3	Abraham (Biblical patriarch) in the New Testament	231	BT180.G6	Glory of God
			231	BT153.S8	Suffering of God
225.92	BS2440	Apostles	231-239	BT65-84	Theology, Doctrinal
226	BS2549	Bible. N.T. Gospels	231.042	BT98-101	God—Proof, Ontological
226.6	BS2620-2628	Bible. N.T. Acts	231.044	BT109-115	Trinity
226.8	BT373-378	Jesus Christ—Parables	231.09	BT98	God—History of doctrines
226.8	BT378.D5	Rich man and Lazarus (Parable)	231.3	BT117-123	Holy Spirit
			231.4	BT133	God—Omnipotence
226.8	BT378.P	Pearl of great price (Parable)	231.4	BT131	God—Omniscience
226.8	BT378.G7	Great supper (Parable)	231.4	BT130-157	God—Attributes
226.8	BT378.M8	Mustard seed (Parable)	231.5	BT135	Providence and government of God
226.8	BT378.G6	Good Samaritan (Parable)			
226.8	BS680.P3	Bible—Parables	231.5	BT95-96.2	Providence and government of God
226.9	BT380-.2	Sermon on the mount			
226.93	BT382	Beatitudes	231.72	BT94	Kingdom of God
227	BS2640-2815.5	Bible. N.T. Pauline Epistles	231.73	BS1199.M5	Miracles
227	BS2630-2815.5	Bible. N.T. Epistles	231.73	BS2545.M5	Miracles
228	BS2820-2827	Four Horsemen of the Apocalypse	231.73	BT97-.2	Miracles
			231.74	BT126-127.5	Revelation
228	BS646	Revelation	231.74	BX8643.R4	Revelation (Mormon theology)
229	BS1691-1830	Bible. O.T. Apocrypha	231.745	BX8643.P7	Prophets (Mormon theology)
229	BS2831-2970	Apocryphal books (New Testament)	231.76	BT155	Covenant theology
			231.765	BT98-102	God—Proof, Cosmological
230	BT19-33	Dogma	231.765	BS651-652	Biblical cosmology

Dewey	LC	Subject Heading	Dewey	LC	Subject Heading
231.765	BS651-652	Creation	234.4	BT790	Regeneration (Theology)
231.765	BX8643.C68	Mormon cosmology	234.5	BT800	Repentance
231.7652	BS651-652	Creationism	234.5	BT263-268	Atonement
231.8	BT160-162	Theodicy	234.5	BT795	Forgiveness of sin
231.8	BT137	God—Goodness	234.7	BT763-764.2	Justification
232	BT306	Jesus Christ—Words	234.8	BT767	Holiness
232	BT198-590	Jesus Christ	234.9	BT809-810.2	Predestination
232.1	BT220	Incarnation	235	BT960-985	Spirits
232.1	BT225	Typology (Theology)	235.2	BT683-694	Saints
232.1	BT230-245	Jesus Christ—Messiahship	235.2	BX577	Relics
232.2	BT210	Logos	235.2	BV890	Relics
232.8	BT198-590	Jesus Christ—Person and offices	235.2	BX575-577.5	Christian saints
			235.2	BX380	Christian saints
232.9	BT232	Son of Man	235.2	BX2315	Relics
232.901	BT300-302	Jesus Christ—Biography	235.24	BX576	Canonization
232.903	BT304-.97	Jesus Christ—Character	235.24	BX2330	Canonization
232.91	BT595-680	Mary, Blessed Virgin, Saint	235.3	BT968.M5	Michael (Archangel)
232.91	BT610-660	Mary, Blessed Virgin, Saint—Theology	235.3	BT960-968	Angels
			235.4	BT850-860	Limbo
232.911	BT620	Immaculate Conception	235.4	BT980-981	Devil
232.917	BT650-660	Visions	236	BT819-891	Eschatology
232.917	BT650-654	Mary, Blessed Virgin, Saint—Apparitions and miracles	236	BT985	Antichrist
			236.2	BT899-940	Future life
			236.21	BT910-912	Eternity
232.921	BT317	Virgin birth	236.22	BT919-925	Immortality
232.923	BT315	Magi	236.23	BT930	Annihilationism
232.95	BT340-500	Jesus Christ—Biography—Public life	236.23	BT919-925	Conditional immortality
			236.24	BT844-849	Paradise
232.954	BS2415-2417	Jesus Christ—Teachings	236.24	BT844-849	Heaven
232.955	BT363-367	Jesus Christ—Miracles	236.25	BT834-838	Hell
232.956	BT410	Jesus Christ—Transfiguration	236.4	BT830	Intermediate state
			236.5	BT840-842	Purgatory
232.957	BT420	Last Supper	236.8	BT870-872	Resurrection
232.96	BT430-470	Jesus Christ—Passion	236.9	BT880-882	Judgment Day
232.96	BT414	Holy Week	236.9	BT875-891	End of the world
232.963	BT465	Holy Cross	236.9	BT890-891	Millennium
232.966	BT587.S4	Holy Shroud	236.9	BT885-886	Second Advent
232.966	BT587	Jesus Christ—Relics	238	BT990	Creeds, Ecumenical
233	BT700-745	Man (Christian theology)	238	BT1029-1040	Catechisms
233	BT700-745	Man (Theology)	238	BT990-1010	Creeds
233	BT704	Woman (Christian theology)	238	BX8068-8070	Catechetics
233	BS661	Man (Theology)	238.2	BX1958-1968	Catholic Church—Catechisms
233.14	BT720	Sin, Original			
233.14	BT710	Fall of man	238.373	BX5939	Episcopal Church—Creeds
233.14	BT715-722	Sin	238.373	BX6074	Episcopal Church—Creeds
233.5	BT708	Sex—Religious aspects—Christianity	238.58	BX7235-7236.2	Congregational churches—Creeds
233.5	BT740-743	Soul	238.6	BX6335	Baptists—Creeds
234	BT759	Salvation outside the church	238.6(1-5)	BX6336	Baptists—Catechisms
234	BT760-769	Grace (Theology)	238.7	BX8335	Methodist Church—[Catechisms/Creeds]
234	BT755	Salvation outside the Catholic Church			
			239	BT1095-1255	Apologetics
234	BT773	Merit (Christianity)	239.09	BT1109-1115	Apologetics—History
234	BT809-810.2	Election (Theology)	239.7	BT1209-1211	Rationalism
234	BT750-810.2	Salvation	240-248	BV1-4	Theology, Practical
234.13	BT123	Baptism in the Holy Spirit	241	BJ1188.5-1278	Christian ethics
234.13	BT767.3	Gifts, Spiritual	241	BV4618	Human acts
234.131	BT732.5-.56	Spiritual healing	241	BV4625-4780	Christian ethics
234.166	BX5949.C6	Confession	241.1	BV4615	Conscience
234.23	BT770-772	Faith	241.1	BX2377	Conscience, Examination of
234.3	BT775	Redemption	241.2	BT95-97	Law (Theology)

Dewey	LC	Subject Heading	Dewey	LC	Subject Heading
241.3	BR115.W2	Evil, Non-resistance to	246.558	CC300-350	Crosses
241.3	BT725	Temptation	246.6	BV165	Colors, Liturgical
241.3	BT721	Sin, Unpardonable	246.6	BX8643.T4	Mormon temples
241.3	BV4726.S2	Sacrilege	246.75	BV301-530	Hymns
241.3	BV4627.H8	Hypocrisy	246.75	BV520	Sunday schools—Hymns
241.3	BV4625	Sin	247.1	BV195-196	Altars
241.3	BV4625-4627	Vices	247.1	BV863.P4	Pews and pew rights
241.3	BV4625-4627	Sins	248	BV4800-4897	Devotional exercises
241.3	BV4626	Deadly sins	248.2	BR110	Experience (Religion)
241.3	BV4627.R4	Revenge	248.2	BR112	Enthusiasm
241.3	BV4627.Q	Quarreling	248.2	BR114	Fanaticism
241.3	BV4630-4647	Vice	248.2	BV4912-4915	Experience (Religion)
241.3	BV4627.S9	Swearing	248.22	BV5095	Mystics
241.3	BV4627.S6	Slander	248.22	BV5070-5095	Mysticism
241.31	BV4625.6-.7	Sin, Venial	248.24	BR110	Conversion
241.4	BR1610	Religious tolerance	248.24	BT780	Conversion
241.4	BV4647.D6	Discretion	248.24	BV4930-4935	Converts
241.4	BV4647.M4	Spiritual works of mercy	248.24	BV4912-4950	Conversion
241.4	BV4647.P5	Piety	248.29	BV5090-5091	Trance
241.4	BV4647.M4	Mercy	248.29	BV5091.R4	Private revelations
241.4	BV4647.M2	Magnanimity	248.29	BV5091.V6	Visions
241.4	BV4647.T4	Temperance (Virtue)	248.29	BV5091.R4	Revelation
241.4	BV4645	Cardinal virtues	248.29	BV5083	Discernment of spirits
241.4	BV4630-4647	Virtue	248.29	BV5091.E3	Ecstasy
241.4	BV4635-4639	Theological virtues	248.3	BV5-530	Worship
241.4	BV4639	Charity	248.309	BV5-8	Worship—History
241.4	BV4625-4627	Virtues	248.30901	BV6	Worship—History—Early church, ca. 30-600
241.4	BV4647.S4	Self-denial			
241.4	BV1518-1533	Virtues	248.34	BX2177-2198	Meditations
241.4	BV4637	Faith	248.34	BV5091.C7	Contemplation
241.4	BV4647.M3	Meekness	248.34	BV4800-4870	Meditations
241.4	BV4647.M4	Corporal works of mercy	248.4	BV4500-4595	Christian life
241.5	BV4720-4730	Commandments of the church	248.47	BV5055	Fasting
			248.47	BV5099	Quietism
241.52	BV4655-4710	Ten commandments	248.47	BV5015-5068	Asceticism
241.54	BV4715	Golden rule	248.470901	BV5023	Asceticism—History—Early church, ca. 30-600
241.62	BV4647.J	Justice (Virtue)			
241.66	BV4647.C5	Chastity	248.470902	BV5025	Asceticism—History—Middle Ages, 600-1500
241.66	BV4647.C5	Virginity			
242	BS617.8	Bible—Devotional use	248.5	BV4520	Witness bearing (Christianity)
242	BV4815	Devotion	248.6	BV772	Stewardship, Christian
242	BV4800-4895	Devotional literature	248.6	BX5165	Tithes
242	BX2177-2198	Devotional literature	248.6	BX8643.T5	Tithes—Mormon Church
242.2	BV287	Prayer groups	248.83	BV4530-4579	Youth—Religious life
242.2	BV283.S3	Schools—Prayers	248.85	BV4580	Aged—Religious life
242.2	BV283.G7	Grace at meals	248.88	BV4593	Working class—Religious life
242.3	BV4810-4812	Devotional calendars	249	BV200	Family—Religious life
242.4	BV4900-4911	Consolation	249	BV1590	Religious education—Home training
242.5	BS680.P64	Bible—Prayers			
242.72	BV194.D	Doxology	250	BV637.8	Small churches
242.74	BT303	Mysteries of the Rosary	250	BV652.9	Church controversies
242.74	BX2310.R7	Rosary	250.91732	BV637	City churches
242.8	BV245-283	Prayer-books	250.91733	BV637.7	Suburban churches
242.802	BX2080	Books of hours	250.91734	BV638-.8	Rural churches
242.802	BX2050-2155	Catholic Church—Prayer-books and devotions	251	BV4235.B56	Biographical preaching
			251	BV4235.L3	Lay preaching
242.82	BV283.B7	Boys—Prayer-books and devotions	251	BV4235.E8	Extemporaneous preaching
			251	BV4235.T65	Topical preaching
246.55	BV150-168	Signs and symbols	251	BV4200-4317	Preaching
246.55	BV150-168	Symbolism	251	BV4235.L43	Lectionary preaching
246.558	BV160	Crosses	251.009	BV4207-4208	Preaching—History

Dewey	LC	Subject Heading	Dewey	LC	Subject Heading
252	BV4307.D5	Dialogue sermons	254.5	BV652.25	Church growth
252	BV4257.5	Communion sermons	254.5	BV820	Church membership
252	BV4254.2	Occasional sermons	254.7	BV636	Church buildings—
252	BV4239-4316	Sermons			Interdenominational use
252.02	BX1756	Catholic Church—Sermons	254.8	BX1950	Catholic Church—Finance
252.03	BX5008	Anglican Communion—	254.8	BV772.5	Church fund raising
		Sermons	254.8	BV770-777	Church finance
252.041	BX8066	Lutheran Church—Sermons	254.8	BV772	Christian giving
252.042	BX9426	Reformed Church—Sermons	254.8	BV771	Tithes
252.046	BX8577	Moravians—Sermons	255.00901	BV761.A1-.A5	Church orders, Ancient
252.05	BX9178	Presbyterian Church—	255.(1-7)	BX2435	Monastic and religious life
		Sermons	255.(1-7)	BX2460-2749	Monasteries
252.058	BX7233	Congregational churches—	255.(1-7)	BX2400-4560	Monasticism and religious
		Sermons			orders
252.06(1-5)	BX6333	Baptists—Sermons	255.(1-7)	BX4668.2-.3	Ex-monks
252.067	BX6123	Adventists—Sermons	255.(1-7)009	BX2460-2749	Monastic and religious
252.091	BX9843	Unitarian Universalist			life—History
		churches—Sermons	255.(1-7)0094	BX2631-2676	Monasticism and religious
252.09134	BX9943	Universalism—Sermons			orders—Europe
252.093	BX8639	Mormon Church—Sermons	255.(1-7)0095	BX2677-2731	Monasticism and religious
252.094	BX8724	New Jerusalem Church—			orders—Asia
		Sermons	255.(1-7)0096	BX2732-2740	Monasticism and religious
252.096	BX7733	Society of Friends—Sermons			orders—Africa
252.097	BX8127	Mennonites—Sermons	255.(1-7)00971	BX2527-2529	Monasticism and religious
252.097	BX8129.A1	Mennonites—Parties and			orders—Canada
		movements	255.(1-7)00972	BX2530-2532	Monasticism and religious
252.098	BX9777	Shakers—Sermons			orders—Mexico
252.1	BV4275	Funeral sermons	255.(1-7)009728	BX2533-2547	Monasticism and religious
252.3	BV3797	Evangelistic sermons			orders—Central America
252.53	BV4315	Children's sermons	255.(1-7)00973	BX2505-2525	Monasticism and religious
252.55	BV4310	Youth sermons			orders—United States
252.6	BV4254.3	Festival-day sermons	255.(1-7)0098	BX2561-2589	Monasticism and religious
252.6	BV4270	Fast-day sermons			orders—South America
252.61	BV40	Advent sermons	255.(1-7)0099	BX2743-2745	Monasticism and religious
252.615	BV4257	Christmas sermons	(3/4)		orders—[New Zealand/
252.63	BV4259	Easter—Sermons			Australia]
252.68	BV4282	New Year sermons	255.(1-7)06	BX2436-2437	Monasticism and religious
252.68	BV4255	Baccalaureate addresses			orders—Rules
252.68	BV4260-4261	Election sermons	255.2	BX3501-3556	Dominicans
252.68	BV4262	Execution sermons	255.(2-3)	BX2820	Friars
252.7	BV4290	Installation (Clergy)	255.3	BX3601-3656	Franciscans
252.7	BX8333	Methodist Church—Sermons	255.3	BX3651-3653	Secular Franciscans
253	BV4000-4470	Pastoral theology	255.4	BX2901-2956	Augustinians
253	BV4335	Pastoral medicine	255.7	CR5547-5575	Orders of knighthood and
253.2	BV4327	Clergy—Political activity			chivalry, Papal
253.2	BV4395.5	Clergy—Divorce	255.791	CR4701-4731	Orders of knighthood and
253.22	BV4396	Clergy—Family relationships			chivalry, Papal
253.25	BV4390	Celibacy	255.791	CR5547-5577	Papal decorations
253.252	BX1912.9	Catholic Church—	255.7914	CR4759-4775	Teutonic Knights
		Clergy—Sexual behavior	255.7914	DK4600.P77	Teutonic Knights
253.5	BV4012.25	Pastoral counseling centers	255.8	BV4405-4408	Monasticism and religious
253.5	BV4012.2	Pastoral counseling			orders, Protestant
253.52	BV4012-.3	Pastoral psychology	255.819	BX385-388	Monasticism and religious
253.53	BV5053	Spiritual direction			orders, Orthodox Eastern
253.53	BX382.5	Spiritual direction	255.819	BX385	Monasticism and religious
253.53	BX2350.7	Spiritual direction			orders
254	BV652-.9	Church management	255.819	BX580-583	Monasticism and religious
254	BV168.S7	Staff, Pastoral			orders
254.4	BV653	Advertising—Churches	255.83	BX5970-5974	Monasticism and religious
254.4	BV652.95-657	Church publicity			orders, Anglican
254.5	BV4523	Church attendance	255.83	BX5178	Anglican orders

Dewey	LC	Subject Heading
255.9(1-7)	BX4200-4563	Monasticism and religious orders for women
255.9(1-7)	BX4200-4556	Sisterhoods
255.972	BX4337-.5	Dominican sisters
255.973	BX4361-4364	Franciscans
255.983	BX5185	Sisterhoods
258.0835	BV4427-4430	Youth in church work
259.082	BV4445.5	Abused women—Pastoral counseling of
261	BV601.3	Church—Catholicity
261	BV601.8	Mission of the church
261.2	BR127-128	Christianity and other religions
261.5	BT738-.5	Sociology, Christian
261.513	BR115.P85	Parapsychology—Religious aspects—Christianity
261.7	BV629-631	Church and state
261.7	BX1790-1795	Church and state—Catholic Church
261.8	HT910-921	Slavery and the church
261.83	HN30-39	Church and social problems
261.8348	BT734-.3	Race
261.8348	BT734-.3	Race—Religious aspects—Christianity
262	BT1010	Covenants (Church polity)
262	BV590-640	Church
262.0011092	BX6.7-.8	Ecumenists
262.0017	BV600	Church renewal
262.009	BR97-99	Ecclesiastical geography
262.01947	BX520-558	Orthodox Eastern Church—Government
262.02	BX1939.A3	Administrators apostolic
262.02	BX1800-1920	Catholic Church—Government
262.02	BX1912	Deacons
262.02	BX1911	Archdeacons
262.03	BX5175-5182.5	Priests
262.03	BX5175-5182.5	Church of England—Clergy
262.03	BX5179	Archdeacons
262.0342	BX5150-5182.5	Church of England—Government
262.0373	BX5950-5968	Episcopal Church—Government
262.0373	BX6076	Episcopal Church—Government
262.041	BX8071-.2	Lutheran Church—Clergy
262.042	BX9425	Reformed Church—Government
262.05	BX9190-9195	Presbyterian Church—Government
262.058	BX7240-7246	Congregational churches—Government
262.06(1-5)	BX6340-6346.3	Baptists—Government
262.07	BX8340-8345.5	Methodist Church—Government
262.091	BX9850	Unitarian Universalist churches—Government
262.094	BX8737	New Jerusalem Church—Government
262.095	BX6958	Christian Science—Government
262.096	BX7740-7746	Society of Friends—Government
262.098	BX9776	Shakers—Government
262.1	BV705	Church officers
262.1	BV652.1	Christian leadership
262.1	BX8659.5	Aaronic Priesthood (Mormon Church)
262.12	BX5179	Archdeacons
262.12	BV669-670.2	Episcopacy
262.12	BX5176-5178	Episcopacy
262.122	BX1905	Catholic Church—Bishops
262.13	BX1805-1810	Popes
262.13	BX958.V7	Papal visits
262.13	BX958.A23	Popes—Abdication
262.13	BX950-961	Papacy
262.13	BX1001-1378	Popes
262.13	BX400-440	Patriarchs and patriarchate
262.13	CR5547-5577	Nobility, Papal
262.13090(1-23)	BX965-1263	Papacy—History—To 1309
262.131	BX1806	Popes—Infallibility
262.14	BV830	Ordination
262.14	BV4423-4425	Deaconesses
262.14	BV685	Ordination
262.14	BV680	Deacons
262.14	BV675.7	Clergy couples
262.14	BV659-683	Priests
262.14	BV659-683	Clergy
262.14	BV676	Women clergy
262.14	BV676	Ordination of women
262.14	BV675	Group ministry
262.14091732	BV637.5	City clergy
262.142	BX1910	Vicars apostolic
262.142	BX1910	Vicars-general
262.142	BX1912-1914.5	Catholic Church—Clergy
262.142	BX1912-1914.5	Priests
262.15	BV687	Laity
262.15	BV677	Lay readers
262.152	BX1920	Laity—Catholic Church
262.26	BV4405-4406	Christian communities
262.3	BX837.5	Episcopal conferences (Catholic)
262.3	BX838	Diocesan pastoral councils
262.(4-5)	BV710	Councils and synods
262.5	BV626	Local church councils
262.52	BX820-838	Councils and synods, Episcopal (Catholic)
262.73	BT972	Communion of saints
262.8	BT91	Church—Authority
262.8	BT88-92	Authority—Religious aspects
262.8	BT20-30	Heresies, Christian
262.9	BV759-763	Ecclesiastical law
262.90901	BV761	Canon law—Early church, ca. 30-600
262.91	BX863	Letters, Papal
262.91	BX860	Encyclicals, Papal
262.91	BX863	Letters, Papal
262.932	BX1939.C665	Clergy (Canon law)
262.932	BX1939.P47	Persons (Canon law)
262.932	BX1939.A	Abbots (Canon law)
262.933	BX1939.B3	Baptism (Canon law)
262.933	BX1939.C72	Confirmation (Canon law)

16

Dewey	LC	Subject Heading	Dewey	LC	Subject Heading
262.933	BX1939.C3	Catechetics (Canon law)	264.02036	BX2307.3	Baptismal water
262.933	BX1939.A	Absolution (Canon law)	264.0207	BX2290	Extreme unction
262.934	BX1939.T65	Trial practice (Canon law)	264.0208	BX2200-2292	Sacraments (Liturgy)
263.04	BX2323	Christian pilgrims and pilgrimages	264.02084	BX2240	Ordination—Catholic Church
			264.02085	BX2250-2254	Marriage service
263.042	BX2320-2321	Christian shrines	264.02085	BX2045.W34	Wake services
263.3	BV107-133	Sunday	264.02086	BX2260-2283	Penance
263.9	BV30-135	Fasts and feasts	264.020862	BX2262-2267	Confession
263.9	BV30-135	Church year	264.020862	BX2262-2267	Confessors
263.9	BV50.A4	All Souls' Day	264.020866	BX2279-2283	Indulgences
263.9	CE81	Fasts and feasts	264.0209	BX2310.A	Agnus Dei (Sacramental)
263.915	BV50.E7	Epiphany	264.0209	BX2295-2310	Sacramentals
263.92	BV53	Palm Sunday	264.02092	BX2305	Consecration of virgins
263.92	BV85-95	Lent	264.02094	BX2340	Exorcism
263.925	BV90-95	Holy Week	264.023	BX2015-2016	Missals
263.925	BV95	Good Friday	264.023	BX2037	Sacramentaries
263.925	BT414	Holy Week	264.024	BX2000-.68	Breviaries
263.93	BV55	Easter	264.0274	BX2040	Stations of the Cross
263.93	BV55	Paschal mystery	264.03	BX5940-5948	Episcopal Church—Liturgy
263.93	BV57	Ascension Day	264.03	BX5943-5945	Episcopal Church—Prayer-books and devotions
263.94	BT122.5	Pentecost			
263.94	BV61-63	Pentecost season	264.03	BX5947-5948	Episcopal Church—Liturgy
263.94	BV60	Pentecost Festival	264.03	BX5123	Ritualism
263.97	BV50.H6	Feast of the Holy Innocents	264.03	BX6075	Episcopal Church—Liturgy
263.97	BV50.A7	Feast of the Assumption of the Blessed Virgin	264.03	BX5149.C5	Lord's Supper
			264.03	BX5145	Church of England—Prayer-Books and devotions
263.97	BV50.I6	Feast of the Immaculate Conception	264.0342	BX5140.5-5147	Church of England—Liturgy
263.97	BV75	Thanksgiving Day	264.035	BX5148-5149	Sacraments—Church of England
263.97	BV64.S3	Feast of the Sacred Heart			
263.97	BV64.J4	Feast of Jesus Christ the King	264.035	BX5949	Episcopal Church Confession
			264.03562	BX5149.C6	
263.98	BV67	All Saints' Day	264.041	BX8067	Lutheran Church—Liturgy
264	BV5-25	Public worship	264.04108	BX8072-8073.5	Sacraments—Lutheran Church
264	BV180-181	Ritualism			
264	BV169-199	Rites and ceremonies	264.042	BX9427-.5	Reformed Church—Liturgy
264	BV196.C	Censers	264.05	BX9185-9187	Presbyterian Church—Liturgy
264	BV169-199	Liturgics	264.05	BX9188-9189	Sacraments—Presbyterian Church
264	BV198-199	Liturgies			
264	BV186.7	Ecumenical liturgies	264.058	BX7237	Congregational churches—Liturgy
264.01	BV185	Liturgies, Early Christian			
264.019	BX350-376	Orthodox Eastern Church—Liturgy	264.05808	BX7238-7239	Sacraments—Congregational churches
264.019	BX377-378	Sacraments—Orthodox Eastern Church	264.06(1-5)	BX6337	Baptists—Liturgy
			264.06708	BX6124.3-.6	Sacraments—Adventists
264.01947	BX560-563	Orthodox Eastern Church—Russia	264.07	BX8337	Methodist Church—Liturgy
			264.0708	BX8338	Sacraments—Methodist Church
264.02	BX1970.A7-.Z	Catholic Church—Liturgy			
264.02	BX2045.E96	Exultets (Liturgy)	264.0913308	BX9854	Sacraments—Unitarianism
264.02	BX1970	Liturgical language	264.0913408	BX9954	Sacraments—Universalism
264.02	BX2347-2348	Catholic Church—Liturgy—Theology	264.09308	BX8655-.3	Sacraments—Mormon Church
264.02	BX2230-2234	Mass	264.09408	BX8736	Sacraments—New Jerusalem Church
264.02	BX2015.5.H	Dog Mass			
264.02 (1-9)	BX1999.8-2047	Catholic Church—Liturgy—Texts	264.095	BX6960	Christian Science—Liturgy
			264.13	BV205-287	Prayer—Christianity
264.02036	BX2237	First communion	264.13	BV228-284	Prayers
264.02036	BX2231.7	Private masses	264.13	BX2048.B5	Benediction
264.02036	BX2215.A1	Eucharistic congresses	264.13	BV197.B5	Benediction
264.02036	BX2215-2239	Lord's Supper	264.13	BV250-254	Pastoral prayers
264.02036	BX2220	Transubstantiation	264.36	BV820	Close and open communion

Dewey	LC	Subject Heading	Dewey	LC	Subject Heading
264.36	BV823-828	Lord's Supper	268.432	BV1474-1475.2	Christian education of children
264.9	BV197.S5	Cross, Sign of the			
264.9	BV875-885	Sacramentals	268.6	BV4560-4579	Sunday school literature
265	BV800-873	Sacraments	268.6	BV1534-1536	Religious education— Teaching methods
265	BV199.R5	Responsive worship			
265.1	BV814	Baptism for the dead	268.635	BV1535	Religious education— Audio-visual aids
265.1	BV803-814	Baptism			
265.12	BV813-.2	Infant baptism	268.67	BV1534.4	Drama in Christian education
265.2	BV815	Confirmation			
265.5	BV835-838	Marriage	268.82	BX895-939	Catholic Church—Education
265.6	BV840-850	Penance	268.82	BX1968	Catechetics
265.62	BV845-847	Confession	268.8373	BX5850-5876	Episcopal Church— Education
265.62	BV845-847	Confessors			
265.62	BX5949.C6	Confession	268.8373	BX6061-6064.5	Episcopal Church— Education
265.85	BV199.F8	Funeral service			
265.9	BV873.F7	Foot washing (Rite)	268.846	BX8561-8564.5	Moravians—Education
265.9	BV199	Occasional services	268.85	BX8917-8925	Presbyterian Church— Education
265.9	BV873.L3	Imposition of hands			
265.92	BV199.D4	Dedication services	268.858	BX7119-7127	Congregational churches— Education
265.92	BV4501	Consecration			
265.94	BV873.E8	Exorcism	268.86(1-5)	BX6219-6227	Baptists—Education
266	BV2082.I6	Missions—Interdenomina- tional cooperation	268.87	BX8219-8227	Methodist Church— Education
266	BV2350-2595	Protestant churches— Missions	268.891	BX9817-9823	Unitarian Universalist churches—Education
266	BV2619-2623	Missions to Jews	268.89134	BX9917-9923	Universalism—Education
266	BV2625-2626.4	Missions to Muslims	268.893	BX8610	Mormon Church— Education
266	BV2637	Missions to lepers			
266	BV2000-3705	Missions	268.894	BX8714	New Jerusalem Church— Education
266	BV2082.A9	Aeronautics in missionary work	268.895	BX6917	Christian Science— Education
266.0083	BV2617	Youth in missionary work			
266.009	BV2400-2595	Protestant churches— Missions—History	268.896	BX7619-7627	Society of Friends— Education
266.0092	BV3700-3705	Missionaries	268.898	BX9761-9764	Shakers—Education
266.0094	BV2855-3145	Missions—European	269.2	BV3793	Evangelistic invitations
266.00941	BV2860-2895	Missions—Great Britain	269.2	BV3750-3799	Evangelistic work
266.00943	BV2950-2957	Missions—Germany	269.2	BV4487.E9	Evangelical academies
266.00944	BV2940-2945	Missions—France	269.2	BX5925	Evangelicalism—Episcopal Church
266.00946	BV3120-3127	Missions—Spain			
266.0095	BV3149-3487	Missions—Asia	269.2092	BV3780-3785	Evangelists
266.00952	BV3440-3457	Missions—Japan	269.24	BV3798-3799	Camp-meetings
266.0096	BV3500-3630	Missions—Africa	269.24	BV3750-3799	Revivals
266.00971	BV2810-2820	Missions—Canada	269.24	BX6475-6476	Church camps—Baptists
266.0099(3-6)	BV3640-3680	Missions—Oceania	269.24	BX8475-8476	Camp-meetings
266.00994	BV3650-3660	Missions—Australia	269.6	BX2375	Parish missions
266.022	BV2650	Home missions	269.6	BX2375-2376	Retreats—Catholic Church
266.2	BV2130-2300	Catholic Church—Missions	269.6	BV5068.R4	Retreats
266.373	BX5969	Episcopal Church—Missions	270	BT1313-1480	Theology—History
266.93	BX8661	Mormon Church—Missions	270	BR	Church history
267	BV900-1450	Church societies	270	BX940-1745	Catholic Church—History
267	BV950-1220	Brotherhoods	270.(1-2)	BR160-240	Church history—Primitive and early church, ca. 30-600
267.16	BJ10.M6	Moral re-armament			
267.3	BV1000-1220	Young Men's Christian associations	270.(1-2)	BS2410	Christianity—Early church, ca. 30-600
267.5	BV1300-1393	Young Women's Christian associations	270.(1-8)	BR160-481	Church history—[By date]
			270.(5-8)	BR290-481	Church history—Modern period, 1500-
268	BV1585	Vacation schools, Religious			
268	BV1500-1578	Sunday schools	270.01	BR138	Church history—Philosophy
268.3	BV1531	Directors of religious education	270.03	BR95	Church history—Dictionaries
			270.05	BR1-9	Church history—Periodicals

Dewey	LC	Subject Heading	Dewey	LC	Subject Heading
270.06	BR41-43	Church history—Congresses	275.9	BR1178-1261	Asia, Southeastern—Church history
270.06	BR21-29	Church history—Societies, etc.	276	BR1359-1470	Africa—Church history
270.092	BR1690-1725	Church history—Biography	276.1	BR1369-1415	Africa, North—Church history
270.092	BR1705	Fathers of the church			
270.092	BR60-67	Fathers of the church	276.6	BR1460-1463	Africa, West—Church history
270.092	BX2325-2333	Christian saints			
270.(1-2)	BR160-240	Church history—Primitive and early church, ca. 30-600	276.7	BR1430	Africa, Central—Church history
270.(1-2)	BS2410	Christianity—Early church, ca. 30-600	276.76	BR1440-1445	Africa, East—Church history
270.(1-8)	BR160-481	Church history—[By date]	276.8	BR1446-1458	Africa, Southern—Church history
270.1092	BR60-67	Apostolic Fathers	277.2	BR610-615	Mexico—Church history
270.3	BR160-270	Church history—Middle Ages, 600-1500	277.28	BR620-625	Central America—Church history
270.38	BX303	Schism—Eastern and Western Church	277.29	BR655	Caribbean Area—Church history
270.(5-8)	BR290-481	Church history—Modern period, 1500-	277.3	BR516-569	United States—Religion
			277.3081	BR520	Great Awakening
270.6	BR307	Reformation—Causes	278	BR660-730	South America—Church history
270.6	BR300-420	Reformation			
270.6	BR430	Counter-Reformation	279.4	BR1480-1483	Australia—Church history
270.6	BR295	Reformation—Early movements	279.9(5-6)	BR1490-1495	Oceania—Church history
			280	BR157	Christian sects
270.82	BR1644-.5	Pentecostalism	280.042	BX1-9.5	Christian union
270.82	BT82.2	Fundamentalism	280.042	BX9.5.L55	Liturgics and Christian union
272	BR1600-1609	Persecution	280.042	BX9.5.P29	Papacy and Christian union
272.2	BX1700-1745	Inquisition	280.042	BX9.5.A37	Ecumenical movement—African influences
273.1	BT1390	Gnosticism			
273.4	BT1350	Arianism	280.042	BX9.5.V45	Veneration of saints and Christian union
273.4	BT1370	Donatists			
273.7	BR1650-1653	Pietism	280.042	BV625	Interdenominational cooperation
273.9	BT82	Modernism			
274-279	BR500-1500	[Region or country]—Church history	280.042	BX9.5.E94	Evangelicalism and Christian union
274.1	BR740-799	Great Britain—Church history	280.0420835	BX9.5.Y68	Youth in the ecumenical movement
274.10902	BR745-754	England—Church history—1066-1485			
			280.4	BX4800-9999	Protestant churches
274.109021	BR749	England—Church history—449-1066	280.4	BX4818-.3	Protestant churches—Relations
274.10903	BR750	England—Church history—1485-	280.4	BX4800-4946	Protestantism
			280.405	BX4800	Protestantism—Periodicals
274.109031	BR755-757	England—Church history—16th century	280.409	BX4804-4807	Protestantism—History
			280.4092	BX4800-9890	Protestants
274.109032	BR756	England—Church history—17th century	280.4094	BX4837-4854	Protestant churches—Europe
274.109033	BR758	Evangelical Revival	280.40941	BX5200-5207	Dissenters, Religious—England
274.10904	BR759	England—Church history—20th century	280.40941	BX4838-4840	Protestant churches—Great Britain
274.3	BR850-856.35	Germany—Church history	280.40943	BX4844-.5	Protestant churches—Germany
274.4	BR748	Celtic Church			
274.4	BR840-849	France—Church history	280.40944	BX4843	Protestant churches—France
274.4	BR794	Celtic Church			
274.6	BR1020-1029	Spain—Church history	280.40945	BX4847	Protestant churches—Italy
274.7	BR930-939	Russia—Church history	280.40946	BX4851	Protestant churches—Spain
274.8	BR970-1019	Scandinavia—Church history	280.4095	BX4857	Protestant churches—Asia
275	BR1060-1357	Asia—Church history	280.40972	BX4833	Protestant churches—Mexico
275.1	BR1280-1297	China—Church history			
275.19	BR1320-1337	Korea—Church history	280.409728	BX4833.5-4834	Protestant churches—Central America
275.2	BR1300-1317	Japan—Church history			
275.4	BR1150-1156	India—Church history			

Dewey	LC	Subject Heading	Dewey	LC	Subject Heading
280.409729	BX4835	Protestant churches—West Indies	283.0972092	BX5619-5620	Church of England—Biography
280.4098	BX4836	Protestant churches—South America	283.415	BX5410-5595	Church of Ireland
281.5	BX100-189	Eastern churches	283.41509	BX5500-5510	Church of Ireland—History
281.62	BX120-129	Armenian Church	283.415092	BX5590-5595	Church of Ireland—Biography
281.8	BT1440	Nestorians	283.42	BX5011-5740	Church of England
281.8	BX150-159	Nestorian Church	283.42	BX5115-5126	Church of England—Parties and movements
281.9	BX200-754	Orthodox Eastern Church	283.42	BX5127-5129.8	Church of England—Relations
281.943(6/9)	BX630-639	Orthodox Eastern Church—[Austria/Hungary]			
281.947	BX460-605	Orthodox Eastern Church	283.4205	BX5011	Church of England—Periodicals
281.94709	BX485-492	Orthodox Eastern Church—History	283.42025	BX5031	Church of England—Directories
281.9495	BX610-619	Orthodox Eastern Church—Greece	283.4209	BX5051-5101	Church of England—History
			283.42092	BX5197-5199	Church of England—Biography
282	BX800-4795	Catholic Church			
282.03	BX841	Catholic Church—Dictionaries	283.429	BX5596-5598	Church of England—Wales
			283.5	BX5661-5680.7	Church of England—Asia
282.05	BX800-806	Catholic Church—Periodicals	283.6	BX5681-5700.9	Church of England—Africa
			283.72	BX5601-5620	Church of England—Canada
282.06	BX808-816	Catholic Church—Societies, etc.	283.72	BX5610-5613	Church of England—Canada—History
282.08996073	BX1407.N4	Afro-American Catholics	283.73	BX5926-5928.5	Episcopal Church—Relations
282.09	BX940-1745	Catholic Church—History	283.7305	BX6051	Episcopal Church—Periodicals
282.092	BX4650-4705	Catholic Church—Biography			
282.0922	BX4654-4662	Martyrs—Legends	283.7308996073	BX5979	Afro-American Episcopalians
282.4	BX1490-1612	Catholic Church—Europe	283.7309	BX6065-6069	Episcopal Church—History
282.41	BX1491-1514	Catholic Church—Great Britain	283.7309	BX5879-5919	Episcopal Church—History
			283.73092	BX6091-6093	Episcopalians—Biography
282.43	BX1534-1539	Catholic Church—Germany	283.73092	BX5990-5995	Episcopalians—Biography
282.44	BX1528-1533	Catholic Church—France	283.73092	BX5800-6093	Episcopalians
282.45	BX1543-1548	Catholic Church—Italy	283.9(3/4)	BX5701-5720.8	Church of England—[New Zealand/Australia]
282.46	BX1583-1588	Catholic Church—Spain			
282.47	BX1558-1560	Catholic Church—Russia	284.1	BX8001-8080	Lutheran Church
282.5	BX1662-1670.7	Catholic Church—East Asia	284.104	BX8001	Lutheran Church—Periodicals
282.5	BX1615-1673	Catholic Church—Asia	284.109	BX8018-8063	Lutheran Church—History
282.56	BX1617-1636	Catholic Church—Middle East	284.1092	BX8079-8080	Lutherans—Biography
			284.14	BX8020-8040.5	Lutheran Church—Europe
282.6	BX1675-1682	Catholic Church—Africa	284.143	BX8020-8023	Lutheran Church—Germany
282.71	BX1419-1424	Catholic Church—Canada	284.173	BX8041-8061	Lutheran Church—United States
282.72	BX1427-1431	Catholic Church—Mexico			
282.728	BX1432-1447	Catholic Church—Central America	284.2	BX9401-9640	Calvinism
			284.2	BX9401-9640	Reformed Church
282.729	BX1448-1459	Catholic Church—West Indies	284.205	BX9401	Calvinism—Periodicals
			284.206	BX9403	Reformed Church—Societies, etc.
282.73	BX1404-1418	Catholic Church—United States	284.209	BX9415	Reformed Church—History
282.73	BX1407.A5	Americanism (Catholic controversy)	284.24	BX9430-9480	Reformed Church—Europe
			284.244	BX9450-9459	Reformed Church—France
282.73	BX4600-4644	Catholic Church—[By region or country]	284.2492	BX9470-9479	Reformed Church—Netherlands
282.8	BX1460-1489	Catholic Church—South America	284.2494	BX9430-9439	Reformed Church—Switzerland
282.9(3/4)	BX1685-1692	Catholic Church—[New Zealand/Australia]	284.25	BX9615	Reformed Church—Asia
			284.26	BX9618-9640	Reformed Church—Africa
283	BX5721-5740	Church of England—Oceania	284.271	BX9596-9598	Reformed Church—Canada
283	BX5001-5009	Anglican Communion	284.273	BX9495-9593	Reformed Church—United States
283.09	BX5005	Anglican Communion—History	284.3	BX4900-4906	Lollards
			284.3	BX4913-4918	Hussites

Dewey	LC	Subject Heading	Dewey	LC	Subject Heading
284.3	BX4929-4946	Anabaptists	285.9	BX9301-9359	Puritans
284.4	BX4872-4883	Waldenses	285.909(4-9)	BX9331-9359	Puritans—[By region or country]
284.5	BX9450-9459	Huguenots			
284.6	BX8551-8593	Moravians	286.(1-5)	BX6201-6495	Baptists
284.606	BX8553	Moravians—Societies, etc.	286.(1-5)03	BX6211	Baptists—Dictionaries
284.609	BX8565-8569	Moravians—History	286.(1-5)06	BX6205	Baptists—Societies, etc.
284.6092	BX8591-8593	Moravians—Biography	286.(1-5)09	BX6231-6328	Baptists—History
284.8	BX1301	Schism, The Great Western, 1378-1417	286.(1-5)4	BX6275-6310	Baptists—Europe
			286.(1-5)5	BX6315-6316	Baptists—Asia
284.84	BX4718.5-4735	Jansenists	286.(1-5)6	BX6320-6322	Baptists—Africa
284.9	BX6195-6197	Arminianism	286.(1-5)71	BX6251-6253	Baptists—Canada
285	BX8901-9225	Presbyterian Church	286.(1-5)73	BX6235-6249	Baptists—United States
285.(1-2)	BX8901-9225	Presbyterianism	286.(1-5)8	BX6271-6273	Baptists—South America
285.(1-2)06	BX8905	Presbyterian Church—Societies, etc.	286.(1-5)9(5-6)	BX6327-6328	Baptists—Oceania
			286.(1-5)94	BX6325-6326	Baptists—Australia
285.(1-2)09	BX8930-9169	Presbyterian Church—History	286.1	BX6388.3-.38	Regular Baptists
			286.1092	BX6493-6495	Baptists—Biography
285.(1-2)4	BX9050-9140	Presbyterian Church—Europe	286.3	BX6390-6408	Seventh-Day Baptists
285.(1-2)41	BX9052-9105	Presbyterian Church—Great Britain	286.6	BX7301-7343	Disciples of Christ
			286.63	BX6751-6793	General Convention of the Christian Church
285.(1-2)5	BX9150-9151	Presbyterian Church—Asia	286.7	BX6101-6193	Millerite movement
285.(1-2)6	BX9160-9162	Presbyterian Church—Africa	286.7	BX6101-6193	Adventists
285.(1-2)71	BX9001-9003	Presbyterian Church—Canada	286.709	BX6115-6117	Adventists—History
			286.7092	BX6191-6193	Adventists—Biography
285.(1-2)8	BX9011-9043	Presbyterian Church—Latin America	286.732	BX6151-6155	Seventh-Day Adventists
			287	BX8901-9225	Calvinistic Methodists
285.(1-2)9(3-6)	BX9168-9169	Presbyterian Church—[New Zealand/Australia/Oceania]	287	BX8201-8495	Methodist Church
			287	BX8201-8495	Methodism
285.092	BX9220-9225	Presbyterians—Biography	287.(1-8)4	BX8275-8310	Methodist Church—Europe
285.1	BX8950-8958	Presbyterian Church in the U.S.A.	287.(1-8)41	BX8276-8293	Methodist Church—Great Britain
285.1	BX8960-8968	Presbyterian Church in the U.S.	287.(1-8)5	BX8315-8316	Methodist Church—Asia
			287.(1-8)6	BX8320-8322	Methodist Church—Africa
285.136	BX8990-8998.38	Reformed Presbyterian Church	287.(1-8)71	BX8251-8253	Methodist Church—Canada
			287.(1-8)73	BX8235-8249	Methodist Church—United States
285.233	BX9075-9095	Church of Scotland			
285.733	BX9551-9593	Reformed Church in the United States	287.(1-8)8	BX8271-8273	Methodist Church—South America
285.8	BX7101-7260	Congregational churches	287.(1-8)9(3/4)	BX8325-8326	Methodist Church—[New Zealand/Australia]
285.8	BX7101-7260	Congregationalism			
285.806	BX7106-7109	Congregational churches—Congresses	287.06	BX8207	Methodist Church—Societies, etc.
285.806	BX7105	Congregational churches—Societies, etc.	287.09	BX8231-8328	Methodist Church—History
			287.092	BX8491-8495	Methodists—Biography
285.809	BX7131-7228	Congregational churches—History	287.63(2-3)	BX8380-8389	Methodist Episcopal Church
			287.8	BX8435-8473	Afro-American Methodists
285.8092	BX7259-7260	Congregationalist—Biography	287.96	HV4330-4470.7	Salvation Army
			287.96	BX9701-9743	Salvation Army
285.84	BX7175-7210	Congregational churches—Europe	289.1	BX9801-9869	Unitarian Universalist churches
285.85	BX7215-7216	Congregational churches—Asia	289.106	BX9805-9807	Unitarian Universalist churches—Congresses
285.86	BX7220-7222	Congregational churches—Africa	289.109	BX9831-9835	Unitarian Universalist churches—History
285.871	BX7151-7153	Congregational churches—Canada	289.1092	BX9867-9869	Unitarians
			289.133	BX9801-9869	Unitarianism
285.873	BX7135-7149	Congregational churches—United States	289.134	BX9901-9969	Universalism
			289.134	BX9901-9996	Restorationism
285.894	BX7225-7226	Congregational churches—Australia	289.13406	BX9905-9907	Universalism—Congresses
			289.13409	BX9931-9935	Universalism—History

Dewey	LC	Subject Heading	Dewey	LC	Subject Heading
289.134092	BX9967-9969	Universalists	289.9	BX7990.H6	Snake cults (Holiness churches)
289.1(4-9)	BX9833-9835	Unitarianism—[By region or country]	289.9	BX7433	Dukhobors
289.173	BX9833	Unitarianism—United States	289.92	BX8525-8528	Jehovah's Witnesses
289.3	BX8601-8695	Mormon Church	289.94	BX8762-8780	Pentecostal churches
289.309	BX8611-8617	Mormon Church—History	291.447	BL590	Fasts and feasts
289.32	BX8627.A3-Z	Lamanites (Mormon Church)	291.13	BL300-325	Mythology
289.32	BX8628.A5	Doctrine and covenants stories	291.13	GN799.R4	Religion, Prehistoric
			291.13094	BL689-980	Mythology, European
289.32	BX8621-8631	Mormon Church—Sacred books	291.144	BF1585-1623	Shamanism
			291.144	BL2370.S5	Shamanism
289.4	BX8701-8749	New Jerusalem Church	291.17	BL60	Religion and sociology
289.405	BX8701	New Jerusalem Church—Periodicals	291.17	BL65.C8	Religion and culture
			291.17	BL55	Religion and civilization
289.406	BX8705	New Jerusalem Church—Congresses	291.175	BL239-265	Religion and science
			291.175	BL65.M4	Medicine—Religious aspects
289.409	BX8715-8719	New Jerusalem Church—History	291.175	BL29	Religious literature
289.4092	BX8747-8749	New Jerusalem Church—Biography	291.175	BL53	Psychology, Religious
289.5	BX6901-6997	Christian Science	291.177	BL65.S8	Religion and state
289.506	BX6905-6907	Christian Science—Congresses	291.177	BL65.P7	Religion and politics
			291.177	BL65.L33	Religion and law
289.506	BX6903	Christian Science—Societies, etc.	291.177	BL65.C58	Civil rights—Religious aspects
289.509	BX6931-6935	Christian Science—History	291.17834	BL65.E68	Equality—Religious aspects
289.5092	BX6990-6996	Christian Science—Biography	291.17834	BL65.R3	Race—Religious aspects
			291.178344	BL458	Sexism in religion
289.(6-7)	BX4950-4951	Plain People	291.21	BL473	Gods
289.605	BX7601	Society of Friends—Periodicals	291.21	BL525	Transmigration
			291.21	GN471	Animism
289.605	BX7601-7795	Society of Friends	291.21	GN472	Fetishism
289.606	BX7606.5-7608	Society of Friends—Congresses	291.211	GN491	Totems
			291.211	GN489	Totemism
289.609	BX7630-7728	Society of Friends—History	291.2114	BL325.M6	Mother goddesses
289.6092	BX7790-7795	Quakers—Biography	291.212	BL438	Sun worship
289.64	BX7675-7710	Society of Friends—Europe	291.212	BL439-443	Animal worship
289.641	BX7676-7693	Society of Friends—Great Britain	291.212	BL441	Serpent worship
			291.212	BL438	Moon worship
289.65	BX7715-7716	Society of Friends—Asia	291.212	BL435-457	Nature worship
289.66	BX7720-7723	Society of Friends—Africa	291.212	BL325.M63	Mountain gods
289.671	BX7650-7653	Society of Friends—Canada	291.212	BL444	Tree worship
289.673	BX7635-7649	Society of Friends—United States	291.212	BL447	Mountain worship
			291.212	BL453	Fire-worshipers
289.68	BX7671-7673	Society of Friends—South America	291.213	BL467	Ancestor worship
			291.213	BL465	Emperor worship
			291.2130937	DG124	Emperor worship, Rome
289.694	BX7725-7726	Society of Friends—Australia	291.215	BL477	Angels
289.709	BX8115-8119	Mennonites—History	291.216	BL480	Satanism
289.7092	BX8101-8143	Mennonites	291.216	BL480	Demonology
289.7092	BX8129.043	Old Order Mennonites	291.216	BL480	Devil
289.7092	BX8141-8143	Mennonites—Biography	291.218	BL485	Idols and images—Worship
289.73092	BX8129.A5-.A6	Amish	291.22	BL290	Soul
289.771	BX8118.5-.7	Mennonites—Canada	291.22	BL256	Man (Theology)
289.773	BX8116-8118	Mennonites—United States	291.23	BL500-547	Eschatology
289.8	BX9751-9793	Shakers	291.23	BL545	Hell
289.806	BX9755	Shakers—Congresses	291.23	BL535-547	Future life
289.809	BX9765-9769	Shakers—History	291.23	BL503	Resurrection
289.809(4-9)	BX9766-9769	Shakers—[By region or country]	291.237	BL515	Reincarnation
			291.3	BL550-620	Worship
289.8092	BX9791-9793	Shakers—Biography	291.3	GN470-474	Worship
289.80973	BX9766-9768	Shakers—United States	291.3	GN475.3	Magic

Dewey	LC	Subject Heading	Dewey	LC	Subject Heading
291.31	BL325.H4	Healing gods	292.2113	BL820.06	Ops (Roman deity)
291.32	BL613	Oracles	292.2114	BL820.E5	Eileithyia (Greek deity)
291.32	BL613	Divination	292.2114	BL820.D54	Diktynna (Greek deity)
291.34	BL570	Sacrifice	292.2114	BL820.M6	Athena (Greek deity)
291.35	BL580-586	Shrines	292.2114	BL820.C5	Ceres (Roman deity)
291.36	BL619.S3	Sacred meals	292.2114	BL820.M65	Mother goddesses, Greek
291.36	BL590	Fasts and feasts	292.2114	BL820.C5	Demeter (Greek deity)
291.37	BL406.C7	Crosses	292.2114	BL820.P7	Persephone (Greek deity)
291.37	BL604.V2	V symbol	292.2114	BL820.F7	Fortuna (Roman diety)
291.37	BL604.S8	Swastika	292.28	BL735	Hell
291.37	BL604.C5	Circle—Religious aspects	292.61	BL815.V4	Vestals
291.37	BL603	Emblems	293	BL830-875	Germanic peoples—Religion
291.37	BL600-620	Symbolism	293.13	BL870.F28	Fafnir (Germanic mythology)
291.38	BL600-619	Ritual	293.2113	BL870.B3	Balder (Norse deity)
291.38	BL600-619	Rites and ceremonies	294	BL2000-2016	Mythology, Indic
291.38	GN473	Rites and ceremonies	294.3	BQ1-9999	Buddhism
291.4	BL624-627	Religious life	294.305	BQ1-10	Buddhism—Periodicals
291.42	BL53	Experience (Religion)	294.309	BQ251-799	Buddhism—History
291.42	BL626	Ecstasy	294.30901	BQ287-296	Buddhism—History—To
291.422	BL625	Mysticism			ca. 100 A.D.
291.43	BL560	Prayers	294.3092	BQ840-845	Buddhists—Biography
291.43	BL560	Prayer	294.3094	BQ700-709	Buddhism—Europe
291.435	BL627	Meditation	294.3095	BQ610-699	Buddhism—East Asia
291.447	BL625	Asceticism	294.30951	BQ620-649	Buddhism—China
291.447	BJ1491	Asceticism	294.309519	BQ650-669	Buddhism—Korea
291.447	BL590	Fasts and feasts	294.30952	BQ670-699	Buddhism—Japan
291.5	BJ47	Religion and ethics	294.30954	BQ330-349	Buddhism—India
291.5	BJ1188-1295	Religious ethics	294.3095493	BQ350-379	Buddhism—Sri Lanka
291.5622	BL65.J87	Religion and justice	294.3095496	BQ380-396	Buddhism—Nepal
291.61	BL635	Priests	294.30958	BQ570-609	Buddhism—Asia, Central
291.61	BL475	Messiah	294.30959	BQ440-509	Indochina—Religion
291.65	BL632	Religious communities	294.309591	BQ416-439	Buddhism—Burma
291.82	BL70-71	Sacred books	294.309593	BQ550-568	Buddhism—Thailand
292.07	BL800-820	Rome—Religion	294.309595	BQ540-549	Buddhism—Malaysia
292.08	BL780-795	Greece—Religion	294.309598	BQ510-539	Buddhism—Indonesia
292.13	BL820.P5	Perseus (Greek mythology)	294.3096	BQ710-719	Buddhism—Africa
292.13	BL700-820	Mythology, Classical	294.309(7-8)	BQ720-760	Buddhism—America
292.13	BL820.P4	Pegasus (Greek mythology)	294.30971	BQ740-749	Buddhism—Canada
292.13	BL820.T6	Titans (Mythology)	294.30973	BQ730-739	Buddhism—United States
292.13	BL820.G7	Gorgons (Greek mythology)	294.3099(3-6)	BQ770-799	Buddhism—Oceania
292.13	BL820.P	Pandora (Greek mythology)	294.32	BQ4170	Buddhism—Catechisms
292.13	BL820.M37	Medea (Greek mythology)	294.32	BQ4170	Buddhism—Creeds
292.13	BL820.A6	Amazons	294.333	BQ5741-5755	Mythology, Buddhist
292.13	BL820.F8	Erinyes (Greek mythology)	294.3372	BQ4600-4610	Buddhism—Relations
292.13	BL820.D	Dryads	294.3375	BL1493	Zen Buddhism—Psychology
292.13	BL820.A8	Jason (Greek mythology)	294.3375	BQ4570.P76	Buddhism—Psychology
292.13	BL820.C	Centaurs	294.3378	BQ5851-5899	Buddhism—Charities
292.13	BL820.M63	Minotaur (Greek mythology)	294.33783	BQ5851-5899	Buddhism and social
292.13	BL820.A63	Amycus (Greek mythology)			problems
292.13	BL820.D25	Daedalus (Greek mythology)	294.3378344	BQ4570.W6	Woman (Buddhism)
292.13	BL820.L25	Ladon (Greek mythology)	294.34	BQ4240	Causation (Buddhism)
292.13	BL820.H5	Heracles (Greek mythology)	294.34	BQ4195-4250	Dharma (Buddhism)
292.13	BL820.G8	Graces, The	294.342	BQ5485-5525	Five Precepts (Buddhism)
292.13	BL820.F8	Furies (Roman mythology)	294.342	BQ4061-4570	Buddhism—Doctrines
292.2113	BL820.B2	Dionysia	294.342	BQ4360	Compassion (Buddhism)
292.2113	BL820.A4	Aesculapius (Greek deity)	294.342	BQ5485-5530	Buddhist precepts
292.2113	BL820.A25	Adonis (Greek deity)	294.342	BQ5485-5530	Buddhism—Doctrines
292.2113	BL870.S29	Saturn (Roman deity)	294.342	BQ4050	Buddhism—Apologetic
292.2113	BL820.P2	Pan (Greek deity)			works
292.2113	BL820.J8	Jupiter (Roman deity)	294.34209	BQ4080-4125	Buddhism—Doctrines—
292.2113	BL820.M26	Marsyas (Greek diety)			History

23

Dewey	LC	Descriptor	Dewey	LC	Subject Heading
294.34211	BQ4690.M3	Maitreya (Buddhist deity)	294.375	BQ141-209	Buddhist education
294.34211	BQ4750.D33	Dakini (Buddhist deity)	294.382	BQ1100-3340	Tripitaka
294.34211	BQ4750.Y35	Yama (Buddhist deity)	294.382	BQ1100-3340	Buddhism—Sacred books
294.34211	BQ4860.A4	Acala (Buddhist deity)	294.39	BQ7530-7950	Dge-lugs-pa (Sect)
294.34211	BQ4890.D33-.D334	Dam-tshig-rdo-rje (Buddhist deity)	294.39	BQ7669	Bka'-rgyud-pa (Sect)
			294.39	BQ8000-9800	Buddhist sects
294.3423	BQ4475-4525	Eschatology, Buddhist	294.39	BQ8000-8049	Abhayagiri (Sect)
294.343	BQ7982.4	Bonpo incantations	294.39	BQ7960-7989	Bonpo (Sect)
294.3435	BL1477.8.D4	Temples, Buddhist—Dedication	294.391	BQ7100-7285	Theravada Buddhism
			294.392	BQ7300-7522	Mahayana Buddhism
294.3435	BQ6300-6388	Buddhist shrines	294.3923	BQ7530-7950	Lamaism
294.3435	BQ6460	Gautama Buddha—Shrines	294.3926	BQ8500-8769	Pure Land Buddhism
294.3435	BQ5130-5137	Temples, Buddhist	294.3927	BQ9250-9519	Zen Buddhism
294.34351	BQ6400-6495	Buddhist pilgrims and pilgrimages	294.4	BL1300-1365	Jains
			294.4	BL1300-1365	Jainism
294.3437	BQ5070-5075	Buddhism—Liturgical objects	294.42	BL1356-1375	Jainism—Doctrines
294.3437	BQ5070-5075	Altars, Buddhist	294.43	BL1376-1380	Worship (Jainism)
294.3437	BQ4570.A4	Amulets (Buddhism)	294.434	BL1375.P	Penance (Jainism)
294.3437	BQ4570.A4	Charms (Buddhism)	294.437	BL1377.3	Jaina mantras
294.3438	BL1477.8.F8	Funeral rites and ceremonies, Buddhist	294.438	BL1355.5	Fasts and feasts—Jainism
			294.4422	BL1378.8	Mysticism—Jainism
294.3438	BQ5035-5065	Chants (Buddhist)	294.4436	BL1375.Y63	Yoga (Jainism)
294.3438	BQ5005	Confirmation (Buddhist rite)	294.482	BL1310-1314.2	Jainism—Sacred books
294.3438	BQ4965-5030	Buddhism—Rituals	294.493	BL1380.D	Digambara (Jaina sect)
294.3438	BQ7699.G36	Gcod (Buddhist rite)	294.5	BL1241.46	Brahmans
294.3438	BQ7982.3	Gcod (Bonpo rite)	294.5	BL1100-1270	Hinduism
294.3438	BQ5700-5720	Fasts and feasts—Buddhism	294.5	BL1100-1245	Brahmanism
294.344	BQ4330	Bodhisattva stages (Mahayana Buddhism)	294.5	BL2000-2030	Hinduism
			294.513	BL1225.M	Manus (Hindu mythology)
294.344	BQ5595-5630	Devotion (Buddhism)	294.517	BL1215.S64	Sociology, Hindu
294.344	BQ4965-5030	Buddhism—Customs and practices	294.5175	BL2015.K3	Karma
			294.52	BL1213.32-1215	Hinduism—Doctrines
294.3443	BQ5595-5630	Prayer—Buddhism	294.5211	BL1214.32.B53	Bhakti
294.34433	BQ5535-5594	Buddhism—Prayer-books and devotions	294.5211	BL1200-1225	God (Hinduism)
			294.52113	BL1225.A42	Adityas (Hindu deities)
294.3444	BQ9288	Spiritual life—Zen Buddhism	294.52113	BL1225.D3	Dattatreya (Hindu deity)
294.3444	BQ5360-5680	Religious life—Buddhism	294.52113	BL1225.D48	Devanarayana (Hindu deity)
294.34447	BQ6200-6240	Asceticism—Buddhism	294.52113	BL1225.A	Aatimna (Hindu deity)
294.35	BJ1289.5.Y6	Youth, Buddhist—Conduct of life	294.52114	BL1225.D8	Durga (Hindu deity)
			294.52114	BL1225.A4	Aditi (Hindu deity)
294.35	BJ1289	Buddhist ethics	294.52114	BL1216	Goddesses, Hindu
294.35	BQ4401-4430	Virtues (Buddhism)	294.5213	BL1171	Hindu saints
294.35	BQ4425-4430	Vice (Buddhism)	294.5213	BL1171	Alvars
294.361	BQ7930	Dalai lamas	294.522	BL1215.S8	Soul (Hinduism)
294.361	BQ5140-5355	Priests, Buddhist	294.522	BL1215.M3	Man (Hinduism)
294.363	BQ4670-4690	Buddhas	294.53	BL1226	Worship (Hinduism)
294.363	BQ935	Gautama Buddha—Enlightenment	294.534	BL1236.76.S23	Sacrifice
			294.535	BL1243.72-.78	Temples, Hindu
294.363	BQ922	Gautama Buddha—Footprints	294.5351	BL1239.32	Hindu pilgrims and pilgrimages
294.363	BQ4180	Buddha (The concept)	294.536	BL1213.D87	Durga-puja (Hindu festival)
294.363	BQ938	Gautama Buddha—Date of death	294.538	BL1239.72-.82	Fasts and feasts—Hinduism
			294.538	BL1226.2	Chants (Hindu)
294.365	BQ12-93	Buddhism—Societies, etc.	294.5422	BL1215.M9	Mysticism—Hinduism
294.3657	BL1478	Profession (Buddhist monastic orders)	294.544	BL1228	Religious life—Hinduism
294.3657	BQ6001-6160	Monasticism and religious orders, Buddhist	294.5441	BL1226.82.M3	Marriage customs and rites, Hindu
			294.5447	BL1215.F3	Fasting (Hinduism)
294.372	BQ5901-5975	Buddhism—Missions	294.55	BL1245.A1	Hindu sects
294.375	BQ171-199	Buddhist education of children	294.5514	BL1282.2-.292	Shaktism
			294.5514	BL1141.2-1142.6	Tantrism

Dewey	LC	Subject Heading	Dewey	LC	Subject Heading
294.5657	BL1238	Monasticism and religious orders, Hindu	296.0972	BM230-232	Judaism—Mexico
			296.09728	BM233-247	Judaism—Central America
294.5921	BL1112.2	Vedas	296.09729	BM248-260	Judaism—West Indies
294.6	BL2017-2018.7	Sikhism	296.0973	BM205-225	Judaism—United States
294.6	BL2020.S5	Sikhs	296.098	BM261-289	Judaism—South America
294.682	BL2017.2-.4	Sikhism—Sacred books	296.099(3/4)	BM443-445	Judaism—[New Zealand/ Australia]
294.69	BL2018.7.K44	Khalsa (Sect)			
294.69	BL2018.7	Sikh sects	296.099(5-6)	BM447-449	Judaism—Oceania
295	BL1500-1590	Zorastrianism	296.1	BM495-532	Rabbinical literature
295	BL1500-1590	Parsees	296.12	BM500-509	Talmud
295.82	BL1510-1525	Zoroastrianism—Sacred books	296.120092	BM177	Tannaim
			296.14	BM511-518	Midrash
296	BM	Judaism	296.16	BM525	Cabala
296.025	BM55-65	Judaism—Directories	296.18	BM729.S85	Summer (Jewish law)
296.03	BM50	Judaism—Dictionaries	296.19	BM516-.5	Aggada
296.05	BM11	Judaism—Periodicals	296.3	BM600-603	Judaism—Doctrines
296.09	BM150-449	Judaism—History	296.3	BM945	Samaritan theology
296.09014	BM165-178	Judaism—History—To 70 A.D.	296.311	BM610	God (Judaism)
			296.31172	BM612.5	Covenants—Judaism
296.0902	BM180-185	Judaism—History— Medieval and early modern period, 425-1789	296.32	BM630	Sin (Judaism)
			296.32	BM729.F3	Faith (Judaism)
			296.336	BM615	Jewish messianic movements
296.09033	BM190-199	Judaism—History— Modern period, 1750-	296.336	BM615	Messiah—Judaism
296.092	BM652	Rabbis	296.36	BJ1279-1287	Ethics, Jewish
296.094	BM290-376	Judaism—Europe	296.36	BJ1286.G64	Golden rule
296.0941	BM292-305	Judaism—Great Britain	296.4	BM656-685	Worship (Judaism)
296.0943	BM316-318	Judaism—Germany	296.41	BM685	Sabbath
296.09436	BM307-309	Judaism—Austria	296.43	BM970	Fasts and feasts— Samaritan religion
296.09438	BM337-339	Judaism—Poland			
296.0944	BM313-315	Judaism—France	296.43	BM690	Religious calendars— Judaism
296.0945	BM322-324	Judaism—Italy			
296.0946	BM354-356	Judaism—Spain	296.43	BM690-720	Fasts and feasts—Judaism
296.09469	BM328-330	Judaism—Portugal	296.431	BM693.H5	High Holidays
296.0947	BM331-333	Judaism—Russia	296.4315	BM695.N5	Rosh ha-Shanah
296.0948	BM340-353	Judaism—Scandinavia	296.432	BM675.A8	Yom Kippur
296.09481	BM348-350	Judaism—Norway	296.432	BM695.A8	Yom Kippur
296.09485	BM351-353	Judaism—Sweden	296.435	BM657.H3	Hanukkah lamp
296.09489	BM342-344	Judaism—Denmark	296.435	BM695.H3	Hanukkah
296.094897	BM334-336	Judaism—Finland	296.435	BM657.M35	Menorah
296.09492	BM325-327	Judaism—Netherlands	296.437	BM675.P3	Passover
296.09493	BM310-312	Judaism—Belgium	296.437	BM695.P3	Passover
296.09494	BM357-359	Judaism—Switzerland	296.437	BM695.P35	Seder
296.09495	BM319-321	Judaism—Greece	296.4391	BM720.S2	Sabbatical year (Judaism)
296.094971	BM373-375	Judaism—Yugoslavia	296.4424	BM707-.4	Confirmation (Jewish rite)
296.09498	BM370-372	Judaism—Romania	296.444	BM713	Marriage customs and rites, Jewish
296.09499	BM364-366	Judaism—Bulgaria			
296.095	BM377-431	Judaism—Asia	296.445	BM712	Mourning customs, Jewish
296.0951	BM423-425	Judaism—China	296.45	BM669	Prayer—Judaism
296.0952	BM426-428	Judaism—Japan	296.45	BM675.D3	Siddurim
296.0953	BM393-395	Judaism—Arabia	296.4615	BM659.S3	Scribes, Jewish
296.0954	BM406-410	Judaism—India	296.4615	BM657.T6	Torah scrolls
296.0955	BM396-398	Judaism—Iran	296.462	BM658.2	Cantors (Judaism)
296.09567	BM386.4-.6	Judaism—Iraq	296.47	BM730	Jewish preaching
296.09569(1/4)	BM387-389	Judaism—[Syria/Palestine]	296.4731	BM746	High Holiday sermons
296.095694	BM390-392	Judaism—Israel	296.4737	BM747.P3	Passover sermons
296.09581	BM400	Judaism—Afghanistan	296.481	BM693.P5	Pilgrim Festivals (Judaism)
296.096	BM432-440	Judaism—Africa	296.61	BM652.5	Pastoral counseling (Judaism)
296.0962	BM434-436	Judaism—Egypt			
296.0968	BM437	Judaism—South Africa	296.65	BM653-655	Synagogues
296.0971	BM227-229	Judaism—Canada	296.67	BM1	Judaism—Societies, etc.

25

Dewey	LC	Subject Heading	Dewey	LC	Subject Heading
296.67	BM21-30	Judaism—Congresses	297.352	BP187.3	Muslim pilgrims and pilgrimages—Saudi Arabia—Mecca
296.68	BM70-135	Jews—Education			
296.7	BM723	Jewish way of life			
296.7	BM650-747	Judaism—Customs and practices	297.362	BP183.6	Ramadan sermons
			297.37	BP184.25	Islamic preaching
296.72	BM729.C6	Consolation (Judaism)	297.37	BP183.6	Islamic sermons
296.73	BM710	Jews—Dietary laws	297.38	BP184.4	Purity, Ritual—Islam
296.8	BM175	Jewish sects	297.38	BM184	Judaism—Liturgy
296.81	BM185-.4	Karaites	297.382	BP178	Prayer—Islam
296.812	BM175.P4	Pharisees	297.385	BP184.9.F8	Funeral rites and ceremonies, Islamic
296.813	BM175.S2	Sadducees			
296.814	BM175.E8	Essenes	297.39	BP190.5.A5	Amulets (Islam)
296.82	BM199.S3	Sabbathaians	297.4	BP189	Sufism
296.82092	BX9680.S3	Sabbatarians	297.4	BP189	Mysticism—Islam
296.8332	BM198	Hasidism	297.4092	BP189.33	Muslim saints
296.834	BM197.8	Humanistic Judaism	297.4382	BP189.62	Sufi meditations
296.8342	BM197.5	Conservative Judaism	297.5	BJ1291-1292	Islamic ethics
297	BP1-223	Islam	297.53	BP179	Fasting (Islam)
297.03	BP40	Islam—Dictionaries	297.53	BP186	Fasts and feasts—Islam
297.05	BP1-9	Islam—Periodicals	297.57	BP188	Religious life—Islam
297.122	BP100-134	Koran	297.57	BP188.3.Y6	Youth, Muslin—Religious life
297.12209	BP134.E5	Egypt in the Koran			
297.122092	BP133.7.A3	Adam (Biblical figure) in the Koran	297.574	BP170.5	Muslim converts
			297.574	BP170.5	Muslim converts from Christianity
297.122092	BP133.7.M67	Moses (Biblical leader) in the Koran			
			297.576	BP190.5.A75	Asceticism—Islam
297.122092	BP133.7.D38	David, King of Israel, in the Koran	297.577	BP190.5.S4	Sex—Religious aspects—Islam
297.12286413	BP134.F58	Food in the Koran	297.61	BP184	Pastoral theology (Islam)
297.124	BP135	Hadith	297.63	BP75-77.5	Muhammad, Prophet, d. 632
297.124	BP193.25-.28	Hadith (Shiites)	297.63	BP75.8	Muhammad, Prophet, d. 632—Miracles
297.18	BP137-.5	Legends, Islamic			
297.2	BP165.5-166.94	Islam—Doctrines	297.65	BP10-15	Islam—Congresses
297.21	BP166.89	Spirits (Islam)	297.72	BP182	Jihad
297.21	BP166.89	Discernment of spirits (Islam)	297.74	BP170.85	Dawah (Islam)
			297.77	BP42-48	Islamic religious education
297.211	BP166.2	Word of God (Islam)	297.81	BP175.S8	Sunnites
297.211	BP166.2	God (Islam)	297.82	BP193	Shiites
297.2115	BP166.6	Revelation (Islam)	297.822	BP195.A8	Assassins (Ismailites)
297.215	BP166.89	Angels (Islam)	297.85	BL1695	Druzes
297.216	BP166.89	Demonology, Islamic	297.87	BP62.N4	Muslims, Black
297.216	BP166.89	Devil (Islam)	297.87	BP221-223	Black Muslims
297.22	BP166.75	Sin (Islam)	297.92	BP340	Babism
297.22	BP166.78	Faith (Islam)	297.93	BP300-395	Bahai faith
297.22	BP166.7	Man (Islam)	297.93435	BP380	Bahai meditations
297.225	BP166.73	Soul (Islam)	299.14122	BL2035	Pakistan—Religion
297.227	BP166.3	Predestination—Islam	299.15	BL1590.R5	Rider-gods
297.227	BP166.3	Free will and determinism (Islam)	299.155	BL2270-2280	Iran—Religion
			299.2	BL1600-1710	Semites—Religion
297.23	BP166.83	Resurrection (Islam)	299.21	BL1625.P3	Panbabylonism
297.23	BP166.87	Paradise (Islam)	299.21	BL1625.M37	Marduk (Babylonian deity)
297.23	BP166.8	Eschatology, Islamic	299.26	BL1671	Baal (Deity)
297.23	BP166.85	Judgment Day (Islam)	299.3	BL2462	Africa, North—Religion
297.246	BP166.4	Prophets, Pre-Islamic	299.31	BL2450.A89	Atum (Egyptian deity)
297.27	BP173.25-.45	Sociology, Islamic	299.31	BL2450.A45	Amon (Egyptian deity)
297.3	BP184.2	Worship (Islam)	299.31	BL2420-2460	Egypt—Religion
297.31	BP176	Pillars of Islam	299.31	BL2450.N45	Neith (Egyptian deity)
297.35	BP187	Muslim pilgrims and pilgrimages	299.31	BL2450.G6	Gods, Egyptian
			299.31	BL2450.O7	Osiris (Egyptian deity)
297.35	BP194.6	Shiite shrines	299.31	BL2450.S27	Satis (Egyptian deity)
			299.5	BL1000-2370	Mythology, Oriental

Dewey	LC	Subject Heading	Dewey	LC	Subject Heading
299.5	BL2050-2150	Asia, Southeastern—Religion	301.071	HM45-47	Sociology—Study and teaching
299.51	BL1800-1975	China—Religion	301.072	GN42-46	Anthropology—Research
299.512	BL1830-1875	Confucianism	301.09	HM19-22	Sociology—History
299.514	BL1900-1940	Taoism	301.09	HM104	Historical sociology
299.5145	BL1290.8	Taoist ethics	301.092	GN20-21	Anthropologists
299.56	BL2200-2228	Japan—Religion	301.7	GN406-498	Society, Primitive
299.56	BL2211.E46	Emperor worship—Japanese	302	HM251-291	Social psychology
299.56	BL2211.D33	Daikokuten (Japanese diety)	302	HM132	Interpersonal relations
299.56	BL2211.E24	Ebisu (Japanese deity)	302.015195	HM253	Sociometry
299.561	BL2216-2227.8	Shinto	302.12	BF323.S63	Social perception
299.56135	BL2224.9-2225.3	Shinto shrines	302.14	RC455.4.S67	Social adjustment
299.56136	BL2224.3	Shinto devotional calendars	302.14	HN49.V64	Voluntarism
299.56138	BL2224.2	Shinto—Rituals	302.2	GN799.T73	Communication, Prehistoric
299.56182	BL2217-.5	Shinto—Sacred books	302.2	P95.8	Communication policy
299.5619	BL2222.H5	Hinomoto (Sect)	302.2	P87-96	Communication
299.6	BL2400-2490	Africa—Religion	302.208996073	P94.5.A37	Afro-Americans—Communication
299.675	BL2490	Voodooism			
299.6869	BL2480.Y6	Egungun (Cult)	302.222	GR780-790	Flower language
299.6869	BL2480.Y6	Sopono (Cult)	302.23	TR835	Microfilm readers
299.7	E98.R3	Indians of North America—Religion	302.23	P95.8	Mass media policy
			302.23	P96.A83	Audiences
299.74	E98.D2	Sun dance	302.23089	P94.5.M55	Ethnic mass media
299.74	E98.D2	Eagle dance	302.2308996073	P94.5.A37	Afro-American mass media
299.74	E98.R2	Wolf ritual	302.2308996073	P94.5.A37	Afro-Americans in mass media
299.8	BL2580-2592	South America—Religion			
299.891	BL2590.B7	Afro-Brazilian cults	302.2308996073	P94.5.A37	Afro-Americans and mass media
299.92	BL2600-2630	Oceania—Religion			
299.924	BL2620.P6	Mythology, Polynesian	302.3	HM291	Social interaction
299.9294	BL740-760	Etruscans—Religion	302.32082	HQ1201-1216	Women—Socialization
299.9295	BL1616.E54	Enki (Sumarian deity)	302.33	HM281-283	Mobs
299.93	BF638-648	New Thought	302.34	GN486.3	Friendship
299.93	BP605.G68	Great White Brotherhood	302.34	HM132.5	Friendship—Sociological aspects
299.93	BP605.N48	New Age movement			
299.934	BP573.R5	Reincarnation	302.34083	HQ784.F7	Friendship in children
299.934	BP500-585	Theosophy	302.4	HM291	Social interaction
299.935	BP595-597	Anthroposophy	302.54	HM136-146	Individualism
299.957	BL2230-2240	Korea—Religion	303.32	GN510	Socialization
300	H	Social sciences	303.32	HQ783	Socialization
300.1	H61-.4	Social sciences—Methodology	303.34	HM141	Leadership
300.5	H1-8	Social sciences—Periodicals	303.34	HM259	Social influence
300.6	H21-29	Social sciences—Congresses	303.36	HM271-276	Authority
			303.372	HM216	Social ethics
300.71	H62-.5	Social sciences—Study and teaching	303.375	HM263	Propaganda
			303.38	HM261	Public opinion
300.72	H62-.5	Social sciences—Research	303.380723	HM261	Public opinion polls
300.724	H62	Social sciences—Experiments	303.4	HM101-121	Social change
			303.44	CB155	Progress
300.9	H51-53	Social sciences—History	303.44	HM101-121	Progress
300.92	H57-59	Social sciences—Biography	303.482	GN345.65	Cross-cultural orientation
301	GN	Anthropology	303.482	GN345.6	Intercultural communication
301	GN	Man	303.482	JV6342	Assimilation (Sociology)
301	HM	Sociology	303.482	HM258	Intercultural communication
301.01	GN33-34.3	Anthropology—Methodology	303.483	T14.5	Technology—Social aspects
301.01	HM24-37	Sociology—Methodology	303.483	T174.5	Technology assessment
301.028	GN34.3.A35	Aerial photography in anthropology	303.483	Q175.5	Science—Social aspects
			303.4833	HC79.I55	Information technology
301.03	HM17	Sociology—Dictionaries	303.6	P96.V5	Violence in mass media
301.05	HM1-7	Sociology—Periodicals	303.6	HM281-283	Violence
301.06	HM13	Sociology—Congresses	303.623	HM281-283	Riots
			303.64	HM281-283	Revolutions

Dewey	LC	Subject Heading	Dewey	LC	Subject Heading
304.2	GF1-900	Human ecology	304.60944949	HB2055-2056	Population geography—Germany
304.2	GF24	Applied human geography			
304.2	GF51-71	Man—Influence of environment	304.60945	HB2059-2060	Population geography—Italy
			304.60945	HB3599-3600	Demography—Italy
304.2	HM206-208	Social ecology	304.60946	HB3619-3620	Demography—Spain
304.20913	GF895	Human ecology—Tropics	304.60946	HB2079-2080	Population geography—Spain
304.209(4-9)	GF500-895	Human ecology—[By region or country]	304.609469	HB3621-3622	Demography—Portugal
304.20973	GF503-504	Human ecology—United States	304.609469	HB2081-2082	Population geography—Portugal
304.25	GF71	Man—Influence of climate	304.6094698	HB2128.5	Population geography—Madeira Islands
304.5	GN365.9	Sociobiology	304.6094698	HB3668.5	Demography—Madeira Islands
304.5	HM121	Heredity			
304.6	GN33.5	Demographic anthropology	304.6094699	HB2127.5	Population geography—Azores
304.6	HB848-3697	Population			
304.6	HB887	Demographic transition	304.6094699	HB3667.5	Demography—Azores
304.6	HB848-3697	Demography	304.60947	HB3607-3608.2	Demography—Russia
304.605	HB848	Demography—Periodicals	304.60947	HB2067-2068.2	Population geography—Russia
304.6072	HB850-.5	Population Research			
304.609	HB851-853	Population—History	304.609481	HB2075-2076	Population geography—Norway
304.6091724	HB884	Developing countries—Population			
			304.609481	HB3615-3616	Demography—Norway
304.6091724	HB2160	Population geography—Developing countries	304.609485	HB3617-3618	Demography—Sweden
			304.609485	HB2077-2078	Population geography—Sweden
304.6091734	HB2371-2578	Rural population			
304.6092	HB855-865	Demography—Biography	304.609489	HB2071-2072	Population geography—Denmark
304.609411	HB3587-3588	Demography—Scotland			
304.609411	HB2047-2048	Population geography—Scotland	304.609489	HB3611-3612	Demography—Denmark
			304.6094897	HB2068.3	Population geography—Finland
304.609415	HB3589-3590	Demography—Ireland			
304.609415	HB2049-2050	Population geography—Ireland	304.6094897	HB3608.3	Demography—Finland
			304.6094912	HB2073-2074	Population geography—Iceland
304.609416	HB3588.5	Demography—Northern Ireland			
			304.6094912	HB3613-3614	Demography—Iceland
304.609416	HB2048.5	Population geography—Northern Ireland	304.609492	HB3605-3606	Demography—Netherlands
			304.609492	HB2065-2066	Population geography—Netherlands
304.60942(9)	HB2045-2046	Population geography—England and Wales			
			304.609493	HB3603-3604	Demography—Belgium
304.60942(9)	HB3585-3586	Demography—England and Wales	304.609493	HB2063-2064	Population geography—Belgium
304.60943	HB3595-3596.5	Demography—Germany	304.6094935	HB2066.5	Population geography—Luxembourg
304.609436	HB3591-3592	Demography—Austria			
304.609436	HB2051-2052	Population geography—Austria	304.6094935	HB3606.5	Demography—Luxembourg
			304.609494	HB2083-2084	Population geography—Switzerland
304.60943648	HB2052.9	Population geography—Liechtenstein			
			304.609494	HB3623-3624	Demography—Switzerland
304.60943648	HB3592.9	Demography—Liechtenstein	304.609495	HB2092.5	Population geography—Greece
304.609437	HB3592.3	Demography—Czechoslovakia			
			304.609495	HB3632.5	Demography—Greece
304.609437	HB2052.3	Population geography—Czechoslovakia	304.6094965	HB2086.5	Population geography—Albania
304.609438	HB3608.7	Demography—Poland			
304.609438	HB2068.7	Population geography—Poland	304.6094965	HB3626.5	Demography—Albania
			304.609497	HB2088.5	Population geography—Yugoslavia
304.609439	HB3592.5	Demography—Hungary			
304.609439	HB2052.5	Population geography—Hungary	304.609497	HB3628.5	Demography—Yugoslavia
			304.609498	HB2091-2092	Population geography—Romania
304.60944	HB3593-3594	Demography—France			
304.60944	HB2053-2054	Population geography—France	304.609498	HB3631-3632	Demography—Romania
			304.609499	HB2087-2088	Population geography—Bulgaria
304.60944949	HB3594.5	Demography—Monaco			

Dewey	LC	Subject Heading	Dewey	LC	Subject Heading
304.609499	HB3627-3628	Demography—Bulgaria	304.6095498	HB3640.3	Demography—Bhutan
304.60951	HB2114	Population geography—China	304.6095498	HB2100.3	Population geography—Bhutan
304.60951	HB3654	Demography—China	304.60955	HB2096.4	Population geography—Iran
304.60951249	HB2116	Population geography—Taiwan	304.60955	HB3636.4	Demography—Iran
			304.609561	HB3633.4	Demography—Turkey
304.60951249	HB3656	Demography—Taiwan	304.609561	HB2093.4	Population geography—Turkey
304.6095125	HB2117	Population geography—Hong Kong			
			304.609567	HB3636.3	Demography—Iraq
304.6095125	HB3657	Demography—Hong Kong	304.609567	HB2096.3	Population geography—Iraq
304.6095126	HB2115	Population geography—Macao	304.6095691	HB2093.7	Population geography—Syria
304.6095126	HB3655	Demography—Macao	304.6095691	HB3633.7	Demography—Syria
304.609517	HB2112.8	Population geography—Mongolia	304.6095692	HB3633.9	Demography—Lebanon
			304.6095692	HB2093.9	Population geography—Lebanon
304.609517	HB3652.8	Demography—Mongolia			
304.609519	HB2112.5-.6	Population geography—Korea	304.6095693	HB2093.5	Population geography—Cyprus
304.609519	HB3652.5-.6	Demography—Korea	304.6095693	HB3633.5	Demography—Cyprus
304.60952	HB2111-2112	Population geography—Japan	304.6095694	HB2094	Population geography—Israel
304.60952	HB3651-3652	Demography—Japan	304.6095694	HB3634	Demography—Israel
304.609533	HB3634.9-3635	Demography—Yemen	304.6095695	HB3634.3	Demography—Jordan
304.609533	HB2094.9-2095	Population geography—Yemen	304.6095695	HB2094.3	Population geography—Jordan
304.6095353	HB2095.3	Population geography—Oman	304.609581	HB3636.6	Demography—Afghanistan
			304.609581	HB2096.6	Population geography—Aghanistan
304.6095353	HB3635.3	Demography—Oman			
304.6095357	HB2095.5	Population geography—United Arab Emirates	304.609591	HB2096.7	Population geography—Burma
304.6095357	HB3635.5	Demography—United Arab Emirates	304.609591	HB3636.7	Demography—Burma
			304.609593	HB2104.55	Population geography—Thailand
304.6095363	HB2095.7	Population geography—Qatar	304.609593	HB3644.55	Demography—Thailand
304.6095363	HB3635.7	Demography—Qatar	304.609594	HB2104.4	Population geography—Laos
304.6095365	HB3635.9	Demography—Bahrain			
304.6095365	HB2095.9	Population geography—Bahrain	304.609594	HB3644.4	Demography—Laos
			304.609595	HB2104.6	Population geography—Malaysia
304.6095367	HB3636	Demography—Kuwait			
304.6095367	HB2096	Population geography—Kuwait	304.609595	HB3644.6	Demography—Malaysia
			304.609596	HB2104.3	Population geography—Cambodia
304.609538	HB2094.7	Population geography—Saudi Arabia			
			304.609596	HB3644.3	Demography—Cambodia
304.609538	HB3634.7	Demography—Saudi Arabia	304.609597	HB2104.5	Population geography—Vietnam
304.60954	HB2099-2100	Population geography—India			
304.60954	HB3639-3640	Demography—India	304.609597	HB3644.5	Demography—Vietnam
304.6095491	HB3640.5	Demography—Pakistan	304.609598	HB2107-2108	Population geography—Indonesia
304.6095491	HB2100.5	Population geography—Pakistan			
			304.609598	HB3647-3648	Demography—Indonesia
304.6095492	HB3640.6	Demography—Bangladesh	304.609599	HB2109-2110	Population geography—Philippines
304.6095492	HB2100.6	Population geography—Bangladesh			
			304.609599	HB3649-3650	Demography—Philippines
304.6095493	HB2096.8	Population geography—Sri Lanka	304.609611	HB2121.5	Population geography—Tunisia
304.6095493	HB3636.8	Demography—Sri Lanka	304.609611	HB3661.5	Demography—Tunisia
304.6095495	HB2131.5	Population geography—Maldives	304.609612	HB2121.6	Population geography—Libya
304.6095495	HB3671.5	Demography—Maldives	304.609612	HB3661.6	Demography—Libya
304.6095496	HB3636.9	Demography—Nepal	304.60962	HB2121.7	Population geography—Egypt
304.6095496	HB2096.9	Population geography—Nepal	304.60962	HB3661.7	Demography—Egypt

29

Dewey	LC	Subject Heading	Dewey	LC	Subject Heading
304.609624	HB2121.8	Population geography—Sudan	304.6096683	HB2125.7	Population geography—Benin
304.609624	HB3661.8	Demography—Sudan	304.6096683	HB3665.7	Demography—Benin
304.60963	HB2122	Population geography—Ethiopia	304.609669	HB2126.7	Population geography—Nigeria
304.60963	HB3662	Demography—Ethiopia	304.609669	HB3666.7	Demography—Nigeria
304.60964	HB2121.3	Population geography—Morocco	304.6096711	HB2125.4	Population geography—Cameroon
304.60964	HB3661.3	Demography—Morocco	304.6096711	HB3665.4	Demography—Cameroon
304.609648	HB2127.4	Population geography—Western Sahara	304.6096715	HB2124.7	Population geography—Sao Tome and Principe
304.609648	HB3667.4	Demography—Western Sahara	304.6096715	HB3664.7	Demography—Sao Tome and Principe
304.609649	HB2129	Population geography—Canary Islands	304.6096718	HB2124.6	Population geography—Equatoria Guinea
304.609649	HB3669	Demography—Canary Islands	304.6096718	HB3664.6	Demography—Equatorial Guinea
304.60965	HB2121.4	Population geography—Algeria	304.6096721	HB2124.9	Population geography—Gabon
304.60965	HB3661.4	Demography—Algeria	304.6096721	HB3664.9	Demography—Gabon
304.609661	HB2126.6	Population geography—Mauritania	304.6096724	HB2125	Population geography—Congo (Brazzaville)
304.609661	HB3666.6	Demography—Mauritania	304.6096724	HB3665	Demography—Congo (Brazzaville)
304.6096623	HB2126.3	Population geography—Mali			
304.6096623	HB3666.3	Demography—Mali	304.609673	HB2124.4	Population geography—Angola
304.6096625	HB2126.4	Population geography—Burkina Faso	304.609673	HB3664.4	Demography—Angola
304.6096625	HB3666.4	Demography—Burkina Faso	304.6096741	HB2125.2	Population geography—Ubangi-Shari
304.6096626	HB2125.9	Population geography—Niger	304.6096741	HB3665.2	Demography—Ubangi-Shari
304.6096626	HB3665.9	Demography—Niger	304.6096743	HB2125.3	Population geography—Chad
304.609663	HB2126.5	Population geography—Senegal	304.6096743	HB3665.3	Demography—Chad
304.609663	HB3666.5	Demography—Senegal	304.6096751	HB2124.5	Population geography—Zaire
304.609664	HB2126.9	Population geography—Sierra Leone	304.6096751	HB3664.5	Demography—Zaire
304.609664	HB3666.9	Demography—Sierra Leone	304.60967571	HB2122.7	Population geography—Rwanda
304.6096651	HB2127	Population geography—Gambia	304.60967571	HB3662.7	Demography—Rwanda
304.6096651	HB3667	Demography—Gambia	304.60967572	HB2122.8	Population geography—Burundi
304.6096652	HB2126.2	Population geography—Guinea	304.60967572	HB3662.8	Demography—Burundi
304.6096652	HB3666.2	Demography—Guinea	304.6096761	HB2122.6	Population geography—Uganda
304.6096657	HB2127.3	Population geography—Guinea-Bissau	304.6096761	HB3662.6	Demography—Uganda
304.6096657	HB3667.3	Demography—Guinea-Bissau	304.6096762	HB2122.5	Population geography—Kenya
304.6096658	HB2129.5	Population geography—Cape Verde	304.6096762	HB3662.5	Demography—Kenya
304.6096658	HB3669.5	Demography—Cape Verde	304.6096771	HB2122.3	Population geography—Djibouti
304.6096662	HB2127.2	Population geography—Liberia	304.6096771	HB3662.3	Demography—Djibouti
304.6096662	HB3667.2	Demography—Liberia	304.6096773	HB2122.2	Population geography—Somalia
304.6096668	HB2126	Population geography—Cote d'Ivoire	304.6096773	HB3662.2	Demography—Somalia
304.6096668	HB3666	Demography—Cote d'Ivoire	304.609678	HB2122.9	Population geography—Tanzania
304.609667	HB2126.8	Population geography—Ghana	304.609678	HB3662.9	Demography—Tanzania
304.609667	HB3666.8	Demography—Ghana	304.609679	HB2123	Population geography—Mozambique
304.6096681	HB2125.8	Population geography—Togo	304.609679	HB3663	Demography—Mozambique
304.6096681	HB3665.8	Demography—Togo	304.60968	HB2123.4	Population geography—South Africa

Dewey	LC	Subject Heading	Dewey	LC	Subject Heading
304.60968	HB3663.4	Demography—South Africa	304.6097283	HB2000	Population geography—Honduras
304.6096881	HB2124.2	Population geography—Namibia	304.6097284	HB2004	Population geography—El Salvador
304.6096881	HB3664.2	Demography—Namibia	304.6097284	HB3544	Demography—El Salvador
304.6096883	HB2123.9	Population geography—Botswana	304.6097285	HB2001	Population geography—Nicaragua
304.6096883	HB3663.9	Demography—Botswana	304.6097285	HB3541	Demography—Nicaragua
304.6096885	HB2123.7	Population geography—Lesotho	304.6097286	HB1997-1998	Population geography—Costa Rica
304.6096885	HB3663.7	Demography—Lesotho	304.6097286	HB3537-3538	Demography—Costa Rica
304.6096887	HB2123.8	Population geography—Swaziland	304.6097287	HB2002-2003	Population geography—Panama
304.6096887	HB3663.8	Demography—Swaziland	304.6097287	HB3542-3543	Demography—Panama
304.6096894	HB2123.6	Population geography—Zambia	304.6097291	HB2009-2010	Population geography—Cuba
304.6096894	HB3663.6	Demography—Zambia	304.6097291	HB3549-3550	Demography—Cuba
304.6096897	HB2124	Population geography—Malawi	304.6097292	HB2013-2014	Population geography—Jamaica
304.6096897	HB3664	Demography—Malawi	304.6097292	HB3553-3554	Demography—Jamaica
304.609691	HB2123.2	Population geography—Madagascar	304.6097293	HB2012	Population geography—Dominican Republic
304.609691	HB3663.2	Demography—Madagascar	304.6097293	HB3552	Demography—Dominican Republic
304.609694	HB2132.5	Population geography—Comoro Islands	304.6097294	HB2011	Population geography—Haiti
304.609694	HB3672.5	Demography—Comoro Islands	304.6097294	HB3551	Demography—Haiti
304.609696	HB2132	Population geography—Seychelles	304.6097296	HB3547-3548	Demography—Bahamas
			304.6097296	HB2007-2008	Population geography—Bahamas
304.609696	HB3672	Demography—Seychelles	304.609729722	HB2016.3	Population geography—Virgin Islands of the United States
304.6096981	HB2133.5	Population geography—Reunion			
304.6096981	HB3673.5	Demography—Reunion	304.609729722	HB3556.3	Demography—Virgin Islands of the United States
304.6096982	HB2133	Population geography—Mauritius			
304.6096982	HB3673	Demography—Mauritius	304.60972973	HB3556.78	Demography—Saint Kitts and Nevis
304.609699	HB2134	Population geography—Kerguelen Islands	304.60972973	HB3556.72	Demography—Anguilla
304.609699	HB3674	Demography—Kerguelen Islands	304.60972973	HB2016.78	Population geography—Saint Kitts and Nevis
304.6097(4-9)	HB1987	Population geography—[United States, By city]	304.60972973	HB2016.72	Population geography—Anguilla
304.6097(4-9)	HB3525	Demography—[United States, By State]	304.60972974	HB2016.74	Population geography—Antigua
304.6097(4-9)	HB3527	Demography—[United States, By City]	304.60972974	HB3556.74	Demography—Antigua
			304.60972975	HB2016.76	Population geography—Monserrat
304.6097(4-9)	HB1985	Population geography—[United States, By state]	304.60972975	HB3556.76	Demography—Montserrat
304.60971	HB1989-1990	Population geography—Canada	304.60972976	HB2017.7	Population geography—Guadeloupe
304.60971	HB3529-3530	Demography—Canada	304.60972976	HB3557.7	Demography—Guadeloupe
304.60972	HB1991-1992	Population geography—Mexico	304.60972977	HB2017.385	Population geography—Saint Eustatius (Netherlands Antilles)
304.60972	HB3531-3532	Demography—Mexico			
304.6097281	HB3539	Demography—Guatemala	304.60972977	HB3557.38	Demography—Saba (Netherlands Antilles)
304.6097281	HB1999	Population geography—Guatemala	304.60972977	HB3557.385	Demography—Saint Eustatius (Netherlands Antilles)
304.6097282	HB3535-3536	Demography—Belize			
304.6097282	HB1995-1996	Population geography—Belize	304.60972977	HB3557.39	Demography—Saint Martin
304.6097283	HB3540	Demography—Honduras	304.60972977	HB2017.39	Population geography—Saint Martin

Dewey	LC	Subject Heading	Dewey	LC	Subject Heading
304.60972981	HB3556.57	Demography—Barbados	304.609881	HB3572.3	Demography—Guyana
304.60972981	HB2016.57	Population geography—Barbados	304.609881	HB2032.3	Population geography—Guyana
304.60972982	HB2017.9	Population geography—Martinique	304.609882	HB2032.7	Population geography—French Guiana
304.60972982	HB3557.9	Demography—Martinique	304.609882	HB3572.7	Demography—French Guiana
304.60972983	HB2017	Population geography—Trinidad and Tobago	304.609883	HB3572.5	Demography—Surinam
304.60972983	HB3557	Demography—Trinidad and Tobago	304.609883	HB2032.5	Population geography—Surinam
304.609729841	HB3556.93	Demography—Dominica	304.609892	HB2033-2034	Population geography—Paraguay
304.609729841	HB2016.93	Population geography—Dominica	304.609892	HB3573-3574	Demography—Paraguay
304.609729843	HB2016.97	Population geography—Saint Lucia	304.609895	HB3577-3578	Demography—Uruguay
304.609729843	HB3556.97	Demography—Saint Lucia	304.609895	HB2037-2038	Population geography—Uruguay
304.609729844	HB3556.99	Demography—Saint Vincent	304.60993	HB2152.5	Population geography—New Zealand
304.609729844	HB2016.99	Population geography—Saint Vincent	304.60993	HB3692.5	Demography—New Zealand
304.609729845	HB2016.95	Population geography—Grenada	304.60994	HB2135-2136	Population geography—Australia
304.609729845	HB3556.95	Demography—Grenada	304.60994	HB3675-3676	Demography—Australia
304.60972986	HB2017.36	Population geography—Bonaire	304.609953	HB2152.8	Population geography—Papua New Guinea
304.60972986	HB2017.35	Population geography—Aruba	304.609953	HB3692.8	Demography—Papua New Guinea
304.60972986	HB2017.37	Population geography—Curacao	304.6099593	HB2153	Population geography—Solomon Islands
304.60972986	HB3557.35	Demography—Aruba	304.6099593	HB3693	Demography—Solomon Islands
304.60972986	HB3557.37	Demography—Curacao			
304.60972986	HB3557.36	Demography—Bonaire	304.6099595	HB2153.4	Population geography—Vanuatu
304.6097299	HB2128	Population geography—Bermuda Islands	304.6099595	HB3693.4	Demography—Vanuatu
304.6097299	HB3668	Demography—Bermuda Islands	304.6099597	HB2153.3	Population geography—New Caledonia
304.60973	HB3505-3527	Demography—United States	304.6099597	HB3693.3	Demography—New Caledonia
304.60973	HB1965-1987	Population geography—United States	304.6099611	HB2153.5	Population geography—Fiji
304.60981	HB2023-2024	Population geography—Brazil	304.6099611	HB3693.5	Demography—Fiji
			304.6099612	HB2153.6	Population geography—Tonga
304.60981	HB3563-3564	Demography—Brazil	304.6099612	HB3693.6	Demography—Tonga
304.60982	HB2019-2020	Population geography—Argentina	304.6099613	HB2153.7	Population geography—American Samoa
304.60982	HB3559-3560	Demography—Argentina	304.6099613	HB3693.7	Demography—American Samoa
304.60983	HB3565-3566	Demography—Chile			
304.60983	HB2025-2026	Population geography—Chile	304.6099614	HB2153.8	Population geography—Western Samoa
304.60984	HB3561-3562	Demography—Bolivia	304.6099614	HB3693.8	Demography—Western Samoa
304.60984	HB2021-2022	Population geography—Bolivia			
304.60985	HB3575-3576	Demography—Peru	304.609962	HB2153.9	Population geography—French Polynesia
304.60985	HB2035-2036	Population geography—Peru	304.609962	HB3693.9	Demography—French Polynesia
304.609861	HB3567-3568	Demography—Colombia			
304.609861	HB2027-2028	Population geography—Colombia	304.6099623	HB2153.65	Population geography—Cook Islands
304.609866	HB3569-3570	Demography—Ecuador	304.6099623	HB3693.65	Demography—Cook Islands
304.609866	HB2029-2030	Population geography—Ecuador	304.609967	HB2152.7	Population geography—Guam
304.60987	HB3579-3580	Demography—Venezuela			
304.60987	HB2039-2040	Population geography—Venezuela	304.609967	HB3692.7	Demography—Guam

Dewey	LC	Subject Heading	Dewey	LC	Subject Heading
304.6099681	HB2152.9	Population geography—Kiribati	305.2309	HQ767.87	Children—History
304.6099681	HB3692.9	Demography—Kiribati	305.23091732	HT206	City children
304.6099711	HB2131	Population geography—Falkland Islands	305.232	HQ779-.5	Baby books
			305.232	HQ774.5	Toddlers
304.6099711	HB3671	Demography—Falkland Islands	305.232	HQ774	Infants
			305.232	HQ774	Infants—Development
304.609973	HB2130.5	Population geography—Tristan da Cunha	305.233	HQ774.5	Preschool children
			305.234	HQ778.6	School-age child care
304.609973	HB2130	Population geography—Saint Helena	305.235	GN483-484	Adolescence
			305.235	HQ799.5-.9	Young adults
304.609973	HB3670	Demography—Saint Helena	305.235	HQ793-799.9	Youth
304.609973	HB3670.5	Demography—Tristan da Cunha	305.23508352	HQ798	Teenage girls
			305.23509(4-9)	HQ799	Youth—[By region or country]
304.60998	HB3695	Demography—Arctic Regions	305.24	HQ799.95-.97	Adulthood
304.60998(1-8)	HB2155	Population geography—Arctic regions	305.244	HQ1059.4-.5	Middle age
			305.26	HQ1060-1064	Aged—Government policy
304.609982	HB2156	Population geography—Greenland	305.26	HQ1060-1064	Aged
			305.26	P96.A38	Aged in mass media
304.609982	HB3696	Demography—Greenland	305.26091734	HQ1060-1064	Rural aged
304.61	HB1953	Population density	305.3	HB1741-1948	Sex distribution (Demography)
304.632	HB901-1108	Fertility, Human			
304.63209(4-9)	HB901-1108	Fertility, Human—[By region or country]	305.3	P96.S48	Sexism in communication
			305.3	HQ77.7-.95	Transsexualism
304.632091724	HB1108	Fertility, Human—Developing countries	305.3	HQ1075-.5	Sex role
			305.3	P96.S5	Sex role in mass media
304.634	HQ759.98	Family demography	305.3097(4-9)	HB1777	Sex distribution (Demography)—[United States, By city]
304.634	HQ760-767.7	Family size			
304.63409(1-9)	HQ762	Family size—[By region or country]	305.3097(4-9)	HB1775	Sex distribution (Demography)—[United States, By state]
304.64	HB1321-1528	Mortality	305.30973	HB1755-1777	Sex distribution (Demography)—United States
304.64021	HB1322	Mortality—Tables			
304.64083	HB1323.C5	Children—Mortality			
304.6408996073	HB1323.B5	Afro-Americans—Mortality	305.31	GN372	Wild men
304.645(4-9)	HB1335-1526	Mortality—[By region or country]	305.31	HQ1088-1090.7	Men's studies
			305.389652	HQ800.3	Bachelors
304.6451724	HB1528	Mortality—Developing countries	305.389654	HQ1058-.5	Widowers
			305.389664	HQ75.8	Gay men
304.666	HQ763-767.52	Birth control	305.4	GN372	Wild women
304.8	GN370	Man—Migrations	305.4	HQ1101-2030.7	Women
304.8	D135-149	Migrations of nations	305.406	HQ1871-2030.7	Women—Societies and clubs
304.8	D145	Lombards			
304.808939	D139	Vandals	305.407	HQ1180-1186	Women's studies
304.82	DS22.7	Golden Horde	305.409	HQ1121-1172	Women—History
305	GN478-491.7	Social structure	305.409	HQ1139	Amazons
305	HM146	Equality	305.409(4-9)	HQ1400-1870.5	Women—[By region or country]
305	HM131-134	Social groups			
305.2	HB1531-1738	Age distribution (Demography)	305.40973	HQ1402-1439	Women—United States
			305.42	HQ1190	Feminist theory
305.209(4-9)	HB1541-1737	Age distribution (Demography)—[By region or country]	305.42	HQ1121-1870.5	Women—Social conditions
			305.48	HQ1871-2030.7	Women—Societies and clubs
305.2097(4-9)	HB1565	Age distribution (Demography)—[United States, By state]			
			305.48696	HQ1172	Jewish women
			305.486971	HQ1170	Muslim women
305.20973	HB1545-1567	Age distribution (Demography)—United States	305.489652	HQ800.2	Single women
			305.489654	HQ1058-.5	Widows
			305.489664	HQ75.3-.6	Abused lesbians
305.23	HQ767.8-792.2	Children	305.5	HT601-1444	Social classes
305.2308996073	E185.86	Afro-American children	305.5072	HT608	Social classes—Research

Dewey	LC	Subject Heading	Dewey	LC	Subject Heading
305.509	HT607	Social classes—History	305.8073	E184-185.98	United States—Race relations
305.5122	GN491.4	Caste			
305.5122	HT713-725	Caste	305.8073	E184.A1	United States—Ethnic relations
305.51220954	DS422.C3	Caste			
305.52	HT647-653	Aristocracy (Social class)	305.8096	GN664.N3	Negritos
305.5223	HT647-653	Nobility	305.83	GN549.G4	Germanic peoples
305.5232	HT657	Gentry	305.83	GN549.T4	Teutonic race
305.55	HT680-690	Middle class	305.892	GN547	Semites
305.5509(4-9)	HT690	Middle class—[By region or country]	305.8924	GN547	Jews
			305.893	HT1581-1589	Black race
305.555	HT421	Farm life	305.8942	GN548	Mongols
305.567	HT851-1444	Slavery	305.896073	E185.61	Afro-Americans—Segregation
305.56709	HT863-867	Slavery—History			
305.567094	HT1155-1240	Slavery—Europe	305.89912	GN664.P2	Papuans
305.5670941	HT1161-1165	Slavery—Great Britain	305.89915	GN666	Australian aborigines—Ethnic identity
305.5670943	HT1181	Slavery—Germany			
305.5670944	HT1176-1180	Slavery—France	305.8995	GN671.B5	Gunantuna (Melanesian people)
305.5670945	HT1191-1194	Slavery—Italy			
305.5670946	HT1216-1220	Slavery—Spain	305.89952	GN669	Micronesians
305.5670947	HT1206-1209	Slavery—Russia	305.90652	HQ800-.4	Single people
305.56709492	HT1196-1203	Slavery—Benelux countries	305.90664	HQ76.5-.8	Gay liberation movement
305.56709494	HT1227-1228	Slavery—Switzerland	305.90691	GN387	Nomads
305.56709495	HT1234	Slavery—Greece	305.906945	HQ998-999	Illegitimacy
305.567095	HT1240.5-1315	Slavery—Asia	306	CB	Culture
305.5670951	HT1241-1244	Slavery—China	306	GN493.3	Social norms
305.5670952	HT1276	Slavery—Japan	306	GN400-406	Culture
305.56709599	HT1271	Slavery—Philippines	306	HN25	Quality of life
305.567096	HT1321-1427	Slavery—Africa	306	HM101-121	Culture
305.5670971	HT1051-1052	Slavery—Canada	306.08	GN492.5	Tribes
305.5670972	HT1053-1054	Slavery—Mexico	306.08	GN380	Indigenous peoples
305.56709728	HT1055-1056	Slavery—Central America	306.2	GN492-495	Political anthropology
305.56709729	HT1071-1119	Slavery—West Indies	306.27	UH750-769	Military social work
305.567098	HT1121-1152	Slavery—South America	306.3	GN448-450.7	Economic anthropology
305.5670994	HT1431	Slavery—Australia	306.3	HM35	Economics—Sociological aspects
305.8	GN495.6	Ethnicity			
305.8	GN496-498	Race relations	306.36	HD6951-6957	Industrial sociology
305.8	GN496-498	Ethnic relations	306.361	HD6951-6957	Quality of work life
305.8	GN495.4	Ethnic groups	306.3613	HD4905-.3	Work ethic
305.8	GN301-673	Ethnology	306.363	HD4871-4875	Indentured servants
305.8	CB195-197	National characteristics	306.365	HT751-815	Serfdom
305.8	HT1501-1595	Race	306.36509(4-9)	HT781-815	Serfdom—[By region or country]
305.8	HT1501-1595	Race relations			
305.8036	HT1581-1589	Black race	306.3650941	HT781	Serfdom—Great Britain
305.8001	GN468	Ethnophilosophy	306.3650943	HT791-801	Serfdom—Germany
305.8001	HM24	Ethnomethodology	306.36509436	HT803	Serfdom—Austria
305.80074	GN35-41	Ethnological museums and collections	306.3650944	HT785	Serfdom—France
			306.3650947	HT807-809	Serfdom—Russia
305.8009	GN345.2	Ethnohistory	306.38	HD7110-.5	Early retirement
305.8009	HT1507	Race relations—History	306.42	GN451-477.7	Intellectual life
305.80094	GN575-585	Ethnic groups—Europe	306.42	HM213	Intellectuals
305.80095	GN625-635	Ethnic groups—Asia	306.43	LB45	Educational anthropology
305.80096	GN643-661	Ethnic groups—Africa	306.43	LC189-214.53	Educational sociology
305.80097	GN550-560	Ethnic groups—North America	306.44	P40	Sociolinguistics
			306.46	HM221	Technology—Sociological aspects
305.80098	GN562-564	Ethnic groups—South America			
			306.482	GN454.6	Gambling
305.80099(5-6)	GN662-671	Ethnic groups—Oceania	306.483	GN454-455	Sports
305.8034	GN537	Caucasian race	306.7	HQ12-449	Sex
305.8034	HT1575-1577	Caucasian race	306.7	HQ801-.83	Man-woman relationships
305.8044	GN645	Mulattoes	306.7	HQ19-30.7	Sexual instinct

Dewey	LC	Subject Heading	Dewey	LC	Subject Heading
306.70816	HQ30.5	Handicapped—Sexual behavior	306.81097(4-9)	HB1147	Marital status—[United States, By city]
306.7082	HQ29	Women—Sexual behavior	306.81097(4-9)	HB1145	Marital status—[United States, By state]
306.7083	HQ784.S45	Children—Sexual behavior	306.810971	HQ559-560	Marriage—Canada
306.70835	HQ27-.5	Young adults—Sexual behavior	306.810972	HQ561-562	Marriage—Mexico
306.70846	HQ30	Aged—Sexual behavior	306.8109728	HQ563-574	Marriage—Central America
306.7088375	HQ27	Students—Sexual behavior	306.8109729	HQ575-587.9	Marriage—West Indies
306.73	HQ801.8	Interracial dating	306.810973	HB1125-1126	Marital status—United States
306.73	HQ801.83	Dating violence			
306.73	HQ12-18	Sex customs	306.810973	HQ535-557	Marriage—United States
306.732	HQ800.15	Celibacy	306.81098	HQ588-610	Marriage—South America
306.735	HQ961-967	Free love	306.810994	HQ705-706	Marriage—Australia
306.735	HX546	Free love	306.82	GN480.3	Endogamy and exogamy
306.736	HQ806	Adultery	306.83	GN480	Double descent (Kinship)
306.74	HQ101-440.7	Prostitution	306.83	GN480-.65	Kinship
306.7409	HQ111-117	Prostitution—History	306.84	HQ1028	Marriage with deceased wife's sister
306.7409(4-9)	HQ141-270.7	Prostitution—[By region or country]	306.84	HQ803	Temporary marriage
306.765	HQ74-.2	Bisexuality	306.84	HQ803	Marriage, Companionate
306.766	HQ75-76.95	Homosexuality	306.84	HQ1018-1019	Remarriage
306.7663	HQ75.3-.6	Lesbianism	306.842	HQ981-996	Group marriage
306.77	HQ76.97-77.2	Transvestites	306.8423	GN480.33-.36	Polygamy
306.77	HQ79	Fetishism (Sexual behavior)	306.8423	GN480.6	Polyandry
306.772	HQ447	Masturbation	306.8423	HQ981-996	Polygamy
306.775	HQ79	Sadism	306.843	HQ1031	Interfaith marriage
306.775	HQ79	Sadomasochism	306.843083	HQ777.9	Children of interracial marriage
306.8	HQ503-1064	Family			
306.8	HQ503-1064	Home	306.846	GN254	Miscegenation
306.81	GN480	Marriage	306.846	E185.62	Miscegenation
306.81	GN480.4	Cross-cousin marriage	306.846	HQ1031	Interracial marriage
306.81	HQ503-1064	Marriage	306.85	GN480-.65	Family
306.81021	HB1111-1317	Marital status—Statistics	306.850896073	E185.86	Afro-American families
306.81087	HQ1036-1043	Handicapped—Marriage	306.859	GN497.5	Matriarchy
306.810872	HQ1040	Deaf—Marriage	306.87	HQ777.22	Second-born children
306.8109	HB1121-1317	Marital status—[By region or country]	306.87	HQ777.2	First-born children
			306.874	HQ759.913	Parents of handicapped children
306.8109	HQ503-518	Marriage—History			
306.8109(4-9)	HQ531-727.9	Marriage—[By region or country]	306.874	HQ759.913	Parents of exceptional children
306.81094	HQ611-662.7	Marriage—Europe	306.874	HQ755.7-759.92	Parenthood
306.810941	HQ613-618.5	Marriage—Great Britain	306.874	HQ755.7-759.92	Parenting
306.810943	HQ625-626.5	Marriage—Germany	306.874	HQ799.15	Parent and teenager
306.810944	HQ623-624	Marriage—France	306.874	HQ755.85	Abused parents
306.810945	HQ629-630	Marriage—Italy	306.8740835	HQ759.64	Teenage parents
306.810946	HQ649-650	Marriage—Spain	306.874084	HQ755.86	Parent and adult child
306.810947	HQ637-638	Marriage—Russia	306.874087	HQ759.912	Handicapped parents
306.8109492	HQ631-636.5	Marriage—Benelux Countries	306.8742	HQ756	Stepfathers
			306.8742	HQ756-.7	Fathers
306.8109494	HQ653-654	Marriage—Switzerland	306.8742	HQ756-.7	Fatherhood
306.8109495	HQ662.5	Marriage—Greece	306.874208653	HQ756	Divorced fathers
306.81095	HQ663-690.5	Marriage—Asia	306.8743	HQ759-.6	Motherhood
306.810951	HQ684	Marriage—China	306.8743	HQ759.48	Working mothers
306.810952	HQ681-682	Marriage—Japan	306.8743	HQ759.5	Surrogate mothers
306.810954	HQ669-670	Marriage—India	306.8743	HQ759.3	Absentee mothers
306.810955	HQ666.4	Marriage—Iran	306.8743	HQ759-.6	Mothers
306.8109567	HQ666.3	Marriage—Iraq	306.87430835	HQ759.4	Teenage mothers
306.81095694	HQ664	Marriage—Israel	306.8745	HQ759.9	Grandparenting
306.8109599	HQ679-680	Marriage—Philippines	306.875	GN63.6	Twins
306.81096	HQ691-697.4	Marriage—Africa	306.875	GN63.6	Triplets
			306.875	GN63.6	Quadruplets

Dewey	LC	Subject Heading	Dewey	LC	Subject Heading
306.875	GN63.6	Quintuplets	307.760973	HT123-.5	Sociology, Urban—United States
306.877	GN480.3	Incest			
306.877	HQ71	Incest	307.76098	HT129	Sociology, Urban—South America
306.88	HQ805	Desertion and non-support			
306.8809(4-9)	HQ831-960.7	Divorce—[By region or country]	307.760994	HT149	Sociology, Urban—Australia
			307.768	HT169.55-.57	Planned communities
306.8809(4-9)	HQ837-960.9	Desertion—[Other regions and countries]	307.768	HT169.55-.57	New towns
			307.774	HQ970-975.7	Communal living
306.880973	HQ833-836	Desertion—United States	310	HA175-4737	Census
306.89	HQ811-960.7	Divorce	310	HA	Statistics
306.9	HQ1073-.5	Death	310	HA154-4737	Vital statistics
306.9	HQ1073-.5	Thanatology	310.0223	GA109.8	Maps, Statistical
307	HM131-134	Community life	310.0723	HA31.2	Sampling (Statistics)
307	HT51-65	Human settlements	310.1	HA30.6	Spatial analysis (Statistics)
307	HT101-395	Cities and towns	310.1	HA29-32	Statistics—Methodology
307.1209(4-9)	HT392-395	Regional planning—[By region or country]	310.3	HA17	Statistics—Dictionaries
			310.5	HA1	Statistics—Periodicals
307.120973	HT392-394	Regional planning—United States	310.72	HA31.3	Correlation (Statistics)
			310.72	HA35	Statistics—Research
307.1216	HT165.5-169.5	City planning	310.9	HA19	Statistics—History
307.121609 (4-9)	HT167-169.54	City planning—[By region or country]	310.92	QA276.17	Statistical consultants
			314	HA1107-1650	Europe—Census
307.12160973	HT167-168	City planning—United States	314.1	HA1121-1170	Great Britain—Census
			314.11	HA1151-1160	Scotland—Census
307.14	GF101-127	Human settlements	314.15	HA1170.1-.5	Ireland—Census
307.14	HN49.C6	Community development	314.16	HA1141-1150	Northern Ireland—Census
307.24	HB1955	Rural-urban migration	314.29	HA1161-1170	Wales—Census
307.26	HB1956-2157	Urban-rural migration	314.3	HA1231-1349	Germany—Census
307.26	HT381	Urban-rural migration	314.36	HA1171-1190	Austria—Census
307.3364	HV4023-4170.7	Slums	314.3648	HA1210.5	Liechtenstein—Census
307.3416	HT170-178	Urban renewal	314.37	HA1191-1200	Czechoslovakia—Census
307.341609 (4-9)	HT178	Urban renewal—[Other regions or countries]	314.38	HA1451-1460	Poland—Census
			314.39	HA1201-1210	Hungary—Census
307.34160973	HT175-177	Urban renewal—United States	314.4	HA1211-1230	France—Census
			314.5	HA1361-1379	Italy—Census
307.72	HT401-485	Sociology, Rural	314.6	HA1541-1560	Spain—Census
307.7209	HT415	Sociology, Rural—History	314.69	HA1571-1580	Portugal—Census
307.74	HT351-352	Suburban life	314.698	HA2285	Madeira Islands—Census
307.76	GN395	Urban anthropology	314.699	HA2280	Azores—Census
307.76	HT101-395	Sociology, Urban	314.7	HA1431-1450.12	Russia—Census
307.76	HT161-165	Garden cities	314.81	HA1501-1520	Norway—Census
307.76	HT156	Inner cities	314.85	HA1521-1540	Sweden—Census
307.76072	HT110	Sociology, Urban—Research	314.89	HA1471-1490	Denmark—Census
307.7609	HT111-150	Sociology, Urban—History	314.897	HA1450.5	Finland—Census
307.760902	D134	Cities and towns, Medieval	314.912	HA1491-1500	Iceland—Census
307.760902	HT115	Cities and towns, Medieval	314.92	HA1381-1390	Netherlands—Census
307.76091724	HT149.5	Sociology, Urban—Developing countries	314.93	HA1391-1410	Belgium—Census
			314.935	HA1411-1420	Luxembourg—Census
307.76093	HT114	Cities and towns, Ancient	314.94	HA1591-1610	Switzerland—Census
307.76094	HT131-145	Sociology, Urban—Europe	314.95	HA1351-1359	Greece—Census
307.760941	HT133	Sociology, Urban—Great Britain	314.965	HA1620.5	Albania—Census
			314.97	HA1631-1635	Yugoslavia—Census
307.760943	HT137	Sociology, Urban—Germany	314.98	HA1641-1650	Romania—Census
307.760944	HT135	Sociology, Urban—France	314.99	HA1621-1630	Bulgaria—Census
307.76095	HT147	Sociology, Urban—Asia	315.1	HA4631-4640	China—Census
307.76096	HT148	Sociology, Urban—Africa	315.1249	HA4646-4650	Taiwan—Census
307.760971	HT127	Sociology, Urban—Canada	315.125	HA4651-4655	Hong Kong—Census
307.760972	HT127.7	Sociology, Urban—Mexico	315.126	HA4641-4645	Macao—Census
307.7609728	HT128	Sociology, Urban—Central America	315.17	HA4630.8	Mongolia—Census
			315.19	HA4630.5-.6	Korea—Census
			315.2	HA4621-4630	Japan—Census

36

Dewey	LC	Subject Heading	Dewey	LC	Subject Heading
315.33	HA4564	Yemen—Census	316.724	HA4716	Congo (Brazzaville)—Census
315.353	HA4565	Oman—Census	316.73	HA4710	Angola—Census
315.357	HA4566	United Arab Emirates—Census	316.741	HA4717	Central African Republic—Census
315.363	HA4567	Qatar—Census	316.743	HA4718	Chad—Census
315.365	HA4568	Bahrain—Census	316.751	HA4711	Zaire—Census
315.38	HA4563	Saudi Arabia—Census	316.7571	HA4695	Rwanda—Census
315.4	HA4581-4590	India—Census	316.7572	HA4696	Burundi—Census
315.491	HA4590.5	Pakistan—Census	316.761	HA4694	Uganda—Census
315.492	HA4590.6	Bangladesh—Census	316.762	HA4693	Kenya—Census
315.493	HA4570.8	Sri Lanka—Census	316.771	HA4691	Djibouti—Census
315.495	HA2300	Maldives—Census	316.773	HA4690	Somalia—Census
315.496	HA4570.9	Nepal—Census	316.78	HA4697	Tanzania—Census
315.498	HA4590.3	Bhutan—Census	316.79	HA4698	Mozambique—Census
315.5	HA4570.2	Iran—Census	316.8	HA4701	South Africa—Census
315.61	HA4556.5	Turkey—Census	316.881	HA4708	Namibia—Census
315.67	HA4569	Iraq—Census	316.883	HA4706	Botswana—Census
315.691	HA4558	Syria—Census	316.885	HA4704	Lesotho—Census
315.692	HA4559	Lebanon—Census	316.887	HA4705	Swaziland—Census
315.693	HA4557	Cyprus—Census	316.89	HA4702	Rhodesia—Census
315.694	HA4560	Israel—Census	316.894	HA4703	Zambia—Census
315.695	HA4561	Jordan—Census	316.897	HA4707	Malawi—Census
315.81	HA4570.6	Afghanistan—Census	316.91	HA4699	Madagascar—Census
315.91	HA4570.7	Burma—Census	316.96	HA2301	Seychelles—Census
315.93	HA4600.55	Thailand—Census	316.981	HA2307	Reunion—Census
315.94	HA4600.4	Laos—Census	316.982	HA2305	Mauritius—Census
315.95	HA4600.6	Malaysia—Census	316.99	HA2309	Kerguelen Islands—Census
315.96	HA4600.3	Cambodia—Census	317.1	HA741-750	Canada—Census
315.97	HA4600.5	Vietnam—Census	317.2	HA761-770	Mexico—Census
315.98	HA4601-4610	Indonesia—Census	317.281	HA811-820	Guatemala—Census
315.99	HA4611-4620	Philippines—Census	317.282	HA791-800	Belize—Census
316.11	HA4684	Tunisia—Census	317.283	HA821-830	Honduras—Census
316.12	HA4685	Libya—Census	317.284	HA841-850	El Salvador—Census
316.2	HA4686	Egypt—Census	317.285	HA831-840	Nicaragua—Census
316.24	HA4687	Sudan—Census	317.286	HA801-810	Costa Rica—Census
316.3	HA4689	Ethiopia—Census	317.287	HA851-854	Panama—Census
316.4	HA4682	Morocco—Census	317.291	HA871-880	Cuba—Census
316.48	HA4737	Western Sahara—Census	317.292	HA891-900	Jamaica—Census
316.49	HA2287	Canary Islands—Census	317.293	HA886-890	Dominican Republic—Census
316.5	HA4683	Algeria—Census			
316.61	HA4730	Mauritania—Census	317.294	HA881-885	Haiti—Census
316.623	HA4727	Mali—Census	317.295	HA901-910	Puerto Rico—Census
316.625	HA4728	Burkina Faso—Census	317.296	HA861	Bahamas—Census
316.626	HA4724	Niger—Census	317.297	HA866-.9	Leeward Islands (West Indies)—Census
316.63	HA4729	Senegal—Census			
316.64	HA4733	Sierra Leone—Census	317.29722	HA911-915	Virgin Islands of the United States—Census
316.651	HA4734	Gambia—Census			
316.652	HA4726	Guinea—Census	317.2976	HA918.7	Guadeloupe—Census
316.657	HA4736	Guinea-Bissau—Census	317.2981	HA865	Barbados—Census
316.658	HA2289	Cape Verde—Census	317.2982	HA918.9	Martinique—Census
316.662	HA4735	Liberia—Census	317.2983	HA867	Trinidad and Tobago—Census
316.668	HA4725	Cote d'Ivoire—Census			
316.67	HA4732	Ghana—Census	317.2986	HA917-.78	Netherlands Antilles—Census
316.681	HA4723	Togo—Census			
316.683	HA4722	Benin—Census	317.299	HA921-930	Bermuda Islands—Census
316.69	HA4731	Nigeria—Census	317.3	HA201-214	United States—Statistics, Vital
316.711	HA4719	Cameroon—Census			
316.715	HA4713	Sao Tome and Principe—Census	317.3	HA201-214	United States—Statistics
			317.3	HA201-730	United States—Census
316.718	HA4712	Equatorial Guinea—Census	317.(4-9)	HA221-730	[United States, By state]—Census
316.721	HA4715	Gabon—Census			

Dewey	LC	Subject Heading	Dewey	LC	Subject Heading
318.1	HA971-990	Brazil—Census	320.54095694	DS149-151	Zionism
318.2	HA941-960	Argentina—Census	320.85	JS113	Municipal home rule
318.3	HA991-1010	Chile—Census	320.85	JS	Municipal government
318.4	HA961-970	Bolivia—Census	320.85	JS	Municipal corporations
318.5	HA1051-1070	Peru—Census	320.9174927	JQ1850	Arab countries—Politics
318.61	HA1011-1020	Colombia—Census			and government
318.66	HA1021-1030	Ecuador—Census	320.932	JC66	Egypt—Politics and
318.7	HA1091-1100	Venezuela—Census			government
318.81	HA1033	Guyana—Census	320.933	JC67	Jews—Politics and
318.82	HA1037	French Guiana—Census			government
318.83	HA1035	Surinam—Census	320.9376	JC81-89	Rome—Politics and
318.92	HA1041-1050	Paraguay—Census			government
318.95	HA1071-1090	Uruguay—Census	320.938	JC75.D	Deme
319.3	HA3171-3190	New Zealand—Census	320.938	JC71-75	Greece—Politics and
319.4	HA3001-3010	Australia—Census			government—To 146 B.C.
319.53	HA4013	Papua New Guinea—Census	320.94	JN12	Europe—Politics and
319.593	HA4014	Solomon Islands—Census			government—20th century
319.595	HA4015.5	Vanuatu—Census	320.94090	D1058-1065	Europe—Politics and
319.597	HA4015	New Caledonia—Census	(44-511)		government—1945-
319.611	HA4016	Fiji—Census	320.940948	D2009	Europe—Politics and
319.612	HA4017	Tonga—Census			government—1989-
319.613	HA4018.5	American Samoa—Census	320.941	JN101-1371	Great Britain—Politics and
319.623	HA4017.5	Cook Islands—Census			government
319.67	HA4012	Guam—Census	320.941090	JN175-231	Great Britain—Politics
319.681	HA4016.7	Kiribati—Census	(3-511)		and government—1485-
319.71	HA2295	Falkland Islands—Census	320.9410902	JN137-158	Great Britain—Politics and
319.73	HA2291	Saint Helena—Census	(1-4)		government—1066-1485
319.82	HA740	Greenland—Census	320.9411	JN1187-1371	Scotland—Politics and
319.89	HA4020-.5	Antarctica			government
320	JA	Political science	320.9415	JN1405-1571.5	Ireland—Politics and
320	J	Political science			government
320	HM33	Political science	320.9416	JN1572	Northern Ireland—Politics
320	B65	Political science			and government
320.011	JC	State, The	320.9429	JN1150-1159	Wales—Politics and
320.011	JC578	Justice			government
320.05	JA1-26	Political science—	320.943	JN3201-4944	Germany—Politics and
		Periodicals			government
320.06	JA35.5	Political science—	320.9436	JN1601-2041	Austria—Politics and
		Congresses			government
320.06	JA27-34	Political science—	320.9437	JN2210-2229	Czechoslovakia—Politics
		Societies, etc.			and government
320.071	JA86-88	Political science—Study	320.9438	JN6750-6769	Poland—Politics and
		and teaching			government
320.09	JA81-84	Political science—History	320.944	JN2301-3007	France—Politics and
320.0975	JK9661-9993	Confederate States of			government
		America—Politics and	320.946	JN8101-8399	Spain—Politics and
		government			government
320.11	JA81-84	Social contract	320.9469	JN8423-8661	Portugal—Politics and
320.11	GN492.6	State, The—Origin			government
320.11	JC336	Social contract	320.947	JN6500-6598	Russia—Politics and
320.12	JC319-323	Geopolitics			government
320.12	CC600-605	Boundary stones	320.948	JN7011-7066	Scandinavia—Politics and
320.12	JC323	Boundaries			government
320.12	JC319-323	Political geography	320.9481	JN7401-7695	Norway—Politics and
320.120973	JK2556	United States—Territories			government
		and possessions	320.9485	JN7721-7995	Sweden—Politics and
320.15	JC327	Sovereignty			government
320.404	JF229	Separation of powers	320.9489	JN7101-7367	Denmark—Politics and
320.533	JC481	Fascism			government
320.54	JC311-314	Nationalism	320.94897	JN7390-7399	Finland—Politics and
320.5409174927	DS38	Panarabism			government

Dewey	LC	Subject Heading	Dewey	LC	Subject Heading
320.94912	JN7370-7379	Iceland—Politics and government	320.95694	JQ1830	Israel—Politics and government
320.9492	JN5701-5999	Netherlands—Politics and government	320.95695	JQ1833	Jordon—Politics and government
320.9493	JN6101-6371	Belgium—Politics and government	320.9581	JQ1760-1769	Afghanistan—Politics and government
320.9494	JN8701-9599	Switzerland—Politics and government	320.9593	JQ1740-1749	Thailand—Politics and government
320.9495	JN5001-5191	Greece—Politics and government	320.9594	JQ950-959	Laos—Politics and government
320.9495	JC91-93	Byzantine Empire—Politics and government	320.9595	JQ751	Burma—Politics and government
320.9496	JN9600-9689	Balkan Peninsula—Politics and government	320.9596	JQ930-939	Cambodia—Politics and government
320.9(5-6)	JQ5995-6651	Oceania—Politics and government	320.9597	JQ800-899	Vietnam—Politics and government
320.95	JQ21-1825	Asia—Politics and government	320.9598	JQ760-779	Indonesia—Politics and government
320.951	JQ1500-1519	China—Politics and government	320.9599	JQ1250-1419	Philippines—Politics and government
320.951249	JQ1520-1539	Taiwan—Politics and government	320.96	JQ1870-3981	Africa—Politics and government
320.9519	JQ1720-1729.5	Korea—Politics and government	320.971	JL1-500	Canada—Politics and government
320.952	JQ1600-1699	Japan—Politics and government	320.971090 (1-33)	JL41-45	Canada—Politics and government—To 1763
320.9533	JQ1842	Yemen—Politics and government	320.97109033	JL48	Canada—Politics and government—1763-1791
320.95353	JQ1843	Oman—Politics and government	320.9710903 (3-4)	JL53	Canada—Politics and government—1791-1841
320.95357	JQ1844	United Arab Emirates	320.97109034	JL55	Canada—Politics and government—1841-1867
320.95363	JQ1845	Qatar—Politics and government	320.971090 (34-511)	JL65	Canada—Politics and government—1867-
320.95365	JQ1846	Bahrain—Politics and government	320.972	JL1200-1299	Mexico—Politics and government
320.95367	JQ1848	Kuwait—Politics and government	320.97281	JL1480-1499	Guatemala—Politics and government
320.9538	JQ1841	Saudi Arabia—Politics and government	320.97282	JL670-679	Belize—Politics and government
320.954	JN5201-5690	Italy—Politics and government	320.97283	JL1520-1539	Honduras—Politics and government
320.954	JQ200-620	India—Politics and government	320.97284	JL1560-1579	El Salvador—Politics and government
320.95491	JQ629	Pakistan—Politics and government	320.97285	JL1600-1619	Nicaragua—Politics and government
320.95492	JQ630-639	Bangladesh—Politics and government	320.97286	JL1440-1459	Costa Rica—Politics and government
320.95493	JQ650-659	Sri Lanka—Politics and government	320.97291	JL1000-1019	Cuba—Politics and government
320.955	JQ1780-1789	Iran—Politics and government	320.97292	JL630-639	Jamaica—Politics and government
320.9561	JQ1800-1809	Turkey—Politics and government	320.972921	JL629.5	Cayman Islands—Politics and government
320.9567	JQ1849	Iraq—Politics and government	320.97293	JL1120-1139	Dominican Republic—Politics and government
320.95691	JQ1826	Syria—Politics and government	320.97294	JL1080-1099	Haiti—Politics and government
320.95692	JQ1828	Lebanon—Politics and government	320.97295	JL1040-1059	Puerto Rico—Politics and government
320.95693	JQ1811	Cyprus—Politics and government			

Dewey	LC	Subject Heading	Dewey	LC	Subject Heading
320.97296	JL610-619	Bahamas—Politics and government	321.030944	JC359	Bonapartism
			321.04094	D1060	European federation
320.97297	JL640-649.7	Leeward Islands (West Indies)—Politics and government	321.04094	JN15	European federation
			321.06	JC352	City-states
			321.06	JC365	States, Small
320.972976	JL820-829	Guadeloupe—Politics and government	321.07	HX806-811	Utopias
			321.08	JV	Colonies
320.972982	JL830-839	Martinique—Politics and government	321.09	JC492	Counterrevolutions
			321.09	JC494	Coups d'etat
320.972983	JL650-659	Trinidad and Tobago—Politics and government	321.094	JC491	Revolutions
			321.1	GN479.6	Patriarchy
320.9729845	JL629.6	Grenada—Politics and government	321.3	JC109-121	Feudalism
			321.3	D131	Feudalism
320.972986	JL770-779	Curacao—Politics and government	321.5	JC419	Oligarchy
			321.5	JC20-89	Theocracy
320.97299	JL590-599	Bermuda Islands—Politics and government	321.6	D226.7	Royal houses
			321.6	JC375-393	Monarchy
320.973	JK	United States—Politics and government	321.6	JC375-392	Despotism
			321.6	JC389	Divine right of kings
320.9730903	JK54-103	United States—Politics and government—To 1775	321.6	JC391	Coronations
			321.60901	GN495.5	Kings and rulers, Ancient
320.97309034	JK320	United States—Politics and government—Civil War, 1861-1865	321.8	JC421-423	Democracy
			321.8042	JF285	Heads of state—Succession
320.97309034	JK321	United States—Politics and government—1865-1877	321.80420973	E176.4	Presidents—United States—Mistresses
320.981	JL2400-2499	Brazil—Politics and government	321.86	JC421-458	Republics
			321.9	JC480-481	Totalitarianism
320.982	JL2000-2099	Argentina—Politics and government	321.9092	JC495	Dictators
			321.92	JC474	Communist state
320.983	JL2600-2699	Chile—Politics and government	321.94	HD3611-4730.9	Corporate state
			321.94	JC478	Corporate state
320.984	JL2200-2299	Bolivia—Politics and government	322.1	K3280-3282	Church and state
			322.4	JC328.3	Civil disobedience
320.985	JL3400-3499	Peru—Politics and government	322.5	JF195	Civil-military relations
			323	JC571-628	Human rights
320.9861	JL2800-2899	Colombia—Politics and government	323	JC571-628	Civil rights
			323	JC571-605	Individualism
320.9866	JL3000-3099	Ecuador—Politics and government	323.044	JC328.3	Government, Resistance to
			323.044	JC585-599	Political persecution
320.987	JL3800-3899	Venezuela—Politics and government	323.0440951	HV6433.I	Red Brigades
320.9881	JL680-689	Guyana—Politics and government	323.0941	JN900-1088	Political rights—Great Britain
320.9882	JL810-819	French Guiana	323.0973	JK1717-2217	Political rights—United States
320.9883	JL780-789	Surinam—Politics and government	323.1	JC312	Minorities
			323.1196073	E185.61	Afro-Americans—Civil rights
320.9892	JL3200-3299	Paraguay—Politics and government	323.34	HQ1236-.5	Women's rights
320.9895	JL3600-3699	Uruguay—Politics and government	323.42	JC575-578	Equality
			323.44	JC585-599	Liberty
320.99711	JL690-699	Falkland Islands—Politics and government	323.442	BL640	Freedom of religion
			323.442	BV741	Freedom of religion
320.9982	JN7380-7389	Greenland—Politics and government	323.442	BV741	Liberty of conscience
			323.445	Z657-659	Book burning
			323.48	JC609	Petition, Right of
321	GN492.7	Kings and rulers	323.480973	JK1731	Petition, Right of
321	JF251-289	Heads of state	323.6	JC328	Treason
321.02	JC355	Federal government	323.6	JF801	Citizenship
321.02	K3285	Federal government	323.6	JC328	Allegiance
321.03094	D352.1	Royal houses	323.60973	JK1758-1759	Patriotism—United States
321.03094	D412.7	Royal houses	323.60973	JK1758	Americanization

Dewey	LC	Subject Heading	Dewey	LC	Subject Heading
324	JF1001-1048	Elections	325.(2438/438)	JV8195	Poland—Emigration and immigration
324.0973	JK524-529	Presidents—United States—Election	325.(244/44)	JV7900-7999	France—Emigration and immigration
324.2	JF2011-2112	Political parties	325.(245/45)	JV8130-8139	Italy—Emigration and immigration
324.241	JN1111-1129	Political parties—Great Britain	325.(246/46)	JV8250-8259	Spain—Emigration and immigration
324.24102	JN1129.T7	Tories, English	325.(2469/469)	JV8260-8269	Portugal—Emigration and immigration
324.273015	JK2063-2075	Nominations for office	325.(247/47)	JV8180-8189	Russia—Emigration and immigration
324.2730154	JK2071-2077	Primaries			
324.2730156	JK2255-2261	Political conventions	325.(2481/481)	JV8210-8219	Norway—Emigration and immigration
324.3	JF2101	Political clubs	325.(2485/485)	JV8220-8229	Sweden—Emigration and immigration
324.5	JF2085	Nominations for office	325.(2489/489)	JV8200-8209	Denmark—Emigration and immigration
324.52	JF2085	Caucus	325.(2492/492)	JV8150-8159	Netherlands—Emigration and immigration
324.54	JF2085	Primaries	325.(2493/493)	JV8160-8169	Belgium—Emigration and immigration
324.60973	JK1846-1929	Suffrage—United States			
324.62	JF831-851	Suffrage	325.(24935/4935)	JV8175	Luxembourg—Emigration and immigration
324.62	JF841	Voting age	325.(2494/494)	JV8280-8289	Switzerland—Emigration and immigration
324.62	JF1031	Voting, Compulsory	325.(2495/495)	JV8110-8119	Greece—Emigration and immigration
324.62	JS215	Suffrage	325.(25/5)	JV8490-8758	Asia—Emigration and immigration
324.62	JF825-1141	Voting	325.(251/51)	JV8700-8709	China—Emigration and immigration
324.6208996073	JK1924-1929	Afro-Americans—Suffrage			
324.6209376	JC85.S8	Suffrage	325.(251249/51249)	JV8710-8719	Taiwan—Emigration and immigration
324.620938	JC75.S8	Suffrage	325.(252/52)	JV8720-8729	Japan—Emigration and immigration
324.620973	JK1965-2217	Elections	325.(254/54)	JV8500-8509	India—Emigration and immigration
324.623	JF847-855	Women—Suffrage	325.(256/56)	JV8739-8751	Middle East—Emigration and immigration
324.63	JF285	Presidents—Election	325.(2599/599)	JV8685	Philippines—Emigration and immigration
324.63	JF1051-1075	Representative government and representation	325.(26/6)	JV8790-9024.5	Africa—Emigration and immigration
324.63	JF1051-1075	Majorities	325.(271/71)	JV7200-7299	Canada—Emigration and immigration
324.6301	B105.R4	Representation (Philosophy)	325.(272/72)	JV7400-7409	Mexico—Emigration and immigration
324.630943	JN3250.C83	Electors (Kurfursten)			
324.65	JF1091-1177	Ballot	325.(27281/7281)	JV7416	Guatemala—Emigration and immigration
324.65	JF1033	Absentee voting	325.(27283/7283)	JV7419	Honduras—Emigration and immigration
324.65	JF1128	Voting-machines	325.(27284/7284)	JV7423	El Salvador—Emigration and immigration
324.65	JF1125	Polling places	325.(27285/7285)	JV7426	Nicaragua—Emigration and immigration
324.650973	JK2214-2217	Ballot	325.(27286/7286)	JV7413	Costa Rica—Emigration and immigration
324.66	JK1994	Elections—Corrupt practices	325.(27287/7287)	JV7429	Panama—Emigration and immigration
324.66	JF1081-1083	Political corruption			
324.66	JF1081-1083	Elections—Corrupt practices			
324.660941	JN1088	Elections—Corrupt practices			
324.660973	JK2249	Elections—Corrupt practices			
324.68	JF247.R4	Recall			
324.680973	JK1533	Recall			
324.680973	JS344.R4	Recall			
324.70973	JK2251-2391	Campaign literature			
324.780973	JK1991-.5	Campaign funds			
324.973	JS426	Special districts—United States			
325.(2/1)	JV6001-9500	Emigration and immigration			
325.(2/1)09	JV6021-6032	Emigration and immigration—History			
325.(241/41)	JV7600-7699	Great Britain—Emigration and immigration			
325.(2411/411)	JV7700-7709	Scotland—Emigration and immigration			
325.(2415/415)	JV7710-7719	Ireland—Emigration and immigration			
325.(243/43)	JV8000-8099	Germany—Emigration and immigration			
325.(2436/436)	JV7800-7899	Austria—Emigration and immigration			

Dewey	LC	Subject Heading	Dewey	LC	Subject Heading
325.(2729/729)	JV7320-7397	West Indies—Emigration and immigration	327.1747	UA12.5	Disarmament—Inspection
			327.2	CD1-724	Diplomatics
325.(27291/7291)	JV7370-7379	Cuba—Emigration and immigration	327.2090(1-5)	CD50-79	Diplomatics—[By region or country]
325.(27293/7293)	JV7395	Dominican Republic—Emigration and immigration	327.4	D2009	Europe—Foreign relations—1989-
325.(27294/7294)	JV7393	Haiti—Emigration and immigration	328	JF501-619	Legislative bodies
			328	JF491-619	Legislation
325.(27295/7295)	JV7380-7389	Puerto Rico—Emigration and immigration	328.23	JF491-497	Referendum
			328.31	JF541-549	Legislative bodies—Upper chambers
325.(273/73)	JV6403-7127	United States—Emigration and immigration	328.310973	JK1154-1259	United States. Congress. Senate
325.(281/81)	JV7460-7469	Brazil—Emigration and immigration	328.32	JF601-619	Legislative bodies—Lower chambers
325.(282/82)	JV7440-7449	Argentina—Emigration and immigration	328.320973	JK1308-1432	United States. Congress. House
325.(283/83)	JV7470-7479	Chile—Emigration and immigration	328.33455	JK1347-1343	Gerrymander
325.(284/84)	JV7450-7459	Bolivia—Emigration and immigration	328.3347	JF1071-1075	Proportional representation
			328.34	JF538	Cloture
325.(285/85)	JV7510-7519	Peru—Emigration and immigration	328.34	JF519	Filibusters (Political science)
			328.369	JF518	Opposition (Political science)
325.(2861/861)	JV7480-7489	Colombia—Emigration and immigration	328.37411	KDC70-90	Legislation—Scotland
			328.37415	KDK38-50	Legislation—Ireland
325.(2866/866)	JV7490-7499	Ecuador—Emigration and immigration	328.37416	KDE42-50	Legislation—Northern Ireland
325.(287/87)	JV7530-7539	Venezuela—Emigration and immigration	328.3742	KD125-180	Legislation—England
			328.3771	KE78-125	Legislation—Canada
325.(2892/892)	JV7500-7509	Paraguay—Emigration and immigration	328.38097(4-9)	JK2498	Lobbying
			328.380973	JK1118	Lobbying
325.(2895/895)	JV7520-7529	Uruguay—Emigration and immigration	328.41	JN500-678	Great Britain. Parliament
			328.73	JK1012-1432	United States. Congress
325.(293/93)	JV9260-9269	New Zealand—Emigration and immigration	328.73025	JK1012	United States. Congress—Directories
325.(294/94)	JV9100-9199	Australia—Emigration and immigration	330	HB1-130	Economics
			330.01	HB131	Economics—Methodology
325.(29(5-6)/9(5-6)	JV9290-9470	Oceania—Emigration and immigration	330.011	HB141	Econometric models
			330.0112	HB3730	Economic forecasting
325.(2-1)	JV6118	Emigration and immigration—Economic aspects	330.015195	HB139-141	Econometrics
			330.025	HB63	Economics—Directories
			330.03	HB61	Economics—Dictionaries
325.(7-8)	JV221-231	America—Colonization	330.05	HB1-9	Economics—Periodicals
325.3	JV1-5399	Colonization	330.06	HB21	Economics—Congresses
325.309	JV61-151	Colonies—History	330.0727	HB137	Economics—Statistical methods
325.32	JC359	Imperialism			
325.341	JV1000-1099	Great Britain—Colonies	330.09	HB75-130	Economics—History
325.344	JV1800-1899	France—Colonies	330.090(1-33)	HB77-83	Economics—History—To 1800
325.345	JV2200-2299	Italy—Colonies			
325.346	JV4000-4099	Spain—Colonies	330.0902	HC41-42	Economic history—Medieval, 500-1500
325.3469	JV4200-4299	Portugal—Colonies			
325.3489	JV3300-3399	Denmark—Colonies	330.09034	HB85	Economics—History—19th century
325.3492	JV2500-2899	Benelux countries—Colonies			
325.352	JV5200-5299	Japan—Colonies	330.0904	HB87	Economics—History—20th century
325.373	JV500-599	United States—Territories and possessions	330.0904	HC54-60.5	Economic history—20th century
325.6	JV246	Africa—Colonization			
326.8	HT1025-1037	Slaves—Emancipation	330.09044	HC59-60.5	Economic history—1945-
327.112	D217	Balance of power	330.122	HB95	Free enterprise
327.117	HF1413.5	Economic sanctions	330.15	HB241	Supply-side economics
327.17	JC361-363	Internationalism	330.1513	HB91	Mercantile system
327.17	JC362	International cooperation	330.155	HD1311-1313	Single tax

Dewey	LC	Subject Heading	Dewey	LC	Subject Heading
330.157	HB201-205	Marginal utility	330.951249	HC430.5	Taiwan—Economic conditions
330.17	HB701-715	Property			
330.9	HC	Economic history	330.9519	HC466-470.2	Korea—Economic conditions
330.9	HF1021-1027	Economic geography			
330.9	HF1021-1027	Commercial geography	330.952	HC461-465	Japan—Economic conditions
330.917241	HC246	Commonwealth countries—Economic conditions	330.9533	HC415.34	Yemen—Economic conditions
330.91732	HT321-325	Urban economics	330.95353	HC415.35	Oman—Economic conditions
330.94	HC240-407	Europe—Economic conditions	330.95357	HC415.36	United Arab Emirates—Economic conditions
330.942	HC251-260	England—Economic conditions	330.95363	HC415.37	Qatar—Economic conditions
330.943	HC281-290.795	Germany—Economic conditions	330.95365	HC415.38	Bahrain—Economic conditions
330.9436	HC261-270	Austria—Economic conditions	330.95367	HC415.39	Kuwait—Economic conditions
330.9437	HC270.2-.295	Czechoslovakia—Economic conditions	330.9538	HC415.33	Saudi Arabia—Economic conditions
330.9438	HC340.3	Poland—Economic conditions	330.954	HC431-440	India—Economic conditions
330.944	HC275	Famine compact, 1765	330.95491	HC440.5	Pakistan—Economic conditions
330.944	HC271-280	France—Economic conditions	330.95492	HC440.8	Bangladesh—Economic conditions
330.945	HC301-310	Italy—Economic conditions	330.95493	HC424	Sri Lanka—Economic conditions
330.946	HC381-390	Spain—Economic conditions	330.95496	HC425	Nepal—Economic conditions
330.9469	HC391-394.5	Portugal—Economic conditions	330.955	HC471-480	Iran—Economic conditions
330.947	HC331-340	Russia—Economic conditions	330.9561	HC491-495	Turkey—Economic conditions
330.948	HC341-380	Scandinavia—Economic conditions	330.9567	HC415.4	Iraq—Economic conditions
330.9481	HC361-370	Norway—Economic conditions	330.95691	HC415.23	Syria—Economic conditions
330.9485	HC371-380	Sweden—Economic conditions	330.95692	HC415.24	Lebanon—Economic conditions
330.9489	HC351-360	Denmark—Economic conditions	330.95694	HC415.25	Israel—Economic conditions
330.9492	HC321-329.5	Netherlands—Economic conditions	330.95695	HC415.26	Jordan—Economic conditions
330.9493	HC311-320	Belgium—Economic conditions	330.9581	HC416-420	Afghanistan—Economic conditions
330.94935	HC330	Luxembourg—Economic conditions	330.9591	HC422	Burma—Economic conditions
330.9494	HC395-400	Switzerland—Economic conditions	330.9593	HC445	Thailand—Economic conditions
330.9495	HC291-300	Greece—Economic conditions	330.9594	HC443	Laos—Economic conditions
330.9496	HC401-407	Balkan Peninsula—Economic conditions	330.9596	HC442	Cambodia—Economic conditions
330.94965	HC402	Albania—Economic conditions	330.9597	HC444	Vietnam—Economic conditions
330.9497	HC407	Yugoslavia—Economic conditions	330.9598	HC446-450	Indonesia—Economic conditions
330.9498	HC405	Romania—Economic conditions	330.9599	HC451-460	Philippines—Economic conditions
330.9499	HC403	Bulgaria—Economic conditions	330.96	HC800-1085	Africa—Economic conditions
330.95	HC411-495	Asia—Economic conditions	330.9611	HC820	Tunisia—Economic conditions
330.951	HC426-430	China—Economic conditions	330.9612	HC825	Libya—Economic conditions

43

Dewey	LC	Subject Heading	Dewey	LC	Subject Heading
330.962	HC830	Egypt—Economic conditions	330.9730896073	E185.8	Afro-Americans—Economic conditions
330.9624	HC835	Sudan—Economic conditions	330.98	HC161-239.5	South America—Economic conditions
330.963	HC845	Ethiopia—Economic conditions	330.981	HC186-190	Brazil—Economic conditions
330.964	HC810	Morocco—Economic conditions	330.982	HC171-180	Argentina—Economic conditions
330.965	HC815	Algeria—Economic conditions	330.983	HC191-195	Chile—Economic conditions
330.96626	HC1020	Niger—Economic conditions	330.984	HC181-185	Bolivia—Economic conditions
330.96652	HC1030	Guinea—Economic conditions	330.985	HC226-230	Peru—Economic conditions
330.96668	HC1025	Cote d'Ivoire—Economic conditions	330.9861	HC196-200	Colombia—Economic conditions
330.9669	HC1055	Nigeria—Economic conditions	330.9866	HC201-204.5	Ecuador—Economic conditions
330.96711	HC995	Cameroon—Economic conditions	330.987	HC236-239.5	Venezuela—Economic conditions
330.96721	HC975	Gabon—Economic conditions	330.9892	HC221-225	Paraguay—Economic conditions
330.96724	HC980	Congo (Brazzaville)—Economic conditions	330.9895	HC231-235	Uruguay—Economic conditions
330.9673	HC950	Angola—Economic conditions	330.993	HC661-670	New Zealand—Economic conditions
330.96743	HC990	Chad—Economic conditions	330.994	HC601-610	Australia—Economic conditions
330.96751	HC955	Zaire—Economic conditions	330.99(5-6)	HC681-688	Islands of the Pacific—Economic conditions
330.967571	HC875	Rwanda—Economic conditions	330.997	HC585-595.5	Islands of the Atlantic—Economic conditions
330.967572	HC880	Burundi—Economic conditions	330.998(1-8)	HC731-740	Arctic regions
330.96761	HC870	Uganda—Economic conditions	330.9982	HC110.5	Greenland—Economic conditions
330.96762	HC865	Kenya—Economic conditions	331	HD4801-8943	Labor
330.96773	HC850	Somalia—Economic conditions	331	HD4801-8943	Work
			331	HD6958.5-6976	Industrial relations
330.9678	HC885	Tanzania—Economic conditions	331.011	HD6971.8	Employee rights
330.9679	HC890	Mozambique—Economic conditions	331.0112	HD5650-5660	Management—Employee particpation
330.968	HC905	South Africa—Economic conditions	331.09(4-9)	HD8045-8942.5	Labor—[By region or country]
330.96887	HC925	Swaziland—Economic conditions	331.094	HD8371-8650.7	Labor—Europe
			331.0941	HD8381-8400	Labor—Great Britain
330.9689	HC910	Rhodesia—Economic conditions	331.0943	HD8441-8460.5	Labor—Germany
			331.0944	HD8421-8440	Labor—France
330.96894	HC915	Zambia—Economic conditions	331.0945	HD8471-8490	Labor—Italy
			331.0946	HD8581-8590	Labor—Spain
330.9691	HC895	Madagascar—Economic conditions	331.0947	HD8521-8530	Labor—Russia
			331.09492	HD8491-8520.5	Labor—Benelux countries
330.971	HC111-120	Canada—Economic conditions	331.09494	HD8601-8610	Labor—Switzerland
			331.09495	HD8650.5	Labor—Greece
330.972	HC131-140	Mexico—Economic conditions	331.0951	HD8731-8740	Labor—China
			331.0952	HD8721-8730	Labor—Japan
330.9728	HC141-148	Central America—Economic conditions	331.0954	HD8681-8690	Labor—India
			331.0955	HD8670.2	Labor—Iran
330.9729	HC151-158.6	West Indies—Economic conditions	331.0956	HD8656-8669	Labor—Middle East
			331.09567	HD8670	Labor—Iraq
330.973	HC101-110	United States—Economic conditions	331.095694	HD8660	Labor—Israel
			331.09581	HD8670.6	Labor—Afghanistan
			331.09599	HD8711-8720	Labor—Philippines
			331.096	HD8771-8837	Labor—Africa
			331.0971	HD8101-8110	Labor—Canada

Dewey	LC	Subject Heading
331.0972	HD8111-8120	Labor—Mexico
331.09728	HD8126-8190	Labor—Central America
331.09729	HD8191-8250	Labor—West Indies
331.0973	HD8051-8085	Labor—United States
331.098	HD8251-8370	Labor—South America
331.0994	HD8841-8850	Labor—Australia
331.11	HD4904.7	Human capital
331.11	HD4801-8943	Working class
331.11	HD4801-8943	Proletariat
331.117	HD2337-2339	Sweatshops
331.1173	HD4905.5	Service, Compulsory non-military
331.1173	HD4871-4875	Service, Compulsory non-military
331.11734	HD4861-4865	Slave labor
331.12	HD5701-5852	Labor market
331.12	HD5701-5852	Labor supply
331.12042	HD7795-8013	Labor policy
331.1209(4-9)	HD5723-5851	Labor market—[By region or country]
331.12094	HD5764-5811.84	Labor market—Europe
331.120941	HD5765-5767.5	Labor market—Great Britain
331.120943	HD5777-5780.5	Labor market—Germany
331.120944	HD5773-5776	Labor market—France
331.120945	HD5782-5785	Labor market—Italy
331.120946	HD5805-5808	Labor market—Spain
331.120947	HD5794-5797	Labor market—Russia
331.1209492	HD5785.5-5793.5	Labor market—Benelux countries
331.1209494	HD5810	Labor market—Switzerland
331.1209495	HD5811.83	Labor market—Greece
331.120951	HD5830	Labor market—China
331.120952	HD5827	Labor market—Japan
331.120954	HD5817-5820	Labor market—India
331.120955	HD5812.56	Labor market—Iran
331.1209561	HD5811.93	Labor market—Turkey
331.1209567	HD5812.55	Labor market—Iraq
331.12095694	HD5812.2	Labor market—Israel
331.1209581	HD5812.6	Labor market—Afghanistan
331.1209599	HD5825	Labor market—Philippines
331.12096	HD5837-5849.3	Labor market—Africa
331.120971	HD5727-5729	Labor market—Canada
331.120972	HD5731	Labor market—Mexico
331.1209728	HD5733-5739	Labor market—Central America
331.1209729	HD5740-5745.9	Labor market—West Indies
331.120973	HD5723-5726	Labor market—United States
331.12098	HD5746-5763	Labor market—South America
331.120994	HD5850	Labor market—Australia
331.123	HD5701-5852	Labor demand
331.124	HD5710.5	Job vacancies
331.125	HD5701.5-.75	Employment (Economic theory)
331.125008997	E98.E6	Indians of North America—Employment
331.1250871	HV1652-1658	Blind—Employment
331.126	HF5549.5.T8	Labor turnover
331.128	HD5860-6000.7	Employment agencies
331.12809(4-9)	HD5871-6000.7	Employment agencies—[By region or country]
331.13	HD5709-.2	Underemployment
331.133	HD4903-.5	Discrimination in employment
331.137	HD5708.7-.75	Disguised unemployment
331.137	HD5707.5-5710.2	Unemployment
331.137	HD5707.5-5710.2	Unemployed
331.137	HD5708.8-.85	Hard-core unemployed
331.137041	HD5708.46-.47	Structural unemployment
331.137042	HD6331-.2	Technological unemployment
331.137044	HD5855-5856	Seasonal unemployment
331.137044	HD6271-.2	Summer employment
331.21	HB522-715	Income
331.21	HD4928.A5	Guaranteed annual wage
331.21	HD4909-5100.7	Wages
331.21091724	HD4967	Wages—Developing countries
331.21094	HD5014-5061.84	Wages—Europe
331.210971	HD4977-4980	Wages—Canada
331.210972	HD4981	Wages—Mexico
331.2109728	HD4983-4989	Wages—Central America
331.2109729	HD4990-4995.9	Wages—West Indies
331.210973	HD4973-4976	Wages—United States
331.21098	HD4996-5013	Wages—South America
331.2153	HD6061-.2	Pay equity
331.216	HD4928.T93	Two-tier wage payment systems
331.216	HD4928.D5	Severance pay
331.2162	HD5111	Overtime
331.2164	HD4928.B6	Bonus system
331.2164	HD4928.G34	Gain sharing
331.2164	HD4928.P5	Piece-work
331.2164	HD4928.S74	Employee stock options
331.2164	HD2970-3110.9	Profit-sharing
331.216409 (4-9)	HD2981-3110.9	Profit-sharing—[By region or country]
331.23	HD4917-4924	Minimum wage
331.2309(4-9)	HD4918-4924	Minimum wage—[By region or country]
331.25	HD2331-2336.35	Telecommuting
331.25	HD7260-7780.8	Work environment
331.25	HD6331-.2	Employees—Effect of technological innovations on
331.252	HD7105-7108.4	Retirement age
331.252	HD7105.3-.35	Old age pensions
331.252912532	BV4382	Clergy—Pensions
331.25291355	UB370-375	Military pensions
331.255	HD4928.E4	Employee discounts
331.255	HD4928.N6	Employee fringe benefits
331.255	HD4928.N6	Cafeteria benefit plans
331.2550973	HD7095-7096	Insurance, Unemployment
331.257	HD5106-5267	Hours of labor
331.257	HD5108-.2	Hours of labor, Staggered
331.2572	HD5109-.2	Hours of labor, Flexible
331.2572	HD5110-.2	Part-time employment
331.2572	HD5110.5-.6	Work sharing
331.2572	HD5111.5-.6	Shift systems
331.25723	HD5106-5267	Eight-hour movement
331.2574	HD5113-.2	Night work
331.2576	HD4928.H	Holiday pay

Dewey	LC	Subject Heading	Dewey	LC	Subject Heading
331.2576	HD5112	Rest periods	331.8924	HD5311	Wildcat strikes
331.2576	HD5114	Weekly rest-day	331.8925	HD5307	General strikes
331.2576	HD5260-5267	Vacations, Employee	331.89250941	HD5366	General strike, Great Britain, 1926
331.25762	HD5115.5-.6	Sick leave			
331.25763	HD6065-.5	Parental leave	331.892509416	HD5368	General strike, Northern Ireland, 1974
331.25763	HD5255-5257.3	Leave of absence			
331.25763	HD5257-.2	Educational leave	331.8927	HD5468	Picketing
331.2596	HD5708.4-.45	Job security	331.89290943	HD5379.C6	Eles (Firm) Strike, Bleidenstadt, Ger., 1975
331.2598	HD5715-.2	Abenteeism (Labor)			
331.2813711	LB2842-2844	Teachers—Salaries, etc.	331.89290952	HD5427	Daiichi Togyo Kabushiki Kaisha Strike, 1970-1975
331.28178	ML3795	Musicians—Salaries, etc.			
331.283	HD4966.A29	Agricultural wages	331.893	HD5461	Boycotts
331.287482	HD4966.C82	Coopers and cooperage	331.893	HD5473	Sabotage
331.31	HD6228-6250.5	Children—Employment	332	HG1655	Acceptances
331.34	HD6276.5-.52	College students—Employment	332	HG	Finance
			332	HG1-9999	Financial institutions
331.34	HD6270-6276	Youth—Employment	332.021	HG176-.5	Finance—Statistics
331.398	HD6279-6283	Aged—Employment	332.024	HG179	Finance, Personal
331.409(4-9)	HD6091-6220.7	Working class women—[By region or country]	332.024092	HG179.5	Financial planners
			332.025	HG64-96	Finance—Directories
331.4133	HD6060-.5	Sex discrimination in employment	332.03	HG151	Finance—Encyclopedias
			332.041	HC79.C3	Capital
331.52	UB356-359	Veterans—Employment	332.041	HB501	Capital
331.542	HD2365-2385	Contracting out	332.0414	HG4028.C4	Capital investments
331.542	HD4871-4875	Contract labor	332.0415	HG7920-7933	Saving and thrift
331.544	HD1521-1542	Migrant agricultural laborers	332.042	HG3891	Capital movements
331.544	HD5855-5856	Casual labor	332.042	HG3879-4000	International finance
331.544	HD5855-5856	Migrant labor	332.05	HG1-61	Finance—Periodicals
331.55	HD4881-4885	Apprentices	332.06	HG63	Finance—Congresses
331.6	HD6304	Minorities—Employment	332.071	HG152-.5	Finance—Study and teaching
331.62	HD6300	Alien labor			
331.7	HB2581-2787	Occupations—Statistics	332.09	HG171	Finance—History
331.702	HF5381-5382.5	Vocational guidance	332.1	HG1501-3550	Banks and banking
331.702	HD4903-.5	Free choice of employment	332.1	HG1616.C34	Bank capital
331.712	HD8038	Professional employees	332.1	HG1656	Bank reserves
331.761385	HE1741-1759	Railroads—Employees	332.10285	HG1710-.5	Electronic funds transfer
331.7622	HD8039.M6-.M7	Miners	332.10285	HG1709	Banks and banking—Computer programs
331.763	HD1521-1542	Agricultural laborers			
331.763	HD1521-1542	Peasantry	332.109(4-9)	HG2401-3542.7	Banks and banking—[By region or country]
331.792	HD8039.M39	White collar workers			
331.8	HD4801-4854	Labor movement	332.10973	HG2401-2626	Banks and banking—United States
331.88	HD6350-6940.7	Trade-unions			
331.8809	HD6451-6481.2	Trade-unions—History	332.110973	HG2559-2565	Federal Reserve banks
331.8809(4-9)	HD6500-6940.7	Trade-unions—[By region or country]	332.12	HG2301-2351	Clearinghouses (Banking)
			332.123	HG1978-2031	Private banks
331.880973	HD6500-6519	Trade-unions—United States	332.152	HG3882-3890	Balance of payments
331.88113711	LB2844.52-.53	Teachers' unions	332.16	HG1722	Bank mergers
331.8892	HD6488-.2	Open and closed shop	332.17	HG1711-1712	Home banking services
331.8892	HD4903-.5	Right to labor	332.17	HG1616.C87	Banks and banking—Customer services
331.8896	HD6972.5	Grievance procedures			
331.89	HD6971.5-.65	Collective bargaining	332.1752	HG1660	Bank deposits
331.8912	HD6490.R4	Trade-unions—Recognition	332.1752	HG1660	Savings accounts
331.8912	HD6490.07	Trade-unions—Organizing	332.1752	HG1660	Bank accounts
331.89143	HD5481-5630.7	Arbitration, Industrial	332.1752	HG1691-1704	Checking accounts
331.8914309 (4-9)	HD5501-5630.7	Arbitration, Industrial—[By region or country]	332.1753	HG1641-1643	Term loans
			332.1753	HG1641-1643	Commercial loans
331.892	HD5306-5474	Strikes and lockouts	332.1753	HG1641-1643	Bank loans
331.892(4-9)	HD5321-5450.7	Strikes and lockouts—[By region or country]	332.1754	HG1616.I5	Bank investments
			332.178	HG1643	Bank credit cards
331.8923	HD5309	Strikes and lockouts, Sympathetic	332.178	HG2251-2256	Safe-deposit boxes
			332.178	HG1643	Affinity credit cards

Dewey	LC	Subject Heading	Dewey	LC	Subject Heading
332.178	HG1643	Check credit plans	332.55	HG1685-1704	Drafts
332.21	HG1881-1966	Savings banks	332.6	HG4529.5	Portfolio management
332.22	HG1951-1956	Postal savings banks	332.6	HG4501-6051	Investments
332.26	HG4301-4480.9	Trust companies	332.6	HG4530	Investment clubs
332.26025	HG4307	Trust companies—Directories	332.609(4-9)	HG4901-5993	Investments—[By region or country]
332.2609	HG4311	Trust companies—History	332.60973	HG4905-5131	Investments—United States
332.2609(4-9)	HG4341-4480.9	Trust companies—[By region or country]	332.62	HG4621	Discount brokers
			332.62	HG4621	Stockbrokers
332.260973	HG4341-4356	Trust companies—United States	332.63	AM237	Collectibles as an investment
332.28	HG1975-1976	Development banks	332.63	N8600	Art as an investment
332.31	HG2041-2051	Land banks	332.632	HG4650-4930.5	Securities
332.31	HG2041-2051	Agricultural cooperative credit associations	332.6322	HG4028.T4	Tender offers (Securities)
			332.6322	HG4661	Stocks
332.32	HG2039.5-2040.5	Mortgage banks	332.63221	HG4028.D5	Dividend reinvestment
			332.63221	HG4028.V3	Valuation
332.32	HG2121-2156	Savings and loan associations	332.63228	HG6043	Stock index futures
			332.63228	HG6042	Stock options
332.34	HG2070-2106	Pawnbroking	332.6323	HB531-549	Interest rates
332.34	HG2070-2106	Pawnbrokers	332.6323	HG4028.B6	Bond transfer
332.37	HG1970-1971	Merchant banks	332.6323	HG4651	Bonds
332.4	GN435.7-450.5	Shell money	332.63232	HG4701-4726	Government securities
332.4	GN436.2	Stone money	332.632320973	HG4931-4955	Government securities—United States
332.4	HG321-329	Mints			
332.4	HG201-1496	Money	332.63233	HG4726	Municipal bonds
332.4	HG235	Shell money	332.63244	HG4655	Mortgages
332.4	HG353.5	Military currency	332.6327	HG4530	Mutual funds
332.401	HG226.6	Quantity theory of money	332.6328	HG6046-6051	Commodity futures
332.4021	HG3854-3858	Money—Tables	332.642	HG4621	Floor traders (Finance)
332.4042	HG258-312	Precious metals	332.642	HG4551-4598	Stock-exchanges
332.4042	HG321	Gold—Minting	332.64273	HG4571-4575.3	Wall Street
332.4042	HG261-315	Coinage	332.644	HG6046-6051	Commodity exchanges
332.4042	HG289	Gold	332.645	HG6001-6051	Speculation
332.40420973	HG551	Gold	332.645	HG6024-6051	Futures
332.40420973	HG551-566	Coinage	332.645	HG3853	Foreign exchange futures
332.4044	HG348-353.5	Paper money	332.645	HG6024.3-.9	Financial futures
332.4044	HG348-353.5	Bank notes	332.6722	HG1723	Bank stocks
332.40440973	HG607-610	Bank notes	332.673	HG4538	Investments, Foreign
332.40440973	HG604	Greenbacks	332.7	HG3746	Documentary credit
332.4048	HG393	Decimal system	332.7	HG3691-3769	Credit
332.4089973	E98.M7	Wampum	332.7	HG3752.3	Accounts receivable loans
332.41	HG229-.5	Purchasing power	332.7	HG3751.5-.9	Credit ratings
332.41	HG229-.5	Prices	332.71	HD1439-1440	Agricultural credit
332.41	HG223	Value	332.72	HD1443	Mortgages
332.414	HG226.5	Demand for money	332.72	HG2039.5-2040.5	Mortgage loans, Reverse
332.42042	HG361-363	Legal tender			
332.4222	HG297	Gold standard	332.722	HG2040.4	Home improvement loans
332.4223	HG301-309	Silver	332.722	HG2040.45	Home equity loans
332.45	HG3810-4000	Foreign exchange	332.742	HG3751-3754.5	Commercial credit
332.45	HG381-421	Coinage, International	332.742	HG3753-3754	Export credit
332.4503	HG3810.5	Foreign exchange—Encyclopedias	332.743	HG3755.5	Installment plan
			332.743	HG3755-3756	Consumer credit
332.4509	HG3811-3815	Foreign exchange—History	332.743	HG3755-3756	Loans, Personal
332.4509(4-9)	HG3901-4000	Foreign exchange—[By region or country]	332.75	HG3773	Receivers
			332.75	HG3705-3711	Credit control
332.49(4-9)	HG451-1496	Money—[By region or country]	332.75	HG3760-3769	Bankruptcy
			332.76	HG1692	Check float
332.490973	HG641-645	Counterfeits and counterfeiting	332.76	HG1692	Check collection systems
			332.76	HG1710.5	Debit cards
332.4973	HG451-645	Money—United States	332.77	HG3745	Letters of credit

Dewey	LC	Subject Heading	Dewey	LC	Subject Heading
332.82	HG1621-1623	Interest rates	333.7309499	HD811-820	Land use—Bulgaria
332.83	HB551	Usury	333.730951	HD921-930	Land use—China
332.84	HG1651-1654	Discount houses (Finance)	333.730951249	HD936-940	Land use—Taiwan
332.84	HG1651-1654	Discount	333.73095125	HD941-945	Land use—Hong Kong
332.9	HG1696-1698	Forgery	333.73095126	HD931-935	Land use—Macao
332.90973	HG335-341	Counterfeits and counterfeiting	333.7309517	HD920.8	Land use—Mongolia
			333.7309519	HD920.5-.6	Land use—Korea
333.14	HD1301-1339	Land, Nationalization of	333.730952	HD911-920	Land use—Japan
333.2	HD1286-1289	Commons	333.7309533	HD854-.5	Land use—Yemen
333.3	HD1241-1339	Land tenure	333.73095353	HD855	Land use—Oman
333.30973	HD251-279	Real property	333.73095357	HD856	Land use—United Arab Emirates
333.31	HD1332-1333.5	Land reform			
333.32	HD1336-1339	Peasantry	333.73095363	HD857	Land use—Qatar
333.33	HD1361-1395.5	Real estate business	333.73095365	HD858	Land use—Bahrain
333.33	HD1334-1335	Consolidation of land holdings	333.73095367	HD859	Land use—Kuwait
			333.7309538	HD853	Land use—Saudi Arabia
333.335	HD1471	Haciendas	333.730954	HD871-880	Land use—India
333.335563	HD1478	Sharecropping	333.73095491	HD880.5	Land use—Pakistan
333.5	HB401	Rent	333.73095492	HD880.6	Land use—Bangladesh
333.7	HF1051-1054	Raw materials	333.73095493	HD860.8	Land use—Sri Lanka
333.7	SH327.5	Fishery resources	333.73095495	HD1029.7	Land use—Maldives
333.7071	GE70-90	Environmental education	333.73095496	HD860.9	Land use—Nepal
333.7071	GE70-90	Environmental education	333.73095498	HD880.3	Land use—Bhutan
333.72	GE195-199	Green movement	333.730955	HD860.2	Land use—Iran
333.72	JA75.8	Green movement	333.7309561	HD846.5	Land use—Turkey
333.72	S900-954	Conservation of natural resources	333.7309567	HD860	Land use—Iraq
			333.73095691	HD848	Land use—Syria
333.72071	S946	Environmental education	333.73095692	HD849	Land use—Lebanon
333.73	HD101-1131	Land use	333.73095693	HD847	Land use—Cyprus
333.7309	HD113-156	Land use—History	333.73095694	HD850	Land use—Israel
333.7309411	HD611-620	Land use—Scotland	333.73095695	HD851	Land use—Jordan
333.7309415	HD621-630	Land use—Ireland	333.7309581	HD860.6	Land use—Afghanistan
333.7309416	HD620.5	Land use—Northern Ireland	333.7309591	HD860.7	Land use—Burma
333.730942	HD601-610	Land use—England	333.7309593	HD890.55	Land use—Thailand
333.730943	HD651-660.5	Land use—Germany	333.7309594	HD890.4	Land use—Laos
333.7309436	HD631-640	Land use—Austria	333.7309595	HD890.6	Land use—Malaysia
333.730943648	HD640.9	Land use—Liechtenstein	333.7309596	HD890.3	Land use—Cambodia
333.7309437	HD640.3	Land use—Czechoslovakia	333.7309597	HD890.5	Land use—Vietnam
333.7309438	HD726-729.5	Land use—Poland	333.7309598	HD891-900	Land use—Indonesia
333.7309439	HD640.5	Land use—Hungary	333.7309599	HD901-910	Land use—Philippines
333.730944	HD641-650	Land use—France	333.7309611	HD974	Land use—Tunisia
333.730944949	HD650.5	Land use—Monaco	333.7309612	HD975	Land use—Libya
333.730945	HD671-680	Land use—Italy	333.730962	HD976	Land use—Egypt
333.730946	HD771-780	Land use—Spain	333.7309624	HD977	Land use—Sudan
333.7309469	HD781-790	Land use—Portugal	333.730963	HD979	Land use—Ethiopia
333.73094698	HD1028.5	Land use—Madeira Islands	333.730964	HD972	Land use—Morocco
333.73094699	HD1028	Land use—Azores	333.7309648	HD1027	Land use—Western Sahara
333.730947	HD711-720	Land use—Russia	333.7309649	HD1028.7	Land use—Canary Islands
333.7309481	HD751-760	Land use—Norway	333.730965	HD973	Land use—Algeria
333.7309485	HD761-770	Land use—Sweden	333.7309661	HD1020	Land use—Mauritania
333.7309489	HD731-740	Land use—Denmark	333.73096623	HD1017	Land use—Mali
333.73094897	HD721-725	Land use—Finland	333.73096625	HD1018	Land use—Burkina Faso
333.73094912	HD741-750	Land use—Iceland	333.73096626	HD1014	Land use—Niger
333.7309492	HD701-710	Land use—Netherlands	333.7309663	HD1019	Land use—Senegal
333.7309493	HD691-700	Land use—Belgium	333.7309664	HD1023	Land use—Sierra Leone
333.73094935	HD710.5	Land use—Luxembourg	333.73096651	HD1024	Land use—Gambia
333.7309494	HD791-800	Land use—Switzerland	333.73096652	HD1016	Land use—Guinea
333.7309495	HD840.5	Land use—Greece	333.73096657	HD1026	Land use—Guinea Bissau
333.73094965	HD810.5	Land use—Albania	333.73096658	HD1028.9	Land use—Cape Verde
333.7309497	HD821-825	Land use—Yugoslavia	333.73096662	HD1025	Land use—Liberia
333.7309498	HD831-840	Land use—Romania	333.73096668	HD1015	Land use—Cote d'Ivoire

Dewey	LC	Subject Heading	Dewey	LC	Subject Heading
333.7309667	HD1022	Land use—Ghana	333.730972973	HD453.8	Land use—Saint Kitts and Nevis
333.73096681	HD1013	Land use—Togo	333.730972973	HD453.2	Land use—Anguilla
333.73096683	HD1012	Land use—Benin	333.730972974	HD453.4	Land use—Antigua
333.7309669	HD1021	Land use—Nigeria	333.730972975	HD453.6	Land use—Montserrat
333.73096711	HD1009	Land use—Cameroon	333.730972976	HD458	Land use—Guadeloupe
333.73096715	HD1003	Land use—Sao Tome and Principe	333.730972977	HD456.8	Land use—Saba (Netherlands Antilles)
333.73096718	HD1002	Land use—Equatorial Guinea	333.730972977	HD456.85	Land use—Saint Eustatius (Netherlands Antilles)
333.73096721	HD1005	Land use—Gabon	333.730972977	HD456.9	Land use—Saint Martin
333.73096724	HD1006	Land use—Congo (Brazzaville)	333.730972981	HD451.5	Land use—Barbados
333.7309673	HD1000	Land use—Angola	333.730972982	HD459	Land use—Martinique
333.73096741	HD1007	Land use—Central African Republic	333.730972983	HD455	Land use—Trinidad and Tobago
333.73096743	HD1008	Land use—Chad	333.7309729841	HD454.3	Land use—Dominica
333.73096751	HD1001	Land use—Zaire	333.7309729843	HD454.7	Land use—Saint Lucia
333.730967571	HD985	Land use—Rwanda	333.7309729844	HD454.9	Land use—Saint Vincent
333.730967572	HD986	Land use—Burundi	333.7309729845	HD454.5	Land use—Grenada
333.73096761	HD984	Land use—Uganda	333.730972986	HD456.5	Land use—Aruba
333.73096762	HD983	Land use—Kenya	333.730972986	HD456.7	Land use—Curacao
333.73096771	HD981	Land use—Djibouti	333.730972986	HD456.6	Land use—Bonaire
333.73096773	HD980	Land use—Somalia	333.73097299	HD1028.3	Land use—Bermuda Islands
333.7309678	HD987	Land use—Tanzania	333.730973	HD170-279	Land use—United States
333.7309679	HD988	Land use—Mozambique	333.730981	HD491-500	Land use—Brazil
333.730968	HD991	Land use—South Africa	333.730982	HD471-480	Land use—Argentina
333.73096881	HD998	Land use—Namibia	333.730983	HD501-510	Land use—Chile
333.73096883	HD996	Land use—Botswana	333.730984	HD481-490	Land use—Bolivia
333.73096885	HD994	Land use—Lesotho	333.730985	HD551-560	Land use—Peru
333.73096887	HD995	Land use—Swaziland	333.7309861	HD511-520	Land use—Colombia
333.7309689	HD992	Land use—Rhodesia	333.7309866	HD521-530	Land use—Ecuador
333.73096894	HD993	Land use—Zambia	333.730987	HD571-580	Land use—Venezuela
333.73096897	HD997	Land use—Malawi	333.7309881	HD540.3	Land use—Guyana
333.7309691	HD989	Land use—Madagascar	333.7309882	HD540.7	Land use—French Guiana
333.7309694	HD1030	Land use—Comoro Islands	333.7309883	HD540.5	Land use—Surinam
333.7309696	HD1029.9	Land use—Seychelles	333.7309892	HD541-550	Land use—Paraguay
333.73096981	HD1030.5	Land use—Reunion	333.7309895	HD561-570	Land use—Uruguay
333.73096982	HD1030.3	Land use—Mauritius	333.730993	HD1120.5	Land use—New Zealand
333.7309699	HD1030.7	Land use—Kerguelen Islands	333.730994	HD1031-1040	Land use—Australia
333.730971	HD311-320	Land use—Canada	333.7309953	HD1122	Land use—Papau New Guinea
333.730972	HD321-330	Land use—Mexico	333.73099593	HD1123	Land use—Solomon Islands
333.73097281	HD351-360	Land use—Guatemala	333.73099595	HD1125	Land use—Vanuatu
333.73097282	HD336-340	Land use—Belize	333.73099597	HD1124	Land use—New Caledonia
333.73097283	HD361-370	Land use—Honduras	333.73099611	HD1126	Land use—Fiji
333.73097284	HD391-400	Land use—El Salvador	333.73099612	HD1127	Land use—Tonga
333.73097285	HD371-380	Land use—Nicaragua	333.73099613	HD1128	Land use—American Samoa
333.73097286	HD341-350	Land use—Costa Rica	333.7309962	HD1129.5	Land use—French Polynesia
333.73097287	HD381-385	Land use—Panama	333.73099623	HD1127.5	Land use—Cook Islands
333.730972875	HD386-390	Land use—Panama Canal Zone	333.7309967	HD1121.5	Land use—Guam
			333.73099681	HD1122.3	Land use—Kiribati
333.73097291	HD411-420	Land use—Cuba	333.7309971	HD1029.5	Land use—Falkland Islands
333.73097292	HD431-440	Land use—Jamaica	333.7309973	HD1029.3	Land use—Tristan da Cunha
333.73097293	HD426-430	Land use—Dominican Republic	333.7309973	HD1029	Land use—Saint Helena
333.73097294	HD421-425	Land use—Haiti	333.730998(1-8)	HD1130	Land use—Arctic regions
333.73097295	HD441-450	Land use—Puerto Rico	333.7309982	HD1130.5	Land use—Greenland
333.73097296	HD406-410	Land use—Bahamas	333.73137	HD1665-1671	Waste lands
333.7309729722	HD450.3	Land use—Virgin Islands of the United States	333.7316	S439-481	Green Revolution
			333.736153	HD1711-1741	Desert reclamation
			333.736153	TC801-957	Desert reclamation
			333.740973	HD241	Grazing

Dewey	LC	Subject Heading	Dewey	LC	Subject Heading
333.75	SD387.043	Old growth forests	335.009(4-9)	HX80-517.5	Socialism—[By region or country]
333.75	SD426-428	Forest reserves			
333.75	SD411-428	Forest conservation	335.1209	HX626-632	Utopian socialism—History
333.76	HD1393	Farms—Valuation	335.1209(4-9)	HX651-780.7	Utopian socialism—[By region or country]
333.76	HD101-1131	Land capability for agriculture	335.1209694	HX742.2	Kibbutzim
333.77	HD1393.5	Industrial districts	335.15	HD6479	Guild socialism
333.7717	HT169.6-.9	Zoning	335.4	HB97.5	Marxian economics
333.780973	E160	National parks and reserves—United States	335.4092	HX518.L4	Communist leadership
			335.412	HB206	Labor theory of value
333.7816	QH75-77	Nature conservation	335.43	HX77	Democratic centralism
333.784	GV191.67.F6	Forest reserves—Recreational use	335.7	HX51-54	Socialism, Christian
			335.82	HD6477	Syndicalism
333.79	HD9502-.5	Energy policy	335.83	HX821-970.7	Anarchism
333.79	TN263.5	Energy minerals	335.8309(4-9)	HX841-970.7	Anarchism—[By region or country]
333.7923	HD9681	Solar energy industries			
333.7924	HD9698-.5	Nuclear industry	336	HJ2240-7395	Taxation
333.7932	HD9685-9695	Electric utilities	336	HJ	Finance, Public
333.8509162	TN264	Marine mineral resources	336.005	HJ9-99.8	Finance, Public—Periodicals
333.850973	HD242.5	Mineral lands	336.014	HJ9103-9695	Local finance
333.91	HD1690-1702	Water resources development	336.014(4-9)	HJ9141-9695	Local finance—[By region or country]
333.9164	GC1000-1023	Marine resources	336.01405	HJ9103	Local finance—Periodicals
333.916416	GC1018	Marine resources conservation	336.01473	HJ9141-9343	Local finance—United States
333.91816	QH75-77	Wetland conservation	336.02	HJ2240-7395	Revenue
333.95	QH75-77	Biosphere reserves	336.09(4-9)	HJ210-240	Finance, Public—History
333.95	QH75-77	Biological diversity conservation	336.1	HS351-929	Freemasons
			336.16	HJ5301-5508	Licenses
333.953	QK86-.4	Plant conservation	336.1609(4-9)	HJ5321-5510	Licenses—[By region or country]
333.95416	SF996.45	Wildlife rehabilitation			
333.95416	QL81.5-84.7	Wildlife conservation	336.160973	HJ5321-5374	Licenses—United States
333.95416	QL83.4	Wildlife reintroduction	336.17	HG6105-6270.9	Lotteries
333.958	QL676.5-.57	Bird refuges	336.170973	HG6126-6134	Lotteries—United States
333.95816	SK351-579	Birds, Protection of	336.2	HJ3241	Tax assessment
334	HD2951-3575	Cooperation	336.20015195	HJ2351.4	Tax revenue estimating
334.06	HD2952	Cooperation—Societies, etc.	336.2009	HJ2250-2279	Taxation—History
			336.2009(4-9)	HJ2361-3192.7	Taxation—[By region or country]
334.09	HD2956	Cooperation—History			
334.1	HD7287.7-.72	Housing, Cooperative	336.20097(4-9)	HJ2391-2442	Taxation—[United States, By state]
334.2	HG2032-2039	Banks and banking, Cooperative	336.200973	HJ2361-2442	Taxation—United States
334.22	HG2032-2039	Credit unions	336.200973	HJ2361	Internal revenue—United States
334.5	HD3271-3575	Consumers' leagues			
334.5	HD3271-3575	Consumer cooperatives	336.2014	HJ9115-9123	Municipal revenue
334.509	HD3281-3410.9	Consumer cooperatives—[By region or country]	336.206	HJ2336-2337	Tax exemption
			336.207	HD2753	Corporations—Taxation
334.6	HD3120-3260.9	Producer cooperatives	336.22	HJ4101-4936	Property tax
334.609(4-9)	HD3131-3260.9	Producer cooperatives—[By region or country]	336.23	HJ4581-4601	Taxation of personal property
			336.2309(4-9)	HJ4120-4460	Property tax—[By region or country]
334.683	HD1483-1491.5	Agriculture, Cooperative			
334.683	HD1492-.5	Collective farms	336.24	HJ4621-4830	Income tax
334.683	HD1493-.5	State farms	336.24240973	HJ4653.C3	Capital gains tax
334.683	HX550.A37	Communism and agriculture	336.24320973	HJ4653.E8	Excess profits tax
334.7	HG9201-9245	Friendly societies	336.27	HJ5711-5715	Turnover tax
334.7	HS1501-1510	Friendly societies	336.271	HJ5730-5731	Excise tax
335	HX1-550	Socialism	336.271	HJ5771-5797	Luxuries—Taxation
335.0071	HX19-.2	Socialism—Study and teaching	336.2713	HJ5711-5721	Sales tax
			336.2714	HJ5711-5715	Value-added tax
335.009	HX21-54	Socialism—History	336.272	HJ5315	Revenue-stamps
			336.276	HJ5801-5823	Inheritance and transfer tax

Dewey	LC	Subject Heading	Dewey	LC	Subject Heading
336.27863371	HD9130-9149	Tobacco industry	338.27633	HD9585.B67-.B675	Borax
336.293	HJ2326-2327	Progressive taxation	338.372072	SH343.4	Fishery research vessels
336.294	HJ2321-2323	Tax incidence	338.3727	SH334	Fisheries subsidies
336.294	HJ3863-3925	Direct taxation	338.4	HD9980-9990	Service industries
336.294	HJ5250-5255	Indirect taxation	338.47004	HD9696.D54-.D544	Digital computer industry
336.29409(4-9)	HJ3925.A-.Z	Direct taxation—[By region or country]	338.4702504	HD9696.D36-.D364	Database industry
336.3	HJ8003-8899	Debts, External	338.47355	HD9743-9744	Defense industries
336.3	HJ8001-8899	Debts, Public	338.47355092	HD8039.M9	Defense industries—Employees
336.3409(4-9)	HJ8101-8899	Debts, Public—[By region or country]	338.473621	RA410-415	Medical economics
336.363	HJ8052	Sinking-funds	338.4738773	HD9711-.2	Aircraft industry
336.368	HJ8061	State bankruptcy	338.4739142	HD9948.3	Lingerie industry
336.39	HJ7461-7977	Expenditures, Public	338.4754786	HD9660.D84-.D844	Dye industry
336.3909(4-9)	HJ7537-7977	Expenditures, Public—[By region or country]	338.476151	HD9665-9675	Nonprescription drug industry
336.390973	HJ7537-7654	Expenditures, Public—United States	338.476153137	HD9675.A7-.A74	Aspirin
336.7(4-9)	HJ285-785	Finance, Public—[United States, By state]	338.4762161	HD9705.5.F35-.F354	Fans (Machinery) industry
336.73	HJ241-785	Finance, Public—United States	338.476218	HD9705-9705.5	Machinery industry
337	HF1351-1532.935	International economic relations	338.4762382	VM298.5-301	Shipbuilding industry
337.(4-9)	HF1451-1647	International economic relations—[By region or country]	338.47624	HD9715-9717.5	Construction industry
			338.4762912	HD9711.5	Aerospace industries
			338.47637143	HD9275-9283.7	Dairy products industry
337.14	HG3896	Euro-bond market	338.476453	HD9939	Drapery industry
338	HD2329	Industrialization	338.4766	HD9650-9660	Chemical industry
338	HD2321-4730.9	Industries	338.4766316	HD9390-9395	Distilling industries
338	HD	Production (Economic theory)	338.476655	HD9490-.5	Oil industries
338	HF1040-1054	Primary commodities	338.476655384	HD9579.D5-.D54	Diesel fuels industry
338.04	HB615	Entrepreneurship	338.476682	HD9660.G58-.G6	Glycerin
338.06	HD56-57.5	Industrial productivity	338.476683	HD9999.A4-.A44	Adhesives industry
338.068	HD30.22	Managerial economics	338.4767	HD9720-9739	Manufactures
338.0919	TL797	Space industrialization	338.4767	HD7406-7510	Factories
338.1	SB107-109	Botany, Economic	338.4767634	HD9971.5.T32-.T324	Disposal tableware industry
338.13	HD1447	Agricultural prices	338.476774742	HD9929.5.A27-.A274	Acrylic fiber industry
338.16	HD1470-1476	Farms, Size of			
338.16	HD1471	Farms	338.47678	HD9662.E42-.E423	Elastomer industry
338.16	HD1401-2210	Farms			
338.163	HD1549	Gleaning	338.476816	HD9801	Electronic office machine industry
338.17	HD9000-9019	Farm produce			
338.17351	HD9070-9093	Cotton growing	338.47681761	HD9995.D54-.D544	Diagnostic equipment industry
338.17498	SD430-557	Timber			
338.1767	SF434.5-435	Dog industry	338.476834	HD9744.F55-.F554	Firearms industry and trade
338.181	HD1428-1431	Agriculture—International cooperation	338.476887221	HD9993-.D65-.D654	Doll industry
338.2025	TN12	Mineral industries—Directories	338.4791	G154.9	Tourist trade
338.203	TN9-10	Mineral industries—Dictionaries	338.5	HB615	Risk
			338.516	HC79.P7	Profit
338.205	TN1-4	Mineral industries—Periodicals	338.516	HB601	Profit
			338.52	HB221-236	Prices
338.206	TN5	Mineral industries—Congresses	338.52	HB143	Shadow prices
			338.52	HF5417	Price cutting
338.2074	TN6	Mineral industries—Exhibitions	338.52	HD6977-7080	Prices
338.209	TN15-124	Mineral industries—History	338.521	HB201-206	Supply and demand
338.2724	HD9540-9559	Coal	338.521	HB201-206	Value
			338.526	HB236	Prices—Government policy

Dewey	LC	Subject Heading	Dewey	LC	Subject Heading
338.542	HB3711-3840	Business cycles	338.740973	HD2771-2798.5	Corporations—United States
338.542	HB3722-3725	Financial crises	338.74098	HD2827-2843	Corporations—South America
338.542	HB3711-3840	Depressions			
338.542	HB3729	Long waves (Economics)	338.740994	HD2930	Corporations—Australia
338.54209(4-9)	HB3741-3840	Business cycles—[By region or country]	338.76313	HD9486-.6	Agricultural machinery industry
338.6	HD2756-.2	Diversification in industry	338.7637143	HD9282	Dried milk industry
338.6041	HG4001-4285	Business enterprises—Finance	338.790896073	E185.8	Afro-Americans in business
338.6042	HD5708.5-.55	Plant shutdowns	338.8042	HD2756-.2	Conglomerate corporations
338.6048	HD41	Competition	338.82	HD2757-2768	Oligopolies
338.6048	HB238	Competition, Imperfect	338.82	HD2709-2932	Monopolies
338.6048	HF1414	Competition	338.83	HG4028.M4	Consolidation and merger of corporations
338.634	HD2336.2-.25	Cottage industries			
338.634	HD2331-2336.35	Home labor	338.83	HD2746.5-.55	Consolidation and merger of corporations
338.634	HD2331-2336.35	Home-based businesses			
338.6420681	HG4027.7	Small business—Finance	338.86	HD2709-2932	Stock companies
338.644	HD2350.8-2356	Big business	338.87	HD2757.5	Cartels
338.65	HD2350.8-2356	Factory system	338.9	HD72-88	Economic development
338.7	HC79.D5	Business relocation	338.9	HD82-85	Autarchy
338.7	HD62.25	Family-owned business enterprises	338.9	HD87-88	Economic policy
			338.901	HD108-.8	Economic development—Methodology
338.7	HD62.27	Couple-owned business enterprises	338.926	T174.3	Technology transfer
338.7	HD5650-5660	Employee ownership	338	T58.7-.8	Industrial capacity
338.7	HF5001-6182.2	Business	339.21	HB401	Rent
338.74	HD59.2	Corporate image	339.23	HB142	Input-output analysis
338.74	HD59	Corporations—Investor relations	339.42	HD6977-7080	Cost and standard of living
			339.46	HC79.P6	Poverty
338.74	HG4001-4285	Corporations—Finance	339.47	HC79.C6	Consumption (Economics)
338.74	HD2709-2932	Corporations	339.47	HB801-843	Consumption (Economics)
338.7409	HD2770-2930.7	Corporations—[By region or country]	339.47092	HC79.C6	Consumers
			339.5	HB3732	Economic stabilization
338.74094	HD2844-2891.84	Corporations—Europe	339.5	HB145	Equilibrium (Economics)
338.740941	HD2845-2847.5	Corporations—Great Britain	340-349	K	Law
338.740943	HD2857-2860.5	Corporations—Germany	340.0207	K183-184.7	Law—Humor
338.740944	HD2853-2856	Corporations—France	340.03	K50-54	Law—Dictionaries
338.740945	HD2862-2865	Corporations—Italy	340.071	K100-103	Law—Study and teaching
338.740946	HD2885-2888	Corporations—Spain	340.0711	LC1101-1261	Law schools
338.7409469	HD2889	Corporations—Portugal	340.09	K325-328	Historical jurisprudence
338.740947	HD2874-2877	Corporations—Russia	340.09	K140-165	Law—History
338.7409492	HD2865.5-2873.5	Corporations—Benelux countries	340.092	K170	Law—Biography
			340.0973	KF338	Lawyer referral service—United States
338.7409495	HD2891.83	Corporations—Greece			
338.740951	HD2910	Corporations—China	340.11	K280-286	Law—Sources
338.740952	HD2907	Corporations—Japan	340.11	KF382	Rule of law—United States
338.740954	HD2897-2900	Corporations—India	340.115	K368-380	Sociological jurisprudence
338.740955	HD2892.56	Corporations—Iran	340.18	BM523.5.S53	Shaving (Jewish law)
338.7409561	HD2891.93	Corporations—Turkey	340.2	K583-591	Comparative law
338.7409567	HD2892.55	Corporations—Iraq	340.52	K190-195	Law, Primitive
338.74095694	HD2892.2	Corporations—Israel	340.550942	KD834-839	Feudal law—England
338.7409598	HD2904	Corporations—Indonesia	340.59	BP140-165	Islamic law
338.7409599	HD2905	Corporations—Philippines	340.9	K7680	Judgments, Foreign
338.74096	HD2917-2929.3	Corporations—Africa	340.912	K7120-7197	Conflict of laws—Persons
338.740971	HD2807-2810	Corporations—Canada	340.913	K7145-7148	Conflict of laws—Juristic persons
338.740972	HD2811	Corporations—Mexico			
338.7409728	HD2813.5-2819	Corporations—Central America	340.915	K7155-7197	Conflict of laws—Domestic relations
338.7409729	HD2820.5-2825.9	Corporations—West Indies	340.917	K7181-7197	Conflict of laws—Parent and child

Dewey	LC	Subject Heading	Dewey	LC	Subject Heading
340.918	K7197	Conflict of laws—Guardian and ward	342.420412	KD4030	England—Foreign relations—Law and legislation
340.92	K7260-7335	Conflict of laws—Obligations	342.42042	KD680-685	Conflict of laws—England
340.92	K7265-7305	Conflict of laws—Contracts	342.42044	KD4000-4010	Separation of powers—England
340.929	K7310	Conflict of laws—Quasi contracts	342.4205	KD4190-4381	Great Britain. Parliament.
340.93	K7315-7335	Conflict of laws—Torts	342.4206	KD4430-4531	Monarchy—Great Britain
340.94	K7200-7218	Conflict of laws—Property	342.4206	KD4462	Prime ministers—Great Britain
340.948	K7550-7582	Conflict of laws—Intellectual property	342.42083	KD4050-4058	Citizenship—England
340.948	K7570-7582	Conflict of laws—Industrial property	342.42083	KD4130-4139	Aliens—England
			342.42085	KD4080-4119	Civil rights—England
340.9482	K7555-7557	Conflict of laws—Copyright licenses	342.4209	KD4746-4840	Local government—Law and legislation—England
340.952	K7230-7245	Conflict of laws—Inheritance and succession	342.421	KD8996-9142	Statutes—London
			342.71	KE4125-4775	Canada—Constitutional law
340.966	K7490-7495	Conflict of laws—Corporations	342.710412	KE4310	Canada—Foreign relations—Law and legislation
340.97	K7340-7512	Conflict of laws—Commercial law	342.710418	KE5006-5010	Police power—Canada
			342.71042	KE470-474	Conflict of laws—Canada
340.97	K7350-7444	Conflict of laws—Contracts	342.7105	KE4533-4665	Canada. Parliament.
340.972	K7350	Conflict of laws—Sales	342.7106	KE4730	Prime ministers—Canada
340.982	K7380-7384	Conflict of laws—Banking	342.71085	KE4381-4430	Civil rights—Canada
340.986	K7470	Conflict of laws—Insurance	342.7109	KE4900-4995	Local government—Law and legislation—Canada
340.996	K7360-7370	Conflict of laws—Negotiable instruments	342.73	KF4501-5130	United States—Constitutional law
341	K540-5570	International law			
341.0711	KF285	Law School Admission Test	342.73	KF4546-4554	United States—Constitutional law
341.2422	HC241.2-.25	European Economic Community literature	342.73024	JK301	Constitutional conventions
341.28	K3375	Colonies—Law and legislation	342.73029	JK	United States—Constitutional history
341.47	K4135	Space law	342.73032	KF4555-4558	United States—Constitutional law—Amendments
341.48	K783-793	Personal property			
341.7	K7051-7054	Law—International unification	342.730413	KF4635	Law—United States—Territories and possessions
342	K3154-3367	Constitutional law	342.730418	KF5399-.5	Police power—United States
342	K3150	Public law	342.730418	KF4695	Police power—United States
342.029	K3161	Constitutional history	342.73042	KF410-418	Conflict of laws—United States
342.0292	JF71-99	Constitutional conventions			
342.0297(4-9)	JK2413-2428	Constitutions, State	342.73042	JK310-331	Secession
342.03288	K970	Reparation	342.73042	JK311-325	States rights
342.041	K3220-3225	Public policy (Law)	342.73042	KF4600-4629	Federal government—United States
342.0418	JK371.P7-.P8	Police power			
342.042	K7000-7720	Conflict of laws	342.73044	JK305	Separation of powers
342.062	K3332-3351	Executive power	342.73044	KF4565-4579	Separation of powers—United States
342.066	K3400-3431	Administrative law			
342.068	K3440-3460	Civil service	342.7305	KF4930-5005	Legislative bodies—United States
342.08	K3290-3304	People (Constitutional law)			
342.08	K3224-3229	People (Constitutional law)	342.730509	JK1033-1059	United States. Congress—History
342.085	K3236-3268	Human rights			
342.085	K3252	Right to life	342.7306	KF5050-5125	Executive departments—United States
342.085	K3236-3268	Civil rights			
342.411	KDC750-785	Scotland—Constitutional law	342.73066	KF5401-5425	Administrative law—United States
342.415	KDK1200-1350	Ireland—Constitutional law	342.73068	KF5336-5398	Civil service—United States
342.416	KDE410-462	Northern Ireland—Constitutional law	342.7308	KF4881-4921	People (Constitutional law)—United States
342.42	KD3931-4645	England—Constitutional law	342.73082	KF4794-.5	Passports—United States
342.42029	KD3931-3966	England—Constitutional history	342.73083	KF4800-4848	Aliens—United States
			342.73083	KF4700-4720	Citizenship—United States

Dewey	LC	Subject Heading	Dewey	LC	Subject Heading
342.730852	KF4865-4869	Church and state—United States	343.0994	K4301-4339	Telecommunication—Law and legislation
342.73087	KF4788	Political parties—United States	343.37604	KJA3210	Taxation (Roman law)
342.730872	KF8201-8228	Indians of North America—Legal status, laws, etc.	343.401	UB590-684	Military law—Europe
			343.41103	KDC807-825	Finance, Public—Law and legislation—Scotland
342.7309	KF5300-5332	Local government—Law and legislation—United States	343.41503	KDK1430-1526	Finance, Public—Law and legislation—Ireland
343.(4-9)01	UB461-736	Military law—[By region and country]	343.41507	KDK550-769	Commercial law—Ireland
			343.41607	KDE235-282	Commercial law—Northern Ireland
343.01	K4720-4760	Military readiness—Law and legislation	343.4201	KD6000-6355	Military readiness—Law and legislation—England
343.014	UB790-795	Military discipline	343.4202	KD1034-1107	Government property—England
343.014	VB840-845	Naval discipline			
343.0143	VB800-807	Courts-martial and courts of inquiry	343.420252	KD1185-1189	Eminent domain—England
343.0143	UB850-857	Courts-martial and courts of inquiry	343.420256	KD1195	Public works—Law and legislation—England
343.019	VB350-785	Naval law	343.4203	KD5280-5752	Finance, Public—Law and legislation—England
343.02	K3558-3560	Government property			
343.02	K3476-3558	Public domain	343.42032	KD5288	Foreign exchange—Law and legislation—England
343.0252	K3511-3512	Eminent domain	343.42032	KD5284-5286	Money—Law and legislation—England
343.03	K4430-4675	Finance, Public—Law and legislation			
343.03	K4650-4675	Local finance—Law and legislation	343.42034	KD5292	Budget—Law and Legislation—England
343.04	K4456-4590	Taxation—Law and legislation	343.42037	KD5300	Debts, Public—Law and legislation—England
343.052	K4501-4550	Income tax—Law and legislation	343.4204	KD5351-5605	Taxation—Law and legislation—England
343.0532	K4568	Inheritance and succession	343.4205242	KD3241-3250	Social security—Law and legislation—England
343.054	K4560-4564	Property tax—Law and legislation	343.42056	KD5641-5694	Tariff—Law and legislation—England
343.0553	K4572-4580	Excise tax—Law and legislation	343.4207	KD2455-2530	Commercial law—England
343.056	K4600-4640	Tariff—Law and legislation	343.42072	KD2225-2226	Competition, Unfair—England
343.07	K3840-4375	Commercial law			
343.08	K3842-3862	Trade regulation	343.420721	KD2218-2220	Antitrust law—England
343.082	HF5833	Advertising laws	343.42075	KD2230-2231	Containers—Law and legislation—England
343.09	K3978-3990	Public utilities—Law and legislation	343.42076	KD2241-2295	Agricultural laws and legislation—England
343.0924	K3496-3501	Water-supply—Law and legislation	343.4207692	KD2310-2315	Fishery law and legislation—England
343.093	K4021-4025	Transportation—Law and legislation	343.42077	KD2331-2370	Mining law—England
343.0942	K3492	Highway law	343.42078	KD2405-2430	Food law and legislation—England
343.0942	K4028-4042	Highway law	(33847664)		
343.095	K4061-4070	Railroad law	343.42078624	KD2435	Construction industry—Law and legislation
343.096	K7449-7460	Conflict of laws—Maritime law	343.4208	KD2204-2231	Trade regulation—England
343.0967	K4198-4200	Harbors—Law and legislation	343.42082	KD2208-2209	Labels—Law and legislation—England
343.0967	K4182-4194	Inland navigation—Law and legislation	343.42082	KD2206	Advertising laws—England
			343.42083	KD2215	Price regulation—England
343.097	K4091-4124	Aeronautics—Law and legislation	343.4209	KD2535-2560	Public utilities—Law and legislation—England
343.098	K4080	Local transit—Law and legislation	343.42093	KD2571-2838	Transportation—Law and legislation—England
343.0992	K4245-4254	Postal service—Law and legislation	343.42093	KD1800-1847	Carriers—Law and legislation—England
			343.420942	KD1040-1048	Highway law—England

54

Dewey	LC	Subject Heading
343.42097	KD1804	Aeronautics, Commercial—Law and legislation—England
343.42(1-9)03	KD5710-5752	Local finance—Law and legislation—England
343.4301	UB620-624	Military law—Germany
343.4401	UB615-619	Military law—France
343.4501	UB640-644	Military law—Italy
343.4601	UB660-664	Military law—Spain
343.46901	UB650-654	Military law—Portugal
343.4701	UB655-659	Military law—Russia
343.49501	UB630-634	Military law—Greece
343.501	UB685-710	Military law—Asia
343.5101	UB690-694	Military law—China
343.5201	UB700-704	Military law—Japan
343.5401	UB695-699	Military law—India
343.601	UB715-729	Military law—Africa
343.7101	KE6800-7240	Military readiness—Law and legislation—Canada
343.7101	UB505-509	Military law—Canada
343.7102	KE5105-5420	Government property—Canada
343.7103	KE5600-6328	Finance, Public—Law and legislation—Canada
343.7107	KE1935-1999	Commercial law—Canada
343.71076	KE1671-1745	Agricultural laws and legislation—Canada
343.7107692	KE1760-1765	Fishery law and legislation—Canada
343.71077	KE1790-1802	Mining law—Canada
343.71078624	KE1915	Construction industry—Law and legislation—Canada
343.7108	KE1591-1660	Trade regulation—Canada
343.71082	KE1610-1614	Advertising laws—Canada
343.71082	KE1616-1618	Labels—Law and legislation—Canada
343.7109	KE2020-2061	Public utilities—Law and legislation—Canada
343.71093	KE2071-2649	Transportation—Law and legislation—Canada
343.71093	KE1099-1135	Carriers—Law and legislation—Canada
343.7201	UB510-514	Military law—Mexico
343.72801	UB515-519	Military law—Central America
343.72901	UB520-524	Military law—West Indies
343.7301	KF5900-6075.5	War and emergency legislation—United States
343.730143	KF7625-7659	Courts-martial and courts of inquiry—United States
343.7302	KF5500-5865	Government property—United States
343.730252	KF5599	Eminent domain—United States
343.730253	KF5675-5677	Land grants—Law and legislation—United States
343.730253	KF5670-5673	Homestead law—United States
343.7303	KF6200-6795	Finance, Public—Law and legislation—United States
343.73032	KF6201-6219	Money—Law and legislation—United States
343.73034	KF6221-6227	Budget—Law and legislation—United States
343.73034	KF6231-6239	Finance, Public—Auditing—Law and legislation
343.73036	KF6251-6708	Internal revenue law—United States
343.73037	KF6241-6245	Debts, Public—Law and legislation—United States
343.7304	KF6329-6330	Tax exemption—Law and legislation—United States
343.7304	KF6271-6636	Taxation—Law and legislation—United States
343.73043	KF6770-6795	Local finance—Law and legislation—United States
343.73052	KF6351-6499	Income tax—Law and legislation—United States
343.7305242	KF3641-3664	Social security—United States
343.730526	KF6598-6609	Indirect taxation
343.73054	KF6525-6558	Property tax—Law and legislation—United States
343.73056	KF6651-6708	Tariff—Law and legislation—United States
343.7307	KF1600-2940	Commercial law—United States
343.7307	KF1659-.1	Small business—Law and legislation—United States
343.73072	KF1631-1657	Monopolies—United States
343.73072	KF1601-1611	Competition, Unfair—United States
343.73072	KF3195-3198	Competition, Unfair—United States
343.73075	KF1665-1666	Weights and measures—Law and legislation—United States
343.73076	KF1681-1755	Agricultural laws and legislation—United States
343.7307692	KF1770-1773	Fishery law and legislation—United States
343.73077	KF1801-1873	Mining law—United States
343.73078	KF1875-1893	United States—Manufactures—Law and legislation
343.73078624	KF1950	Construction industry—Law and legislation—United States
343.7308	KF1085-1087	Commodity exchanges—Law and legislation—United States
343.73082	KF1614-1617	Advertising laws—United States
343.73082	KF1619-1620	Labels—Law and legislation
343.73093	KF1091-1137	Carriers—Law and legislation—United States
343.73093	KF2161-2654	Transportation—Law and legislation—United States
343.730942	KF5521-5536	Highway law—United States
343.801	UB530-589	Military law—South America

55

Dewey	LC	Subject Heading	Dewey	LC	Subject Heading
343.8201	UB530-534	Military law—Argentina	344.4209	KD4650	Emblems, National—England
343.8301	UB545-549	Military law—Chile			
343.86101	UB550-554	Military law—Colombia	344.42092	KD3753-3755	Archives—Law and legislation—England
343.8701	UB585-589	Military law—Venezuela			
343.9401	UB730-734	Military law—Australia	344.42092	KD3746	Library legislation—England
343.9(5-6)01	UB735-736	Military law—Oceania	344.42093	KD3736	Museums—Law and legislation—England
344	K1701-2000	Social legislation			
344.01	K1701-1841	Labor laws and legislation	344.42097	KD3720-3731	Performing arts—Law and legislation—England
344.01712	K4360-4375	Professions—Law and legislation	344.42099	KD3527	Gambling—Law and legislation—England
344.01893	K2320	Injunctions			
344.0316	K1960-2000	Public welfare—Law and legislation	344.42099	KD3525	Sports—Law and legislation—England
344.04	K3566-3597	Public health laws	344.42099	KD3523	Amusements—Law and legislation—England
344.0411	RA1056.5	Medical personnel—Malpractice	344.429071	KD9460	Law—Wales—Study and teaching
344.042	K3651-3654	Alcohol—Law and legislation	344.71	KE3098-3542	Social legislation—Canada
344.04232	K3626-3633	Food law and legislation	344.710189	KE928-936	Labor contract—Canada
344.04633	SB970-.4	Pesticides—Government policy	344.71041	KE3575-3635	Public health laws—Canada
344.049	K3615-3617	Veterinary hygiene—Law and legislation	344.71041	KE3646-3660	Medical laws and legislation—Canada
344.05242	K1861-1929	Social security—Law and legislation	344.7104232	KE1867-1906	Food law and legislation—Canada
344.063635	K3550-3553	Public housing—Law and legislation	344.7104233	KE3714-3725	Drugs—Law and legislation—Canada
344.07	K3740-3762	Educational law and legislation	344.7107	KE3805-3917	Educational law and legislation—Canada
344.09	K3770	Research—Law and legislation	344.71097	KE3968	Law and art—Canada
344.411	KDC635-674	Social legislation—Scotland	344.73	KF3300-3771	Social legislation—United States
344.411041	KDC690-695	Medical laws and legislation—Scotland	344.7301	KF3301-3580	Labor laws and legislation—United States
344.415	KDK800-895	Social legislation—Ireland	344.7301542	KF898-905	Contracts for work and labor—United States
344.415041	KDK926-932	Medical laws and legislation—Ireland	344.7301712	KF2900-2940	Professions—Law and legislation—United States
344.416	KDE320-348	Social legislation—Northern Ireland	344.730316	KF3720-3745	Public welfare—Law and legislation—United States
344.42	KD3000-3315	Social legislation—England	344.7303288	KF9763	Victims of crimes—United States
344.4201	KD3001-3177	Labor laws and legislation—England			
344.4201542	KD1638-1642	Labor contract—England	344.7304	KF3775-3816	Public health laws—United States
344.420316	KD3291-3315	Public welfare—Law and legislation	344.73041	KF3821-3829	Medical laws and legislation—United States
344.4204	KD3395-3413	Medical laws and legislation—England	344.73042	KF3945-3965	Product safety—Law and legislation—United States
344.4204	KD3351-3375	Public health laws—England	344.7304232	KF1900-1944	Food law and legislation—United States
344.42042	KD3466-3480	Alcohol—Law and legislation—England	344.73047	KF3970	Accident law—United States
344.4204233	KD3460-3462	Drugs—Law and legislation—England	344.73048	KF3832	Sterilization, Eugenic—Law and legislation—United States
344.42047	KD3510	Accident law—England			
344.42049	KD3420-3422	Veterinary hygiene—Law and legislation—England	344.73049	KF3835-3838	Veterinary hygiene—Law and legislation—United States
344.420533	KD3492	Weapons—Law and legislation—England	344.7305	KF4850-4856	Internal security—United States
344.420535	KD6340	Civil defense—Law and legislation—England	344.7305	KF3901-3925	Alcohol—Law and legislation—United States
344.4207	KD3600-3689	Educational law and legislation	344.730533	KF3941-3942	Weapons—Law and legislation—United States

Dewey	LC	Subject Heading
344.7305348	KF3750	Disaster relief—Law and legislation—United States
344.730535	KF7685	Civil defense—Law and legislation—United States
344.7305377	KF3975-3977	Fire prevention—Law and legislation—United States
344.730542	KF1241	Contracts, Aleatory—United States
344.730542	KF3992	Lotteries—Law and legislation—United States
344.7306	KF5865	Public works—Law and legislation—United States
344.73063635	KF5721-5740	Housing—Law and legislation—United States
344.730655168	KF5594	Weather control—Law and legislation—United States
344.7307	KF4192-.5	School employees—Legal status, laws, etc.—United States
344.7307	KF4195-4223	Educational law and legislation—United States
344.7307	KF4101-4257	Educational law and legislation—United States
344.73074	KF4225-4257	Education, Higher—Law and legislation—United States
344.73076	KF4125-4143	Education—Finance—Law and legislation—United States
344.73078	KF4175-4190	Teachers—Legal status, laws, etc.—United States
344.73079	KF4150-4166	Students—Legal status, laws, etc.—United States
344.7309	KF5150	Emblems, National—United States
344.73092	KF4325	Archives—Law and legislation—United States
344.73092	KF4315-4319	Library legislation—United States
344.73093	KF4305	Museums—Law and legislation—United States
344.73094	KF4310-4312	Historic buildings—Law and legislation—United States
344.73099	KF3987	Amusements—Law and legislation—United States
344.73099	KF3989	Sports—Law and legislation—United States
345	K5011-5316	Criminal law
345.01	K5036-5048	Criminal jurisdiction
345.01	K5423	Criminal jurisidiction
345.04	K5064-5083	Criminal liability
345.05	K5401-5570	Criminal procedure
345.05	HV7231-9960	Criminal justice, Administration of
345.05072	HV7419.5	Criminal justice, Administration of—Research
345.0509(4-9)	HV9950-9960	Criminal justice, Administration of—[By region or country]
345.050973	HV9950-9956	Criminal justice, Administration of—United States
345.052	JF781	Extradition
345.06	K5465-5490	Evidence, Criminal

Dewey	LC	Subject Heading
345.072	K5425	Indictments
345.075	K5492	Jury
345.075	K5460-5492	Trials
345.0772	K5510-5560	Sentences (Criminal procedure)
345.08	K5575-5582	Juvenile courts
345.411	KDC910-920	Criminal law—Scotland
345.415	KDK1750-1782	Criminal law—Ireland
345.41675	KDE550-557	Criminal procedure—Northern Ireland
345.42	KD7850-8090	Criminal law—England
345.4205	KD8220-8464	Criminal procedure—England
345.429	KD9490	Criminal law—Wales
345.42907	KD9423	Trials—Wales
345.71	KE8801-9112	Criminal law—Canada
345.73	KF9201-9479	Criminal law—United States
345.7301	JK1548.P8	Public defenders
345.7302	KF221.B74	Trials (Bribery)—United States
345.730207	KF221.C6	Trials (Conspiracy)—United States
345.730231	KF224.W	Watergate Trial, Washington, D.C., 1973
345.730233	KF6334	Tax evasion—United States
345.73025	KF9304-9329	Offenses against the person—United States
345.73026	KF9350-9379	Offenses against property—United States
345.73052	KF9635	Extradition—United States
345.730522	KF9630	Searches and seizures—United States
345.730527	KF9625	Arrest—United States
345.73056	KF9632	Bail—United States
345.7306	KF9660-9678	Evidence, Criminal—United States
345.7307	KF219-224	Trials—United States
345.73072	KF9645-9650	Arraignment—United States
345.73072	KF9640-9642	Indictments—United States
345.73075	KF9680	Jury—United States
345.73077	KF9695	Pardon—United States
345.730773	KF9725	Capital punishment—United States
346	K623-968	Civil law
346.015	K670-709	Domestic relations
346.02	K1024-1132	Contracts
346.02	K840-917	Contracts
346.02	K830-968	Obligations (Law)
346.023	HD3860-3861	Public contracts
346.029	K920	Quasi contracts
346.03	K923-968	Torts
346.043	JK318	Squatter sovereignty
346.044	K3478-3486	Natural resources—Law and legislation
346.045	K3531-3544	Regional planning—Law and legislation
346.048	K1500-1578	Industrial property
346.048	K1401-1578	Intellectual property
346.0482	K1411-1485	Copyright
346.0482	Z649.T7	Copyright—Transfer
346.052	K805-821	Inheritance and succession

Dewey	LC	Subject Heading	Dewey	LC	Subject Heading
346.07	K1010-1014	Business law	346.42064	KD2061-2062	Nonprofit organizations— Law and legislation—England
346.07	K1001-1388	Commercial law	346.42066	KD2057-2127	Corporation law—England
346.082	HG1725-1778	Banking law	346.420682	KD2049-2054	Partnership—England
346.082	K1066-1088	Banking law	346.42073	KD1740-1742	Loans—Law and legislation—England
346.086	K1241-1287	Insurance law			
346.086	HG9733-9735	Insurance, Fire—Law and legislation	346.42074	KD1752	Suretyship and guaranty— England
346.08632	HG8901-8914	Insurance, Life—Law and legislation	346.42078	KD2141-2164	Bankruptcy—England
			346.42082	KD1715-1737	Banking law—England
346.092	K1112-1116	Investments—Law and legislation	346.42086	KD1851-1913	Insurance law—England
			346.420862	KD1845-1847	Insurance, Marine—England
346.092	K1100-1108	Security (Law)	346.42092	KD1774-1787	Investments—Law and legislation—England
346.096	K1054-1065	Negotiable instruments			
346.411012	KDC350-378	Persons (Law)—Scotland	346.42096	KD1695-1699	Negotiable instruments— England
346.411052	KDC462-470	Inheritance and succession—Scotland			
346.415012	KDK185-205	Persons (Law)—Ireland	346.71004	KE457	Equity—Canada
346.41502	KDK370-437	Contracts—Ireland	346.71012	KE498-606	Persons (Law)—Canada
346.41503	KDK450-469	Torts—Ireland	346.71015	KE531-606	Domestic relations—Canada
346.415052	KDK360-365	Inheritance and succession—Ireland	346.7102	KE1328-1332	Agency (Law)—Canada
			346.7102	KE850-1225	Contracts—Canada
346.416012	KDE90-98	Persons (Law)—Northern Ireland	346.71025	KE970-972	Bailments—Canada
			346.7103	KE1232-1309	Torts—Canada
346.416052	KDE145-151	Inheritance and succession— Northern Ireland	346.71043	KE625-754	Real property—Canada
			346.71045	KE5258-5284	Regional planning—Law and legislation—Canada
346.42004	KD674	Equity—England			
346.42012	KD723-785	Persons (Law)—England	346.71047	KE765-781	Personal property—Canada
346.42015	KD750-785	Domestic relations—England	346.71048	KE2771-2998	Intellectual property— Canada
346.4202	KD1554-1920	Contracts—England			
346.42025	KD1679-1685	Bailments—England	346.71052	KE806-833	Inheritance and succession—Canada
346.42029	KD1924	Quasi contracts—England			
346.42029	KD2022	Power of attorney—England	346.71064	KE1351-1361	Unincorporated societies—Canada
346.4203	KD1941-1980	Torts—England			
346.42043	KD821-1195	Real property—England	346.71066	KE1369-1465	Corporation law—Canada
346.420432	KD833-960	Land tenure—Law and legislation—England	346.71073	KE1030-1034	Loans—Law and legislation—Canada
346.420432	KD841-960	Estates (Law)—England	346.71078	KE1491-1506	Bankruptcy—Canada
346.4204364	KD1010-1016	Mortgages—England	346.71082	KE991-1026	Banking law—Canada
346.420437	KD810-815	Possession (Law)—England	346.71086	KE1141-1220	Insurance law—Canada
346.42045	KD1125-1162	Zoning law—England	346.71092	KE1060-1089	Investments—Law and legislation—Canada
346.42046	KD1035	Natural resources—Law and legislation—England			
			346.71092	KE1042-1056	Securities—Canada
346.4204691	KD1070	Water—Law and legislation—England	346.71096	KE980-986	Negotiable instruments— Canada
346.42047	KD1205-1465	Personal property—England	346.73004	KF398-400	Equity—United States
346.42048	KD1450	Business names—England	346.73012	KF465-553	Persons (Law)—United States
346.42048	KD1261-1450	Intellectual property— England	346.73015	KF501-553	Domestic relations—United States
346.42048	KD1238-1450	Intangible property—England			
346.420482	KD1281-1325	Copyright—England	346.7302	KF801-1241	Contracts—United States
346.420484	KD1345	Design protection—England	346.73025	KF939-951	Bailments—United States
346.420486	KD1361-1413.3	Patent laws and legislation—England	346.73029	KF1244-.5	Quasi contracts—United States
346.4205	KD1497	Estate planning—England	346.73029	KF1341-1348	Agency (Law)—United States
346.42052	KD1500-1534	Inheritance and succession—England	346.7303	KF1246-1329	Torts—United States
			346.73043	KF566-698	Real property—United States
346.4206	KD2228	Trade associations—Law and legislation—England	346.73044	KF5505-5510	Conservation of natural resources—United States
346.42064	KD2046-2054	Unincorporated societies— England	346.73045	KF5691-5710	City planning and redevelopment law— United States

Dewey	LC	Subject Heading	Dewey	LC	Subject Heading
346.7304691	KF5551-5590	Water resources development—Law and legislation	347.42	KD720-721	Civil law—England
			347.4201	KD4645	Courts—England
			347.42013	KD327-332	Judicial statistics—England
346.73047	KF701-720	Personal property—United States	347.4203	KD7132-7216	Appellate courts—England
			347.4205	KD6850-7640	Procedure (Law)—England
346.73048	KF2971-3193	Intellectual property—United States	347.42055	KD318	Forms (Law)—England
			347.4207	KD370-379.5	Trials—England
346.730482	KF2986-3080	Copyright—United States	347.4209	KD7645-7647	Arbitration and award—England
346.730484	KF3086	Design protection—United States			
			347.42901	KD9480-9484	Courts—Wales
346.730486	KF3091-3193	Patent laws and legislation—United States	347.71	JL87-111	Executive departments—Canada
346.73052	KF753-780	Inheritance and succession—United States	347.71	KE495	Civil law—Canada
			347.7101	KE8200-8605	Courts—Canada
346.7306	KF1355-1480	Associations, institutions, etc.—Law and legislation	347.7101	KE4775	Courts—Canada
			347.71013	KE198-206	Judicial statistics—Canada
346.73064	KF1361-1381	Unincorporated societies—United States	347.7105	KE8341-8605	Procedure (Law)—Canada
			347.7107	KE225-237	Trials—Canada
346.73064	KF1388-1390	Nonprofit organizations—Law and legislation—United States	347.7109	KE8618	Arbitration and award—Canada
346.73064	KF1661	Trade associations—Law and legislation—United States	347.7301	JK1606	Courts—United States
			347.7301	KF101-153	Courts—United States
			347.73012	KF5130	Judicial power—United States
346.73066	KF1384-1480	Corporation law—United States	347.73013	KF180-185	Judicial statistics—United States
346.73066	KF1396-1477	Corporations—Law and legislation—United States	347.7305	KF8741-8752	Appellate procedure—United States
346.73067	KF1480	Corporations, Government—Law and legislation—United States	347.7305	KF8700-9075	Procedure (Law)—United States
346.7307	KF1970-2105	Business law—United States	347.7305	KF8810-9075	Civil procedure—United States
346.73073	KF1035-1040	Loans—Law and legislation—United States	347.73051	KF8816-8821	Court rules—United States
			347.73051	KF8858-8861	Jurisdiction—United States
346.73074	KF1045	Suretyship and guaranty—United States	347.73052	KF8890-8896.5	Parties to actions—United States
346.73078	KF1501-1548	Bankruptcy—United States	347.73053	KF8863-8865	Actions and defenses—United States
346.73082	KF966-1032	Banking law—United States			
346.73086	KF1146-1238	Insurance law—United States	347.7306	KF8931-8969	Evidence (Law)—United States
346.73092	KF1066-1084	Investments—Law and legislation—United States	347.7307	KF8910-8986	Trials—United States
			347.73072	KF8866-8885	Pleading—United States
346.73092	KF1046-1062	Security (Law)—United States	347.73072	KF8900-8902	Pre-trial procedure—United States
346.73096	KF956-962	Negotiable instruments—United States	347.73075	KF8911-8925	Trial practice—United States
			347.730752	KF8971-8984	Jury—United States
347.012	JF711	Judicial review	347.73077	KF8990-9002	Judgments—United States
347.012	K3367	Judicial power	347.7309	KF9085-9086	Arbitration and award—United States
347.035	K5495	Appellate procedure			
347.05	K2201-2385	Civil procedure	347.731(4-6)	KF8771-8807	Courts—United States—Officials and employees
347.05	K2100-2385	Procedure (Law)			
347.07	K540-546	Trials	348.022	K7010-7011	Statutes
347.09	K7690	Conflict of laws—Arbitration and award	348.41504	KDK61-80	Law reports, digests, etc.—Ireland
347.41103	KDC110-113	Appellate courts—Scotland	348.416041	KDE55-60	Law reports, digests, etc.—Northern Ireland
347.41105	KDC840-915	Procedure (Law)—Scotland			
347.41107	KDC184-188	Trials—Scotland	348.42022	KD125-150	Statutes—England
347.41505	KDK1580-1713	Procedure (Law)—Ireland	348.42041	KD187-291	Law reports, digests, etc.—England
347.41507	KDK102-106	Trials—Ireland			
347.41605	KDE510-530	Procedure (Law)—Northern Ireland	348.429022	KD9407	Statutes—Wales

Dewey	LC	Subject Heading	Dewey	LC	Subject Heading
348.429041	KD9410-9417	Law reports, digests, etc.—Wales	349.561	KKX	Law—Turkey
			349.5645	KJN	Law—Cyprus
348.71041	KE132-156	Law reports, digests, etc.—Canada	349.7	KDZ	Law—North America
			349.71	KE	Law—Canada
348.7301	KF16-22	Bills, Legislative—United States	349.71	KE335-355	Lawyers—Canada
348.73022	KF50-70	Statutes—United States	349.71071	KE273-322	Law—Study and teaching—Canada
348.73041	KF255	Law reporting—United States	349.71072	KE250-259	Legal research—Canada
			349.711	KEB	Law—British Columbia
348.7(4-9)	KF165	Uniform state laws	349.71(1-9)	KEZ	Law—[Canada, cities]
349.411	KDC	Law—Scotland	349.7123	KEA	Law—Alberta
349.411	KDC225-247	Lawyers—Scotland	349.7124	KES	Law—Sasketchewan
349.411003	KDC152	Law—Scotland—Dictionaries	349.7127	KEM	Law—Manitoba
			349.713	KEO	Law—Ontario
349.415	KDK	Law—Ireland	349.714	KEQ	Law—Quebec
349.415	KDK120-134	Lawyers—Ireland	349.7151	KEN0-599	Law—New Brunswick
349.41503	KDK84	Law—Ireland—Dictionaries	349.716	KEN7400-7999	Law—Nova Scotia
349.416	KDE	Law—Northern Ireland	349.717	KEP	Law—Prince Edward Island
349.42	KD	Law—England	349.718	KEN1200-1799	Law—Newfoundland
349.42	KD460-472	Lawyers—England	349.7188	KDZ4000-4499	Law—St. Pierre and Miquelon
349.42	KD8850-9355	Statutes—England			
349.42	KD5020-5025	Commonwealth countries	349.7191	KEY	Law—Yukon Territory
349.4203	KD313	Law—England—Dictionaries	349.72	KGF	Law—Mexico
349.42071	KD419-452	Law—Study and teaching—England	349.7281	KGD	Law—Guatemala
			349.7282	KGA	Law—Belize
349.42072	KD392-400	Legal research—England	349.7283	KGE	Law—Honduras
349.4209	KD530-632	Law—England—History	349.7284	KGC	Law—El Salvador
349.4234	KDG	Law—Channel Islands	349.7285	KGG	Law—Nicaragua
349.42341	KDG220-380	Law—Jersey (Channel Islands)	349.7286	KGB	Law—Costa Rica
			349.7287	KGH	Law—Panama
349.42342	KDG421-440	Law—Guernsey (Channel Islands)	349.729	KGJ-KGZ	Law—West Indies
			349.7291	KGN	Law—Cuba
349.4279	KDG26-170	Law—Isle of Man	349.7292	KGT0-499	Law—Jamaica
349.429	KD9400-9500	Law—Wales	349.7293	KGQ	Law—Dominican Republic
349.42903	KD9420	Law—Wales—Dictionaries	349.7294	KGS	Law—Haiti
349.43	KK	Law—Germany	349.7295	KGV	Law—Puerto Rico
349.436	KJJ	Law—Austria	349.7296	KGL0-499	Law—Bahamas
349.43648	KKJ	Law—Liechtenstein	349.729722	KGZ0-499	Law—Virginia Islands of the United States
349.437	KJP	Law—Czechoslovakia			
349.438	KKP	Law—Poland	349.729725	KGL4000-4499	Law—British Virgin Islands
349.439	KKF	Law—Hungary	349.72973	KGJ7000-7499	Law—Anguilla
349.44	KJV	Law—France	349.72973	KGW2000-2499	Law—Saint Kitts and Nevis
349.44949	KKL	Law—Monaco	349.72974	KGK0-499	Law—Antiguilla
349.45	KKH	Law—Spain	349.72975	KGT2000-2499	Law—Montserrat
349.4585	KKK1000-1499	Law—Malta	349.72976	KGR5000-5499	Law—Guadeloupe
349.46	KKT	Law—Spain	349.72976	KGR3000-3499	Law—West Indies, French
349.469	KKQ	Law—Portugal	349.72977	KGW7000-7499	Law—Saint Eustatius
349.481	KKN	Law—Norway	349.72977	KGW0-499	Law—Saba (Netherlands Antilles)
349.485	KKV	Law—Sweden			
349.489	KJR	Law—Denmark	349.72977	KGW8000-8499	Law—Saint Martin
349.4897	KJT	Law—Finland	349.72981	KGL1000-1499	Law—Barbados
349.4912	KKG	Law—Iceland	349.72982	KGT1000-1499	Law—Martinique
349.492	KKM	Law—Netherlands	349.72983	KGX0-499	Law—Trinidad and Tobago
349.493	KJK	Law—Belgium	349.729841	KGP2000-2499	Law—Dominica
349.4935	KKK0-499	Law—Luxembourg	349.729843	KGW3000-3499	Law—Saint Lucia
349.494	KKW	Law—Switzerland	349.729844	KGW5000-5499	Law—Saint Vincent
349.495	KKE	Law—Greece	349.729845	KGR4000-4499	Law—Grenada
349.4965	KJG	Law—Albania	349.72986	KGR1000-1499	Law—Netherlands Antilles
349.497	KKZ	Law—Yugoslavia	349.72986	KGL2000-2499	Law—Bonaire
349.498	KKR	Law—Romania	349.72986	KGP0-499	Law—Curacao
349.499	KJM	Law—Bulgaria	349.72986	KGK1000-1499	Law—Aruba

Dewey	LC	Subject Heading	Dewey	LC	Subject Heading
349.7299	KDZ2000-2499	Law—Bermuda	349.796	KFI0-599	Law—Idaho
349.73	KF	Law—United States	349.797	KFW0-599	Law—Washington
349.73	KF297-338	Lawyers—United States	349.798	KFA1200-1799	Law—Alaska
349.7303	KF156	Law—United States—Dictionaries	349.8	KH	Law—South America
			349.81	KHD	Law—Brazil
349.73071	KF261-292	Law—United States—Study and teaching	349.82	KHA	Law—Argentina
			349.83	KHF	Law—Chile
349.73072	KF240-247	Legal research—United States	349.84	KHC	Law—Bolivia
			349.85	KHQ	Law—Peru
349.7308996073	KF299.A35	Afro-American lawyers	349.861	KHH	Law—Columbia
349.7309	KF350-374	Law—United States—History	349.866	KHK	Law—Ecuador
			349.87	KHW	Law—Venezuela
349.7(4-9)	KFX	Law—[United States, cities]	349.882	KHM	Law—French Guiana
349.741	KFM0-599	Law—Maine	349.883	KHS	Law—Surinam
349.742	KFN1200-1799	Law—New Hampshire	349.892	KHP	Law—Paraguay
349.743	KFV0-599	Law—Vermont	349.895	KHU	Law—Uruguay
349.744	KFM2400-2999	Law—Massachusetts	349.969	KFH0-599	Law—Hawaii
349.745	KFR0-599	Law—Rhode Island	349.9711	KHL	Law—Falkland Islands
349.746	KFC3600-4199	Law—Connecticut	349.982	KDZ3000-3499	Law—Greenland
349.747	KFN5000-6199	Law—New York (State)	350	JF	Public administration
349.748	KFP0-599	Law—Pennsylvania	351	JF1501-1521	Civil service
349.749	KFN1800-2399	Law—New Jersey	351.056	JS7435-7520	Local government—Middle East
349.75	KFZ8600-9199	Law—Confederate States of America	351.4	JS3000-6949.8	Local government—Europe
349.751	KFD0-599	Law—Delaware	351.41	JN309-678	Public administration—Great Britain
349.752	KFM1200-1799	Law—Maryland			
349.753	KFD1200-1799	Law—Washington, D.C.	351.41	JS3001-4295	Local government—Great Britain
349.754	KFW1200-1799	Law—West Virginia			
349.755	KFV2400-2999	Law—Virginia	351.43	JS5301-5598	Local government—Germany
349.756	KFN7400-7999	Law—North Carolina	351.436	JS4501-4655	Local government—Austria
349.757	KFS1800-2399	Law—South Carolina	351.439	JS4661-4696	Local government—Hungary
349.758	KFG0-599	Law—Georgia	351.44	JS4801-5250	Local government—France
349.759	KFF0-599	Law—Florida	351.45	JS5701-5925	Local government—Italy
349.761	KFA0-599	Law—Alabama	351.46	JS6301-6335	Local government—Spain
349.762	KFM6600-7199	Law—Mississippi	351.469	JS6341-6375	Local government—Portugal
349.763	KFL0-599	Law—Louisiana	351.47	JS6051-6109	Local government—Russia
349.764	KFT1200-1799	Law—Texas	351.485	JS6251-6285	Local government—Sweden
349.766	KFO1200-1799	Law—Oklahoma	351.489	JS6151-6185	Local government—Denmark
349.767	KFA3600-4199	Law—Arkansas	351.492	JS5931-5998	Local government—Netherlands
349.768	KFT0-599	Law—Tennessee			
349.769	KFK1200-1799	Law—Kentucky	351.493	JS6001-6048	Local government—Belgium
349.771	KFO0-599	Law—Ohio	351.494	JS6401-6889	Local government—Switzerland
349.773	KFI1200-1799	Law—Illinois			
349.774	KFM4200-4799	Law—Michigan	351.496	JS6899.5-6949.8	Local government—Balkan Peninsula
349.775	KFW2400-2999	Law—Wisconsin			
349.776	KFM5400-5999	Law—Minnesota	351.5	JS6950-7520	Local government—Asia
349.777	KFI4200-4799	Law—Iowa	351.51	JS7351-7365	Local government—China
349.778	KFM7800-8399	Law—Missouri	351.52	JS7371-7385	Local government—Japan
349.781	KFK0-599	Law—Kansas	351.54	JS7001-7090	Local government—India
349.782	KFN0-599	Law—Nebraska	351.599	JS7301-7335	Local government—Philippines
349.783	KFS3000-3599	Law—South Dakota			
349.784	KFN8600-9199	Law—North Dakota	351.6	JS7525-7819	Local government—Africa
349.786	KFM9000-9599	Law—Montana	351.71	JL1-500	Public administration—Canada
349.787	KFW4200-4799	Law—Wyoming			
349.788	KFC1800-2399	Law—Colorado	351.71	JS1701-1800	Local government—Canada
349.789	KFN3600-4199	Law—New Mexico	351.72	JS2101-2143	Local government—Mexico
349.791	KFA2400-2999	Law—Arizona	351.728	JS2145-2219	Local government—Central America
349.792	KFU0-599	Law—Utah			
349.793	KFN600-1199	Law—Nevada	351.729	JS1840-2058	Local government—West Indies
349.794	KFC0-1199	Law—California			
349.795	KFO2400-2999	Law—Oregon	351.73063	JK631-868	Civil service

Dewey	LC	Subject Heading	Dewey	LC	Subject Heading
351.7(4-9)	JS300-1583	Local government—United States	352.283	JS113	Decentralization in government
351.75	JK9717-9719	Executive departments—Confederate States of America	352.283	JF225	Delegation of powers
			352.293	JF341	Ministerial responsibility
			352.33	JF1525.D4	Public administration—Decision making
351.8	JS2300-2778	Local government—South America	352.35	JF1621	Administrative responsibility
351.824	Z551-656	Copyright	352.448	HJ6603-7390	Customs administration
351.93	JS8331-8399	Local government—New Zealand	352.44809(4-9)	HJ6622-7390	Customs administration—[By region or country]
351.94	JS8001-8310	Local government—Australia	352.4480973	HJ6622-6731	Customs administration—United States
351.9(5-6)	JS8450-8490	Local government—Oceania	352.48	HJ2005-2216	Budget
352.1309(4-9)	JK2443-2525	Public administration—[United States, By state]	352.5	JF1525.P7	Government property
			352.530973	HJ2050-2053	United States—Appropriations and expenditures
352.1309(4-9)	JK2701-9593	State governments—[United States, By state]			
352.130973	JK2403-9593	State governments—United States	352.63	JS148-153	Civil service
			352.63	HD8001-8013	Civil service
352.133	JK2441	Interstate agreements	352.63	JK765-770	Civil service—Personnel management
352.14	JS	Local government			
352.1406	JS42	Local government—Societies, etc.	352.63	HD5713.5-.6	Public service employment
			352.630971	JL106-111	Civil service—Canada
352.14071	JS49	Local government—Study and teaching	352.630973	JK771-794	United States—Official and employees—Salaries, etc.
352.1409	JS55-67	Local government—History	352.630973	JK681	Civil service reform
352.150973	JS411	County government—United States	352.885	JF1621	Government liability
			353	JK404-1685	Public administration—United States
352.16	JS261	Boroughs			
352.16092	JS148-155	Municipal officials and employees	353.00074	JK4	Freedom Train
			353.15	JV443	Civil service, Colonial
352.16097(4-9)	JS422	Metropolitan government—United States	353.15	JV412-461	Colonies—Administration
			353.15092	JV431	Viceroyalty
352.16097(4-9)	JS504-1583	Municipal government—[U.S. by city]	353.36	HV7935-8025	Police administration
			353.549	JF1671	Civil service—Pensions
352.23	JF286	Heads of state—Term of office	353.596	RA405	Death—Proof and certification
352.23	JF255	Presidents	353.606	RA10-388	Health boards
352.230973	JK511-609	Presidents—United States	353.60604	RA239-299	Health boards—Europe
352.232130973	JK2447-2454	Governors—United States	353.60605	RA303-340	Health boards—Asia
352.23216	JS143-163	Mayors	353.60606	RA345-352	Health boards—Africa
352.2330941	JN331-389	Great Britain—Kings and rulers	353.60607(4-9)	RA15-182	Health boards—[United States, by state]
352.235	JF251-289	Executive power	353.60607(4-9)	RA13	Health boards—[United States, cities]
352.238	J80-82	Presidents—Messages			
352.2380973	J82	Presidents—United States—Messages	353.606071	RA184-186	Health boards—Canada
			353.606072	RA187-188	Health boards—Mexico
352.2390973	JK2459	Lieutenant governors—United States	353.6060728	RA191	Health boards—Central America
352.2390973	JK609.5	Vice-Presidents—United States	353.606073	RA11-182	Health boards—United States
352.24	JF331-341	Cabinet system	353.60608	RA198-235	Health boards—South America
352.240973	JK610-616	Cabinet officers			
352.250973	JS342-343	Municipal government by commission	353.606094	RA371-372	Health boards—Australia
			353.88284	LB2331.6-.615	Universities and colleges—Accreditation
352.266	HD3840-4420.8	Government ownership	354.094	JN	Public administration—Europe
352.266	HD3850	Corporations, Government			
352.266	HD4421-4730.9	Municipal ownership	354.37	QC875	Meteorological services
352.2660973	HD3881-4420.8	Corporations, Government—United States	354.7299	JL131-179	Canada. Parliament

Dewey	LC	Subject Heading	Dewey	LC	Subject Heading
355	U130-135	Military art and science—Officers' handbooks	355.032	UA16	Military missions
355	U	Military art and science	355.03305	UA830	East Asia—Strategic aspects
355.0021	UA19	Military statistics	355.0335	UA11	Military policy
355.003	U24-26	Military art and science—Dictionaries	355.07	U390-395	Military research
355.006	U7	Military art and science—Congresses	355.0973	U410.E9	Hazing
355.0071	U400-714	Military education	355.113	UB280-285	Military passes
355.00710(4-9)	U407-714	Military education—[By region or country]	355.12	UB400-405	Military dependents
			355.123	U22	Morale
355.007104	U505-630	Military education—Europe	355.13323	UB820-825	Military police
355.0071041	U510-549.3	Military education—Great Britain	355.13325	UB810-815	Corporal punishment
355.0071043	U570-574.54	Military education—Germany	355.1334	UB780-789	Military offenses
355.00710436	U550-554	Military education—Austria	355.1334	UB789	Insubordination
355.007105	U635-660	Military education—Asia	355.1334	UB788	Desertion, Military
355.0071051	U640-644	Military education—China	355.1334	UB787	Mutiny
355.0071052	U650-654	Military education—Japan	355.134	UB430-435	Military decorations
355.0071054	U645-649	Military education—India	355.1342	UB430-435	Decorations of honor
355.0071055	U655-659	Military education—Iran	355.13420941	UB435.G	Distinguished Conduct Medal (Great Britain)
355.007106	U670-695	Military education—Africa	355.13420973	UB433	Medal of Honor
355.0071071	U440-444	Military education—Canada	355.13420973	UB433	Distinguished Service Cross (U.S.)
355.0071072	U445-449	Military education—Mexico	355.13420973	VB333	Navy Cross (Medal)
355.00710728	U450-454	Military education—Central America	355.13420973	UC533	United States. Army—Medals, badges, decorations, etc.
355.00710729	U455-459	Military education—West Indies	355.14	UC480-485	Military uniforms
355.0071073	U408-439	Military education—United States	355.14	UC530-535	Insignia
			355.15	UC590-595	Flags
355.007108	U465-499	Military education—South America	355.15	UC590-595	Standards, Military
			355.15	UC590-595	Guidons
355.0071094	U700-704	Military education—Australia	355.17	U350-355	Weddings, Military
355.0074	U13	Military museums	355.17	U350-365	Military ceremonies, honors, and salutes
355.0074	U13	Military art and science—Exhibitions	355.22	UA17.5	Manpower
355.009	D25-.4	Military history	355.223	UB320-345	Recruiting and enlistment
355.009	U27-43	Military art and science—History	355.2230973	UB323	United States. Army—Recruiting, enlistment, etc.
355.00901	U29-35	Military art and science—History—To 500	355.2236	UB320-338	Advertising—Recruiting and enlistment
355.00902	D128	Military history—Medieval	355.22362	UB320-325	Military service, Voluntary
355.00903	D214	Military history—Modern	355.22363	UB340-355	Draft
355.0092	U750-773	Soldiers	355.224	UB341-342	Conscientious objectors
355.0092	U1-145	Soldiers	355.225	UB350-355	Draft
355.0092	U51-55	Generals	355.26	UA18	Industrial mobilization
355.0092	U51-55	Military art and science—Biography	355.28	UC15	Requisitions, Military
			355.28	UA910-915	Armed forces—Mobilization
355.02	U	War	355.3008996073	E185.63	United States—Armed Forces—Afro-Americans
355.0213	U21	Militarism			
355.0213	UA10	Militarism	355.306073	UB233	United States—Armed Forces—Headquarters
355.0215	UA11.5	Limited war	355.30942	DA49-69.3	Great Britain—History, Military
355.0217	U162.6	Deterrence (Strategy)			
355.0217	U263	Nuclear warfare	355.30943	DD99-104	Germany—History, Military
355.0217	U264	No first use (Nuclear strategy)	355.30943	DD106	Germany—History, Naval
355.0217	U263	Nuclear crisis stabililty	355.30943	DD354	Prussia (Germany)—History, Military
355.0218	U241	Counterinsurgency	355.309436	DB42-44	Austria—History, Military
355.0218	D25.5	Guerrillas	355.30944	DC44-47	France—History, Military
355.0218	U240	Guerrilla warfare	355.30945	DG480-484	Italy—History, Military
355.031	UA12	Mutual security program, 1951-			

Dewey	LC	Subject Heading	Dewey	LC	Subject Heading
355.30946	DP76-78	Spain—History, Military	355.34506	UH205	Medicine, Military—Congresses
355.309469	DP547	Portugal—History, Military			
355.30947	DK50-54	Soviet Union—History, Military	355.345071	UH398-399	Medicine, Military—Study and teaching
355.309492	DJ124	Netherlands—History, Military	355.34509	UH215-324	Medicine, Military—History
355.309492	DH113	Netherlands—History, Military	355.345092	UH341-347	Medicine, Military—Biography
355.309493	DH540-545	Belgium—History, Military	355.345092	UH400	Physicians
355.309494	DQ59	Switzerland—History, Military	355.345094	UH255-295	Medicine, Military—Europe
			355.345094	UH321-322	Medicine, Military—Australia
355.309495	DF765	Greece—History, Military	355.3450941	UH257-264	Medicine, Military—Great Britain
355.309495	DF543	Byzantine Empire—History, Military			
			355.3450943	UH273-274	Medicine, Military—Germany
355.309497	DR1250-1251	Yugoslavia—History, Military	355.3450944	UH271-272	Medicine, Military—France
355.309498	DR219	Romania—History, Military	355.3450945	UH279-280	Medicine, Military—Italy
355.309499	DR70	Bulgaria—History, Military	355.3450946	UH287-288	Medicine, Military—Spain
355.30951	DS775.4	China—History, Military—1912-1949	355.34509469	UH283-284	Medicine, Military—Portugal
			355.3450947	UH285-286	Medicine, Military—Russia
355.30951	DS777.65	China—History, Military	355.3450948	UH286.5	Medicine, Military—Scandinavia
355.309561	DR448	Turkey—History, Military			
355.30971	F1028	Canada—History, Military	355.34509495	UH275-276	Medicine, Military—Greece
355.30973	UA24.A7	United States. Army—Appropriations and expenditures	355.345095	UH299-313	Medicine, Military—Asia
			355.3450951	UH301-302	Medicine, Military—China
			355.3450952	UH305-306	Medicine, Military—Japan
355.30973	E181	United States—History, Military	355.3450954	UH303-304	Medicine, Military—India
			355.345096	UH315-319	Medicine, Military—Africa
355.30973	UA24-39	United States. Army	355.3450971	UH226-227	Medicine, Military—Canada
355.30973	UA23-25	United States. Army—History	355.3450972	UH228-229	Medicine, Military—Mexico
			355.34509728	UH230-231	Medicine, Military—Central America
355.30973	UA24-39	United States. Army			
355.30973	E181	United States. Army—History	355.34509729	UH232-233	Medicine, Military—West Indies
355.309730216	U11	United States. Army—Registers	355.3450973	UH223-224	Medicine, Military—United States
355.30975	UA580-585	Confederate States of America. Army	355.345098	UH234-254	Medicine, Military—South America
355.31	UA	Armies	355.3450982	UH236-237	Medicine, Military—Argentina
355.33041	UB210	Command of troops	355.3450983	UH243-244	Medicine, Military—Chile
355.33041	UB210	Leadership	355.34509861	UH245-246	Medicine, Military—Colombia
355.3308351	UB418.B69	Boys as soldiers			
355.332	UB410-415	Armies—Officers	355.3450987	UH254	Medicine, Military—Venezuela
355.3320973	UB408-.5	United States—Armed Forces—Warrant officers	355.345099(5-6)	UH323-324	Medicine, Military—Oceania
355.3320973	UB412-414	United States. Army—Officers	355.3460973	U56-59	United States—Armed Forces—Officers' clubs
355.3410973	UC723	United States—Armed Forces—Messes	355.347	UH20-25	Chaplains
355.3432	UB250-271	Military intelligence	355.3480973	UA45	United States—Armed Forces—Women's reserves
355.3432092	UB270-271	Spies	355.35	UA12.8	Guard troops
355.3434	UB275-277	Psychological warfare	355.35	U370-375	Garrisons
355.345	UH490-495	Military nursing	355.350973	U173	United States. Army—Field service
355.345	UH201-551	War—Relief of sick and wounded	355.350975	U173.5	Confederate States of America. Army—Field service
355.345	UH420-425	Pharmacy, Military			
355.345	UH600-629.5	Military hygiene			
355.345	UH650-655	Veterinary service, Military	355.351	U230	Riots
355.345	UH201-515	Medicine, Military	355.352	UA14	Armies, Colonial
355.345021	UH215-325	War—Casualties (Statistics, etc.)	355.354	G539	Soldiers of fortune
			355.37	UA13	Militia

Dewey	LC	Subject Heading	Dewey	LC	Subject Heading
355.370973	UA42-560	United States—National Guard	355.3709791	UA70-79	Arizona—National Guard
355.370973	UA42-560	United States—Militia	355.3709792	UA480-489	Utah—National Guard
355.370973	UA42-560	United States—Armed Forces—Reserves	355.3709793	UA320-329	Nevada—National Guard
355.37097(4-9)	UA50-549	United States—Armed Forces—Reserves [By state]	355.3709794	UA90-99	California—National Guard
			355.3709795	UA410-419	Oregon—National Guard
			355.3709796	UA160-169	Idaho—National Guard
355.3709741	UA230-239	Maine—National Guard	355.3709797	UA510-519	Washington (State)—National Guard
355.3709742	UA330-339	New Hampshire—National Guard	355.3709798	UA60-69	Alaska—National Guard
355.3709743	UA490-499	Vermont—National Guard	355.3709969	UA159.1-.9	Hawaii—National Guard
355.3709744	UA250-259	Massachusetts—National Guard	355.4	D25	Battles
			355.4	U865	Swordplay
355.3709745	UA430-439	Rhode Island—National Guard	355.4	U161-163	Operational art (Military science)
355.3709746	UA100-109	Connecticut—National Guard	355.4	U167.5.A35	Advanced guard (Military science)
355.3709747	UA360-369	New York (State)—National Guard	355.4	U250-255	Military maneuvers
355.3709748	UA420-429	Pennsylvania—National Guard	355.4	U280-285	Staff rides
			355.40973	U253	United States. Army—Maneuvers
355.3709749	UA340-349	New Jersey—National Guard	355.41	UG447.7	Smoke screens
355.3709751	UA110-119	Delaware—National Guard	355.41	UG449	Camouflage (Military science)
355.3709752	UA240-249	Maryland—National Guard	355.411	U168	Integrated logistic support
355.3709753	UA120-129	Washington (D.C.)—National Guard	355.411	U168	Logistics
			355.413	U220	Military reconnaisance
355.3709754	UA520-529	West Virginia—National Guard	355.413	U190	Scouts and scouting
355.3709755	UA500-509	Virginia—National Guard	355.42	U164-167.5	Tactics
355.3709756	UA370-379	North Carolina—National Guard	355.42	U161-163	Strategy
			355.422	U167.5.R34	Raids (Military science)
355.3709757	UA440-449	South Carolina—National Guard	355.422	U210	Skirmishing
355.3709758	UA150-159	Georgia—National Guard	355.422	U200	Landing operations
355.3709759	UA140-149	Florida—National Guard	355.422	U262	Commando troops
355.3709761	UA50-59	Alabama—National Guard	355.422	U215	Rearguard action (Military science)
355.3709762	UA280-289	Mississippi—National Guard	355.422	U167	Amicicide (Military science)
355.3709763	UA220-229	Louisiana—National Guard	355.422	U167.5.E57	Envelopment (Military science)
355.3709764	UA470-479	Texas—National Guard	355.422	U167.5.L5	Lightning war
355.3709766	UA400-409	Oklahoma—National Guard	355.422	U190-195	Guard duty
355.3709767	UA80-89	Arkansas—National Guard	355.423	U167.5.W5	Winter warfare
355.3709768	UA460-469	Tennessee—National Guard	355.423	U167.5.J8	Jungle warfare
355.3709769	UA210-219	Kentucky—National Guard	355.423	U205	Stream crossing, Military
355.3709771	UA390-399	Ohio—National Guard	355.424	UH87-100	Animals—War use
355.3709772	UA180-189	Indiana—National Guard	355.44	UG443-449	Siege warfare
355.3709773	UA170-179	Illinois—National Guard	355.44	UG446	Intrenchments
355.3709774	UA260-269	Michigan—National Guard	355.45	UA10.7	Civilian-based defense
355.3709775	UA530-539	Wisconsin—National Guard	355.450973	UA23	United States—Defenses
355.3709776	UA270-279	Minnesota—National Guard	355.450975	UA580-585	Confederate States of America—Defenses
355.3709777	UA190-199	Iowa—National Guard			
355.3709778	UA290-299	Missouri—National Guard	355.46	U261	Amphibious warfare
355.3709781	UA200-209	Kansas—National Guard	355.46	U260	Combined operations (Military science)
355.3709782	UA310-319	Nebraska—National Guard			
355.3709783	UA450-459	South Dakota—National Guard	355.47	UA985-997	Military geography
			355.47	UA985-997	Maps, Military
355.3709784	UA380-389	North Dakota—National Guard	355.48	U310	War games
			355.48	U313	Imaginary wars and battles
355.3709786	UA300-309	Montana—National Guard	355.48	U280-285	Staff rides
355.3709787	UA540-549	Wyoming—National Guard	355.480285	U310	Computer war games
355.3709789	UA350-359	New Mexico—National Guard	355.480285	U310	AGATE (Computer war game)
			355.5	U290-295	Military training camps

Dewey	LC	Subject Heading	Dewey	LC	Subject Heading
355.5	U300-305	Bombing and gunnery ranges	355.8094	UC158-233	Europe—Armed Forces—Supplies and stores
355.5	U110-115	Military art and science—Soldiers' handbooks	355.80941	UC184-187	Great Britain—Armed Forces—Supplies and stores
355.5	U320-325	Physical education and training, Military	355.80943	UC180-183	Germany—Armed Forces—Supplies and stores
355.5071	U715-717	Soldiers—Education, Non-military	355.8095	UC234-245	Asia—Armed Forces—Supplies and stores
355.50973	U408.3	Experimental Volunteer Army Training Progam	355.80952	UC241	Japan—Armed Forces—Supplies and stores
355.50973	U323	United States. Army—Physical training	355.8096	UC247-253	Africa—Armed Forces—Supplies and stores
355.5470973	U113	United States. Army—Handbooks, manuals, etc.	355.80971	UC90-93	Canada—Armed forces—Supplies and stores
355.6	UB	Military administration	355.80972	UC94-97	Mexico—Armed forces—Supplies and stores
355.605	UB1	Military administration—Periodicals	355.809728	UC98-99	Central America—Armed Forces—Supplies and stores
355.609	UB15	Military administration—History	355.80973	UC523	United States. Army—Equipment
355.60943	UB73-74	Germany—Armed Forces—Management	355.80973	UF523-563	United States. Army—Ordnance and ordnance stores
355.60947	UB85-86	Russia—Armed Forces—Management			
355.60951	UB101-102	China—Armed Forces—Management	355.8098	UC106-154	South America—Armed Forces—Supplies and stores
355.60952	UB105-106	Japan—Armed Forces—Management	355.80994	UC255-256	Australia—Armed Forces—Supplies and stores
355.60973	UA23.2-.6	United States. Dept. of Defense	355.81	U825	Helmets
355.60973	UB23-25	United States—Armed Forces—Management	355.81	UC570-575	Tents
355.60973	UB163	United States. Army—Records and correspondence	355.81	UC460-465	Armies—Equipment
355.62	UC700-780	Armies—Commissariat	355.824	U167.5.H3	Flexible weapons (Hand-to-hand fighting)
355.620973	UC40-44	United States. Army—Commissariat	355.8241	U875	Catapult
355.620975	UC85-86	Confederate States of America. Army—Commissariat	355.8241	U850-863	Sabers
			355.8241	U877-878	Bow and arrow
			355.8241	U875	Ballista
355.6212	UC260	Armed forces—Procurement	355.8241	U850-872	Swords
355.62120973	UC260-267	United States—Armed Forces—Procurement	355.82420975	UD383.5	Confederate States of America. Army—Firearms
355.62120973	UC263	United States. Army—Procurement	355.825119	U264	Nuclear weapons
355.62137	UC260-267	Surplus military property	355.83	UC330-335	Airlift, Military
355.622	UA17	Armies, Cost of	355.83	UC340-345	Motorization, Military
355.622	UA17	War, Cost of	355.83	UC320-325	Transports
355.640973	UC70-75	United States. Army—Pay, allowances, etc.	355.83	UC330-335	Airdrop
			355.83	UH500-505	Transportation, Military
355.685	UB240-245	Military inspectors general	355.85	UA940-945	Communications, Military
355.6850973	UB243	United States. Army—Inspection	355.88	UH440-445	Medical supplies
			356.1	UD	Infantry
355.693	UH80-85	Postal service	356.106	UD1	Infantry—Societies, etc.
355.7	UB390-395	Military reservations	356.109	UD15	Infantry—History
355.7	UF540-545	Arsenals	356.10973	UA28-29	United States. Army. Infantry
355.71	UC400-440	Barracks	356.10973	UD23	United States. Army. Infantry
355.71	UC410	Soldiers—Billeting	356.114	UD330-335	Sniping (Military science)
355.72	UH460-485	Military hospitals	356.114	UD330-335	Sharpshooting (Military science)
355.75	UA	Armories			
355.8	U800-897	Weapons	356.114	UD310-315	Marching
355.8	UC260-267	Military supplies	356.1154	UD157-302	Infantry drill and tactics
			356.11547	UD330-335	Shooting, Military
			356.118	UD370-375	Infantry—Equipment

Dewey	LC	Subject Heading	Dewey	LC	Subject Heading
356.1182	UD380-415	Firearms	358.12	UF628	Antitank weapons
356.1182	UD390	Firearms—Sights	358.12	UF	Artillery
356.118241	UD400	Bayonets	358.12006	UF1	Artillery—Societies, etc.
356.118241	UD420-425	Swords	358.1203	UF9	Artillery—Dictionaries
356.118241	UD340-345	Bayonets	358.12074	UF6	Military museums
356.1182425	UD390-395	Assault rifles	358.1209	UF15	Artillery—History
356.1182425	UD390-395	Rifles	358.1209(4-9)	UF21-124	Artillery—[By region or country]
356.11824250973	UD395.M17	M1 carbine			
356.1182432	UD410-415	Pistols	358.12094	UF55-95	Artillery—Europe
356.1182436	UD410-415	Revolvers	358.120941	UF57-64	Artillery—Great Britain
356.164	UD460-465	Mountain warfare	358.120943	UF73-74	Artillery—Germany
356.164	UD470-475	Ski troops	358.120944	UF71-72	Artillery—France
356.166	UD480-485	Parachute troops	358.120945	UF79-80	Artillery—Italy
356.1660973	UD483	United States—Armed Forces—Airborne troops	358.120946	UF87-88	Artillery—Spain
			358.1209469	UF83-84	Artillery—Portugal
356.1660973	UD483	United States—Armed Forces—Parachute troops	358.120947	UF85-86	Artillery—Russia
			358.120948	UF86.5	Artillery—Scandinavia
356.4	UD460-465	Military maneuvers	358.1209495	UF75-76	Artillery—Greece
357	UE	Cavalry	358.12095	UF99-113	Artillery—Asia
357.04144	UE440-445	Cavalry—Uniforms	358.120951	UF101-102	Artillery—China
357.0482	UE420-425	Sabers	358.120952	UF105-106	Artillery—Japan
357.048241	UE420-425	Swords	358.120954	UF103-104	Artillery—India
357.06	UE1	Cavalry—Societies, etc.	358.12096	UF115-119	Artillery—Africa
357.09	UE15	Cavalry—History	358.120971	UF26-27	Artillery—Canada
357.09(4-9)	UE21-124	Cavalry—[By region or country]	358.1209728	UF30-31	Artillery—Central America
			358.1209729	UF32-33	Artillery—West Indies
357.094	UE55-95	Cavalry—Europe	358.120973	UA32-33	United States. Army—Artillery
357.0941	UE57-64	Cavalry—Great Britain			
357.0943	UE73-74	Cavalry—Germany	358.120973	UF23	United States. Army—Artillery
357.0944	UE71-72	Cavalry—France			
357.0945	UE79-80	Cavalry—Italy	358.120973	UF23-25	Artillery—United States
357.0946	UE87-88	Cavalry—Spain	358.12098	UF34-54	Artillery—South America
357.09469	UE83-84	Cavalry—Portugal	358.120982	UF36-37	Artillery—Argentina
357.0947	UE85-86	Cavalry—Russia	358.120983	UF43-44	Artillery—Chile
357.0948	UE86.5	Cavalry—Scandinavia	358.1209861	UF45-46	Artillery—Colombia
357.09495	UE75-76	Cavalry—Greece	358.120987	UF54	Artillery—Venezuela
357.095	UE99-113	Cavalry—Asia	358.12099(3/4)	UF121-122	Artillery—[New Zealand/Australia]
357.0951	UE101-102	Cavalry—China			
357.0952	UE105-106	Cavalry—Japan	358.12099(5-6)	UF123-124	Artillery—Oceania
357.0954	UE103-104	Cavalry—India	358.124	UF157-302	Artillery drill and tactics
357.096	UE115-119	Cavalry—Africa	358.1240973	UF160-162	United States. Army—Artillery—Drill and tactics
357.0971	UE26-27	Cavalry—Canada			
357.0972	UE28-29	Cavalry—Mexico	358.125	UF340-345	Target practice
357.09728	UE30-31	Cavalry—Central America	358.128	UF845	Telescopes
357.09729	UE32-33	Cavalry—West Indies	358.128	UF560-565	Ordnance, Rapid-fire
357.0973	UE23-25	Cavalry—United States	358.1280287	UF890	Ordnance testing
357.098	UE34-54	Cavalry—South America	358.1282	UF765	Grenades
357.0982	UE36-37	Cavalry—Argentina	358.1282	UF700-770	Ammunition
357.0983	UE43-44	Cavalry—Chile	358.1282	UF656	Recoilless rifles
357.09861	UE45-46	Cavalry—Colombia	358.1282	UF620	Machine-guns
357.0987	UE54	Cavalry—Venezuela	358.1282	UF563.A77	Trench mortars
357.0994	UE121-122	Cavalry—Australia	358.1282	UF520-780	Ordnance
357.099(5-6)	UE123-124	Cavalry—Oceania	358.1282	UF560-565	Howitzers
357.10973	UA30-31	United States. Army. Cavalry	358.1282	UF780	Electric detonators
357.184	UE157-302	Cavalry drill and tactics	358.12822	UF470-475	Howitzers
357.2	UC600-695	Remount service	358.1282356	UF767	Rockets (Ordnance)
357.2	UC600-695	Horses	358.128251	UF767	Projectiles, Aerial
357.2	UE460-475	War horses	358.1282513	UF750-770	Projectiles
357.2	UE460-475	Horses	358.128255	UF740-745	Cartridges
357.2	UE460-475	Horsemanship	358.120972	UF28-29	Artillery—Mexico
358.12	UF400-445	Artillery, Field and mountain	358.1382	UF625	Antiaircraft guns

Dewey	LC	Subject Heading	Dewey	LC	Subject Heading
358.16	UG448	Coast defenses	358.4383	UG1230-1235	Attack helicopters
358.16	UF450-455	Artillery, Coast	358.44	TL685.7	Supersonic transport planes
358.174	UF625	Surface-to-air missiles	358.44	TL685.7	Jet transports
358.175482	UG1312.I2	Intercontinental ballistic missiles	358.45	UG760-765	Aerial reconnaissance
			358.45	UG1242.R4	Reconnaissance aircraft
358.1883	UG446.5	M1 (Tank)	358.450941	UG765.G	Aerial reconnaissance, British
358.1883	UG446.5	Armored personnel carriers			
358.1883	UG446.5	Half-track vehicles, Military	358.450973	UG763	Aerial reconnaissance, American
358.1883	UG446.5	Tanks (Military science)			
358.22	UG375	Obstacles (Military science)	358.8	UG1500-1530	Space surveillance
358.22	UG360-390	Military field engineering	358.8	UG1530	Space warfare
358.22	UG	Military engineering	359	VA37-42	Navies
358.2206	UG5	Military engineering—Congresses	359	V	Naval art and science
			359	V	War
358.2206	UG1	Military engineering—Societies, etc.	359	VA	Naval districts
			359.003	V23-24	Naval art and science—Dictionaries
358.22071	UG157	Military engineering—Study and teaching			
			359.003	V23-24	Naval art and science—Terminology
358.2209	UG15	Military engineering—History			
			359.005	V1-5	Naval art and science—Periodicals
358.22092	UG	Military engineers			
358.22092	UG127-128	Tank engineers	359.006	V7	Naval art and science—Congresses
358.2209(4-9)	UG21-124	Military engineering—[By region or country]			
			359.0071	V400-695	Naval education
358.23	UG370	Demolition, Military	359.00710(4-9)	V411-695	Naval education—[By region or country]
358.24	UG570-613.5	Signals and signaling			
358.25	UC270-360	Transportation, Military	359.007104	V500-623	Naval education—Europe
358.25	UC300-305	Pack transportation	359.0071041	V510-530	Naval education—Great Britain
358.250973	UC273	United States. Army—Transporation			
			359.0071043	V570-574.54	Naval education—Germany
358.32	V795	Ships of the line	359.007105	V625-650	Naval education—Asia
358.34	UG447-.5	Gases, Asphyxiating and poisonous—War use	359.0071051	V630-634	Naval education—China
			359.0071052	V640-644	Naval education—Japan
358.34	UG447-.65	Chemical warfare	359.0071054	V635-639	Naval education—India
358.34	UG447.5.M8	Mustard gas	359.0071055	V645-649	Naval education—Iran
358.38	UG447.8	Biological warfare	359.007106	V660-680	Naval education—Africa
358.4	UG630	Air warfare	359.0071071	V440-444	Naval education—Canada
358.4	UG622-1425	Air forces	359.0071072	V445-449	Naval education—Mexico
358.4	UG630-670	Aeronautics, Military	359.00710728	V450-453	Naval education—Central America
358.4006	UG623	Air forces—Congresses			
358.4006	UG622	Air forces—Societies, etc.	359.00710729	V455-458	Naval education—West Indies
358.4009	UG625	Air forces—History			
358.40092	UG626-.2	Air pilots, Military	359.0071073	V411-437	Naval education—United States
358.400942	DA89.5	England. Royal Air force			
358.400973	UG633-634.5	United States. Air Force	359.0071073	V415	Midshipmen
358.414	UG1180-1185	Air forces—Insignia	359.007108	V465-496	Naval education—South America
358.414	UG730-735	Air defenses			
358.41422	UG700	Air interdiction	359.0071094	V690-694	Naval education—Australia
358.4183	UG1240-1242	Airplanes, Military	359.0074	V13	Naval museums
358.42	UG1242.A28	Dauntless (Dive bomber)	359.009	D27	Naval history
358.428251	UG1312.C7	Cruise missiles	359.009	VD23-25	Sailors—United States
358.428251	UG1282.N48	Neutron bomb	359.009	V25-55	Naval art and science—History
358.4283	UG1242.A25	Antisubmarine aircraft			
358.4283	UG1242.A28	Dive bombers	359.00901	D95	Naval history, Ancient
358.42830973	UG1242.B6	B-52 bomber	359.0092	VD15	Sailors—History
358.43	UG1242.A28	Attack planes	359.0092	V61-65	Naval biography
358.4303	UG1242.F5	Night fighter planes	359.0092	VD	Sailors
358.43092	UG626-.2	Fighter pilots	359.0092	VD21-124	Sailors—[By region or country]
358.434	UG700-705	Fighter plane combat			
358.4383	TL685.3	Fighter planes	359.0094	D436	Naval history, Modern—20th century
358.4383	UG1242.F5	Fighter planes			

Dewey	LC	Subject Heading	Dewey	LC	Subject Heading
359.00947	DK55-59	Russia—History, Naval	359.32	V799-800	Armored vessels
359.07	V390-395	Naval research	359.32	V890	Floating batteries
359.13323	VB920-925	Military police	359.32	V750-995	Warships
359.13325	VB910	Corporal punishment	359.32	VF440	Warships—Turrets
359.1334	VB870-875	Desertion, Naval	359.32092	VK221	Ships—Manning
359.1334	VB850-880	Naval offenses	359.3220948	V46	Viking ships
359.1334	VB860-867	Mutiny	359.3220973	V880	United States. Navy—Boats
359.1334	VB880	Insubordination	359.3253	V820-.5	Battle cruisers
359.1342	VB330-335	Military decorations	359.3254	V825-.5	Destroyers (Warships)
359.1342	VC345	Insignia	359.3258	V830-840	Torpedo-boats
359.15	V300-305	Flags	359.331	VB190	Admirals
359.150973	V303-304	Flags—United States	359.332	VB310-315	Navies—Officers
359.17	V310	Naval ceremonies, honors, and salutes	359.3320973	V133	United States. Navy—Officers' handbooks
359.2236	VB260-275	Recruiting and enlistment	359.3320973	V123	United States. Navy—Petty officers' handbooks
359.22360973	VB263	United States. Navy—Recruiting, enlistment, etc.	359.3320973	VB313-314	United States. Navy—Officers
359.30942	DA70-89.1	Great Britain—History, Naval	359.3320973	VB308	United States—Armed Forces—Warrant officers
359.30943	DD358	Prussia (Germany)—History, Naval	359.3380973	VG803	United States. Navy—Machinist's mates
359.309436	DB45	Austria—History, Naval	359.3380973	VD150-155	United States. Navy—Sailors' handbooks
359.30944	DC49-53	France—History, Naval			
359.30946	DP80-81	Spain—History, Naval	359.3380973	V143-144	United States. Navy—Sailors' handbooks
359.309469	DP550-551	Portugal—History, Naval			
359.309492	DJ130-138	Netherlands—History, Naval	359.3380973	VG903	United States. Navy—Yeomen
359.309492	DH121	Netherlands—History, Naval			
359.309493	DH551	Belgium—History, Naval	359.3380973	VG913	United States. Navy—Draftsmen
359.309495	DF544	Byzantine Empire—History, Naval	359.3380973	VG953	United States. Navy—Boatswains
359.309497	DR1252-1253	Yugoslavia—History, Naval	359.34	VG60-65	Postal service
359.309498	DR225	Romania—History, Naval	359.340973	VG63	United States. Navy—Postal service
359.30951090 (45-5)	DS777.7	China—History, Naval—1949-			
359.309561	DR451	Turkey—History, Naval	359.342	VG500-505	Journalism, Military
359.30971	F1028.5	Canada—History, Naval	359.3420973	VG503	Journalism, Military—United States
359.30973	E182	United States. Navy—History			
359.30973	E182	United States—History, Naval	359.3432	VB230-250	Intelligence service
			359.3432092	VB250	Spies
359.30973	VA49-395	United States. Navy—Organization	359.34320973	VG1020	United States. Navy—Intelligence specialists
359.30975	VA393-395	Confederate States of America. Navy—Organization	359.345	VG100-475	Medicine, Naval
			359.345	VG280-285	Dentistry, Naval
			359.345	VG270-275	Pharmacy, Military
359.30975	E591-600	Confederate States of America—History, Naval	359.345	VG470-475	Naval hygiene
359.30975	E591-600	Confederate States of America. Navy—History	359.345071	VG230-235	Medicine, Naval—Study and teaching
359.309561	DR451	Turkey—History, Naval	359.345092	VG226-228	Medicine, Naval—Biography
359.30971	F1028.5	Canada—History, Naval	359.34509(4-9)	VG121-224	Medicine, Naval—[By region or country]
359.30973	E182	United States. Navy—History			
359.30973	E182	United States—History, Naval	359.345094	VG155-196	Medicine, Naval—Europe
			359.3450941	VG157-164	Medicine, Naval—Great Britain
359.30973	VA49-395	United States. Navy—Organization			
359.30975	VA393-395	Confederate States of America. Navy—Organization	359.3450943	VG173-174.5	Medicine, Naval—Germany
			359.3450944	VG171-172	Medicine, Naval—France
			359.3450945	VG179-180	Medicine, Naval—Italy
			359.3450946	VG187-188	Medicine, Naval—Spain
			359.3450948	VG186.5	Medicine, Naval—Scandinavia
359.310973	VD403	United States. Navy—Small-boat service	359.345095	VG199-213	Medicine, Naval—Asia
			359.3450952	VG205-206	Medicine, Naval—Japan

358 - 359

69

Dewey	LC	Subject Heading	Dewey	LC	Subject Heading
359.345096	VG215-219	Medicine, Naval—Africa	359.609495	VB75-76	Naval art and science—Greece
359.3450971	VG126-127	Medicine, Naval—Canada			
359.3450972	VG128-129	Medicine, Naval—Mexico	359.6095	VB99-113	Naval art and science—Asia
359.34509728	VG130-131	Medicine, Naval—Central America	359.60951	VB101-102	Naval art and science—China
359.3450973	VG123-125	Medicine, Naval—United States	359.60952	VB105-106	Naval art and science—Japan
359.345098	VG134-154	Medicine, Naval—South America	359.6096	VB115-119	Naval art and science—Africa
359.3450993	VG222.5	Medicine, Naval—New Zealand	359.60971	VB26-27	Naval art and science—Canada
359.3450994	VG221-222	Medicine, Naval—Australia	359.60972	VB28-29	Naval art and science—Mexico
359.347	VG20-25	Chaplains, Military			
359.3470973	VG23	United States. Navy—Chaplains	359.609728	VB30-31	Naval art and science—Central America
359.350973	V175	United States. Navy—Field service	359.609729	VB32-33	Naval art and science—West Indies
359.37	VA45	Naval reserves	359.60973	VB23-25	Naval art and science—United States
359.370941	VA460	Navy-yards and naval stations—Great Britain	359.6098	VB34-54	Naval art and science—South America
359.370971	VA402	Naval militia—Canada	359.60982	VB36-37	Naval art and science—Argentina
359.4	D27	Naval battles			
359.41	V215	Warships—Camouflage	359.60983	VB43-44	Naval art and science—Chile
359.41	V215	Camouflage (Military science)	359.609861	VB45-46	Naval art and science—Colombia
359.41	V245	Naval maneuvers			
359.410973	V245	United States. Navy—Maneuvers	359.60994	VB121-122	Naval art and science—Australia
359.411	V179	Logistics, Naval	359.6099(5-6)	VB123-124	Naval art and science—Pacific Islands
359.413	V190	Naval reconnaissance			
359.42	V167-178	Naval tactics	359.610973	VB258	United States. Navy—Personnel management
359.42	V160-165	Naval strategy			
359.422	VF520-530	Fire control (Naval gunnery)	359.62120973	VC260-267	United States. Navy—Procurement
359.422	VF550	Range-finding	359.6220973	VA53	United States. Navy—Appropriations and expenditures
359.450947	VG185-186	Medicine, Naval—Russia			
359.4509729	VG132-133	Medicine, Naval—West Indies	359.6220973	VC503	United States. Navy—Accounting
359.48	V250	War games, Naval	359.6229	VA20-25	Navies, Cost of
359.48	V253	Imaginary wars and battles	359.6850973	VB223	United States. Navy—Inspection
359.50973	V263	United States. Navy—Physical training			
359.50973	V435-436	Training-ships	359.7	V230	Navy-yards and naval stations
359.547	VF310-315	Target practice	359.70973	VA66	Navy-yards and naval stations—United States
359.6	VB	Naval art and science			
359.609(4-9)	VB21-124	Naval art and science—[By region or country]	359.710973	VC423	United States. Navy—Barracks and quarters
359.6094	VB55-96	Naval art and science—Europe	359.72	VG410-450	Hospitals, Naval and marine
359.60941	VB57-64	Naval art and science—Great Britain	359.8	V396-.5	Military oceanography
359.60943	VB73-74.5	Naval art and science—Germany	359.80287	VF540	Ordnance testing
			359.80941	VC184-187	Great Britain. Royal Navy
359.60944	VB71-72	Naval art and science—France	359.80973	VC263	United States. Navy—Supplies and stores
359.60945	VB79-80	Naval art and science—Italy	359.80973	VC20-65	United States. Navy
359.60946	VB87-88	Naval art and science—Spain	359.80973	VC50-65	United States. Navy—Pay, allowances, etc.
359.609469	VB83-84	Naval art and science—Portugal	359.80973	VF353-420	United States. Navy—Ordnance and ordnance stores
359.60947	VB85-86	Naval art and science—Russia	359.81	VC300-345	Military uniforms
			359.82	V880	Steel boats

Dewey	LC	Subject Heading	Dewey	LC	Subject Heading
359.82	VF	Ordnance, Naval	359.94	VG90-95	Naval aviation
359.8209	VF15	Ordnance, Naval—History	359.940973	VG93	United States. Navy—Aviation
359.8209(4-9)	VF21-124	Ordnance, Naval—[By region or country]	359.9435	V874-875	Aircraft carriers
359.82094	VF55-96	Ordnance, Naval—Europe	359.94834	VG90-95	Airplanes, Military—Turrets
359.820941	VF57-64	Ordnance, Naval—Great Britain	359.96	VE	Marines
			359.9609	VE15	Marines—History
359.820943	VF73-74.5	Ordnance, Naval—Germany	359.961342	VE345	Marines—Insigna
359.820944	VF71-72	Ordnance, Naval—France	359.9614	VE400-405	Marines—Uniforms
359.820945	VF79-80	Ordnance, Naval—Italy	359.96309(4-9)	VE21-124	Marines—[By region or country]
359.820946	VF87-88	Ordnance, Naval—Spain			
359.8209469	VF83-84	Ordnance, Naval—Portugal	359.963094	VE55-96	Marines—Europe
359.820947	VF85-86	Ordnance, Naval—Russia	359.9630941	VE57-64	Marines—Great Britain
359.820948	VF86.5	Ordnance, Naval—Scandinavia	359.9630943	VE73-74.5	Marines—Germany
			359.9630944	VE71-72	Marines—France
359.82095	VF101-113	Ordnance, Naval—Asia	359.9630945	VE79-80	Marines—Italy
359.820952	VF105-106	Ordnance, Naval—Japan	359.9630946	VE87-88	Marines—Spain
359.8209561	VF111-112	Ordnance, Naval—Turkey	359.9630947	VE85-86	Marines—Russia
359.82096	VF115-119	Ordnance, Naval—Africa	359.9630948	VE86.5	Marines—Scandinavia
359.820971	VF26-27	Ordnance, Naval—Canada	359.963095	VE99-113	Marines—Asia
359.820972	VF28-29	Ordnance, Naval—Mexico	359.9630952	VE105-106	Marines—Japan
359.8209728	VF30-31	Ordnance, Naval—Central America	359.963096	VE115-119	Marines—Africa
			359.9630971	VE26-27	Marines—Canada
359.8209729	VF32-33	Ordnance, Naval—West Indies	359.9630972	VE28-29	Marines—Mexico
			359.96309728	VE30-31	Marines—Central America
359.820973	VF23-25	Ordnance, Naval—United States	359.96309729	VE32-33	Marines—West Indies
			359.9630973	VE23-25	United States. Marine Corps
359.82098	VF34-54	Ordnance, Naval—South America	359.963098	VE34-54	Marines—South America
			359.9630993	VE122.5	Marines—New Zealand
359.820982	VF36-37	Ordnance, Naval—Argentina	359.9630994	VE121-122	Marines—Australia
359.820983	VF43-44	Ordnance, Naval—Chile	359.9633	VE150-155	Marines—Handbooks, manuals, etc.
359.8209861	VF45-46	Ordnance, Naval—Colombia			
359.820993	VF122.5	Ordnance, Naval—New Zealand	359.965	VE430-435	Military training camps
			359.9650973	VE160-162	United States. Marine Corps—Drill and tactics
359.820994	VF121-122	Ordnance, Naval—Australia			
359.820973	VF440	Ridgway's revolving battery	359.9671	VE420-425	Marines—Barracks and quarters
359.820973	VF347	United States. Navy—Weapons systems	359.96824	VE350-390	Marines—Firearms
359.824	VD360-390	Firearms	359.9709073	V437	United States. Coast Guard
359.8240973	VD360-390	United States. Navy—Firearms	359.970973	VG53	United States. Coast Guard
359.8240973	VF350-420	United States. Navy—Firearms	359.98170973	VF347	United States. Navy—Fire control technicians (Missile)
			359.98170973	VF347	AEGIS (Weapons system)
359.82424	VF410.G3-.G34	Gatling guns	359.981782	V990-995	Fleet ballistic missile weapons systems
359.82424	VF410	Machine-guns			
359.82424	VF410.G2-.G24	Gardner machine-gun	359.9830973	VG73	United States. Navy—Communication systems
359.82425	VD370	Rifles			
359.82432	VD390	Pistols	359.984	VG86-88	Underwater demolition teams
359.82436	VD390	Revolvers	359.9840973	VG87	Underwater demolition teams—United States
359.8251	VF480-500	Projectiles			
359.8251	VF509	Depth charges	359.985	VC550-580	Transportation, Military
359.82517	V850-855	Torpedoes	359.985	V865	Naval auxiliary vessels
359.83	V880	Motor vehicles, Amphibious	359.985	VC530-535	Military sealift
359.88	VG290-295	Medical supplies	359.9850973	VC553	United States. Navy—Transportation
359.93	V214.5	Submarine boat combat			
359.93	V210-214.5	Submarine warfare	361	HV1-696	Social service
359.933	V857-859	Submarines (Ships)	361.006	HV6	Social service—Societies, etc.
359.9330973	V858	United States. Navy—Submarine forces	361.025	HV7	Social service—Directories
359.9383	V857-859	Submarine boats	361.05	HV59-63	Institutional care
359.93834	V857.5	Nuclear submarines	361.1	HN	Social problems

Dewey	LC	Subject Heading	Dewey	LC	Subject Heading
361.10285	HV29.2-.5	Information storage and retrieval systems—Social service	362.11	RK3-.5	Dental clinics
			362.11068	RA971-.8	Hospitals—Administration
			362.11072	RA964.5	Hospitals—Research
361.105	HN1	Social problems—Periodicals	362.1109(4-9)	RF6	Hospitals, Ophthalmic and aural—[By region or country]
361.106	HN3	Social problems—Congresses	362.1109(4-9)	RK3.5	Dental clinics—[By region or country]
361.10723	HN29	Social surveys			
361.109	HN8-19	Social problems—History	362.1109(4-9)	RA980-993	Hospitals—[By region or country]
361.3	HV7428	Social work with criminals			
361.3023	HV10.5	Social service—Vocational guidance	362.110902	RA964	Hospitals, Medieval
			362.11091734	RA975.R87	Rural hospitals
361.3071	HV11-.8	Social work education	362.1109174927	RA990.5	Hospitals—Arab countries
361.308664	HV1449	Social work with gays	362.11094	RA985-989	Hospitals—Europe
361.3092	HV40.54	Social workers—Supervision of	362.110941	RA986-988	Hospitals—Great Britain
			362.11095	RA990	Hospitals—Asia
361.322	H61.28	Focused group interviewing	362.11096	RA991	Hospitals—Africa
361.4	HV45	Social group work	362.110971	RA983	Hospitals—Canada
361.6	HV	Public welfare	362.110973	RJ27.2-.3	Pediatric clinics—United States
361.7	HV40-69	Charity organization			
361.7	HV544	Bazaars (Charities)	362.110973	RD705.5	Orthopedic hospitals—United States
361.7	HV687-694	Charities, Medical			
361.7	HV1-4959	Charities	362.110973	RA981-982	Hospitals—United States
361.70681	HV41.2-.9	Fund raising	362.11099(5-6)	RA993	Hospitals—Oceania
361.709	HV16-25	Social service—History	362.110993	RA992.5-.7	Hospitals—New Zealand
361.75	HV530	Church charities	362.110994	RA992-.3	Hospitals—Australia
361.77	HV560-583	Red Cross	362.12	RA974-.5	Hospitals—Outpatient services
361.77	UH535-537	Red Cross			
361.77	VG457	Red Cross	362.12	RC660.7	Diabetes clinics
361.7709(4-9)	HV575-580	Red Cross—[By region or country]	362.12	RA966	Clinics
			362.12	RZ242	Chiropractic clinics
361.91734	HV67	Social service, Rural	362.12	RA960-993	Dispensaries
361.9(4-9)	HV85-520.5	Social service—[By region or country]	362.12	RA974-.5	Public hospitals—Outpatient services
361.97(4-9)	HV98-99	Social service—[United States, By state or city]	362.12	RJ27-28	Pediatric clinics
			362.14	RA645.3-.37	Home care services
361.973	HV85-99	Social service—United States	362.16	RA960-993	Sanatoriums
			362.16	RA997-999	Nursing homes
362.(3-4)	HV888-907	Handicapped children—Services for	362.16	RA997-999	Long-term care facilities
			362.1608697	UB380-385	Soldiers' homes
362.(3-4)	HV1551-3024	Handicapped	362.1608697	UB356-375	Veterans
362.0425	HD7255-7256	Rehabilitation counselors	362.16092	RA997-998	Volunteer workers in long-term care facilities
362.1	HV687-694	Sick			
362.1	RA390-392	Missions, Medical	362.172	RC455.2.R43	Psychiatric referral
362.10425	HV687-688	Medical social work	362.172	R727.5	Medical referral
362.104258	RA413-.7	Health maintenance organizations	362.174	RA975.5.I56	Intensive care units
			362.1756	R726.8	Hospices (Terminal care)
362.104258	RA413-.5	Managed care plans (Medical care)	362.177	RA427.5-.6	Medical screening
			362.1783	RD129.5	Donation of organs, tissues, etc.
362.108697	UB368-369.5	Veterans—Medical care			
362.108996073	RA448.5.N4	Afro-Americans—Medical care	362.1783	RD127-128.5	Tissue banks
			362.1783	RD128	Musculoskeletal banks
362.11	RX6-.5	Homeopathy—Hospitals and dispensaries	362.1783	RE89	Eye banks
			362.1783092	RD129.5	Organ donors
362.11	RF5-6	Hospitals, Ophthalmic and aural	362.1784	RM172	Blood banks
			362.18	RA645.5-.9	Emergency medical services
362.11	RG12-16	Hospitals, Gynecologic and obstetric	362.18	RA975.5.E5	Hospitals—Emergency service
362.11	RA960-996	Public hospitals	362.18	RA975.5.T83	Trauma centers
362.11	RZ302-304	Osteopathic hospitals	362.188	RA996.5	Airplane ambulances
362.11	RA960-996	Hospitals	362.188	RA995-996	Ambulance service
362.11	RD705-706	Orthopedic hospitals			

Dewey	LC	Subject Heading	Dewey	LC	Subject Heading
362.1968	HV3004-3009.5	Day care centers for the developmentally disabled	362.298	HV5810	Cocaine habit
			362.299	HV5822.G5	Glue-sniffing
362.1968	HV1570-.5	Developmentally disabled	362.3	HV3004-3009	Mental retardation
362.1968	HV891-901	Developmentally disabled children	362.(3-4)	HV888-907	Handicapped children—Services for
362.1969792	P96.A39	AIDS (Disease) in mass media	362.(3-4)	HV1551-3024	Handicapped
			362.30973	HV3006-3008	Mentally handicapped—[By region or country]
362.196995	RC309-.5	Tuberculosis—Hospitals			
362.2	HV4975-4977	Insanity	362.38	HV891-901	Day care centers for mentally handicapped children
362.2	RA790-.95	Mental health			
362.2	RA790-.95	Mental health services	362.385	HV3004-3008	Mental retardation facilities
362.20425	HV689-690	Psychiatric social work	362.4083	HV903-907	Disfigured children
362.20846	RC451.4.A5	Aged—Mental health services	362.408697	UB360-366	Veterans, Disabled
			362.41	HV1571-2349	Blind
362.21	RC439.4	Violence in psychiatric hospitals	362.41	HV1597-.2	Blind-deaf—Services for
			362.4109(4-9)	HV1783-2220.5	Blind—[By region or country]
362.22	RC455	Community psychiatry	362.410973	HV1783-1796	Blind—United States
362.22	RA790.55	Community psychology	362.418	HV1631.5	Visually handicapped—Means of communication
362.28021	HB1323.S8	Suicide—Statistics			
362.2881	RC480.6	Psychiatric hospitals—Emergency service	362.418	HV1701	Blind, Apparatus for the
			362.418071	HV1780-.6	Guide dog schools
362.29	HV4997-5840	Substance abuse	362.42	HV2350-2990.5	Hearing impaired
362.29(3-8)	HV5800-5840	Drug abuse	362.42	HV2350-2990.5	Deaf
362.29(3-8)09 (4-9)	HV5825-5840	Drug abuse—[By region or country]	362.4209(4-9)	HV2510-2990.5	Deaf—[By region or country]
			362.420973	HV2510-2561	Deaf—United States
362.29(3-8)0973	HV5825-5833	Drug abuse—United States	362.4283	HV2503	Video recordings for the hearing impaired
362.29(3-8)7	HV5800-5840	Drug abuse—Prevention			
362.29083	HV4999.Y68	Youth—Substance use	362.4283	HV2402	Interpreters for the deaf
362.290834	HV4999.C45	School children—Substance use	362.48	HV1568.7-.8	Day care centers for the handicapped
362.2909(4-9)	HV4999.2-5000	Substance abuse—[By region or country]	362.48	HV3011-3024	Physically handicapped—Services for
362.292	HV5053-5055	Alcoholism and crime	362.4809(4-9)	HV3023-3024	Physically handicapped—[By region or country]
362.292	HV5001-5722	Alcoholism			
362.29201	B105.D78	Drunkenness (Philosophy)	362.480973	HV3023	Physically handicapped—United States
362.29205	HV5001-5002	Alcoholism—Periodicals			
362.2920709	HV5020-5025	Temperance—History	362.5	HV4480-4630	Tramps
362.29209(4-9)	HV5285-5722	Alcoholism—[By region or country]	362.5	HV1-4630	Poverty
			362.5	HV4023-4470.7	Poor
362.2920973	HV5285-5298	Alcoholism—United States	362.5091724	HV4173	Poor—Developing countries
362.2923	HV5132	Adult children of alcoholics	362.5091732	HV4023-4470.7	Urban poor
362.2923	HV5132	Children of alcoholics	362.509(4-9)	HV4041-4173	Poor—[By region or country]
362.2923	HV5132	Alcoholics' spouses	362.5094	HV4084-4131.84	Poor—Europe
362.2923	HV5132	Alcoholics—Family relationships	362.50941	HV4085-4087.5	Poor—Great Britain
			362.50943	HV4097-4100.5	Poor—Germany
362.2928	HV5001-5720	Temperance	362.50944	HV4093-4096	Poor—France
362.2928	HV5006	Temperance—Societies, etc.	362.50945	HV4102-4105	Poor—Italy
362.29286	HV5275-5283	Alcoholism counseling	362.50946	HV4125-4128	Poor—Spain
362.293	HV5813	Morphine habit	362.50947	HV4114-4117	Poor—Russia
362.293	HV5800-5840	Narcotic habit	362.509492	HV4105.5-4113.5	Poor—Benelux countries
362.293	HV5816	Opium habit	362.5095	HV4131.85-4156.5	Poor—Asia
362.293	HV5822.H4	Heroin			
362.294	HV5822.5.L9	LSD (Drug)	362.50951	HV4150	Poor—China
362.295	HV5822.M3	Marihuana	362.50952	HV4147	Poor—Japan
362.296	HV5725-5770	Ex-smokers	362.50954	HV4137-4140	Poor—India
362.296	HV5740-5745	Cigarette habit	362.5096	HV4157-4169.3	Poor—Africa
362.296	HV5725-5770	Tobacco habit	362.50971	HV4047-4050	Poor—Canada
362.296	HV5725-5770	Smoking	362.50972	HV4051	Poor—Mexico
362.29609(4-9)	HV5755-5770	Smoking—[By region or country]	362.509728	HV4053-4059	Poor—Central America
			362.509729	HV4060-4065.9	Poor—West Indies
362.2960973	HV5755-5768	Smoking—United States	362.50973	HV4043-4046	Poor—United States

Dewey	LC	Subject Heading	Dewey	LC	Subject Heading
362.5098	HV4066-4083	Poor—South America	363.107	HD7273	Safety appliances
362.50994	HV4170	Poor—Australia	363.11	HD7262-.5	Industrial accidents
362.585	HV61	Almshouses	363.11	T54	Hazardous occupations
362.6	HV1597.5	Blind aged	363.11	T55-.3	Industrial safety
362.6	HV1450-1493	Old age	363.1172	HD7395.C5	Protective clothing
362.6	HV1450-1494	Aged	363.119371	LB2864.6.A25	School accidents
362.6091734	HV1450-1494	Rural aged	363.122	HE1779-1795	Railroad accidents
362.609(4-9)	HV1457-1494	Aged—[By region or country]	363.123	VK1265	Submarine disasters
362.61	HV1454-.2	Old age homes	363.123	VK1250-1299	Steamboat disasters
362.68	HV1455-.2	Day care centers for the aged	363.123	VK1250-1299	Shipwrecks
362.7	HV701-1420.5	Child welfare	363.12309(4-9)	VK1270-1294	Shipwrecks—[By region or country]
362.705	HV701	Child welfare—Periodicals			
362.7083	HV1423	Young men	363.124	TL867	Space vehicle accidents
362.7083	HV1425	Young women	363.125	HE5613.5-5614.6	Traffic safety
362.708691	HV873-887	Street children	363.125	RA772.T7	Traffic accidents
362.709(4-9)	HV741-804	Child welfare—[By region or country]	363.12514	HE5620.D7	Drinking and traffic accidents
			363.1257	LB2865	School safety patrols
362.70973	HV741-743	Child welfare—United States	363.19	HF5415.9	Product recall
362.712	HQ778.5-.7	Day care centers	363.192	HD9000.9	Food adulteration and inspection
362.713	HV697-700	Aid to families with dependent children	363.192064	TX501-597	Food adulteration and inspection
362.73	HV835-847	Foundlings			
362.73	HV873-875.7	Abandoned children	363.1929064	SF255	Dairy inspection
362.73	HV959-1420.5	Orphans	363.1929064	SH335	Fish inspection
362.7309(4-9)	HV880-887	Abandoned children—[By region or country]	363.2	HV7981	Constables
			363.2	HV7551-8280.7	Police
362.730973	HV880-885	Abandoned children—United States	363.2	HV7936.D78	Police—Drug testing
			363.2025	HV7900	Police—Directories
362.732	HV862-866	Group homes for children	363.20284	HV7936.E7	Riot helmets
362.732	HV959-1420.5	Orphanages	363.20284	HV7936.E7	Handcuffs
362.73209(4-9)	HV971-1420.5	Orphanages—[By region or country]	363.20284	HV7936.E7	Nonlethal weapons
			363.20284	HV7936.E7	Tear gas munitions
362.7320973	HV971-995	Orphanages—United States	363.20284	HV7936.E7	Truncheons
362.734	HV875.5	Intercountry adoption	363.2071	HV7923	Police—Study and teaching
362.734	HV874.8-875.7	Adoption	363.209	HV7903-7909	Police—History
362.809(4-9)	HQ301-440.7	Church work with prostitutes	363.2091734	HV7965-7985	Police, Rural
362.8292	HV697-700.5	Abused wives—Services for	363.209(4-9)	HV8130-8280.7	Police—[By region or country]
362.829209(4-9)	HV699-700	Abused wives—Services for—[By region or country]	363.2094	HV8194-8261.84	Police—Europe
			363.20941	HV8195-8197.5	Police—Great Britain
362.8294	HV700.7	Unmarried fathers	363.20943	HV8207-8210	Police—Germany
362.83	HV697-700	Maternal and infant welfare	363.20944	HV8203-8206	Police—France
362.83	HV1442-1448	Women—Services for	363.20945	HV8212-8215	Police—Italy
362.8394	HV700.5	Unmarried mothers	363.20946	HV8235-8238	Police—Spain
362.8496073	HV3181-3185	Afro-Americans—Services for	363.209469	HV8239	Police—Portugal
362.858	HV3025-3163	Sailors—Services for	363.20947	HV8224-8227	Police—Russia
362.86	VB280-285	Military pensions	363.209492	HV8215.5-8223.5	Police—Benelux countries
362.87	HV640-.5	Refugees, Political	363.209495	HV8241.83	Police—Greece
362.87	HV640-.5	Refugees	363.2095	HV8241.85-8263	Police—Asia
362.87	HV6322-.7	Disappeared persons	363.20951	HV8260	Police—China
362.88	HV6250-.4	Victims of crimes	363.20952	HV8257	Police—Japan
362.880723	HV6250	Victims of crimes surveys	363.20954	HV8247-8250	Police—India
362.88082	HV6250.4.W65	Women—Crimes against	363.20956	HV8241.9-8242.56	Police—Middle East
362.88083	HV6250.4.Y68	Youth—Crimes against			
362.880846	HV6250.4.A34	Aged—Crimes against	363.209599	HV8255	Police—Philippines
362.88088375	HV6250.4.S78	Students—Crimes against	363.2096	HV8267-8279.3	Police—Africa
362.8808996073	HV6250.4.E75	Afro-Americans—Crimes against	363.20971	HV8157-8160	Police—Canada
			363.20972	HV8161	Police—Mexico
362.883	RC560.R36	Rape victims	363.209728	HV8163-8169	Police—Central America
363	HD3840-4420.8	Public works	363.209729	HV8170-8175.9	Police—West Indies
363.	HV8067	Vice control	363.20973	HV8130-8148	Police—United States
363.107	HV675-677	Accidents—Prevention	363.2098	HV8176-8193	Police—South America

Dewey	LC	Subject Heading
363.20994	HV8280	Police—Australia
363.22	HV7936.P75	Police psychiatrists
363.22	HV7936.P75	Police psychologists
363.22	HV8079.2-.3	Police social work
363.22	HV8080.D54	Police divers
363.22	HV8012	Police chiefs
363.22019	HV7936.J63	Police—Job stress
363.22082	HV8023	Policewomen
363.232	HV8080.A6	Arrest (Police methods)
363.232	HV8080.P2	Police patrol—Field interrogation
363.232	HV8080.P2	Police patrol—Surveillance operations
363.2332	HV8079.5-.55	Traffic police
363.23320284	HV8079.5	Radar in speed limit enforcement
363.24	HV6071	Legal photography
363.24	HV6074	Fingerprints
363.24	HV7936.C8	Police communication systems
363.24	HV7936.R53	Police reports
363.25	HV8073-8077.5	Chemistry, Forensic
363.25	HV8073-8079.3	Criminal investigation
363.25092	P96.D4	Detectives in mass media
363.254	HV8078-.5	Lie detectors and detection
363.254092	HV8078	Polygraph operators
363.256	HV7936.C88	Crime analysis
363.2562	HV8077.5.F6	Footprints
363.2562	HV8077	Forensic ballistics
363.2565	HV8074-8076	Writing—Identification
363.2565	HV8077	Firearms—Identification
363.258	HV6065-6079	Criminals—Identification
363.258	HV8073.4	Police artists
363.258	HV8073-.8	Identification
363.25906	HV8079.O73	Organized crime investigation
363.25947	HV8079.D76	Drunk driving—Investigation
363.25953	HV8079.S48	Sex crimes—Investigation
363.259532	HV8079.R35	Rape—Investigation
363.259552	HV8079.R62	Robbery investigation
363.2595553	HV8079.S67	Wife abuse—Investigation
363.2595554	HV8079.C46	Child abuse—Investigation
363.2595554	HV8079.C48	Child sexual abuse—Investigation
363.25962	HV8079.A98	Automobile theft investigation
363.25963	HV8079.F7	Fraud investigation
363.25968	HV8079.C65	Computer crimes—Investigation
363.25968	HV8079.W47	White collar crime investigation
363.25977	HV8079.N3	Drug traffic—Investigation
363.283	HV7961	Secret service
363.289	HV8081-8099	Private investigators
363.289	HV8290-8291	Watchmen
363.289	HV8290-8291	Campus police
363.289	HV8290-8291	Private security services
363.289	HV8290-8291	Police, Private
363.33	HV7435-7439	Gun control
363.348	HV553-639	Disaster relief

Dewey	LC	Subject Heading
363.34809(4-9)	HV555	Disaster relief—[By region or country]
363.3481	VK1259	Refloating of ships
363.3481	TL553.8	Search and rescue operations
363.3492	HV635.5-636	Storms
363.34929	HV625-626	Droughts
363.34938	HV609-610	Floods
363.3495	HV599-600	Earthquakes
363.34988	HV639	War relief
363.35	UA926-929	Civil defense
363.37	HV620	Fires
363.37092	TH9128	Fire fighters—Physical training
363.46	HQ767-.4	Abortion
363.46	RG734-.5	Abortion services
363.46	PN4784.A18	Abortion in the press
363.460973	PN4888.A2	Abortion in the press
363.47	HQ471	Pornography—Social aspects
363.47	HQ471-472	Pornography
363.5	HD7285-7391	Housing
363.5	HD7287.8-.82	Home ownership
363.506	HD7287.8-.82	Homeowners' associations
363.5091724	HD7391	Housing—Developing countries
363.5091732	HD7289.4-.42	Urban homesteading
363.5091734	HD7289	Housing, Rural
363.509(4-9)	HD7291-7391	Housing—[By region or country]
363.5094	HD7332-7357.7	Housing—Europe
363.50941	HD7333-7335.5	Housing—Great Britain
363.50943	HD7339-.5	Housing—Germany
363.50944	HD7338	Housing—France
363.50945	HD7341	Housing—Italy
363.50946	HD7351	Housing—Spain
363.50947	HD7345	Housing—Russia
363.509492	HD7342-7344.5	Housing—Benelux countries
363.509494	HD7353	Housing—Switzerland
363.509495	HD7357.5	Housing—Greece
363.5095	HD7359.6	Housing—Asia
363.50951	HD7368	Housing—China
363.50952	HD7367	Housing—Japan
363.50954	HD7361	Housing—India
363.50955	HD7359.2	Housing—Iran
363.509561	HD7358.25	Housing—Turkey
363.509567	HD7359	Housing—Iraq
363.5095694	HD7358.45	Housing—Israel
363.509599	HD7366	Housing—Philippines
363.5096	HD7372-7378.4	Housing—Africa
363.50971	HD7305	Housing—Canada
363.50972	HD7306	Housing—Mexico
363.509728	HD7307-7313	Housing—Central America
363.509729	HD7314-7319.9	Housing—West Indies
363.50973	HD7293-7304	Housing—United States
363.5098	HD7320-7331	Housing—South America
363.50994	HD7379	Housing—Australia
363.5908996073	HD7288.72U	Afro-Americans—Housing
363.6	HD2763-2768	Public utilities
363.68	SB481-485	Parks
363.68	SB481-484	National parks and reserves

Dewey	LC	Subject Heading	Dewey	LC	Subject Heading
363.68068	SB481-485	Parks—Management	364.09728021	HV7317-7323	Criminal statistics—Central America
363.680973	SB482-483	Parks—United States			
363.7	TD194.5-.58	Environmental impact statements	364.09729021	HV7324-7329.9	Criminal statistics—West Indies
363.7	TD194.6	Environmental impact analysis	364.0973021	HV7245-7300	Criminal statistics—United States
363.7063	QH541.15.M64	Environmental monitoring	364.097(4-9)021	HV7250-7300	Criminal statistics—[United States, By state]
363.728	TD796.5	Compost			
363.7288	TS214	Scrap metals	364.098021	HV7330-7341	Criminal statistics—South America
363.73874	QC981.8.G56	Global warming			
363.7392	QC882	Smaze	364.0994021	HV7389	Criminal statistics—Australia
363.7392	QC882.4-.46	Aerosols	364.0995021	HV7368-7381	Criminal statistics—Asia
363.7392	QC882.6	Smoke plumes	364.1	HV6275	Conspiracies
363.7394	GC1080-1581	Marine pollution	364.1	HV6705-6738	Crimes without victims
363.7396	TD878-880	Soil pollution	364.106	HV6437-6439	Gangs
363.75	HD9999.U5-.U54	Undertakers and undertaking	364.106	HV6441-6453	Mafia
363.75	RA626-630	Cemeteries	364.10660973	HV6448	Black Hand (United States)
363.75	RA622-623.6	Undertakers and undertaking	364.109(4-9)	HV6774-7220.5	Criminals—[By region or country]
363.8	HC79.F3	Famines			
363.8	HV630-635	Famines	364.10973	HV6774-6795	Criminals—United States
363.8	HD9000-9019	Food supply	364.131	HV6254-6322.7	Political crimes and offenses
363.8	TX341-641	Nutrition	364.131	HV6275	Treason
363.8071	TX364-365	Nutrition—Study and teaching	364.131	HV6285	Sedition
			364.1323	HV6301-6321	Bribery
363.83	HV868	Milk programs	364.132309(4-9)	HV6303-6321	Bribery—[By region or country]
363.882	HV696.F6	Food stamps			
363.883	HV696.F6	Food relief	364.13230973	HV6306-6316	Bribery—United States
363.883	HV694	Diet kitchens	364.133	HJ6619	Smugglers
363.9	HB883.5	Population policy	364.1330973	HJ6690-6710	Smugglers—United States
363.92	HQ750-755.5	Eugenics	364.134	HV6326	Perjury
363.96	HQ766.2-.4	Birth control—Moral and ethical aspects	364.134	HV6455-6471	Lynching
			364.1340973	JK1543	Contempt of court
363.96091724	HB884.5	Population assistance	364.135	HV6252	Transnational crime
364	HV6001-7220.5	Criminology	364.13809041	D625-626	War crimes
364	HV6251-6773.3	Crime	364.142	HV6419-6433	Offenses against public safety
364	HV6001-7220.5	Crime			
364	P96.C74	Crime in mass media	364.143	HV6486-6491	Disorderly conduct
364.109(4-9)	HV6774-7220.5	Criminals—[By region or country]	364.143	HV6474-6485	Riots
			364.143	HV6474-6485	Mobs
364.10973	HV6774-6795	Criminals—United States	364.147	HV6422-6425	Traffic violations
364.05	HV6001-6006	Criminology—Periodicals	364.148	HV4480-4630.7	Vagrancy
364.071	HV6024	Criminology—Study and teaching	364.15	HV6493-6633	Offenses against the person
			364.151	HV6322.7	Genocide
364.072	HV6024.5	Criminology—Research	364.1522	HV6543-6548	Suicide
364.09	HV6021-6023	Criminology—History	364.1522	HV6547	Mass suicide
364.09(4-9)021	HV7245-7400	Criminal statistics—[By region or country]	364.1523	HV6499-6542	Murder
			364.1523	HV6537-6541	Infanticide
364.094021	HV7342-7367.7	Criminal statistics—Europe	364.152309(4-9)	HV6518-6535	Murder—[By region or country]
364.0941021	HV7343-7345.5	Criminal statistics—Great Britain			
			364.15230973	HV6518-6534	Murder—United States
364.0943021	HV7349-.5	Criminal statistics—Germany	364.1524	HV6499-6535	Assassination
364.0944021	HV7348	Criminal statistics—France	364.1524	HV6278	Assassination
364.0945021	HV7351	Criminal statistics—Italy	364.153	HQ71-72	Sex offenders
364.0946021	HV7361	Criminal statistics—Spain	364.153	HQ71-72	Sex crimes
364.0947021	HV7355	Criminal statistics—Russia	364.153	HV6584-6589	Seduction
364.0951021	HV7378	Criminal statistics—China	364.153	HV6558-6569	Sex crimes
364.0952021	HV7377	Criminal statistics—Japan	364.1532	HV6558-6569	Rape
364.0954021	HV7371	Criminal statistics—India	364.1532	HV6558-6569	Gang rape
364.096021	HV7382-7388.4	Criminal statistics—Africa	364.154	HV6595-6604	Kidnapping
364.0971021	HV7315	Criminal statistics—Canada	364.154	HV6571-6574	Abduction
364.0972021	HV7316	Criminal statistics—Mexico	364.1552	HV6646-6665	Cattle stealing

Dewey	LC	Subject Heading	Dewey	LC	Subject Heading
364.1552	HV6441-6453	Brigands and robbers	364.6	HV9051-9230.7	Social work with juvenile delinquents
364.1552	HV6646-6665	Mugging	364.6	HV7231-9960	Punishment
364.1555	HV6618	Assault and battery	364.601	HV9261-9430.7	Criminals—Rehabilitation
364.1555(3-4)	HV6626-.23	Family violence	364.63	HV9278	Parole
364.15553	HV6626-.23	Wife abuse	364.63	HV9278	Probation
364.15554	HV6626.5-.54	Child abuse	364.65	HV8692	Pardon
364.156	HV6631	Libel and slander	364.66	HV8551-8586	Executions and executioners
364.16	HV6635-6700	Offenses against property	364.66	HV8555	Guillotine
364.162	HV6646-6665	Burglary	364.66	HV8569	Crucifixion
364.162	N8795	Art thieves	364.66	HV8696	Electrocution
364.162	HV6653	Thieves	364.66	HV8579-8581	Hanging
364.162	HV6675-6685	Embezzlement	364.66	HV8552-8555	Beheading
364.163	CC140	Forgery of antiquities	364.67	HQ770.4	Corporal punishment
364.163	HV6675-6685	Forgery	364.67	HV8593-8599	Torture
364.163	HV6691-6699	Fraud	364.67	HV8609	Branding (Punishment)
364.164	HV6640	Bombings	364.67	HV8609-8621	Corporal punishment
364.164	HV6638-.5	Arson	364.67	HV8613-8621	Flagellation
364.164	HV6666-6669	Vandalism	364.68	HV9277.5	Community service (Punishment)
364.16409(4-9)	HV6638.5	Arson—[By region or country]			
364.165	HV6688	Extortion	364.68	HV9277	Fines (Penalties)
364.168	HV6772-6773.3	Computer crimes	364.68	HV9276.5	Alternatives to imprisonment
364.168	HV6763-6771	Securities fraud	365	HV8705-8749	Imprisonment
364.168	HV6763-6771	Securities theft	365	HV8708-8719	Prison sentences
364.168	HV6763-6771	Corporations—Corrupt practices	365	HV8301-9960	Prisons
			365.021	HV8482-8488	Prisons—Statistics
364.168	HV6763-6771	Insurance crimes	365.068	HV8756-8763	Prison administration
364.172	HV6708-6722	Gambling	365.09	HV8497-8654	Prisons—History
364.17206	HV6711	Casinos	365.3	HV8647-8649	Galleys
364.1791	HV6549-6555	Poisoning	365.34	HV8748-8749	Workhouses
364.187	HV4749-4755	Horses	365.34	HV8935-8962	Penal colonies
364.2	HV6001-6197	Criminal anthropology	365.34	HV9279	Community-based corrections
364.2	HV6189	War and crime	365.34	HV9051-9230.7	Reformatories
364.22	HV6177	Cities and towns	365.34082	HV8738	Reformatories for women
364.24	HV6047	Criminal behavior—Genetic aspects	365.48	VB890-895	Military prisons
			365.48	UB800-805	Military prisons
364.24	HV6133	Insane, Criminal and dangerous	365.6	HV9051-9230.7	Status offenders
			365.6	HV8884	Prison visits
364.24	HV6163	Crime and age	365.6	HV9025	Prison violence
364.24	HV6121-6125	Heredity	365.64	HV9025	Prison homocide
364.25	HV6166	Reading disability and crime	365.64	HV8935-8962	Prisoners, Transportation of
364.25	HV6166	Education and crime	365.641	HV8657-8658	Escapes
364.256	HV6441-6453	Vendetta	365.643	HV8766-8778	Prison discipline
364.256	HV6174	Begging	365.65	HV8888-8931	Prison industries
364.309(4-9)	HV6774-7220.5	Criminals—[By region or country]	365.65	HV8888-8931	Convict labor
			365.66	HV8833-8844	Prison nurses
364.30973	HV6774-6795	Criminals—United States	365.66	HV8833-8844	Prison physicians
364.3	HV6441-6453	Outlaws	365.7	HV8971-8978	Prison reformers
364.3	HV6001-7220.5	Criminals	365.9(4-9)	HV9441-9649	Prisons—[By region or country]
364.3	HV6049	Recidivism			
364.3	HV6080-6113	Criminal psychology	365.94	HV9636-9775.7	Prisons—Europe
364.36	HV9051-9230.7	Juvenile delinquency	365.941	HV9641-9650	Prisons—Great Britain
364.36	HV9051-9230.7	Juvenile delinquents	365.943	HV9671-9680.5	Prisons—Germany
364.36071	HV9068	Juvenile delinquency—Study and teaching	365.944	HV9661-9670	Prisons—France
			365.945	HV9686-9695	Prisons—Italy
364.3609(4-9)	HV9101-9230.7	Juvenile delinquency—[By region or country]	365.946	HV9741-9745	Prisons—Spain
			365.947	HV9711-9715	Prisons—Russia
364.360973	HV9103-9106	Juvenile delinquency—United States	365.9492	HV9696-9710.5	Prisons—Benelux countries
			365.9495	HV9776-831	Prisons—Greece
364.4	HV7936.C58	Crime stoppers programs	365.951	HV9816-9820	Prisons—China
364.4	HV7431	Crime prevention	365.952	HV9811-9815	Prisons—Japan

Dewey	LC	Subject Heading	Dewey	LC	Subject Heading
365.954	HV9791-9795	Prisons—India	367.9(4-9)	HS2721-3200	Clubs—[By region or country]
365.956	HV9776.5-9785.2	Prisons—Middle East	367.973	HS2721-2725	Clubs—United States
365.9599	HV9806-9810	Prisons—Philippines	368	HG8082	Self-insurance
365.96	HV9836-9868.5	Prisons—Africa	368	HG8054.5	Risk (Insurance)
365.971	HV9501-9510	Prisons—Canada	368	HG8011-9999	Insurance
365.972	HV9511-9515	Prisons—Mexico	368.0065	HG8075-8107	Insurance companies
365.9728	HV9516-9550	Prisons—Central America	368.092	HG9970	Insurance, Automobile
365.9729	HV9551-9575.95	Prisons—West Indies	368.093	HG9972	Insurance, Aviation
365.973	HV9456-9481	Prisons—United States	368.094	HG8059	Insurance, Business
365.98	HV9576-9635	Prisons—South America	368.096	HG9986	Homeowner's insurance
365.994	HV9871-9875	Prisons—Australia	368.11	HG9651-9899	Insurance, Fire
366	HS	Societies	368.110021	HG9663	Insurance, Fire—Statistics
366.0025	HS17	Societies—Directories	368.11009	HG9660	Insurance, Fire—History
366.003	HS12	Societies—Encyclopedias	368.11009(4-9)	HG9751-9899	Insurance, Fire—[By region or country]
366.005	HS1	Societies—Periodicals			
366.006	HS5	Societies—Congresses	368.1100973	HG9751-9780	Insurance, Fire—United States
366.009	HS25-35	Societies—History, organization, etc.			
			368.11014	HG9711-9715	Fire insurance claims adjusters
366.1	HS351-929	Freemasonry			
366.(1-5)	HS155-158	Secret societies—Rituals	368.121	HG9966-9969	Insurance, Agricultural
366.(1-5)	HS101-330.7	Secret societies	368.122	HG9979	Insurance, Disaster
366.(1-5)	GN495.2	Secret societies	368.1222	HG9983	Insurance, Flood
366.(1-5)03	HS121-123	Secret societies—Directories	368.1226	HG9981	Insurance, Earthquake
366.(1-5)05	HS101-106	Secret societies—Periodicals	368.22	HE961-971	Insurance, Marine
366.(1-5)06	HS110	Secret societies—Congresses	368.23	HE961-971	Insurance, Marine
			368.23	HG9903-9905	Insurance, Inland marine
366.(1-5)09	HS125-148	Secret societies—History, organization, etc.	368.3	HG8058	Insurance, Group
			368.32	HG9271	Insurance, Child
366.(1-5)09(4-9)	HS201-330.7	Secret societies—[By region or country]	368.32	HG8751-9271	Insurance, Life
			368.3200151	HG8779-8793	Insurance, Life—Mathematics
366.(1-5)0973	HS203-206	Secret societies—United States			
			368.32009(4-9)	HG8941-9200.5	Insurance, Life—[By region or country]
366.1025	HS381-390	Freemasons—Directories			
366.105	HS351-359	Freemasons—Periodicals	368.3201	HG8783-8785	Mortality—Tables
366.108996073	HS875-895	Afro-American freemasonry	368.362	HG9251-9262	Industrial life insurance
366.109	HS403-420	Freemasons—History	368.366	HG9466-9479	Insurance, Burial
366.109(4-9)	HS501-680.7	Freemasons—[By region or country]	368.37	HG8790-8793	Annuities
			368.382	HG9371-9399	Insurance, Health
366.10973	HS503-539	Freemasons—United States	368.382	HD7105.2-.25	Insurance, Disability
366.12	HS455-459	Freemasonry—Rituals	368.3827	HG9389	Insurance, Hospitalization
366.3	HS951-1179	Independent Order of Odd Fellows	368.384	HG9301-9343	Insurance, Accident
			368.4	HG8205-8220	Insurance, Government
366.3025	HS963-975	Independent Order of Odd Fellows—Directories	368.4	HD7088-7250.7	Social security
			368.4009	HD7121-7250.7	Social security—[By region or country]
366.305	HS951-953	Independent Order of Odd Fellows—Periodicals			
366.309	HS987-991	Independent Order of Odd Fellows—History	368.400973	HD7123-7126	Social security—United States
366.309(4-9)	HS1041-1051	Independent Order of Odd Fellows—[By region or country]	368.424	HG9291-9295	Insurance, Maternity
			368.5	HG9990	Insurance, Liability
			368.5	HG9956-9969	Insurance, Casualty
366.30973	HS1041-1045	Independent Order of Odd Fellows—United States	368.562	HG9995	Insurance, Products liability
			368.564	HG8053.5-8054.45	Insurance, Malpractice
366.46	U260	Unified operations (Military science)	368.5642	HG8054	Insurance, Physicians' liability
366.6027	HS159-160	Insignia	368.5728	HG9970.A4-.A68	Insurance, No-fault automobile
367	HS2501-3371	Clubs			
367	HQ1871-2030.7	Women—Societies and clubs	368.83	HG9997	Insurance, Surety and fidelity
367.025	HS2507-2515	Clubs—Directories	368.84	HG9997	Insurance, Surety and fidelity
367.05	HS2501-2503	Clubs—Periodicals	368.852	HG9992	Mortgage guarantee insurance
367.4	HS3250-3270	Youth—Societies and clubs			

Dewey	LC	Subject Heading	Dewey	LC	Subject Heading
368.854	HG1662	Deposit insurance	370.72	LB1028.24	Action research in education
368.88	HG9999	Insurance, Title	370.72	LB1028-.25	Education—Research
368.9(4-9)	HG8501-8745	Insurance—[By region or country]	370.723	LB2823	Educational surveys
			370.74	L797-898	Education—Museums
368.973	HG8501-8540	Insurance—United States	370.8968073	LC2667-2688	Hispanic Americans—Education
369	HS2301-2460.7	Patriotic societies	370.9	LA	Education—History
369.1	HS2321-2330	Patriotic societies—United States	370.901	LA31-81	Education, Ancient
			370.902	LA91-98	Education, Medieval
369.42	HS3301-3325	Boys—Societies and clubs	370.91724	LC2601-2611	Education—Developing countries
369.42	HV877-878	Boys	370.91732	LC5101-5143	Education, Urban
369.42	HV878	Boys—Societies and clubs	370.91732	LC5101-5143	Urban schools
369.43	HS3312-3316	Boy Scouts	370.91734	LC5146-5148	Education, Rural
369.46	HV879-887	Girls	370.9174927	LA1490-1493	Education—Arab countries—History
369.463	HS3353.G5	Girl Scouts			
369.463	HS3359	Daisy Girl Scouts	370.92	LA2301-2397	Educators
370	LC1035-.8	Basic education	370.92	LB51-875	Educators
370	L	Education	370.92	LA2301-2397	Teachers
370	P96.E29	Education in mass media	370.9(3-9)	LA190-2284	Education—History
370.1	LB125-875	Education—Philosophy	370.9(3-9)	L111-791	Education—[By region or country]
370.1	LB41	Education—Aims and objectives			
			370.932	LA37	Education, Egyptian
370.111	LC213-.3	Compensatory education	370.938	LA77	Education, Minoan
370.111	LC5161-5163	Fundamental education	370.938	LA75	Education, Greek
370.112	LC1001-1024	Education, Humanistic	370.94	L341-551	Education—Europe
370.112	LB41.5	Education—Forecasting	370.941	L341-359	Education—Great Britain
370.11209024	LA106-108	Education, Humanistic	370.9415	L346-348	Education—Ireland
370.113	HD5715-.5	Occcupational training	370.943	L401-410	Education—Germany
370.113	LC1041-1047	Vocational education	370.9436	L361-366	Education—Austria
370.113	LC1041-1047	Technical education	370.9437	L385-387	Education—Czechoslovakia
370.113	LC1037-.8	Career education	370.9439	L381-383	Education—Hungary
370.113082	LC1500-1506	Women—Vocational education	370.944	L391-396	Education—France
			370.945	L421-426	Education—Italy
370.113087	LC4219.7	Physically handicapped children—Vocational education	370.946	L511-516	Education—Spain
			370.9469	L521-526	Education—Portugal
			370.947	L451-466	Education—Russia
370.11308996073	LC2780	Afro-Americans—Vocational education	370.9481	L491-496	Education—Norway
			370.9485	L501-506	Education—Sweden
370.114	LC251-301	Character	370.9489	L471-476	Education—Denmark
370.114	LC251-318	Moral education	370.94912	L481	Education—Iceland
370.116	LB2283-2286	Educational exchanges	370.9492	L441-446	Education—Netherlands
370.1163	LB2283-2285	Teacher exchange programs	370.9493	L431-436	Education—Belgium
370.117	LC201.5-.7	Native language and education	370.9494	L531-536	Education—Switzerlad
			370.9495	L411-416	Education—Greece
370.117	LC1099-.5	Multicultural education	370.9497	L549-550	Education—Yugoslavia
370.1175	LC3701-3743	Education, Bilingual	370.9498	L545-546	Education—Romania
370.14	LB1033.5	Nonverbal communication in education	370.9499	L541-542	Education—Bulgaria
			370.95	L561-642	Education—Asia
370.15	LB1051-1091	Educational psychology	370.951	L571-573	Education—China
370.1522	LB1063-1064	Memory	370.9519	L613-614	Education—Korea
370.153	LB1060.2	Behavior modification	370.952	L611-612	Education—Japan
370.157	LB1062	Creative thinking	370.954	L577-578	Education—India
370.158	LB1139.S88	Student adjustment	370.95491	L578.5-.6	Education—Pakistan
370.207	LA23	Humor in education	370.955	L615-616	Education—Iran
370.21	LB2846	Educational statistics	370.9561	L539-540	Education—Turkey
370.5	L7-101	Education—Periodicals	370.9567	L627-628	Education—Iraq
370.6	L106-107	Education—Congresses	370.95694	L631-632	Education—Israel
370.71	LB2157	Student teachers	370.957	L617-620	Education—Siberia
370.711	LB1762-1765	Examinations	370.959(4-7)	L585-586	Education—Indochina
370.711	LB1731	Teachers—In-service training			
370.711	LB1705-2286	Teachers—Training of			
370.711	LB1805-2151	Teachers colleges			

Dewey	LC	Subject Heading	Dewey	LC	Subject Heading
370.9598	L597-598	Education—Indonesia	371.23	LB3034	School year
370.96	L651-742	Education—Africa	371.232	LC5701-5760	Summer schools
370.97(4-9)	L116-219	Education—[United States, By state]	371.25	LB3061.8	Track system (Education)
			371.251	LB3013.2	Class size
370.971	L221-223	Education—Canada	371.254	LB3061	Ability grouping in education
370.972	L227-229	Education—Mexico	371.255	LB1029.N6	Nongraded schools
370.9728	L231-249	Education—Central America	371.256	LB1029.06	Open plan schools
370.9729	L251-267	Education—West Indies	371.27	LB3060.77	Examinations—Scoring
370.973	L111-219	Education—United States	371.27	LB3060.65	Examinations—Design and construction
370.98	LA540-609	Education—South America—History	371.27	LB3060.57	Examinations—Study guides
370.98	L291-335	Education—South America	371.271	LB3060.32.D65	Domain-referenced tests
370.99(3-6)	L750-791	Education—[New Zealand/ Australia/Oceania]	371.271	LB3060.3	Achievement tests
			371.271	LB3051-3059	Examinations—Questions
371	L	Schools	371.271	LB3050-3060	Examinations
371.00973	LD	Schools—United States	371.271	LB3060.32.N67	Norm-referenced tests
371.01	LC	Public schools	371.271	LB3060.32.035	Objective tests
371.02	LC47-57	Private schools	371.271	LB3051-3060.87	Educational tests and measurements
371.04	LB1029.F7	Free schools			
371.042	LC40	Home schooling	371.271	LB3060.32.M85	Multiple-choice examinations
371.071	BV1580-1583	Week-day church schools	371.272	LB3051-3063	Grading and marking (Students)
371.071	LC427-629	Church schools			
371.1	LB1775-1785	Teaching	371.2913	LC142-145	Dropouts
371.1	LB2832-2844.47	Teachers	371.2914	LB3064	Students, Transfer of
371.1	LB1025-1050.7	Teaching	371.294	LC142-148.5	School attendance
371.100882971	LC905.T42	Muslim teachers	371.294	LB3081-3087	School attendance
371.1023	LB1033	Teacher-student relationships	371.3	LB1027.3	Education—Experimental methods
371.1024	LB3013	Classroom management	371.3	LB1027	Educational innovations
371.103	LC225.5	Parent-teacher conferences	371.30281	LB1048	Homework
371.104	LC72-.5	Teaching, Freedom of	371.32	LB3045-3048	Textbooks
371.104	LB2836	Teachers—Tenure	371.32	LB3045.6	Textbook bias
371.104	LB2843.L4	Teachers—Leaves of absence	371.32	LT	Textbooks
			371.33	LB1028.4	Media programs (Education)
371.104	LC72-.5	Academic freedom	371.33	LB1043.6	Displays in education
371.11	LB1755-1779	Teachers	371.3331	LB1044.5-.6	Radio in education
371.12	LB1771-1773	Teachers—Certification	371.334	LB1028.5-.7	Computer-assisted instruction
371.14	LB2844.1	Teachers, Part-time			
371.1412	LB2844.1.W6	Teachers—Workload	371.334	LB1028.5	Programmed instruction
371.144	LB2844.1.P7	Teachers, Probationary	371.334	LB1028.43	Education—Data processing
371.148	LB1032	Team learning approach in education	371.334	LB1028.75	Interactive video
			371.334	LB1029.A85	Teaching machines
371.19206	LC230-235	Parents' and teachers' associations	371.335	LB1043.5	Overhead projection
			371.335	LB1043-1044.9	Audio-visual education
371.2	LB3011-3095	School management and organization	371.335	LB1043.5-1044	Visual aids
			371.3352	LB1043.67	Pictures in education
371.2	LB2806.3	School management teams	371.3352	LB1043.8	Filmstrips in education
371.201	LB2831.5-2844.4	School personnel management	371.33523	LB1044.75	Video tapes in education
			371.33523	LB1044.75	Video tapes
371.201	LB2831.5-.585	School employees	371.3358	LB1044.7	Television in education
371.2011	LB2831.7-.776	School superintendents	371.337	LB1029.T6	Educational toys
371.2011	LB2831.8-.876	School administrators	371.337	LB1029.G3	Educational games
371.2012	LB2831.9-.976	School principals	371.35	LC5800-5808	Distance education
371.203	LB2806.4	School supervision	371.36	LB1029.U6	Unit method of teaching
371.206	LC241-245	Educational fund raising	371.37	LB1039	Recitation (Education)
371.206	LB2824-2830	Education—Finance	371.382	LB1029.L3	Dalton laboratory plan
371.207	LC71.2	Educational planning	371.384	LB1047	School field trips
371.219	LC130-139	School enrollment	371.384	LB1047	Outdoor education
371.223	LB2848-2849	Scholarships	371.39	LB1029.M7	Monitorial system of education
371.22308996073	LC2707	Afro-Americans—Scholar-ships, fellowships, etc.			

Dewey	LC	Subject Heading	Dewey	LC	Subject Heading
371.392	LB1029.M75	Montessori method of education	371.897	LB3621	Student publications
371.393	LB2806.2	Performance contracts in education	371.897	TR818	School photography
			371.9	LC4704-4706	Learning disabilities
371.394	LC41	Tutors and tutoring	371.9	LC4818-.53	Learning disabled
371.3943	LB1049	Independent study	371.9	LC3950-3990.4	Special education
371.396	LC6501-6560	Forums (Discussion and debate)	371.91	LC4001-4100	Handicapped children—Education
371.397	LB1029.S5	Simulated environment (Teaching method)	371.91	LC4201-4580	Physically handicapped children—Education
371.397	LB1029.S53	Education—Simulation methods	371.911	HV1618-1782	Blind—Education
			371.912	HV2417-2500	Deaf—Education
371.4	LB2341	Deans (Education)	371.9144	LB1050.5	Dyslexia
371.4	LB1027.5-.8	Educational counseling	371.9144	LC4708-4710	Dyslexic children
371.4047	LB1027.5	Peer counseling of students	371.92	LC4601-4700	Mentally handicapped children—Education
371.46	LB3013.4	School social work	371.926	LC4661-4700.4	Slow learning children
371.46	LB3013.5	Visiting teachers	371.94	LC4165-4184	Mentally ill children—Education
371.5	LB3025	Discipline of children			
371.5	LB3011-3095	School discipline	371.9573	LC4604	Mentally handicapped children—Education (Secondary)
371.543	LB3089-.4	Student suspension			
371.58	LB3249	School vandalism	372	LB1555-1601	Education, Elementary
371.59	LB3092-3095	Student government	372	LB1501-1547	Education, Primary
371.6	LB3205-3295	School buildings	372.11	LB1775.6	Early childhood educators
371.6	LB3205-3325	School facilities	372.11	LB1776	Elementary school teachers
371.61	LB3251	School grounds	372.11	LB1537	Education, Primary—Activity programs
371.61	LB3253	Campus parking	372.12	LB2822.5	Elementary school administration
371.63	LB3261-3281	Schools—Furniture, equipment, etc.	372.12012	LB2831.9-.976	Elementary school principals
371.71	LB3401-3495	School hygiene	372.12913	LC145.5-.8	Elementary school dropouts
371.71	LB3401-3495	School health services	372.182996073	LC2771	Afro-Americans—Education (Elementary)
371.713	LB1027.55	School psychology			
371.716	LB3473-3479	School breakfast programs	372.21	LB1775.5	Preschool teachers
371.716	LB3473-3479	School children—Food	372.21	LB1139.2-.4	Early childhood education
371.716	LB3473-3479	School milk programs	372.21	LB1140-.5	Education, Preschool
371.78	LB3013.3	School violence	372.218	LB1141-1499	Kindergarten
371.8	LB3604	Students—Language	372.4	LB1140.5.R4	Reading (Preschool)
371.8	LB3602-3618	Students	372.4	LB1181.2	Reading (Kindergarten)
371.8	LB3604-3615	Hazing	372.4	LB1525-.8	Reading (Primary)
371.8	LB3605	Student activities	372.4	LB1525	Reading (Elementary)
371.81	LA186	Student movements	372.4	LB1573	Reading (Elementary)
371.822	LC1401-2571	Women—Education	372.4	LB1050	Reading
371.8246	LC5451-5493	Aged—Education	372.40284	LB1050.37	Reading machines
371.82621	JC393	Education of princes	372.414	LB1050.43	Reading readiness
371.82623	LC5001-5060	Working class—Education	372.43	LB1050.5	Reading—Remedial teaching
371.82655	LB3613.M3	Married students	372.452	LB1573.5	Oral reading
371.82694	LC4051-4100	Socially handicapped children—Education	372.462	LB1573.37	Reading (Elementary)—Whole-word method
371.826942	LC5144-.3	Homeless students	372.465	LB1573.3	Reading—Phonetic method
371.82697	UB356-359	Veterans—Education	372.47	LB1050.45	Reading comprehension
371.8279	LC3991-4000	Gifted children	372.48	LB1050.46	Reading—Ability testing
371.829	LC3701-3740	Minorities—Education	372.5	LB1595-1599	Manual training
371.829	LC3800-3806	Ethnic schools	372.6	LB1576	Language arts (Elementary)
371.82991497	LC3503-3520	Gypsies—Education	372.632	LB1574	Spelling ability
371.82995	LC3001-3501	Asians—Education	372.634	LB1590	Penmanship
371.82996073	LC2699-2913	Blacks—Education	372.634	LB1536	Penmanship
371.82996073	LC2701-2853	Afro-Americans—Education	372.677	LB1042	Storytelling
371.85	LJ	Greek letter societies	373.0025	L900-991	Education—Directories
371.871	LB3226-3228	Student housing	373.11	LB1777-.4	High school teachers
371.871	LB3226-3229	Dormitories	373.12012	LB2831.9-.976	High school principals
371.872	LB2864	School children—Transportation			

Dewey	LC	Subject Heading	Dewey	LC	Subject Heading
373.1219	LC146	High school enrollment	378.161	LB2351-2359	Universities and colleges—Admission
373.12913	LC146.5-.8	High school dropouts	378.1616	LB2351.5-.52	College applications
373.182996073	LC2779	Afro-Americans—Education (Secondary)	378.1617	LB2351-2360	Universities and colleges—Entrance requirements
373.222	LC58-.7	Preparatory schools	378.1618	LB2359.5	College credits
373.236	LB1623	Junior high schools	378.1662	LB2353	Universities and colleges—Examinations
373.236	LB1623	Middle schools	378.1662	LB2353-.28	Universities and colleges—Examinations
373.238	LB1603-1694	High schools			
373.238	LB1627.7	High school equivalency certificates	378.1662	LB2367	Universities and colleges—Examinations
373.241	LB2818	Magnet schools	378.170281	LB2395	Note-taking
373.242	LC1001-1021	Classical education	378.175	LC6201-6401	University extension
373.246	TT161-170.7	Manual training	378.177	LB2393.5	Seminars
373.73	LD7501	High schools—United States	378.1796	LB2393	Lecture method in teaching
373.0025	L900-991	Education—Directories	378.194	LB2343	Faculty advisors
374	LC5201-6660	Adult education	378.19822	LC1551-1651	Women—Education (Higher)
374	LC5201-6660	Continuing education			
374.012	LB1029.R4	Remedial teaching	378.1982996073	LC2781	Afro-Americans—Education (Higher)
374.1822	LC1660-1666	Adult education of women			
374.22	HV547	Self-help groups	378.199	LB2361-2365	Universities and colleges—Curricula
374.8	LC5501-5560	Evening and continuation schools	378.2	LB2381-2391	Degrees, Academic
375	LB1570-1571	Education—Curricula	378.2	LB2383	Bachelor of arts degree
378	LB2300-2411	Universities and colleges	378.2	LB2385	Master of arts degree
378.0025	L900-991	Education—Directories	378.2	LB2386	Doctor of philosophy degree
378.009	LA173-186	Education, Higher	378.241	LB2366-2367	Examinations
378.00902	LA177	Education, Medieval	378.242	LB2369	Dissertations, Academic
378.013	LC1051-1071	Professional education	378.28	LB2389	Academic costume
378.013076	LC1070-1071	Examinations	378.3	LB2337.2-2340.8	Student aid
378.01308996073	LC2785	Afro-Americans—Professional education	378.34	LB2338-2339	Scholarships
			378.362	LB2340-.4	Student loan funds
378.016	LB2375-2378	Student exchange programs	378.38	LB2342-.2	College costs
378.016	LB2375-2378	Educational exchanges	378.4	LF	Universities and colleges—Europe
378.052	LB2328.4	Urban universities and colleges			
			378.5	LG21-395	Universities and colleges—Asia
378.052	LB2329	Municipal universities and colleges			
			378.6	LG401-681	Universities and colleges—Africa
378.053	LB2329.5	State universities and colleges			
			378.7	LE	Universities and colleges—America
378.071	LC427-629	Church colleges			
378.07122	LC487	Catholic universities and colleges	378.71	LE3-5	Universities and colleges—Canada
			378.73	LD13-7251	Universities and colleges—United States
378.1	LB2801-2997	School management and organization			
378.104	LB2331.5	University cooperation	379	LC71-188	Education and state
378.106	LB2335.95-2337	Educational fund raising	379.111	LB1027.9	School choice
378.106	LB2336-2337	Endowments	379.121	LB2825-2826.6	Federal aid to education
378.106	LB2342	Universities and colleges—Finance	379.123	LB2813	County school systems
			379.13	LB2824-2830	School bonds
378.111	LB2341	College administrators	379.130973	HG4951-4953	School bonds
378.12	LB2331.7-.74	Universities and colleges—Faculty	379.152	LB2809	State departments of education
378.12	LB1778	College teachers			
378.1543	LB2328	Junior colleges	379.1531	LB2831	School boards
378.1543	LB2328	Community colleges	379.1535	LB2832.2	Public school closings
378.15430973	LD6501	Junior colleges—United States	379.1535	LB2861	Schools—Centralization
			379.1535	LB2862	Schools—Decentralization
378.155	LB2372.E3	Education—Graduate work	379.1535	LB2823.2	School closings
378.155	LB2371	Universities and colleges—Graduate work	379.1535	LB2817-.5	School districts
378.161	LB2341	Student registration	379.156	LB3045.66	Sexism in textbooks

Dewey	LC	Subject Heading	Dewey	LC	Subject Heading
379.158	LB2806.22	Educational accountability	380.10951	HF3831-3840	China—Commerce
379.158	LB2822.75	Educational evaluation	380.10952	HF3821-3830	Japan—Commerce
379.158	LB2810-.5	Accreditation (Education)	380.10954	HF3781-3790	India—Commerce
379.23	LC129-139	Education, Compulsory	380.10955	HF3770.2	Iran—Commerce
379.24	LC149-160	Literacy	380.10956	HF3756-3770.2	Middle East—Commerce
379.26	LC213-.3	Educational equalization	380.109567	HF3770	Iraq—Commerce
379.26	LC212.8-.83	Sex discrimination in education	380.1095694	HF3760	Israel—Commerce
379.26	LC212.5-.73	Segregation in education	380.10958	HF3770.22-.27	Asia, Central—Commerce
379.26	LC212-.863	Discrimination in education	380.109599	HF3811-3820	Philippines—Commerce
379.263	LC214.5-.53	Busing for school integration	380.1096	HF3871-3937	Africa—Commerce
379.263	LC214-.3	School integration	380.10971	HF3221-3230	Canada—Commerce
379.263	LC212.6-.63	De facto school segregation	380.10972	HF3231-3240	Mexico—Commerce
379.28	LC107-120	Religion in the public schools	380.109728	HF3241-3310	Central America—Commerce
379.32	LB2828	State aid to private schools	380.109729	HF3311-3369	West Indies—Commerce
379.941	LA630-669.5	Education—Great Britain—History	380.10973	HF3021-3031	United States—Commerce—History
379.947	LA830-838	Education—Russia—History	380.10973	HF3000-3163	United States—Commerce
380.1	HF5484-5495	Warehouses	380.10973	HF3001-3006	United States—Commerce—Statistics
380.1	HF	Commerce	380.1098	HF3371-3480	South America—Commmerce
380.1	HF5446-5456	Canvassing			
380.1	HF1040-1044	Commercial products	380.10994	HF3941-3950	Australia—Commerce
380.1	HF5415.6-.9	Physical distribution of goods	380.13	HF1410-1411	Commercial policy
380.1	HF5416	Product coding	380.141	HD9000-9019	Farm produce—Marketing
380.1	HF5438-5439	Selling	380.141	S571.5	Roadside marketing
380.1	HF5410-5417.5	Marketing	380.141	S571-.5	Farm produce—Marketing
380.1	HF5415.3	Market surveys	380.14133	HF2651.G8	Grain trade
380.1021	HF1016-1017	Commercial statistics	380.141351	HD9070-9089	Cotton trade
380.1025	HF54	Commerce—Directories	380.141351	HD9870-9889	Cotton trade
380.103	HF1001-1002.5	Commerce—Encyclopedias	380.141383	HD9210-9211	Spice trade
380.105	HF1-53	Commerce—Periodicals	380.1415	HD9220-9235	Vegetable trade
380.106	HF294-343	Boards of trade	380.14159	SB442.8-445	Florists
380.106	HF294-343	Commercial associations	380.14162	HD9433	Cattle trade
380.1071	HF1101-1186	Business education	380.1417	HD9275-9283.7	Dairy products—Marketing
380.10710(4-9)	HF1131-1186	Business education—[By region or country]	380.14224	HD9540-9559	Coal trade
380.107104	HF1140-1165	Business education—Europe	380.1424	HD9506-9624	Metal trade
			380.1431	HD9030-9049	Grain trade
380.107105	HF1171	Business education—Asia	380.144	HT975-1445	Slave-trade
380.107106	HF1176	Business education—Africa	380.145004	HF5468.2	Computer stores
380.1071073	HF1131-1134	Business education—United States	380.14502504	HF5415.126	Database marketing
			380.145388342	HF5439.A8	Selling—Automobiles
380.1071108	HF1135	Business education—Latin America	380.145388342	HD9710-.37	Automobiles—Marketing
			380.145391	HD9940-9949.5	Fashion merchandising
380.1071094	HF1181-1182	Business education—Australia	380.1456151	HF5439.D75	Selling—Drugs
			380.145769	NE62	Prints—Marketing
380.1072	HF5415.2-5415.34	Marketing research	380.145808	PN161	Authorship—Marketing
			380.14580802	PN161	Queries (Authorship)
380.1089926	HF370	Phoenicians	381.092	HF5439.25-.8	Sales personnel
380.109	HF351-499	Boards of trade—History	381.092	HF5439.25-.8	Sales executives
380.1094	HF3491-3750.7	Europe—Commerce	381.092	HF5441-5444	Traveling sales personnel
380.10941	HF3501-3530.5	Great Britain—Commerce	381.092	HF5457-5459	Peddlers and peddling
380.10943	HF3561-3570.5	Germany—Commerce	381.1	HF5495	Stores or stock-room keeping
380.10944	HF3551-3560	France—Commerce	381.1	HF5415.1265	Telemarketing
380.10945	HF3581-3590	Italy—Commerce	381.1	HF5415.126	Multilevel marketing
380.10946	HF3681-3690	Spain—Commerce	381.1	HF5415.126	Direct marketing
380.10947	HF3621-3630	Russia—Commerce	381.1	HF5428-5429.6	Retail trade
380.109492	HF3591-3620.5	Benelux countries—Commerce	381.1	HF5429.7-5430.6	Shopping centers
			381.1	HF5429.7-5430.6	Shopping malls
380.109494	HF3701-3710	Switzerland—Commerce	381.1092	HD8039.M39	Clerks (Retail trade)
380.109495	HF3750.5	Greece—Commerce	381.12	HF5468	Chain stores
			381.141	HF5460-5469.5	Department stores

Dewey	LC	Subject Heading	Dewey	LC	Subject Heading
381.142	HF5465.5-5467	Mail-order business	383.49	HE6041-6055	Postal service—History
381.147	HF5469.25-.55	Convenience stores	383.49(4-9)	HE6300-7496	Postal service—[By region or country]
381.149	HF5429.2-.215	Discount houses (Retain trade)	383.492	HE6061	Postal service—Biography
381.15	HF5429.2-.215	Outlet stores	383.4973	HE6300-6500	Postal service—United States
381.17	HF5476-5477	Auctions	384	HE9723-9737	Signals and signaling
381.18	HF5469.7-5481	Markets	384.1	HE7601-8635	Telegraph
381.18	HF5469.7-5481	Fairs	384.1	HE7709-7741	Cables, Submarine
381.18	HF5481	Fairs	384.1	TK5601-5681	Cables, Submarine
381.192	HF5482.15	Flea markets	384.1025	HE7621	Telegraph—Directories
381.195	HF5482.3	Garage sales	384.106	HE7603	Telegraph—Societies, etc.
381.2	HF5419-5422	Wholesale trade	384.109(4-9)	HE7761-8630.7	Telegraph—[By region or country]
381.2092	HF5422	Commission merchants	384.10973	HE7761-7798	Telegraph—United States
381.2092	HF5419-5422	Brokers	384.13	HE7681-7691	Telegraph—Rates
381.3	HF5415	Rationing	384.14	HE7669-7679	Cipher and telegraph codes
381.3	HF5415.5	Consumer affairs departments	384.15	TK5301-5481	Telegraph lines
381.45002	Z278-550	Booksellers and bookselling	384.51	HE9719-9721	Artificial satellites in telecommunication
381.457(3-6)	N8610-8660	Art dealers	384.52	HE8660-8688	Telegraph, Wireless
382	HF4050	East-West trade	384.53	HE9713-9715	Celluar radio
382	HF1371-1385	International trade	384.54	HE8689.7.F34	Fairness doctrine (Broadcasting)
382	HF1417.5	Foreign trade promotion	384.54	HE8697.P57	Pirate radio broadcasting
382.17	HF1014	Balance of trade	384.54	PN1990-1992.92	Broadcasting
382.5	HF1419-1420	Imports	384.54	HE8690-8699	Radio broadcasting
382.6	HF1414.4-1417.3	Exports	384.54089	PN1991.8.E84	Ethnic radio broadcasting
382.6	HF1425	Dumping (International trade)	384.55	HE8700.7-.72	Low power television
382.63	HF2701	Export subsidies	384.55	HE8700-.95	Television broadcasting
382.64	HF1414.5-.55	Export controls	384.5532	HE8700.65-.66	Television programs—Rating
382.7	HF1715-1718	Drawbacks			
382.7	HF1701-2701	Tariff	384.5532	PN1992-.92	Television programs
382.7	HF1721-1733	Tariff preferences	384.555	HE8700.7-.72	Satellite master antenna television
382.709(4-9)	HF1745-2580.9	Tariff—[By region or country]			
382.70973	HF1750-1757	Tariff—United States	384.556	TK6680	Closed-circuit television
382.9	HF1721-1733	Reciprocity	384.558	TR882.3	Camcorders
382.9	HF1430	Nontariff trade barriers	384.558	TK6685	Videodisc players
383.1	HE6000-7500	Postal service	384.6	HE8701-9685	Telephone companies
383.1	HE6182-6228	Postmarks	384.6	HE8701-9685	Telephone
383.1	HE5999	Mail receiving and forwarding services	384.609(4-9)	HE8801-9685	Telephone companies—[By region or country]
383.1	HE6149	Postal service—Unclaimed mail	384.60973	HE8801-8846	Telephone companies—United States
383.1025	HE6031	Postal service—Directories			
383.1071	HE6036	Postal service—Study and teaching	385	HE1001-5600	Railroads
			385.021	HE2271-2273	Railroads—Statistics
383.1202	HE6148	Franking privilege	385.025	HE1009	Railroads—Directories
383.12020973	HE6448	Franking privilege—United States	385.05	HE1001	Railroads—Periodicals
			385.06	HE1003	Railroads—Societies, etc.
383.122	HE6184.P65	Postcards	385.068	HE1621-1813	Railroads—Management
383.125	HE6171-6173	Parcel post	385.09	HE1021	Railroads—History
383.1250973	HE6471-6473	Parcel post—United States	385.092	HD8039.R1-.R45	Railroads—Employees
383.143	HE6175-.5	Railway mail service	385.092	HE1811	Railroad conductors
383.1430973	HE6475-.3	Railway mail service—United States	385.09(4-9)	HE2701-3560	Railroads—[By region or country]
383.144	HE6184.A35	Aerogrammes			
383.144	HE6238	Air mail service	385.0941	HE3011-3040	Railroads—Great Britain
383.1450973	HE6455-6456	Rural free delivery—United States	385.09415	HE3041-3050	Railroads—Ireland
			385.0943	HE3071-3080.5	Railroads—Germany
383.23	HE6125-6148	Postal rates	385.09436	HE3051-3059.2	Railroads—Austria
383.23	HE6182-6228	Postage stamps	385.09437	HE3059.3	Railroads—Czechoslovakia
383.41	HE6246-6278	Postal service—International cooperation	385.09438	HE3060.5	Railroads—Poland

Dewey	LC	Subject Heading	Dewey	LC	Subject Heading
385.09439	HE3059.5	Railroads—Hungary	385.096751	HE3434	Railroads—Zaire
385.0944	HE3061-3070	Railroads—France	385.0967571	HE3421	Railroads—Rwanda
385.0945	HE3091-3100	Railroads—Italy	385.0967572	HE3422	Railroads—Burundi
385.0946	HE3191-3200	Railroads—Spain	385.096761	HE3420	Railroads—Uganda
385.09469	HE3201-3210	Railroads—Portugal	385.096762	HE3419	Railroads—Kenya
385.0947	HE3131-3140.2	Railroads—Russia	385.096773	HE3417	Railroads—Somalia
385.09481	HE3171-3180	Railroads—Norway	385.09678	HE3423	Railroads—Tanzania
385.09485	HE3181-3190	Railroads—Sweden	385.09679	HE3424	Railroads—Mozambique
385.09489	HE3151-3160	Railroads—Denmark	385.0968	HE3426	Railroads—South Africa
385.094912	HE3161-3170	Railroads—Iceland	385.096881	HE3432.3	Railroads—Namibia
385.09492	HE3121-3130	Railroads—Netherlands	385.096883	HE3431	Railroads—Botswana
385.09493	HE3111-3120	Railroads—Belgium	385.096885	HE3429	Railroads—Lesotho
385.09494	HE3211-3220	Railroads—Switzerland	385.096887	HE3430	Railroads—Swaziland
385.09497	HE3241-3245	Railroads—Yugoslavia	385.096894	HE3428	Railroads—Zambia
385.09498	HE3251-3260	Railroads—Romania	385.096897	HE3432	Railroads—Malawi
385.09499	HE3231-3240	Railroads—Bulgaria	385.09691	HE3425	Railroads—Madagascar
385.0951	HE3281-3290	Railroads—China	385.0971	HE2801-2810	Railroads—Canada
385.09519	HE3360.5	Railroads—Korea	385.0972	HE2811-2820	Railroads—Mexico
385.0952	HE3351-3360	Railroads—Japan	385.097281	HE2836-2840	Railroads—Guatemala
385.09538	HE3380.3	Railroads—Saudi Arabia	385.097282	HE2825.5	Railroads—Belize
385.0954	HE3291-3300	Railroads—India	385.097283	HE2841-2845	Railroads—Honduras
385.095491	HE3300.5	Railroads—Pakistan	385.097284	HE2851-2855	Railroads—El Salvador
385.095492	HE3300.6	Railroads—Bangladesh	385.097285	HE2846-2850	Railroads—Nicaragua
385.095493	HE3300.3	Railroads—Sri Lanka	385.097286	HE2831-2835	Railroads—Costa Rica
385.09594	HE3320.4	Railroads—Laos	385.09729	HE2856-2889	Railroads—West Indies
385.09595	HE3321-3330	Railroads—Malaysia	385.0973	HE2704-2791	Railroads—United States
385.09597	HE3320.3	Railroads—Vietnam	385.0979	HE2763	Pacific railroads
385.09598	HE3331-3340	Railroads—Indonesia	385.0979	HE1062	Pacific railroads
385.09599	HE3341-3350	Railroads—Philippines	385.0979	HE2763	Pacific railroads—Early projects
385.09611	HE3413	Railroads—Tunisia			
385.09612	HE3414	Railroads—Libya	385.098	HE2891-3000	Railroads—South America
385.0962	HE3401-3410	Railroads—Egypt	385.0981	HE2921-2930	Railroads—Brazil
385.09624	HE3415	Railroads—Sudan	385.0982	HE2901-2910	Railroads—Argentina
385.0963	HE3416	Railroads—Ethiopia	385.0983	HE2931-2940	Railroads—Chile
385.0964	HE3411	Railroads—Morocco	385.0984	HE2911-2920	Railroads—Bolivia
385.09648	HE3458.2	Railroads—Western Sahara	385.0985	HE2971-2980	Railroads—Peru
385.0965	HE3412	Railroads—Algeria	385.09861	HE2941-2950	Railroads—Colombia
385.09661	HE3452	Railroads—Mauritania	385.09866	HE2951-2960	Railroads—Ecuador
385.096623	HE3449	Railroads—Mali	385.0987	HE2991-3000	Railroads—Venezuela
385.096625	HE3450	Railroads—Burkina Faso	385.09881	HE2962	Railroads—Guyana
385.096626	HE3446	Railroads—Niger	385.09882	HE2964	Railroads—French Guiana
385.09663	HE3451	Railroads—Senegal	385.09883	HE2963	Railroads—Surinam
385.09664	HE3455	Railroads—Sierra Leone	385.09892	HE2966-2970	Railroads—Paraguay
385.096651	HE3456	Railroads—Gambia	385.09895	HE2981-2990	Railroads—Uruguay
385.096652	HE3448	Railroads—Guinea	385.0993	HE3550.5	Railroads—New Zealand
385.096657	HE3458	Railroads—Guinea-Bissau	385.0994	HE3461-3550	Railroads—Australia
385.096662	HE3457	Railroads—Liberia	385.1	HE2231-2261	Railroads—Finance
385.096668	HE3447	Railroads—Cote d'Ivoire	385.2	HE1821-2591	Railroads—Traffic
385.09667	HE3454	Railroads—Ghana	385.22	HE1826	Demurrage (Car service)
385.096681	HE3445	Railroads—Togo	385.22	HE2556	Railroads—Baggage handling
385.096683	HE3444	Railroads—Benin	385.22	HE2561-2591	Railroads—Passenger traffic
385.09669	HE3453	Railroads—Nigeria	385.22	HE1951-2100	Railroads—Fares
385.096711	HE3442	Railroads—Cameroon	385.22	TF653	Railroads—Passenger traffic
385.096715	HE3436	Railroads—Sao Tome and Principe	385.24	HE2321.L7	Cattle—Transportation
385.096718	HE3435	Railroads—Equatoria Guinea	385.24	HE2321.L7	Railroads—Livestock transportaton
385.096721	HE3438	Railroads—Gabon	385.24	HE2301-2547	Freight and freightage
385.096724	HE3439	Railroads—Congo (Brazzaville)	385.24	HE2321.E8	Explosives—Transportation
			385.24	HE2301-2547	Railroads—Freight
385.09673	HE3433	Railroads—Angola	385.24	TF970	Electric railroads—Freight
385.096743	HE3441	Railroads—Chad	385.312	HE1617-1618	Railroads—Crossings

Dewey	LC	Subject Heading	Dewey	LC	Subject Heading
385.312	TF240-268	Railroads—Track	387.5092	VK205	Ship captains
385.314	HE1613-1614	Railroad stations	387.5092	VK221	Merchant marine—Officers
385.37	HE1830	Railroads—Cars	387.5092	VK139-140	Merchant mariners— Biography
385.4183	UG1240	Stealth aircraft			
385.5(4-6)	TF670-1124	Railroads, Local and light	387.50973	HE745-767	Merchant marine—United States
385.52	TF675	Railroads, Narrow-gage			
385.54	TF677	Railroads, Industrial	387.50973	VK23-25	Merchant marine—United States
385.6	HE4051-4071	Mountain railroads			
386	HE380.8-560	Waterways	387.52	VK571	Great circle sailing
386.0971	HE399-401.25	Waterways—Canada	387.52	VK570	Optimum ship routing
386.0973	HE392.8-398	Waterways—United States	387.54	HE594	Shipping—Rates
386.098	HE401.5-402	Waterways—Latin America	387.54	HE603-605	Shipping—Finance
386.229	GN440.2	Dugout canoes	387.54	VK381-397	Merchant marine—Signaling
386.229	GN440.2	Canoes and canoeing	387.54044	VK149	Seafaring life
386.229	GN440.2	Outrigger canoes	387.54044	VK361-365	Mooring of ships
386.4	HE526	Canals	387.54044	VK361	Coaling
386.42	HE528-545	Canals, Interoceanic	387.544	HE593-597	Freight and freightage
386.6	HE5751-5870	Ferries	387.544	VK237	Load-line
387.1	HE550-560	Harbors	387.544	VK235	Cargo handling
387.1	VK321-369.8	Harbors	387.544	VK235	Stowage
387.1	SH337.5	Fishing ports	387.5442	HE566.R64	Roll-on/roll-off ships
387.1	VK369-.8	Harbors of refuge	387.5448	HE595.L7	Cattle—Transportation
387.1	TC203-327	Harbors	387.55	HE971	Salvage
387.12	VK321	Roadsteads	387.55	VK1491	Salvage
387.13	HF1418-.5	Free ports and zones	387.7	HE9785	Local service airlines
387.15	HE550-560	Docks	387.7	HE9795-9796	Airplanes, Company
387.15	HE951-953	Docks	387.7	HE9761-9900	Aeronautics, Commercial
387.15	VK361-365	Docks	387.705	HE9761-.9	Aeronautics, Commercial— Periodicals
387.15	VK369-.8	Marinas			
387.2	GN440.1	Ships	387.709	HE9774-9775	Aeronautics, Commercial— History
387.2	HE565	Tonnage			
387.20216	HE565-566	Ship registers	387.709(4-9)	HE9801-9900	Aeronautics, Commercial— [By region or country]
387.2044	HE566.P3	Paddle steamers			
387.2044	HE599-601	Steamboats—Passenger accommodation	387.7094	HE9842-9867.7	Aeronautics, Commercial— Europe
387.2044	HE945	Steamboat lines	387.70941	HE9843-9845.5	Aeronautics, Commercial— Great Britain
387.2045	GC67	Oceanographic submersibles			
387.245	HE566.T3	Tankers	387.70943	HE9849-.5	Aeronautics, Commercial— Germany
387.245	VK235-237	Ships—Cargo			
387.29	VK1473	Life-boats	387.70944	HE9848	Aeronautics, Commercial— France
387.5	HE730-943	Merchant marine			
387.5	HE561-971	Shipping	387.70945	HE9851	Aeronautics, Commercial— Italy
387.5	VK	Merchant marine			
387.5023	VK160	Merchant marine— Vocational guidance	387.70946	HE9861	Aeronautics, Commercial— Spain
387.505	HE561	Shipping—Periodicals	387.70947	HE9855	Aeronautics, Commercial— Russia
387.505	VK1-4	Merchant marine— Periodicals	387.709492	HE9852-9854.5	Aeronautics, Commercial— Benelux countries
387.506	HE564	Shipping—Societies, etc.			
387.506	HE562	Shipping—Congresses	387.709494	HE9863	Aeronautics, Commercial— Switzerland
387.506	VK5	Merchant marine— Congresses	387.709495	HE9867.5	Aeronautics, Commercial— Greece
387.50681	HE740-743	Shipping bounties and subsidies	387.7095	HE9869.22- 9869.27	Aeronautics, Commercial— Asia
387.509	VK15-20	Merchant marine—History			
387.509(4-9)	HE745-943	Merchant marine—[By region or country]	387.70951	HE9878	Aeronautics, Commercial— China
387.509(4-9)	VK21-124	Merchant marine—[By region or country]	387.70952	HE9877	Aeronautics, Commercial— Japan
387.5092	HD8039.S4	Sailors	387.70954	HE9871	Aeronautics, Commercial— India
387.5092	HD8039.L8	Stevedores			

Dewey	LC	Subject Heading
387.70955	HE9869.2	Aeronautics, Commercial—Iran
387.70956	HE9868.2-.95	Aeronautics, Commercial—Middle East
387.709567	HE9869	Aeronautics, Commercial—Iraq
387.7095694	HE9868.45	Aeronautics, Commercial—Israel
387.709599	HE9876	Aeronautics, Commercial—Philippines
387.7096	HE9882-9888.4	Aeronautics, Commercial—Africa
387.70971	HE9815	Aeronautics, Commercial—Canada
387.70972	HE9816	Aeronautics, Commercial—Mexico
387.709728	HE9817-9823	Aeronautics, Commercial—Central America
387.709729	HE9824-9829.9	Aeronautics, Commercial—West Indies
387.70973	HE9803-9814	Aeronautics, Commercial—United States
387.7098	HE9830-9841	Aeronautics, Commercial—South America
387.70994	HE9889	Aeronautics, Commercial—Australia
387.712	HE9783-.75	Airlines—Rates
387.736	HE9797-.5	Airports
387.7364	HE9797.4.S56	Airport slot allocation
387.742	HE9787-.5	Aeronautics, Commercial—Passenger traffic
387.744	TL720.7	Aeronautics, Commercial—Freight
388	HE	Transportation
388.01	HE147.5-149	Transportation—Theory
388.021	HE191.4-.5	Transportation—Statistics
388.042	HE1831-2220	Transportation—Rates
388.044	HE5880-5990	Express service
388.044	HE199-.5	Freight and freightage
388.04409(4-9)	HE5893-5990	Express service—[By region or country]
388.0440973	HE5893-5904.5	Express service—United States
388.049	HE195.4-.5	Transportation—Rates
388.05	HE1-8	Transportation—Periodicals
388.06	HE11	Transportation—Congresses
388.071	HE191.9-192	Transportation—Study and teaching
388.09	HE159-181	Transportation—History
388.092	HE151.4-.5	Transportation—Biography
388.1	HE331-380	Roads
388.1	HE336.R68	Route choice
388.10937	DG28-29	Roads, Roman
388.12	HE336.B8	Bus lanes
388.12	HE336.B8	High occupancy vehicle lanes
388.12091734	HE336.R85	Rural roads
388.122	HE336.T64	Toll roads
388.132	HE374-377	Bridges
388.228	HE5746-5749	Coaching
388.310723	HE369-373	Traffic surveys
388.312	HE369-373	Traffic regulations
388.314	HE336.C64	Traffic congestion
388.314	HE336.H48	Highway capacity
388.322	HE5601-5725	Bus lines
388.324	HE5601-5725	Trucking
388.32409(4-9)	HE5623-5725	Trucking—[By region or country]
388.341	HD9709.5	Wagons
388.341	SF304.5-307	Coaching
388.341	SF304.5-307	Driving of horse-drawn vehicles
388.34232	HE5601-5725	Taxicabs
388.3472	HE5736-5739	Bicycles
388.4	HE305-311	Urban transportation
388.4	TA1205-1207	Urban transportation
388.411	HE331-380	Streets
388.413212	HE5620.C3	Car pools
388.413212	HE5620.R53	Ridesharing
388.413214	HE5601-5725	Cab and omnibus service
388.42	HE5351-5600	Electric railroads
388.42	HE3601-4043	Railroads, Local and light
388.4205	HE3601	Railroads, Local and light—Periodicals
388.4209(4-9)	HE3651-4043	Railroads, Local and light—[By region or country]
388.44	HE4201-5300	Railroads, Elevated
388.4409(4-9)	HE4401-5260	Railroads, Elevated—[By region or country]
388.440973	HE4401-4491	Railroads, Elevated—United States
388.46	HE4351	Street-railroads—Finance
388.46	HE4341-4345	Street-railroads—Fares
388.47	TA1225	Terminals (Transportation)
388.57	TJ898.5	Coal slurry pipelines
390	GT	Manners and customs
390	GN494	Taboo
390	GT	Rites and ceremonies
390.008822	BX2790	Church vestments
390.008822	BX1925	Church vestments
390.008823	BX5180	Church vestments
390.082	GT2520-2540	Women
390.08342	GT2540	Girls
390.09143	GT3490	Mountain life
390.091734	GT3470	Country life
390.0952	GT3412	Geishas
390.23	GT3510-3530	Courts and courtiers
390.23	GT5350-5490	Nobility—Social life and customs
390.23	GT5010-5090	Nobility—Social life and customs
390.24	GT5650-5680	Peasantry—Social life and customs
390.406927	GT6550-6710	Criminals
390.463	S521	Farm life
390.463	GT5810-5856.995	Harvesting
390.478	GT3650	Troubadours
390.478	GT3650	Minstrels
391	GT500-2370	Fashion
391	GT49	Beauty, Personal
391	GT1747-1748	Disguise
391	GT500-2370	Costume

Dewey	LC	Subject Heading	Dewey	LC	Subject Heading
391	GT525	Clothing and dress—Social aspects	392.12	GT2460-2465	Birth customs
391	GT500-2350	Clothing and dress	392.13	HQ768-777.95	Child rearing
391	GT529	Cold weather clothing	392.3	GT2420	Home
391	GN418-419	Clothing and dress	392.3	GT5870-5899	Domestication
391.0088296	GT540	Costume, Jewish	392.36	GR490-497	Dwellings
391.009	GT530-596	Costume—History	392.36	GT445	Lamps
391.00901	GT530-560	Costume—History—To 500	392.36	GT420-425	Heating
391.00902	GT575	Costume—History—Medieval, 500-1500	392.36	GT165-476	Dwellings
391.00903(1-3)	GT585	Costume—History—[16th/18th] century	392.36	GT450	Furniture
			392.36	GT445	Lanterns
391.009(4-9)	GT601-1605	Costume—[By region or country]	392.36	GT440-445	Lighting
			392.36	GT472	Sanitation, Household
391.0094	GT720-1330	Costume—Europe	392.36	GT170	Dwellings—Social aspects
391.0095	GT1370-1570	Costume—Asia	392.36	GT476	Toilets
391.00952	GT1560	Kimonos	392.36009(4-9)	GT201-384	Dwellings—[By region or country]
391.0096	GT1580-1589	Costume—Africa	392.3600941	GT285-294	Dwellings—Great Britain
391.0097	GT603-648	Costume—North America	392.36009415	GT294.5-.6	Dwellings—Ireland
391.0098	GT675-716	Costume—South America	392.3600943	GT298.9-300.5	Dwellings—Germany
391.0099(3-6)	GT1590-1599	Costume—[New Zealand/Australia/Oceania]	392.36009436	GT295-296	Dwellings—Austria
			392.36009439	GT296.5-.6	Dwellings—Hungary
391.024	GT1850	Peasantry	392.3600944	GT297-298	Dwellings—France
391.04204	BV167	Church vestments	392.3600945	GT303-304	Dwellings—Italy
391.08997	E59.C6	Indians—Costume	392.3600946	GT323-324	Dwellings—Spain
391.412	GT2170	Gloves	392.36009469	GT325-326	Dwellings—Portugal
391.412	GT2190	Muffs	392.3600947	GT311-312	Dwellings—Russia
391.413	GT2128	Hosiery	392.36009481	GT319-320	Dwellings—Norway
391.413008997	E98.C8	Moccasins	392.36009485	GT321-322	Dwellings—Sweden
391.42	GT2073	Underwear	392.36009489	GT315-316	Dwellings—Denmark
391.42	GT2075	Crinolines	392.360094912	GT317-318	Dwellings—Iceland
391.42	GT2075	Corsets	392.36009492	GT307-308	Dwellings—Netherlands
391.43	GT2110	Head-gear	392.36009494	GT327-328	Dwellings—Switzerland
391.43	GT2112	Veils	392.36009495	GT301-302	Dwellings—Greece
391.43	GT2110	Hats	392.36009496	GT331-341	Dwellings—Balkan Peninsula
391.434	GN419.5	Masks	392.360095	GT349-350	Dwellings—Asia
391.434	GT1747-1748	Masks	392.360095	GT343-372	Dwellings—Asia
391.44	GT2280	Pins and needles	392.3600951	GT365-366	Dwellings—China
391.44	GT2150	Fans	392.36009519	GT369-370	Dwellings—Korea
391.44	GT2220	Staffs (Sticks, canes, etc.)	392.3600952	GT367-368	Dwellings—Japan
391.44	GT2210	Umbrellas and parasols	392.3600954	GT351-352	Dwellings—India
391.44	GT2120	Neckties	392.360095493	GT352.5-.6	Dwellings—Sri Lanka
391.44	GT2370	Eyeglasses	392.3600955	GT347-348	Dwellings—Iran
391.44	GT2220	Staffs (Sticks, canes, etc.)	392.36009561	GT345-346	Dwellings—Turkey
391.5	GT2320	Beard	392.36009567	GT346.5-.6	Dwellings—Iraq
391.5	GT2310	Wigs	392.360095691	GT344-.2	Dwellings—Syria
391.5	GT2318	Mustache	392.36009593	GT355-356	Dwellings—Thailand
391.63	GT2340	Perfumes	392.36009595	GT357-358	Dwellings—Malaysia
391.63	GT2340-2341	Cosmetics	392.36009598	GT359-360	Dwellings—Indonesia
391.65	GN419.2	Mutilation	392.36009599	GT361-362	Dwellings—Philippines
391.65	GN419.15	Body marking	392.360096	GT373-377	Dwellings—Africa
391.7	GT2265	Earrings	392.3600962	GT375-376	Dwellings—Egypt
391.7	GT2270	Rings	392.3600971	GT228-229	Dwellings—Canada
391.7	GT2250-2280	Gems	392.3600972	GT231-232	Dwellings—Mexico
391.7	GT2260	Necklaces	392.360097281	GT239-240	Dwellings—Guatemala
391.7	GT2250-2281	Jewelry	392.360097282	GT235-236	Dwellings—Belize
392	GT2420	Family	392.360097283	GT241-242	Dwellings—Honduras
392	GT3005.3-.4	Sitting customs	392.360097284	GT246-.5	Dwellings—El Salvador
392	GT3000.3-.5	Sleeping customs	392.360097285	GT243-244	Dwellings—Nicaragua
392.1	GN484	Circumcision	392.360097286	GT237-238	Dwellings—Costa Rica
392.12	GN482.1	Birth customs	392.360097287	GT245-.5	Dwellings—Panama
			392.360097291	GT251-252	Dwellings—Cuba

Dewey	LC	Subject Heading	Dewey	LC	Subject Heading
392.360097292	GT255-256	Dwellings—Jamaica	394.1	GT2850-2930	Drinking customs
392.360097294	GT253-254	Dwellings—Haiti	394.12	GT2940-2947	Drinking cups
392.360097295	GT257-.5	Dwellings—Puerto Rico	394.12	GT2905-2916	Tea
392.360097296	GT249-250	Dwellings—Bahamas	394.12	GT2870	Condiments
392.3600973	GT205-227	Dwellings—United States	394.12	GT2865-2866	Food of animal origin
392.3600981	GT265-266	Dwellings—Brazil	394.12	GT2952	Toothpicks
392.3600982	GT261-262	Dwellings—Argentina	394.12	GT2995	Lying down position
392.3600983	GT267-268	Dwellings—Chile	394.12	GT2918	Coffee
392.3600984	GT263-264	Dwellings—Bolivia	394.12	GT2870	Salt
392.3600985	GT277-278	Dwellings—Peru	394.12	GT2870	Spices
392.36009861	GT269-270	Dwellings—Colombia	394.120952	GT2910-2916	Japanese tea ceremony
392.36009866	GT271-272	Dwellings—Ecuador	394.13	GT2940-2947	Drinking cups
392.3600987	GT281-282	Dwellings—Venezuela	394.14	GT3020	Smoking
392.36009892	GT275-276	Dwellings—Paraguay	394.14	GT3010	Narcotics
392.36009895	GT279-280	Dwellings—Uruguay	394.14	GT3030	Snuff
392.3600993	GT381-382	Dwellings—New Zealand	394.14	GT3020-3030	Tobacco
392.3600994	GT379-380	Dwellings—Australia	394.15	GT2955	Picnicking
392.360099(5-6)	GT383-384	Dwellings—Oceania	394.2	GT3920-4995	Fasts and feasts
392.4	GN480.1	Bridal price	394.2	GT2800	Wedding anniversaries
392.4	GT2600-2640	Love	394.23	GT5020	Heralds
392.4	GT2650	Betrothal	394.25	GT4180-4299	Carnivals
392.4	HQ1017	Dowry	394.26	GT4403	Kwanzaa
392.4	GN484.43	Betrothal	394.26	GT4380-4499	Harvest festivals
392.4	GT2620	Courtly love	394.26	GT3930-4995	Holidays
392.4	B105.E5	Engagement (Philosophy)	394.26	GT3930-4995	Festivals
392.5	GT2660-2800	Marriage customs and rites	394.2608997	E98.P86	Powwows
392.5	GR465	Marriage	394.261	GT4995.G	Groundhog Day
392.5	GT2797	Wedding cakes	394.2614	GT4905-4908	New Year
392.5	GT2810	Chastity belts	394.262	GT4995.A6	April Fools' Day
392.5	HQ745	Marriage service	394.262	GT4995.P3	Saint Patrick's Day
392.50882971	GT2695.M8	Marriage customs and rites, Islamic	394.262	HQ759.2	Mother's Day
392.50902	GT2680	Marriage customs and rites, Medieval	394.262	GT4504-.995	Spring festivals
			394.2627	GT4945	May Day
392.509(4-9)	GT2701-2796	Marriage customs and rites—[By region or country]	394.2627	GT4945	May-pole
			394.2635	DC167	Bastille Day
392.6	GN484.3	Sex customs	394.264	GT4995.A4	All Souls' Day
393	GR455	Dead	394.2646	GT4965	Halloween
393	GN486	Funeral rites and ceremonies	394.2649	GT4975	Thanksgiving Day
393	GR455	Death	394.266	GT4995.P45	Pentecost Festival
393	GT3150-3390	Dead	394.266	GT4995.A8	Ascension Day
393	GT3353	Body snatching	394.2663	GT4985	Christmas
393	GT3150-3390.5	Funeral rites and ceremonies	394.2663	GT4989	Christmas trees
393	GT3150-3390.5	Death	394.2667	GT4930	Holy Week
393.0901	GT3170	Funeral rites and ceremonies, Ancient	394.2667	GT4935	Easter
			394.2667	GT4987.5	Advent calendars
393.1	GT3380	Ship burial	394.26973	E231	Patriots' Day
393.1	GT3150-3390.5	Burial	394.26973	E642	Memorial Day
393.1	GN486	Burial	394.26973	E312.6	Washington's Birthday
393.1	GT3320	Cemeteries	394.26973	JK1761	Flag Day
393.2	GT3330	Cremation	394.26975	E645	Confederate Memorial Day
393.3	GT3340	Embalming	394.3	GT5810-5850	Hunting customs
393.4	GT3350	Scaffold burial	394.3	GR480-485	Games
393.9	GT3370	Widow suicide	394.3	GT5904-5905	Fishing
393.9	GT3370	Sati	394.3	GN454.8-455	Games
394	GT3085	Oaths	394.3	GN454-456	Toys
394	GT2640	Kissing	394.308996073	GR103	Afro-American children's games
394	GT3050	Salutations			
394	GT3050	Gifts	394.4	D127	Coronations
394	GT3080	Swearing	394.4	GT5050	Coronations
394.1	GT2850-2960	Food habits	394.40973	JK536	Inauguration Day
			394.5	GT3980-4099	Processions

Dewey	LC	Subject Heading	Dewey	LC	Subject Heading
394.5	GT3980-4099	Pageants	398.20441	PQ781-841	Folk literature, French
394.5	GT3980-4096	Parades	398.20451	PQ4186-4199	Folk literature, Italian
394.53	GT5220-5285	Travel	398.20461	PQ6155-6167	Folk literature, Spanish
394.53	GT5220	Transportation	398.20469	PQ9121-9128	Folk literature, Portuguese
394.6	GT4580-4699	Fairs	398.2048	PA3285	Folk literature, Greek
394.7	CR	Chivalry	398.2049155	PK6426	Folk literature, Persian
394.7	UB880	Courts of honor	398.204924	PJ5048	Folk literature, Hebrew
394.8	UB880	Courts of honor	398.204927	PJ7580	Folk literature, Arabic
394.8	CR4571-4595	Dueling	398.204927	PJ7680	Folk literature, Arabic
395	BJ1801-2195	Etiquette	398.204951	PL2445-2446	Folk literature, Chinese
395.03	BJ1815	Etiquette—Dictionaries	398.204956	PL748-749	Folk literature, Japanese
395.05	BJ1801	Etiquette—Periodicals	398.204957	PL968.2-.4	Folk literature, Korean
395.06	BJ19	Ethics—Congresses	398.209	PN905-1008	Folk literature—History
395.09	BJ1821	Etiquette—History			and criticism
395.142	BJ1855	Etiquette for men	398.20902	PN683-687	Legends
395.144	BJ1856	Etiquette for women	398.20973	PS451-478	Folk literature, American
395.22	BJ2051-2065	Wedding etiquette	398.21	BF1552	Fairies
395.23	BJ2071-2075	Mourning etiquette	398.21	GR75.S6	Snow White (Tale)
395.3	BJ2021-2078	Entertaining	398.245	GR75.L56	Little Red Riding Hood (Tale)
395.3	BJ2021-2028	Hospitality	398.27	GN492.3	Political customs and rites
395.4	BJ2100-2115	Letter writing	398.32	GR940-941	Geographical myths
395.5	GT5810-5895	Hunting	398.32	GR650-690	Geographical myths
395.5	BJ2137-2156	Travel etiquette	398.3209143	GR660	Mountains
395.52	GT6010-6070	Commerce	398.32091693	GR680	Rivers
395.52	GT6110-6390	Professions	398.33	GR930	Seasons
395.52	HF5389	Business etiquette	398.33	GR930	Days
395.53	BJ2018-2019	Church etiquette	398.354	GR462	Sex—Folklore
395.53	GT3770-3896	Hotels	398.355	GR890-910	Occupations—Folklore
395.54	BJ2041	Table etiquette	398.355	GR950.L4	Lanterns
395.59	BJ2120-2128	Conversation	398.362	GR625	Stars
395.59	BJ2195	Telephone etiquette	398.362	GR625	Sun
396.70944	DC611.P961	Courts of love	398.363	GR630	Lightning
398	GR72.3	Folklore—Performance	398.363	GR630	Thunderstorms
398	GR	Folklore	398.364	GR690	Wells
398.08997	E59.F6	Indians—Folklore	398.364	GR690	Springs—Folklore
398.092	GR50	Folklorists	398.365	GR800	Rocks
398.09(4-9)	GR100-390	Folklore—[By region or	398.368	GR780-790	Plants
		country]	398.368	GR780	Botany—Folklore
398.094	GR135-263	Folklore—Europe	398.368216	GR785	Trees—Folklore
398.095	GR265-345	Folklore—Asia	398.369	GR820-830	Animals, Mythical
398.096	GR350-360	Folklore—Africa	398.36957	GR750	Insects
398.097	GR101-118	Folklore—North America	398.3697	GR745	Fishes—Folklore
398.098	GR130-133	Folklore—South America	398.36979	GR740	Reptiles
398.099(3-6)	GR365-385	Folklore—[New Zealand/	398.3699772	GR720	Dogs
		Australia/Oceania]	398.41	GR933	Thirteen (The number)
398.2	GR550-552	Fairy tales	398.41	GR81	Superstition
398.2	GR72-390	Folk literature	398.45	GR555	Trolls
398.2	PZ8	Fairy tales	398.45	GR549-552	Fairies
398.2	PN1341-1347	Folk poetry	398.45	GR540	Incantations
398.2	GR74-76	Tales	398.45	GR560	Ghouls and ogres
398.2042	PR951-981	Folk literature, English	398.45	GR600	Amulets
398.20431	PT881-951	Folk literature, German	398.45	GR825-830	Monsters
398.2043931	PT6200-6230	Folk literature, Flemish	398.45	GR540	Demonology
398.2043931	PT5351-5395	Folk literature, Dutch	398.45	GR910	Mermaids
398.2043936	PT6540-6545	Folk literature, Afrikaans	398.45	GR600	Talismans
398.204394	PT4829-4830	Folk literature, Low German	398.45	GR530	Witchcraft
398.204395	PT7088-7089	Folk literature, Scandinavian	398.45	GR525	Ghouls and ogres
398.20439691	PT7420-7438	Folk literature, Icelandic	398.45	GR830.V3	Vampires
398.204397	PT9509-9542	Folk literature, Swedish	398.45	GR600	Charms
398.2043981	PT7900-7930	Folk literature, Danish	398.45	GR500-510	Supernatural
398.2043982	PT8600-8635	Folk literature, Norwegian	398.45	GR540	Exorcism

Dewey	LC	Subject Heading	Dewey	LC	Subject Heading
398.469	GR830.D7	Dragons	411.70943	CN950-957	Inscriptions—Germany
398.469	GR830.U6	Unicorns	411.709436	CN910-915	Inscriptions—Austria
398.47	GR580	Ghosts	411.70944	CN945-948	Inscriptions—France
398.8	PN6110.C4	Nursery rhymes	411.70945	CN1010-1015	Inscriptions—Italy
398.8	GR485	Counting-out rhymes	411.70946	CN1090-1095	Inscriptions—Spain
398.8	PZ8.3	Nursery rhymes	411.70947	CN1060-1065	Inscriptions—Russia
398.9	PN6299-6308	Maxims	411.7095	CN1150-1230	Inscriptions—Asia
398.9	PN6400-6525	Proverbs	411.70951	CN1160-1161	Inscriptions—China
398.9	PN6269-6278	Aphorisms and apothegms	411.70952	CN1180-1181	Inscriptions—Japan
399.08997	E98.W2	Scalping	411.70954	CN1170-1175	Inscriptions—India
398.8	PN6110.C4	Nursery rhymes	411.7095694	CN1193-1194	Inscriptions—Israel
398.8	GR485	Counting-out rhymes	411.7096	CN1300-1320	Inscriptions—Africa
400	P1-410	Language and languages	411.70972	CN877-878	Inscriptions—Mexico
401.3	PM8008	Language, Universal	411.709728	CN882-884	Inscriptions—Central America
401.3	PM7801-7895	Lingua francas			
401.4	P305-.18	Vocabulary	411.70973	CN870-872	Inscriptions—United States
401.409	P326	Historical lexicology	411.7098	CN886-888	Inscriptions—South America
401.41	P302-.87	Discourse analysis	411.70994	CN1340-1345	Inscriptions—Australia
401.41	P99-.4	Semiotics	412	P721-725	Indo-European languages—Etymology
401.43	P325-.5	Semantics			
401.4309	P325.5.H57	Semantics, Historical	412	P321-324.5	Language and languages—Etymology
401.9	P99.4.P72	Pragmatics			
401.9	P37	Psycholinguistics	413	P361	Polyglot glossaries, phrase books, etc.
401.93	P118-.7	Language acquisition			
401.93	P118.2	Second language acquisition	413	P361	Dictionaries, Polyglot
403	P29	Language and languages—Dictionaries	413	P761-769	Indo-European languages—Lexicography
405	P1-10	Language and languages—Periodicals	413	PB331	Dictionaries, Polyglot
			413.028	P501	Indo-European philology—Periodicals
407.1	P51-59	Language and languages—Study and teaching			
			414	P583-610	Indo-European languages—Phonology
407.1	P53.44	Immersion method (Language teaching)	414.8	P221-232	Phonetics
409	P375-381	Linguistic geography	414.8	P223	Tone (Phonetics)
410	P123	Comparative linguistics	415	P575-769	Indo-European languages—Grammar, Comparative
410	P121-149	Linguistics			
410	P501-769	Indo-European philology	415	P671-675	Indo-European languages—Syntax
410	P501-769	Indo-European languages			
410.1	P128.M48	Metalanguage	415	P151-299	Grammar, Comparative and general
410.18	P147	Functionalism (Linguistics)			
410.6	P505	Indo-European languages—Congresses	415	P207	Language and languages—Grammars
410.92	P121-141	Linguists	415	P611-627	Indo-European languages—Morphology
411	P211-214	Alphabets			
411	P226	Transliteration	415	P270-288	Parts of speech
411.7	CN	Inscriptions	415	P241-259	Morphemics
411.7	CN120-730	Inscriptions, Ancient	415	P631-663	Indo-European languages—Parts of speech
411.7	Z105-115.5	Paleography			
411.701	CN40-42	Inscriptions—Philosophy	417.2	P409	Jargon (Terminology)
411.703	CN70	Inscriptions—Dictionaries	417.2	P409-410	Slang
411.705	CN1	Inscriptions—Periodicals	417.2	PM9001-9021	Languages, Secret
411.706	CN15	Inscriptions—Congresses	417.22	PM7801-7895	Pidgin languages
411.7071	CN50	Inscriptions—Study and teaching	417.24	P128.E94	Linguistics, Experimental
			417.7	P35	Linguistic paleontology
411.7074	CN25-30	Inscriptions—Collectors and collecting	417.7	P140	Historical linguistics
			418	PB73	Polyglot glossaries, phrase books, etc.
411.709	CN870-1355	Inscriptions—[By region or country]			
			418	P408	Colloquial language
411.709	CN55	Inscriptions—History	418.020285	P307-310	Machine translating
411.7094	CN900-1130	Inscriptions—Europe	418.4	LB1050.55	Silent reading
411.70941	CN960-997	Inscriptions—Great Britain	418.4	LB1050.53	Developmental reading

91

Dewey	LC	Subject Heading	Dewey	LC	Subject Heading
419	HV2477-2480	Finger spelling	427.9411	PE2101-2364	Scots language
419	E98.S5	Sign language	428.1	PE1144-1146	Spellers
420	PE1001-3729	English language	428.6	PE1417	Readers
420	PE	English philology	428.6	PE1117-1130	Readers
420.71	PE1065-1069	English language—Study and teaching	429	PE101-123	English language—Old English, ca. 450-1100—Philology
421	PE1151	Phonetic spelling	429	PE101-299	English language—Old English, ca. 450-1100
421	PE1151	Phonetic alphabet			
421.5	PE1133-1168	English language—Phonology	429.2	PE261-269	English language—Old English, ca. 450-1100—Etymology
421.509	PE1133	English language—Phonology, Historical	429.3	PE275-285	English language—Old English, ca. 450-1100—Dictionaries
422	PE1571-1599	English language—Etymology			
423	PE1704	English language—Dictionaries	429.3028	PE274-285	English language—Old English, ca. 450-1100—Lexicography
423.028	PE1601-1693	English language—Lexicography			
423.1	PE1591	English language—Synonyms and antonyms	429.5	PE129-231	English language—Old English, ca. 450-1100—Grammar
425	PE1171	English language—Morphology	429.7	PE287-299	English language—Old English, ca. 450-1100—Dialects
425	PE1199-1359	English language—Parts of speech			
425	PE1097-1105	English language—Grammar	430	PF3001-5999	German language
425	PE1112	English language—Grammar—1950-	430	PF	Germanic languages
427	PE3729.U	Pig Latin	430	PD	Germanic languages
427	PE3701-3729	English language—Slang	430.042	PD571-599	Germanic languages—Etymology
427	PE1700-3601	English language—Dialects	430.043	PD625-660	Germanic languages—Dictionaries
427.009031	PE1079-1081	English language—Early modern, 1500-1700	430.043028	PD601-660	Germanic languages—Lexicography
427.009032	PE1079-1081	English language—Early modern, 1500-1700	430.045	PD99-321	Germanic languages—Grammar
427.009033	PE1083	English language—18th century	430.047	PD700-777	Germanic languages—Dialects
427.009034	PE1085	English language—19th century	430.05	PD1-9	Germanic languages—Periodicals
427.02	PE524-531	English language—Middle English, 1100-1500—Philology	430.071	PD65-69	Germanic languages—Study and teaching
427.02	PE501-685	English language—Middle English, 1100-1500	430.71	PF3065-3069	German language—Study and teaching
427.022	PE561-569	English language—Middle English, 1100-1500—Etymology	431.5	PF3131-3168	German language—Phonology
427.023	PE575-585	English language—Middle English, 1100-1500—Dictionaries	432	PF3571-3599	German language—Etymology
427.023028	PE574-585	English language—Middle English, 1100-1500—Lexicography	433	PF3620-3693	German language—Dictionaries
427.025	PE529-531	English language—Middle English, 1100-1500—Grammar	433.028	PF3601-3693	German language—Lexicography
427.027	PE688	English language—Middle English, 1100-1500—Dialects	435	PF3171-3197	German language—Morphology
427.73	PE2801-3102	English language—United States	435	PF3097-3400	German language—Grammar
427.9	PE1079-1087	English language—History	435	PF3199-3335	German language—Parts of speech
427.9	PM7891	Pidgin English	437	PF3051-3060	German language—History
427.9	PM7875.G8	Sea Islands Creole dialect	437	PF5971-5999	German language—Slang
			437	PF5000-5951	German language—Dialects

92

Dewey	LC	Subject Heading	Dewey	LC	Subject Heading
437	PD51-60	Germanic languages—History	439.317	PF951-979	Dutch language—Slang
			439.317	PF700-979	Dutch language—Dialects
437.01	PF3801-3991	German language—Old High German, 750-1050	439.32	PF571-599	Dutch languages—Etymology
			439.36	PF861-884	Afrikaans language
437.01	PF3801-3823	German language—Old High German, 750-1050—Philology	439.4	PF5601-5844	Low German language
			439.4	PF3992-4000	Old Saxon language
437.015	PF3831-3931	German language—Old High German, 750-1050—Grammar	439.(5-6)	PD1501-5929	Scandinavian languages
			439.(5-6)	PD1501-1541	Scandinavian philology
			439.(5-6)071	PD1535-1539	Scandinavian languages—Study and teaching
437.02	PF4043-4350	German language—Middle High German, 1050-1500	439.(5-6)2	PD1801-1819	Scandinavian languages—Etymology
437.023	PF4333-4345	German language—Middle High German, 1050-1500—Dictionaries	439.(5-6)3028	PD1823	Scandinavian languages—Lexicography
437.023028	PF4327-4345	German language—Middle High German, 1050-1500—Lexicography	439.(5-6)5	PD1559-1701	Scandinavian languages—Grammar
			439.(5-6)7	PD1850-1893	Scandinavian languages—Dialects
437.025	PF4061-4171	German language—Middle High German, 1050-1500—Grammar	439.6	PD2201-2392	Old Norse philology
			439.6	PD2201-2392	Old Norse language
			439.62	PD2361-2369	Old Norse language—Etymology
437.09	PF4501-4596	German language—Early modern, 1500-1700	439.63028	PD2376-2385	Old Norse language—Lexicography
439.(5-6)	PD1501-5929	Scandinavian languages	439.65	PD2229-2331	Old Norse language—Grammar
439.(5-6)	PD1501-1541	Scandinavian philology			
439.(5-6)071	PD1535-1539	Scandinavian languages—Study and teaching	439.67	PD2387-2392	Old Norse language—Dialects
439.(5-6)2	PD1801-1819	Scandinavian languages—Etymology	439.67	PD2483-2489	Old Norse Language—Dialects
439.(5-6)3028	PD1823	Scandinavian languages—Lexicography	439.69	PD2401-2447	Icelandic language
439.(5-6)5	PD1559-1701	Scandinavian languages—Grammar	439.69071	PD2407	Icelandic language—Study and teaching
439.(5-6)7	PD1850-1893	Scandinavian languages—Dialects	439.692	PD2431	Icelandic language—Etymology
439.1	PJ5111-5119	Yiddish language	439.693	PD2437	Icelandic language—Dictionaries
439.13	PJ5117	Yiddish language—Dictionaries	439.695	PD2411-2423	Icelandic language—Grammar
439.15	PJ5115-5116.5	Yiddish language—Grammar	439.697	PD2447	Icelandic language—Slang
439.2	PF1401-1497	Frisian language	439.699	PD2483	Faroese language
439.2	PF1401-1411	Frisian language—Philology	439.7	PD5001-5929	Swedish language
439.31	PF1-979	Dutch language	439.7	PD5001-5071	Swedish philology
439.31	PF1-979	Dutch philology	439.7071	PD5065	Swedish language—Study and teaching
439.31	PF1001-1184	Dutch language			
439.31071	PF1019	Dutch language—Study and teaching	439.72	PD5571-5599	Swedish language—Etymology
439.31071	PF65-69	Dutch language—Study and teaching	439.73	PD5625-5693	Swedish language—Dictionaries
439.3109	PF1015	Dutch language—History			
439.3109	PF51-60	Dutch language—History	439.73028	PD5611-5693	Swedish language—Lexicography
439.3115	PF131-168	Dutch language—Phonology			
439.312	PF1161-1167	Dutch language—Etymology	439.75	PD5101-5400	Swedish language—Grammar
439.313	PF620-693	Dutch language—Dictionaries			
439.313	PF1175-1184	Dutch language—Dictionaries	439.77	PD5700-5929	Swedish language—Dialects
439.313028	PF601-693	Dutch language—Lexicography	439.81	PD3001-3071	Danish philology
			439.81	PD3001-3929	Danish language
439.315	PF171-197	Dutch language—Morphology	439.81071	PD3065	Danish—Study and teaching
439.315	PF1033-1125	Dutch language—Grammar	439.812	PD3571-3599	Danish language—Etymology
439.315	PF199-335	Dutch language—Parts of speech	439.813	PD3625-3693	Danish language—Dictionaries
439.315	PF97	Dutch language—Grammar			

Dewey	LC	Subject Heading	Dewey	LC	Subject Heading
439.813028	PD3601-3693	Danish language—Lexicography	449.2	PC3283-3286	Provencal language—Etymology
439.815	PD3101-3400	Danish language—Grammar	449.3028	PC3287-3295	Provencal language—Lexicography
439.817	PD3700-3929	Danish language—Dialects			
439.817	PD3901-3929	Danish language—Slang	449.5	PC3219-3273	Provencal language—Grammar
439.82	PD2501-2999	Norwegian philology			
439.82	PD2571-2699	Norwegian language	449.7	PC3299	Provencal language—Slang
439.82071	PD2611-2612	Norwegian language—Study and teaching	449.77	PC3296	Provencal language—Dialects
439.822	PD2683-2684	Norwegian language—Etymology	449.9	PC3801-3899	Catalan language
			449.92	PC3883-3886	Catalan language—Etymology
439.823	PD2688-2695	Norwegian language—Dictionaries	449.93028	PC3887-3895	Catalan language—Lexicography
439.823028	PD2687-2695	Norwegian language—Lexicography	449.95	PC3819-3873	Catalan language—Grammar
439.825	PD2619-2673	Norwegian language—Grammar	450	PC1001-1977	Italian philology
			450	PC1001-1977	Italian language
439.827	PD2696-2699	Norwegian language—Dialects	450.71	PC1065	Italian language—Study and teaching
439.827	PD2699	Norwegian language—Slang	452	PC1571-1580	Italian language—Etymology
439.9	PD1101-1211	Gothic language	453	PC1620-1645	Italian language—Dictionaries
439.9	PD1270	Vandal language	453.028	PC1620-1693	Italian language—Lexicography
439.93	PD1193	Gothic language—Dictionaries			
439.95	PD1119-1167	Gothic language—Grammar	455	PC1099-1400	Italian language—Grammar
440	PC	Romance philology	457	PC1951-1977	Italian language—Slang
440	PC2001-3761	French language	457	PC1700-1977	Italian language—Dialects
440	PC2001-2071	French philology	457	PC1851-1874	Gallo-Italian dialects
440	PC	Romance languages	457.994972	PC890	Dalmatian language (Romance)
440.05	PC1-5	Romance languages—Periodicals	459	PC601-799	Romanian language
440.071	PC35-39	Romance languages—Study and teaching	459	PC601-872	Romanian philology
			459.071	PC619	Romanian language—Study and teaching
440.71	PC2065	French language—Study and teaching	459.11	PC785	Abbreviations, Romanian
441.5	PC2131-2151	French language—Phonology	459.2	PC761-767	Romanian language—Etymology
442	PC2761	French language—Etymology			
442	PC2571-2591	French language—Etymology	459.3028	PC775-784	Romanian language—Lexicography
443.028	PC2766	French language—Lexicography	459.5	PC631-725	Romanian language—Grammar
443.028	PC2620-2693	French language—Lexicography	459.7	PC799	Romanian language—Slang
445	PC2721-2746	French language—Grammar	459.9	PC901-949	Raeto-Romance language
445	PC2101-2400	French language—Grammar	459.9071	PC907	Raeto-Romance language—Study and teaching
445	PC2201-2321	French language—Parts of speech	459.92	PC931	Raeto-Romance language—Etymology
445	PC2171-2175	French language—Morphology	459.93	PC937	Raeto-Romance language—Dictionaries
447	PC2700-3761	French language—Dialects	459.95	PC911-923	Raeto-Romance language—Grammar
447.0(1-2)	PC2801-2896	French language—To 1500			
447.0(1-2)3028	PC2887-2895	French language—To 1500—Lexicography	459.97	PC941-949	Raeto-Romance language—Dialects
447.0(1-2)5	PC2821-2873	French language—To 1500—Grammar	459.97	PC949	Raeto-Romance language—Slang
447.01(1-2)2	PC2883-2886	French language—To 1500—Etymology	460	PC4001-4977	Spanish language
447.9	PM7831-7875	Creole dialects	460	PC4001-4071	Spanish philology
448.6	PC2113-2117	French language—Readers	460.71	PC4065	Spanish language—Study and teaching
449	PC3371-3420	Langue d'oc			
449	PC3201-3299	Provencal language	462	PC4571-4580	Spanish language—Etymology
449	PC3081-3148	Franco-Provencal dialects			

Dewey	LC	Subject Heading	Dewey	LC	Subject Heading
463.028	PC4620-4693	Spanish language—Lexicography	487.311	CN455	Inscriptions, Byzantine
463	PC4620-4645	Spanish language—Dictionaries	487.4	PA600-895	Greek language, Hellenistic (300 B.C.-600 A.D.)
465	PC4099-4400	Spanish language—Grammar	487.4	CN750-753	Inscriptions, Christian
467	PC4951-4977	Spanish language—Slang	487.4	PA695-895	Greek language, Biblical
467	PC4700-4941	Spanish language—Dialects	487.43	PA881	Greek language, Biblical—Dictionaries
469	PC5001-5041	Portuguese philology			
469	PC5001-5498	Portuguese language	487.45	PA813-857	Greek language, Biblical—Grammar
469.0071	PC5035-5039	Portuguese language—Study and teaching	489	PA500-581	Greek language—Dialects
			489	PA1000-1179	Greek language, Medieval and late
469.2	PC5301-5315	Portuguese language—Etymology	489.3	PA201-1179	Greek language
469.3	PC5325-5348	Portuguese language—Dictionaries	489.3	PA1000-1179	Greek language, Modern
			489.3071	PA231-241	Greek language—Study and teaching
469.3028	PC5320-5348	Portuguese language—Lexicography	489.3071	PA1041-1049	Greek language, Modern—Study and teaching
469.5	PC5061-5231	Portuguese language—Grammar	489.315	PA1061-1072	Greek language, Modern—Phonology
469.7	PC5350-5498	Portuguese language—Dialects	489.315	PA265-281	Greek language—Phonology
469.709	PC5498	Portuguese language—Slang	489.32	PA1111-1114.5	Greek language, Modern—Etymology
469.794	PC5411-5414	Galician dialect			
470	PA2001-2995	Latin language	489.32	PA421-430	Greek language—Etymology
470	PA2001-2067	Latin philology	489.33	PA441-465	Greek language—Dictionaries
470	PA2420-2915	Italic languages and dialects			
470.71	PA2061-2067	Latin language—Study and teaching	489.33	PA1123-1145	Greek language, Modern—Dictionaries
471	CN510-740	Inscriptions, Latin	489.33	PA1031	Greek language, Modern—Dictionaries
472	PA2341-2350	Latin language—Etymology			
473	PA2361-2390	Latin language—Dictionaries	489.33028	PA431-465	Greek language—Lexicography
473.028	PA2351-2390	Latin language—Lexicography	489.35	PA283-287	Greek language—Morphology
475	PA2161-2281	Latin language—Parts of speech	489.35	PA303-361	Greek language—Parts of speech
475	PA2285-2297	Latin language—Syntax	489.35	PA367-379	Greek language—Syntax
475	PA2133-2158	Latin language—Morphology	489.35	PA1091-1097	Greek language, Modern—Syntax
475	PA2111-2131	Latin language—Phonology			
475	PA2071-2310	Latin language—Grammar	489.35	PA1081-1089	Greek language, Modern—Parts of speech
477	PA2600-2748	Latin language, Vulgar	489.35	PA251-379	Greek language—Grammar
477	PA2510-2519	Latin language, Preclassical to ca. 100 B.C.	489.35	PA1051-1099	Greek language, Modern—Grammar
477	PA2300-2309	Latin language, Postclassical	489.35	PA1076	Greek language, Modern—Morphology
480	PA1-199	Classical philology			
480	PA550-554	Aeolic Greek dialect	489.37	PA1151-1159	Greek language, Modern—Dialects
480	PA	Classical languages			
480	PA530-539	Doric Greek dialect	490	PJ	Oriental languages
480.03	PA31	Classical languages—Dictionaries	490.071	PJ65-69	Oriental languages—Study and teaching
481.0932	CN440-441	Inscriptions, Greek—Egypt	490.2	PJ183	Oriental languages—Etymology
481.1	CN350-455	Inscriptions, Greek			
481.1	CN1000-1005	Inscriptions, Greek	490.3028	PJ187	Oriental languages—Lexicography
481.109(3-9)	CN380-455	Inscriptions, Greek—[By region or country]	490.5	PJ120-171	Oriental languages—Grammar
481.1094959	CN420	Inscriptions, Greek—Crete			
481.1095	CN400	Inscriptions, Greek—Asia	491.1	PK1-9201	Indo-Iranian languages
481.10953	CN440-441	Inscriptions, Greek—Middle East	491.1	PK1-17	Indo-Iranian philology
481.109561	CN410-415	Inscriptions, Greek—Turkey	491.1	PK1231-1239	Maharashtri language
481.1095693	CN430	Inscriptions, Greek—Cyprus	491.1071	PK11-13	Indo-Iranian philology—Study and teaching
485	PA111	Classical languages—Grammar, Comparative			

Dewey	LC	Subject Heading	Dewey	LC	Subject Heading
491.13	PK75-77	Indo-Iranian languages—Dictionaries	491.5	PK6001-6996	Iranian philology
491.13	PK1537	Indo-Aryan languages, Modern—Dictionaries	491.51	PK6121-6129	Old Persian language
			491.5111	PK6128	Old Persian inscriptions
491.13	PK14	Indo-Iranian languages—Dictionaries	491.52	PK6101-6109	Avestan language
			491.53	PK6135	Iranian languages, Middle
491.15	PK1511-1523	Indo-Aryan languages, Modern—Grammar	491.55	PK6201-6399	Persian language
			491.5511	PK6395	Abbreviations, Persian
491.15	PK21-41	Indo-Iranian languages—Grammar	491.56	PK6871-6879	Dari language
			491.6	PB3001-3029	Gaulish language
491.(2-4)	PK101-2899	Indo-Aryan languages	491.6	PB1001-1095	Celtic philology
491.(2-4)	PK119	Devanagari alphabet	491.6	PB1001-1095	Celtic languages
491.(2-4)	PK101-119	Indo-Aryan philology	491.6	PB2001-2060	Brythonic languages
491.2	PK401-976	Sanskrit language	491.6071	PB1011	Celtic languages—Study and teaching
491.2	PK401-418	Sanskrit philology			
491.22	PK901-919	Sanskrit language—Etymology	491.62	PB1101-1113	Gaelic philology
			491.62	PB1201-1299	Irish language
491.23	PK925-969	Sanskrit language—Dictionaries	491.6(2-3)	PB1501-1599	Gaelic language
			491.6(2-3)071	PB1111	Gaelic philology—Study and teaching
491.23028	PK920-969	Sanskrit language—Lexicography			
			491.6(2-3)071	PB1511	Gaelic language—Study and teaching
491.25	PK501-811	Sanskrit language—Grammar			
491.29	PK201-379	Vedic language	491.6(2-3)2	PB1583-1584	Gaelic language—Etymology
491.292	PK361-369	Vedic language—Etymology	491.6(2-3)3028	PB1587-1595	Gaelic language—Lexicography
491.293	PK375-379	Vedic language—Dictionaries			
491.295	PK231-313	Vedic language—Grammar	491.6(2-3)3028	PB1187-1189	Gaelic language—Lexicography
491.3	PK1201-1429	Prakrit languages			
491.33	PK1223-1225	Prakrit languages—Dictionaries	491.6(2-3)5	PB1521-1573	Gaelic language—Grammar
			491.6(2-8)071	PB2005	Brythonic languages—Study and teaching
491.35	PK1206-1215	Prakrit languages—Grammar			
491.37	PK1001-1095	Pali language	491.6(2-8)2	PB1083-1085	Celtic languages—Etymology
491.37	PK1001-1095	Pali philology	491.6(2-8)2	PB2021	Brythonic languages—Etymology
491.372	PK1083-1086	Pali language—Etymology			
491.373	PK1089-1095	Pali language—Dictionaries	491.6(2-8)3028	PB2023	Brythonic languages—Lexicography
491.373028	PK1087-1093	Pali language—Lexicography	491.6(2-8)3028	PB1087-1089	Celtic languages—Lexicography
491.375	PK1017-1073	Pali language—Grammar			
491.4	PK1501-2845	Indo-Aryan languages, Modern	491.6(2-8)5	PB1019-1071	Celtic languages—Grammar
			491.6(2-8)5	PB2009-2015	Brythonic languages—Grammar
491.4(1-9)	PK1550-2899	Indo-Aryan languages, Modern—Dialects			
			491.64	PB1801-1847	Manx language
491.41	PK2781-2794	Sindhi language	491.66	PB2101-2199	Welsh language
491.42	PK2631-2639	Panjabi language	491.67	PB2501-2549	Cornish language
491.43	PK1931-1939	Hindi language	491.67071	PB2507	Cornish language—Study and teaching
491.43	PK1931-1937	Hindustani language			
491.439	PK1975-1987	Urdu language	491.675	PB2511-2547	Cornish language—Grammar
491.44	PK1651-1695	Bengali language	491.68	PB2800-2849	Breton language
491.45	PK2561-2569	Oriya language	491.68071	PB2807	Breton language—Study and teaching
491.451	PK1550-1599	Assamese language			
491.454	PK1821-1824	Magahi language	491.685	PB2811-2847	Breton language—Grammar
491.46	PK2351-2378	Marathi language	491.7	PG2001-2847	Russian language
491.47	PK1841-1847	Gujarati language	491.7	PG2001-2069	Russian philology
491.479	PK2701-2709	Rajasthani language	491.7071	PG2065-2069	Russian language—Study and teaching
491.487	PK1836	Divehi language			
491.49	PK2591-2610	Pahari languages	491.715	PG2131-2161	Russian language—Phonology
491.495	PK2595-2599	Nepali language			
491.497	PK2896-2899	Romany language	491.72	PG2571-2591	Russian language—Etymology
491.499	PK7070	Khowar language			
491.499	PK7001-7070	Dardic languages	491.73	PG2625-2693	Russian language—Dictionaries
491.499	PK7021-7029	Kashmiri language			
491.499	PK7045.M3	Maiya language	491.73028	PG2601-2693	Russian language—Lexicography
491.5	PK6001-6996	Iranian languages			

Dewey	LC	Subject Heading	Dewey	LC	Subject Heading
491.75	PG2097-2127	Russian language—Grammar	491.87	PG5201-5399	Slovak language
			491.87	PG5201-5223	Slovak philology
491.75	PG2171-2197	Russian language—Morphology	491.873	PG5375-5384	Slovak language—Dictionaries
491.75	PG2199-2321	Russian language—Parts of speech	491.875	PG5231-5325	Slovak language—Grammar
			491.877	PG400	Slavic languages—Slang
491.77	PG2700-2850	Russian language—Dialects	491.877	PG350-400	Slavic languages—Dialects
491.7709	PG2850	Russian language—Slang	491.88	PG5631-5698	Sorbian languages
491.79	PG3801-3899	Ukrainian language	491.91	PG8201-8208	Prussian language
491.793	PG3888-3894.5	Ukranian language—Dictionaries	491.913	PG8206	Prussian language—Dictionaries
491.793028	PG3887-3894.5	Ukranian language—Lexicography	491.92	PG8501-8693	Lithuanian language
			491.92	PG8501-8693	Lithuanian philology
491.795	PG3819-3881	Ukrainian language—Grammar	491.93	PG8801-8993	Latvian language
			491.93	PG8801-8993	Latvian philology
491.8	PG1-9198	Slavic languages	491.991	PG9501-9599	Albanian language
491.8	PG1-41	Slavic philology	491.991	PG9501-9513	Albanian philology
491.8042	PG301-319	Slavic languages—Etymology	491.992	PK8001-8454	Armenian language
491.8043028	PG320-335	Slavic languages—Lexicography	491.9927	PK8451-8499	East Armenian dialect
			491.998	P1001	Anatolian languages
491.8045	PG59-97	Slavic languages—Grammar	491.998	P945	Hittite language
491.8071	PG35-39	Slavic languages—Study and teaching	492	PJ3001-9278	Semitic languages
			492	PJ990	Afroasiatic languages
491.81	PG801-823	Bulgarian philology	492.04071	PJ3011-3013	Semitic languages—Study and teaching
491.81	PG801-993	Bulgarian language			
491.813	PG975-984	Bulgarian language—Dictionaries	492.0411	PJ3081-3095	Inscriptions, Semitic
			492.042	PJ3065	Semitic languages—Etymology
491.815	PG831-925	Bulgarian language—Grammar	492.043	PJ3004	Semitic languages—Dictionaries
491.81701	PG601-698	Church Slavic language			
491.817015	PG661-698	Church Slavic language—Grammar	492.043028	PJ3071-3075	Semitic languages—Lexicography
491.819	PG1161-1164	Macedonian language	492.045	PJ3021-3041	Semitic languages—Grammar
491.82	PG1201-1223	Serbo-Croatian philology			
491.82	PG1224-1399	Serbo-Croatian language	492.047	PJ4121-4129	Semitic languages, Northwest
491.823	PG1374-1384	Serbo-Croatian language—Dictionaries	492.1	PJ3101-3595	Akkadian language
			492.111	PJ3191-3225	Cuneiform writing
491.825	PG1229-1313	Serbo-Croatian language—Grammar	492.2	PJ5201-5329	Aramaic language
			492.211	PJ5208-5209	Inscriptions, Aramaic
491.827	PG1399	Serbo-Croatian language—Slang	492.29	PJ5271-5279	Samaritan Aramaic language
			492.3	PJ5401-5411	Syriac philology
491.83	PG331-335	Slavic languages—Dictionaries	492.3	PJ5701-5809	Syriac language
491.84	PG1801-1899	Slovenian language	492.32	PJ5483	Syriac language—Etymology
491.84	PG1801-1813	Slovenian philology	492.33	PJ5490-5493	Syriac language—Dictionaries
491.843	PG1888-1894.5	Slovenian language—Dictionaries			
			492.35	PJ5419-5471	Syriac langue—Grammar
491.843028	PG1887-1894.5	Slovenian language—Lexicography	492.37	PJ5401	Mandailing dialect
			492.4	PJ4501-4541	Hebrew philology
491.845	PG1819-1881	Slovenian language—Grammar	492.4	PJ4501-4937	Hebrew language
			492.411	CN745	Inscriptions, Jewish
491.85	PG6001-6790	Polish language	492.411	PJ5034.4-.9	Inscriptions, Hebrew
491.85	PG6001-6790	Polish philology	492.415	PJ4576-4583	Hebrew language—Phonology
491.853028	PG6625-6638	Polish language—Lexicography			
			492.42	PJ4801-4819	Hebrew language—Etymology
491.857	PG6700-6790	Polish language—Dialects	492.42	PJ4931-4933	Hebrew language—Etymology
491.86	PG4601-4771	Czech language	492.43	PJ4825-4847	Hebrew language—Dictionaries
491.86	PG4001-4771	Czech philology			
491.863	PG4625-4693	Czech language—Dictionaries	492.43	PJ4935-4937	Hebrew language—Dictionaries
491.867	PG4700-4771	Czech language—Dialects			

Dewey	LC	Subject Heading	Dewey	LC	Subject Heading
492.43028	PJ4934-4937	Hebrew language—Lexicography	493.13028	PJ1401-1439	Egyptian language—Lexicography
492.43028	PJ4820-4847	Hebrew language—Lexicography	493.15	PJ1121-1201	Egyptian language—Grammar
492.45	PJ4601-4677	Hebrew language—Morphology	493.17	PJ1801-1921	Egyptian language—Demotic, ca. 650 B.C.-450 A.D.
492.45	PJ4553-4731	Hebrew language—Grammar	493.2	PJ2001-2187	Coptic language
492.47	PJ4901-4950	Hebrew language, Talmudic	493.2071	PJ2019	Coptic language—Study and teaching
492.47	PJ4855-4937	Hebrew language—Dialects			
492.475	PJ4911-4925	Hebrew language—Grammar	493.22	PJ2161	Coptic language—Etymology
492.6	PJ4171-4187	Phoenician language	493.23028	PJ2181	Coptic language—Lexicography
492.67	PJ4150	Ugaritic language			
492.7	PJ6001-6071	Arabic philology	493.25	PJ2029-2113	Coptic language—Grammar
492.7	PJ6001-7144	Arabic language	493.3	PJ2369-2399	Berber languages
492.7071	PJ6065-6069	Arabic language—Study and teaching	493.3	PJ2377	Rif language
			493.3	PJ2340-2349	Berber languages
492.71	CN1153	Inscriptions, Islamic	493.32	PJ2347	Berber languages—Etymology
492.711	PJ6123	Arabic alphabet			
492.711	PJ7593-7600	Inscriptions, Arabic	493.33	PJ2349	Berber languages—Dictionaries
492.72	PJ6172-6199	Arabic language—Etymology			
492.73	PJ6031	Arabic language—Dictionaries	493.35	PJ2345	Berber languages—Grammar
			493.5	PJ2401-2413	Cushitic languages
492.75	PJ6101-6599	Arabic language—Grammar	493.5	PJ2465	Afar language
492.77	PJ6821-6830	Arabic language—Dialects—Iraq	493.52	PJ2409	Cushitic languages—Etymology
492.77	PJ6841-6880	Arabic language—Dialects—Arabian Peninsula	493.53	PJ2413	Cushitic languages—Dictionaries
492.77	PJ6771-6799	Arabic language—Dialects—Egypt	493.54	PJ2531-2534	Somali language
			493.55	PJ2405	Cushitic langues—Grammar
492.77	PJ6751-6760	Arabic language—Dialects—Spain	493.57	PJ2425-2594	Cushitic languages—Dialects
			493.7	PL8117	Daba language
492.77	PJ6701-6901	Arabic language—Dialects	494	PL1-9	Altaic lanugages
492.77	PJ6810	Arabic language—Dialects—Lebanon	494.1	PL450	Tungus-Manchu languages
			494.1	PL481.E92	Even language
492.77	PJ6811-6820	Arabic language—Dialects—Syria	494.1	PL471-479	Manchu language
			494.1	PL451-459	Evenki language
492.77	PJ6805-6808	Arabic language—Dialects—Palestine	494.23	PL400-431	Mongolian languages
			494.23	PL401-409	Mongolian language
492.8	PJ8991-8999	Ethiopian languages	494.3	PL21-29	Turkic languages
492.81	PJ9001-9087	Ethiopic language	494.31	PL31	Old Turkic language
493.1	PJ1001-1109	Egyptian philology	494.332	PL364.Z9.D	Dolgan dialect
493.1	PJ1001-1479	Egyptian language	494.35	PL101-199	Turkish language
493.1	PJ1091	Hieroglyphics	494.357	PL51-56	Turkic languages, Southeast
493.11	PJ1105	Egyptian language—Writing, Hieratic	494.361	PL311-314	Azerbaijani language
			494.364	PL331-334	Turkmen language
493.111	PJ1091-1097	Egyptian language—Writing, Hieroglyphic	494.37	PL41-45	Turkic languages, Northeast
493.111	PJ1051-1109	Egyptian language—Writing	494.37	PL61-65	Turkic languages, Northwest
493.111	PJ1501-1819	Egyptian language—Inscriptions			
493.111	PJ1501-1921	Egyptian language—Papyri	494.38	PL65.B2	Karachay-Balkar language
493.111	PH1091-1097	Hieroglyphics	494.387	PL65.T3	Tatar language
493.111	PJ1107	Egyptian language—Writing, Demotic	494.388	PL65.C74	Crimean Tatar language
			494.5	PH	Finno-Ugric languages
			494.5	PH1-11	Finno-Ugric philology
493.12	PJ1350-1371	Egyptian language—Etymology	494.5071	PH11	Finno-Ugric languages—Study and teaching
493.13	PJ1423-1439	Egyptian language—Dictionaries	494.51	PH1251-1254	Ob-Ugric languages
			494.511	PH2001-2800	Hungarian language
493.13	PJ1031	Egyptian language—Dictionaries	494.5113	PH2625-2693	Hungarian language—Dictionaries

Dewey	LC	Subject Heading	Dewey	LC	Subject Heading
494.5113028	PH2601-2693	Hungarian language—Lexicography	495.4	PL3601-3651	Tibetan language
			495.4	PL3551-4001	Tibeto-Burman languages
494.5115	PH2097-2410	Hungarian language—Grammar	495.4	PL3651.D96	Dzongkha language
			495.6	PL501-700	Japanese language
494.5117	PH2800	Hungarian language—Slang	495.611	PL750-751	Inscriptions, Japanese
			495.63	PL674.5-677.6	Japanese language—Dictionaries
494.53	PH1001-1004	Permic languages			
494.54	PH501-509	Karelian language	495.65	PL531.3-532.5	Japanese language—Grammar
494.54	PH561-569	Votic language			
494.54	PH91-98	Finnic languages	495.67	PL525.2	Japanese language—To 794
494.54	PH581-589	Livonian language	495.67	PL525.5	Japanese language—Edo period, 1600-1868
494.54	PH541-549	Veps language			
494.541	PH101-123	Finnish philology	495.67	PL525-.6	Japanese language—Meiji period, 1868-1912
494.541	PH101-293	Finnish language			
494.5415	PH131-225	Finnish language—Grammar	495.7	PL901-949	Korean language
494.545	PH601-629	Estonian language	495.711	PL969.2-.4	Inscriptions, Korean
494.55	PH21-41	Finno-Ugric languages—Grammar	495.73	PL935-.6	Korean language—Dictionaries
494.55	PH701-729	Lapp language	495.8	PL3921-3969	Burmese language
494.56	PH751-779	Mordvin language	495.91	PL4111-4251	Thai language
494.56	PH801-807	Mari language	495.922	PL4371-4379	Vietnamese language
494.6	PL495	Ainu language	495.93	PL4281-4587	Austroasiatic languages
494.6	PM1-95	Hyperborean languages	495.93	PL4301-4309	Mon-Khmer languages
494.8	PL4601-4794	Dravidian languages	495.95	PL4501-4509	Munda languages
494.8	PL4601	Dravidian philology	496	PL8000-8008	African languages
494.811	PL4751-4759	Tamil language	496.071	PL8004	African languages—Study and teaching
494.812	PL4711-4719	Malayalam language			
494.814	PL4641-4649	Kannada language	496.1	PL8541	Nama languge
494.82	PL4627	Gadaba language (Dravidian)	496.3	PL8026.N44	Niger-Congo languages
			496.32	PL8134	Diola language
494.827	PL4771-4779	Telugu language	496.322	PL8181-8184	Fula language
495	PL4051-4054	Karen language	496.33	PL8221	Grebo language
495	PL3521-3529	Sino-Tibetan languages	496.337	PL8164.Z9	Fon dialect
495.1	PL1891-1900	Mandarin dialects	496.3374	PL8161-8164	Ewe language
495.1	PL1001-2244	Chinese language	496.3378	PL8191	Ga language
495.115	PL1201-1219	Chinese language—Phonology	496.3385	PL8046.A63	Akan language
			496.3385	PL8167.F4	Fanti language
495.12	PL1281-1315	Chinese language—Etymology	496.348	PL8204	Gbandi language
			496.35	PJ4149	Mossi languages
495.13	PL1420-1498	Chinese language—Dictionaries	496.361	PL8024.A33	Adamawa languages
			496.361	PL8205	Gbaya language
495.13028	PL1401-1498	Chinese language—Lexicography	496.3642	PL8147	Efik language
			496.39	PL8025	Bantu languages
495.15	PL1099-1241	Chinese language—Grammar	496.391	PL8025	Bisa language
			496.392	PL8701-8704	Swahili language
495.17	PL1501-1940	Chinese language—Dialects	496.395	PL8207.G55	Gisu language
			496.3957	PL8201	Ganda language
495.17	PL1861-1870	Hsiang dialects	496.396	PL8167.F3	Fang language
495.17	PL1081	Chinese language—Middle Chinese, 1200-1919	496.3962	PL8141	Duala language
			496.397	PL8771	Venda language
495.17	PL1077	Chinese language—To 600	496.397	PL8801-8804	Yao language
			496.3977	PL8689	Sotho language
495.17	PL1079	Chinese language—Ancient Chinese, 600-1200	496.3986	PL8841-8844	Zulu language
			496.5	PL8008	African languages—Grammar
495.17	PL1931-1940	Wu dialects	496.5	PL8041	Acoli language
495.17	PL1083	Chinese language—Modern Chinese, 1919-	496.5	PL8571-8574	Nubian languages
			496.5	PL8197	Gambai dialect
495.17	PL1731-1740	Cantonese dialects	496.5	PL8127	Daza language
495.4	PL3881-3884	Naga languages	496.5	PL8131	Dinka language
495.4	PL4001.G2	Garo language	497	E98.P6	Picture-writing, Indian

Dewey	LC	Subject Heading
497	PM1-7356	Indians of North America—Languages
497	PM5071-5079	Indians of the West Indies—Languages
497.1	PM50-94	Eskimo languages
497.12	PM50-64	Inuit language
497.19	PM31-34	Aleut language
497.2	PM2006-2009	Navajo language
497.3	PM1971-1974	Muskogean languages
497.3	PM635	Arapaho language
497.3	PM1885	Mohegan language
497.3	PM600-609	Algonquian languages
497.3	PM851-854	Ojibwa language
497.4152	PM3961-3969	Mayan lanuagages
497.45	PM2321	Shoshonean languages
497.45	PM1351	Hopi language
497.45	PM2175	Pima languages
497.45	PM2515	Ute language
497.452	PM4061-4069	Nahuatl Language
497.52	PM1001	Crow language
497.52	PM1021-1024	Dakota language
497.55	PM781-784	Cherokee language
497.55	PM1381-1384	Iroquoian languages
497.55	PM1881-1884	Mohawk language
497.57	PM1343	Hokan-Coahuiltecan languages
497.9	PM2711	Zuni language
497.9	PM3001-4566	Indians of Central America—Languages
498	PM5001-7356	Indians of South America—Languages
498.38	PM7171-7179	Tupi languages
499.12	PL6601-6621	Papuan languages
499.15	PL7001-7101	Australian languages
499.2	PL5021-6571	Austronesian languages
499.21	PL5501-6135	Philippine languages
499.211	PL6051-6059	Tagalog language
499.22	PL5221-5224	Balinese language
499.221	PL5071-5079	Indonesian languge
499.222	PL5161-5169	Javanese language
499.28	PL5101-5129	Malay language
499.4	PL6401-6551	Polynesian languages
499.442	PL6465	Maori language
499.444	PL6515	Tahitian language
499.48	PL6531	Tonga language (Tonga Islands)
499.5	PL6201-6209	Melanesian languages
499.5	PL6235	Fijian language
499.52	PL6191-6195	Micronesian languages
499.92	PH5001-5259	Basque language
499.92	PH5001-5022	Basque philology
499.93	P943	Elamite language
499.94	P1078	Etruscan language
499.9411	CN479	Inscriptions, Etruscan
499.95	PJ4001-4041	Sumerian language
499.9511	PJ4051-4075	Cuneiform inscriptions, Sumerian
499.953	PJ4037	Sumerian language—Dictionaries
499.955	PJ4011-4025	Sumerian language—Grammar
499.96	PK9001-9201	Caucasian languages
499.962	PK9051	Abkhazo-Adyghian languages
499.962	PK9201.A2	Abazin language
499.9623	PK9201.A3	Abkhaz language
499.9624	PK9201.K3	Kabardian language
499.964	PK9201.D3	Dargwa language
499.964	PK9051	Daghestan languages
499.965	PK9106-9115	Georgian language—Grammar
499.969	PK9101-9151	Georgian language
499.99	PM8001-9021	Languages, Artificial
499.992	PM8201-8298	Esperanto
500	Q	Science
500.2	Q	Physical sciences
500.5	QB495-500.268	Space sciences
501	Q174-175.32	Science—Philosophy
501	Q174-175.32	Science—Methodology
501.4	Q179	Science—Terminology
501.4	Q179	Science—Nomenclature
502.2	Q222	Scientific illustration
502.5	Q145	Scientists—Directories
502.84	Q184-185.7	Scientific apparatus and instruments
502.85	Q183.9	Science—Data processing
503	Q123	Science—Dictionaries
505	Q1-9	Science—Periodicals
506	Q10-99	Science—Societies, etc.
507.1	Q181-183.4	Science—Study and teaching
507.2	Q180	Research
507.2	Q183-.4	Laboratories
507.4	Q105	Science—Exhibitions
507.8	Q182.3	Science projects
508	Q148-149	Scientific surveys
508	QH	Natural history
508.014	QH83	Natural history—Terminology
508.022	QH46.5	Natural history illustration
508.0222	QH46	Natural history—Pictorial works
508.03	QH13	Natural history—Dictionaries
508.06	QH1-7	Natural history—Periodicals
508.071	QH51-58	Nature study
508.071	QH51-58	Natural history—Study and teaching
508.072	QH75-77	Research natural areas
508.074	QH70	Natural history museums
508.092	QH26-35	Naturalists
509	Q125-127	Science—History
509.01	Q124.95	Science, Ancient
509.02	Q124.97	Science, Medieval
509.0(24-31)	Q125.2	Science, Renaissance
509.2	Q141-143	Scientists—Biography
509.(4-9)	Q127-.2	Science—[By region or country]
510	QA	Mathematics
510.1	QA8-10.5	Mathematics—Philosophy
510.1	QA9	Metamathematics
510.284	QA71-90	Mathematical instruments
510.284	QA73	Slide-rule
510.284	QA75	Calculators
510.3	QA5	Mathematics—Dictionaries

Dewey	LC	Subject Heading	Dewey	LC	Subject Heading
510.5	QA1	Mathematics—Periodicals	512.56	QA372.5	Differential-algebraic equations
510.71	QA11-20	Mathematics—Study and teaching	512.7	QA171.5	Lattices, Distributive
510.9	QA21-27	Mathematics—History	512.7	QA241-247.5	Number theory
510.901	QA22	Mathematics, Ancient	512.7	QA141.15	Number concept
510.902	QA23	Mathematics, Medieval	512.72	QA242-244	Congruences and residues
510.902	QA32	Mathematics, Medieval	512.72	QA242	Diophantine equations
510.92	QA28-29	Mathematicians	512.72	QA242	Numbers, Divisibility of
510.9(4-9)	QA27	Mathematics—[By region or country]	512.72	QA246	Numbers, Prime
			512.73	QA165	Partitions (Mathematics)
510.931	QA27.C	Mathematics, Chinese	512.74	QA341	Algebraic functions
510.935	QA22	Mathematics, Babylonian	512.74	QA244	Fermat's theorem
510.938	QA22	Mathematics, Greek	512.74	QA242	Diophantine analysis
511.3	QA9.65	Decidability (Mathematical logic)	512.922	QA55-59	Logarithms
511.3	QA267-268.5	Machine theory	512.923	QA242	Factors (Algebra)
511.3	BC131-135	Logic, Symbolic and mathematical	512.923	QA161.F3	Factors (Algebra)
			512.924	QA221-224	Approximation theory
511.3	QA9-10.3	Logic, Symbolic and mathematical	512.925	QA165	Permutations
			512.925	QA165	Combinations
511.3	QA9.5	Lambda calculus	512.94	QA211-218	Equations
511.3	QA9.54	Proof theory	512.94	QA211-218	Equations, Theory of
511.3	QA9.4-.5	Nonclassical mathematical logic	512.942	QA215	Equations, Cubic
511.324	QA10-.3	Algebraic logic	512.942	QA161	Equations, Quadratic
511.324	QA10.3	Algebra, Boolean	512.942	QA245	Equations, Binomial
511.33	QA171.5	Lattice theory	512.942	QA215	Equations, Quartic
511.42	QA275	Least squares	512.942	QA161.B5	Binomial theorem
511.43	QA275	Error analysis (Mathematics)	512.9432	QA191	Determinants
511.5	QA90	Nomography (Mathematics)	512.9434	QA188-196	Matrices
511.5	QA166-.24	Graph theory	512.944	QA243	Forms (Mathematics)
511.6	QA164-167.2	Combinatorial analysis	512.944	QA201	Forms (Mathematics)
511.64	QA165	Magic squares	513	QA101-141.8	Arithmetic
511.66	QA306	Maxima and minima	513	GN476.1	Arithmetic
511.801	QA9.7	Model theory	513	QA248-.5	Arithmetic—Foundations
511.801	QA9.7	Forcing (Model theory)	513.0284	QA75	Abacus
512	QA150-272.5	Algebra	513.211	QA115	Addition
512	QA246	Numerical functions	513.211	QA113	Counting
512	QA251	Algebra, Universal	513.212	QA115	Subtraction
512.0071	QA159	Algebra—Study and teaching	513.213	QA115	Multiplication
512.02	QA162	Algebra, Abstract	513.214	QA115	Division
512.2	QA174-183	Group theory	513.23	QA119	Square root
512.2	QA215	Equations, Abelian	513.23	QA119	Roots, Numerical
512.2	QA176	Representations of groups	513.23	QA49	Square root
512.3	QA211	Galois theory	513.23021	QA51	Factor tables
512.3	QA247-.45	Algebraic fields	513.26	QA117	Fractions
512.3	QA171	Infinite groups	513.26071	QA135-139	Fractions—Study and teaching
512.3	QA171	Galois theory			
512.3	QA247.45	Division algebras	513.26	QA242	Decimal fractions
512.3	QA214	Galois theory	513.5	QA141-.8	Numeration
512.4	QA247	Rings (Algebra)	513.56	QA141.5	Duodecimal system
512.4	QA251.3	Dedekind rings	513.57	QA141.8.S4	Sexadecimal system
512.4	QA247	Ideals (Algebra)	513.6	QA247.35	Modular arithmetic
512.4	QA171	Group extensions (Mathematics)	514	QA611-614.97	Topology
			514	QA611.5	Ergodic theory
512.5	QA190-201	Substitutions, Linear	514.23	QA612.3-.77	Homology theory
512.5	QA199.5	Multilinear algebra	514.3	QA611.234	Hewitt-Nachbin spaces
512.55	QA387	Lie groups	514.3	QA611.28	Metric spaces
512.55	QA326	Operator algebras	514.3	QA689	Generalized spaces
512.55	QA252.3	Lie algebras	514.72	QA613.6-.66	Differential topology
512.56	QA247.4	Difference algebra	514.72	QA613.62	Foliations (Mathematics)
			514.74	QA614-.97	Global analysis (Mathematics)

Dewey	LC	Subject Heading	Dewey	LC	Subject Heading
514.74	QA614.83	Hamiltonian systems	516.04	QA473-475	Geometry, Modern
514.74	QA614.92	Index theorems	516.1	QA601-608	Transformations (Mathematics)
515	QA303-316	Calculus			
515	QA297-299.4	Numerical analysis	516.15	QA482	Triangle
515	QA299.82	Nonstandard mathematical analysis	516.15	QA484	Circle
			516.15	QA491	Prisms
515.24	QA295	Processes, Infinite	516.15	QA485	Parabola
515.24	QA9	Infinite	516.15	QA482	Polygons
515.243	QA295	Series, Infinite	516.15	QA465	Mensuration
515.243	QA295	Partial sums (Series)	516.183	QA608	Line geometry
515.2433	QA403-.3	Harmonic analysis	516.2	QA451-469	Euclid's Elements
515.2433	QA403.3	Wavelets (Mathematics)	516.2	QA608	Congruences (Geometry)
515.2433	QA403.5-404.5	Fourier analysis	516.22	QA451-485	Geometry, Plane
515.25	QA331-355	Functions	516.23	QA491	Geometry, Solid
515.26	QA295	Inequalities (Mathematics)	516.23	QA457	Geometry, Solid
515.35	QA871	Perturbation (Mathematics)	516.24	QA531-538	Trigonometry
515.35	QA871	Stability	516.24021	QA55	Trigonometry—Tables
515.35	QA370-380	Differential equations	516.242	QA533	Plane trigonometry
515.35	TA347.D45	Differential equations	516.244	QA535	Spherical trigonometry
515.353	QA374-377	Differential equations, Partial	516.3	QA551-563	Geometry, Analytic
			516.35	QA564-609	Geometry, Algebraic
515.354	QA372	Differential equations, Linear	516.352	QA571-573	Surfaces
515.37	QA381	Differential invariants	516.36	QA615-639	Geometry, Infinitesimal
515.37	QA381	Differential forms	516.36	QA641-672	Surfaces
515.38	QA373	Differential-difference equations	516.36	QA631-638	Surfaces
			516.36	QA641-672	Geometry, Differential
515.4	QA312	Integrals, Generalized	516.375	QA689	Finsler spaces
515.4	QA308-311	Integrals	516.375	QA689	G-spaces
515.42	QA313	Ergodic theory	516.5	QA501-521	Projection
515.52	QA246	Euler's numbers	516.6	QA501-521	Geometry, Descriptive
515.52	QA353.G3	Gamma functions	516.9	QA473	Inversions (Geometry)
515.53	QA408	Hankel functions	519.2	QA273-274.8	Probabilities
515.53	QA405	Harmonic functions	519.2	QA273	Games of chance (Mathematics)
515.54	QA405	Mathieu functions			
515.55	QA164.8	Generating functions	519.2	QA273-274.8	Chance
515.55	QA353.G44	Generating functions	519.23	QA274-.8	Stochastic processes
515.56	QA351	Functions, Zeta	519.233	QA274.75	Diffusion processes
515.623	QA355	Numerical differentiation	519.233	QA274.7-.76	Markov processes
515.624	QA299.3-.4	Numerical integration	519.24	QA273.6	Distribution (Probability theory)
515.625	QA431	Difference equations			
515.63	QA433	Vector analysis	519.3	QA269-272.5	Game theory
515.64	QA402.3-.37	Control theory	519.3	T57.92	Game theory
515.64	QA315-316	Calculus of variations	519.4	QA297	Numerical calculations
515.64	QA402.35	Nonlinear control theory	519.4	QA402.2	Decomposition method
515.7	QA319-329.9	Functional analysis	519.5	QA278.8	Nonparametric statistics
515.7	QA324	Theory of distribution (Functional analysis)	519.5	QA276-280	Mathematical statistics
			519.52	QA276.6	Sampling (Statistics)
515.723	QA432	Laplace transformation	519.535	QA278.6	Latent structure analysis
515.7242	QA329.42	Partial differential operators	519.535	QA278.65	Discriminant analysis
515.7248	QA321.5	Nonlinear functional analysis	519.5354	QA278.5	Factor analysis
515.73	QA322	Linear topological spaces, Ordered	519.537	QA273-281	Correlation (Statistics)
			519.538	QA279-.2	Analysis of variance
515.73	QA331	Analytic functions	519.542	QA279.4-.7	Decision-making
515.8	QA331.5	Functions of real variables	519.544	QA276.8	Estimation theory
515.9	QA646	Conformal mapping	519.55	QA280	Time-series analysis
515.9	QA360	Conformal mapping	519.7	QA402.5	Programming (Mathematics)
515.9	QA331.7	Functions of complex variables	519.72	T57.74-.79	Linear programming
			519.76	T57.8-.825	Nonlinear programming
515.93	QA333-337	Riemann surfaces	519.82	QA274.8	Queuing theory
515.983	QA343	Elliptic functions	520	QB25-26	Astrology
516	QA440-699	Geometry	520	QB	Astronomy

Dewey	LC	Subject Heading	Dewey	LC	Subject Heading
520	QB136	Space astronomy	523.019	QB463-464.2	Nuclear astrophysics
520.1	QB14.5	Astronomy—Philosophy	523.02	QB450-.5	Cosmochemistry
520.151	QB47	Astronomy—Mathematics	523.1	QB63	Constellations
520.21	QB149	Statistical astronomy	523.1	QB980-991	Cosmology
520.216	QB6	Astrographic catalog and chart	523.112	QB856-858.8	Galaxies
			523.1125	QB790-792	Interstellar matter
520.223	QB65	Stars—Atlases	523.1125	QB791	Cosmic dust
520.228	QB67	Astronomical models	523.1126	QB791.3	Dark matter (Astronomy)
520.3	QB14	Astronomy—Encyclopedias	523.1135	QB855.5	Planetary nebulae
520.5	QB1	Astronomy—Periodicals	523.115	QB860	Quasars
520.71	QB61-62.7	Astronomy—Study and teaching	523.12	QB632	Earth—Origin
			523.12	QB980-991	Cosmogony
520.9	QB15-34	Astronomy—History	523.18	QB991.I54	Inflationary universe
520.901	GN799.A8	Astronomy, Prehistoric	523.18	QB991.B54	Big bang theory
520.901	QB16-22	Astronomy, Ancient	523.19	QB991.E53	End of the universe
520.902	QB23-26	Astronomy, Medieval	523.2	QB500.5-785	Solar system
520.90(23-31)	QB29	Astronomy, Renaissance	523.3	QB592	Lunar geology
520.92	QB35-36	Astronomers—Biography	523.3	QB591	Moon—Surface
520.931	QB17	Astronomy, Chinese	523.3	QB580-595	Moon
520.935	QB19	Astronomy, Assyro-Babylonian	523.3	QB592	Lunar soil
			523.3	QB391-399	Lunar theory
520.938	QB21	Astronomy, Greek	523.3021	QB399	Moon—Tables
521	QB349-421	Celestial mechanics	523.3021	VK563-567	Moon—Tables
521.3	QB355-357	Orbits	523.38	QB579	Lunar eclipses
521.4	QB362.T9	Two-body problem	523.4	QB603.R55	Planetary rings
521.4	QB361-407	Perturbation (Astronomy)	523.4	QB600-701	Planets
521.4	QB362.F47	Few-body problem	523.4	QB361-389	Planetary theory
521.4	QB362.M3	Many-body problem	523.41	QB371	Mercury (Planet)
521.9	QB165	Nutation	523.41	QB611	Mercury (Planet)
522	QB84.5-135	Lenses	523.42	QB621	Venus (Planet)
522	QB51.3.I45	Imaging systems in astronomy	523.42	QB372	Venus (Planet)
			523.42	QB621	Venus (Planet)—Surface
522	QB105	Solar compass	523.423	QB372	Venus (Planet)—Orbit
522	QB807	Astrometry	523.423	QB509-513	Venus (Planet), Transit of
522.1	QB4-.9	Astronomy—Observations	523.43	QB376	Mars (Planet)
522.2	QB88	Telescopes	523.43	QB641	Mars (Planet)
522.2	QB88	Reflecting telescopes	523.44	QB651	Asteroids
522.2	QB84.5-115	Astronomical instruments	523.44	QB516	Asteroids
522.29	QB81-84	Astronomical observatories	523.44	QB377-379	Asteroids
522.29	QB500.267-.268	Orbiting astronomical observatories	523.45	QB661	Jupiter (Planet)
			523.45	QB384	Jupiter (Planet)
522.4	QB105	Quadrant	523.46	QB384	Saturn (Planet)
522.5	QB107	Chronometers	523.46	QB671	Saturn (Planet)
522.5	QB107	Astronomical clocks	523.47	QB681	Uranus (Planet)
522.62	QB135	Astronomical photometry	523.47	QB387	Uranus (Planet)
522.63	QB121-.5	Astronomical photography	523.481	QB691	Neptune (Planet)
522.67	QB465	Astronomical spectroscopy	523.481	QB388	Neptune (Planet)
522.68	QB480	Radar in astronomy	523.482	QB701	Pluto (Planet)
522.682	QB479.2	Radio telescopes	523.51	QB738	Meteoroids
522.682	QB475-479.55	Radio astronomy	523.51	QB740-753	Meteors
522.683	QB470	Infrared astronomy	523.51	QB754.8-759	Meteorites
522.6862	QB471.7.B85	Gamma ray bursts	523.58	QB529	Solar wind
522.6863	QB472-473	X-ray astronomy	523.6	QB717-732	Comets
522.7	QB140-237	Spherical astronomy	523.63	QB357	Comets—Orbits
522.9	QB163	Aberration	523.642	QB723.H2	Halley's comet
522.9	QB155-156	Refraction, Astronomical	523.7	QB520-545	Sun
523	QB802	Zodiac	523.7021	QB374	Sun—Tables
523	QB15-26	Zodiac	523.72	QB524-526	Solar activity
523.01	QB460-466	Astrophysics	523.72	QB531	Solar radiation
523.019	QB462.6	Molecular astrophysics	523.72	QB539.N6	Solar noise storms
523.019	QB462.7-.72	Plasma astrophysics	523.72	QB539.M23	Solar magnetic fields

Dewey	LC	Subject Heading	Dewey	LC	Subject Heading
523.73	QB526.C9	Solar cycle	526.103	QB279	Geodesy—Encyclopedias
523.73	QB523	Sun—Rotation	526.109	QB280.5	Geodesy—History
523.73	QB551	Sun—Rotation	526.3	GA23	Area measurement
523.75	QB525	Sunspots	526.3	QB301-328	Surveys
523.75	QB529	Sun—Corona	526.3	QB303	Base measuring
523.75	QB516.F6	Solar flares	526.3	TA590	Topographical surveying
523.76	QB539.I5	Sun—Internal structure	526.30287	QB291	Arc measures
523.78	QB541-545	Solar eclipses	526.33	QB311	Triangulation
523.8	QB6	Stars—Observations	526.33	TA583	Triangulation
523.8	QB799-903	Stars	526.6	QB201-205	Geodetic astronomy
523.80216	QB6	Stars—Catalogs	526.61	QB231-237	Latitude
523.81	QB814	Stars—Masses	526.62	QB225-229.5	Longitude
523.82	QB817	Stars—Radiation	526.63	QB207	Azimuth
523.83	QB812	Stellar oscillations	526.63	TA597	Azimuth
523.83	QB810	Stars—Rotation	526.7	QB330-339	Gravity
523.841	QB821-830	Double stars	526.7	QB341	Gravitation
523.841	QB821-830	Multiple stars	526.8	GA110-115	Map projection
523.841	QB421	Double stars	526.9	GA51-87	Surveys
523.844	QB833-841	Variable stars	526.9	TA625	Route surveying
523.8444	QB835.E4	Eclipsing binaries—Orbits	526.9	TA611	Surveys—Plotting
523.8446	QB843.D85	Dwarf Novae	526.9	TA501-625	Surveying
523.85	QB851-855.9	Stars—Clusters	526.9	TA515-531	Surveyors
523.87	QB121	Stars—Photographic measurements	526.90284	TA579-581	Measuring-tapes
			526.90284	TA579	Surveyors' chains
523.88	QB895	Stars, New	526.90284	TA562-581	Surveying—Instruments
523.88	QB843.R42	Red giants	526.9071	TA535-538	Surveying—Study and teaching
523.88	QB843.E2	Early stars			
523.88	QB843.D9	Dwarf stars	526.98	TA616	Topographical drawing
523.88	QB843.R4	Red dwarfs	526.982	TR693-696	Photogrammetry
523.88	QB806	Stars—Evolution	526.982	TA592-593.9	Photographic surveying
523.88	QB841	Stars, New	526.982	TA593	Photogrammetry
523.88	QB843.N12	N stars	527	VK563	Azimuth
523.88	QB806	Stars—Formation	527	VK549-587	Nautical astronomy
523.887	QB843.W5	White dwarfs	527.015308	VK572	Mile, Nautical
523.8874	QB843.N4	Neutron stars	527.021	VK563-567	Navigation—Tables
523.8875	QB843.B55	Kerr black holes	527.0284	VK584.A7	Artificial horizons (Nautical instruments)
523.8875	QB843.B55	Black holes (Astronomy)			
523.9	QB175-185	Transits	527.1	VK565	Latitude
523.98	QB401-407	Satellites	527.2	VK565-567	Longitude
523.986	QB405	Saturn (Planet)—Ring system	528	QB8	Nautical almanacs
523.9881	QB407	Neptune (Planet)—Satellites	528	QB7-9	Ephemerides
523.99	QB175-185	Eclipses	529	CE	Chronology
525	QB630-638.8	Earth	529	QB209-224	Time
525	QB630-638.8	Astronomical geography	529.0218	QB223	Time—Systems and standards
525.317	QB216	Sun—Rising and setting			
525.35	QB633	Earth—Rotation	529.03	CE4	Chronology—Dictionaries
525.5	QB637.2-.8	Seasons	529.05	CE1	Chronology—Periodicals
526	GA101-1999	Cartography	529.06	CE1.5	Chronology—Congresses
526	GA1-87	Mathematical geography	529.09	CE6	Chronology—History
526.021	GA4	Mathematical geography—Tables	529.0935	CE33	Calendar, Assyro-Babylonian
526.0221	GA130	Map drawing	529.1	QB217	Time, Equation of
526.0284	QB331	Gravimeters (Geophysical instruments)	529.223	QB65	Astronomy—Charts, diagrams, etc.
526.09	GA201-246	Cartography—History	529.3	CE73	Calendars
526.0973	GA405	Cartography—United States	529.3	CE91-92	Perpetual calendars
526.097(4-9)	GA409-460	Cartography—[United States, By state]	529.30935	CE33	Chronology, Assyro-Babylonian
526.1	QB275-343	Geodesy	529.309376	CE46	Calendar, Roman
526.10285	QB297	Geodesy—Computer programs	529.30938	CE42	Chronology, Greek
			529.325	CE31-39.5	Chronology, Oriental

Dewey	LC	Subject Heading	Dewey	LC	Subject Heading
529.326	CE35	Calendar, Jewish	530.475	QC183	Brownian movements
529.327	CE59	Calendar, Islamic	530.475	QC185	Diffusion
529.42	CE75	Calendar, Julian	530.7	QC53-55	Physical instruments
529.44	CE83	Easter	530.7	QC100.5-.8	Measuring instruments
529.44	CE81-83	Church calendar	530.7	QC53	Recording instruments
529.7	QB215	Dialing	530.7	QC107	Weighing-machines
529.7	QB215	Sundials	530.7	QC107	Scales (Weighing instruments)
529.7	QB213	Time measurements			
529.7	QB214	Hour-glasses	530.8	G86	Mile, Roman
530	QC	Physics	530.8	QC100-111	Testing
530	QC170-197	Matter	530.8	T50-51	Mensuration
530	QC120-168.86	Mechanics	530.81	QC81-114	Weights and measures
530.01	QC5.56-6.4	Physics—Philosophy	530.8109	QC83-86	Weights and measures—History
530.03	QC5	Physics—Encyclopedias			
530.06	QC1	Physics—Congresses	530.812	QC90.8-94	Metric system
530.071	QC30-48	Physics—Study and teaching	530.812	QC91-94	Decimal system
			531	QC176-.9	Solid state physics
530.071	QC29	Physics—Vocational guidance	531.01515	QA801-871	Mechanics, Analytic
			531.11	QA801-935	Motion
530.072	QC51	Physical laboratories	531.11	QA861-863	Dynamics, Rigid
530.078	QC35-37	Physics—Laboratory manuals	531.11	QA845-871	Dynamics
530.09	QC6.9-9	Physics—History	531.11	QC122-168	Motion
530.092	QC15-16	Physicists	531.112	QA841-842	Kinematics
530.11	QC173.5-.65	Relativity (Physics)	531.1134	QC189-.2	Viscosity
530.11	QC173.59.S65	Space and time	531.1134	QC197	Friction
530.12	QC173.96-174.52	Quantum theory	531.12	QA821-835	Statics
530.12	QC174.17.B6	Bound states (Quantum mechanics)	531.12	QA839	Moments of inertia
			531.14	QC111-114	Specific gravity
530.122	QC174.3-.35	Matrix mechanics	531.14	QC178	Gravitational fields
530.122	QC174.17.H4	Heisenberg uncertainty principle	531.14	QC178	Gravitation
			531.16	QA851-855	Dynamics of a particle
530.122	QC174.17.D44	Density matrices	531.32	QA865-867.5	Oscillations
530.124	QC174.2-.26	Wave mechanics	531.32	QA935-939	Vibration
530.13	QC174.7-175.36	Statistical mechanics	531.324	QA862.P4	Pendulum
530.133	QC174.4-.43	Quantum statistics	531.33	QA935	Wave-motion, Theory of
530.138	QC175.2-.25	Transport theory	531.34	QA862.G9	Gyroscopes
530.14	QC174.17.P7	Few-body problem	531.381	QA931-939	Strains and stresses
530.14	QC173.68-.75	Field theory (Physics)	531.382	QC191	Elastic waves
530.142	QC794.6.G7	Grand unified theories (Nuclear physics)	531.382	QA935	Elastic plates and shells
			531.382	QC191	Elastic solids
530.1423	QC174.17.S9	Supergravity	531.382	QA935	Elastic waves
530.143	QC174.45-.52	Quantum field theory	531.382	QA935	Elastic solids
530.143	QC174.52.D43	Degree of freedom	531.382	QC191	Elasticity
530.1435	QC793.3.F5	Gauge fields (Physics)	531.382	QA931-939	Elasticity
530.144	QC174.17.P7	Many-body problem	531.385	QA931-939	Plasticity
530.15	QC19.2-20.85	Mathematical physics	531.385	QC191	Plasticity
530.15071	QC20.8-.82	Mathematical physics—Study and teaching	531.6	QC72-73.8	Force and energy
			532	QA901-930	Fluids
530.411	QC176.8.L3	Lattice dynamics	532	QC138-168.86	Fluids
530.416	QC176.8.E9	Exciton theory	532	QC141-159	Liquids
530.416	QC174.1	Tunneling (Physics)	532	TC160-179	Hydraulics
530.4175	QC176.82-.9R37	Thin films	532.051	QA913	Boundary layer
530.42	QA911-930	Fluid dynamics	532.0525	QA929	Laminar flow
530.42	QC175.4-.47	Superfluidity	532.25	QA907	Floating bodies
530.427	QC183	Surface tension	532.25	QC147	Floating bodies
530.44	QC717-.8	Plasma (Ionized gases)	532.5	QA913	Kinematics
530.44	QC702-721	Ionization of gases	532.5	QA911-930	Hydrodynamics
530.444	QC701.7-702.7	Ionization	532.5	QC175.3-.36	Kinetic theory of liquids
530.474	QC175.16.P5	Phase transformations (Statistical physics)	532.5	QC150-159	Hydrodynamics
			532.5	QC150-159	Fluid dynamics
530.475	QC318.M3	Mass transfer	532.5	QA913	Rotating masses of fluid

Dewey	LC	Subject Heading	Dewey	LC	Subject Heading
532.5	TC171-179	Hydrodynamics	535.420284	QC425	Prisms
532.510284	TC177	Flow meters	535.47	QC411	Interference (Light)
532.52	TC173	Nozzles	535.52	QC440-446	Polarization (Light)
532.52	TC173	Water jets	535.6	QC494-496.9	Color
532.54	TC175-.2	Channels (Hydraulic engineering)	535.6	QC494-496.9	Colors
			535.6019	BF789.C7	Color—Psychological aspects
532.59	QA913	Turbulence	535.84	QC454.E46	Emission spectroscopy
532.59	QA925	Vortex-motion	535.84	QC465	Spectroscope
532.59	QA927	Gravity waves	535.84	QC454.A8	Atomic absorption spectroscopy
532.59	TC172	Wave makers			
532.59	TC172	Water waves	535.840284	QC451	Spectrum analysis—Instruments
532.593	QA913	Wakes (Fluid dynamics)			
532.593	QA927	Nonlinear wave equations	535.842	QC457	Infrared spectra
532.593	QC168.85.D46	Detonation waves	535.842	QC457	Infrared spectroscopy
532.593	QA927	Wave-motion, Theory of	535.843	QC454.L63	Light beating spectroscopy
532.593	QC157	Waves	535.844	QC459-.5	Ultraviolet spectroscopy
532.595	QC159	Vortex-motion	535.846	QC454.R36	Raman effect
533	QC161-166.5	Pneumatics	536	QC251-338.5	Heat
533	QC161-166.5	Gases	536.2	QC319.8-338.5	Heat—Transmission
533.2	QC167.5-168.86	Gas dynamics	536.41	QC281.5.E9	Expansion (Heat)
533.2	QA930	Gas dynamics	536.412	QC164	Expansion of gases
533.5	QC166-.5	Vacuum	536.42	QC303	Fusion
533.50284	QC166	Vacuum-gages	536.42	QC303	Solidification
533.6	QC161-166.5	Air	536.44	QC304	Evaporation
533.61	QC168	Aerostatics	536.50287	QC270-278.6	Temperature measurements
533.62	QA930	Aerodynamics	536.50287	QC270-278.6	Thermometers
533.7	QC175-.16	Kinetic theory of gases	536.520287	QC277	Pyrometers
534	QC220-246	Sound	536.56072	QC277.9-278.6	Low temperature research
534.0284	QC228.3	Sound—Equipment and supplies	536.57	QC276-277	High temperatures
			536.6	QC290-297	Calorimeters
534.0287	QC243	Sound—Measurement	536.7	QC310.15-319	Thermodynamics
534.204	QC233	Echo	537	QC669-675.8	Electromagnetic theory
534.208	QC243	Sound-waves—Damping	537	QC501-721	Electricity
534.208	QC235	Sound-waves—Damping	537	QC759.6-761.3	Electromagnetism
534.208	QC233	Absorption of sound	537.0284	QC543-544	Electric apparatus and appliances
534.23	QC242-.5	Underwater acoustics			
534.5	QC235-241	Vibration	537.0287	QC535-537	Electric measurements
534.5	QC231	Kinematics	537.072	QC541	Electric laboratories
534.55	QC244	Ultrasonic waves	537.0724	QC533-534	Electricity—Experiments
535	QC350-467	Light	537.0724	QC527	Electricity—Experiments
535	QC350-467	Optics	537.092	QC514-515	Electricians
535.014	QC459.5	Far ultraviolet radiation	537.2	QC570-596.9	Electrostatics
535.014	QC459-.5	Ultraviolet radiation	537.21	QC581.E4	Electric charge and distribution
535.028	QC370.5-379	Optical instruments			
535.0284	QC367	Optical measurements	537.24	QC584-585.8	Dielectrics
535.12	QC402	Light, Corpuscular theory of	537.240287	QC584	Dielectric measurements
535.13	QC403	Light, Wave theory of	537.2448	QC596-.9	Ferroelectricity
535.2	QC392-449.5	Physical optics	537.2448	TK7872.F44	Ferroelectric devices
535.2	QC403	Coherence (Optics)	537.5	QC685-689.55	Quantum electronics
535.2	QC446.15-.3	Nonlinear optics	537.5	QC703.7	Exploding wire phenomena
535.220287	QC391	Photometry	537.52	QC705	Electric arc
535.323	QC425	Reflection (Optics)	537.534	QC660.5-665	Electric waves
535.323	QC385	Reflection (Optics)	537.534	QC676-678.6	Radio waves
535.324	QC385	Lenses	537.534	QC665.P6	Radio waves—Polarization
535.324	QC425	Refraction, Double	537.5352	QC482.S6	X-ray spectroscopy
535.326	QC437	Absorption of light	537.54	QC611	Photoelectricity
535.35	QC476.4-480.2	Luminescence	537.54	QC612.P5	Photoconductivity
535.352	QC477-.4	Fluorescence	537.54	QC715.15	Photoemission
535.357	QC480	Electroluminescence	537.56	QC793.5.E62-.E629	Electron optics
535.4	QC414.8-417	Diffraction			
535.4	QC431-435	Dispersion	537.6	QC612.H3	Hall effect

Dewey	LC	Subject Heading	Dewey	LC	Subject Heading
537.6	QC623	Electric currents—Heating effects	539.72112	QC793.5.E462-.E4629	Electrons
537.6	QC641	Electric currents, Alternating	539.72112	QC793.5.E628	Electrons—Polarization
537.6	QC601-641	Electric currents	539.72123	QC793.5.P72-.P729	Antiprotons
537.6	QC630-648	Electrodynamics	539.7213	QC793.5.N462-.N4622	Neutrons
537.62	QC610.3-635	Electric conductivity			
537.62	QC611	Electric resistance	539.7213	QC793.5.N4629	Neutron sources
537.62	TK3301-3351	Electric conductors	539.7215	QC793.5.N42-.N429	Neutrinos
537.6223	QC611.8.W53	Wide gap semiconductors	539.7216	QC793.5.S72-.S729	Strange particles
537.6223	QC611.8.M25	Diluted magnetic semiconductors			
537.6223	QC611.8.N35	Narrow gap semiconductors	539.7216	QC793.5.H32-.H329	Hadrons
537.6223	QC611.8.O7	Organic semiconductors	539.72162	QC793.5.M42-.M429	Kaons
537.6223	QC611.8.D66	Doped semiconductors			
537.6226	QC610.9-611.8	Semiconductors	539.72162	QC793.5.M42-.M429	Mesons
537.623	QC611.9-.98	Superconductivity			
537.65	QC621-625	Thermoelectricity	539.72167	QC793.5.Q252-.Q2529	Quarks
537.67	QC679-680.5	Quantum electrodynamics			
538	QC760-.3	Electromagnets	539.7217	QC173	Photon beams
538	QC750-776	Magnetism	539.7217	QC793.5.P42-.P429	Photons
538.0287	QC761	Magnetic measurements			
538.0287	QC818-849	Magnetic measurements	539.7222	QC480-482.3	X-rays
538.362	QC762	Deuteron magnetic resonance spectroscopy	539.7222	QC484.3	Bremsstrahlung
			539.7222	QC793.5.G322	Gamma ray sources
538.362	QC762	Nuclear magnetic resonance	539.7223	QC484.8-485.9	Cosmic rays
538.364	QC763	Electron paramagnetic resonance	539.7223	QC485	Solar cosmic rays
			539.7232	QC793.5.A22-.A229	Alpha rays
538.4	QC757	Magnets			
538.4	QC754.2.M33	Magnetic induction	539.7234	QC702.7.H42	Heavy ions
538.42	QC771	Diamagnetism	539.725	Q172.5.S95	Symmetry
538.6	QC718.5.M36	Magnetohydrodynamics	539.725	QC174.17.S9	Symmetry (Physics)
538.6	QC809.M3	Magnetohydrodynamics	539.725	QC794.6.E9	Spin excitations
538.7	QC811-849	Geomagnetism	539.725	QC793.3.S9	Symmetry (Physics)
538.7	QC809.M25	Cosmic magnetic fields	539.725	QC795.8.E5	Energy levels (Quantum mechanics)
538.70223	QC822	Geomagnetism—Maps			
538.727	QE501.4.P35	Paleomagnetism	539.73	QC787.E39	Electron accelerators
538.744	QC835	Magnetic storms	539.73	QC787.P3	Particle accelerators
538.748	QC845	Earth currents	539.73	QC793.3.B4	Particle beams
538.766	QC809.V3	Van Allen radiation belts	539.73	TK9340	Particle accelerators
538.766	QC809.M35	Magnetosphere	539.732	QC787.E4	Electrostatic accelerators
538.768	QC970-972.5	Auroras	539.733	QC787.L5	Linear accelerators
538.79	QC818	Geomagnetic observatories	539.735	QC787.S9	Synchrotrons
539.14	QC173.4.A87	Atomic structure	539.736	QC787.S83	Superconducting Super Collider
539.2	QC665.T7	Electromagnetic waves—Transmission			
539.2	QC665.E4	Electromagnetic fields	539.74	QC793.3.S8	Nuclear structure
539.2	QC665.D5	Electromagnetic waves—Diffraction	539.75	QC794	Annihilation reactions
			539.752	QC795.8.H3	Half-life (Nuclear physics)
539.2	QC474-492	Radiation	539.752	QC795.8.D4	Decay schemes (Radioactivity)
539.2	QC476.S6	Radiation sources			
539.6	QC173	Molecules	539.752	QC794.95-798	Radioactivity
539.6	QC179	Molecules	539.752	QC793.3.D4	Decay schemes (Radioactivity)
539.7	QC173	Atoms			
539.7	QC770-798	Nuclear physics	539.7544	QC794.8.W4	Weak interactions (Nuclear physics)
539.7	QC791.9-792.8	Nuclear energy			
539.72	QC793-.5	Particles (Nuclear physics)	539.7546	QC794.8.E4	Electromagnetic interactions
539.721	QC793.5.F42-.F429	Fermions	539.756	QC794.8.P4	Photonuclear reactions
			539.757	QC794.6.C6	Collisions (Nuclear physics)
539.7211	QC793.5.L42-.L429	Leptons (Nuclear physics)	539.758	QC794.6.S3	Scattering amplitude (Nuclear physics)

Dewey	LC	Subject Heading	Dewey	LC	Subject Heading
539.758	QC794.6.S3	Scattering (Physics)	541.372	QD565	Electrolytes—Conductivity
539.762	QC789.7-790.8	Nuclear fission	541.372	QD117.E45	Electrophoresis
539.764	QC790.95-791.8	Nuclear fusion	541.372	QD272.E43	Electrophoresis
539.764	QC791.7-.775	Controlled fusion	541.372	QD79.E44	Electrophoresis
539.77	QC787.C6	Neutron counters	541.3722	QD562.I65	Dissociation
539.77	QC787.C6	Nuclear counters	541.3722	QD561-562	Ionization
539.770284	QC785.5-787	Radioactivity—Instruments	541.3723	QD562.I63	Ion exchange
539.772	QC787.I6	Ionization chambers	541.3724	QD571-572	Electrodes
539.774	QC787.G4	Geiger-Muller counters	541.38	QD601-608	Radiochemistry
539.775	QC787.S34	Scintillation counters	541.38	QD601-608	Nuclear chemistry
540	QD	Chemistry	541.382	QD625-655	Radiation chemistry
540.112	QD23.3-26.5	Alchemy	541.388	QD466.5	Isotopes
540.112	QD13	Alchemy	541.39	QD501-505.5	Chemical reaction, Conditions and law of
540.14	QD7	Chemistry—Nomenclature			
540.3	QD4-5	Chemistry—Dictionaries	541.392	QD503	Phase rule and equilibrium
540.6	QD1	Chemistry—Societies, etc.	541.393	QD63.O9	Electrolytic oxidation
540.71	QD40-49	Chemistry—Study and teaching	541.393	QD63.R4	Electrolytic reduction
			541.393	QD63.R4	Reduction (Chemistry)
540.72	QD51-64	Chemical laboratories	541.395	QD505	Catalysis
540.724	QD43	Chemistry—Experiments	541.395	QD505	Phase-transfer catalysts
540.9	QD11-18	Chemistry—History	542	QD535	Dewar flasks
540.92	QD21-22	Chemists	542	QD53-54	Chemical apparatus
541	QD450-801	Chemistry, Physical and theoretical	542	QD54.C4	Centrifuges
			542.4	QD63.D6	Distillation
541.0421	QD478	Organic solid state chemistry	542.4	QD87	Blowpipe
541.0421	QD478	Solid state chemistry	542.6	QD63.F5	Filters and filtration
541.0424	QD581	Plasma chemistry	543	QD71-142	Chemistry, Analytic
541.06	QD450	Chemistry, Physical and theoretical—Societies, etc.	543.005	QD71	Chemistry, Analytic—Periodicals
541.2	QD461	Molecular theory	543.0858	QC450-467	Spectrum analysis
541.2	QD461	Atomic theory	543.0871	QC115-116	Electrochemical analysis
541.22	QD461	Molecular structure	543.0896	QD79.C45	Gas chromatography
541.222	QD463-464	Molecular weights	544	QD81-98	Chemistry, Analytic—Qualitative
541.224	QD471	Radicals (Chemistry)			
541.224	QD471	Free radicals (Chemistry)	544.2	QD79.T38	Thermal analysis
541.224	QP527	Free radicals (Chemistry)	544.6	QD95-96	Spectrum analysis
541.224	RB170	Free radicals (Chemicals)	545	QD101-117	Chemistry, Analytic—Quantitative
541.2252	QD471	Tautomerism			
541.24	QD467	Periodic law	545.2	QD111	Volumetric analysis
541.242	QD463-464	Atomic weights	545.4	QD117.T4	Thermal analysis
541.242	QD466	Atomic mass	545.896	QD117.C515	Gas chromatography
541.28	QD462-464	Quantum chemistry	546	QD146-197	Chemistry, Inorganic
541.33	QD506-509	Surface chemistry	546.06	QD146	Chemistry, Inorganic—Societies, etc.
541.34	QD541-543	Activity coefficients			
541.34	QD541-549	Solution (Chemistry)	546.2	QD181.H1	Hydrogen
541.3415	QD543	Osmosis	546.212	QD181.H1	Deuterium
541.342	QD543	Solubility	546.22	GB855	Water chemistry
541.35	QD701-731	Photochemistry	546.22	QD169.W3	Water
541.36	QD510-536	Thermochemistry	546.22	QD142	Water—Analysis
541.361	QD516	Combustion	546.24	QD167	Inorganic acids
541.361	QD516	Explosions	546.3	QD171-172	Metals
541.361	QD516	Flame	546.34	QD189-193	Salts
541.364	QD517	Dissociation	546.343	QD191	Double salts
541.3686	QD515	Cryochemistry	546.38	QD172.A4	Alkalies
541.3686072	QD536	Low temperature research	546.41	QD172.R2	Earths, Rare
541.37	QD551-575	Electrochemistry	546.41	QD172.R2	Rare earth metals
541.37	QD273	Electrochemistry	546.431	QD181.U7	Uranium
541.372	QC541-543	Electrolytes	546.6	QD172.T6	Transition metal compounds
541.372	QD549	Electrolytes	546.621	QE391.I7	Iron
541.372	QD553-585	Electrolytes	546.663	QD181.H6	Mercury
541.372	QD561-562	Ions	546.678	QD181.T7	Thallium

Dewey	LC	Subject Heading	Dewey	LC	Subject Heading
546.6812	QD181.C1	Carbon dioxide	549.528	QE364.2.R3	Radioactive substances
546.7	QD161-169	Nonmetals	549.62	QE391.T6	Topaz
546.711	QD181.N1	Nitrogen	549.62	QE391.G37	Garnet
546.712	QD181.P1	Phosphorus	549.68	QE394.07	Opals
546.716	QD181.S3	Antimony	549.68	QE391.Q2	Quartz
546.721	QD181.01	Oxygen	549.68	QE391.F3	Feldspar
546.721	QD181.01	Active oxygen	549.72	QE394.T8	Turquoise
546.73	QD165	Halogen compounds	549.72	QE389.64	Phosphate minerals
546.731	QD181.F1	Fluorine	549.74	QE390.2.T85	Tungsten ores
546.734	QD181.I1	Iodine	549.782	QE391.D6	Dolomite
546.751	QD181.H4	Helium	550	QC801-809	Cosmic physics
546.752	QD181.N5	Neon	550	QE500-511.7	Geophysics
546.755	QD181.X1	Xenon	550	QC801-809	Geophysics
546.756	QD181.R2	Radon	550.284	QE49.5	Earth science instruments
547	QD241-441	Chemistry, Organic	551	QE	Geology
547.005	QD241	Chemistry, Organic—	551	QE28.2	Physical geology
		Periodicals	551.014	QE7	Geology—Terminology
547.05	QD410-412.5	Organometallic compounds	551.0223	QE36	Geology—Maps
547.2	QD262	Organic compounds—	551.0228	QE43	Geological modeling
		Synthesis	551.0285	QE48.8	Geology—Computer
547.23	QD281.R4	Electrolytic reduction			programs
547.23	QD281.09	Oxidation	551.06	QE1	Geology—Societies, etc.
547.23	QD281.09	Electrolytic oxidation	551.071	QE40-48	Geology—Study and
547.28	QD341	Condensation products			teaching
		(Chemistry)	551.0723	QE61-350	Surveys
547.28	QD281.P6	Polymerization	551.0723	QE61-350.62	Geological surveys
547.28	QD281.P6	Addition polymerization	551.074	QE51	Geological museums
547.41	QD305.H5-.H9	Hydrocarbons	551.09	QE11-13	Geology—History
547.413	QD305.H8	Acetylene compounds	551.09	QE28.3	Historical geology
547.413	QD305.H8	Acetylene	551.092	QE21-22	Geologists
547.59	QD399-406	Heterocyclic compounds	551.11	QE509	Earth—Internal structure
547.6	QD330-341	Aromatic compounds	551.12	QE509	Earth temperature
547.61	QD341.H9	Hydrocarbons	551.136	QE511.7	Sea-floor spreading
547.611	QD341.H9	Benzene	551.(2-3)	QE500-639.5	Geodynamics
547.62	QD412	Halogen compounds	551.21	QE521.5-527.5	Volcanoes
547.632	QD341.P5	Phenols	551.22	QE531-541	Seismology
547.7	QD380-388	Polymers	551.22	QE531-541	Earthquakes
547.72	QD421-.7	Alkaloids	551.22	QE539	Elastic waves
547.75	QD431-.7	Proteins	551.220287	QE541	Seismometry
547.75	QD431-.7	Amino acids	551.23	GB1198.5-.8	Geysers
547.756	QD431-.7	Peptides	551.23	GB1198-.4	Hot springs
547.78	QD320-327	Carbohydrates	551.23	QE545	Volcanic gases
547.781	QD320-327	Sugars	551.23	QE528	Hot springs
547.7813	QD321	Glucose	551.302	QE570	Weathering
547.7813	QD321	Dextrose	551.302	QE571-597	Erosion
547.7813	QD321	Fructose	551.303	QE571-597	Sedimentation and
547.8434	QD419-.7	Gums and resins			deposition
548	QD901-999	Crystallography	551.307	QE599	Landslides
548.5	QD921-926	Crystal growth	551.307	QE599	Rockslides
548.5	QD901-999	Crystallization	551.307	QC929.A8	Avalanches
548.7	QD911-919	Lattice theory	551.307	QE599	Debris avalanches
548.7	QD911-919	Crystallography,	551.307	QE598-600.3	Earth movements
		Mathematical	551.307	QE598-600.3	Mass-wasting
548.842	QD945	Dislocations in crystals	551.31	GB2401-2597	Ice
549	QE351-399.2	Mineralogy	551.31	GB2401-2598	Ice sheets
549.012	QE388	Minerals—Classification	551.31028	GB2401.72.A37	Aerial photography in
549.05	QE351	Mineralogy—Periodicals			glaciology
549.1	QE367-369	Mineralogy, Determinative	551.312	GB2401-2598	Glaciers
549.13	QE371	Mineralogical chemistry	551.312	GB641-648	Rock glaciers
549.2	QE389.1	Native element minerals	551.313	QE575-579	Glacial erosion
549.4	QE389.4	Halide minerals	551.315	GB581-588	Glacial landforms

Dewey	LC	Subject Heading	Dewey	LC	Subject Heading
551.342	GB2401-2597	Icebergs	551.4609	GC96-97.8	Estuaries
551.343	GB2401-2598	Sea ice drift	551.461	GC481-711	Oceanography—Atlantic Ocean
551.353	TC175.2	Sediment transport	551.465	GC771-871	Oceanography—Pacific Ocean
551.372	QE597	Wind erosion			
551.375	GB649.S3	Sand waves	551.467	GC721-761	Oceanography—Indian Ocean
551.375	GB631-638	Sand dunes			
551.38	QC929.H6	Frost	551.468	GC401-455	Oceanography—Arctic Ocean
551.397	QB754.8-759	Meteorite craters			
551.41	GB621-628	Swamps	551.469	GC461-462	Oceanography—Antarctic Ocean
551.41	GB400-649	Geomorphology			
551.41	GB400-649	Landforms	551.47	GC228.5-.6	Ocean circulation
551.41	GB621-628	Bogs	551.4701	GC296.G9	Gulf Stream
551.41028	GB400.42.A35	Aerial photography in geomorphology	551.4701	GC296.8.E	El Nino Current
			551.4701	GC229-299	Ocean currents
551.415	GB611-618	Arid regions	551.4702	GC205-226	Ocean waves
551.415	GB611-618	Deserts	551.4702	GC211-222	Waves
551.415	GB611-618	Desertification—Control	551.47022	GC225-226	Storm surges
551.415	GB611-618	Desertification	551.4708	GC300-376	Tides
551.42	GB471-478	Islands	551.4708	GC308-309	Tidal currents
551.424	GB461-468	Reefs	551.4708	GC376	Bores (Tidal phenomena)
551.424	GB461-468	Coral reefs and islands	551.4708	QC883.2.A8	Atmospheric tides
551.424	QE565-566	Coral reefs and islands	551.48	GB651-2998	Water-supply
551.43	GB448	Slopes (Physical geography)	551.48	GB651-2998	Hydrology
551.432	GB501-555	Mountains	551.48	GB651-2998	Water
551.434	GB571-578	Mesas	551.48028	GB656.2.A37	Aerial photography in hydrology
551.434	GB571-578	Plateaus			
551.44	GB454.F5	Fjords	551.482	GB2201-2398	Lagoons
551.44	GB454.I54	Inlets	551.482	GB1601-1798.9	Lakes
551.442	GB561-568	Arroyos	551.483	GB1201-1399.5	Rivers
551.442	GB561-568	Valleys	551.483	GB1207	Streamflow
551.442	GB561-568	Floodplains	551.4830287	GB1201-1398	Stream measurements
551.447	GB599-609.2	Karst	551.484	GB1401-1597	Waterfalls
551.447	GB601-608	Caves	551.489	GB1203	Flood routing
551.447	GB609.2	Sinkholes	551.489	GB1399-.5	Floods
551.45	GB561-568	Watersheds	551.4890112	GB1399.2	Flood forecasting
551.453	GB561-568	Savannas	551.49	GB1001-1199.8	Groundwater
551.453	GB571-578	Plains	551.498	GB1198-.4	Springs
551.453	GB591-598	Alluvial plains	551.5	QC883-.2	Weather, Influence of the moon on
551.453	GB571-578	Prairies			
551.453	GB571-578	Steppes	551.5	QC851-999	Meteorology
551.456	GB591-598	Deltas	551.5	QC851-999	Atmosphere
551.458	GB451-460	Seashore	551.5014	QC854.2	Meteorology—Terminology
551.46	GC	Oceanography	551.50284	QC880	Densitometer (Meteorological instrument)
551.46	VK	Hydrography			
551.4601	GC160-177	Ocean temperature	551.50284	QC875.5-876.7	Meteorological instruments
551.4601	GC121-127	Salinity	551.505	QC851	Meteorology—Periodicals
551.4601	GC109-149	Chemical oceanography	551.509	QC855-857	Meteorology—History
551.4601	GC175	Deep-sea temperature	551.5092	QC858	Meteorologists—Biography
551.4601	GC100-103	Seawater	551.51	QC973.4.R35	Atmospheric radio refractivity
551.460284	GC41	Oceanographic instruments	551.511	QC879.6-.85	Atmospheric chemistry
551.4607	GC65-78	Underwater exploration	551.5113	QC882.5	Dust
551.4607	VK588-597	Hydrographic surveying	551.513	QC881.2.T75	Troposphere
551.46072	GC66	Manned undersea research stations	551.514	QC973.4.M33	Magnetospheric radio wave propagation
551.46072	GC57-59	Oceanography—Research	551.514	QC879	Atmosphere, Upper— Radiosonde observations
551.4608	GC87.6	Submarine trenches			
551.4608	QE39	Submarine geology	551.514	QC879-.59	Atmosphere, Upper
551.46083	GC380-399	Marine sediments	551.5142	QC881.2.O9	Ozone layer
551.46083	GC87-.6	Ocean bottom	551.5145	QC881.2.I6	Ionosphere
551.46084	GC83-87.6	Submarine topography	551.5145	QC881.2.E2	E region
551.4609	GC96-97.8	Estuarine oceanography			

Dewey	LC	Subject Heading	Dewey	LC	Subject Heading
551.5145	QC879	F region	551.5771	QC926.5-.57	Acid precipitation (Meteorology)
551.517	QC880.4.A8	Atmospheric circulation			
551.518	QC930.5-959	Winds	551.5773	QC929.2-.28	Droughts
551.518	QC935	Winds aloft	551.5784	QC929.S7	Snow
551.5183	QC935	Jet stream	551.5787	QC929.H15	Hail
551.5183	QC939.T7	Trade winds	551.6	QC980-999	Weather
551.5184	QC939.M7	Monsoons	551.6	QC851-999	Climatology
551.5185	QC939.L37	Sea breeze	551.605	QC980	Weather—Periodicals
551.5185	QC939.M8	Mountain wave	551.63	QC875	Automatic meteorological stations
551.52	QC880.4.T5	Atmospheric thermodynamics	551.63	QC875	Meteorological stations
551.5246	GC190-.5	Ocean-atmosphere interation	551.63	QC994.95-999	Weather forecasting
551.525	QC901-912.2	Atmospheric temperature	551.632	QC877.5	Television weathercasting
551.5271	QC910.2-911.82	Solar radiation	551.632	QC877.5	Weather broadcasting
551.5271	QC910.2-913.2	Sunshine	551.632	QC877.5	Weather reporting, Radio
551.5272	QC809.T4	Terrestrial radiation	551.633	QC996.5	Statistical weather forecasting
551.5273	QC912.3	Atmospheric radiation			
551.5276	QC913-.2	Atmospheric radioactivity	551.634	QC996	Numerical weather forecasting
551.5276	QC883.2.S6	Cosmic physics			
551.54	QC885-896	Atmospheric pressure	551.635	QC972.6-973.8	Radio meteorology
551.540284	QC886-887	Barometers	551.6353	QC973.45-.8	Radar meteorology
551.55	QC940.6-959	Storms	551.6353	QC973.8.W	Weather radar networks
551.55	QC880.4.T8	Atmospheric turbulence	551.6362	QC997.75	Nowcasting (Meteorology)
551.55	QC880.4.S65	Squalls	551.6365	QC999	Almanacs
551.55	QC880.4.S65	Squall lines	551.6365	QC997	Long-range weather forecasting
551.5512	QC880.4.A5	Air masses			
551.5512	QC880.4.F7	Fronts (Meteorology)	551.6418	QC931	Wind forecasting
551.5512	QC880.4.F7	Occluded fronts (Meteorology)	551.64513	QC951	Cyclone forecasting
			551.65162	QC993.83-994.9	Marine meteorology
551.5512	QC981.8.A5	Cold waves (Meteorology)	551.66	QC883.7-.86	Micrometeorology
551.5513	QC940.6-959	Cyclones	551.68	QC926.6-928.74	Weather control
551.552	QC944-948	Hurricanes	551.68	QC948	Typhoon modification
551.552	QC948	Typhoons	551.68	QC928.6	Rain-making
551.553	QC957	Waterspouts	551.69	QC884-.2	Paleoclimatology
551.553	QC955-.5	Tornadoes	551.6913	QC993.5	Tropics—Climate
551.554	QC968-.2	Thunderstorms	551.69143	QC993.6	Mountain climate
551.554	QC929.H15	Hailstorms	551.69154	QC993.7	Arid regions climate
551.559	QC958-959	Dust storms	551.691732	QC981.7.U7	Urban climatology
551.56	QC974.5-976	Meteorological optics	551.694	QC989	Europe—Climate
551.561	QC966.7.A84	Atmospheric ionization	551.695	QC990	Asia—Climate
551.563	QC960.5-969	Atmospheric electricity	551.696	QC991	Africa—Climate
551.5632	QC966-.7	Lightning	551.6971	QC985-.5	Canada—Climate
551.567	QC976.R2	Rainbow	551.6972	QC986	Mexico—Climate
551.57	GB2801-2998	Hydrometeorology	551.69729	QC987	West Indies—Climate
551.57	QC915	Moisture index	551.6973	QC983-984	United States—Climate
551.57	QC920	Water	551.698	QC988	South America—Climate
551.57	QC915-929	Moisture	551.6994	QC992	Australia—Climate
551.571	QC915-917	Humidity	551.7	QE501.4.P3	Paleogeography
551.572	QC915-917	Evaporation (Meteorology)	551.7	QE640-699	Geology, Stratigraphic
551.572	QC915.5-.7	Evapotranspiration	551.701	QE508	Radioactive dating
551.574	QC921.6.C6	Condensation (Meteorology)	551.701	QE508	Geological time
551.5741	QC921.6.C6	Atmospheric nucleation	551.701	QE508	Earth—Age
551.5744	QC929.D5	Dew	551.72	QE654-674	Geology, Stratigraphic—Paleozoic
551.575	QC929.F7	Ice fog			
551.575	QC929.F7	Fog	551.76	QE675-688	Geology, Stratigraphic—Mesozoic
551.576	QC920.7-924	Clouds			
551.577	QC929	Precipitation (Meteorology)	551.78	QE690-699	Geology, Stratigraphic—Cenozoic
551.577	QC924.5-926.2	Rain and rainfall			
551.5770284	QC926	Rain gauges	551.792	QE697-698	Glacial epoch
551.5770284	QC926	Precipitation gauges	551.8	QE604	Rock deformation
			551.8	QE511.4-.48	Plate tectonics

Dewey	LC	Subject Heading	Dewey	LC	Subject Heading
551.872	QE606-.5	Faults (Geology)	560.172	QE725-730	Paleontology—Paleozoic
551.875	QE606-.5	Folds (Geology)	560.1723	QE726	Paleontology—Cambrian
551.88	QE611-.5	Dikes (Geology)	560.174	QE728	Paleontology—Devonian
551.88	QE611-.5	Veins (Geology)	560.176	QE731-734	Paleontology—Mesozoic
551.88	QE611-.5	Intrusions (Geology)	560.1766	QE733	Paleontology—Jurassic
551.88	QE611-.5	Necks (Geology)	560.177	QE734	Paleontology—Cretaceous
551.9	QE514-516.5	Geochemistry	560.178	QE735-741.3	Paleontology—Cenozoic
552	QB420-499	Petrology	560.1784	QE737	Paleontology—Eocene
552	QE420-499	Rocks	560.1785	QE738	Paleontology—Oligocene
552	QE420-499	Petrology	560.1787	QE739	Paleontology—Miocene
552.005	QE420	Petrology—Periodicals	560.5	QE701	Paleontology—Periodicals
552.0094	QE451	Petrology—Europe	560.75	QE718	Fossils—Collection and
552.0095	QE452	Petrology—Asia			preservation
552.0096	QE453	Petrology—Africa	560.94	QE753-755	Paleontology—Europe
552.00971	QE445.5-446	Petrology—Canada	560.95	QE756	Paleontology—Asia
552.00972	QE446.5-.6	Petrology—Mexico	560.96	QE757	Paleontology—Africa
552.009728	QE447	Petrology—Central America	560.971	QE748	Paleontology—Canada
552.009729	QE448	Petrology—West Indies	560.972	QE749	Paleontology—Mexico
552.00973	QE444-445	Petrology—United States	560.9728	QE751	Paleontology—Central
552.0098	QE449	Petrology—South America			America
552.00993	QE454.5-.6	Petrology—New Zealand	560.9729	QE750	Paleontology—West Indies
552.00994	QE453.5-454	Petrology—Australia	560.973	QE746-747	Paleontology—United States
552.0099(5-6)	QE455	Petrology—Oceania	560.98	QE752	Paleontology—South America
552.09981	QE456	Petrology—Arctic regions	560.994	QE758	Paleontology—Australia
552.09989	QE456.5	Petrology—Antarctic regions	560.9981	QE744	Paleontology—Arctic regions
552.1	QE461-462	Rocks, Igneous	560.9989	QE760	Paleontology—Antarctic
552.22	QE461	Lava			regions
552.23	QE461-462	Volcanic ash, tuff, etc.	561	QE980-983	Angiosperms, Fossil
552.3	QE462.G7	Granite	561.16	QE991	Petrified forests
552.3	QE462.D56	Diorite	561.194	QE943-945	Paleobotany—Europe
552.4	QE475	Rocks, Metamorphic	561.195	QE946	Paleobotany—Asia
552.4	QE475.A2	Metamorphism (Geology)	561.196	QE947	Paleobotany—Africa
552.5	QE471-.15	Rocks, Sedimentary	561.1971	QE938	Paleobotany—Canada
552.5	QE471.15.S25	Sandstone	561.1972	QE939	Paleobotany—Mexico
552.5	QE471-.15	Sedimentology	561.19728	QE941	Paleobotany—Central
552.5	QE471.15.S5	Shale			America
552.5	QE471.3	Clay	561.19729	QE940	Paleobotany—West Indies
552.5	QE472	Sedimentary structures	561.1973	QE936-937	Paleobotany—United States
552.58	QE471.15.D6	Dolomite	561.198	QE942	Paleobotany—South America
552.58	QE471.15.C3	Rocks, Carbonate	561.1993	QE948.2	Paleobotany—New Zealand
553	TN260	Geology, Economic	561.1994	QE948	Paleobotany—Australia
554	QE260-288	Geology—Europe	561.199(5-6)	QE949	Paleobotany—Oceania
555	QE289-319	Geology—Asia	561.1998(1-8)	QE934	Paleobotany—Arctic regions
556	QE320-339	Geology—Africa	561.19989	QE950	Paleobotany—Antarctic
557	QE71-217	Geology—North America			regions
557.1	QE185-199	Geology—Canada	561.3	QE983	Dicetyledons, Fossil
557.2	QE201-203	Geology—Mexico	561.5	QE975-978	Gymnosperms, Fossil
557.28	QE210-217	Geology—Central America	562	QE770-832	Invertebrates, Fossil
557.29	QE220-226	Geology—West Indies	565	QE815-832	Arthropoda, Fossil
557.3	QE72-182	Geology—United States	566	QE841-899	Vertebrates, Fossil
557.(4-9)	QE81-182	Geology—[United States,	567.9	P96.M6	Dinosaurs in mass media
		By state]	567.9	QE862.D5	Dinosaurs
558	QE230-251	Geology—South America	569	QE881-882	Mammals, Fossil
559.4	QE340-348	Geology—Australia	569	QL707	Extinct mammals
559.81	QE70	Geology—Arctic regions	569.5	QE882.C5	Dolphins, Fossil
559.82	QE70	Geology—Arctic regions	569.8	QE882.P7	Primates, Fossil
559.89	QE350	Geology—Antartica	569.9	GN284.6	Java man
560	QL88-.15	Extinct animals	569.9	GN283.9	Homo habilis
560	QE701-996.5	Paleontology	569.9	GN284-.7	Homo erectus
560	QE760.8-899.2	Animals, Fossil	569.9	GN284.4	Solo man
560.171	QE724	Paleontology—Precambrian	569.9	GN282-286.7	Fossil man

Dewey	LC	Subject Heading	Dewey	LC	Subject Heading
569.9	GN284.7	Peking man	571.6072	QH583-.2	Cytology—Research
569.9	GN285	Neanderthals	571.629	QR77.35	Bacteria cell surfaces
569.9	GN307-499	Man, Primitive	571.63435	QH657	Gravity
569.9	GN700-890	Man, Prehistoric	571.6345	QH652-.7	Cells—Effect of radiation on
569.9	GN785-786	Lake-dwellers and lake-dwellings	571.63455	QH651	Light—Physiological effect
			571.638	QH585.2-.45	Cell culture
569.9	GN799.W66	Women, Prehistoric	571.64	QH509	Biological transport
569.9	GN282.5	Missing link	571.64	QH601-602	Cell membranes
570	QH301-705	Biology	571.658	QH603.R5	Ribosomes
570.1	QH325-349	Life (Biology)	571.66	QH595	Cell nuclei
570.1	QH331	Biology—Philosophy	571.672	QR78	Flagella (Microbiology)
570.1	QP81-87	Life (Biology)	571.7	QH508	Biological control systems
570.151	QH323.5	Biomathematics	571.7236	QK725	Plant cells and tissues
570.228	QH324.8	Biological models	571.7236	QK725	Plant cell development
570.282	QH201-278.5	Microscopy	571.72366	QK725	Plant chromosomes
570.282	QH211-212	Microscopes	571.742	QK898.H67	Plant hormones
570.2825	QH212.E4	Electron microscopy	571.75	QP90.4	Homeostasis
570.2825	QH212.E4	Electron microscopes	571.77	QH527	Biological rhythms
570.2827	QH236.2	Freeze fracturing	571.77	QP84.6	Biological rhythms
570.2827	QH237	Stains and staining (Microscopy)	571.77	QP84.6	Sleep-wake cycle
			571.772	QK761	Biological rhythms in plants
570.284	QH324	Biological apparatus and supplies	571.782	QK761	Dormancy in plants
			571.8	QH511	Growth
570.285	QH324.2	Biology—Data processing	571.8	QH471-489	Reproduction
570.71	QH315-320	Biology—Study and teaching	571.82	QK731-745	Growth (Plants)
			571.835	QH607	Cell differentiation
570.72	QH321-323.2	Biological laboratories	571.844	QH605-.3	Cell division
570.72	QH315-320	Biology—Research	571.844	QH605.2	Mitosis
570.9	QH305-.2	Biology—History	571.845	QH605	Meiosis
570.92	QH26-31	Biologists	571.845	QK658	Pollen
571	QP	Physiology	571.847	QK929	Spores (Botany)—Dispersal
571.014	QP13	Physiology—Terminology	571.86	QL951-991	Embryology
571.0284	QP55	Physiological apparatus	571.860724	QL961	Embryology, Experimental
571.05	QP1	Physiology—Periodicals	571.862	QK740	Germination
571.071	QP39-47	Physiology—Study and teaching	571.864	QH485	Fertilization (Biology)
			571.8642	QK926	Pollination
571.0919	QH327-328	Space biology	571.8642	QK828	Fertilization of plants
571.1	QP31-33	Physiology, Comparative	571.8642	QK926	Fertilization of plants by insects
571.3	QH351	Morphology			
571.3	QL799-.5	Morphology (Animals)	571.876	QL981	Metamorphosis
571.3	QL801-950.9	Anatomy, Comparative	571.884	QH489	Generations, Alterating
571.4	QH505	Biophysics	571.889	QH499	Regeneration (Biology)
571.43	QH513	Biomechanics	571.8892	QK840	Regeneration (Botany)
571.435	QP82.2.G7	Gravity	571.89	QH475-479	Reproduction, Asexual
571.437	QP82.2.P7	Atmospheric pressure—Physiological effect	571.9	RB113	Physiology, Pathological
			571.936	QH671	Death
571.444	QP82.2.N6	Noise—Physiological effect	571.9379	RB131-.5	Suppuration
571.45	QP82.2.N64	Nonionizing radiation	571.939	QH671	Cell death
571.464	QP82.2.C6	Cold—Physiological effect	571.939	QP87	Death
571.4645	QH324.9.C7	Cryobiology	571.96	QR180-189.5	Immunology
571.49	QP82.2.C5	Weather—Physiological effect	571.96	QR185.2	Natural immunity
			571.960724	QR180-183.5	Experimental immunology
571.49	QP82.2.P6	Pollution—Physiological effect	571.964	QR186-.3	Immune response
			571.9644	QR187.5	Interferon
571.49	QP82.2.A4	Altitude, Influence of	571.9644	QR187.5	Interferon inducers
571.49	QP801.P38	Pesticides—Physiological effect	571.9645	QR186.5-.6	Antigens
			571.9648	QR184-.4	Immunogenetics
571.5	QL807	Histology	571.966	QR185.8.T2	T cells
571.6	QH573-671	Cells	571.9677	QR187-.3	Antigen-antibody reactions
571.6	QH573-671	Cytology	571.972	QR188	Allergy
571.6	QH631-647	Cell physiology	571.973	QR186.82-.83	Autoantibodies

Dewey	LC	Subject Heading	Dewey	LC	Subject Heading
571.973	QR188.3	Autoimmunity	572.8	QH506	Molecular biology
571.974	QR188.35	Immunodeficiency	572.8	QP620-625	Nucleic acids
571.992	QR201.E75	Epstein-Barr virus diseases	572.82	QK728	Plant molecular biology
571.992445	QR201.P26	Papillomavirus diseases	572.86	QH447-.8	Genes
571.99247	QR201.P33	Parvovirus infections	572.86	QH447	Genomes
571.992562	QR201.A72	Arbovirus infections	572.86	QP619.D53	DNA Ligases
571.993	QR201.B34	Bacterial diseases	572.86	QP616.D56	DNA topoisomerase II
571.99327	QR353.5.R4	Rickettsia	572.86	QP616.D56	DNA topoisomerase I
571.99353	QR201.S68	Staphylococcal infections	572.86	QP624-.75	DNA
571.995	QR245-248	Pathogenic fungi	572.8633	QH445.2	Gene mapping
572	QD415-436	Biochemistry	572.8633	QP625.N89	Nucleotide sequence
572	QH345	Biochemistry	572.865	QH450-.6	Genetic regulation
572	QH613	Histochemistry	572.877	QH443-450.6	Genetic recombination
572	QP501-801	Biochemistry	572.88	QP623.5.M47	Messenger RNA
572	QP550-801	Bioorganic chemistry	572.88	QP623-.5	RNA
572.2	QK861-899	Botanical chemistry	572.8845	QH450.2	Genetic transcription
572.4	QH521	Metabolism	572.886	QP623.5.T73	Transfer RNA
572.4	QH634.5	Cell metabolism	573.1	QL835-841	Cardiovascular system
572.42	QK881-897	Plants—Metabolism	573.1555	QL868	Spleen
572.42	QK867-898	Plants—Nutrition	573.16	QL841	Lymphatics
572.435	QP517.P45	Photobiochemistry	573.17	QL838	Heart—Anatomy
572.4358	QH641	Bioluminescence	573.18	QL835	Blood-vessels
572.437	QH517	Electrophysiology	573.185	QL835	Arteries
572.437	QP341	Electrophysiology	573.186	QL835	Veins
572.4372	QK845	Electrophysiology of plants	573.2	QL845-855	Respiratory organs
572.46	QK882	Photosnythesis	573.22	QL848	Lungs
572.47	QH633	Cell respiration	573.3	QL856-867	Digestive organs
572.472	QK891	Plants—Respiration	573.35	QL857	Mouth
572.51	QP533	Minerals in the body	573.355	QL857	Lips
572.51	QP531-535	Bioinorganic chemistry	573.356	QL858	Teeth
572.515	QP534	Trace elements in the body	573.357	QL946	Tongue
572.516	QP535.C2	Calcium	573.359	QL861	Esophagus
572.516	QP535.C2	Calcium in the body	573.36	QL862	Stomache
572.52	QP532	Metals in the body	573.37	QL863	Intestines
572.5238224	QP913.N2	Salt—Physiological effect	573.377	QL866	Pancreas
572.53	QP913.O1	Oxygen—Physiological effect	573.378	QL863	Duodenum
			573.38	QL867	Gallbladder
572.53	QP535.O1	Active oxygen in the body	573.38	QL867	Liver
572.539	QP535.H1	Water in the body	573.4	QL868	Endocrine glands
572.54	QP535.N1	Nitrogen in the body	573.4	QL868	Endocrinology, Comparative
572.548	QP801.A48	Amines in the body	573.4	QL865-868	Glands
572.56	QP701-702	Carbohydrates	573.44	QP801.H7	Hormones
572.565	QP702.S85	Sugar in the body	573.45	QL868	Pituitary gland
572.565	QP702.S85	Sugars	573.49	QL872-875	Excretory organs
572.57	QP752.F35	Fatty acids in human nutrition	573.49	QL872	Bladder
			573.49	QL872-881	Urinary organs
572.57	QP752.F35	Fatty acids	573.496	QL873	Kidneys
572.57	QP751-752	Lipids	573.5	QL941-943	Skin
572.57	QP752.E84	Essential fatty acids	573.5	QL941-943	Dermis
572.59	QP670-671	Pigments (Biology)	573.5	QP88.5	Dermis
572.592	QK898.P7	Plant pigments	573.5	QL941-943	Epidermis
572.633	QP551	Amino acid sequence	573.5	QP88.5	Epidermis
572.645	QH450.5	Genetic translation	573.58	QL942	Hair
572.65	QP561-563	Amino acids	573.59	QL942	Nails (Anatomy)
572.65	QP552.P4	Peptides	573.59	QL942	Toenails
572.65	QP572.P4	Peptide hormones	573.6	QL876-881	Generative organs
572.65	QP572.V28	Vasoactive intestinal peptides	573.65	QL878	Generative organs, Male
			573.658	QL878	Prostate
572.69	QP552.C34	Carrier proteins	573.66	QL881	Generative organs, Female
572.7	QP601-619	Enzymes	573.665	QL881	Ovaries
572.72	QK898.E58	Plant enzymes	573.667	QL881	Uterus

Dewey	LC	Subject Heading	Dewey	LC	Subject Heading
573.679	QL944	Mammary glands	577	QH540-549.5	Ecology
573.7	QL821-831	Musculoskeletal system	577	QK900-938	Plants—Habitat
573.701	B105.M65	Movement (Philosophy)	577	QH514.15.E27	Ecotones
573.75	QL831	Muscles	577.071	QH541.2-.264	Environmental education
573.76	QL821	Bones	577.14	QH343.7-344	Biogeochemistry
573.76	QL821-827	Skeleton	577.14	TD193-.5	Environmental chemistry
573.76	QM101-117	Bones	577.15	QH541.3	Biological productivity
573.78	QL825	Joints	577.18	QH353	Biological invasions
573.78356	QL827	Ligaments	577.22	QH543-.2	Bioclimatology
573.79	QL950.7	Leg	577.27	QK750-751	Plants, Effect of pollution on
573.798	QP310.F5	Animal flight	577.273	TD195.A34	Agricultural pollution
573.8	QL921-939	Nervous system	577.2752	QK751	Plants, Effect of acid
573.85	QL939	Sympathetic nervous system			precipitation on
573.85	QL939	Nerves	577.276	QK751	Plants, Effect of air
573.86	QL938.H56	Hippocampus (Brain)			pollution on
573.86	QL933-937	Meninges	577.277	QH543.5-.6	Radioecology
573.86	QL937	Cerebellum	577.3	QH541.5.F6	Forest ecology
573.86	QL933-937	Medulla oblongata	577.34	QH541.5.R27	Rain forest ecology
573.869	QL938.S6	Spinal cord	577.38	QH541.5.S55	Shrubland ecology
573.87	QL698.8	Bird navigation	577.38	QH541.5.M6	Moor ecology
573.87	QL945-949	Sense organs	577.4	QH541.5.R3	Range ecology
573.87	QL782	Animal navigation	577.4	QH541.5.P7	Grassland ecology
573.88	QL949	Eye	577.4	QH541.5.P7	Grasslands
573.88	QL949	Eyelids	577.44	QH541.5.P7	Prairie ecology
573.88	QL949	Optic nerve	577.46	QH541.5.M4	Meadow ecology
573.88	QL949	Pupil (Eye)	577.48	QH541.5.P7	Savanna ecology
573.88	QL949	Retina	577.54	QH541.5.D4	Desert ecology
573.89	QL948	Ear, External	577.55	QH541.5.R62	Roadside ecology
573.89	QL948	Middle ear	577.55	S441-482	Agricultural ecology
573.89	QL948	Eustachian tube	577.554	QH541.5.G37	Garden ecology
573.89	QL948	Ear	577.554	QH541.5.H67	Household ecology
575	QK641-707	Botany—Anatomy	577.56	HT241-243	Urban ecology
575	QK710-899	Plant physiology	577.56	QH541.5.C6	Urban ecology (Biology)
575.49	QK645-650	Shoots (Botany)	577.57	QH541.5.S6	Soil ecology
575.54	QK644	Roots (Botany)	577.583	QH541.5.S26	Sand dune ecology
575.57	QK649	Leaves	577.6	QH541.5.F7	Freshwater ecology
575.6	QK658-659	Plants, Sex in	577.6	QH541.5.W3	Aquatic ecology
575.6	QK830	Plants, Flowering of	577.63	QH541.5.L27	Lagoon ecology
575.6	QK653	Double flowers	577.63	QH541.5.L3	Lake ecology
575.6	QK830	Double flowers	577.639	QH541.5.S22	Salt lake ecology
575.6	QK825-830	Plants—Reproduction	577.64	QH541.5.S7	Stream ecology
575.6	QK827-830	Plants, Sex in	577.68	QH541.5.S9	Swamp ecology
575.633	QK653-661	Flowers—Anatomy	577.68	QH541.5.M3	Wetland ecology
575.633	QK653-661	Flowers—Morphology	577.687	QH541.5.B63	Bog ecology
575.65	QK828	Pollination	577.69	QH541.5.S35	Tide pool ecology
575.75	QK871	Plants, Motion of fluids in	577.69	QH541.5.S35	Seashore ecology
575.76	QK871	Plants—Absorption of water	577.7	QH541.5.D35	Deep-sea ecology
575.8	QK873	Evapotranspiration	577.78	QH541.5.S87	Sublittoral ecology
575.8	QK876	Gases from plants	577.786	QH541.5.E8	Estuarine ecology
576.15	QR100-130	Microbial ecology	577.789	QH541.5.C7	Coral reef ecology
576.5	QH426-470	Genetics	577.83	QK911	Plant competition
576.54	QH401-411	Variation (Biology)	577.83	QH546.3	Competition (Biology)
576.549	QH465-.5	Mutagens	577.852	QH548.3	Mutualism (Biology)
576.549	QH460-468	Mutation (Biology)	577.88	QH352	Population biology
576.58	QH455	Population genetics	578.09	QH84-198	Biogeography
576.8	QH359-425	Evolution (Biology)	578.09(4-9)	QH101-199	Natural history—[By region
576.82	QH375	Natural selection			or country]
576.83	QH325	Spontaneous generation	578.094	QH135-178	Natural history—Europe
576.84	QE721.2.E97	Extinction (Biology)	578.095	QH179-193	Natural history—Asia
576.84	QH78	Extinction (Biology)	578.096	QH194-195	Natural history—Africa
576.87	QH372	Coevolution	578.0971	QH106-.2	Natural history—Canada

Dewey	LC	Subject Heading	Dewey	LC	Subject Heading
578.0972	QH107	Natural history—Mexico	579.2562	QR398	Arboviruses
578.09728	QH108	Natural history—Central America	579.2569	QR414.5-.6	Retroviruses
			579.2569	QR372.058	Oncogenic DNA viruses
578.09729	QH109	Natural history—West Indies	579.26	QR342-.2	Bacteriophages
578.0973	QH104-105	Natural history—United States	579.27	QR343	Fungal viruses
			579.28	QR351	Plant viruses
578.098	QH111-130	Natural history—South America	579.3	QR75-99.5	Bacteria
			579.3	QR201	Pathogenic bacteria
578.0994	QH197	Natural history—Australia	579.3	QR	Bacteriology
578.4	QH546	Adaptation (Biology)	579.3028	QR65-69	Bacteriology—Technique
578.4	QP82-.2	Adaptation (Physiology)	579.3072	QR64-.8	Bacteriological laboratories
578.42	QH543.2	Acclimatization	579.3138	QR81.7	Bacteria—Evolution
578.42	QH544	Phenology	579.3149	QR89.5	Anaerobic bacteria
578.68	QH75-77	Endangered species	579.31755	QR111	Bacteriology, Agricultural
578.68	QL81.5-84.77	Endangered species	579.31755	QR351	Bacteriology, Agricultural
578.738	QH87.5	Moors and heaths	579.332	QR82.P78	Pseudomonas
578.748	QH87.7	Savannas	579.355	QR82.S78	Streptococcus
578.754	QH88	Deserts	579.362	QR82.B3	Bacillus (Bacteria)
578.754	QH88	Desert biology	579.4	QL366-369.2	Protozoa
578.757	QH84.8	Soil biology	579.432	QL368.A5	Amoeba
578.76	QH90-100	Aquatic biology	579.5	QK600-635	Fungi
578.76	QH96-100	Freshwater biology	579.5135	QK602	Fungi—Genetics
578.763	QH98	Lakes	579.562	QR151	Yeast
578.768	QH87.3	Wetlands	579.6	QK617	Mushrooms, Edible
578.768	QH87.3	Marshes	579.6	QK600-635	Mushrooms, Hallucinogenic
578.768	QH87.3	Swamps	579.7	QK580.7-597.7	Lichens
578.77	QH91.75	Marine parks and reserves	579.8	QK564-580.5	Algae
578.77	QH91-95.59	Marine biology	579.82	QL368.F5	Flagellata
578.77	QH95.9	Brackish water biology	579.89	QL948	Labyrinth (Ear)
578.77072	QH91.6-.65	Marine laboratories	580	QK495	Angiosperms
578.773	QH92-93.9	Marine biology—Atlantic Ocean	580	QK	Botany
			580	QK	Plants
578.774	QH95-.55	Marine biology—Pacific Ocean	580.12	QK91-97	Botany—Classification
			580.14	QK96	Botany—Nomenclature
578.775	QH94-.7	Marine biology—Indian Ocean	580.14	QK10	Botany—Terminology
			580.222	QK98	Botany—Pictorial works
578.776	QH90.8.P5	Plankton	580.223	QK63	Vegetation mapping
578.777	QH95.58	Marine biology—Antarctic Ocean	580.3	QK9	Botany—Dictionaries
			580.6	QK1	Botany—Societies, etc.
578.7789	QH95.8	Coral reef biology	580.71	QK51-57	Botany—Study and teaching
579	QR	Microbiology	580.723	QK62	Vegetation surveys
579	QR	Microorganisms	580.73	QK71-73	Botanical gardens
579.012	QR12	Microbiology—Classification	580.74	QK79-.5	Botany—Exhibitions
579.014	QR11	Microbiology—Terminology	580.74	QK75-77	Herbaria
579.0222	QR54	Microbiology—Pictorial works	580.75	QK61	Plants—Collection and preservation
579.028	QR65-69	Microbiology—Technique	580.92	QK26-31	Botanists
579.05	QR1	Microbiology—Periodicals	580.94	QK281-339	Botany—Europe
579.072	QR61-63	Microbiology—Research	580.95	QK341-379	Botany—Asia
579.09	QR21-22	Microbiology—History	580.956	QK353	Botany—Middle East
579.092	QR30-31	Microbiologists	580.959	QK360-368	Botany—Asia, Southeastern
579.138	QR13	Microorganisms—Evolution	580.96	QK381-424	Botany—Africa
579.165	QR201	Pathogenic microorganisms	580.971	QK201-203	Botany—Canada
579.17	QR130	Space microbiology	580.972	QK211	Botany—Mexico
579.1757	QR111-113	Soil microbiology	580.9728	QK215-222	Botany—Central America
579.176	QR105.5	Freshwater microbiology	580.9729	QK225-231	Botany—West Indies
579.177	QR106-.5	Marine microbiology	580.973	QK115-195	Botany—United States
579.2	QR355-502	Viruses	580.97(4-9)	QK145-195	Botany—[United States, By state]
579.2445	QR406-.2	Papovaviruses			
579.247	QR408-.2	Parvoviruses	580.98	QK241-274	Botany—South America
579.25	QR395	RNA viruses	580.994	QK431-461	Botany—Australia

Dewey	LC	Subject Heading	Dewey	LC	Subject Heading
580.998	QK474-.3	Botany—Arctic regions	584.9	QK495.G74	Deepwater rice
580.9989	QK474.4	Botany—Antarctica	584.9	QK495.G74	Grasses
581.35	QK981.3	Plant biochemical genetics	584.9	QK495.G74	Durum wheat
581.35	QK981.4	Plant genetic regulation	585	QK494-.5	Gymnosperms
581.38	QK980-989	Plants—Evolution	585.2	QK494.5.P66	Eastern hemlock
581.498	QK776	Roots (Botany)	585.2	QK494.5.P66	Fir
581.63	QK98.4	Plants, Useful	585.2	QK494.5.P66	Douglas fir
581.632	QK98.5	Plants, Edible	585.4	QK494.5.C975	Eastern redcedar
581.632	QK98.5	Wild plants, Edible	585.5	QK494.5.T3	Dawn redwood
581.634	QK99	Botany, Medical	586	QK504-635	Cryptogams
581.634	QK99	Medicinal plants	587	QK520-532	Pteridophyta
581.636	QK98.7	Dye plants	588	QK532.4-563.87	Bryophytes
581.659	QK617	Mushrooms, Poisonous	590	QL	Zoology
581.659	QK100	Poisonous plants	590.14	QL10	Zoology—Terminology
581.68	QK86	Endangered plants	590.222	QL46	Zoology—Pictorial works
581.7	QK900-938	Plant ecology	590.6	QL1	Zoology—Societies, etc.
581.73	QK938.F6	Forest plants	590.71	QL51-58	Zoology—Study and teaching
581.73	QK938.F6	Forest ecology	590.724	QL52.6	Zoology—Experiments
581.73	QK938.F6	Timberline	590.73	QL73	Menageries
581.73	QK108-474.5	Forest plants	590.73	QL76-77.5	Petting zoos
581.74	QK938.P7	Grasslands	590.73	QL76-77.5	Zoos
581.744	QK938.P7	Prairies	590.74	QL71	Zoological museums
581.746	QK938.M4	Meadow plants	590.752	QL63	Taxidermy
581.748	QK936	Tropical plants	590.92	QL26-31	Ethologist
581.7538	QK937	Mountain plants	590.9(4-9)	QL101-345	Zoogeography
581.754	QK922	Desert plants	590.9(4-9)	QL155-339	Zoology—[By region or country]
581.754	QK938.D4	Desert plants			
581.76	QK932-.7	Freshwater plants	590.98	QL105	Zoology—Arctic regions
581.76	QK930-935	Aquatic plants	591.47	QL759	Animal defenses
581.76	QK102-105	Aquatic plants	591.47	QL940	Animal weapons
581.76	QK105	Freshwater plants	591.472	QL767	Protective coloration (Biology)
581.7786	QK108-474.5	Estuarine plants	591.477	QL401-432	Shells
581.7786	QK938.E	Estuarine plants	591.479	QL768	Animal tracks
581.9	QK101-474.5	Phytogeography	591.5	QL785.3	Extrasensory perception in animals
582.13	QK	Flowers			
582.16	QK474.8-494	Trees	591.5	QL750-795	Animal behavior
583	QK495.A12	Dicotyledons	591.5	QL785-.27	Animal psychology
583	QK108-474.5	Dicotyledons	591.5092	QL26-31	Zoologists
583.45	QK495.M73	Fig	591.512	QL781	Instinct
583.46	QK495.F14	English oak	591.513	QL785	Animal intelligence
583.46	QK495.F14	Durmast oak	591.513	QL785	Cognition in animals
583.685	QK495.M27	Hibiscus	591.5(3-4)	QL756.5-.57	Animals—Food
583.75	QK917	Carnivorous plants	591.53	QL756.57	Cannibalism in animals
583.765	QK495.M9	Guava	591.56	QL775	Social hierarchy in animals
583.766	QK495.M9	Eucalyptus	591.562	QL761	Sexual selection in animals
583.79	QK495.E92	Coca	591.562	QL761	Sexual behavior in animals
583.84	QK495.A6853	Ginseng	591.563	QL761.5	Familial behavior in animals
583.849	QK495.U48	Dill	591.563	QL762	Parental behavior in animals
583.86	QK495.V84	Grapes	591.563	QL763.2	Imprinting (Psychology)
583.94	QK495.C98	Dodder	591.563	QL763.5	Play behavior in animals
583.95	QK495.G4	African violets	591.564	QL756-.15	Animals—Habitations
583.952	QK495.S7	Eggplant	591.5648	QL756.15	Animal burrowing
583.99	QK495.C74	Daisies	591.565	QL755	Hibernation
583.99	QK495.C74	Dandelions	591.59	QL776	Animal communication
584.32	QK495.L72	Easter lily	591.59	QL776	Human-animal communication
584.32	QK495.L72	Daylilies			
584.34	QK495.A484	Daffodils	591.594	QL765	Animal sounds
584.352	QK495.A26	Agave	591.594	QL765	Sound production by animals
584.38	QK495.I75	Dwarf irises	591.594	QL765	Voice
584.5	QK495.P17	Date palm	591.6	SF84-.45	Zoology, Economic
584.9	QK495.G74	Fescue	591.6	SB922-998	Zoology, Economic

Dewey	LC	Subject Heading	Dewey	LC	Subject Heading
591.609(4-9)	SB993.3-.34	Zoology, Economic—[By region or country]	597.072	QL618.5-.55	Fishes—Research
			597.073	QL78.5	Marine aquariums, Public
591.60973	SB993.3-32	Zoology, Economic—United States	597.073	QL78-79	Aquariums, Public
			597.073	SF456-458.83	Aquariums
591.65	QL100	Dangerous animals	597.09(4-9)	QL619-637	Fishes—Geographical distribution
591.65	QL100	Poisonious animals			
591.65	QL757	Parasitology	597.135	QL638.99	Fishes—Genetics
591.65	QL757	Parasites	597.1477	QL639	Scales (Fishes)
591.7	QH540-549.5	Animal ecology	597.1479	QL639.4	Fishes—Locomotion
591.73	QL112	Forest animals	597.1479	QL639	Fins
591.74	QL115.3-.5	Grassland fauna	597.1568	QL639.5	Fishes—Migration
591.754	QL116	Desert animals	597.165	QL618.7	Dangerous fishes
591.76	QL141-149	Freshwater animals	597.165	QL618.7	Poisonous fishes
591.77	QL120-149	Aquatic animals	597.168	QL676.7	Rare birds
591.773	QL127-135	Aquatic animals—Atlantic Ocean	597.168	QL676.8	Extinct birds
			597.177073	SF457.1	Marine aquariums
591.7732	QL126	Aquatic animals—Arctic Ocean	597.1788	QL618.3	Fish populations
			597.3	QL638.95.S7	Hammerhead sharks
591.774	QL138	Aquatic animals—Pacific Ocean	597.36	QL638.9	Dogfish
			597.562	QL639.2	Fishes—Spawning
591.775	QL137	Aquatic animals—Indian Ocean	597.6798	QL638.S9	Dwarf sea horse
			597.75	QL638.P4	Darters (Fishes)
591.777	QL126.5	Aquatic animals—Antarctic Ocean	597.89	QL668.E2-.E275	Frogs
			597.9	QL641-669	Reptiles
591.788	QL752	Animal populations	597.9165	QL645.7	Dangerous reptiles
592	QL360-599	Invertebrates	597.92	QL666.C584	Desert tortoise
592.3	QL386-394	Worms	597.96	QL666.064	Cobras
592.64	QL391.A6	Earthworms	597.96	QL666.069	Eastern diamondback rattlesnake
593.4	QL370.7-374.2	Sponges			
593.5	QL375-379	Coelenterata	597.96	QL666.06-.694	Snakes
593.8	QL380-.8	Ctenophora	597.98	QL666.C925	Crocodiles
593.9	QL381-385.2	Echinodermata	597.98	QL666.C925	Alligators
594	QL401-445.2	Shellfish	598	QL671-699	Ornithology
594	QL401-432	Mollusks	598	QL671-699	Birds
594.32	QL430.5.H34	Abalones	598.073	QL677.8	Aviaries
594.4	TC201	Shipworms	598.147	QL697	Feathers
595	QL434-599.82	Arthropoda	598.1479	QL698.7	Birds—Flight
595.3	QL435-445.2	Crustacea	598.1594	QL698.5	Birdsongs
595.38	QL444.M33	Decapoda (Crustacea)	598.165	QL677.75	Dangerous birds
595.4	QL451-459.2	Arachnida	598.(4-9)	QL678-695.5	Birds—Geographical distribution
595.66	QL449.6-.65	Millipedes			
595.7	QL461-599.82	Insects	598.41	QL696.A52	Ducks
595.7072	QL468.5	Entomology—Research	598.415	QL696.A52	Eider
595.726	QL508.A2	Desert locust	598.47	QL696.S473	Adelie penguin
595.726	QL508.A2	Migratory locust	598.47	QL696.S473	Emperor penguin
595.733	QL520-.42	Dragonflies	598.53	QL696.C34	Emus
595.733	QL520-.42	Damselflies	598.625	QL696.G27	Pheasants
595.76	QL596.S35	Douglas fir beetle	598.65	QL696.C63	Eared dove
595.7649	QL596.S3	Dung beetles	598.65	QL696.C67	Dodo
595.78	QL561.T55	Clothes moths	598.71	QL696.P7	African gray parrot
595.78	QL561.S2	Ailanthus moth	598.832	QL696.P235	Dippers (Birds)
595.78139	QL561.L3	Eastern tent caterpillar	598.842	QL696.P288	Eastern bluebird
595.789	QL541-562.4	Butterflies	598.883	QL696.P2438	Dusky seaside sparrow
595.796	QL568.F7	Fire ants	598.942	QL696.F32	African fish eagle
595.796	QL568.F7	Ants	598.942	QL696.F32	Eagles
595.799	QL563-569.4	Bees	598.96	QL696.F34	Falcons
595.799	QL568.A6	Honeybee	599	QL700-739.8	Mammals
595.799	QL568.A6	Africanized honeybee	599.168	QL706.8-.83	Rare mammals
596	QL605-739.8	Vertebrates	599.1788	QL708.6	Mammal populations
597	QL614-639.8	Fishes	599.31	QL737.T8	Aardvark
597.012	QL618	Fishes—Classification	599.336	QL737.M242	Elephant shrews

Dewey	LC	Subject Heading	Dewey	LC	Subject Heading
599.35	QL737.R6	Dancing mice	601.48	T8	Technology—Abbreviations
599.356	QL737.R638	Dwarf hamsters	601.9	R726.5-.8	Medicine and psychology
599.356	QL737.R666	Hamsters	602.2	T11.8	Technical illustration
599.3592	QL737.R634	Guinea pigs	602.75	T325	Trademarks
599.3596	QL737.R656	Dormice	603	T9-10	Technology—Dictionaries
599.3596	QL737.R656	Edible dormouse	604.2	T351-385	Mechanical drawing
599.35987	QL737.R66	Desert kangaroo rat	604.2	T355	Structural drawing
599.36	QL737.R68	Abent squirrel	604.2	T359	Freehand technical sketching
599.364	QL737.R68	Eastern chipmunk	604.20284	T375-377	Drawing instruments
599.53	QL737.C434	Dall Porpoise	604.2068	T352	Drawing-room management
599.53	QL737.C432	Dolphins	604.24	T352	Drawing-room practice
599.638	QL737.U56	Giraffe	604.245	T369	Perspective
599.64	QL737.U53	Antelopes	604.245	T362-369	Projection
599.642	QL737.U5	Elands	604.25	T379	Blueprints
599.642	QL737.U53	African buffalo	604.7	T55.3.H3	Hazardous substances
599.643	QL737.U53	American bison	605	T1-5	Technology—Periodicals
599.65	QL737.U55	Deer	606	T6	Technology—Congresses
599.657	QL737.U55	Elk	607.1	T61-173	Technical education
599.665	QL737.U62	African wild ass	607.10(4-9)	T71-170	Technical education—[By region or country]
599.67	QL737.P98	Elephants			
599.674	QL737.P98	African elephant	607.2	T65	Research
599.7	QL737.C2	Carnivora	607.2	T175-178	Research, Industrial
599.756	QL737.C23	Tigers	607.34	T391-999	Exhibitions
599.77	QL737.C2	Dogs	608	T201-339	Inventions
599.775	QL737.C22	Foxes	608	T201-342	Patents
599.79	QL737.P63	Eared seals	608.0228	T324	Models (Patents)
599.794	QL737.P64	Elephant seals	608.7	T221-323.7	Patents—History
599.8	QL737.P9-.P968	Primates	609	T14.7-33	Technology—History
599.83	QL737.P93	Demidoff's galago	609	T15-31	Inventions—History
599.88	QL737.P96	Apes	609.2	T39-40	Inventors
599.884	QL737.P96	Gorilla	610	R	Medicine
599.9	GN49-298	Physical anthropology	610.089927	R143	Medicine, Arab
599.90835	GN63	Adolescence	610.1	R723-.5	Medicine—Philosophy
599.938	GN281-.4	Man—Origin	610.14	R123	Medicine—Terminology
599.938	GN281-289	Human evolution	610.21	RA407-409.5	Medical statistics
599.94	GN51-59	Anthropometry	610.222	R120	Medicine—Pictorial works
599.94	QM24	Human anatomy—Variation	610.25	R711-713.97	Physicians—Directories
599.940846	GN59.A35	Aged—Anthropometry	610.28	R856-857	Biomedical engineering
599.943	GN209	Teeth	610.284	R856-858	Medical instruments and apparatus
599.943	GN209	Dental anthropology			
599.945	GN199	Albinos and albinism	610.284	RC75	Medical thermometers
599.945	GN197	Color of man	610.284	RM889	Electric apparatus and appliances
599.945	GN191-199	Skin			
599.945	GN192	Dermatoglyphics	610.285	R858-859.7	Medical informatics
599.945	GN192	Fingerprints	610.3	R121	Medicine—Dictionaries
599.947	GN70	Ribs	610.5	R5-101	Medicine—Periodicals
599.947	GN231-232	Posture	610.6	R729.5	Medicine—Practice
599.947	GN70	Skeleton	610.6	R728	Medical offices
599.948	GN181-190.5	Brain	610.6	R106	Medicine—Congresses
599.948	GN71-131	Craniology	610.6	R10-99.7	Medicine—Societies, etc.
599.948	GN71-131	Skull	610.6952	RA972	Interns (Medicine)
599.948	GN131	Eye-sockets	610.6952	RA972	Residents (Medicine)
599.949	GN66-69	Proportion (Anthropometry)	610.6952	R707-.4	Physicians
599.949	GN66	Somatotypes	610.696	R727.3-.45	Physician and patient
599.949	GN69.3-.5	Midgets	610.71	R735-845	Medicine—Study and teaching
599.949	GN69.3-.5	Dwarfs			
600	T	Technology	610.711	R735-845	Medical colleges
601	T14	Technology—Philosophy	610.72	R860-862	Medical laboratories
601.12	T174	Technological forecasting	610.73	RT	Nursing
601.4	T9-10	Technology—Terminology	610.7301	RT84.5	Nursing—Philosophy
601.4	T11-.3	Technology—Language			

Dewey	LC	Subject Heading	Dewey	LC	Subject Heading
610.73019	RT86	Nursing—Psychological aspects	610.941	R486-498.4	Medicine—Great Britain
			610.9415	R498.6-.9	Medicine—Ireland
610.73025	RT25	Nurses—Directories	610.943	R509-512.5	Medicine—Germany
610.73028	RT90.5	Team nursing	610.9436	R499-502	Medicine—Austria
610.730285	RT50.5	Nursing—Data processing	610.9438	R535-538	Medicine—Poland
610.7306	RT3	Nursing—Congresses	610.944	R504-507	Medicine—France
610.7306	RT1	Nursing—Societies, etc.	610.945	R517-520	Medicine—Italy
610.73069	RT48-.6	Nursing assessment	610.946	R555-558	Medicine—Spain
610.73069	RT86.7-.75	Nursing—Practice	610.9469	R559-562	Medicine—Portugal
610.73069	RT48.6	Nursing diagnosis	610.947	R531-534	Medicine—Russia
610.730692	RT82.8	Nurse practitioners	610.9481	R547-550	Medicine—Norway
610.730693	RT62	Practical nursing	610.9485	R551-554	Medicine—Sweden
610.730698	RT84	Nurses' aides	610.9489	R539-542	Medicine—Denmark
610.730699	RT86.4	Nurse and physician	610.94912	R543-546	Medicine—Iceland
610.730699	RT86.3	Nurse and patient	610.9492	R526-529	Medicine—Netherlands
610.73071	RT71-81	Nursing—Study and teaching	610.9493	R521-524	Medicine—Belgium
610.730711	RT71-81	Nursing schools	610.9494	R563-566	Medicine—Switzerland
610.73072	RT81.5	Nursing—Research	610.9495	R513-516	Medicine—Greece
610.7309	RT31	Nursing—History	610.95	R581	Medicine, Oriental
610.73092	RT34-37	Nurses	610.95	R581-644	Medicine—Asia
610.7309(4-9)	RT4-17	Nursing—[By region or country]	610.951	R601-604	Medicine—China
			610.9519	R627-630	Medicine—Korea
610.732	RT104	Private duty nursing	610.952	R623-626	Medicine—Japan
610.733	RT90.7	Primary nursing	610.9538	R591-594	Medicine—Saudi Arabia
610.734	RT97	Public health nursing	610.954	R605-608	Medicine—India
610.7343	RT98	Visiting nurses	610.95491	R604.2-.5	Medicine—Pakistan
610.7349	RT108	Disaster nursing	610.95493	R608.2-.5	Medicine—Sri Lanka
610.736	RF52.5	Otolaryngological nursing	610.955	R631-634	Medicine—Iran
610.736	RL125	Dermatologic nursing	610.9561	R640-643	Medicine—Turkey
610.7361	RT120.E4	Emergency nursing	610.957	R635-638	Medicine—Asiatic Russia
610.7361	RT120.I5	Intensive care nursing	610.959(3-7)	R609-612	Medicine—Indochina
610.7361	RT87.T45	Terminal care	610.9598	R614-617	Medicine—Indonesia
610.7361	RT87.T45	Hospice care	610.9599	R618-621	Medicine—Philippines
610.7362	RJ245-247	Pediatric nursing	610.96	R651-654	Medicine—Africa
610.7365	RC954	Geriatric nursing	610.971	R461-464	Medicine—Canada
610.73677	RD99-.35	Surgical nursing	610.972	R465-468	Medicine—Mexico
610.73677	RE88	Ophthalmic nursing	610.9728	R469-472	Medicine—Central America
610.73677	RD753	Orthopedic nursing	610.9729	R473-476	Medicine—West Indies
610.73678	RG105	Gynecologic nursing	610.973	R151-363	Medicine—United States
610.73678	RG951	Maternity nursing	610.97(4-9)	R155-363	Medicine—[United States, by state]
610.7368	RC440	Psychiatric nursing			
610.7368	RC350.5	Neurological nursing	610.98	R480-483	Medicine—South America
610.7368	RD596	Neurological nursing	610.993	R675-678	Medicine—New Zealand
610.7368	RJ502.3	Adolescent psychiatric nursing	610.994	R671-674	Medicine—Australia
			610.99(5-6)	R681-684	Medicine—Oceania
610.73691	RC674	Cardiovascular system—Diseases—Nursing	611	QM	Human anatomy
			611.0022	QM25	Human anatomy—Atlases
610.73692	RC735.5	Respiratory organs—Diseases—Nursing	611.0074	QM51	Anatomical museums
			611.0078	QM34	Human anatomy—Laboratory manuals
610.73698	RC266	Cancer—Nursing			
610.73699	RC180.8	Poliomyelitis—Nursing	611.013	QM601-695	Embryology, Human
610.737	R728.8	Medical assistants	611.018	QM551-575	Tissues
610.82	R692	Women physicians	611.018	QM550-577.8	Histology
610.8996073	R695	Afro-Americans in medicine	611.018	QP88-.6	Tissues
610.8996073	R695	Blacks in medicine	611.0182	QM563	Elastic tissue
610.9	R131-684	Medicine—History	611.0182	QM565	Adipose tissues
610.901	R135-138.5	Medicine, Ancient	611.0183	QM567	Cartilage
610.902	R141-144	Medicine, Medieval	611.0184	QM569	Bone marrow
610.92	R134-.5	Physicians—Biography	611.0188	QM575	Nerve tissue
610.935	R135	Medicine, Persian	611.1	QM178-197	Cardiovascular system
610.94	R484-575	Medicine—Europe	611.11	QM181	Pericardium

Dewey	LC	Subject Heading	Dewey	LC	Subject Heading
611.12	QM181	Heart—Anatomy	611.712	QM113	Ribs
611.12	QM181	Myocardium	611.715	QM105	Skull
611.13	QM191	Pulmonary artery	611.716	QM105	Jaws
611.13	QM191	Aorta	611.717	QM101	Clavicle
611.13	QM191	Blood-vessels	611.718	QM117	Femur
611.13	QM191	Arteries	611.718	CC400	Fibula (Archaeology)
611.14	QM191	Veins	611.72	QM131-142	Joints
611.2	QM251-265	Respiratory organs	611.72	QM141	Ligaments
611.21	QM505	Frontal sinus	611.72	QM563	Ligaments
611.21	QM505	Nasopharynx	611.73	QM151-170	Muscles
611.22	QM255	Glottis	611.73	QM571	Muscles
611.22	QM255	Larynx	611.74	QM563	Fasciae (Anatomy)
611.22	QM255	Epiglottis	611.74	QM563	Connective tissues
611.24	QM261	Lungs	611.74	QM170	Tendons
611.3	QM301-367	Alimentary canal	611.77	QM484	Dermis
611.3	QM301-367	Gastrointestinal system	611.77	QM481-484	Skin
611.3	QM301-367	Digestive organs	611.77	QM484	Epidermis
611.31	QM306	Mouth	611.77	QM561	Epidermis
611.313	QM503	Tongue	611.78	QM488	Nails (Anatomy)
611.314	QM311	Teeth	611.78	QM488	Eyelashes
611.316	QM325-371	Salivary glands	611.78	QM488	Hair
611.317	QM306	Lips	611.8	QM451-471	Nervous system
611.32	QM535	Throat	611.8	QM501-511	Sense organs
611.32	QM331	Pharnyx	611.81	QM455	Hypothalamus
611.32	QM331	Tonsils	611.81	QM455	Medulla oblongata
611.32	QM331	Esophagus	611.81	QM455	Cerebellum
611.33	QM341	Stomache	611.81	QM455	Hippocampus (Brain)
611.34	QM345	Intestines	611.81	QM469	Meninges
611.341	QM345	Duodenum	611.82	QM465	Spinal cord
611.345	QM345	Appendix (Anatomy)	611.83	QM471	Nerves
611.347	QM345	Colon (Anatomy)	611.83	QM471	Sympathetic nervous system
611.36	QM351	Liver	611.84	QM511	Eye
611.36	QM352	Gallbladder	611.84	QM511	Retina
611.37	QM353	Pancreas	611.84	QM511	Optic nerve
611.38	QM367	Peritoneum	611.84	QM511	Eyelids
611.4	QM325-371	Glands	611.84	QM511	Pupil (Eye)
611.4	QM576	Endocrine glands	611.85	QM507	Ear
611.4	QM371	Endocrine glands	611.85	QM507	Labyrinth (Ear)
611.41	QM371	Spleen	611.85	QM507	Middle ear
611.42	QM197	Lymphatics	611.85	QM507	Eustachian tube
611.45	QM371	Adrenal glands	611.85	QM507	Ear, External
611.47	QM371	Pituitary gland	611.9	QM531-549	Anatomy, Surgical and topographical
611.49	QM495	Breast			
611.49	QM495	Mammary glands	611.91	QM535	Head
611.6	QM416-421	Generative organs	611.92	QM535	Chin
611.61	QM401-413	Urinary organs	611.92	QM535	Face
611.61	QM404	Kidneys	611.93	QM535	Neck
611.62	QM411	Bladder	611.95	QM543	Abdomen
611.63	QM416	Prostate	611.97	QM548	Hand
611.63	QM416	Generative organs, Male	611.97	QM548	Arm
611.64	QM416	Penis	611.97	QM548	Forearm
611.65	QM421	Fallopian tubes	611.97	QM548	Fingers
611.65	QM421	Generative organs, Female	611.97	QM548-549	Extremities (Anatomy)
611.65	QM421	Ovaries	611.98	QM548-549	Extremities (Anatomy)
611.66	QM421	Uterus	611.98	QM549	Toes
611.7	QM100-170	Musculoskeletal system	611.98	QM549	Leg
611.71	QM101-117	Human skeleton	611.98	QM549	Foot
611.71	QM101-117	Skeleton	612	QP34-38	Human physiology
611.711	QM111	Spinal canal	612	QP34-38	Human biology
611.711	QM111	Vertebrae	612	RC1151.B54	Biological rhythms—Effect of space flight on
611.711	QM111	Spine			

Dewey	LC	Subject Heading	Dewey	LC	Subject Heading
612.0083	RJ125-137	Children—Physiology	612.42	QP115	Lymphatics
612.01426	QP135	Body temperature	612.44	QP188.P3	Parathyroid glands
612.0145	RC1150-1151	Space flight—Physiological effect	612.45	QP188.A3	Adrenal glands
			612.45	QP188.A28	Adrenal cortex
612.02	QP572.M44	Melatonin	612.46	QP159	Excretion
612.044	QP301-310	Exercise—Physiological aspects	612.46	QP247-250.8	Urinary organs
			612.46	QP211	Excretion
612.11	QP91-99.5	Blood	612.463	QP249	Kidneys
612.1111	QP96.5	Hemoglobin	612.492	QP188.P58	Pituitary gland
612.115	QP91	Fibrin	612.6	QP84	Human growth
612.115	QP93.5-.7	Blood—Coagulation	612.6	QP84	Growth
612.115	QP93.5-.7	Blood coagulation factors	612.6	QP251-285	Human reproduction
612.116	QP99	Blood plasma	612.6	QP251-285	Reproduction
612.11825	QP98	Blood groups	612.6	QP251-285	Generative organs
612.14	QP105-.4	Blood pressure	612.61	QP255	Semen
612.14	QP101	Pulse	612.61	QP253-257	Generative organs, Male
612.17	QP111-114	Heart	612.62	QP259-281	Generative organs, Female
612.17	QP113.2	Myocardium	612.63	QP251-281	Conception
612.17	QP108	Coronary circulation	612.647	RG613	Fetus—Growth
612.18	QP109	Vasomotor system	612.647	RG610-621	Fetus—Physiology
612.2	QP121-125	Lungs	612.65	GN63	Child development
612.2	QP121-125	Respiratory organs	612.65	RJ131-137	Child development
612.2	QP107	Pulmonary circulation	612.65	RJ131-137	Children—Growth
612.2	QP121-125	Respiration	612.654	RJ134	Infants—Development
612.2	QP306	Larynx	612.661	QP84.4	Puberty
612.22	QP913.C1	Carbon dioxide—Physiological effect	612.661	RJ140	Teenagers—Growth
			612.661	RJ140-145	Youth—Physiology
612.3	QP141-185.3	Nutrition	612.662	RJ145	Menarche
612.3	QP145-159	Digestion	612.664	QP188.M3	Mammary glands
612.3	QP151-156	Gastrointestinal system	612.664	QP246	Lactation
612.3	RJ206-235	Children—Nutrition	612.67	QP86	Old age
612.312	QP146	Tonsils	612.68	QP85	Longevity
612.313	QP188.S2	Salivary glands	612.68	RA776.75	Longevity
612.313	QP191	Saliva	612.7	QP301-336	Musculoskeletal system
612.315	QP146	Esophagus	612.74	QP321-322	Muscles
612.32	QP151	Stomache	612.744	QP321	Fatigue
612.32	QP193	Stomache—Secretions	612.76	QP301-336	Locomotion
612.32	QP193	Gastric juice	612.76	QP301-310	Animal locomotion
612.33	QP156	Intestines	612.76	QP301-336	Human mechanics
612.33	QP156	Duodenum	612.78	QP306	Voice
612.34	QP195	Pancreas—Secretions	612.78	QP306	Speech
612.34	QP188.P26	Pancreas	612.7921	QP221	Perspiration
612.34	QP572.I5	Insulin	612.8	QP431-495	Senses and sensation
612.35	QP185	Liver	612.8042	QP356.3	Neurochemistry
612.35	QP185	Gallbladder	612.81	QP351-430	Nervous system
612.38	QP165	Intestinal absorption	612.81	QP361-375.5	Nerves
612.38	QP165	Absorption (Physiology)	612.82	QP406	Memory
612.39	QP171-177	Metabolism	612.82	QP376-430	Brain
612.391	QP139	Thirst	612.821	QP425-427	Sleep
612.391	QP141	Hunger	612.825	QP383-.17	Cerebral cortex
612.4	QP187-.6	Endocrinology, Comparative	612.8262	QP572.H9	Hypothalamic hormones
612.4	QP187-.6	Endocrine glands	612.827	QP379	Cerebellum
612.4	QP187-.6	Endocrinology	612.828	QP377	Medulla oblongata
612.4	QP187.7	Exocrine glands	612.83	QP370-375	Spinal cord
612.4	QP190-246.5	Secretion	612.83	QP330	Spine
612.4	QP186-246	Glands	612.84	QP476	Pupil (Eye)
612.405	QP572.P74	Prolactin	612.84	QP475-495	Eye
612.405	QP572.P7	Progesterone	612.84	QP474-495	Vision
612.405	QP572.S4	Hormones, Sex	612.843	QP479	Retina
612.405	QP572.T4	Testosterone	612.846	QP477.5	Eye—Movements
612.41	QP187	Spleen	612.85	QP460-469.3	Hearing

Dewey	LC	Subject Heading
612.85	QP460-471.2	Ear
612.85	RF294-.5	Audiometry
612.854	QP461	Eustachian tube
612.854	QP461	Middle ear
612.858	QP471	Vestibular apparatus
612.858	QP471-.2	Labyrinth (Ear)
612.86	QP455-458	Chemical senses
612.86	QP458	Odors
612.86	QP458	Nose
612.86	QP458	Smell
612.87	QP456	Taste
612.88	QP401	Pain
612.88	QP451	Touch
612.9	QM540	Back
612.92	QP311	Jaws
613	RA427.8	Health promotion
613	RA421-790	Medicine, Preventive
613	RA780	Hygiene
613	RA773-790	Health
613	RA770.5	Hygiene
613.04	RA418.5.F3	Family—Health and hygiene
613.0432	RJ240	Immunization of children
613.08996073	RA448.5.N4	Afro-Americans—Health and hygiene
613.091732	RA566.7	Urban health
613.091734	RA771-.7	Rural health
613.092	RA424.4-.5	Hygienists
613.122	RA794-954	Health resorts
613.192	RA782	Breathing exercises
613.193	RM843	Sun-baths
613.194	GV450	Nudism
613.19406	GV451-.4	Nudist camps
613.2	RA784	Diet
613.2	RA784	Nutrition
613.23	TX551	Food—Caloric content
613.25	RM222.2	Low-calorie diet
613.25	RM226-228	Fasting
613.25	RM222.2	Reducing diets
613.26	RM232	Egg-free diet
613.26	RM237.87	Wheat-free diet
613.26	RM237.85	Sugar-free diet
613.26	RM234.5	Milk-free diet
613.26	RM237.5	Raw food diet
613.262	RM236	Vegetarianism
613.262	TX392-.8	Vegetarianism
613.263	RM237.6	High-fiber diet
613.263	TX553.F53	Fiber in human nutrition
613.269	RJ216	Breast feeding
613.282	QP561	Amino acids in human nutrition
613.282	RM237.65	High-protein diet
613.283	RM237.59	High-carbohydrate diet
613.283	RM237.73	Low-carbohydrate diet
613.283	RM237.58	Complex carbohydrate diet
613.283	TX553.C28	Food—Carbohydrate content
613.283	TX553.S8	Sugars in human nutrition
613.284	RM237.7	Low-fat diet
613.284	RM237.75	Low-Cholesterol diet
613.284	TX553.C43	Food—Cholesterol content
613.285	RM237.8	Salt-free diet
613.285	RM237.56	High-calcium diet
613.286	TX553.V5	Vitamins
613.287	RA793-954	Mineral waters
613.4	RL87	Skin—Care and hygiene
613.41	RA780	Baths
613.62	RC967	Industrial hygiene
613.62	RC968-969	Occupational health services
613.62092	RC963	Industrial hygienists
613.6209(4-9)	HD7651-7780.8	Industrial hygiene—[By region or country]
613.66	GV1111	Self-defense
613.69	RC1040-1045	Traffic accidents
613.69	TL553.7	Survival after airplane accidents, shipwrecks, etc.
613.7	QP303	Kinesiology
613.70287	GV436	Physical fitness—Testing
613.7042	GV443	Physical education for children
613.706	GV428-433	Physical fitness centers
613.71	GV501.5	Step aerobics
613.71	GV460-548	Exercise
613.71	QP301-336	Exercise
613.71	RA781.17	Aquatic exercises
613.71	RA781.15	Low impact aerobic exercises
613.71	RA781.15	Aerobic exercises
613.71	RA781-.85	Exercise
613.71081	GV482.5	Exercise for men
613.713	GV546.3	Weight lifting
613.7130284	GV547.4	Dumbbells
613.714	GV539	Rings (Gymnastics)
613.714	GV536	Uneven parallel bars
613.714	GV464	Musico-callisthenics
613.716	GV838.53.E94	Aquatic exercises
613.78	RA781.5	Posture
613.79	RA785	Relaxation
613.79	RA786-.3	Sleep
613.79	RA785	Rest
613.9071	HQ51	Sex instruction for girls
613.9071	HQ53	Sex instruction for children
613.9071	HQ41	Sex instruction for boys
613.9071	HQ54-.4	Sex instruction for the handicapped
613.9071	HQ55	Sex instruction for the aged
613.9071	HQ56-59	Sex instruction
613.9072	HQ60	Sexology—Research
613.94	RG136-137.6	Contraception
613.9432	RG136.85	Antifertility vaccines
613.9432	RG137.4-.6	Contraceptive drugs
613.9432	RG137.5	Oral contraceptives
613.9432	RG137-.6	Contraceptives
613.9432	RG137.2	Spermicides
613.9434	RG136.5	Natural family planning
613.9435	RG137.3	Intrauterine contraceptives
613.9435	RG137.2	Contraceptives, Vaginal
613.95	RA788	Hygiene, Sexual
614	RA	Public health
614.072	RA440.85-.87	Public health—Research
614.091724	RA441.5	Public health—Developing countries
614.09(4-9)	RA442-558	Public health—[By region or country]
614.094	RA483-523	Public health—Europe

Dewey	LC	Subject Heading	Dewey	LC	Subject Heading
614.095	RA525-541	Public health—Asia	614.43	RA639-641	Animals as carriers of disease
614.096	RA545-552	Public health—Africa			
614.097	RA443-450	Public health—North America	614.43	RA639.3	Vector control
614.0971	RA449-450	Public health—Canada	614.432	RA639.5	Insects as carriers of disease
614.0972	RA451-452	Public health—Mexico	614.4322	RA641.T7	Tsetse-flies
614.09728	RA453-454	Public health—Central America	614.4323	RA640	Mosquitoes as carriers of disease
614.09729	RA455-456	Public health—West Indies	614.4323	RA640	Mosquitoes—Control
614.0973	RA445-448.5	Public health—United States	614.433	RA641.T5	Tick-borne diseases
614.098	RA457-482	Public health—South America	614.433	RA641.M5	Mites as carriers of disease
			614.45	RA975	Isolation (Hospital care)
614.1	RA1063	Death, Apparent	614.46	RA655-758	Quarantine
614.1	RA1063.3	Brain death	614.4609(4-9)	RA664-758	Quarantine—[By region or country]
614.1	RA1063.4	Autopsy			
614.1	RA1063	Death—Causes	614.46094	RA700-737	Quarantine—Europe
614.1	RA1062	Dental jurisprudence	614.46095	RA738-751	Quarantine—Asia
614.1	RA1148	Psychology, Forensic	614.46096	RA753-755	Quarantine—Africa
614.1	RA1057	Chemistry, Forensic	614.46097	RA664-677	Quarantine—North America
614.1	RA1001-1171	Medical jurisprudence	614.460971	RA671	Quarantine—Canada
614.1	RA1151-1152	Forensic psychiatry	614.460972	RA673	Quarantine—Mexico
614.1021	RA1018.5-.56	Medical jurisprudence—Statistics	614.4609728	RA675	Quarantine—Central America
			614.4609729	RA677	Quarantine—West Indies
614.107	RA1027-.5	Medical jurisprudence—Study and teaching	614.460973	RA665-667	Quarantine—United States
			614.46098	RA678-699	Quarantine—South America
614.109	RA1021-1022	Medical jurisprudence—History	614.460994	RA756	Quarantine—Australia
			614.46099(5-6)	RA758	Quarantine—Oceania
614.10973	RA1063.4	Forensic pathology	614.47	RA638	Vaccination
614.4	RA648.5-654	Epidemics	614.48	RA766.S8	Steam as a disinfectant
614.4	RA648.5-654	Epidemiology	614.48	RA761-767	Fumigation
614.4	RA404	Diseases—Reporting	614.48	RA766.G6	Glycerin
614.42	RA652.2.P82	Public health surveillance	614.48	RA766.H9	Hydrogen peroxide
614.42	RA407.3-408	Health surveys	614.48	RA766.R2	Radiation sterilization
614.42	RA791-954	Medical geography	614.5	RA643-644	Communicable diseases
614.42(4-9)	RA801-954	Medical geography—[By region or country]	614.5	RA601.5	Foodborne diseases
			614.5112	RA644.T8	Typhoid fever
614.42(4-9)	RA650-650.9	Epidemics—[By region or country]	614.5112	RA644.T8	Typhoid fever—Vaccination
			614.5123	RA644.D6	Diphtheria—Prevention
614.424	RA650.6	Epidemics—Europe	614.514	RA644.C3	Cholera
614.424	RA845-887	Medical geography—Europe	614.516	RA644.A57	Amebiasis
614.425	RA650.7	Epidemics—Asia	614.518	RA644.I6	Influenza
614.425	RA891-934	Medical geography—Asia	614.523	RA644.M5	Measles
614.426	RA650.8	Epidemics—Africa	614.524	RA644.R8	Rubella
614.426	RA943-949	Medical geography—Africa	614.532	RA644.M2	Malaria
614.42(7-8)	RA650-.55	Epidemics—America	614.541	RA644.Y4	Yellow fever
614.4271	RA809-810	Medical geography—Canada	614.542	RA644.T7	Tuberculosis—Vaccination
614.4272	RA811-812	Medical geography—Mexico	614.542	RA644.T7	Tuberculosis
614.42728	RA813-814	Medical geography—Central America	614.543	RA644.W6	Whooping cough
			614.547	RA644.H45	Herpes genitalis
614.42729	RA815-816	Medical geography—West Indies	614.547	RA644.V4	Sexually transmitted diseases—Prevention
614.4273	RA804-807	Medical geography—United States	614.547	RA644.V4	Sexually transmitted diseases
614.428	RA817-844	Medical geography—South America	614.55	RA643-644	Parasitic diseases
			614.5552	RA644.F5	Filariasis
614.4293	RA952.5	Medical geography—New Zealand	614.56	RA641.D6	Dogs as carriers of disease
			614.56	RA639-641	Zoonoses
614.4294	RA951-952	Medical geography—Australia	614.563	RA644.R3	Rabies
			614.57	RA644.V55	Virus diseases
614.4294	RA650.9.A8	Epidemics—Australia	614.571	RA644.D4	Dengue
614.429(5-6)	RA953-954	Medical geography—Oceania	614.5732	RA644.P7	Plague—Vaccination
			614.59	RA571	Soil pollution

Dewey	LC	Subject Heading	Dewey	LC	Subject Heading
614.59	RA576	Smog	615.1901	RS189-190	Drugs—Analysis
614.59	TD884	Smoke	615.3137	RM666.A82	Aspirin
614.59241	RA644.P8	Pneumonia	615.321	RM666.A4	Alkaloids
614.5939	RA645.N87	Nutritionally induced diseases	615.321	RM666.H33	Herbs—Therapeutic use
			615.321	RS431.E73	Exgot alkaloids
614.5939	RA645.N87	Nutrition disorders	615.321	RS160-167	Pharmacognosy
614.5939	RA645.N87	Malnutrition	615.32369	RM666.C375	Castor oil
614.59462	RA645.D5	Diabetes	615.32379	RS165.C5	Coca
614.59832	RA644.E52	Epidemic encephalitis	615.328	RM259	Vitamin therapy
614.59834	RA645.M82	Multiple sclerosis	615.329	RM265-267	Antibiotics
614.59836	RA645.C47	Cerebral palsy	615.329	RM409	Antibacterial agents
614.5993	RA645.A44	Allergy	615.329	RM666.B2	Bacitracin
614.599392	RA644.A25	AIDS-related complex	615.3295654	RM666.P35	Penicillin
614.5996	RK52-.45	Dental public health	615.3295654	RS165.P38	Penicillin
614.6	RA619-640	Dead	615.36	RM283-298	Hormone therapy
614.6	RA625-630	Burial	615.37	RM282.T7	Transfer factor (Immunology)
614.6	RA631-636.7	Cremation	615.37	RM270-282	Immunotherapy
614.832	RC141.E6	Epidemic encephalitis	615.37	RM270-282	Serotherapy
615.1	RM300-671.5	Drugs	615.37	RM370-373	Immunopharmacology
615.1	RM300-671.5	Pharmacology	615.37	RM373	Immunosuppressive agents
615.1	RM671-.5	Drugs, Nonprescription	615.372	QR189.5.B33	Bacterial vaccines
615.1	RS	Pharmacy	615.372	QR189.5.E53	Enterobacterial vaccines
615.1	RS153-185	Materia medica	615.372	QR189-.5	Vaccines
615.10128	RS189	Drugs—Standards	615.372	RM281	Vaccination
615.1014	RS55	Pharmacy—Terminology	615.375	RM278	Antitoxins
615.10151	RS57	Pharmaceutical arithmetic	615.39	RM171.4-.45	Blood products
615.1025	RS74-76	Pharmacists—Directories	615.39	RM171.4	Recombinant blood proteins
615.105	RS21	Pharmacy—Periodicals	615.39	RM171.7	Blood plasma substitutes
615.106	RS1	Pharmacy—Societies, etc.	615.39	RM175-176	Plasma exchange (Therapeutics)
615.106	RS3	Pharmacy—Congresses			
615.1068	RS100-.4	Pharmacy management	615.39	RM171-174	Blood—Transfusion
615.1071	RS101-121	Pharmacy—Study and teaching	615.39	RM177	Blood platelets—Transfusion
			615.39	RM298.P5	Placental extracts
615.10710(4-9)	RS110-121	Pharmacy—Study and teaching—[By region or country]	615.39	RM171.5	Blood coagulation factors
			615.42	RS201.E4	Elixirs
			615.42	RS201.S6	Solutions (Pharmacy)
615.1072	RM301.25-.27	Pharmacology, Experimental	615.42	RS201.S8	Syrups
615.1072	RS122	Pharmacy—Research	615.43	RS201.T2	Tablets (Medicine)
615.1074	RS123	Pharmaceutical museums	615.43	RS201.P5	Pills
615.1078	RS93	Pharmacy—Laboratory manuals	615.43	RS201.C3	Capsules (Pharmacy)
			615.43	RS201.P8	Powders (Pharmacy)
615.1083(2-4)	RJ560-570	Pediatric pharmacology	615.45	RS201.O3	Ointments
615.10846	RC953.7	Geriatric pharmacology	615.45	RS201.E5	Emulsions (Pharmacy)
615.108996073	RS122.5	Afro-American pharmacists	615.5	R733	Alternative medicine
615.109	RS61-68	Pharmacy—History	615.5	RC90	Iatrogenic diseases
615.1092	HD8039.D7	Drugstore employees	615.5	R727.43	Patient compliance
615.1092	RS71-73	Pharmacists	615.5	RM	Therapeutics
615.1092	RS122.95	Pharmacy technicians	615.5014	RM38	Therapeutics—Terminology
615.11	RS139-141.9	Pharmacopoeias	615.505	RM16	Therapeutics—Periodicals
615.13	RS151.2-.9	Dispensatories	615.506	RM21	Therapeutics—Congresses
615.13	RS125-131.9	Medicine—Formulae, receipts, prescriptions	615.506	RM1	Therapeutics—Societies, etc.
			615.507	RT90-.3	Patient education
615.14	RM139	Prescription writing	615.5071	RM108-.5	Therapeutics—Study and teaching
615.14	RM138	Drugs—Prescribing			
615.14	RS200-201	Drugs—Dosage forms	615.5072	RM111	Therapeutics, Experimental
615.18	RS424	Drug stability	615.509	RM41-47	Therapeutics—History
615.18	RS159.5	Drugs—Packaging	615.53	RZ414	Medicine, Chronothermal
615.18	RS159	Drugs—Preservation	615.53	RV1-9	Medicine, Botanic
615.19	RS400-431	Pharmaceutical chemistry	615.53	RV431	Dispensatories, Eclectic
615.19	RS192-210	Pharmaceutical technology	615.53	RV11-431	Medicine, Eclectic
615.1901	RM301.27	Drugs—Testing			

Dewey	LC	Subject Heading	Dewey	LC	Subject Heading
615.5305	RV15	Medicine, Eclectic—Periodicals	615.6	RM163-176	Injections
			615.6	RM162	Oral medication
615.5306	RV21	Medicine, Eclectic—Congresses	615.6	RM169	Injections, Hypodermic
			615.6	RS201.P37	Parenteral solutions
615.53071	RV100-181	Medicine, Eclectic—Study and teaching	615.6	RS199.5-210	Drug delivery systems
			615.6	RS201.B54	Bioadhesive drug delivery systems
615.5309	RV61	Medicine, Eclectic—History			
615.532	RZ420	Electrohomeopathy	615.6	RS201.C64	Drugs—Controlled release
615.532	RX601-675	Homeopathy—Materia medica and therapeutics	615.6	RS201.V43	Drugs—Vehicles
			615.6	RS210	Drug delivery devices
615.532	RX81	Homeopathy—Attenuations, dilutions, and potencies	615.7	RM301.5	Pharmacokinetics
			615.7042	RM302.5	Drugs—Side effects
			615.7045	RM302-.4	Drug interactions
615.532	RX671-675	Pharmacy, Homeopathic	615.71	RM349	Cardiotonic agents
615.532	RX	Homeopathy	615.71	RM345-349	Cardiovascular agents
615.532025	RX46	Homeopathic physicians—Directories	615.711	RM666.D5	Digitalis
			615.711	RS165.D5	Digitalis
615.53205	RX11	Homeopathy—Periodicals	615.716	RM347	Myocardial depressants
615.53206	RX1	Homeopathy—Societies, etc.	615.72	RM388-.7	Respiratory agents
615.53206	RX21	Homeopathy—Congresses	615.72	RM388-.7	Pulmonary pharmacology
615.532071	RX91-101	Homeopathy—Study and teaching	615.72	RM390	Expectorants
			615.73	RM355-365	Gastrointestinal agents
615.53209	RX51	Homeopathy—History	615.73	RM365	Antacids
615.532092	RX61-66	Homeopathic physicians—Biography	615.7308996073	RT83.5	Afro-American nurses
			615.731	RM359	Emetics
615.533	RZ301-397.5	Osteopathic medicine	615.731	RM666.T2	Tartar emetic
615.533023	RZ336	Osteopathic medicine—Vocational guidance	615.732	RM357	Laxatives
			615.761	RM377	Diuretics
615.533025	RZ333	Osteopathic physicians—Directories	615.761	RS431.D58	Diuretics
			615.766	RM386	Aphrodisiacs
615.53305	RZ311	Osteopathic medicine—Periodicals	615.773	RM312	Neuromuscular blocking agents
615.53306	RZ313	Osteopathic medicine—Congresses	615.773	RM312	Musculoskeletal system—Effect of drugs on
615.53306	RZ301	Osteopathic medicine—Societies, etc.	615.78	RM315-334	Neuropsychopharmacology
			615.78	RM315-334	Neuropharmacology
615.533071	RZ337-338	Osteopathic medicine—Study and teaching	615.78	RM315-334	Psychopharmacology
			615.782	RM325	Sedatives
615.5330711	RZ337-338	Osteopathic schools	615.782	RM325	Hypnotics
615.53309	RZ321-325	Osteopathic medicine—History	615.782	RM325	Barbiturates
			615.7822	RM328	Narcotics
615.533092	RZ331-332	Osteopathic physicians—Biography	615.7822	RM666.M8	Morphine
			615.7827	RM666.C266	Cannabis
615.534	RZ201-275	Chiropractic	615.783	RM319	Analgesics
615.534	RZ260-275	Diseases—Chiropractic treatment	615.785	RM332-.3	Stimulants
			615.788	RM330	Central nervous system depressants
615.534025	RZ233	Chiropractors—Directories			
615.53405	RZ211	Chiropractic—Periodicals	615.788	RM666.L88	LSD (Drug)
615.53406	RZ213	Chiropractic—Congresses	615.788	RM332-.3	Antidepressants
615.53406	RZ201	Chiropractic—Societies, etc.	615.788	RM315-334	Psychotropic drugs
615.534071	RZ237-238	Chiropractic—Study and teaching	615.7882	RM333	Tranquilizing drugs
			615.7883	RM324.8	Hallucinogenic drugs
615.53409	RZ221-225	Chiropractic—History	615.8043	RC87	Resuscitation
615.534092	RZ231-232	Chiropractors—Biography	615.82	RD736.M25	Manipulation (Therapeutics)
615.535	RZ433-445	Naturopathy	615.82	RM725-727	Exercise therapy
615.535092	RZ440	Naturopaths	615.82	RM724	Manipulation (Therapeutics)
615.542	RJ434	Respiratory therapy for children	615.82	RM695-893	Physical therapy
			615.82	RM695-931	Therapeutics, Physiological
615.542	RJ52-53	Children—Diseases—Treatment	615.82	RM695-951	Medicine, Physical
615.58	RM260-263	Chemotherapy	615.82025	RM697	Physical therapists—Directories
615.6	RM147-180	Drugs—Administration			

126

Dewey	LC	Subject Heading	Dewey	LC	Subject Heading
615.8206	RM695	Physical therapy—Societies, etc.	615.90071	RA1198-.3	Toxicology—Study and teaching
615.8206	RM696	Physical therapy—Congresses	615.90072	RA1199-.5	Toxicology—Research
615.82071	RM706-707	Physical therapy—Study and teaching	615.90083	RA1225	Poisoning, Accidental, in children
615.820846	RC953.8.E93	Exercise therapy for the aged	615.902	RA1229-.5	Industrial toxicology
615.82092	RM699.5-.7	Physical therapists	615.907	RA1199.4.A38	Acute toxicity testing
615.822	RA780.5	Massage	615.907	RA1199-.5	Toxicity testing
615.822	RM723.A27	Acupressure	615.907	RA1221-1223	Analytical toxicology
615.822	RM719-727	Mechanotherapy	615.908	RA1224.5	Toxicological emergencies
615.822	RM721-723	Massage	615.91	RA577	Gases, Asphyxiating and poisonous
615.822083	RJ53.A27	Acupressure for children	615.91	RA1247.M8	Mustard gas
615.83	RM862.7	Ultrasonic waves—Therapeutic use	615.91	RA1247.C17	Carbon monoxide
615.831	RM835-844	Phototherapy	615.91	RA1245-1247	Gases, Asphyxiating and poisonous
615.831	RM838	Light—Physiological effect	615.942	RA1242.S53	Poisonous snakes—Venom
615.831	RM835-844	Light, Colored	615.954	RA1258-1260	Food—Toxicology
615.831	RM840	Color—Therapeutic use	615.954	RA1242.S48	Seafood poisoning
615.831	RZ414.6	Color—Therapeutic use	615.954	SH177.R4	Paralytic shellfish poisoning
615.832	RM865-868.5	Thermotherapy	616	RC	Internal medicine
615.8323	RM874	Diathermy	616	RC31-80	Clinical medicine
615.8325	RM868-.5	Fever therapy	616.003	RC41	Internal medicine—Dictionaries
615.836	RC735.I5	Respiratory therapy	616.00835	RJ550	Adolescent medicine
615.836	RM827	Compressed air—Therapeutic use	616.0088791	RC965.P46	Entertainers—Diseases
615.836	RM161	Respiratory therapy	616.009	R702	Diseases and history
615.836	RM666.08	Oxygen therapy	616.01	QR177	Drug resistance in microorganisms
615.836	RM824-827	Aerotherapy	616.01	QR46-48	Body, Human—Microbiology
615.842	RM845-862.5	Radiotherapy	616.01	QR46	Medical microbiology
615.842	RM845-862.5	Radiation—Dosage	616.014	QR46	Medical bacteriology
615.8423	RM859	Radium—Therapeutic use	616.025	RC86-88.9	Medical emergencies
615.845	RM869-890	Electrotherapeutics	616.025	RA645.5-.7	Emergency medical technicians
615.845	RM862.E4	Electron beams—Therapeutic use	616.025	RC86-88.9	Emergency medicine
615.845	RM886	Electrolysis in medicine	616.025	RA645.5-.8	Emergency medical personnel
615.845	RZ422	Magnetic healing	616.0252	RC86-88.9	First aid in illness and injury
615.851	RZ403.S56	Silva Mind Control	616.028	RC86-88.9	Critical care medicine
615.851	RZ400-408	Mental healing	616.029	R726.8	Terminally ill
615.851092	RZ407-408	Healers	616.029	R726.8	Terminal care
615.8515	RM735-.7	Occupational therapy	616.042	RB155.8	Gene therapy
615.85153	RM736.7	Recreational therapy	616.042	RB155-.8	Medical genetics
615.85154	ML3919-3920	Music therapy	616.042	RB155.5-.8	Genetic disorders
615.85155083	RJ505.D3	Dance therapy for children	616.042	RB155.5-.8	Human chromosome abnormalities
615.85156	RM735.7.H35	Handicraft—Therapeutic use	616.042	RL793	Mole (Dermatology)
615.853	RM801-822	Hydrotherapy	616.044	RC108	Chronic diseases
615.854	RM214-258	Dietetics	616.044	RB156	Chronic diseases
615.854	RM214-258	Diet therapy	616.047	RB129	Fever
615.854	RM214-258	Diet in disease	616.047	RB153-154	Infection
615.855	RM149	Parenteral therapy	616.047	RC69	Symptomatology
615.855	RM149	Parenteral solutions	616.047	RB150.S5	Shock
615.855	RM170-180	Intravenous therapy	616.047	RB144-.5	Edema
615.882	GN477-.7	Traditional medicine	616.047	RB48.5	Endocrine manifestations of general diseases
615.882	GR880	Traditional medicine	616.047	RC144.G3	Gas gangrene
615.886	RM671-.5	Patent medicines	616.047	RD153	Gangrene
615.892	RC73.2	Acupuncture points	616.047	RD628	Gangrene
615.892	RM184-.5	Acupuncture	616.047	RD641	Abscess
615.892083	RJ53.A27	Acupuncture for children			
615.9	RA1190-1270	Toxicology			
615.9	RA1190-1270	Poisoning			
615.9	RA1190-1270	Poisons			

Dewey	LC	Subject Heading	Dewey	LC	Subject Heading
616.04706	RX211	Fever—Homeopathic treatment	616.11	RC685.E5	Endocarditis
616.04706	RV211	Fever—Eclectic treatment	616.12	RC685.C18	Cardiogenic shock
616.0472	RC73-.2	Pain	616.12	RC681-688	Heart—Diseases
616.0472	RB127	Pain	616.12043	RC687	Congenital heart disease
616.0478	RB150.F37	Chronic fatigue syndrome	616.1206	RC684.A35	Adrenergic beta blockers
616.07	RB	Pathology	616.1206	RC684.A34	Adrenergic alpha blockers
616.0705	RB1	Pathology—Periodicals	616.120645	RC684.E4	Electric countershock
616.0706	RB3	Pathology—Congresses	616.12075	RC683.5.B63	Body surface mapping
616.07071	RB123-124	Pathology—Study and teaching	616.12075	RC683.5.E94	Treadmill exercise tests
			616.1207543	RC683.5.U5	Echocardiography
616.0709	RB15-.2	Pathology—History	616.1207543	RC683.5.U5	Two-dimensional echocardiography
616.075	RB37-56.5	Diagnosis, Laboratory			
616.075	RC71.6	Diagnosis, Noninvasive	616.1207543	RC683.5.U5	Doppler echocardiography
616.075	RC80	Prognosis	616.1207547	RC683.5.E5	Electrocardiography
616.075	RC71.5	Diagnosis, Differential	616.1207547	RC683.5.A45	Ambulatory electrocardiography
616.075	R837.E9	Medicine—Examinations			
616.075	RC71-78.7	Diagnosis	616.1207572	RC683.5.A5	Angiocardiography
616.0751	RC65	Medical history taking	616.122	RC685.A6	Angina pectoris
616.0754	RC78.7.D53	Diagnostic imaging	616.123	RC685.C6	Coronary heart disease
616.0754	RC76-.5	Physical diagnosis	616.123025	RC685.C173	Cardiac arrest
616.0754	RC75	Body temperature	616.1237	RC685.I6	Myocardial infarction
616.0754028	RC76.3	Stethoscopes	616.124	RC685.M92	Myocarditis
616.07543	RC78.7.U4	Diagnosis, Ultrasonic	616.124	RC685.M9	Myocardium—Diseases
616.07543	R857.U48	Ultrasonics in medicine	616.125	RC685.V2	Mitral valve insufficiency
616.07543	RC78.7.D86	Duplex ultrasonography—Diagnostic use	616.125	RC685.V2	Heart valves—Diseases
			616.128	RC685.A65	Arrhythmia
616.07545	RC78.7.E5	Endoscopy	616.128	RC685.V43	Ventricular fibrillation
616.07547	RC77-.5	Electrodiagnosis	616.128	RC685.A65	Palpitation
616.07548	RC78.7.N83	Magnetic resonance imaging	616.13	RC694.5.I53	Arteritis
616.0756	RB112.5	Clinical biochemistry	616.13	RC691-697	Arteries—Diseases
616.0756	RB52	Body fluids—Analysis	616.13	RC691-701	Blood-vessels—Diseases
616.0756	RM40	Clinical chemistry	616.13	RC685.H93	Hypotension
616.07561	RB45-15	Blood—Analysis	616.13075	RC691.5-.6	Blood-vessels—Diseases—Diagnosis
616.0757	RC78-.5	Diagnosis, Radioscopic			
616.0757	RC78.7.T6	Tomography	616.1307543	RC691.6.D87	Duplex ultrasonography—Diagnostic use
616.07572	RC78-.5	Radiography, Medical			
616.07572	RC78.7.F5	Diagnosis, Fluoroscopic	616.1307572	RC691.6.A53	Angiography
616.07575	R895-920	Nuclear medicine	616.131	RC694	Peripheral vascular diseases
616.0758	RB43-.6	Medical microscopy	616.131	RC694.5.I53	Vasculitis
616.0758	RB46.7	Electron microscopic immunocytochemistry	616.132	RC685.H8	Hypertension
			616.132	RC685.H8	Essential hypertension
			616.132	RC918.R38	Renal hypertension
616.0759	RB57	Autopsy	616.132075	RC683.5.A43	Ambulatory blood pressure monitoring
616.078	RA1063-.5	Death			
616.0796	QR184.2	Human immunogenetics	616.133	RC693	Aneurysms
616.08	RC49-52	Medicine, Psychosomatic	616.138	RC691	Aorta—Diseases
616.1	RB144-.5	Blood circulation disorders	616.138	RC693	Aortic aneurysms
616.1	RC666-701	Cardiovascular system—Diseases	616.14	RC695-697	Veins—Diseases
			616.142	RC696	Phlebitis
616.10092	RC666.7-.72	Cardiologists	616.143	RC695-697	Varicose veins
616.1043	RC701	Cardiovascular system—Abnormalities	616.15	RC647.B5	Blood platelet disorders
			616.15	RC633-647.5	Blood—Diseases
616.106	RX311-316	Cardiovascular system—Diseases—Homeopathic treatment	616.15027	RB145	Hematology, Experimental
			616.15027	RC636	Hematology, Experimental
			616.152	RC641-.7	Anemia
616.106	RV251-256	Cardiovascular system—Diseases—Eclectic treatment	616.152	RC641.7.F36	Fanconi's anemia
			616.152	RC641.7.R44	Renal anemia
			616.157	RB144-.5	Hemorrhage
616.1075	RC670-.5	Cardiovascular system—Diagnosis	616.157	RC647.C55	Blood coagulation disorders
			616.157	RC647.D5	Disseminated intravascular coagulation
616.11	RC685.P5	Pericardium			

Dewey	LC	Subject Heading	Dewey	LC	Subject Heading
616.1572	RC642	Hemophilia	616.33	RC799-869	Gastrointestinal system
616.2	RC737-.5	Apnea	616.33	RC816-840	Stomache—Diseases
616.2	RC705-779	Respiratory organs— Diseases	616.33	RC840.G3	Gastroenteritis
			616.3307545	RC804.G3	Gastroscopy
616.2	RC740	Respiratory infections	616.332	RC827	Indigestion
616.201	RC746	Croup	616.332	RC815.2	Indigestion disorders
616.202	RC590	Hay fever	616.333	RC831	Gastritis
616.202	RC589-596	Respiratory allergy	616.34	RC860-862	Colon—Diseases
616.203	RC150-.9	Influenza	616.3407545	RC804.D79	Duodenoscopy
616.203	RC150	Asian flu	616.3407572	RC804.R6	Duodenum—Radiography
616.204	RC204	Whooping cough	616.342	RC866.D43	Fecal incontinence
616.205	RF361	Cold (Disease)	616.342	RC866.D43	Defecation disorders
616.206	RC735.H54	High-frequency ventilation (Therapy)	616.3423	RC862.M3	Malabsorption syndromes
			616.3428	RC861	Constipation
616.206	RX321-326	Respiratory organs— Diseases—Homeopathic treatment	616.343	RC821	Peptic ulcer
			616.344	RC862.E5	Enteritis
			616.3447	RC862.C6	Colitis
616.206	RV261-266	Respiratory organs— Diseases—Eclectic treatment	616.35	RC865	Hemorrhoids
			616.35	RC864-866	Proctology
			616.362	RC845-848	Liver—Diseases
616.2075	RC734.P84	Pulmonary function tests	616.362075	RC847-.5	Liver function tests
616.212	RF341-437	Nose—Diseases	616.3623	RC848.C4	Chronic active hepatitis
616.21207545	RF345	Nasoscopy	616.3623	RC848.H42	Hepatitis
616.22	RF526	Vocal cords—Diseases	616.3624	RC848.A42	Alcoholic liver diseases
616.2207545	RF514-.5	Laryngoscopy	616.3625	RC851	Jaundice
616.234	RC778	Bronchitis	616.365	RC849-853	Gallbladder—Diseases
616.238	RC591	Asthma	616.37	RC857-858	Pancreas—Diseases
616.24	RC776.03	Respiratory organs— Obstructions	616.37	RC858.C95	Cystic fibrosis
			616.39	RA1116	Starvation
616.24	RC756-776	Lungs-Diseases	616.39	RB147	Metabolism—Disorders
616.24	RC776.F33	Farmer's lung	616.39	RC622	Nutritionally induced diseases
616.241	RC771-772	Pneumonia			
616.244	RD137	Respiratory organs— Foreign bodies	616.39	RC623	Malnutrition
			616.39	RC620-627	Nutrition disorders
616.248	RC776.E5	Emphysema, Pulmonary	616.39	RC623.5-627	Deficiency diseases
616.249	RC776.P85	Pulmonary embolism	616.39	RC623.7	Avitaminosis
616.25	RC751	Pleurisy	616.39	RC627.5-632	Metabolism—Disorders
616.3	RC799-869	Digestive organs—Diseases	616.39043	RC627.8	Metabolism, Inborn errors of
616.306	RV271-276	Digestive organs— Diseases—Eclectic treatment	616.398	RC628-.5	Obesity
			616.3992	RB147	Acidosis
			616.3992	RC630	Water-electrolyte imbalances
616.306	RX331-336	Digestive organs— Diseases—Homeopathic treatment	616.3998	RC632.L33	Lactose intolerance
			616.3999	RC629-.5	Gout
			616.4	RC648-665	Endocrinology
616.307572	RC804.A5	Digestive organs— Radiography	616.4	RC648-665	Endocrine glands—Diseases
			616.44	RC655-657	Thyroid gland—Diseases
616.31	RC811	Gastrointestinal system— Motility—Disorders	616.442	RC656-.3	Goiter
			616.443	RC657.5.G7	Graves' disease
616.31	RC815-.6	Mouth—Diseases	616.444	RC657	Hypothyroidism
616.31	RC815-.6	Oral medicine	616.45	RC659	Addison's disease
616.31	RF460-547	Throat—Diseases	616.45	RC659	Adrenal glands—Diseases
616.31075	RF476	Throat—Examination	616.462	RC660-662.4	Diabetes
616.313	RC168.M8	Mumps	616.462	RC660-662.18	Non-insulin-dependent diabetes
616.314	RF491	Tonsillitis			
616.32	RC815.7	Esophagus—Diseases	616.462	RC658.5	Diabetes
616.32	RC815.7	Esophageal varices	616.46200835	RJ420.D5	Diabetes in adolescence
616.32	RF485	Pharyngitis	616.47	RB140-.5	Growth disorders
616.32	RF481-499	Pharnyx—Diseases	616.47	RC658-.7	Pituitary gland—Diseases
616.32	RF545	Esophagus—Foreign bodies	616.47	RC658.3	Acromegaly
616.32	RF481-499	Tonsils—Diseases	616.5	RL	Dermatology
616.32043	RC815.7	Esophagus—Abnormalities	616.5	RL701-751	Neurocutaneous disorders

Dewey	LC	Subject Heading	Dewey	LC	Subject Heading
616.5	RL241	Occupational dermatitis	616.692	RC889	Infertility, Male
616.5	RL247	Photosensitivity disorders	616.692	RC889	Impotence
616.50014	RL39	Dermatology—Terminology	616.693	RC884	Climacteric, Male
616.50025	RL43	Dermatologists—Directories	616.694	RC883	Hermaphroditism
616.500284	RL55	Dermatology—Apparatus and instruments	616.7	RC925-935	Muscles—Diseases
			616.7	RD701-811	Orthopedics
616.5005	RL26	Dermatology—Periodicals	616.7	RD762	Posture disorders
616.5006	RL31	Dermatology—Congresses	616.700284	RE73	Optical instruments
616.5006	RL1	Dermatology—Societies, etc.	616.7005	RD711	Orthopedics—Periodicals
616.50071	RL77	Dermatology—Study and teaching	616.70232	RD727-728	Orthopedists
			616.7025	RD750	Orthopedic emergencies
616.5009	RL46	Dermatology—History	616.70284	RD757.S45	Orthopedic shoes
616.50092	RL46.2-.3	Dermatologists	616.70754	RD734-.5	Orthopedics—Diagnosis
616.5027	RL79	Dermatology, Experimental	616.709	RD725-726	Orthopedics—History
616.506	RV381-391	Dermatology	616.71	RC930-931	Bones—Diseases
616.506	RX561-581	Dermatology	616.71	RC931.F5	Fibrous dysplasia of bone
616.51	RL231-241	Skin—Inflammation	616.71043	RD763	Skull—Abnormalities
616.51	RL244	Contact dermatitis	616.71043	RD779-789	Leg—Abnormalities
616.521	RL242-249	Atopic dermatitis	616.71043	RD775-789	Extremities (Anatomy)— Abnormalities
616.521	RL251	Eczema			
616.523	RL221	Carbuncle	616.712	RC931.064	Osteitis
616.523	RL221	Furuncle	616.716	RC931.073	Osteoporosis
616.524	RL283	Impetigo	616.722	RC933	Arthritis
616.526	RL321	Psoriasis	616.7223	RC931.067	Osteoarthritis
616.53	RL131	Acne	616.7227	RC933	Rheumatoid arthritis
616.544	RL471	Warts	616.723	RC927-.5	Rheumatism
616.544	RL451	Scleroderma (Disease)	616.723	RC927.5.N65	Nonarticular rheumatism
616.544	RL435	Ichthyosis	616.723	RC927.3	Fibromyalgia
616.544	RL435	Keratosis	616.73	RD771.I58	Spine—Instability
616.545	RL675	Bedsores	616.73043	RD768-771	Spine—Abnormalities
616.546	RL91	Dandruff	616.73062	RZ265.S64	Spinal adjustment
616.546	RL91	Beard	616.74	RD925-927	Muscles—Diseases
616.546	RL431	Hupertrichosis	616.74	RD688	Muscles—Diseases
616.546	RL155-.5	Baldness	616.74	RC935.A8	Muscular atrophy
616.547	RD563	Nails, Ingrowing	616.76	RC935.T4	Tendinitis
616.55	RL793	Mole (Dermatology)	616.76	RC935.B8	Bursitis
616.57	RL780	Ringworm	616.77	RC924-.5	Connective tissues— Diseases
616.57	RL764.S28	Scabies			
616.6	RC901.8	Urinary tract infections	616.8	RC394.D35	Brain—Degeneration
616.6	RC901.75	Urination disorders	616.8028	RC350.N49	Neurological intensive care
616.6	RC900-923	Urinary organs—Diseases	616.804075	RC348-349	Neurologic examination
616.6	RC870-923	Urology	616.8047543	RC386.6.U45	Ultrasonic encephalography
616.6075	RC901	Urinary organs—Examination	616.8047547	RC386.6.A45	Ambulatory electroencephalography
616.61	RC902-918	Kidneys—Diseases			
616.61	RC902	Nephrology	616.8047547	RC386.6.E43	Electroencephalography
616.61075	RC904-.5	Kidneys—Diseases— Diagnosis	616.806	RC350.N48	Neural stimulation
			616.806	RV241-246	Nervous system— Diseases—Eclectic treatment
616.612	RC907	Bright's disease			
616.614	RC918.R4	Chronic renal failure			
616.62	RC892	Urethra—Diseases	616.806	RX281-301	Nervous system— Diseases—Homeopathic treatment
616.62	RG484-485	Bladder—Diseases			
616.62	RC919-921	Bladder—Diseases			
616.622	RC916	Urinary organs—Calculi	616.8(1-4)	RC346-429	Neurology
616.635	RC915	Uremia	616.8(1-4)	RC386-395	Brain—Diseases
616.65	RC899	Prostate—Diseases	616.8(1-4)	RC346-429	Nervous system—Diseases
616.65	RC875-899.5	Andrology	616.81	RC388.5	Cerebrovascular disease
616.65043	RC881.5-883.5	Generative organs— Abnormalities	616.81	RC394.I5	Cerebral infarction
			616.82	RC376	Meningitis
616.66	RC896	Penis—Diseases	616.82	RC124	Meningitis
616.67	RC897	Scrotum—Diseases	616.831	RC523-.2	Alzheimer's disease
616.692	RC889	Infertility	616.833	RC382	Parkinsonism, Symptomatic

Dewey	LC	Subject Heading	Dewey	LC	Subject Heading
616.833	RC382	Parkinsonism	616.8582	RC569.5.V55	Violence
616.834	RC377	Multiple sclerosis	616.8582	RC552.S4	Self-mutilation
616.835	RC180-181	Poliomyelitis	616.8582	RC569.5.S48	Self-injurious behavior
616.836	RC388	Cerebral palsied	616.8582	RC569.5.S45	Self-destructive behavior
616.837	RC406.P3	Paraplegics	616.85822	RC569.5.F3	Family violence
616.84	RC394.M46	Memory disorders	616.85822	RC569.5.F3	Wife abuse
616.845	RC394.C77	Convulsions	616.858223	RC569.5.C55	Child abuse
616.849	RB150.C6	Coma	616.858223	RC569.5.P75	Psychological child abuse
616.849	RC569.5.E5	Enuresis	616.8583	RC560.V68	Voyeurism
616.8491	RB128	Tension headache	616.8583	RC560.S45	Sexual aversion disorders
616.8491	RB128	Headache	616.8583	RC560.A97	Autoerotic asphyxia
616.8491	RC392	Headache	616.8583	RC558.5	Lesbianism
616.8491	RC392	Cluster headache	616.8583	RC556-560	Psychosexual disorders
616.8498	RC547-549	Sleep disorders	616.8583	RC560.S43	Sex addition
616.8498	RC549	Narcolepsy	616.8583	RC558-.5	Homosexuality
616.8498	RC548-.5	Insomnia	616.85832	RC560.I45	Impotence
616.852	RC530-552	Neuroses	616.85835	RC560.S23	Sadomasochism
616.8521	RC552.P67	Post-traumatic stress disorder	616.85835	RC553.M36	Masochism
616.8521	RC552.03	Occupational neuroses	616.85836	RC560.C46	Child sexual abuse
616.8521	RC560.R36	Rape trauma syndrome	616.85836	RC560.I53	Incest
616.85223	RC535	Panic disorders	616.85836	RJ506.C48	Child sexual abuse
616.85223	RC531	Anxiety	616.8584	RC569.5.I46	Impulsive personality
616.85225	RC552.A44	Agoraphobia	616.8584	RC533	Compulsive behavior
616.85225	RC535	Phobias	616.85841	RC569.5.G35	Compulsive gambling
616.85227	RC533	Obsessive-compulsive disorders	616.85843	RC569.5.P9	Pyromania
616.8523	RC553.D5	Dissociative disorders	616.858445	RA1136-1137	Suicide
616.85232	RC394.A5	Amnesia	616.858445	RC569	Suicide
616.85236	RC569.5.M8	Multiple personality	616.858445	RC569	Suicidal behavior
616.8524	RC532	Hysteria	616.8585	RC553.N36	Narcissism
616.8524	RC552.S66	Somatization disorder	616.85852	RC569.5.B67	Borderline personality disorder
616.8526	RC567.5	Coffee habit	616.8588	RC569.7-571	Mental retardation
616.8526	RC552.E18	Eating disorders	616.858842	RC571	Down's syndrome
616.8526	RC552.C65	Compulsive eating	616.858843	RC391	Hydrocephalus
616.852600835	RJ506.E18	Eating disorders in adolescence	616.858848043	RC657	Cretinism
616.85262	RC552.A5	Anorexia nervosa	616.86	RC563-568	Substance abuse
616.85263	RC552.B84	Bulimia	616.86	RM316	Designer drugs
616.8527	RC537-545	Affective disorders	616.861	RC526	Delirium tremens
616.8527	RC537-545	Depression, Mental	616.861	RC525-527	Alcoholic psychoses
616.852700835	RJ506.D4	Depression in adolescence	616.861	RC564.7-565.9	Alcoholism
616.852700846	RC537.5	Depression in old age	616.8610019	HV5045	Alcoholism—Psychological aspects
616.8528	RC552.N5	Neurasthenia	616.8619	RC569.5.C63	Codependency
616.853	RC372-374.5	Epilepsy	616.8632	RC568.06	Opium habit
616.853	RC374.5	Petit mal epilepsy	616.8632	RC568.06	Morphine habit
616.85300835	RJ496.E6	Epilepsy in adolescence	616.8632	RC568.058	Opioid habit
616.855	RC423-428.8	Speech disorders	616.8632	RC566	Narcotic habit
616.855	RC423-428.8	Communicative disorders	616.8634	RC553.H3	Hallucinations and illusions
616.855	RC423-428.5	Language disorders	616.8635	RC568.C2	Cannabis
616.855	RC424.7	Articulation disorders	616.8635	RC568.C2	Hashish
616.855	RF510-540	Voice disorders	616.8647	RC568.C6	Cocaine habit
616.85506	RC423-428.8	Speech therapy	616.865	RC567	Tobacco habit
616.8552	RC425-.7	Aphasia	616.865	RC567	Nicotine
616.8552	RC425.5	Agrammatism	616.865	RC567	Smoking
616.8553	RC394.W6	Dyslexia	616.865	RC567	Tobacco—Physiological effect
616.8554	RC424	Stuttering	616.865	RM666.T6	Tobacco—Physiological effect
616.858	RC554-569.5	Personality disorders	616.87	RC400-406	Spinal cord—Diseases
616.858	RC555	Antisocial personality disorders	616.87	RC416	Neuritis
616.8582	RA1146	Self-mutilation	616.87	RC420	Sciatica

Dewey	LC	Subject Heading	Dewey	LC	Subject Heading
616.87	RC422.C26	Carpal tunnel syndrome	616.8917	RC510	Group psychoanalysis
616.87	RF341	Smell disorders	616.8917	RC489.024	Object constancy (Psychoanalysis)
616.89	RC455.4.C6	Psychiatry, Comparative			
616.89	RC466.8-467.95	Clinical psychology	616.8917	RC500-510	Psychoanalysis
616.89	RC440.7	Mental health care teams	616.8917	RC489.025	Object relations (Psychoanalysis)
616.89	RC435-571	Psychology, Pathological			
616.89001	RC455.2.M4	Psychiatry—Methodology	616.8918	RC489.N3	Narcotherapy
616.890028	RC473.P7	Projective techniques	616.892	RC512-528	Psychoses
616.8900835	RJ503	Adolescent psychopathology	616.895	RC516	Manic-depressive psychoses
616.8900835	RJ503	Adolescent psychiatry	616.898	RC514	Schizophrenia
616.89008996073	RC451.5.N4	Afro-Americans—Mental health	616.898	RC514	Paranoid schizophrenia
			616.8982	RC553.A88	Autism
616.890092	RC440.5	Psychiatric aides	616.8983	RC521-524	Dementia
616.89025	RC480.6	Psychiatric emergencies	616.8983	RC524	Senile dementia
616.89075	RC473.M5	Minnesota Multiphasic Personality Inventory	616.9(01-6)	RC109-216	Communicable diseases
			616.91	RC106	Exanthemata
616.89075	RC455.2.C4	Mental illness—Classification	616.912	RC183-.9	Smallpox
			616.914	RC125	Chickenpox
616.89075	RC469-473	Psychodiagnostics	616.915	RC168.M4	Measles
616.89075	RC473.R6	Rorschach Test	616.916	RC182.R8	Rubella
616.890932	RJ502.5	Infant psychiatry	616.917	RC182.S2	Scarlatina
616.891	RC439.2	Psychiatric day treatment	616.92	RC114-.7	Virus diseases
616.891	RC480.52	Psychiatry—Differential therapeutics	616.92	RC116.S8	Staphylococcal infections
			616.92	RC116.M8	Mycobacterial diseases
616.8910028	RC480.7	Interviewing in psychiatry	616.92	RC115-116	Bacterial diseases
616.8914	RC489.E24	Eclectic psychotherapy	616.921	RC137	Dengue
616.8914	RC481	Client-centered psychotherapy	616.9222	RC199-.9	Typhus fever
			616.9232	RC171-179	Black death
616.8914	RC455.2.E8	Psychotherapy—Moral and ethical aspects	616.9232	RC171-179	Plague
			616.9244	RC182.R3	Relapsing fever
616.8914	RC489.C68	Countertransference (Psychology)	616.925	RC114.6	Slow virus diseases
			616.925	RC147.G6	Mononucleosis
616.8914	RC475-489	Psychotherapy	616.925	RC141.5	Epstein-Barr virus diseases
616.8914	RC489.T45	Psychotherapy—Termination	616.927	RC182.S12	Salmonellosis
616.8914	RC489.S86	Supportive psychotherapy	616.9272	RC187-197	Typhoid fever
616.8914	RC480.55	Single-session psychotherapy	616.928	RC206-216	Yellow fever
616.8914	RC489.P68	Problem-solving therapy	616.9313	RC138-.9	Diphtheria
616.8914	RC489.E93	Existential psychotherapy	616.9318	RC185	Tetanus
616.8914	RC489.F27	Psychotherapy—Failure	616.932	RC126-134	Cholera
616.8914	RC489.I45	Impasse (Psychotherapy)	616.935	RC140	Dysentery
616.8914	RC489.M85	Multiple psychotherapy	616.936	RC118.7	Protozoan diseases
616.891400835	RJ505.T47	Adolescent psychotherapy—Termination	616.936	RC156-166	Malaria
			616.936	RC121.A5	Amebiasis
616.891400835	RJ503	Adolescent psychotherapy	616.9363	RC186.T82	African trypanosomiasis
616.89140092	RC455.2.A28	Psychotherapy patients—Abuse of	616.951	RC200-203	Sexually transmitted diseases
616.89142	RC489.C6	Cognitive-analytic therapy	616.9513	RC201-.9	Syphilis
616.89142	RC489.B4	Behavior therapy	616.9518	RC203.H45	Herpes genitalis
616.89142	RC489.B4	Aversion therapy	616.953	RC148	Rabies
616.89142	RC489.C63	Cognitive therapy	616.956	RC121.A6	Anthrax
616.89145	RC489.T7	Transactional analysis	616.959	RC113.5	Zoonoses
616.89152	RC488-.6	Group psychotherapy	616.96	QR251-255	Medical parasitology
616.891523	RC489.P7	Psychodrama	616.96	RC119-.7	Parasitic diseases
616.89156	RC488.6	Divorce therapy	616.96	RC226-248	Blood—Parasites
616.89156	RC488.5-.6	Family psychotherapy	616.964	RC184.T6	Echinococcosis
616.89156	RC488.5-.6	Marital psychotherapy	616.9652	RC142.5	Filariasis
616.89162	RC490-499	Therapeutics, Suggestive	616.9652	RC142.5	Elephantiasis
616.89165	RC487	Occupational therapy	616.968	RC119.5	Ectoparasitic infestations
616.891653	RC489.R4	Recreational therapy	616.969	RC117	Mycoses
616.891655	RC489.D3	Dance therapy	616.97	RC583-598	Allergy
616.891656	RC489.A7	Art therapy	616.97	RC588.C45	Antiallergic agents

Dewey	LC	Subject Heading	Dewey	LC	Subject Heading
616.975	RC596	Food allergy	616.99434	RC280.D5	Digestive organs—Cancer
616.9750654	RC588.D53	Food allergy—Diet therapy	616.994347	RC280.C6	Colon—Cancer
616.9758	RC598.D7	Drug allergy	616.99446	RC644	Hodgkin's disease
616.978	RC600	Autoimmune diseases	616.99449059	RD667.5	Mastectomy
616.979	RC606-607	Immunological deficiency symdromes	616.9947	RC280.B6	Osteosarcoma
			616.99477	RC280.S5	Skin—Cancer
616.9792	RC607.A26	AIDS (Disease)	616.99477	RC280.S5	Basal cell carcinoma
616.979200835	RJ387.A25	AIDS (Disease) in adolescence	616.99477	RC280.M37	Melanoma
			616.9948	RC280.N4	Neuroblastoma
616.979201	QR414.6.H58	HIV (Viruses)	616.9948	RD663	Nervous system—Tumors
616.98	RB152	Environmentally induced diseases	616.99481	RC280.B7	Brain—Cancer
			616.99481	RD663	Brain—Tumors
616.9802	RC1030-1035	Transportation medicine	616.99485	RC280.E2	Ear—Tumors
616.980213	RC1050-1097	Aviation medicine	616.99495	RC280.A2	Abdomen—Cancer
616.980213	RC1076.J48	Jet lag	616.99495	RC280.A2	Abdomen—Tumors
616.980214	RC1120-1160	Space medicine	616.995	RC306-320.5	Tuberculosis
616.98022	RC1000-1020	Submarine medicine	616.995061	RC311.3.C45	Tuberculosis—Chemotherapy
616.98023	RC970-971	Medicine, Military	616.9950654	RC311.D5	Tuberculosis—Diet therapy
616.98024	RC981-986	Medicine, Naval	616.995075	RC311.2	Tuberculin test
616.9803	RC963-969	Medicine, Industrial	616.998	RC154-.9	Leprosy
616.9803	RC963-969	Work environment	617	RX366-376	Surgery, Homeopathic
616.988	RA791-954	Medical climatology	617.01	RD98.3	Surgical wound infections
616.9881	RC955-958	Circumpolar medicine	617.01	RD98-.4	Surgery—Complications
616.9883	RC960-962	Tropical medicine	617.01	RD98.4	Postoperative pain
616.9892	RC103.M6	Motion sickness	617.024	RD110-.5	Ambulatory surgery
616.9893	RC103.A4	Mountain sickness	617.024	RD111-114	Surgery, Minor
616.9894	RC103.C3	Decompression sickness	617.03	RM930-950	Medical rehabilitation
616.9897	RA1231.R2	Radioactive substances—Toxicology	617.03	RM950	Rehabilitation technology
			617.044	RD156	War wounds
616.991	RC182.R4	Rheumatic fever	617.0901	GN477.5-.7	Surgery, Primitive
616.992	RC254-282	Tumors	617.1	RD96.15	Blunt trauma
616.992	RC268.55	Radiation carcinogenesis	617.1027	RC1200-1245	Sports medicine
616.992	RD651-678	Tumors	617.1062	RZ270-275	Wounds and injuries—Chiropractic treatment
616.994	RC254-282	Oncology			
616.994	RC261-282	Cancer	617.11	RA1085	Fires—Casualties
616.9940072	RC267	Cancer—Research	617.11	RD96.4-.55	Burns and scalds
616.994042	RC268.4-.44	Cancer—Genetic aspects	617.11	RD96.45	Chemical burns
616.99405	RC268-.15	Cancer—Prevention	617.11	RD96.4-.55	Burn care teams
616.994059	RD651-678	Cancer—Surgery	617.122	RA1091	Electrical injuries
616.99406	RC271.C5	Antineoplastic agents	617.122	RD96.5	Electrical burns
616.99406	RC271.P54	Plasma exchange (Therapeutics)	617.14	RA1121	Wounds and injuries
			617.14	RC87	Wounds and injuries
616.99406	RC271.H55	Cancer—Hormone therapy	617.145	RD96.3	Gunshot wounds
616.99406	RC270.8-271	Cancer—Treatment	617.15	RD104.S77	Stress fractures (Orthopedics)
616.99406	RC271.I45	Cancer—Immunotherapy			
616.99406	RX261.C3	Cancer—Homeopathic treatment	617.15	RD101-104	Fractures
			617.15	RD104.A95	Avulsion fractures
616.994061	RC271.D68	Doxorubicin	617.15	RD101	Fractures, Spontaneous
616.994071	RC268.5-.7	Carcinogenesis	617.155	RD529	Skull—Fractures
616.994071	RC268.57	Viral carcinogenesis	617.157	RD558	Elbow—Fractures
616.994071	RC268.6-.7	Carcinogens	617.158	RD549-.5	Pelvic bones—Fractures
616.994071	RC268.48	Cancer—Etiology	617.158	RD551-563	Extremities (Anatomy)—Fractures
616.99419	RC643	Lymphocytic leukemia			
616.99419	RC643	Leukemia	617.16	RD557.5	Shoulder joint—Dislocation
616.99419	RC643	Chronic lymphocytic leukemia	617.16	RD106	Dislocations
616.99419	RC280.H47	Hematological oncology	617.18	RA1071-1082	Asphyxia
616.99419	RC643	Acute leukemia	617.18	RC87.3	Asphyxia
616.99424	RC280.L8	Lungs—Cancer	617.18	RA1076	Drowning
616.99431	RC280.M6	Mouth—Cancer	617.1806	RC87.9	Artificial respiration
616.99432	RC280.E8	Esophagus—Cancer	617.300222	RD733.2	Orthopedics—Pictorial works
616.99432	RC280.E8	Esophagus—Tumors			

Dewey	LC	Subject Heading	Dewey	LC	Subject Heading
617.41	RD597-598.7	Cardiovascular system—Surgery	617.5109	RF25-26	Otolaryngology—History
			617.51092	RF37-38	Otolaryngologists
617.412	RD598.35.C37	Cardiomyoplasty	617.514	RD529	Craniotomy
617.412	RD598.35.C35	Cardiac catheterization	617.52044	RD523	Face—Wounds and injuries
617.412	RD598-.35	Heart—Surgery	617.52059	RD523-527	Face—Surgery
617.4120592	RD598.35.T7	Heart—Transplantation	617.520592	RD119.5.F33	Facelift
617.4120592	RD598.35.A78	Heart, Artificial	617.52306	RV341-347	Nose—Diseases—Eclectic treatment
617.4120645	RC684.P3	Pacemaker, Artificial (Heart)			
617.4120645	RC684.P3	Cardiac pacing	617.52306	RX451	Nose—Diseases—Homeopathic treatment
617.413	RD598.5	Arterial catheterization			
617.413	RD598.5	Dissecting aortic aneurysms	617.531044	RF547	Throat—Wounds and injuries
617.413	RD598.5	Angioplasty	617.531059	RF484.5	Tonsillectomy
617.413	RD598.5-.7	Blood-vessels—Surgery	617.533059	RF517	Tracheotomy
617.413	RD598.35.C67	Coronary artery bypass	617.533059	RF516-517	Larynx—Surgery
617.413059	RC693	Dissecting aortic aneurysms	617.54	RC941	Chest pain
617.414059	RM182-190	Veins—Puncture	617.54	RC941	Chest—Diseases
617.44	RD599.5.A37	Adrenalectomy	617.5406	RV293	Chest—Dieases—Eclectic treatment
617.440592	RD123.5	Bone marrow—Transplantation			
			617.5406	RX360	Chest—Diseases—Homeopathic treatment
617.440592	RD599.5.P58	Pituitary gland—Transplantation			
			617.548	RD539.5	Esophagectomy
617.462059	RD580-581	Bladder—Surgery	617.548044	RD539.5	Esophagus—Wounds and injuries
617.463	RD585.5	Vasectomy			
617.463	RD585.5	Sterilization reversal	617.548059	RD539.5	Esophagus—Surgery
617.463	RD590	Circumcision	617.55	RC944	Abdomen—Diseases
617.463059	RD572	Castration	617.55	RC946	Pelvis—Diseases
617.47	RD701-789	Orthopedic surgery	617.55	RD540-548	Acute abdomen
617.47044	RD680-688	Musculoskeletal system—Wounds and injuries	617.55044	RD540-548	Abdomen—Wounds and injuries
617.470592	RD755.5-.7	Orthopedic implants	617.55059	RD540-547	Digestive organs—Surgery
617.471	RD103.B65	Bone wiring (Orthopedics)	617.55059	RD540-548	Abdomen—Surgery
617.471059	RD103.E88	External skeletal fixation (Surgery)	617.5506	RV297	Pelvis—Diseases—Eclectic treatment
617.471059	RD684	Bones—Surgery	617.553059	RD540.5	Gastrostomy
617.4710592	RD123	Bone-grafting	617.553059	RD540.5-.57	Gastrectomy
617.4720592	RD549	Artificial hip joints	617.553059	RD540.5-.57	Stomache—Surgery
617.4720592	RD549	Total hip replacement	617.5545	RD542	Appendectomy
617.4770592	RD121	Skin-grafting	617.5565	RD546-547	Gallbladder—Surgery
617.48044	RD592.5-596	Nervous system—Wounds and injuries	617.559059	RD621-626	Hernia
			617.564	RD771.B217	Backache
617.48059	RD592.5-596	Nervous system—Surgery	617.574	RD756.2-.22	Artificial arms
617.481	RD594-.15	Psychosurgery	617.574059	RD557	Arm—Amputation
617.481044	RD594-.15	Brain—Wounds and injuries	617.575059	RD778-.5	Hand—Surgery
617.481059	RD594-.15	Brain—Surgery	617.58	RC951	Extremities (Anatomy)—Diseases
617.482044	RD533	Spine—Wounds and injuries			
617.482059	RD594.3	Spinal cord—Surgery	617.58	RD756-.42	Artificial limbs
617.51	RF	Otolaryngology	617.58	RD553	Phantom limb
617.51	RC936	Head—Diseases	617.58044	RD551-563	Extremities (Anatomy)—Wounds and injuries
617.510025	RF28	Otolaryngologists—Directories			
			617.58059	RD551-563	Extremities (Anatomy)—Surgery
617.51005	RF11	Otolaryngology—Periodicals			
617.51006	RF1	Otolaryngology—Societies, etc.	617.58059	RD553	Amputation
			617.580592	RD551-563	Extremities (Anatomy)—Transplantation
617.51006	RF16	Otolaryngology—Congresses			
617.51044	RF50	Otolaryngology—Wounds and injuries	617.5820592	RD561	Total knee replacement
			617.5820592	RD561	Artificial knee
617.51059	RF51-52	Otolaryngology, Operative	617.584059	RD562	Excision of ankle
617.5106	RV291	Head—Diseases—Eclectic treatment	617.585	RD563	Podiatry
			617.585	RC951	Foot—Diseases
617.51075	RF48-.5	Otolaryngology—Diagnosis	617.585043	RD786-789	Toes—Abnormalities
617.51075	RF48-.5	Otolaryngologic examination	617.585043	RD781-789	Foot—Abnormalities

Dewey	LC	Subject Heading	Dewey	LC	Subject Heading
617.585044	RD781	Foot—Dislocation	617.632	RK361-450	Periodontal disease
617.585044	RD563	Foot—Wounds and injuries	617.632	RK401-410	Gums—Diseases
617.585059	RD563	Foot—Surgery	617.634	RK320.E53	Dental enamel microabrasion
617.5850592	RD563	Foot—Reimplantation	617.634	RK340-341	Dental enamel—Diseases
617.5850592	RD563	Foot—Amputation	617.6342	RK351-356	Endodontics
617.585075	RD563	Foot—Examination	617.643	RK527-528	Orthodontics, Corrective
617.6	RK328	Dental calculus	617.643	RK520-528	Orthodontics
617.6	RK328	Dental plaque	617.643	RK523	Malocclusion
617.6	RK328	Dental deposits	617.64300284	RK527-528	Orthodonic appliances
617.6	RK	Dentistry	617.645	RK55.C5	Pedodontics
617.60014	RK28	Dentistry—Terminology	617.645	RK361-450	Periodontics
617.60019	RK53	Dentistry—Psychological aspects	617.66	RK531-.5	Teeth—Extraction
			617.67	RK331	Dental caries
617.60023	RK60-.5	Dentistry—Vocational guidance	617.672	RK515	Dental drilling
			617.672	RK515	Dental cavity preparation
617.60025	RK37	Dentists—Directories	617.675	RK653	Dental metallurgy
617.600284	RK681-686	Dental instruments and apparatus	617.675	RK519.A4	Dental amalgams
			617.675	RK517-519	Fillings (Dentistry)
617.6005	RK16	Dentistry—Periodicals	617.675	RK653	Gold alloys
617.6006	RK1	Dentistry—Societies, etc.	617.675	RK653.5	Dental ceramic metals
617.6006	RK21	Dentistry—Congresses	617.675	RK655	Dental ceramics
617.60071	RK60.8	Dental health education	617.69	RK652.7-.8	Dental bonding
617.60071	RK71-231	Dentistry—Study and teaching	617.69	RK641-667	Prosthodontics
			617.69	RK656	Denture attachments
617.600710(4-9)	RK86-231	Dentistry—Study and teaching—[By region and country]	617.69	RK667.T57	Tissue-integrated prostheses
			617.692	RK656-666	Dentures, Immediate
			617.692	RK656-666	Overlay dentures
617.60072	RK80	Dentistry—Research	617.692	RK656-666	Dentures
617.600723	RK52-.45	Dental surveys	617.692	RK664-666	Partial dentures
617.60076	RK57	Dentistry—Examinations, questions, etc.	617.692	RK665	Partial dentures, Removable
			617.692	RK666	Bridges (Dentistry)
617.6008996073	RK60.45	Afro-Americans in dentistry	617.692	RK666	Crowns (Dentistry)
617.60092	RK	Dentists	617.6920592	RK667.I45	Implant dentures
617.601	RK61	Teeth—Care and hygiene	617.695	RK652.7-.8	Dental adhesives
617.601	RK60.7-.8	Preventive dentistry	617.695	RK652.7-.8	Dental cements
617.601	RK60.7-.8	Dental Prophylaxis	617.695	RK652.5-655	Dental materials
617.601	RK60.7	Teeth—Polishing	617.7	RE	Ophthalmology
617.6023	RK58-59.3	Dentistry—Practice	617.70014	RE20	Ophthalmology—Terminology
617.60232	RK	Dentists	617.70025	RE22	Ophthalmologists—Directories
617.60233	RK60.5	Dental auxiliary personnel			
617.6044	RK490-493	Teeth—Wounds and injuries	617.700284	RE73	Ophthalmology—Instruments
617.605	RK529-535	Mouth—Surgery	617.7005	RE6	Ophthalmology—Periodicals
617.605	RK513	Dentistry, Operative—Complications	617.7006	RE1	Ophthalmology—Societies, etc.
617.605	RK503	Dentistry, Operative—Positioning	617.7006	RE11	Ophthalmology—Congresses
			617.70071	RE56	Ophthalmology—Study and teaching
617.605	RK501-519	Dentistry, Operative			
617.60592	RK533	Teeth—Transplantation	617.70232	RE31-36	Ophthalmologists
617.606	RK701-715	Dentistry—Formulae, receipts, prescriptions	617.7026	RE48	Ophthalmologic emergencies
			617.7043	RE906	Eye—Abnormalities
617.606	RK318-320	Dental therapeutics	617.7059	RE80-87	Eye—Surgery
617.6071073	RK91-97	Dentistry—Study and teaching—United States	617.706	RX410-431	Eye—Diseases—Homeo-pathic treatment
617.60901	RK29-34	Dentistry—History	617.706	RV321-331	Eye—Diseases—Eclectic treatment
617.60901	RK31	Dentistry, Ancient			
617.63	RK305	Focal infection, Dental	617.7061	RE994	Ophthalmic drugs
617.63	RK301-493	Teeth—Diseases	617.7061	RE994	Ocular pharmacology
617.63	RK351	Focal infection, Dental	617.7075	RE75-79	Eye—Examination
617.630754	RK308-310	Teeth—Diseases—Diagnosis	617.707547	RE79.E39	Electroculography
617.632	RK410	Gingivitis	617.707547	RE79.E4	Electroretinography
617.632	RK450.P4	Periodontitis	617.707572	RE79.R3	Eye—Radiography

135

Dewey	LC	Subject Heading	Dewey	LC	Subject Heading
617.709	RE26-30	Ophthalmology—History	617.84	RF220-229	Middle ear—Diseases
617.71043	RD772	Hip joint—Dislocation, Congenital	617.85	RF210	Tympanic membrane—Diseases
617.712	RE95	Vision, Monocular	617.86	RF230	Eustachian tube—Diseases
617.712	RE91	Low vision	617.87	RF235	Mastoid process—Diseases
617.712	RE91-95	Blindness	617.882	RF260-275	Labyrinth (Ear)—Diseases
617.713	RE831-840	Eye—Wounds and injuries	617.8820592	RF305	Cochlear implants
617.719	RE336-340	Cornea—Diseases	617.89	RF300-310	Hearing aids
617.719	RE328	Sclera—Diseases	617.9	RD736.T7	Orthopedic traction
617.7190592	RE336	Artificial corneas	617.9	RD757.S5	Orthopedic slings
617.72	RE350-355	Uvea—Diseases	617.9	RD757.W4	Wheelchairs
617.732	RE725-780	Neuroophthalmology	617.9	RD756	Crutches
617.735	RE551-661	Retina—Diseases	617.9	RD755-757	Orthopedic apparatus
617.735	RE603	Retinal detachment	617.93	RD113-.4	Bandages and bandaging
617.735	RE661.D5	Diabetic retinopathy	617.93	RD113-.4	Surgical dressings
617.74	RE651	Thrombosis	617.95	RD118-120.5	Surgery, Plastic
617.74	RE835	Eye—Foreign bodies	617.95	RD120.6-129.8	Transplantation of organs, tissues, etc.
617.74	RE96	Eye—Inflammation			
617.74	RE96	Eye—Infections	617.95	RD130	Prosthesis
617.741	RE871	Glaucoma	617.960083	RD139	Pediatric anesthesia
617.742	RE401-461	Crystalline lens—Diseases	617.9600846	RD145	Geriatric anesthesia
617.742	RE451	Cataract	617.9682	RG732-733	Anesthesia in obstetrics
617.746	RE501	Vitreous body—Diseases	617.97	RD145	Aged—Surgery
617.75	RE91-95	Vision disorders	617.98	RD137-139	Children—Surgery
617.75	RE51	Eyestrain	617.99	RD151-498	Surgery, Military
617.75	RE940-981	Optometry	617.99	RD151-498	Surgery, Naval
617.7522	RE940-981	Eyeglasses	617.99094	RD268-441	Surgery, Military—Europe
617.7522	RE961-962	Ophthalmic lenses	617.99095	RD445-476	Surgery, Military—Asia
617.7523	RE977.C6	Contact lenses	617.99096	RD481-489	Surgery, Military—Africa
617.7524	RE988	Intraocular lenses	617.990971	RD216	Surgery, Military—Canada
617.755	RE925-939	Eye—Refractive errors	617.990972	RD221	Surgery, Military—Mexico
617.755	RE925-939	Eye—Accomodation and refraction	617.9909728	RD224-225	Surgery, Military—Central America
617.755	RE932	Astigmatism	617.9909729	RD231-232	Surgery, Military—West Indies
617.755	RE48	Eyestrain			
617.759	RE921	Color blindness	617.990973	RD200-214	Surgery, Military—United States
617.759075	RE918-921	Color vision—Testing			
617.762	RE731-780	Eye—Movement disorders	617.99098	RD235-267	Surgery, Military—South America
617.762	RE731-780	Eye—Muscles			
617.762	RE760	Eye—Paralysis	617.990993	RD493.5	Surgery, Military—New Zealand
617.762	RE738	Diplopia			
617.764	RE201-216	Lacrimal apparatus—Diseases	617.990994	RD493	Surgery, Military—Australia
			617.99099(5-6)	RD498	Surgery, Military—Oceania
617.771	RE121-155	Eyelids—Diseases	618	RC48.6	Women—Diseases
617.773	RE321	Conjunctivitis	618	RG831	Puerperal convulsions
617.773	RE320	Acute hemorrhagic conjunctivitis	618.07	RG77	Gynecologic pathology
			618.1	RG	Gynecology
617.773	RE310-326	Conjunctiva—Diseases	618.1	RG316	Endometrium—Diseases
617.78	RE711	Eye-sockets—Diseases	618.1	RG483.P44	Pelvic pain
617.79	RE986-988	Eyes, Artificial	618.10014	RG47	Gynecology—Terminology
617.8	RF110-320	Otology	618.10019	RG103.5	Gynecology—Psychological aspects
617.8	RF286-320	Audiology			
617.8	RF286-320	Deafness	618.10025	RG32-33	Gynecologists—Directories
617.8	RF110-320	Ear—Diseases	618.1005	RG26	Gynecology—Periodicals
617.8	RF293.5	Deafness, Noise induced	618.1006	RG1	Gynecology—Societies, etc.
617.8	RF286-320	Hearing disorders	618.1006	RG31	Gynecology—Congresses
617.800284	RF298-310	Audiology—Instruments	618.1009	RG51-67	Gynecology—History
617.8006	RF286	Audiology—Societies, etc.	618.1025	RG158	Gynecologic emergencies
617.80071	RF62	Otolaryngology—Study and teaching	618.1059	RG104.5	Gynoplasty
			618.1075	RG304-.5	Uterus—Diseases—Diagnosis
617.8059	RF126-127	Ear—Surgery			

Dewey	LC	Subject Heading	Dewey	LC	Subject Heading
618.1075	RG107-.5	Gynecologic examination	618.3	RG580.M34	Malnutrition in pregnancy
618.107543	RG107.5.E48	Endoscopic ultrasonography	618.3025	RG571-591	Obstetrical emergencies
618.107545	RG107.5.L34	Laparoscopy	618.31	RG586	Ectopic pregnancy
618.1092	RG71-76	Gynecologists	618.32	RG631-633	Perinatal death
618.12	RG421-433	Fallopian tubes—Diseases	618.32	RG629.G76	Fetal growth retardation
618.12059	RG138	Sterilization of women	618.32	RG631-633	Fetal death
618.12059	RG138	Sterilization reversal	618.32	RG600-650	Fetus
618.14	RG310-315	Cervix uteri—Diseases	618.32	RG600-650	Perinatology
618.14	RG361	Uterus—Rupture	618.32	RG629.G75	Fetal growth disorders
618.14	RG301-391	Uterus—Diseases	618.32	RG626-629	Fetus—Diseases
618.142	RG411	Pelvic inflammatory disease	618.32	RG627.6.D79	Fetus—Effect of drugs on
618.143	RG314	Cervix erosion	618.32	RG627.6.M34	Fetal malnutrition
618.145	RG104-.7	Generative organs, Female—Surgery	618.32	RG613.7	Fetus—Immunology
			618.3204275	RG628.3.A48	Amniocentesis
618.145	RD585	Sterilization reversal	618.32043	RG626-629	Fetus—Abnormalities
618.1453	RG391	Hysterectomy	618.32075	RG628-.3	Prenatal diagnosis
618.15	RG268-272	Vagina—Diseases	618.32075	RG628-.3	Fetal monitoring
618.16	RG261-266	Vulva—Diseases	618.3207543	RG628.3.U58	Fetus—Ultrasonic imaging
618.17	RG159-208	Endocrine gynecology	618.326	RG580.D5	Diabetes in pregnancy
618.172	RG165	Premenstrual syndrome	618.326	RG615	Fetus—Metabolism
618.172	RG161-186	Menstruation disorders	618.3261	RG618	Perinatal cardiology
618.172	RG161-186	Menstrual cycle	618.3261	RG580.H47	Blood diseases in pregnancy
618.172	RG181	Dysmenorrhea	618.3261043	RJ269	Fetal heart—Abnormalities
618.172	RG734	Menstrual regulation	618.3261075	RG628.3.H42	Fetal heart rate monitoring
618.175	RG186	Menopause	618.326107543	RG628.3.E34	Echocardiography
618.178	RG133.5-135	Human reproductive technology	618.3268	RG580.E64	Epilepsy in pregnancy
			618.3268	RG580.S75	Substance abuse in pregnancy
618.178	RG201-205	Infertility, Female			
618.178	RG134	Artificial insemination, Human	618.3268	RG580.D76	Drug abuse in pregnancy
			618.34	RG591	Placenta
618.178059	RG135	Fertilization in vitro, Human	618.392	RG648	Miscarriage
618.19	RG491-499	Breast—Diseases	618.397	RG649	Labor, Premature
618.19059	RD539.8	Mammaplasty	618.4	RG663	Underwater childbirth
618.190592	RD539.8	Augmentation mammaplasty	618.4	RG662	Active childbirth
618.2	RG133	Conception	618.4	RG631-633	Stillbirth
618.2	RG	Obstetrics	618.4	RG620	Fetus—Respiration and cry
618.2	RG519-520	Uterus, Pregnant	618.4	RG651-791	Labor (Obstetrics)
618.2	RG551-591	Pregnancy	618.4	RG661.5	Childbirth at home
618.2	RG950	Midwives	618.4	RG734	Labor, Induced (Obstetrics)
618.20019	RG560	Pregnancy—Psychological aspects	618.42	RG671-693	Fetal presentation
			618.45	RG661-662	Natural childbirth
618.20025	RG504-505	Obstetricians—Directories	618.5	RG701-721	Labor (Obstetrics)—Complications
618.200284	RG545	Obstetrics—Apparatus and instruments			
			618.54	RG580.H5	Uterine hemorrhage
618.20072	RG155	Obstetrics—Research	618.54	RG711	Uterine hemorrhage
618.200835	RG556.5	Teenage pregnancy	618.54	RG821	Uterine hemorrhage
618.20284	RG739	Obstetrical forceps	618.56	RG715	Placenta praevia
618.206	RX476	Obstetrics, Homeopathic	618.58	RG719	Umbilical cord—Prolapse
618.206	RV361-365	Obstetrics, Eclectic	618.7	RG801-871	Postnatal care
618.2075	RG563-564	Pregnancy—Signs and diagnosis	618.7	RG801-871	Puerperal disorders
			618.71	RG861-866	Lactation disorders
618.207543	RG527.5.U48	Ultrasonics in obstetrics	618.73	RC867.5	Peritonitis
618.209	RG529	Obstetrics—Case studies	618.75	RG576	Eclampsia
618.209	RG511-518	Obstetrics—History	618.75	RG575-576	Toxemia of pregnancy
618.2092	RG509-510	Obstetricians	618.76	RG852	Postpartum depression
618.24	RG559	Pregnancy—Nutritional aspects	618.76	RG851	Puerperal psychoses
			618.76	RG850-852	Postpartum psychiatric disorders
618.24	RJ91	Prenatal influences			
618.25	RG696-698	Multiple birth	618.8	RG725-791	Obstetrics—Surgery
618.25	RG567	Multiple pregnancy	618.82	RG741	Obstetrical extraction
618.3	RG580.A44	AIDS (Disease) in pregnancy	618.83	RG781	Craniotomy

Dewey	LC	Subject Heading	Dewey	LC	Subject Heading
618.86	RG761	Cesarean section	618.92462083	RJ420.D5	Diabetes in children
618.92	RJ	Pediatrics	618.92462083	RJ420.D5	Diabetes in youth
618.92	RJ	Children—Diseases	618.9247	RJ420.P58	Dwarfism, Pituitary
618.92	RJ135	Failure to thrive syndrome	618.92521	RJ516.E35	Eczema in children
618.92	RJ320.S93	Sudden infant death syndrome	618.926	RJ466-478.5	Pediatric urology
618.9200019	RJ47.5-.53	Pediatrics—Psychosomatic aspects	618.92614	RJ476.R46	Acute renal failure in children
			618.9271	RJ482.B65	Bone diseases in children
			618.92716	RJ128	Children—Metabolism
618.9200025	RJ29	Pediatricians—Directories	618.92748	RJ482.D78	Duchenne muscular dystrophy
618.920005	RJ16	Pediatrics—Periodicals	618.9277	RJ520.C64	Collagen diseases in children
618.920006	RJ1	Pediatricians—Societies, etc.			
618.920006	RJ21	Pediatrics—Congresses	618.9277	RJ482.C65	Connective tissue diseases in children
618.920009	RJ36-42	Pediatrics—History			
618.9200092	RJ43	Pediatricians	618.928	RJ486-496	Pediatric neurology
618.920025	RJ370	Pediatric emergencies	618.928043	RJ496.B7	Brain-damaged children
618.920028	RJ370	Pediatric intensive care	618.928043	RJ290-.5	Nervous system—Abnormalities
618.920042	RJ47.3-.4	Genetic disorders in children			
618.920062	RJ53.E95	Exercise therapy for children	618.92836	RJ496.C4	Cerebral palsied children
618.9200653	RJ53.F5	Fluid therapy for children	618.92842	RJ301	Paralysis
618.9200654	RJ53.D53	Diet therapy for children	618.92842	RJ496.P2	Paralysis
618.9201	RJ268.8	Neonatal gastroenterology	618.92845	RJ496.C7	Febrile convulsions
618.9201	RJ61	Infants—Care	618.92849	RJ476.E6	Enuresis
618.9201	RJ253.5	Neonatal emergencies	618.9285223	RJ506.A58	Anxiety in children
618.9201	RJ281	Birth weight, Low	618.9285225	RJ506.P38	Phobias in children
618.9201	RJ251-325	Neonatology	618.928527	RJ506.D4	Depression in infants
618.9201	RJ253.5	Neonatal intensive care	618.928527	RJ506.D4	Depression in children
618.92011	RJ250-.3	Infants (Premature)	618.928527	RJ506.D4	Affective disorders in children
618.920232	RJ33.5-.8	Pediatrics—Practice	618.92853	RJ496.E6	Epilepsy in children
618.9206	RV375-377	Children—Diseases—Eclectic treatment	618.928553	RJ496.A5	Dyslexic children
			618.928554	RJ496.S8	Stuttering in children
618.9206	RX501-531	Children—Diseases—Homeopathic treatment	618.92858	RJ506.B44	Behavior disorders in children
			618.928582	RJ506.S39	Self-destructive behavior in children
618.920977	RE48.2.C5	Pediatric ophthalmology			
618.92097773	RJ296	Conjunctivitis, Infantile	618.9285836	RC560.I53	Incest victims
618.92098	RJ478-.5	Adolescent gynecology	618.9285836	RJ507.S49	Sexually abused children
618.92098	RJ476.5-478.5	Sexual disorders in children	618.928588	RJ506.F73	Fragile X syndrome
618.92107572	RJ423.5.D54	Digital subtraction angiography	618.9285884	RJ506.M4	Mental retardation
			618.92858842	RJ506.D68	Down's syndrome
618.9212	RJ421-426	Pediatric cardiology	618.928589	RJ506.H9	Attention-deficit hyperactivty disorder
618.921207543	RJ423.5.U46	Echocardiography			
618.9215	RJ411-416	Pediatric hematology	618.9289	RJ499-520	Child psychiatry
618.9215	RJ269.5-271	Neonatal hematology	618.9289	RJ506.C65	Conduct disorders in children
618.922	RJ256	Asphyxia neonatorum	618.9289	RJ499-520	Child psychopathology
618.922	RJ312	Respiratory insufficiency in children	618.9289027	RJ500.2	Child psychopathology—Research
618.922	RJ274	Hyaline membrane disease	618.928914	RJ504-505	Child psychotherapy
618.922	RJ431-436	Pediatric respiratory diseases	618.928917	RJ504.2	Child analysis
618.92238	RJ436.A8	Asthma in children	618.928917	RJ503	Adolescent analysis
618.9231	RJ460-463	Pediatric oral medicine	618.928982	RJ506.A9	Autism in children
618.9232	RJ456.E83	Esophagus—Atresia	618.929	RJ275	Neonatal infections
618.9233	RJ267	Colic	618.9292	RJ406.B32	Bacterial diseases in children
618.9233	RJ446-456	Pediatric gastroenterology	618.92925	RJ401-406	Virus diseases in children
618.92342	RJ456.F43	Fecal incontinence in children	618.9297	RJ386-.5	Allergy in children
			618.92975	RJ386.5	Food allergy in infants
618.923623	RJ272	Hepatitis, Neonatal	618.92975	RJ386.5	Food allergy in children
618.923625	RJ276	Jaundice, Neonatal	618.929792	RJ387.A25	AIDS (Disease) in infants
618.9239	RJ399.M26	Malnutrition in children	618.929792	RJ387.A25	AIDS (Disease) in children
618.92395	RJ396	Rickets	618.9299419	RJ416.A25	Acute myelocytic leukemia in children
618.924	RJ418-420	Pediatric endocrinology			
618.92442	RJ420.G65	Endemic goiter in children	618.97	RC952-954.6	Geriatrics
618.9245	RJ420.A27	Adrenal glands	618.97	RC952-954.6	Aged—Diseases

Dewey	LC	Subject Heading	Dewey	LC	Subject Heading
618.9789	RC451.4.A5	Geriatric psychiatry	620.009496	TA95.A2	Engineering—Balkan Peninsula
619	R850-854	Medicine, Experimental			
619.98	R853.H8	Human experimentation in medicine	620.009497	TA95.Y8	Engineering—Yugoslavia
			620.00951	TA101-102	Engineering—China
620	TA	Engineering	620.00952	TA105-106	Engineering—Japan
620.001171	TA168	Systems engineering	620.00954	TA103-104	Engineering—India
620.00148	TA11	Engineering—Notation	620.0095491	TA104.5-.6	Engineering—Pakistan
620.00151	TA329-348	Engineering mathematics	620.0095493	TA104.7-.8	Engineering—Sri Lanka
620.00151535	TA347.F5	Finite element method	620.00955	TA107-108	Engineering—Iran
620.00212	TA180-181	Specifications	620.009561	TA111-112	Engineering—Turkey
620.00212	TA180-182	Engineering—Specifications	620.009567	TA113.I7	Engineering—Iraq
620.00218	TA368	Standards, Engineering	620.0095694	TA113.I75	Engineering—Israel
620.00228	TA177	Engineering models	620.00957	TA109-110	Engineering—Asiatic Russia
620.0023	TA157-158.3	Engineers	620.009598	TA113.I55	Engineering—Indonesia
620.0025	TA12	Engineering firms—Directories	620.009599	TA113.P6	Engineering—Philippines
			620.0096	TA115-119	Engineering—Africa
620.00284	T13	Engineering—Supplies	620.00962	TA117-118	Engineering—Egypt
620.00284	TA165	Engineering instruments	620.00971	TA26-27	Engineering—Canada
620.00284	TA213-215	Engineering—Equipment and supplies	620.00972	TA28-29	Engineering—Mexico
			620.009728	TA30-31	Engineering—Central America
620.003	TA9	Engineering—Dictionaries			
620.0042	TA174	Engineering design	620.009729	TA32-33	Engineering—West Indies
620.0044	TA191	Engineering inspection	620.00973	TA23-25	Engineering—United States
620.005	TA1-4	Engineering—Periodicals	620.00981	TA41-42	Engineering—Brazil
620.006	TA5	Engineering—Congresses	620.00982	TA36-37	Engineering—Argentina
620.006	TA216-217	Engineering firms	620.00983	TA43-44	Engineering—Chile
620.006	TA157	Engineering firms	620.00984	TA38-39	Engineering—Bolivia
620.0068	TA190-194	Engineering—Management	620.00985	TA52	Engineering—Peru
620.00681	TA177.4-185	Engineering economy	620.009861	TA45-46	Engineering—Colombia
620.0072	TA160-.6	Engineering—Research	620.009866	TA47	Engineering—Ecuador
620.0072	TA416-417	Engineering laboratories	620.00987	TA54	Engineering—Venezuela
620.0072	TA416-417	Engineering experiment stations	620.009881	TA48	Engineering—Guyana
			620.009882	TA50	Engineering—French Guiana
620.00727	TA340	Engineering—Statistical methods	620.009883	TA49	Engineering—Surinam
			620.009892	TA51	Engineering—Paraguay
620.00728	TA337-338	Engineering—Graphic methods	620.009895	TA53	Engineering—Uruguay
			620.00993	TA122.5-.6	Engineering—New Zealand
620.008996073	TA157	Afro-American engineers	620.00994	TA121-122	Engineering—Australia
620.009	TA15-19	Engineering—History	620.0099(5-6)	TA123-124	Engineering—Oceania
620.0092	TA139-140	Engineers—Biography	620.00998	TA125-.5	Engineering—Arctic regions
620.009(4-9)	TA21-127	Engineering—[By region or country]	620.1	TA350-359	Mechanics, Applied
			620.106	TA357-359	Fluid dynamics
620.00941	TA57-64	Engineering—Great Britain	620.1064	TC174	Water hammer
620.00943	TA73-74.5	Engineering—Germany	620.1064	TA357.5.C38	Cavitation
620.009436	TA65-.2	Engineering—Austria	620.1064	TA357.5.M59	Mixing
620.009437	TA65.3-.4	Engineering—Czechoslovakia	620.1064	TA357.5.U57	Unsteady flow (Fluid dynamics)
620.009439	TA65.5-66	Engineering—Hungary			
620.00944	TA71-72.5	Engineering—France	620.1064	TA357.5.M84	Multiphase flow
620.00945	TA79-80	Engineering—Italy	620.10640287	TA357.5.M43	Fluid dynamic measurements
620.00946	TA87-88	Engineering—Spain	620.11	TA401-492	Materials
620.009469	TA83-84.5	Engineering—Portugal	620.110287	TA401-492	Testing
620.00947	TA85-86	Engineering—Russia	620.1103	TA402	Materials—Dictionaries
620.00948	TA88.5	Engineering—Scandinavia	620.1105	TA401	Materials—Periodicals
620.009481	TA81-82	Engineering—Norway	620.11072	TA404.2	Materials—Research
620.009485	TA89-90	Engineering—Sweden	620.112	TA405	Strength of materials
620.009489	TA69-70	Engineering—Denmark	620.112	TA410-417.7	Strength of materials
620.0094897	TA95.F5	Engineering—Finland	620.112	TA410	Buckling (Mechanics)
620.009492	TA77-78	Engineering—Netherlands	620.1121	TA418.58	Thermal stresses
620.009493	TA67-68	Engineering—Belgium	620.11223	TA418.74-.76	Corrosion and anti-corrosives
620.009494	TA91-92	Engineering—Switzerland	620.11233	TA418.22	Materials—Creep
620.009495	TA75-76	Engineering—Greece	620.11233	TA652	Plastic analysis (Engineering)

Dewey	LC	Subject Heading	Dewey	LC	Subject Heading
620.1126	TA418.45	Hard materials	621.09(4-9)	TJ21-127	Mechanical engineering—[By region or country]
620.1126	TA418.42	Hardness			
620.1126	TA409	Fracture mechanics	621.1	TJ268-748	Steam engineering
620.1126	TA354.5	Penetration mechanics	621.1	TJ461-740	Steam-engines
620.11260287	TA413-.5	Testing-machines	621.1	TJ268-280.7	Steam
620.11260287	TA413-.5	Fatigue testing machines	621.1071	TC157-.5	Hydraulic engineering—Study and teaching
620.1127	TA417.2-.55	Non-destructive testing			
620.11274	TA417.4	Ultrasonic testing	621.109(4-9)	TC21-127	Hydraulic engineering—[By region or country]
620.11295	TA418.12	Photoelasticity			
620.1(2-9)	TA401-492	Building materials	621.165	TJ735-740	Steam-turbines
620.12	TA419-424.6	Timber	621.183	TJ320-358	Furnaces
620.136	TA439	Expansive concrete	621.183	TJ281-393	Steam-boilers
620.136	TA439-446	Concrete	621.1830289	TJ350-357	Steam-boilers—Safety appliances
620.14	TA447	Drain-tiles			
620.143	TA455.F5	Fire-clay	621.185	TJ415-444	Steam-pipes
620.144	TA450	Glass	621.185	TJ427	Steam-pipe coverings
620.16	TA479.S7	Steel, Stainless	621.185	TJ370-372	Pressure gages
620.16	TA486	Corrosion resistant alloys	621.194	TJ290-291	Boiler-plates
620.160287	TA459-492	Metals—Testing	621.2	TC	Hydraulic engineering
620.166	TA460	Metals—Fatigue	621.2	TJ836-935	Hydraulic machinery
620.17	TA472-473	Steel, Galvanized	621.2	TJ855-857	Hydraulic motors
620.176	TA473	Steel—Fatigue	621.2	TJ1435	Hydraulic jacks
620.18	TA479.3	Nonferrous metals	621.203	TC9	Hydraulic engineering—Dictionaries
620.18	TA478	Nonmetallic steel			
620.182	TA480.C7	Copper	621.20422	TC147	Ocean wave power
620.185	TA480.T5	Tin	621.20422	TC147	Water-power
620.186	TA480.A6	Aluminum alloys	621.20422	TC147	Tidal power
620.186	TA480.A6	Aluminum, Structural	621.20424	TJ844	Hydraulic fluids
620.188	TA480.N6	Nickel	621.20424	TJ843	Oil hydraulic machinery
620.18923	TA480.S5	Silver	621.205	TC1	Hydraulic engineering—Periodicals
620.18932	TA480.T54	Titanium			
620.192	TA455.P58	Polymers	621.2072	TC158	Hydraulic laboratories
620.1923	TA455.P5-.P55	Plastics	621.209	TC15-20	Hydraulic engineering—History
620.2	TA365-367	Acoustical engineering			
620.23	TD891-893.6	Noise pollution	621.2092	TC139-140	Hydraulic engineers—Biography
620.23	TD893.6.T7	Transportation noise			
620.23	TD892	Noise barriers	621.21	TJ840-890	Water-power
620.4162	TC1501-1800	Ocean engineering	621.21	TJ860-880	Water-wheels
620.416205	TC1501	Ocean engineering—Periodicals	621.21	TJ859	Water mills
			621.3	TK	Electric engineering
620.416206	TC1505	Ocean engineering—Congresses	621.30221	TK431	Electric drafting
			621.3025	TK12	Electric engineering—Directories
620.5	T174.7	Nanotechnology			
621	TJ163.6-.95	Power (Mechanics)	621.303	TK9	Electric engineering—Dictionaries
621	TJ	Mechanical engineering			
621.01	TJ14	Mechanical engineering—Philosophy	621.305	TK1-4	Electric engineering—Periodicals
621.025	TJ11-13	Mechanical engineers—Directories	621.306	TK5	Electric engineering—Congresses
621.042	TJ807-830	Renewable energy sources	621.3071	TK165-213	Electric engineering—Study and teaching
621.05	TJ1-4	Mechanical engineering—Periodicals			
			621.3074	TK6	Electric engineering—Museums
621.06	TJ5	Mechanical engineering—Congresses			
			621.309	TK15-18	Electric engineering—History
621.071	TJ158-159	Mechanical engineering—Study and teaching			
			621.309(4-9)	TK21-127	Electric engineering—[By region or country]
621.09	TJ15-20	Mechanical engineering—History			
			621.31	TK3001-3511	Electric power
621.092	TJ139-140	Mechanical engineers—Biography	621.31	TK153	Electric power factor
			621.31	TK1001-1841	Electric power
			621.31	TK4001-9971	Electric power

Dewey	LC	Subject Heading
621.31042	TK2000-2891	Electric machinery
621.31042	TK2271	Eddy currents (Electric)
621.3121	TJ164	Power-plants
621.3121	TK1041-1078	Cogeneration of electric power and heat
621.3121	TK1191-1841	Electric power-plants
621.3121	TK1001-1841	Electric power production
621.31210287	TK1831	Electric power-plants—Testing
621.312132	TJ395-444	Steam power plants
621.312134	TK1081	Tidal power-plants
621.312134	TK1081-1083	Hydroelectric power plants
621.3124	TK2896	Direct energy conversion
621.31242	TK2941	Storage batteries
621.31242	TK2896-2986	Electric batteries
621.312429	TK2931	Fuel cells
621.31244	TK1085-1087	Solar power plants
621.31244	TK2960	Solar cells
621.31244	TK1545	Solar power plants
621.3126	TK1751	Electric substations
621.313	TK2411-2491	Electric generators
621.313	TK2796	Electric current converters
621.313	TK2796	Rotary converters
621.3132	TK2441	Gramme dynamos
621.3132	TK2611-2699	Electric machinery—Direct current
621.3133	TK2711-2799	Electric machinery—Alternating current
621.3137	TK7872.R35	Electric current rectifiers
621.314	TK2551	Electric transformers
621.314	TK7872.T7	Electronic transformers
621.316	TK2484	Brushes, Carbon
621.316	TK2477	Armatures
621.317	TK2861	Differential relays
621.317	TK2821-2846	Electric switchgear
621.317	TK2842	Electric circuit-breakers
621.317	TK2851	Electric rheostats
621.317	TK2861	Electric contactors
621.319	TK3001-3521	Electric power distribution
621.319	TK3001-3521	Electric power transmission
621.319	TK3091	Electric power failures
621.31912	TK3111	Electric power distribution—Direct current
621.31913	TK1141-1168	Electric currents, Alternating
621.31913	TK3141-3171	Electric power transmission—Alternating current
621.31913	TK3141-3171	Electric power distribution—Alternating current
621.31913	TK3144	Electric power distribution—High tension
621.3192	TK454.2	Electric network topology
621.3192	TK3001-3521	Electric circuits
621.3192	TK3201-3261	Electric lines
621.3192	TK454.2	Electric networks, Active
621.3192	TK3226	Electric networks
621.3192	TK454.2	Electric networks, Passive
621.3192	TK3242-3243	Electric lines—Poles and towers
621.31921	TK3226	Transients (Electricity)
621.31923	TK3251-3261	Underground electric lines
621.31924092	TK139-140	Electricians
621.31933	TK3201-3285	Electric wiring
621.31933	TK3301-3351	Electric wire
621.31933	TK3271-3285	Electric wiring, Interior
621.31934	TK3301-3351	Electric cables
621.32	TH7700-7975	Lighting
621.32	TK4125-4399	Electric lighting
621.320284	TK4198	Electric light fixtures
621.3209(4-9)	TK4134-4156	Electric lighting—[By region or country]
621.3229	SB476	Garden lighting
621.3229	TK4188	Exterior lighting
621.3229	TK4399.S6	Electric signs
621.324	TH7910-7970	Gas-lighting
621.3240284	TH7960-7967	Gas-fixtures
621.325	TK4321-4335	Electric lamps, Arc
621.325	TK4311-4335	Electric lighting, Arc
621.326	TK4351-4367	Incandescent lamps
621.326	TK4341-4367	Electric lighting, Incandescent
621.3273	TK4386	Fluorescent lamps
621.3275	TK4383	Neon tubes
621.3275	TK4383	Neon lamps
621.33	TF880-900	Electric railroads—Wires and wiring
621.33	TF863-952	Electric railroads—Design and construction
621.33	TF858-859	Railroads—Electrification
621.33	TF935	Electric railway motors
621.33	TF930	Electric controllers
621.330284	TF920-952	Electric railroads—Equipment and supplies
621.3309(4-9)	TF1021-1127	Electric railroads—[By region or country]
621.36	TA1501-1820	Photonics
621.362	TA1570	Infrared technology
621.362	TA1570	Infrared sources
621.366	TA1705	Ruby lasers
621.366	TA1671-1715	Lasers
621.366	TA1693	Free electron lasers
621.3663	TA1695	Gas lasers
621.3664	TA1690	Dye lasers
621.367	TA1637	Image processing
621.3692	QC447.9-448.2	Fiber optics
621.3693	TA1660	Integrated optics
621.37	TK401	Electric testing
621.37	TK275-399	Electric measurements
621.373	TK301-399	Electric meters
621.373	TK393	Recording instruments
621.3743	QC615	Voltameter
621.3743	TK321	Voltmeter
621.3743	TK331	Voltameter
621.3744	TK331	Voltameter
621.381	TK7800-8360	Electronics
621.381	TK7870	Electronic systems
621.3810221	TK7866	Electronic drafting
621.3810223	TK7866	Electronics—Charts, diagrams, etc.
621.3810228	TK7870	Miniature electronic equipment
621.3810284	TK7869-7872	Electronic apparatus and appliances

Dewey	LC	Subject Heading	Dewey	LC	Subject Heading
621.3810284	TK7870	Electronic instruments	621.384133	TK6565.R426	Electric resistors
621.3810287	TK7878-7879.4	Electronic measurements	621.384135	TK6565.A6	Radio—Antennas
621.38105	TK7800	Electronics—Periodicals	621.38416	TK9956	Amateur radio stations
621.38106	TK7801	Electronics—Congresses	621.38418	TK6563-6564	Radio—Receivers and
621.381072	TK7855	Electronics—Research			reception
621.3810728	TK7825	Electronics—Graphic methods	621.384191	TL696.B4	Radio beacons
621.3813	TK7876	Microwave devices	621.3842	TK5811-5865	Telegraph, Wireless—
621.38131	TK7876	Microwave transmission lines			Marconi system
621.381331	QC661	Wave guides	621.3842	TK5700-5865	Telegraph, Wireless
621.381334	TK7871.75	Magnetrons	621.38454	TK6570.C5	Citizens band radio
621.3815	TK7867-7868	Electronic circuits	621.3848	TK6573-6595	Radar
621.38151	TK7871.7-.84	Electron Tubes	621.3848	TK6592.D6	Doppler radar
621.381512	TK7872.V3	Vacuum-tubes	621.3848	TK6592.M67	Moving target indicator radar
621.381513	TK7871.8-.84	Gas tubes	621.38483	TK6587	Radar transmitters
621.38152	TK7871.85-.99	Semiconductor wafers	621.385	TK6391-6397	Telephone switchboards
621.38152	TK7871.99.M4	Metal insulator	621.385	TK6001-6571.5	Telephone
		semiconductors	621.385025	TK6011	Telephone—Directories
621.381522	TK7871.89.S95	Diodes, Switching	621.38505	TK6001	Telephone—Periodicals
621.381522	TK7871.89.A94	Diodes, IMPATT	621.3857	TK6397	Telephone switching
621.381528	TK7871.96.B55	Bipolar transistors			systems, Electronic
621.3815282	TK7871.92	Junction transistors	621.387	TK6401-6505	Telephone systems
621.381531	TK7868.P7	Printed circuits	621.38784	TK6381-6383	Telephone wire
621.3815322	TK2699	Electric inverters	621.38784	TK6201-6285	Telephone lines
621.3815322	TK7872.I65	Electric inverters	621.38784	TK6381-6383	Telephone cables
621.381533	TK7872.07	Feedback oscillators	621.388	TK6630-6720	Television
621.381535	TK7871.2-.58	Transistor amplifiers	621.38800284	TK6650-6655	Television—Equipment
621.381535	TK7871.2-.58	Amplifiers (Electronics)			and supplies
621.381537	TK7868.S9	Switching circuits	621.388005	TK6630.A1	Television—Periodicals
621.381542	TK8300-8360	Photoelectric cells	621.38804	TK6670	Color television
621.381542	TK8314	Photoelectric multipliers	621.3883	TK7881.65	Digital audiotape recorders
621.3815422	TK7872.L56	Liquid crystal displays			and recording
621.381548	TK7872.S5	Signal generators	621.38833	TK6655.V5	Video cassette recorders
621.3815483	TK7878.7	Cathode ray oscilloscope	621.38833	TK6655.V5	Videocassette recorders
621.382	TK5103.7-.8	Digital communications	621.38835	TK6676	Television, Master antenna
621.382	TK5101-5105.9	Telecommunication	621.38928	TK7241	Electric alarms
621.38216	TK5105	Packet switching (Data	621.38928	TK7882.E2	Electronic surveillance
		transmission)	621.38932	TK7881.6	Magnetic recorders and
621.38216	TK5105-.42	Data transmission systems			recording
621.38224	TK5101	Random noise theory	621.39	TK7888.3-.4	Electronic digital computers
621.38234	TK5984	Magnetic tapes	621.39	TK7885-7895	Computers
621.38235	TK6710-7620	Facsimile transmission	621.39	TK7885-7895	Computer engineering
621.3825	TK5104-.2	Artificial satellites in	621.390288	TK7887	Computers—Maintenance
		telecommunication			and repair
621.3827	TK5103.59	Optical communications	621.3919	TK7888	Electronic analog computers
621.3828	TA1770	Acoustooptical devices	621.395	TK7888.4	Logic circuits
621.3828	TK5981-5990	Electro-acoustics	621.395	TK7872.L64	Logic devices
621.38284	TK5986	Electrostatic microphone	621.395	TK7874-.8	Digital integrated circuits
621.383	TK5105-5865	Telegraph	621.395	TK7888.4	Electronic digital
621.38305	TK5107	Telegraph—Periodicals			computers—Circuits
621.38405	TK6540	Radio—Periodicals	621.395	TK7874	Linear integrated circuits
621.384(1-5)	TK6540-6571.5	Radio	621.397	TK7895.M4	Cache memory
621.384(1-5) 0284	TK6560-6565	Radio—Equipment and supplies	621.3973	TK7895.M4	Random access memory
			621.3973	TK7895.M4	Read-only memory
621.384(1-5) 0288	TK6553	Radio—Repairing	621.39732	TK7895.M4	Semiconductor storage devices
621.38411	TK6553	Radio—Interference	621.3976	TK7887.55	Data tape drives
621.38412	TK6565.07	Oscillators, Electric	621.3976	TK7882.C56	Compact discs
621.38412	TK6565.A55	Amplifiers (Electronics)	621.39763	TK7872.M25	Magnetic bubble devices
621.384131	TK6561-6562	Radio—Transmitters and	621.39767	TK7895.M4	Optical storage devices
		transmission	621.398	TK7887.5	Computer interfaces
621.384132	TK6565.V3	Vacuum-tubes	621.3981	TK7868.I58	Interface circuits

Dewey	LC	Subject Heading	Dewey	LC	Subject Heading
621.39814	TK7887.8.M63	Modems	621.4835	TK9151.6-.7	Remote handling (Radioactive substances)
621.39814	TK7887.6	Analog-to-digital converters	621.4838	TK9360	Reactor fuel reprocessing
621.3984	TA167	Man-machine systems	621.484	TK9204	Fusion reactors
621.3985	TK7887.8.T4	Computer terminals	621.484	TK9360	Thermonuclear fuels
621.399	TK7882.S65	Speech synthesis	621.485	TK9230	Nuclear propulsion
621.4	TJ250-255	Engines	621.48	TK9001-9401	Nuclear engineering
621.4	TJ	Motors	621.51	TJ990-992	Air-compressors
621.402	TK4601-4661	Electric heating	621.51	TJ990-992	Compressors
621.4021	TJ265	Thermodynamics	621.51	TJ981-1009	Compressed air
621.4024	TH1715-1718	Insulation (Heat)	621.51	TJ950-1030	Pneumatic machinery
621.4025	TJ262	Heat pumps	621.55	TJ940-.5	Vacuum technology
621.4025	TJ255-265	Heat-engines	621.55	TJ940.5	Vacuum pumps
621.4028	TK4601	Microwave heating	621.56	TP490-497	Refrigeration and refrigerating machinery
621.4028	TK4601	Induction heating	621.56	TP480-482	Low temperature engineering
621.406	TJ266-267.5	Turbomachines	621.57	TP496-497	Refrigerators
621.406	TJ266-267.5	Turbines	621.6	TJ901	Ejector pumps
621.43	TJ751-805	Internal combustion engines	621.65	TJ915	Reciprocating pumps
621.43	TJ254.7	Combustion chambers	621.66	TJ917	Rotary pumps
621.433	TJ778	Gas-turbines	621.69	TJ899-927	Pumping machinery
621.4335	TJ779	Free piston engines	621.8	TJ	Machinery
621.43560228	TL844	Rockets (Aeronautics)—Models	621.80287	TJ148	Machinery—Testing
621.437	TJ787	Carburetors	621.81	TJ181-210	Mechanical movements
621.45	TJ820-828	Wind power	621.81	TJ177	Machinery—Vibration
621.453	TJ823-828	Windmills	621.815	TJ227-240	Machine design
621.46	TK2435	Electric motors—Design and construction	621.822	TJ1071	Roller bearings
621.46	TK2511-2541	Electric motors	621.822	TJ1061-1073.7	Bearings (Machinery)
621.46	TK2681	Electric motors	621.822	TJ1073.R8	Rubber bearings
621.46	TK2781-2789	Electric motors, Alternating current	621.824	TJ210	Springs (Mechanism)
621.46	TK2781-2789	Electric motors	621.833	TJ184-204	Gearing
621.47	TJ809-812.8	Solar energy	621.8332	TJ193-196	Gearing, Bevel
621.47072	TJ811-.5	Solar energy—Research	621.8333	TJ192	Gearing, Spiral
621.472	TJ812	Solar collectors	621.8333	TJ200	Gearing, Worm
621.473	TJ812.5	Solar engines	621.837	TJ181.5	Wheels
621.48	TK9001-9401	Nuclear energy	621.84	TJ533	Pistons
621.480284	TK9178-9183	Nuclear power plants—Instruments	621.85	TJ1045-1119	Power transmission
621.480289	TK9152-.16	Nuclear engineering—Safety measures	621.85	TJ1103	Pulleys
621.480289	TK9152-.16	Radiation—Safety measures	621.852	TJ1100-1119	Belts and belting
621.4805	TK9001	Nuclear engineering—Periodicals	621.862	TJ1350-1383	Hoisting machinery
621.483	QC786.4-786.8	Nuclear reactors	621.864	VM811	Capstan
621.483	TK1078	Nuclear power plants	621.864	VM811	Windlasses
621.483	TK9203.H4	Steam generating heavy water reactors	621.867	TJ1385-1418	Conveying machinery
621.483	TK9202-9230	Nuclear reactors	621.8672	TJ930-934	Pipelines
621.4830285	QC783.3-.4	Nuclear reactors—Computer programs	621.8676	TJ1376	Escalators
621.4833	TK9360	Nuclear fuels	621.87	TJ1363-1365	Cranes, derricks, etc.
621.4833	TK9207	Nuclear fuel rods	621.873	TJ1363-1365	Electric cranes
621.48335	TK9360	Spent reactor fuels	621.873	TJ1365	Gantry cranes
621.48336	TK9212	Nuclear reactors—Cooling	621.877	TJ1370-1380	Elevators
621.4834	TK9203.H4	Heavy water reactors	621.88	TJ1320-1340	Fasteners
621.4834	TK9203.S86	Superheating reactors	621.882	TJ1338-1340	Screws
621.4834	TK9203.B6	Boiling water reactors	621.882	TJ1330-1333	Bolts and nuts
621.4834	TK9203.B7	Liquid metal fast breeder reactors	621.89	TJ1075-1081	Lubrication and lubricants
			621.890284	TJ1081	Oil filters
621.4834	TK9203.S65	Solid fuel reactors	621.9	GN436.8-437	Tools
			621.9	TJ1180-1313	Tools
			621.902	TJ1180-1313	Machine-tools
			621.904	TJ1005-1007	Pneumatic tools
			621.91	TJ1205-1210	Planing-machines
			621.91	TJ1225-1227	Milling-machines
			621.914	TJ1345	Crushing machinery

Dewey	LC	Subject Heading	Dewey	LC	Subject Heading
621.92	TJ1280-1298	Grinding and polishing	622.09497	TN95.Y8	Mines and mineral resources—Yugoslavia
621.923	TJ1290	Emery-wheels			
621.93	TJ1233-1255	Saws	622.0951	TN101-102	Mines and mineral resources—China
621.93	TJ1233	Hacksaws			
621.93	TJ1230-1240	Cutting machines	622.0952	TN105-106	Mines and mineral resources—Japan
621.942	TJ1218-1222	Lathes			
621.952	TA745-747	Rock-drills	622.0954	TN103-104	Mines and mineral resources—India
621.952	TJ1260-1270	Drilling and boring			
621.952	TJ1260	Drill presses	622.095491	TN104.5-.6	Mines and mineral resources—Pakistan
621.973	TJ1201.H3	Hammers			
621.98	TJ1465	Pneumatic presses	622.095493	TN104.7-.8	Mines and mineral resources—Sri Lanka
621.984	TJ1335	Taps and dies			
621.984	TS253	Dies (Metal-working)	622.0955	TN107-108	Mines and mineral resources—Iran
622	TN	Mines and mineral resources			
622	TN	Mining engineering	622.09561	TN111-112	Mines and mineral resources—Turkey
622.0284	TN345-347	Mining machinery			
622.071	TN165-213	Mining schools and education	622.09567	TN113.I7	Mines and mineral resources—Iraq
622.092	TN139-140	Mining engineers	622.095694	TN113.I75	Mines and mineral resources—Israel
622.09(4-9)	TN21-127	Mines and mineral resources—[By region or country]	622.0957	TN109-110	Mines and mineral resources—Asiatic Russia
622.0941	TN57-64	Mines and mineral resources—Great Britain	622.09598	TN113.I55	Mines and mineral resources—Indonesia
622.0943	TN73-74.5	Mines and mineral resources—Germany	622.09599	TN113.P6	Mines and mineral resources—Philippines
622.09436	TN65-.2	Mines and mineral resources—Austria	622.096	TN115-119	Mines and mineral resources—Africa
622.09437	TN65.3-.4	Mines and mineral resources—Czechoslovakia	622.0962	TN117-118	Mines and mineral resources—Egypt
622.09439	TN65.5-66	Mines and mineral resources—Hungary	622.0971	TN26-27	Mines and mineral resources—Canada
622.0944	TN71-72.5	Mines and mineral resources—France	622.0972	TN28-29	Mines and mineral resources—Mexico
622.0945	TN79-80	Mines and mineral resources—Italy	622.09728	TN30-31	Mines and mineral resources—Central America
622.0946	TN87-88	Mines and mineral resources—Spain	622.09729	TN32-33	Mines and mineral resources—West Indies
622.09469	TN83-84.5	Mines and mineral resources—Portugal	622.0973	TN23-25	Mines and mineral resources—United States
622.0947	TN85-86	Mines and mineral resources—Russia	622.0981	TN41-42	Mines and mineral resources—Brazil
622.0948	TN88.5	Mines and mineral resources—Scandinavia	622.0982	TN36-37	Mines and mineral resources—Argentina
622.09481	TN81-82	Mines and mineral resources—Norway	622.0983	TN43-44	Mines and mineral resources—Chile
622.09485	TN89-90	Mines and mineral resources—Sweden	622.0984	TN38-39	Mines and mineral resources—Bolivia
622.09489	TN69-70	Mines and mineral resources—Denmark	622.0985	TN52	Mines and mineral resources—Peru
622.094897	TN95.F5	Mines and mineral resources—Finland	622.09861	TN45-46	Mines and mineral resources—Colombia
622.09492	TN77-78	Mines and mineral resources—Netherlands	622.09866	TN47	Mines and mineral resources—Ecuador
622.09494	TN91-92	Mines and mineral resources—Switzerland	622.0987	TN54	Mines and mineral resources—Venezuela
622.09495	TN75-76	Mines and mineral resources—Greece	622.09881	TN48	Mines and mineral resources—Guyana
622.09496	TN95.A2	Mines and mineral resources—Balkan Peninsula	622.09882	TN50	Mines and mineral resources—French Guiana

Dewey	LC	Subject Heading	Dewey	LC	Subject Heading
622.09883	TN49	Mines and mineral resources—Surinam	622.35	TN950-997	Stone
622.09892	TN51	Mines and mineral resources—Paraguay	622.3516	TN967	Dolomite
			622.352	TN970	Granite
622.09895	TN53	Mines and mineral resources—Uruguay	622.353	TN957	Sandstone
			622.36	TN948.D5	Diatomaceous earth
622.0993	TN122.5-.6	Mines and mineral resources—New Zealand	622.3622	TN939	Sand
			622.3622	TN939	Sand and gravel plants
622.0994	TN121-122	Mines and mineral resources—Australia	622.3632	TN900-909	Salt mines and mining
			622.3632	TN900-909	Salt
622.099(5-6)	TN123-124	Mines and mineral resources—Oceania	622.3633	TN917	Borax
			622.3635	TN946	Gypsum
622.0998	TN125-.5	Mines and mineral resources—Arctic regions	622.3636	TN919	Potassium salts
			622.364	TN913-914	Phosphate mines and mining
			622.364	TN911	Nitrates
622.14	TN273	Mine surveying	622.3662	TN948.P5	Pigments
622.18	TN270-271	Prospecting	622.3668	TN890	Sulphur
622.1828	TN271.P4	Petroleum—Prospecting	622.367	TN941-943	Fire-clay
622.23	TN279	Percussion drilling	622.3672	TN930	Asbestos
622.23	TN279-281	Rock-drills	622.3674	TN933	Mica
622.23	TN279	Blasting	622.368	TN945	Cement
622.23	TN281.5	Rotary drilling	622.373	TN923-929.7	Mineral waters
622.24	TN281	Boring	622.38	TN980-997	Precious stones
622.25	TN283	Shaft sinking	622.384	TN997.S24	Sapphires
622.26	TN285	Tunneling	622.386	TN997.E5	Emeralds
622.28	TN289	Mine timbering	622.387	TN997.A35	Agates
622.292	TN277	Quarries and quarrying	622.387	TN997.G3	Garnet
622.292	TN291	Strip mining	622.42	TN301-306	Mine ventilation
622.2927	TN278	Hydraulic mining	622.47	TN306.5-309	Mine lighting
622.33	TN850	Bitumen	622.473	TN307	Electric lamps, Portable
622.334	TN799.9-844.7	Coal	622.473	TN307	Safety-lamps
622.334	TN799.9-844.7	Coal mines and mining	622.48	TN343	Electricity in mining
622.335	TN820-823	Anthracite coal	622.5	TN318	Mine water
622.337	TN853	Asphalt	622.6	TN342	Shuttle cars (Mine haulage)
622.338	TN870	Oil fields—Production methods	622.66	TN338	Gasoline locomotives
			622.66	TN336	Mine railroads
622.3381	TN871.5	Oil well drilling rigs	622.77	TN530	Magnetic separation of ores
622.3381	TN871.2-.3	Oil well drilling	622.8	TN277	Quarries and quarrying—Safety measures
622.33819	TN871.3	Oil well drilling, Submarine			
622.3382	TN871	Oil reservoir engineering	622.8	TN295	Coal mines and mining—Safety measures
622.3382	TN860-879	Petroleum			
622.3382	TN871.37	Secondary recovery of oil	622.8	TN311-320	Coal mine accidents
622.3382	TN871	Gushers	622.8	TN311-320	Mine accidents
622.3385	TN880-884	Gas wells	622.80284	TN297	Gas masks
622.3385	TN880-884	Gas engineering	622.82	TN315	Mine fires
622.3385	TN880-884	Natural gas	622.82	TN313	Mine explosions
622.339	TN885	Amber	622.82	TN313-315	Combustion, Spontaneous
622.34	TN400-580	Metals	622.82	TN305-306	Firedamp
622.34	TN400-580	Ores	622.82	TN305-306	Mine gases
622.341	TN400-409	Iron mines and mining	622.89	TN297	Mine rescue work
622.342	TN410-439	Precious metals	623.042	UG487	Infrared radiation—Military applications
622.3422	HD9536	Gold mines and mining			
622.3422	TN422	Gold dredging	623.043	UG485	Electronics in military engineering
622.3422	TN420-429	Gold ores			
622.3422	TN410-429	Gold mines and mining	623.043	UG485	Electronic countermeasures
622.3423	HD9536	Silver mines and mining	623.043	UG485	Electronic counter-countermeasures
622.3423	TN430-439	Silver mines and mining			
622.344	TN450-459	Lead ores	623.1	UG403	Intrenchments
622.3453	TN470-479	Tin ores	623.1	UG403	Fortification, Field
622.3453	TN470-479	Tin mines and mining	623.1	UG400-442	Fortification
622.347	TN490.B6	Bismuth ores	623.26	V856-.5	Mines and minelaying
622.3483	TN490.C6	Cobalt ores	623.263	QB384	Saturn (Planet)—Orbit

Dewey	LC	Subject Heading	Dewey	LC	Subject Heading
623.4409	U800-897	Armor	623.810287	VM155	Ships—Measurement
623.441	GN799.W3	Weapons, Prehistoric	623.81071	VM165-276	Naval architecture—Study and teaching
623.441	GN498.S5	Shields			
623.441	GN498.B78	Bow and arrow	623.810951	VM101	Junks
623.441	GN498.S55	Slings	623.81245	VM455.3	Chemical carriers (Tankers)
623.441	GN498	Spears	623.81821	VM146	Marine steel
623.441	GN498.B78	Arrowheads	623.81821	VM146-147	Ships, Iron and steel
623.441	U872	Lances	623.81833	VM148	Ships, Concrete
623.441074	U804	Armor—Exhibitions	623.8184	VM142-144	Ships, Wooden
623.4410901	U805	Armor, Ancient	623.82	VK	Ships
623.44109(4-9)	U818-823.5	Armor—[By region or country]	623.82	VM320-361	Boatbuilding
			623.8201	VM298	Ship models
623.45115	UG490	Mines (Military explosives)	623.8201043	VM298	Sailing ships—Models
623.452	TP268-299	Explosives, Military	623.8202	VM352	Rafts
623.452	UF860-880	Military fireworks	623.8202	VM353	Dugout canoes
623.46	UF850-857	Range-finding	623.82023	VM331-333	Yachts
623.46	UF853	Position-finders	623.8204	VM362	Hydrofoil boats
623.46	UF854	Firearms—Sights	623.8205	TC1662	Remote submersibles
623.46	UF855	Telescopic sights	623.820681	VM299.5-.7	Shipbuilding subsidies
623.51	UF820-840	Ballistics	623.821	GN799.B62	Boats, Prehistoric
623.51021	VF550	Ballistics—Tables	623.821	VM17	Ships, Medieval
623.51021	UF820	Ballistics—Tables	623.822	VM311.C3	Catamarans
623.510284	UF830	Ballistic instruments	623.8223	VM351-361	Sailboats
623.55	UF800-805	Gunnery	623.8226	VM371	Dhows
623.558	UF848-856	Fire control (Gunnery)	623.8226	VM331	Skipjacks
623.5580284	UF849	Fire control (Gunnery)—Optical equipment	623.8226	VM453	Oceanographic research ships
623.62	UG330	Military roads	623.8232	VM464	Tugboats
623.63	UG345	Armored trains	623.8232	VM464	Towboats
623.63	UG345	Military railroads	623.8243	VM381-383	Passenger ships
623.67	UG335	Pontoon bridges	623.82436	VM461-.5	River steamers
623.67	UG335	Military bridges	623.82436	VM396	Inland waterway vessels
623.68	UG340	Tunneling	623.82436	VM460	Lake steamers
623.71	UG470-474	Maps, Military	623.82436	VM461-.5	River boats
623.72	TR785	Photography, Military	623.8245	VM393.B7	Bulk carrier cargo ships
623.72	UG476	Photographic interpretation (Military science)	623.8245	VM393.R64	Roll-on/roll-off ships
			623.8245	VM391-395	Cargo ships
623.73	UA940-945	Communications, Military	623.8245	VM457	Ore carriers
623.7312	UG582.H4	Heliograph	623.8245	VM459	Refrigerator ships
623.7314	TA1750	Electrooptical devices	623.8245	VM455	Tankers
623.732	UG590-613.5	Military telegraph	623.8245	VM455.3	Chemical carriers (Tankers)
623.73(2-3)	UG590-610.5	Military telecommunication	623.8257	VM365-367	Submarines (Ships)
623.7341	UG611-.5	Radio, Military	623.826	VM466.035	Offshore support vessels
623.7348	UG612-.5	Radar—Military applications	623.827	VM987	Diving bells
623.746	TL685.3	Airplanes, Military	623.828	VM451	Ice-breaking vessels
623.746	UG630-635	Airplanes, Military—Turrets	623.828	VM453	Deep-sea drilling ships
623.7472	UG615-620	Tracked landing vehicles	623.829	TC765	Canal-boats
623.7472	UG615-620	Automobiles, Military	623.829	VM466.B3	Barges
623.76	UG480	Electricity in military engineering	623.83	TC363	Floating harbors
			623.84	VM341-349	Planing hulls
623.8	VM600-881	Marine engineering	623.84	VM308	Figureheads of ships
623.8071	VM725-728	Marine engineering—Study and teaching	623.843	VM320-361	Steel boats
			623.8432	VM965	Underwater welding and cutting
623.809	VM615-619	Marine engineering—History			
623.809(4-9)	VM621-724	Marine engineering—[By region or country]	623.8501	VM821	Marine compressors
			623.8503	VM471-479	Ships—Electric equipment
623.81	VM340-349	Launches	623.8504	VM325	Boats and boating—Electronic equipment
623.81	VM	Ships			
623.81	VM340-349	Motorboats	623.8504	VM480-.5	Ships—Electronic equipment
623.81	VM159	Stability of ships	623.852	VM491-493	Ships—Lighting
623.81	VM157	Displacement (Ships)	623.852	VM493	Search-lights

Dewey	LC	Subject Heading	Dewey	LC	Subject Heading
623.852	VM815	Ships' lights	623.890284	VK581	Logs (Nautical instruments)
623.853	VM481-482	Ships—Heating and ventilation	623.890289	VK200	Navigation—Safety measures
623.8535	VM485	Marine refrigeration	623.89071	VK401-529	Navigation—Study and teaching
623.8535	VM485	Cold storage on shipboard	623.89(2-3)	VK573-587	Nautical instruments
623.854	VM505	Distilled water	623.892(2-9) +	VK1521-1624	Pilots and pilotage—
623.854	VM505	Seawater—Distillation	(4-9)		[By region or country]
623.8542	VM503-505	Ships—Water-supply	623.8922	VK1500-1661	Pilots and pilotage
623.8561	VK381-397	Signals and signaling	623.8922	VK798-997	Pilot guides
623.8561	V280-285	Signals and signaling	623.8922	VK798	Notices to mariners
623.85641	VM325	Radio on boats	623.892209	VK1515	Pilots and pilotage—History
623.85642	VK397	Telegraph, Wireless—Installation on ships	623.892216 (3-7)	VK804-997	Pilot guides—[By body of water]
623.8567	VG70-85	Communications, Military	623.89223	VK810-880	Pilot guides—Atlantic Ocean
623.86	VM781	Deck machinery	623.8922334	VK819-821.8	Pilot guides—Baltic Sea
623.86	VM781-861	Ships—Equipment and supplies	623.8922336	VK839-844	Pilot guides—English Channel
623.86	VM831	Davits	623.8922336	VK815-818	Pilot guides—North Sea
623.86	VM801	Davits	623.892234	VK947-948	Pilot guides—United States
623.862	VM791	Anchors	623.892236	VK947-948	Pilot guides—United States
623.862	VM841-845	Steering-gear	623.892238	VK853-874	Pilot guides—Mediterranean Sea
623.862	VM532	Sails			
623.862	VM531-533	Masts and rigging	623.89224	VK915-956	Pilot guides—Pacific Ocean
623.8620901	GN799.C49	Cordage, Prehistoric	623.892244	VK917	Pilot guides—North Pacific Ocean
623.865	VK1479	Line-throwing rockets			
623.865	VK1477	Life-preservers	623.892248	VK925	Pilot guides—South Pacific Ocean
623.865	VK1481.L55	Line-throwing guns			
623.87	VM595-989	Marine engineering	623.89225	VK885-901	Pilot guides—Indian Ocean
623.87	VM731-779	Marine engines	623.89229	HE617-720	Inland navigation
623.8722	VM741-750	Steam-boilers, Marine	623.89229	TC601-791	Inland navigation
623.87236	VM770	Marine diesel motors	623.89229	TC769	Canals—Steam-navigation
623.8726	VM345-347	Electric boats	623.89229	HE623-720	Inland navigation—[By region or country]
623.8728	VM774-777	Nuclear ships	(4-9)		
623.8728	VM317	Nuclear ships	623.8922973	HE623-633	Inland navigation—United States
623.8728	VM774-777	Marine nuclear reactor plants			
623.873	VM753-757	Propellers	623.893	VK562	Artificial satellites in navigation
623.874	VM779	Ships—Fuel			
623.88	VK541-547	Seamanship	623.893	VK560	Electronics in navigation
623.88	VM531-533	Marlin spike seamanship	623.8932	VK397	Radio—Installation on ships
623.880971	VK525-529	Nautical training-schools	623.8932	VK397	Radio in navigation
623.88203	VK543	Sailing	623.8932	VK560-561	Loran
623.888	V810	Damage control (Warships)	623.8932	VK577	Compass
623.888	VK200	Merchant marine—Safety measures	623.8932	VK577	Radio compass
623.8882	VM533	Knots and splices	623.8932	VK577	Gyro compass
623.8884	VK371-378	Collisions at sea—Prevention	623.8938	VK388	Sonar
			623.8938	VK560	Sonar
623.8884	VK371	Rule of the road at sea	623.8938	VK584.S6	Sounding and soundings
623.8886	VK1250-1294	Ships—Fires and fire prevention	623.8938	VK584.S6	Echo sounding
			623.8942	VK1000-1246	Lighthouses
623.8887	VK1460-1481	Life-saving apparatus	623.894209	VK1015	Lighthouses—History
623.8887	VK1300-1481	Life-saving	623.89420916347	VK1025.D	Drum Point Lighthouse (Md.)
623.888709	VK1315	Life-saving—History	623.894209(4-9)	VK1021-1124	Lighthouses—[By region or country]
623.888709 (4-9)	VK1321-1424	Life-saving—[By region or country]	623.89420971	VK1026-1027	Lighthouses—Canada
623.89	SH343.8	Fisheries navigation	623.89420973	VK1023-1025	Lighthouses—United States
623.89	VK560	Hyperbolic navigation	623.894209751	VK1025.H	Harbor of Refuge Lighthouse (Del.)
623.89	VK583.5	Inertial navigation systems			
623.89	VK560	Decca navigation	623.8943	VK1000-1246	Lightships
623.890284	VK583	Quadrant	623.8944	VK1150-1246	Buoys—[By region or country]
623.890284	VK583	Sextant			

Dewey	LC	Subject Heading	Dewey	LC	Subject Heading
623.8944	VK1000-1246	Buoys	624.206	TG5	Bridges—Congresses
623.8944	VK1000-1249	Beacons	624.209	TG15-20	Bridges—History
624.1	TA630-901	Structural engineering	624.209(4-9)	TG21-127	Bridges—[By region or country]
624.10285	TA641	Structural engineering—Computer programs	624.25	TG260-270	Structural analysis (Engineering)
624.10289	TA656.5	Safety factor in engineering	624.25	TG265-267	Moments of inertia
624.105	TA630	Structural engineering—Periodicals	624.25	TG300-304	Bridges—Design and construction
624.1072	TA638.2	Structural engineering—Research	624.250299	TG313	Bridges—Design and construction—Estimates
624.15	TA775-787	Foundations	624.252	TG304	Snow loads
624.151	TA703-705.4	Engineering geology	624.252	TG265-267	Strains and stresses
624.15109 (3-4)	TA705.2-.4	Engineering geology—[By region or country]	624.252	TG265	Flexure
624.15136	TA710-711.5	Soil mechanics	624.252	TG265	Buckling (Mechanics)
624.152	TA715-772	Earthwork	624.257	TG260	Structural frames
624.152	TA730-748	Excavation	624.28	TG325	Bridges—Abutments
624.152	TA740-747	Rock excavation	624.283	TG325.6	Bridges—Floors
624.152	TA748	Blasting	624.284	TG320	Bridges—Foundations and piers
624.152	TH5281	Shoring and underpinning			
624.152	TH5101	Excavation	624.284	TG325	Retaining walls
624.1520284	TA725	Earthmoving machinery	624.32	TG365-370	Trestles
624.1520284	TA725	Scrapers (Earthmoving machinery)	624.32	TG365	Bridges, Wooden
			624.33	TG413-416	Bridges, Continuous
624.154	TA780-787	Piling (Civil engineering)	624.33	TG355	Girders, Continuous
624.157	TC198	Coffer-dams	624.35	TG385	Bridges, Cantilever
624.162	TA760-772	Embankments	624.37	TG350-362	Girders
624.164	TA760-772	Retaining walls	624.38	TG375-380	Bridges, Truss
624.171	TA645-656.5	Structural analysis (Engineering)	624.38	TG375	Bridges, Wooden
			624.5	TG400	Suspension bridges
624.172	TA654.4	Snow loads	624.6	TG327-340	Bridges, Arched
624.172	TA648.2	Dead loads (Mechanics)	624.63	TG330	Bridges, Brick
624.176	TA654-656.5	Structural dynamics	624.63	TG330	Bridges, Stone
624.1762	TA654.6	Earthquake engineering	624.63	TG335-340	Bridges, Concrete
624.1762	TA658.44	Earthquake resistant design	624.8	TG420	Drawbridges
624.1771	TA658-.8	Structural design	624.87	TG450	Pontoon bridges
624.1772	TA660.S6	Slabs	625.1	TF	Railroad engineering
624.17723	TA660.S67	Steel I-beams	625.1	TF	Railroads
624.17723	TA492.G5	Girders	625.1	TF16	Horse railroads
624.1773	TA660.T8	Trusses	625.1	TF200-320	Railroads—Design and construction
624.1773	TA660.F7-.F73	Structural frames			
624.1779	TA492.S25	Sandwich construction	625.10021	TF205	Railroad engineering—Tables
624.182	TA684-695	Building, Iron and steel	625.100212	TF195	Railroads—Specifications
624.1821	TA684-695	Steel, Structural	625.10025	TF12	Railroads—Directories
624.183	TA670-683.94	Masonry	625.100284	TF340-499	Railroads—Equipment and supplies
624.1833	TA680-683.94	Portland cement			
624.1834	TA680-683.94	Concrete construction	625.100288	TF542	Railroads—Snow-plows
624.1834	TA683.5.S4	Shells, Concrete	625.100288	TF530-548	Railroads—Maintenance and repair
624.1834	TA683.5.W34	Concrete walls			
624.18341	TA683-683.94	Reinforced concrete construction	625.100289	TF610	Railroads—Safety measures
			625.1005	TF1-4	Railroads—Periodicals
624.183412	TA665	Prestressed construction	625.1006	TF5	Railroads—Congresses
624.183412	TA683.9-.94	Prestressed concrete construction	625.10072	TF171-183	Railroads—Research
			625.10074	TF6	Railroad museums
624.18923	TA668	Plastics in building	625.1009	TF15-20	Railroads—History
624.19	TA800-820	Tunneling	625.10092	TF139-140	Railroad engineers
624.19	TA712	Underground construction	625.1009(4-9)	TF21-127	Railroads—[By region or country]
624.2	TG	Bridges			
624.20288	TG315	Bridges—Maintenance and repair	625.103	TF694	Monorail railroads
			625.11	TF210-217	Railroads—Surveying
624.205	TG1-4	Bridges—Periodicals			

Dewey	LC	Subject Heading	Dewey	LC	Subject Heading
625.11299	TF193	Railroads—Design and construction—Costs	625.733	TE210-212	Roads—Foundations
			625.734	TE215	Road drainage
625.12	TF220-226	Railroads—Earthwork	625.7342	TE213	Culverts
625.15	TF890	Electric railroads—Third rail	625.74	TE230	Roads, Earth
625.15	TF258-262	Railroads—Rails	625.76	TE220-.63	Roads—Maintenance and repair
625.15	TF262	Railroads—Continuous rails			
625.15	TF872	Electric railroads—Rails	625.763	TD868-870	Snow removal
625.163	TF592	Railroads—Switching	625.77	TE178.8	Roadside rest areas
625.163	TF263	Railroads—Crossings	625.77	TE177	Roadside improvement
625.165	TF615-640	Railroads—Signaling	625.794	TE228	Electronic traffic controls
625.18	TF590-593	Railroads—Yards	625.8	TE250-278.8	Pavements
625.18	TF300-308	Railroad terminals	625.8	TE200-205	Road materials
625.19	TF857	Electric railroads, Miniature	625.82	TE233	Roads, Gravel
625.19	TF197	Railroads—Models	625.82	TE255	Roads, Brick
625.2	TF371-499	Railroads—Cars	625.83	TE245	Roads, Plank
625.2	TF920-952	Electric railroads—Cars	625.83	TE253	Pavements, Wooden
625.21	TF413	Draft-gear	625.84	TE278-.8	Pavements, Concrete
625.22	TF542	Snow removal	625.84	TE278-.8	Roads, Concrete
625.22	TF485	Cabooses (Railroads)	625.85	TE221	Bituminous materials
625.23	TF455-461	Railroads—Passenger-cars	625.85	TE210.5.B5	Bitumen
625.23	TF457	Pullman cars	625.85	TE266-276	Pavements, Asphalt
625.23	TF656	Railroads—Baggage handling	625.86	TE243	Roads, Macadamized
			625.88	TE304	Trails
625.23	TF459	Sleeping-cars (Railroads)	625.88	TE303	Trails
625.24	TF470-481	Railroads—Freight-cars	625.88	TE301	Bicycle trails
625.24	TF662-667	Railroads—Freight	625.88	TE280-295	Sidewalks
625.24	TF477	Refrigerator cars	625.888	TE298	Curbs
625.25	TF949.B7	Electric railroads—Brakes	625.889	TE279.3	Driveways
625.25	TF420-430	Air-brakes	627	TC401-558	Water resources development
625.26	TJ603-695	Locomotives			
625.263	TF975	Electric locomotives	627.1	TC601-791	Canals, Interoceanic
625.263	TF980	Electro-diesel locomotive	627.109(4-9)	TC615-727	Inland navigation—[By region or country]
625.266	TJ619-.7	Diesel locomotives			
625.39	TC771-772	Ship-railroads	627.13	TC601-791	Canals
625.(4-6)	TF670-1124	Railroads, Local and light	627.133	TC759	Embankments
625.4	TF1600	Magnetic levitation vehicles	627.1353	TC763	Canals—Lifts
625.42	TF845-851	Subways	627.1370962	TC791	Suez Canal (Egypt)
625.44	TF840-841	Railroads, Elevated	627.2	TC353-365	Harbors
625.5	TF835	Railroads, Cable	627.24	TC337	Embankments
625.66	TF701-1124	Street-railroads	627.24	TC337	Dikes (Engineering)
625.66	TF830	Horse railroads	627.24	TC337	Levees
625.7	TE	Roads	627.24	TC330-340	Shore protection
625.7	TE	Highway engineering	627.24	TC333	Breakwaters
625.7	TE206-209.5	Roads—Location	627.24	TC335	Sea-walls
625.7	TE176.5	Traffic circles	627.31	TC361	Dry docks
625.70212	TE180	Roads—Specifications	627.31	TC357	Warves
625.70284	TE223-227	Road-rollers	627.31	TC355-365	Docks
625.70284	TE223-227	Road machinery	627.31	TC357	Piers
625.705	TE1-4	Roads—Periodicals	627.38	TC328	Marinas
625.706	TE5	Roads—Congresses	627.4	TC167	Flood dams and reservoirs
625.7071	TE191	Roads—Study and teaching	627.42	TC533	Embankments
625.709	TE15-19	Roads—History	627.42	TC533	Levees
625.709143	TE229.8	Mountain roads	627.5	TC801-937	Reclamation of land
625.709152	TE229.5	Forest roads	627.5	TC970-978	Reclamation of land
625.7091734	TE229-.9	Rural roads	627.509(4-9)	TC815-927	Reclamation of land—[By region or country]
625.709(4-9)	TE21-127	Roads—[By region or country]			
			627.52	TC930-933	Irrigation canals and flumes
625.723	TE209-.5	Roads—Surveying	627.52	TC933	Flumes
625.725	TE175	Roads—Design and construction	627.54	TC970-978	Drainage
			627.54	TC970	Ditches
625.732	TE208-.5	Soil surveys	627.54	TC343-345	Reclamation of land

Dewey	LC	Subject Heading	Dewey	LC	Subject Heading
627.54	TC975	Marshes	628.164	TD441-449	Filters and filtration
627.7	TC195-201	Underwater construction	628.165	TD458	Water—Aeration
627.7	TC1800	Underwater pipelines	628.167	TD478-480.7	Saline water conversion
627.73	TC187	Dredging spoil	628.16723	TD479.6	Nuclear saline water conversion plants
627.73	TC188	Dredges			
627.73	TC187-188	Dredging	628.16725	TD479.7	Solar saline water conversion plants
627.75	TC193	Underwater drilling			
627.8	TC540-558	Dams	628.1674	TD480.5	Saline water conversion—Electrodialysis process
627.8	TC547	Arch dams			
627.8	TC540-558	Flood dams and reservoirs	628.16744	TD480.4	Saline water conversion—Reverse osmosis process
627.8	TC542.5	Dams—Earthquake effects			
627.8	TC540	Dams—Design and construction	628.168	TD426-.8	Groundwater—Pollution
			628.168	TD419-428	Water—Pollution
627.82	TC547	Concrete dams	628.168	TD427.V55	Viral pollution of water
627.83	TC543	Earth dams	628.1682	TD427.O7	Organic water pollutants
627.86	TC167	Reservoirs	628.1682	TD427.D4	Detergent pollution of rivers, lakes, etc.
627.882	TC553	Sluice gates			
627.883	TC555	Spillways	628.16833	TD427.P4	Oil pollution of water
627.922	TC375-381	Lighthouses	628.16836	TD196.C45	Chemical spills
628	TD159-168	Municipal engineering	628.16836	TD899.P4	Petroleum waste
628	TD	Sanitary engineering	628.16837	TD800	Petroleum waste
628	TD169-171.8	Environmental protection	628.16846	TD930.2	Feedlot runoff
628.025	TD12	Sanitary engineers—Directories	628.1685	TD427.R3	Radioactive substances in rivers, lakes, etc.
628.05	TD1-4	Sanitary engineering—Periodicals	628.1685	TD427.R3	Radioactive pollution of water
			628.2	TD682	Sewers, Concrete
628.09	TD15-20	Sanitary engineering—History	628.2	TD678-688	Sewer design
			628.21	TD657-.5	Urban runoff
628.092	TD139-140	Sanitary engineers—Biography	628.212	TD665	Storm sewers
			628.3	TD745-758.5	Sewage—Purification
628.09(4-9)	TD21-127	Sanitary engineering—[By region or country]	628.3	TD511-780	Sewerage
			628.3	TD730-737	Sewage
628.1	TD201-500	Water-supply	628.309	TD515-520	Sewerage—History
628.1	TD201-500	Municipal water supply	628.309(4-9)	TD521-627	Sewerage—[By region or country]
628.109(4-9)	TC415-527	River engineering—[By region or country]			
			628.351	TD746.5	Sewage lagoons
628.109	TD215-220	Water-supply—History	628.36	TD741-780	Sewage disposal
628.109(4-9)	TD221-327	Water-supply—[By region or country]	628.3623	TD760	Sewage irrigation
			628.364	TD769.7	Sewage sludge—Conditioning
628.11	TD418	Rain-water (Water-supply)			
628.112	TC401-558	Rivers	628.37	TD770-.3	Sewage sludge—Incineration
628.112	TC401-558	River engineering			
628.114	TD405-414	Wells	628.42	TD899.M5	Acid mine drainage
628.114	TD412	Percussion drilling	628.42	TD812-.4	Radioactive waste disposal
628.114	TD412	Boring	628.44	TD813-870	Litter (Trash)
628.13	TD388-.5	Water conservation	628.44	TD785-812.5	Refuse and refuse disposal
628.13	TD489	Water towers	628.44	TD793.95	Source reduction (Waste management)
628.13	TD388-.5	Water conservation projects			
628.13	TD395	Dew-ponds	628.44072	TD793.3	Refuse and refuse disposal—Research
628.132	TD396	Reservoir sedimentation			
628.132	TD395-397	Reservoirs	628.440973	TD788-.4	Refuse collection—United States
628.144	TD485-487	Pumping stations			
628.144	TD481-493	Water—Distribution	628.442	TD794	Refuse collection
628.15	TD491	Electrolytic corrosion	628.44564	TD795-.7	Sanitary landfills
628.15	TD491	Water-pipes	628.4457	TD796-.2	Incineration
628.15	TD398	Aqueducts	628.4458	TD794.5	Recycling (Waste, etc.)
628.16	TD365-.5	Water quality management	628.46	TD813-870	Street cleaning
628.16	TD370-375	Water quality	628.460284	TD860	Street cleaning—Equipment and supplies
628.162	TD429	Water reuse			
628.162	TD434	Water treatment plants	628.4609(4-9)	TD815-849	Street cleaning—[By region or country]
628.162	TD429.5-477	Water—Purification			

Dewey	LC	Subject Heading
628.5	TD172-193.5	Pollution
628.5	TD878-880	Soil protection
628.5028	TD192	Pollution control equipment
628.5072	TD178.5-.7	Pollution—Research
628.509	TD179	Pollution—History
628.509(4-9)	TD179.5-191	Pollution—[By region or country]
628.5094	TD186-.5	Pollution—Europe
628.5095	TD187-.5	Pollution—Asia
628.5096	TD188-.5	Pollution—Africa
628.50971	TD182-.4	Pollution—Canada
628.50972	TD182.6-.7	Pollution—Mexico
628.50973	TD180-181	Pollution—United States
628.5098	TD185-.5	Pollution—South America
628.5099(3-6)	TD189.5.A8	Pollution—[New Zealand/Australia/Oceania]
628.50998	TD190-.5	Pollution—Arctic regions
628.51	TD896-899	Factory and trade waste
628.51	TD895	Factory sanitation
628.53	TD883	Air quality
628.53	TD881-890	Air—Pollution
628.532	TD884	Smoke prevention
628.532	TD887.H3	Halocarbons
628.532	TD885.5.G73	Greenhouse gases
628.532	TD885	Flue gases
628.535	TD887.R3	Radioactive pollution of the atmosphere
628.55	TD879.P4	Oil pollution of soils
628.55	TD879.P37	Soils—Pesticide content
628.7	TD920-931	Sanitation, Rural
628.72	TD927	Water-supply, Rural
628.742	TD929-930.4	Sewerage, Rural
628.742	TD929-930.4	Sewage disposal, Rural
628.742	TD929	Drainage, House
628.742	TD778	Septic tanks
628.744	TD929-930.4	Refuse and refuse disposal, Rural
628.92	TH9448-9449	Fires
628.922	TH2274	Fire-escapes
628.922072	TH9120	Fire prevention—Research
628.9225	TH9271	Fire detectors
628.9225	TH9271-9275	Fire alarms
628.925	TH9111-9599	Fire extinction
628.9252	TH9336	Fire sprinklers
628.9252	TH9332-9334	Water towers
628.9252	TH9365	Hydrants
628.9252	TH9311-9334	Fire extinction—Water-supply
628.9254	TH9338	Fire extinction—Chemical systems
628.9254	TH9362	Fire extinguishers
628.9259	TH9371-9377	Fire engines
628.9259	TH9391	Fireboats
629.(437/457)	TL4030	Space vehicles—Tracking
629.04	TA1001-1280	Transportation engineering
629.040289	TA1250	Signal lights
629.0405	TA1001-1004	Transportation engineering—Periodicals
629.04071	TA1163	Transportation engineering—Study and teaching
629.0409	TA1015	Transportation engineering—History
629.0409(4-9)	TA1021-1127	Transportation engineering—[By region or country]
629.040973	TA1023-1025	Transportation engineering—United States
629.1	TL500-4050	Aerospace engineering
629.13	TL570-578	Flight
629.13	TL721	Aeronautics—Flights
629.13	TL500-830	Aeronautics
629.1300148	TL509	Aeronautics—Abbreviations
629.1300222	TL549	Aeronautics—Pictorial works
629.1300272	TL513	Aeronautics—Patents
629.1300284	TL589-.5	Aeronautical instruments
629.1300289	TL553.5	Aeronautics—Safety measures
629.13006	TL505	Aeronautics—Congresses
629.13006	TL500-504	Aeronautics—Societies, etc.
629.130072	TL567.R47	Research aircraft
629.130072	TL566-568	Aeronautical laboratories
629.130074	TL506	Aeronautical museums
629.13009	TL515-532	Aeronautics—History
629.13009(4-9)	TL521-532	Aeronautics—[By region or country]
629.130092	TL539-540	Aeronautics—Biography
629.132	TL570-578	Flight
629.1323	TL574.N6	Aerodynamic noise
629.1323	TL570-574	Aerodynamics
629.13230287	TL573	Aerodynamic measurements
629.132306	TL571.5	Aerodynamics, Hypersonic
629.13232	TL574.U5	Unsteady flow (Aerodynamics)
629.13236	TL574.S7	Stability of airplanes
629.132362	TL574.F6	Flutter (Aerodynamics)
629.132362	TL570	Aeroelasticity
629.132362	TL574.V5	Vibration (Aeronautics)
629.132364	TL574.M6	Rolling (Aerodynamics)
629.132364	TL574.M6	Yawing (Aerodynamics)
629.13237	TL574.B6	Boundary layer
629.1324	TL557.F6	Fog—Control
629.1324	TL556-558	Meteorology in aeronautics
629.1325071	TL712-.8	Flight training
629.1325071	TL711.S8	Student flying
629.13251	TL586-589	Navigation (Aeronautics)
629.13252	TL712	Air pilots
629.13252	TL710-713.5	Airplanes—Piloting
629.13252	TL711.H65	Holding patterns (Aeronautics)
629.1325212	TL711.T3	Airplanes—Take-off
629.1325213	TL711.L3	Airplanes—Landing
629.1325213	TL696.L33	Ground controlled approach
629.1325214	TL711.B6	Instrument flying
629.1325214	TL711.N5	Night flying
629.1326	TL589.5	Automatic pilot (Airplanes)
629.13322	TL609-639	Balloons
629.13322	TL638	Hot air balloons
629.13322	TL620	Balloon ascensions
629.13324	TL650-668.1	Airships
629.13332	TL759-.7	Kites
629.13333	TL760-769	Gliders (Aeronautics)

Dewey	LC	Subject Heading	Dewey	LC	Subject Heading
629.13334	TL670-723	Airplanes	629.2	TL	Motor vehicles
629.13334	TL670-724	Flying-machines	629.221	TL237-.2	Automobiles—Models
629.133340422	TL686.G	Lear jet aircraft	629.222	TL236.7	Dune buggies
629.133347	TL684-.3	Seaplanes	629.222	TL1-230.5	Automobiles
629.13335	TL685	Vertically rising aircraft	629.2220294	TL12	Automobiles—Catalogs
629.133352	TL716-.9	Helicopters	629.22203	TL9	Automobiles—Encyclopedias
629.13431	TL671.6	Airframes	629.22205	TL1-5	Automobiles—Periodicals
629.13432	TL672-673	Airplanes—Wings	629.22206	TL6	Automobiles—Congresses
629.13432	TL673.S9	Airplanes—Wings, Swept-back	629.222074	TL7	Automobiles—Museums
			629.22209	TL15	Automobiles—History
629.13433	TL673.F6	Flaps (Airplanes)	629.22209(4-9)	TL21-127	Automobiles—[By region or country]
629.13433	TL677.E6	Elevators (Airplanes)			
629.13435	TL701-704.7	Airplanes—Motors	629.222092	TL139-140	Automobile engineers—Biography
629.134351	TL704.7	Airplanes—Fuel			
629.134353	TL709-.5	Airplanes—Jet propulsion	629.2220941	TL57-64	Automobiles—Great Britain
629.134353	TL709.5.I5	Airplanes—Turbojet engines—Air intakes	629.2220943	TL73-74.5	Automobiles—Germany
			629.2220944	TL71-72.5	Automobiles—France
629.134353	TL709.5.C55	Aircraft gas-turbines—Combustion chambers	629.2220947	TL85-86	Automobiles—Russia
			629.2220952	TL105-106	Automobiles—Japan
629.1343532	TL709.3.T8	Airplanes—Turbine-propeller engines	629.2220973	TL23-25	Automobiles—United States
			629.22233	TL232	Trolley buses
629.1343533	TL709.3.T83	Airplanes—Turbojet engines	629.22233092	TL232.3	Bus drivers
			629.22234	TL235.8	Ambulances
629.134355	TL708	Airplanes—Nuclear power plants	629.2234	TL230	Vans
			629.224	TL230	Dump trucks
629.13436	TL705-708	Propellers, Aerial	629.224	TL230-.5	Trucks
629.134381	TL682-683	Airplanes—Landing gear	629.224092	TL230.3	Truck drivers
629.134386	TL753	Parachutes—Rigging	629.2252	TL233-.8	Traction-engines
629.134386	TL750-758	Parachutes	629.2252	TL233-.8	Farm tractors
629.134386	TL750-758	Parachuting	629.2272	TL410-438	Bicycles
629.1344	RA615.2	Aeronautics—Sanitation	629.2275	TL439-448	Motorcycles
629.1344	TL697.08	Airplanes—Oxygen equipment	629.2275	TL443	Minibikes
			629.228	TL236	Automobiles, Racing
629.13442	TL681.P7	Airplanes—Pressurization	629.2292	TL200	Automobiles, Steam
629.13442	TL681.A5	Airplanes—Air conditioning	629.2293	TK4058-4059	Electric driving
629.13445	TL681.C3	Aircraft cabins	629.23	TL240-278	Automobiles—Design and construction
629.13452	TL671.7	Airplanes—Inspection			
629.13453	TL671.7	Airplanes—Flight testing	629.231	TL245	Automobiles—Aerodynamics
629.135	TL695-696	Avionics	629.25	TL214.P6	Motor vehicles—Pollution control devices
629.135	TL692-696	Aeronautics—Communication systems			
			629.25	TL214.P6	Automobiles—Pollution control devices
629.1351	TL696.L3	Landing aids (Aeronautics)			
629.1352	TL589.2.C58	Gyro compass	629.252	TL210-.7	Automobiles—Motors
629.1352	TL589.2.A3	Accelerometers	629.2548	TL272	Automobiles—Electric equipment
629.1352	TL696.C7	Radio compass			
629.1352	TL696.D5	Radio direction finders	629.2549	TL272.5-.55	Motor vehicles—Electronic equipment
629.1352	TL695-696	Aids to air navigation			
629.1354	TL690-691	Electricity in aeronautics	629.26	TL255-256.5	Automobiles—Bodies
629.1355	TL693-696	Radio in aeronautics	629.2772	TL271-.5	Automobiles—Heating and ventilation
629.1355	TL693-696	Airplanes—Electronic equipment			
			629.282	TL285-295	Automobiles—Testing
629.1355	TL693.R2	Airplanes—Radio equipment	629.283	TL154	Automobile parking
629.136	TL725-733	Airports	629.283	TL152.5-.55	Automobile driving
629.136	TL725.3.B8	Airport buildings	629.283092	TL152.5-.55	Automobile drivers
629.136	TL557.V5	Airports—Visibility	629.286	TL153	Service stations
629.136	TL726.15	International airports	629.287	TL152-.2	Automobiles—Maintenance and repair
629.1361	TL725.6	Seaplane bases			
629.1363	TL725.3.R8	Runways (Aeronautics)	629.287	TL152.2	Automobiles—Conservation and restoration
629.1366	TL725.3.C64	Airport control towers			
629.1366	TL725.3.T7	Air traffic control	629.295	TL480	Lunar surface vehicles
629.1366092	HD8039.A425	Air traffic controllers	629.295	TL475-480	Roving vehicles (Astronautics)

Dewey	LC	Subject Heading	Dewey	LC	Subject Heading
629.4	TL787-4050	Astronautics	629.83	TJ216	Feedback control systems
629.4	TL1050-1060	Astrodynamics	629.89	TJ217.5	Intelligent control systems
629.40212	TL869	Space vehicles—Specifications	629.892	TJ210.2-211.49	Robotics
			629.892	TJ210.2-211.49	Robots
629.4071	TL845-848	Astronautics—Study and teaching	630	GN407.4-.8	Traditional farming
			630	SB1-317	Crops
629.40724	TL794.3	Astronautics—Experiments	630	S494.5.A47	Agropastoral systems
629.409(4-9)	TL789.8	Astronautics—[By region or country]	630	SB45.65	Crop science literature
			630	S560-575	Farms
629.41	TL790	Space flight	630-638	S1-954	Agriculture
629.433	TL784.C63	Rockets (Aeronautics)—Guidance systems	630.11	S439-481	Agricultural systems
			630.23	S494.5.A4	Agriculture—Vocational guidance
629.437	TL694.T35	Aerospace telemetry			
629.437	TL4030	Space vehicles—Tracking	630.2515	S600	Meteorology, Agricultural
629.442	TL795.7	Space colonies	630.289	S565	Agriculture—Safety measures
629.442	TL797	Space stations			
629.450284	TL1098	Space tools	630.5	SB1-13	Crops—Periodicals
629.45071	TL1085	Space flight training	630.5	S1-19	Agriculture—Periodicals
629.453	TL1065-1080	Navigation (Astronautics)	630.6	S533.F66	4-H clubs
629.453	TL1070	Astronautical charts	630.6	S20	Agriculture—Societies, etc.
629.454	TL799.M6	Space flight to the moon	630.6	SB16	Crops—Congresses
629.455	TL943	Planetary quarantine	630.68	S560-572	Farm management
629.455	TL789-790	Interplanetary voyages	630.7	S530-539	Agricultural education
629.4552	TL799.V45	Space flight to Venus	630.72	SB51-56	Crops—Research
629.4553	TL799.M3	Space flight to Mars	630.71	S531-539	Agriculture—Study and teaching
629.4555	TL799.J8	Space flight to Jupiter			
629.457	TL4030	Space vehicles—Tracking	630.711	S537-539	Agricultural colleges
629.458	TL1090-1095	Space vehicles—Piloting	630.715	S544-545	Agricultural extension work
629.46	TL796-798	Artificial satellites	630.715092	S533-534	County agricultural agents
629.46	TL798.G4	Geodetic satellites	630.72	S539.5-542	Agriculture—Research
629.47	TL795-.5	Space ships	630.723	S494.5.E8	Agricultural surveys
629.472	TL950-954	Space vehicles—Materials	630.723	S441-451	Agricultural surveys
629.474	TL3000-3285	Space vehicles—Electronic equipment	630.724	S541-543	Agricultural experimental stations
629.474	TL1100-1102	Space vehicles—Electric equipment	630.74	S550-559	Agricultural exhibitions
			630.74	S549	Agricultural museums
629.474	TL1082	Astronautical instruments	630.9	S419-481	Agriculture—History
629.47445	TL1102.B3	Space vehicles—Batteries	630.901	GN799.A4	Agricultural implements, Prehistoric
629.475	TL780-785.8	Rockets (Aeronautics)			
629.47522	TL784.C63	Liquid propellant rockets—Control systems	630.901	GN799.A4	Agriculture—Origin
			630.901	S421-431	Agriculture, Prehistoric
629.47524	TL785	Solid propellants	630.911	SB109.7	Cold regions agriculture
629.4753	TL783.5	Nuclear rockets	630.911	S604.33	Cold regions agriculture
629.4754	TL783.57	Photon rockets	630.9154	S612-619	Arid regions agriculture
629.4755	TL783.54-.63	Electric rocket engines	630.91732	S494.5.U72	Urban agriculture
629.4755	TL783.6	Plasma rockets	630.92	HD8039.P496	Plantation workers
629.4755	TL783.63	Ion rockets	630.9(4-9)	S439-481	Agricultural geography
629.477	TL1530	Space cabin atmospheres	630.945632	S431	Agriculture—Rome
629.477	TL1500-1575	Life support systems (Space environment)	631	S671-760	Agricultural engineering
			631.27	NA8390-8392	Fences
629.4772	TL1550	Space suits	631.27	S790-.3	Fences
629.4773	TL1565	Space vehicles—Water-supply	631.27	S723	Gates
			631.3	S687-689	Drill (Agricultural implement)
629.4774	TL945	Space vehicles—Sterilization	631.3	S676.5	Agricultural instruments
			631.3	S671-760	Agricultural machinery
629.478	TL4000-4050	Ground support systems (Astronautics)	631.3	S695-697	Mowing machines
			631.3	S695-697	Sickles
629.8	TA165	Automatic control	631.3	S699-701	Threshing machines
629.8	TJ212.2-225	Automatic machinery	631.3	S671-760	Farm equipment
629.8043	TK2851	Electric controllers	631.3	S675.3	Agricultural mechanics
629.82	TJ1560	Vending machines	631.3	S676-.3	Agricultural implements

Dewey	LC	Subject Heading	Dewey	LC	Subject Heading
631.3	S683-685	Plows	631.55	SB185.8	Harvesting time
631.3	TJ1480-1496	Agricultural machinery	631.58	S494.5.P47	Permaculture
631.37	S494.5.E5	Agriculture and energy	631.58	S603.7	Multiple cropping
631.37	S715.C64	Cotton-picking machinery	631.58	S603.7	Double cropping
631.372	S711-713	Power transmission	631.58	S603.5	Intercropping
631.372	S711-713	Farm tractors	631.5814	S604	No-tillage
631.373	S711-713	Farm trucks	631.5818	S602.87	Shifting cultivation
631.4	S590-599.9	Soil science	631.582	S603	Crop rotation
631.4	S593	Soils—Analysis	631.583	SB415-416.3	Solar greenhouses
631.4	S590-599.9	Soils	631.583	SB415-416.3	Greenhouses
631.4	S589.8-.85	Potting soils	631.584	S605.5	Organic farming
631.4	S590-592	Soil management	631.585	SB126.5-.57	Hydroponics
631.4	S590-599.9	Land capability for agriculture	631.586	SB110	Dry farming
			631.587	S599-.9	Soils, Irrigated
631.4	S589.8	Plant growing media	631.587	S612-619	Irrigation
631.41	S592.6.A34	Soils—Agricultural chemical content	631.587	S612-619	Irrigation farming
			631.6	S612-619	Desert reclamation
631.41	S592.5-.6	Soil chemistry	631.6	S604.8-621.5	Reclamation of land
631.41	S583-587.5	Agricultural chemistry	631.62	S594	Drain-gages
631.417	S592.7-.85	Soil biochemistry	631.62	S621	Drainage
631.42	S595	Alkali lands	631.64	S621.5.P59	Plants for land reclamation
631.42	S592.575	Soil acidity	631.64	S621.5.S3	Sand dune planting
631.42	S592.575	Acid sulphate soils	631.8	S662-.5	Liquid fertilizers
631.42	S592.57-.575	Acid soils	631.8	S631-667	Fertilizers
631.43	S589-.6	Agricultural physics	631.8	S633	Garden fertilizers
631.432	S594	Soil moisture	631.826	S592.85	Peat soils
631.432	S594	Moisture index	631.84	S587.5.N5	Nitrogen in agriculture
631.45	S627.P55	Plants for soil conservation	631.84	S651-.3	Nitrogen fertilizers
631.45	S622-627	Soil conservation	631.842	S651-.3	Nitrates
631.45	S627.P76	Soil conservation projects	631.847	S654.5	Biofertilizers
631.451	S604.5-.64	Agricultural conservation	631.85	S647	Phosphatic fertilizers
631.451	S661.5	Mulching	631.85	S659	Bone-meal
631.455	S627.H5	Hillside planting	631.86	S654	Organic fertilizers
631.47	S592.14-.147	Soil surveys	631.86	S654	Organic wastes as fertilizer
631.49154	S592.17.D47	Desert soils	631.86	S587.45	Natural products in agriculture
631.49154	S599-.9	Desert soils			
631.49154	S592.17.A73	Arid soils	631.861	S655	Manures
631.51	S604	Tillage	631.861	S655	Farm manure
631.52	SB123-.5	Plant breeding	631.869	S657	Sewage
631.52	SB123-.25	Selection (Plant breeding)	631.87	S661.2.M3	Marine algae as fertilizer
631.52	SB119-124	Plant propagation	631.874	S661	Green manuring
631.52	SB106.O74	Crops—Evolution	631.875	S661	Compost
631.52	SB106.I47	Crop improvement	631.913	SB111	Tropical crops
631.521	SB114	Seed adulteration and inspection	632	SB601	Plant parasites
			632.09(4-9)	SB605	Garden pests—[By region or country]
631.521	SB113.2-118.45	Seed technology			
631.521	SB113.2-118.45	Seeds	632.11	QK756	Plants—Frost resistance
631.523	SB108-109	Plant introduction	632.19	SB745	Plants, Effect of acid precipitation on
631.5233	SB123.57	Crops—Genetic engineering			
631.5233	SB123.57	Transgenic plants	632.19	SB745	Plants, Effect of air pollution on
631.5233	SB106.B56	Plant biotechnology			
631.5233	SB123.57	Plant genetic engineering	632.19	SB745	Crops—Effect of air pollution on
631.53	SB121	Planting (Plant culture)			
631.53	S600.7.P53	Planting time	632.19	SB745	Crops—Effect of acid precipitation on
631.53	SB185.8	Planting time			
631.531	SB121	Sowing	632.2	SB767	Galls (Botany)
631.536	SB121	Seedlings—Transplanting	632.3	SB599-989	Plant diseases
631.54	SB123.65	Grafting	632.4	SB733	Fungal diseases of plants
631.54	SB125	Disbudding	632.4	SB733	Fungi in agriculture
631.55	S600.7.H37	Harvesting time	632.43	SB741.M65	Mildew
631.55	SB129	Harvesting	632.446	SB741.D68	Downy mildew diseases

Dewey	LC	Subject Heading	Dewey	LC	Subject Heading
632.5	SB610-615	Weeds—Control	633.88	SB293-295	Medicinal plants
632.5	SB610-615	Weeds	633.88384	SB295.G5	Ginseng
632.52	SB610-615	Parasitic plants	633.88393	RS165.C3	Quinine
632.(6-7)	SB599-999	Agricultural pests	633.8858	SB295.E63	Ephedra
632.(6-7)	SB599-1100	Pests	633.895	SB289-291	Gums and resins
632.(6-7)06	SB599.2	Agricultural pests—Congresses	633.8952	SB289-291	Rubber plants
			633.898	SB292	Pesticidal plants
632.68	SB995	Bird pests	634	SB354-399	Fruit
632.69	SB993.5-994	Mammal pests	634	SB354-402	Orchards
632.7	SB818-945	Insect pests	634.3	SB369	Citrus fruits
632.752	SB939	Scale insects	634.32	SB370.G7	Grapefruit
632.9	SB950-989	Plants, Protection of	634.37	SB365	Fig
632.9	SB950-989	Pests—Control	634.5	SB401.M32	Macadamia nut
632.93	SB979.5-985	Plant quarantine	634.5	SB401	Nuts
632.94	SB952.8-955	Pesticides—Application	634.57	SB401	Cashew nut
632.94	SB955	Fumigation	634.62	SB364	Date palm
632.94	SB953	Spraying and dusting in agriculture	634.62	SB364	Date
			634.713	SB386.B6	Blackberries
632.95	SB950.9-970.4	Pesticides	634.737	SB386.B7	Blueberries
632.95	SB951.145.N37	Natural pesticides	634.8	SB387-399	Grapes
632.95042	SB957	Pesticide resistance	634.9	SD	Forests and forestry
632.95042	SB750	Plants—Disease and pest resistance	634.9	SD391-535	Trees
			634.90284	SD388	Forest machinery
632.9517	SB951.5-.54	Insecticides	634.906	SD1	Forests and forestry—Societies, etc.
632.952	SB951.3	Fungicides	634.9071	SD250-381.5	Forestry schools and education
632.954	SB951.4	Herbicides	634.9072	SD356-.54	Forests and forestry—Research
632.96	SB975-989	Pests—Biological control	634.909(4-9)	SD11-115	Forests and forestry—[By region or country]
632.96	SB975	Biological pest control agents	634.90973	SD11-12	Forests and forestry—United States
633	SB183-187	Seed crops	634.9097(4-9)	SD12	Forests and forestry—[United States, By state]
633.1	SB189-192	Grain	634.92	SD387.S52	Short rotation forestry
633.1	SB188-192	Winter grain	634.92	SD387.C58	Clearcutting
633.11	HD9049.W3-.W5	Durum wheat industry	634.93	SD411-428	Forest protection
633.11	SB191.W5	Durum wheat	634.93	SD411	Forests and forestry—Safety measures
633.2	SB195	Silage	634.93	SD421.375	Fire lookout stations
633.2	SB197-202	Grasses	634.95	SD392	Silvicultural systems
633.2	SB193-207	Forage plants	634.953	SD396.5	Forest thinning
633.202	SB199	Meadows	634.956	SD409	Reforestation
633.202	SB199	Pastures	634.956	SD409	Afforestation
633.202	SB193-.55	Rangelands	634.956	SD399.5	Forest genetics
633.21	SB201.K4	Kentucky bluegrass	634.9565	SD391	Tree planting
633.28	SB413.R43	Red fescue	634.96	SB761	Forest insects
633.3	SB203-205	Legumes	634.9617	SD425	Floods
633.3	SB205.F3	Faba bean	634.9618	SD421	Forest fires—Prevention and control
633.5	SB241-261	Fiber plants	634.9618	SD421.43	Aeronautics in wildfire control
633.571	SB261.M3	Abaca (Fiber)	634.9618	SD421	Forest fire detection
633.577	HD9019.A43-.A434	Agave products industry	634.9618	SD420.5-421.5	Forest fires
633.58	SB281-283	Matwork plants	634.9721	SD397.E54	English oak
633.6	SB215-239	Sugar	634.9721	SD397.D87	Durmast oak
633.71	SB273-278	Tobacco	634.973766	SD397.E8	Eucalyptus
633.73	SB269	Coffee	634.9753	SD397.E27	Eastern hemlock
633.74	SB267	Cacao	634.9754	SD397.F5	Fir
633.75	SB295.065	Opium poppy	634.9754	SD397.D7	Douglas fir
633.75	SB295.06	Opium			
633.75	RS165.H3	Hashish			
633.79					
633.81	SB301-303	Aromatic plants			
633.8(3-4)	SB305-307	Spice plants			
633.85	SB298-299	Oilseed plants			
633.86	SB285-287	Dye plants			
633.88	SB293-295	Mushrooms, Hallucinogenic			

Dewey	LC	Subject Heading	Dewey	LC	Subject Heading
634.9758	SD397.R3	Redwood	635.9647	SB433-.34	Lawns
634.9758	SD397.D37	Dawn redwood	635.965	SB419-.3	Indoor gardening
634.98	HD9750-9769	Forest products	635.965	SB419-.3	Indoor gardens
634.98	SD537-538.83	Logging	635.965	SB419-.3	House plants
634.98	SD538-557	Lumbering	635.9671	SB473.2	Patio gardening
634.99	SB172	Multipurpose trees	635.9671	SB419.5	Balcony gardening
634.99	SB170-171	Tree crops	635.9671	SB419.5	Roof gardening
634.99	S494.5.A45	Agroforestry	635.9672	SB459	Rock gardens
634.99	SD387.W6	Woodlots	635.9674	SB423	Water gardens
635	SB118.48-.75	Nurseries (Horticulture)	635.9678	SB419-.3	Window gardening
635	SB175-177	Food crops	635.973	SB428.5	Everlasting flowers
635	SB450.9-467	Gardens	635.973	SB447	Everlasting flowers
635	SB473	Backyard gardens	635.975	SB431	Foliage plants
635	SB317.5-319.77	Horticultural crops	635.976	SB437	Hedges
635	SB450.9-467.8	Gardening	635.977	SB435-437	Ornamental trees
635	SB320-353.5	Vegetables	635.977	SB436	Trees in cities
635	SB320-353.5	Vegetable gardening	635.977	SB435-437	Tree planting
635.0284	SB454.8	Garden tools	635.97713	SB435-437	Flowering woody plants
635.043	SB454.3.P7	Planting time	635.97715	SB435	Ornamental evergreens
635.0484	SB453.5	Organic gardening	635.9772	SB435-.8	Dwarf trees
635.1	SB209-211	Root crops	635.9772	SB433.5	Gardens, Miniature
635.1	SB351.R65	Root crops	635.9772	SB433.5	Bonsai
635.25	SB341	Onions	635.9775	SB435	Evergreens
635.61	SB339	Melons	635.97752	SB413.E27	Eastern hemlock
635.642	SB349	Tomatoes	635.9823	SB415	Greenhouse gardening
635.646	SB351.E5	Eggplant	635.9823	SB414.6-416.3	Greenhouse plants
635.677	SB191.P64	Popcorn	635.9824	QH68	Terrariums
635.7	SB351.H5	Herbs	635.986	SB418-.4	Hanging baskets
635.7	SB351.H5	Herb gardens	635.986	SB418-.4	Container gardening
635.8	SB353-.5	Fungi, Edible	635.986	SB415	Plants, Potted
635.9	SB403-450	Flowers	636	GN407.6-.7	Domestic animals
635.9	SB431.7	Ornamental grasses	636	SF1-140	Livestock
635.9	SB403-450.87	Flower gardening	636	SF	Animal culture
635.9	SB403-450.87	Floriculture	636	SF	Small animal culture
635.9	SB403-450.87	Plants, Ornamental	636.0811	SF411.5	Pet shows
635.9074	SB441-.75	Flower shows	636.082	S494	Breeding
635.92	SB603.5	Garden pests	636.082	S494	Inbreeding
635.9312	SB422	Annuals (Plants)	636.082	SF105	Inbreeding
635.932	SB434	Perennials	636.082	SF105-109	Animal breeding
635.93334	SB413.D4	Delphinium	636.082	SF105.27-.275	Rare breeds
635.933685	SB413.H6	Hibiscus	636.082	SF41	Domestication
635.933734	SB410.9-411.7	Roses	636.0821	SF756.5	Domestic animals—
635.933734	SB411	Rose gardens			Genetic engineering
635.93375	SB432.7	Carnivorous plants	636.0821	SF756.5	Veterinary genetics
635.93379	SB413.G35	Dwarf pelargoniums	636.0821	SF756.5	Domestic animals—
635.93399	SB413.D13	Dahlias			Genetic engineering
635.93399	SB299.S9	Sunflowers	636.0821	SF756.5	Veterinary genetics
635.93399	SB413.D	Daisies	636.0821	SF140.B54	Animal biotechnology
635.93434	SB413.D12	Daffodils	636.08245	SF105.5	Artificial insemination
635.93438	SB413.I8	Dwarf irises	636.0832	QL83.2	Wildlife rescue
635.9344	SB409	Dendrobium	636.0832	HV4746	Dog rescue
635.9345	SB413.P17	Palms	636.0832	HV4701-4959	Animal welfare
635.9373	SB429	Ferns, Ornamental	636.084	SF94.5-99	Animal feeding
635.951	SB439-.26	Native plant gardening	636.0845	SF84.82-98	Range management
635.9525	SB427.5	Desert plants	636.0845	SF84.82-85.6	Rangelands
635.9525	SB427.5	Desert gardening	636.0845	SF140.P38	Pastoral systems
635.9525	SB439.8	Drought-tolerant plants	636.085	SF94.5-99	Animal nutrition
635.9528	SB459	Alpine gardens	636.0852	SF98.F	Fiber in animal nutrition
635.9543	SB434.7	Gardening in the shade	636.0855	SF99.M33	Marine algae as feed
635.9543	SB434.7	Shade-tolerant plants	636.0855	SF99.W34	Organic wastes as feed
635.9642	SB433-.34	Turfgrasses	636.0855	SF99.Y4	Yeast as feed

Dewey	LC	Subject Heading	Dewey	LC	Subject Heading
636.0855	SF98.F	Feeds—Fiber content	636.089639	SF851-855	Nutrition disorders in animals
636.0855	SF99.D5	Distillers feeds	636.08967	SF910.5	Veterinary orthopedics
636.0855	SF99.F37	Feathers as feed	636.089682	SF799	Meningitis
636.0855	SF99	Bone-meal	636.08969	SF781-809	Communicable diseases in animals
636.0855	SF98.P46	Pesticide residues in feeds	636.0896956	SF787	Anthrax
636.0855	SF97.7	Feeds—Flavor and odor	636.0896959	SF740	Zoonoses
636.0855	SF94.5-99	Feeds	636.089696	SF810	Domestic animals—Parasites
636.0855	SF99.F5	Fish meal as feed			
636.08556	SF99.A37	Agricultural wastes as feed	636.0896964	SF810.H8	Echinococcosis
636.08557	SF98.A5	Antibiotics in animal nutrition	636.0896992	SF910.T8	Veterinary oncology
			636.0897	SF911-914.4	Veterinary surgery
636.08557	SF98.M4	Medicated feeds	636.089715	SF914.4	Fractures in animals
636.08557	SF98.A2	Feed additives	636.089796	SF914	Veterinary anesthesia
636.0882	SF180	Draft animals	636.08982	SF887	Veterinary obstetrics
636.0885	SF405.5-407	Laboratory animals	636.1	SF360.6-361.75	Domestic asses
636.0886	SF170-180	Working animals	636.1	SF277-359.7	Horses
636.0887	SF411-459	Pets	636.1	SF290-291	Horse farms
636.0887	SF414.2	Pets—Housing	636.101	SF277-359.7	Foals
636.0887	SF414.3	Pet boarding facilities	636.10811	SF294.5-297.7	Horse shows
636.089	SF600-1100	Veterinary medicine	636.10811	SF295.185-.187	Show horses
636.089	SF604.4-.7	Veterinary hospitals	636.10811	SF295.7	Event horses
636.089014	SF610	Veterinary medicine—Terminology	636.10837	SF309.9	Bridles
			636.10837	SF309.9	Bits (Bridles)
636.089025	SF611	Veterinarians—Directories	636.109	SF293.M56	Miniature horses
636.08906	SF600-604	Veterinary medicine—Societies, etc.	636.12	SF343	Harness racehorses
			636.13	SF309.65-.653	Dressage horses
636.08906	SF605	Veterinary medicine—Congresses	636.13	SF293.S72	Standardbred horse
			636.13	SF293.P5	Pinto horse
636.0890711	SF756.3-.37	Veterinary colleges	636.13037	SF309.9	English saddles
636.089073	SF774.5	Veterinary nursing	636.13037	SF309.9	Western saddle
636.08909	SF615-724	Veterinary medicine—History	636.14	SF312	Coach horses
			636.15	SF311-.3	Draft horses
636.089092	SF612-613	Veterinarians	636.16	SF315.2.C4	Chincoteague pony
636.0891	SF761-767	Veterinary anatomy	636.16	SF315	Ponies
636.0892	SF768-.2	Veterinary physiology	636.182	SF361	Donkeys
636.0893	SF600-1100	Animal health	636.182092	SF361	Donkey breeders
636.0894	SF740	Veterinary public health	636.183	SF362	Mules
636.08944	SF780.9	Veterinary epidemiology	636.2	SF191-219	Cattle
636.089448	SF757.15	Veterinary disinfection	636.2	SF191-219	Cows
636.089456	SF740	Animals as carriers of disease	636.20812	SF101-103.5	Cattle brands
			636.20812	SF101-103.5	Livestock brands
636.08951	SF915-918	Pharmacy	636.20886	SF961-967	Cattle—Diseases
636.08951	SF916.5	Veterinary prescriptions	636.208969	SF961-967	Cattle—Infections
636.0895329	SF918.A5	Antibiotics in veterinary medicine	636.208969	SF967.E3	East Coast fever
			636.208969	SF962	Blackleg in cattle
636.0895372	SF918.V32	Veterinary vaccines	636.213	SF207	Beef cattle
636.0895892	SF914.5	Veterinary acupuncture	636.2142	SF221-250	Dairying
636.0896	SF600-1100	Domestic animals—Diseases	636.2142	SF221-250	Dairy farming
			636.2142	SF251-262.5	Milk
636.0896	SF600-1100	Livestock—Diseases	636.2142	SF208	Dairy cattle
636.0896	SF600-1100	Animals—Diseases	636.2142	SF221-250	Dairy farms
636.0896014	SF780.3	Veterinary bacteriology	636.2142	SF259	Homogenized milk
636.08960194	SF780.4	Veterinary virology	636.21420284	SF247	Dairying—Equipment and supplies
636.0896025	SF778	Veterinary emergencies			
636.08960252	SF914.3	First aid for animals	636.21420681	SF261	Dairying—Accounting
636.0896028	SF778	Veterinary critical care	636.21420688	SF261	Dairy products—Marketing
636.0896075	SF771-774	Veterinary medicine—Diagnosis	636.2142071	SF241-245	Dairying—Study and teaching
636.08960759	SF769	Veterinary autopsy			
636.089612	SF811	Veterinary cardiology	636.21420711	SF241-245	Dairy schools

Dewey	LC	Subject Heading	Dewey	LC	Subject Heading
636.2(2-8)	SF198-199	Cattle breeds	636.7532	SF429.S39	Scottish deerhound
636.224	SF199.G8	Guernsey cattle	636.7533	SF429.A4	Afghan hounds
636.225	SF199.D4	Dexter cattle	636.7538	SF429.D25	Dachshunds
636.226	SF211	Dual-purpose cattle	636.755	SF429.D33	Dandie Dinmont terrier
636.226	SF199.D38	Devon cattle	636.8	SF441-450	Cats
636.23	SF199.E2	East Prussian cattle	636.80822	SF443	Cats—Pedigrees
636.28	SF199.A3	Africander cattle	636.826	SF449.A28	Abyssinian cat
636.292	SF401.A45	American bison	636.832	SF449.P4	Persian cat
636.29401	SF401.D3	Deer farming	636.9322	SF451-455	Rabbits
636.3	SF376.5	Lambs	636.9322	SF455.D8	Dutch rabbits
636.3	SF371-379	Sheep	636.9322	SF455.D85	Dwarf rabbits
636.30833	SF379	Sheep-shearing	636.93560887	SF459.H3	Dwarf hamsters as pets
636.308969	SF969.E	Epizootic catarrh in sheep	636.93592	SF401.G85	Guinea pigs
636.39	SF380-388	Goats	636.965701	SF401.E4	Elk farming
636.4	SF391-397.4	Swine	636.97	SF403-405	Fur-bearing animals
636.408969	SF977.P5	Swine plague	636.9701	SF402-405	Fur farming
636.483	SF393.D9	Duroc Jersey swine	636.97662701	SF405.M6	Mink farming
636.5	SF481-513	Chickens	637	SF250.5-275	Dairy products
636.5082	SF492-493	Poultry—Breeding	637.124	SF250	Milking
636.5082	SF495-497	Poultry—Hatcheries	637.1240284	SF247	Milking machines
636.5082	SF495	Eggs—Incubation	637.14	SF250.5-275	Dairy processing
636.5082	SF492-493	Poultry—Breeding	637.141	SF259	Milk—Sterilization
636.508(4-5)	SF494	Poultry—Feeding and feeds	637.141	SF259	Milk—Pasteurization
636.50896	SF995-.4	Poultry—Diseases	637.143	SF259	Dried milk
636.5142	SF490-.8	Eggs—Production	637.143	SF259	Dairy products—Drying
636.5142	SF490-.8	Eggs	637.2	SF263-269.5	Butter
636.592	SF507	Turkeys	637.3	SF270-274	Cheese
636.597	SF504.7-505.63	Ducks	637.354	SF272.P3	Parmesan cheese
636.6	SF461	Aviculture	638	SF518	Insect rearing
636.6	SF461	Cage birds	638.1	SF521-539	Bee culture
636.63	SF502.8-503.52	Game fowl	638.12	SF521-539	Honeybee
636.63082	SF508-510	Game bird culture	638.16	SF539	Honey
636.7	SF421-440.2	Dogs	638.16	SF539	Bee products
636.707	SF421-435	Puppies	638.17	TP678	Beeswax
636.70811	SF425.7	Dogs—Obedience trials	638.2	SF541-560	Silk
636.70811	SF425.3	Show dogs	638.2	SF541-560	Silkworms
636.70811	SF425-.8	Dog shows	638.2	SF559.5-560	Silkworms, Non-mulberry
636.70822	SF423	Dogs—Pedigrees	638.2	SF541-560	Sericulture
636.7083	SF427.46	Dog walking	639.0901	GN799.H84	Hunting, Prehistoric
636.70831	SF428	Kennels	639.2	SH364	Sea otter
636.70833	SF427.55	Pet grooming salons	639.2	SH	Fisheries
636.70835	SF431	Dogs—Training	639.2028	SH334.5-344.8	Fishery technology
636.70837	SF427.15	Dog collars	639.20284	SH344.8.H6	Fishhooks
636.70886	HV8025	Police dogs	639.20284	SH344.6.T67	Fish traps
636.70886	SF428.8	Watchdogs	639.20284	SH344-.8	Fisheries—Equipment and supplies
636.70886	SF428.73	Search dogs			
636.70886	SF428.7	Sled dogs	639.20284	SH344.8.N4	Fishing nets
636.70886	SF428.55	Rescue dogs	639.20289	SH343.9	Fisheries—Safety measures
636.70886	SF428.6	Livestock protection dogs	639.206	SH3	Fisheries—Congresses
636.70896	SF991.D5	Distemper	639.2068	SH328-329	Fishery management
636.70896	SF991-992	Dogs—Diseases	639.2071	SH332-.2	Fishery schools
636.72	SF429.D3	Dalmatian dog	639.2072	SH343.5	Exploratory fishing
636.73	SF429.G75	Great Pyrenees	639.2072	SH332-.2	Fishery research stations
636.73	SF428.2	Working dogs	639.209	SH211	Fisheries—History
636.73	SF429.E8	Eskimo dogs	639.209163	SH213-.77	Fisheries—Atlantic Ocean
636.736	SF429.D6	Doberman pinschers	639.209164	SH214-215	Fisheries—Pacific Ocean
636.752	SF428.5	Bird dogs	639.209165	SH216-.55	Fisheries—Indian Ocean
636.7524	SF429.E47	English cocker spaniel	639.2092	HD8039.F65	Fishers
636.7524	SF429.E7	English springer spaniels	639.2092	SH20	Fish culturists
636.7526	SF429.S5	Setters (Dogs)	639.2094	SH253-293	Fisheries—Europe
636.753	SF429.H6	Hounds	639.20941	SH255-260	Fisheries—Great Britain

Dewey	LC	Subject Heading	Dewey	LC	Subject Heading
639.209415	SH261-262	Fisheries—Ireland	639.909(4-9)	SK361-579	Wildlife management areas—[By region or country]
639.20945	SH277-278	Fisheries—Italy			
639.20946	SH285-286	Fisheries—Spain	639.9094	SK503-543	Wildlife management areas—Europe
639.209469	SH281-282	Fisheries—Portugal			
639.20947	SH283-284	Fisheries—Russia	639.90941	SK505-511	Wildlife management areas—Great Britain
639.209481	SH279-280	Fisheries—Norway			
639.209485	SH287-288	Fisheries—Sweden	639.9095	SK553-567	Wildlife management areas—Asia
639.209489	SH267-268	Fisheries—Denmark			
639.209492	SH275-276	Fisheries—Netherlands	639.9096	SK571-575	Wildlife management areas—Africa
639.209495	SH273-274	Fisheries—Greece			
639.2095	SH295-307	Fisheries—Asia	639.90971	SK470-471	Wildlife management areas—Canada
639.20951	SH297-298	Fisheries—China			
639.209519	SH302.5-.7	Fisheries—Korea	639.90972	SK473	Wildlife management areas—Mexico
639.20952	SH301-302	Fisheries—Japan			
639.209561	SH291-292	Fisheries—Turkey	639.909728	SK475	Wildlife management areas—Central America
639.20971	SH223-229	Fisheries—Canada			
639.20972	SH231	Fisheries—Mexico	639.909729	SK477	Wildlife management areas—West Indies
639.209728	SH232	Fisheries—Central America			
639.209729	SH233	Fisheries—West Indies	639.90973	SK361-465	Wildlife management areas—United States
639.20973	SH221-222	Fisheries—United States			
639.20973	SH11	Fisheries—United States	639.9098	SK479-501	Wildlife management areas—South America
639.2098	SH234-251	Fisheries—South America			
639.20993	SH318.5	Fisheries—New Zealand	639.90994	SK577	Wildlife management areas—Australia
639.20994	SH317-318	Fisheries—Australia			
639.2099(5-6)	SH319	Fisheries—Oceania	639.92	SH157.85.A7	Artificial reefs
639.209982	SH268.G83	Fisheries—Greenland	639.92	SH153	Fishways
639.22	SH400-.8	Seafood gathering	639.92	SH157.8-.85	Fish habitat improvement
639.2743	SH351.E4	Eel fisheries	639.95	SK357	Game reserves
639.2745	SH351.S3	Sardine fisheries	639.96	SH171-179	Fish kills
639.28	SH381-385	Whaling	639.96	SH175	Fishes—Parasites
639.29	SH360-363	Sealing	639.964	SH171-179	Fishes—Infections
639.3	SH151-179	Fish-culture	639.964	SH171-179	Fishes—Pathogens
639.305	SH1	Fisheries—Periodicals	639.964	SH177.R4	Red tide
639.32	SH399.C6	Coral fisheries	639.964	SH171-179	Fishes—Diseases
639.3789	SH185	Frog culture	639.977	SH327.7	Fishery conservation
639.392	SH399.T9	Turtle fisheries	639.978	QL676.5-.57	Bird attracting
639.4	SH365-380.92	Shellfish culture	640	TX	Home economics
639.4	SH400.4-.8	Shellfish gathering	640.284	TX298-299	Home economics—Equipment and supplies
639.409(4-9)	SH365-367	Shellfish culture—[By region or country]	640.3	TX11	Home economics—Encyclopedias
639.41	SH371	Oyster fisheries			
639.41	SH379.5	Oyster shell	640.46	HD8039.D5	Domestics
639.412	SH377.5	Mother-of-pearl	640.46	HD6072-.2	Domestics
639.412	SH375-377	Pearl fisheries	640.46	TX331-334	Domestics
639.42	SH371-374.52	Mussel fisheries	640.5	TX1	Home economics—Periodicals
639.42	SH372.5-.52	Mussels			
639.4832	SH371.5-.52	Abalone culture	640.6	TX5	Home economics—Congresses
639.4832	SH371.5-.52	Abalone fisheries			
639.56	SH380.4-.45	Crab culture	640.71	TX165-286	Home economics—Study and teaching
639.75	SF597.E3	Earthworm culture			
639.8	SH138	Mariculture	640.73	TX335	Consumer education
639.8	SH20.5-191	Aquaculture	640.9	TX15-19	Home economics—History
639.809	SH21	Aquaculture—History	640.92	HQ756.6	Househusbands
639.809(4-9)	SH34-133	Aquaculture—[By region or country]	640.9(4-9)	TX21-127	Home economics—[By region or country]
639.89	SH393	Seagrasses	641	TX341-357	Groceries
639.9	GE140-160	Environmental degradation	641.013	TX631-641	Gastronomy
639.9	SK351-579	Wildlife management areas	641.2	TX951	Beverages
639.906	SK352	Wildlife management—Congresses	641.3	TX341-641	Food
			641.3	TX553.A3	Food additives
639.9092	SK354	Wildlife managers	641.302	TX369	Natural foods

Dewey	LC	Subject Heading	Dewey	LC	Subject Heading
641.31	TX356	Marketing (Home economics)	641.5943	TX721	Cookery, German
641.331	TX393	Flour	641.5944	TX719-.2	Cookery, French
641.331	TX393	Cereals as food	641.5952	TX724.5.J3	Cookery, Japanese
641.331	TX395	Cereals, Prepared	641.5972	TX716.M4	Cookery, Mexican
641.3318	TX558.R5	Rice	641.612	TX552	Canned foods
641.3373	TX415	Coffee	641.612	TX821	Cookery (Canned foods)
641.3382	TX819	Condiments	641.65	TX801-807	Cookery (Vegetables)
641.3383	TX406-407	Spices	641.6565	TX558.L4	Legumes as food
641.35	TX391	Vegetable juices	641.657	TX406-407	Herbs
641.35655	TX401.2.S69	Tofu	641.66	TX749-.5	Cookery (Meat)
641.357	TX415	Herbal teas	641.665	TX750-.5	Cookery (Poultry)
641.36	TX371-389	Meat	641.692	TX747	Cookery (Seafood)
641.36	TX743-759.5	Food of animal origin	641.692	TX747	Cookery (Fish)
641.36	TX555-556	Meat	641.71	TX690	Roasting (Cookery)
641.37143	TX556.M5	Dried skim milk	641.73	TX691	Steaming (Cookery)
641.38	TX560.H7	Honey	641.73	TX693	Stews
641.392	TX385-388	Seafood	641.73l	TX685	Boiling (Cookery)
641.392	TX385	Fish as food	641.76	TX687	Broiling
641.4	TX599-612	Canning and preserving	641.77	TX689.5	Stir frying
641.4	TX599-613	Food—Preservation	641.81	TX740.5	Garnishes (Cookery)
641.44	TX609	Dried foods	641.812	GN432	Tapa
641.44	TX609	Drying apparatus—Food	641.812	TX740	Appetizers
641.44	TX609	Food—Drying	641.814	TX819.S27	Salad dressing
641.453	TX610	Frozen foods	641.814	TX819	Sauces
641.47	TX599-612	Food preservatives	641.815	HD8039.B2	Bakers and bakeries
641.494	TX612.F5	Fishery products—	641.815	HD9057-9058	Bakers and bakeries
		Preservation	641.815	TX770.B55	Biscuits
641.5	TX642-840	Cookery	641.815	TX770.B55	Scones
641.5	TX151-162	Recipes	641.815	TX769-770	Bread
641.5028	TX657.S3-.S8	Stoves	641.815	TX770.M83	Muffins
641.5071	TX661-669	Cookery—Study and	641.815	TX770.P34	Pancakes, waffles, etc.
		teaching	641.815	TX770.P56	Pita bread
641.509	TX645	Cookery—History	641.82	TX740	Entrees (Cookery)
641.5092	TX649	Cooks	641.821	TX693	Casserole cookery
641.52	TX733	Breakfasts	641.822	TX394.5	Pasta products
641.53	TX735	Luncheons	641.822	TX809.N65	Noodles
641.54	TX737	Dinners and dining	641.83	TX807	Salads
641.563	TX551-560	Dietaries	641.83	TX740	Salads
641.563	TX551-560	Diet	641.84	TX818	Sandwiches
641.5636	TX837-838	Vegetarian cookery	641.853	TX783-799	Confectionery
641.5636	TX837-838	Vegetarianism	641.853	TX783-793	Candy
641.5676435	TX739.2.H35	Hanukkah cookery	641.86	TX773	Desserts
641.5676437	TX739.2.P37	Passover cookery	641.86(2-3)	TX795	Ice cream, ices, etc.
641.568	TX739.2.C45	Christmas cookery	641.864	TX773	Puddings
641.568	TX739.2.E37	Easter cookery	641.8653	TX771-.2	Cake
641.568	TX739-.2	Holiday cookery	641.8654	TX772	Cookies
641.568	TX739.2.T45	Thanksgiving cookery	641.8659	TX771	Coffee cakes
641.57	TX820	Quantity cookery	641.8659	TX773	Pastry
641.57	VC370-375	Cookery, Marine	641.87	TX815-817	Beverages
641.57	UC720-735	Cookery, Military	641.874	TX951	Bartending
641.578	TX823	Outdoor cookery	641.874	TX951	Cocktails
641.5784	TX840.B3	Barbecue cookery	641.874	TX951	Martinis
641.58	TX840.C65	Convection oven cookery	641.877	TX817.C5	Cocoa
641.586	TX827	Stoves, Electric	642	TX871-885	Table
641.587	TX840.P7	Pressure cookery	642	TX727-739.2	Menus
641.5882	TX657.064	Microwave ovens	642.4	TX901-921	Caterers and catering
641.5882	TX832	Microwave cookery	642.4	TX731-739	Entertaining
641.589	TX840.W65	Wok Cookery	642.5	TX901-910	Coffeehouses
641.589	TX840.F6	Food processor cookery	642.(6-8)	TX851-885	Entertaining
641.589	TX724.5.C	Wok cookery	642.6	TX885	Carving (Meat, etc.)
641.592	GN407-411.5	Food	642.7	TX871-885	Table setting and decoration

Dewey	LC	Subject Heading	Dewey	LC	Subject Heading
643.16	TH9739	Burglar alarms	649.122	RJ101-103	Infants—Care
643.16	TH9701-9745	Burglary protection	649.132	HQ775	Boys
643.2	GV777.7	Boat living	649.155	HQ773.5	Gifted children
643.2	GV811.65	Sailboat living	649.64	HQ770.4	Discipline of children
643.2	TH4819.P7	Prefabricated houses	650.01513	HF5691-5716	Business mathematics
643.2	TX1100-1105	Mobile home living	650.1	HF5386	Success in business
643.3	TX653-655	Kitchens	650.1	HF5384.5	Career plateaus
643.4	TX855-859	Dining rooms	650.1	HF5381-5382.5	Career development
643.6	TK7018-7301	Household appliances, Electric	650.14	HF5382.7-.75	Job hunting
645	TX311-317	Interior decoration	650.14	HF5383	Applications for positions
645.4	GN415.C8	Cradles	650.14	HF5383	Resumes (Employment)
645.8	SB473.5	Garden ornaments and furniture	651	HF5735-5746	Filing systems
646.05	TT490	Clothing trade—Periodicals	651.2	HF5548-.115	Office equipment and supplies
646.2	TT720-730	Clothing and dress—Repairing	651.29	HF5371	Business—Forms
646.2	TT700-715	Sewing	651.3	HF5546-5548	Office Management
646.2040284	GN799.P5	Pins and needles, Prehistoric	651.3741	R728	Medical secretaries
646.2044	TJ1501-1519	Sewing machines	651.3743	HE9751-9756	Messengers
646.2044	TT713	Machine sewing	651.53	HF5735-5746	Card system in business
646.21	TT390	Drapery	651.53	HF5738	Electronic filing systems
646.3	TX340	Clothing and dress	651.7	HF5717-5734.7	Business communication
646.402	TT570-630	Men's furnishing goods	651.73	HD9999.T34-.T344	Telephone answering services
646.406	TT635-645	Children's clothing	651.74	HF5548	Dictating machines
646.4060832	TT637	Layettes	651.74	HF5548	Dictograph
646.40608341	TT603	Boy's clothing	651.74	HF5719	Business report writing
646.408	TT550	Clothing and dress—Alteration	651.74	HF5718.3-5734	Business writing
			651.75	HF5721-5734	Commercial correspondence
646.7042	TT950-979	Beauty culture	651.8	HF5548.125-.6	Office practice—Automation
646.724	TT950-979	Barbering	651.8	HF5548.33	Electronic data interchange
646.724	TT967	Electric shavers	652.1	Z40-104.5	Writing
646.724	TT970	Shaving	652.1	Z43-45	Penmanship
646.724	TT975	Hairweaving	652.3	Z49-50.5	Typewriters
646.724	TT973	Hair—Dyeing and bleaching	652.5	HF5548.115	Word processing
646.724	TT975	Braids (Hairdressing)	652.8	Z102.5-104.5	Cryptography
646.7240284	TT969	Shampoos	653	Z53-104.5	Shorthand
646.7240284	TT967	Razors	657	HF5680-5681	Account books
646.7240284	TT969	Hair preparations	657	HF5681.G55	Going concern (Accounting)
646.7248	TT975	Wigs	657	HF5601-5689.8	Accounting
646.727	RL94	Manicuring	657.0284	HF5679	Accounting machines
646.75	GV546.5-.56	Bodybuilding	657.071	HF5630	Accounting—Study and teaching (Internship)
647	TX955	Building management	657.2	HF5601-5689.8	Bookkeeping
647	TX147	Institution management	657.3	HF5681.B2	Financial statements
647.92	TX957-959	Apartment houses	657.3	HF5667.65	Financial statements, Unaudited
647.94	TX901-941	Tourist camps, hostels, etc.	657.3	HF5681.B2	Funds-flow statements
647.94	TX901-946	Hotels	657.42	HF5686.C8	Cost accounting
647.94	TX907-910	Youth hostels	657.42	HF5686.C8	Direct costing
647.940683	TX911.3.P4	Hotels—Personnel management	657.45	HF5667-5668.25	Auditing
647.95	TX945-.5	Restaurants	657.458	HF5668-.25	Auditing, Internal
647.950683	TX911.3.P4	Restaurants—Personnel management	657.46	HF5681.D39	Deferred tax
			657.61	HJ9701-9995	Finance, Public—Accounting
648	TH6025	Electronics in sanitary engineering	657.72	HF5681.A2	Accounts current
648	TH6014-7696	Sanitation, Household	657.72	HF5681.A3	Accounts receivable
648.1	TT583	Pressing of garments	657.73	HF5681.V3	Valuation
648.1	TT980-999	Laundries	657.73	HF5681.D5	Depreciation
648.5	TX324	House cleaning	657.74	HF5681.N65	Employee fringe benefits—Accounting
649.10248	HQ769.5	Babysitting	657.74	HF5681.A27	Accounts payable

Dewey	LC	Subject Heading	Dewey	LC	Subject Heading
657.8333	HG1706-1708	Banks and banking—Accounting	658.5	TS155-194	Production management
			658.5	TS155-194	Factory management
657.95	HF5686.C7	Corporations—Accounting	658.5036	T57.95	Decision-making
658	HD28-70	Management	658.515	T58.8	Industrial efficiency
658	T55.4-60.8	Management science	658.542	T60.7	Motion study
658.019	HD58.7	Organizational behavior	658.5421	T60.4-.47	Time study
658.1	HD2747	Liquidation	658.544	T57.72	Fatigue
658.1511	HF5657.4	Managerial accounting	658.562	HD62	Standardization
658.152	HD39-40.7	Capital	658.562	T59-.2	Standardization
658.15224	HG177-.5	Fund raising	658.562	TS156-.6	Quality control
658.15224	HG4028.S7	Going public (Securities)	658.567	HD9975	Waste products
658.15244	HG4028.C45	Cash management	658.567	TP995-996	Waste products
658.155	HD61	Risk management	658.568	HD3656-3790.9	Factory inspection
658.1552	HD47.3	Cost control	658.56809	HD3661-3790.9	Factory inspection—[By
658.1554	HD47.4	Cost effectiveness	(4-9)		region or country]
658.3	HF5549-.5	Personnel management	658.7	TS161	Materials management
658.3	HF5549.5.C35	Career development	658.72	HD39.5	Industrial procurement
658.301	HF5549.5.M3	Manpower planning	658.788	HF5761-5780	Shipment of goods
658.302	HF5549.12	Supervision of employees	658.788	HF5761-5780	Delivery of goods
658.306	HF5549.5.J6	Job analysis	658.7884	HF5770	Cartons
658.306	HF5549.5.J613	Job descriptions	658.8106	HF5438.8.M4	Sales meetings
658.3111	HF5549.5.R44	Employees—Recruiting	658.812	HF5415.5-.55	Customer relations
658.3112	HF5549.5.E5	Employment tests	658.816	HF5417	Price fixing
658.3112	HF5549.5.D7	Employees—Drug testing	658.816	HF5417	Price maintenance
658.31124	HF5549.5.I6	Employment interviewing	658.816	HF5416.5-5417	Pricing
658.312	HF5549.5.S4	Seniority, Employee	658.82	HF5438.8.P74	Sales presentations
658.31242	HF5549.5.I53	Employee orientation	658.83	HF5415.3	Market surveys
658.3125	HF5549.5.R3	Employees—Rating of	658.83	HF5415.2-5415.34	Marketing research
658.3126	HF5549.5.P7	Promotions			
658.314	HF5549.5.M63	Employee motivation	659.1	HD59.3	Advocacy advertising
658.3142	HF5549.5.I5	Incentives in industry	659.1	HF5801-6182	Advertising
658.3151	HF5549.5.C8	Employees—Counseling of	659.1025	HF5804-5808	Advertising—Directories
658.3155	HF5549.5.G7	Grievance procedures	659.103	HF5803	Advertising—Encyclopedias
658.32021	HF5705-5707	Wages—Tables	659.105	HF5801-5802	Advertising—Periodicals
658.3822	HF5549.5.A4	Alcoholism and employment	659.1071	HF5814-5815	Advertising—Study and teaching
658.3822	HF5549.5.D7	Drugs and employment			
658.383	TX901-946.5	Food service	659.109	HF5811-5813	Advertising—History
658.383068	TX911.3.M27	Food service management	659.111	HF5826.5	Advertising media planning
658.4	HD57.7	Leadership	659.1122	HF5804-5808	Advertising departments
658.4	HD2741-2749	Corporate governance	659.1125	HF6178-6182	Advertising agencies
658.4012	HD30.28	Strategic planning	659.13	HF6146.D75	Advertising drinking glasses
658.4013	HD62.15	Total quality management	659.132	HF5851	Advertising cards
658.4013	HD66-.2	Quality circles	659.132	HF5843-.5	Posters
658.402	HD50-.5	Delegation of authority	659.132	HF5871-6141	Advertising, Newspaper
658.402	HD66-.2	Work groups	659.132	HF5825	Advertising layout and typography
658.402	HD50	Decentralization in management			
			659.13209	HF5901-6097	Advertising, Newspaper—[By region or country]
658.403	HD30.23	Decision-making	(4-9)		
658.4032	T57.85	Network analysis (Planning)	659.133	HF5861-5863	Commercial catalogs
658.4034	T57.9	Queuing theory	659.133	HF5861-5863	Advertising, Direct-mail
658.4052	HD58.6	Negotiation in business	659.143	HF6146.T42	Television advertising
658.406	HD58.8	Organizational change	659.152	HF5845-5849	Display of merchandise
658.408	HD60-.5	Social responsibility of business	659.157	HF5828	Advertising, Point-of-sale
			659.157	HF5845-5849	Show-windows
658.409	HD38.2-.25	Executive ability	659.17	HF6146.P75	Prize contests in advertising
658.46	HD69.C6	Business consultants	659.193877	HF6161.A38	Advertising—Airlines
658.47	HD38.7	Business intelligence	659.19658311	HF6125.5	Help-wanted advertising
658.473	HF5549.5.E43	Employee theft	659.2	HD59-.6	Public relations
658.5	HD38.5	Business logistics	660	TP155-156	Chemical engineering
658.5	HF5415.15-.157	Product management	660	TP	Chemistry, Technical
658.5	T56	Production control			

Dewey	LC	Subject Heading
660.03	TP9	Chemistry, Technical—Encyclopedias
660.05	TP1	Chemistry, Technical—Periodicals
660.06	TP5	Chemistry, Technical—Congresses
660.072	TP165-183	Chemical engineering laboratories
660.072	TP187-197	Research, Industrial—Laboratories
660.09	TP15-20	Chemistry, Technical—History
660.28	TP155.5-.6	Chemical plants
660.2804	TP149	Chemicals—Safety measures
660.281	TP155.7-.75	Chemical processes
660.283	TP157-159	Chemical engineering—Equipment and supplies
660.28424	TP248.25.M46	Membrane separation
660.28424	TP248.25.M45	Membrane reactors
660.284245	TP156.F5	Filters and filtration
660.284248	TP156.E8	Extraction (Chemistry)
660.28425	TP156.D5	Distillation
660.284292	TP156.F65	Fluidization
660.294514	TP156.E6	Emulsions
660.2961	TP265-267	Fire
660.297	TP250-261	Electrochemistry, Industrial
660.6	TP248.13-.65	Biotechnology
660.6	TP248.27.M53	Microbial biotechnology
660.62	QR53-.5	Industrial microbiology
660.63	TP248.3	Biochemical engineering
660.65	QH442.2	Cloning
660.65	QH442-.6	Genetic engineering
660.65	QH442.2	Molecular cloning
660.65	TP248.6	Genetic engineering
661	TP200-248	Chemicals
661.03	TP222-223	Alkalies
661.0431	TP245.U7	Uranium
661.0681	TP245.C4	Carbon
661.0721	TP245.O9	Oxygen
661.0731	TP245.F6	Fluorine
661.2	TP213-217	Acids
661.2	TP213-217	Inorganic acids
661.63	TP240	Sulphites
661.65	TP237-238	Nitrates
661.8	TP247-248	Organic compounds
661.803	TP953	Coal-tar
661.806	TP958-959	Essence and essential oils
661.807	TP247.5	Solvents
661.86	TP247.2	Organic acids
662.1	TP300-301	Firecrackers
662.1	TP300-301	Fireworks
662.2	TP267.5-301	Explosives
662.20289	TP297	Explosives—Safety measures
662.26	TP276	Guncotton
662.26	TP272	Gunpowder
662.27	TP285	Dynamite
662.3383	TN858-859	Oil-shales
662.5	TP310	Matches
662.6	TP315-360	Fuel
662.65	TP324	Fuelwood
662.65	TP323	Briquets (Fuel)
662.66	TP692.2	Gasoline, Synthetic
662.6692	TP358	Gasohol
662.6692	TP358	Alcohol as fuel
662.74	TP331	Charcoal
663	TP500-660	Beverages
663.1	TP593	Alcohol
663.2	TP544-559	Wine and wine making
663.223	TP559.P8	Port wine
663.223	TP559.P8	Madeira wine
663.224	TP555	Champagne (Wine)
663.42	TP568-587	Beer
663.5	TP589-618	Liquors
663.52	TP605	Whiskey
663.53	TP599	Brandy
663.55	TP611	Liqueurs
663.59	TP607.R9	Rum
663.62	TP628-636	Carbonated beverages
663.93	TP645	Coffee
664.001579	QR115-129	Food—Microbiology
664.001579	QR115-129	Food—Bacteriology
664.02	TX761-799	Bakers and bakeries
664.024	TP248.65.F66	Food—Biotechnology
664.024	TP371.44	Fermented foods
664.02852	TP372.2	Cold storage
664.02853	TP372.3	Frozen foods
664.0288	TP371.8	Radiation preservation of food
664.1	TP375-414.5	Sugar—Manufacture and refining
664.1	TP375-414.5	Syrups
664.123	TP390-391	Beet sugar
664.2	TP415-416	Starch
664.3	TP669-699	Oils and fats
664.32	TP684.M3	Margarine
664.34	TP676	Lard oil
664.34	TS1980-1981	Lard
664.68	HD9330.B2-.B23	Baking powder
664.7207	TS2120-2159	Flour-mills
664.7207	TS2120-2159	Flour
664.7207	TS2120-2159	Meal
664.756	TP434-435	Cereals, Prepared
664.76	TS2158	Feed mills
664.805	TP443-444	Vegetables—Drying
664.9	TS1950-1982	Animal products
664.9029	TS1960-1967	Slaughtering and slaughter-houses
664.94	SH334.9-336.5	Fishery processing
664.94(1-8)	SH335-337	Fishery products—Preservation
665.1	TP669-695	Waxes
665.2	TP676	Fish oils
665.3	TP680-684	Vegetable oils
665.332	TP977-979.5	Turpentine
665.353	TP684.C275	Castor oil
665.355	TP684.C7	Coconut oil
665.4	TP685-699	Mineral oils
665.5	TP690-692.5	Petroleum products
665.5	TP690-692.5	Petroleum
665.5	TP355	Petroleum as fuel

Dewey	LC	Subject Heading	Dewey	LC	Subject Heading
665.53	TP690-692.5	Petroleum—Refining	668.406	TP1101	Plastics—Societies, etc.
665.533	TP690.4	Cracking process	668.406	TP1105	Plastics—Congresses
665.53827	TP692.2	Gasoline	668.4071	TP1127-1129	Plastics—Study and teaching
665.5383	TP692.4.K4	Kerosene	668.409	TP1116-1118	Plastics—History
665.5384	TP343	Diesel fuels	668.41	TP1135	Plastics machinery
665.542	TP692.5	Petroleum—Storage	668.412	TP1150	Plastics—Molding
665.542	TP692.5	Oil storage tanks	668.413	TP1175.E9	Plastics—Extrusion
665.544	TN879.5-.6	Petroleum pipelines	668.415	TP1160	Plastics—Welding
665.(7-8)	TP242-244	Gases	668.4225	TP1180.P6	Polyesters
665.7	TP700-764	Gas manufacture and works	668.4227	TS1927.S55	Silicone rubber
665.7	TP350	Natural gas	668.423	TP1180.P57	Polycarbonates
665.7	TP700	Gas	668.423	TP1180.A33	Acetal resins
665.7	TP751-764	Gas	668.4233	TP1180.S7	Styrene
665.744	TN880.5	Natural gas pipelines	668.44	TP1180.C5	Celluloid
665.744	TP757	Gas-pipes	668.44	TP1180.C6	Cellulose
665.744	TP757	Gas distribution	668.492	TP1183.L3	Laminated plastics
665.75	TP345-350	Gas as fuel	668.493	TP1183.F6	Plastic foams
665.772	TP759	Coal gasification	668.55	TP983-986	Cosmetics
665.773	TP759	Oil gasification	668.92	TP156.P6	Polymerization
665.776	TP359.B48	Biogas	669	TN600-799	Metallurgy
665.822	TP245.H4	Helium	669.0282	TN677-.5	Blast furnaces
666.1	TP845-869	Glass manufacture	669.0282	TN677-.5	Metallurgical furnaces
666.1092	HD8039.G5	Glass-workers	669.0282	TN677-.5	Smelting furnaces
666.122	TP859	Glass blowing and working	669.0283	TN688	Hydrometallurgy
666.156	QC375	Glass, Optical	669.0284	TN681-687	Electrometallurgy
666.19	TP865-868	Glassware	669.0284	TN686.5.E4	Electroslag process
666.192	TP866	Bottles	669.05	TN600-605	Metallurgy—Periodicals
666.3	TP785-842	Pottery	669.071	TN675.3	Metallurgy—Study and teaching
666.427	TP823	Glazes			
666.427	TP812	Glazes	669.09	TN615-620	Metallurgy—History
666.43	TP841-842	Kilns	669.09(4-9)	TN621-655	Metallurgy—[By region or country]
666.733	TP839	Drain-tiles			
666.737	TP826-833	Brickmaking	669.141	TN756-757	Iron alloys
666.86	TP870	Artificial minerals	669.1413	TN713-718	Blast furnaces
666.88	TP873-.5	Precious stones, Artificial	669.142	TN755	Steel-works
667.0283	TT310	Paint mixing	669.1422	TN740-742	Open-hearth furnaces
667.1	TP990-992.5	Cleaning compounds	669.1423	TN736-738	Bessemer process
667.12	TP932-.6	Dry cleaning	669.(2-7)	TN758-799	Nonferrous metals
667.14	TP894-895	Bleaching	669.22	TN760-769	Gold—Metallurgy
667.2	TP897-929	Dyes and dyeing	669.3	TN780	Copper—Metallurgy
667.2	TP890-929	Dyes and dyeing—Chemistry	669.72	TS551-552	Light metals
667.29	TP934-937.5	Pigments	669.722	TN775	Aluminum—Metallurgy
667.4	TP946-950	Ink	669.725	TN895-897	Alkalies
667.4	Z247	Printing ink	669.8	TN672	Precipitation hardening
667.6	TP934-937.5	Paint	669.9	TN690	Physical metallurgy
667.6	TT360	Sign painting	669.92	HG325-329	Assaying
667.6	TT300-380	Painting, Industrial	669.92	TN550-580	Assaying
667.72	TP940	Polishes	669.92	TN565	Metallurgical analysis
667.9	TA418.76	Protective coatings	669.95	TN689-693	Metallography
667.9	TP156.C57	Coating processes	669.95	TN690	Alloys
668.12	TP990-992.5	Soap	670	T55.4-60.8	Industrial engineering
668.2	TP973	Glycerin	670	TS	Manufactures
668.3	TP967-970	Glue	670.21	T57.35	Industrial engineering—Statistical methods
668.3	TP967-970	Adhesives			
668.37	TP977-979.5	Gums and resins	670.288	TS192	Plant maintenance
668.374	TP977-979.5	Gums and resins, Synthetic	670.420151	TJ1165	Shop mathematics
668.374	TP1180.E6	Epoxy resins	670.427	T59.5	Automation
668.4	TP1101-1185	Plastics	670.9	T55.6	Industrial engineering—History
668.4027	TP1114	Plastics—Patents			
668.403	TP1110	Plastics—Encyclopedias	670.92	T56.3	Industrial engineers
668.405	TP1103	Plastics—Periodicals	670.941	TS57-64	Great Britain—Manufactures

Dewey	LC	Subject Heading	Dewey	LC	Subject Heading
670.943	TS73-74.5	Germany—Manufactures	670.99(5-6)	TS123-124	Oceania—Manufactures
670.9436	TS65-.2	Austria—Manufactures	671	TS200-770	Metal-work
670.9437	TS65.3-.4	Czechoslovakia—Manufactures	671.0284	TS215	Metal-working machinery
			671.05	TS200	Metal-work—Periodicals
670.9439	TS65.5-66	Hungary—Manufactures	671.2	TS228.99-240	Founding
670.944	TS71-72.5	France—Manufactures	671.2	TS228.97-239	Founding
670.945	TS79-80	Italy—Manufactures	671.32	TS340	Roll-mill
670.946	TS87-88	Spain—Manufactures	671.332	TS225	Forging
670.9469	TS83-84.5	Portugal—Manufactures	671.36	TS320	Tempering
670.947	TS85-86	Russia—Manufactures	671.37	TN695-697	Powder metallurgy
670.948	TS88.5	Scandinavia—Manufactures	671.52	TS227-228.96	Welding
670.9481	TS81-82	Norway—Manufactures	671.521	TK4660	Electroslag welding
670.9485	TS89-90	Sweden—Manufactures	671.521	TK4660	Electric welding
670.9489	TS69-70	Denmark—Manufactures	671.529	TS228.9	Pressure welding
670.94897	TS95.F5	Finland—Manufactures	671.7	TS653-719	Metals—Finishing
670.9492	TS77-78	Netherlands—Manufactures	671.732	TS213	Plating
670.9493	TS67-68	Belgium—Manufactures	671.732	TS670-693	Electroplating
670.9494	TS91-92	Switzerland—Manufactures	671.732	TS662-693	Plating
670.9495	TS75-76	Greece—Manufactures	671.823	TS250	Sheet-metal
670.9496	TS95.A2	Balkan Peninsula—Manufactures	672	TS300-360	Steel-works
			673.3	TS564-589	Brass
670.9497	TS95.Y8	Yugoslavia—Manufactures	673.3	TS570	Bronze
670.951	TS101-102	China—Manufactures	674	TS800-915	Lumber
670.952	TS105-106	Japan—Manufactures	674.0284	TS850-851	Saws
670.954	TS103-104	India—Manufactures	674.2	TS850	Sawmills
670.95491	TS104.5-.6	Pakistan—Manufactures	674.386	TS932-934	Wood—Chemistry
670.95493	TS104.7-.8	Sri Lanka—Manufactures	674.82	HD9750-9769	Coopers and cooperage
670.955	TS107-108	Iran—Manufactures	674.82	TS890	Coopers and cooperage
670.9561	TS111-112	Turkey—Manufactures	674.83	TS870	Veneers and veneering
670.9567	TS113.I7	Iraq—Manufactures	674.834	TS870	Plywood
670.95694	TS113.I75	Israel—Manufactures	674.835	TS869	Laminated wood
670.957	TS109-110	Asiatic Russia—Manufactures	675	TS940-1047	Leather
			675.2	HD9778-.5	Hides and skins
670.9598	TS113.I55	Indonesia—Manufactures	675.2	TS967	Hides and skins
670.9599	TS113.P6	Philippines—Manufactures	675.23	TS940-1047	Tanning
670.96	TS115-119	Africa—Manufactures	675.3	TS1060-1070	Fur
670.962	TS117-118	Egypt—Manufactures	676	TS1080-1268	Papermaking
670.971	TS26-27	Canada—Manufactures	676	TS1080-1268	Paper products
670.972	TS28-29	Mexico—Manufactures	676	TS1080-1268	Paper
670.9728	TS30-31	Central America—Manufactures	676	Z247	Paper
			676.02821	TS1485-1487	Carding
670.9729	TS32-33	West Indies—Manufactures	676.09	TS1090-1096	Papermaking—History
670.973	TS23-25	United States—Manufactures	676.12	TS1171-1177	Wood-pulp
			676.234	TS1118.F5	Paper finishing
670.981	TS41-42	Brazil—Manufactures	676.235	TS1118.F5	Paper coatings
670.982	TS36-37	Argentina—Manufactures	676.2823	TS1228-1268	Stationery
670.983	TS43-44	Chile—Manufactures	676.2848	TH8461-8463	Wallpaper
670.984	TS38-39	Bolivia—Manufactures	677	TP890-933	Textile chemistry
670.985	TS52	Peru—Manufactures	677	TS1760-1770	Dry-goods
670.9861	TS45-46	Colombia—Manufactures	677	TS1540-1549	Textile fibers
670.9866	TS47	Ecuador—Manufactures	677	TS1300-1865	Textile fabrics
670.987	TS54	Venezuela—Manufactures	677.028	TS1488	Sizing (Textile)
670.9881	TS48	Guyana—Manufactures	677.02822	GN432	Spinning
670.9882	TS50	French Guiana—Manufactures	677.02822	TS1480-1487	Spinning
			677.028242	GN432	Weaving
670.9883	TS49	Surinam—Manufactures	677.028242	TS1490-1500	Weaving
670.9892	TS51	Paraguay—Manufactures	677.028242092	HD8039.T4	Weavers
670.9895	TS53	Uruguay—Manufactures	677.028242092	GN432	Weavers
670.993	TS122.5-.6	New Zealand—Manufactures	677.02825	TP934-945	Finishes and finishing
			677.02825	TS1510	Textile finishing
670.994	TS121-122	Australia—Manufactures	677.02854	TS1493	Looms

Dewey	LC	Subject Heading	Dewey	LC	Subject Heading
677.02862	TS1550-1590	Yarn	684.13	TS880	Tables
677.02862	TS1590	Thread	684.13	TS880	Chairs
677.02862	TS1600-1631	Yarn	684.14	TS880	Desks
677.11	TS1700-1735	Flax	684.14	TT197.5.D4	Desks
677.21	TS1542	Cotton	684.16	TT197	Chests
677.31	TS1547	Wool	684.16	TT197	Cabinetwork
677.31	TS1600-1631	Woolen and worsted manufacture	684.18	TT197.5.09	Outdoor furniture
			685.1	TS1030-1035	Saddlery
677.39	TS1546	Silk	685.24	TT525	Fur garments
677.39	TS1640-1688	Satin	685.31	TS989-1025	Boots
677.39	TS1640-1688	Silk	685.31	TS989-1025	Shoes
677.4	TS1688	Synthetic fabrics	685.310092	HD8039.B7-.B72	Shoemakers
677.46	TS1688	Rayon	685.4	TS2160	Gloves
677.4743	TS1548.7.P58	Polyester fibers	686.071	Z122-.5	Printing—Study and teaching
677.6	TS1828	Nonwoven fabrics	686.09	Z124-242	Printing—History
677.617	TS1675	Velvet	686.2	Z244	Print finishing processes
677.617	TS1680	Plush	686.2	Z116.A2-265.5.A5	Printing
677.62	TS1825	Felt			
677.63	TS1825	Felt	686.20278	Z235-236	Printers' marks
677.64	TS1780	Tapestry	686.20284	Z256	Rollers (Printing)
677.643	TS1772-1779.5	Carpets	686.20284	Z249	Paper-cutting machines
677.682	TS1520	Waterproofing of fabrics	686.20299	Z245	Printing industry—Estimates
677.71	TS1784-1787	Rope	686.2092	Z231-234	Printers
677.71	TS1784-1787	Cordage	686.221	Z252	Electrotyping
678.2	TS1870-1935	Rubber industry and trade	686.224	Z250	Printing—Specimens
678.24	TS1891	Vulcanization	686.225	Z242.9-264	Printing
678.32	TS1912	Tires, Rubber	686.2252	Z253.5	Magazine design
678.35	TS1920	Rubber bands	686.2252	Z246	Printing—Layout
678.72	TS1925-1927	Rubber, Articifical	686.22542	Z253	Linotype
679.7	TS2255	Nicotine	686.22542	Z253	Monotype
679.7	TS2220-2283	Tobacco industry	686.22544	TR1010	Phototypesetting
679.72	TS2260	Cigars	686.22544416	Z253.53-.532	Desktop publishing
681.11(3-4)	TS540-549	Horology	686.22544416	Z286.D47	Desktop publishing
681.11(3-4)	TS540-549	Clock and watch making	686.2255	Z254	Proofreading
681.145	HF5688-5689	Calculators	686.23042	Z258	Color-printing
681.4092	RE940-981	Opticians	686.2316	TP901	Silk-printing
681.428	TP867	Mirrors	686.2316	TT273	Screen process printing
681.6	TS1262-1266	Pens	686.232	TR925-997	Photomechanical processes
681.62	Z249-.4	Printing-press	686.2325	TR930-937	Collotype
681.753	TL589.2.06	Optical gyroscopes	686.2325	TR940-950	Photolithography
681.76041	TS283	Pressure vessels	686.2327	TR975	Photoengraving—Halftone process
683	TS400-455	Hardware			
683.3	TS519-531	Locksmithing	686.2327	TR970-977	Photoengraving
683.32	TH9735	Locks and keys	686.2327	TR980	Photogravure
683.32	TH2279	Locks and keys	686.233	Z252.5.N46	Nonimpact printing
683.32	TS519-531	Locks and keys	686.3	Z266-276	Bookbinding
683.4	HV8059	Firearms ownership	686.3	Z272	Endpapers
683.4	TS532-537.5	Firearms	686.30092	Z269-.3	Bookbinders
683.4	TS535-.4	Gunsmithing	686.4	TR920-923	Photographic reproduction of plans, drawings, etc.
683.422	TS536.6.B6	Rifles, Bolt action			
683.436	TS537	Revolvers	686.4	TR824-835	Photocopying
683.82	TS380-.4	Cutlery	686.4	Z48	Fluid copying processes
684	N8550-8553	Picture frames and framing	686.4	Z48	Copying processes
684.00288	TT199	Furniture—Repairing	686.42	TR921	Blueprinting
684.08	TT152-153.7	Workshops	686.42	TR415	Blueprinting
684.1	TS880-889	Furniture	686.43	Z265	Micrographics
684.1	TS880-889	Furniture making	686.43	Z265-.5	Documents on microfilm
684.1	TT194-199.4	Furniture making	686.44	TR1035-1050	Electrophotography
684.104	TT194-199.4	Furniture	686.45	TR470	Photostat
684.13	TT197.5.D5	Dining room furniture	687	TT498	Clothing factories
684.13	TT197.5.T3	Tables	687	TT490-695	Clothing trade

Dewey	LC	Subject Heading	Dewey	LC	Subject Heading
687	TT507	Clothing and dress	690.1822	TH2278	Fire doors
687.043	TT590	Garment cutting	690.1823	TH2261-2276	Windows
687.043	TT520	Garment cutting	690.1832	TH5667-5680	Staircases
687.044	TT570-630	Tailoring	690.21	TH895	Snow loads
687.112	TT500-560	Dressmaking	690.21	TH845-895	Strains and stresses
687.113	TT605	Trousers	690.22	TH443	Building—Accidents
687.141	TT595-600	Coats	690.24	TH3351-3361	Buildings—Maintenance
687.142	TT530	Coats	690.24	TH3401-3411	Buildings—Remodeling for other use
687.147	TT530-535	Cloaks			
687.16	TT626	Livery	690.24	TH4816.2	Buildings—Additions
687.19	TT616	Neckties	690.24	TH3401-3411	Buildings—Repair and reconstruction
687.19	TT657	Kerchiefs			
687.2	TT669-678	Underwear	690.5	TH1097	Air raid shelters
687.21	TT675	T-shirts	690.52	TH4311-4315	Commercial buildings—Design and construction
687.22	TT677	Foundation garments			
687.22	TT669-670	Lingerie	690.53	TH4461	Granaries—Design and construction
687.3	TT679-695	Hosiery			
687.42	TT650-665	Millinery	690.535	TH4451-4499	Warehouses—Design and construction
688.1	TT154-.5	Models and modelmaking			
688.42	TS2270	Tobacco-pipes	690.54	TH4541	Drug factories
688.6	TS2001-2035	Carriage and wagon-making	690.54	TH4532	Distilleries
688.7221	TS2301.T7	Dolls	690.54	TH4511-4591	Factories—Design and construction
688.752	TJ1570	Slot machines			
688.8	TS197.5	Containers	690.54	TH4511-4591	Factories
688.8	TS195-198.8	Packaging	690.54	TH4581-4591	Power-plants
690	TH6057.T23	Tall buildings	690.61	TH4224	Pagodas—Design and construction
690	TH	Building			
690.025	TH12-13	Building—Directories	690.8	TH4805-4890	House construction
690.0284	TH900-915	Construction equipment	690.8	TH4805-4890	Dwellings
690.0284	TH915	Building—Equipment and supplies	690.8370473	TH4818.A3	Earth houses
			690.8370473	TH4819.E27	Earth sheltered houses
690.05	TH1-4	Building—Periodicals	690.8370473	TH1421	Earth construction
690.06	TH5	Building—Congresses	690.86	TH4920	Farmhouses
690.071	TH165-213	Building—Study and teaching	690.872	TH4835	Vacation homes
			690.873	TH4840	Log cabins
690.09	TH15-19	Building—History	690.892	TH4911-4935	Farm buildings
690.09(4-9)	TH21-127	Building—[By region or country]	690.892	TH4935	Silos
			690.8922	TH4930	Dairy barns
690.0973	TH23-25	Building—United States	690.893	TH4970	Decks (Architecture, Domestic)
690.1	TH2060	Buildings—Joints			
690.1	TH2025-3000	Building—Details	692.3	TH425	Buildings—Specifications
690.11	TH2101	Foundations	692.5	TH434-437	Building—Estimates
690.11	TH5201	Foundations	693.1	TH1201	Building, Stone
690.12	TH2201-2251.5	Walls	693.1	TH1199-1301	Masonry
690.12	TH2235-2238.7	Exterior walls	693.1	TH5311-5701	Masonry
690.12	TH2245	Concrete walls	693.1	TH5401-5440	Stonemasonry
690.12	TH2249	Stone walls	693.21	TH1301	Building, Brick
690.13	TH2252-2253	Columns	693.3	TH1077-1083	Tile construction
690.146	TH2170-.7	Domes	693.5	TH1461-1501	Concrete construction
690.15	TH2281-2288	Chimneys	693.54	TH1501	Reinforced concrete construction
690.15	TH2391-2495	Roofs			
690.15	TH2409	Flat roofs	693.6	TH8135-8139	Plaster
690.15	TH2416-2417	Roofs, Shell	693.71	TH1610-1635	Building, Iron and steel
690.15	TH2180	Towers	693.82	TH1061-1093	Building, Fireproof
690.15	TH2431-2459	Roofing	693.82	TH9111-9599	Fire prevention
690.16	TH2521-2529	Flooring	693.82	TH1061-1093	Fireproofing
690.17	TH2531-2533	Ceilings	693.82	TH1065	Fire resistant materials
690.182	TH2276	Blinds	693.834	TH1725	Soundproofing
690.1822	TH2278	Screen doors	693.834	TH1725	Factories—Soundproofing
690.1822	TH2279	Door fittings	693.852	TH1095	Buildings—Earthquake effects
690.1822	TH2278	Doors			

167

Dewey	LC	Subject Heading	Dewey	LC	Subject Heading
693.854	TH1097	Building, Bombproof	700	NX	Arts
693.892	TH9031	Dampness in buildings	700.08996073	N6538.N5	Afro-American artists
693.892	TH9031	Waterproofing	700.3	NX70	Arts—Encyclopedias
693.898	TH9057-9092	Lightning protection	700.3	NX80	Arts—Dictionaries
693.898	TH9057-9092	Lightning-conductors	700.411	BH301.A94	Avant-garde (Aesthetics)
693.91	TH1431	Building, Ice and snow	700.4112	N6490	Modernism (Art)
693.96	TH1560	Glass construction	700.4145	ND1267	Primitivism in art
693.97	TH1098	Buildings, Prefabricated	700.42	BH301.L3	Landscape
694	HD9716.C3-.C33	Carpentry	700.421734	N8205	Pastoral art
694	TH5601-5695	Carpentry	700.4548	N7720	Dance of death
694.0284	TH5618	Miter-gages	700.46	BH301.N3	Nature (Aesthetics)
694.1	TH5611	Carpentry drafting	700.5	NX1-9	Arts—Periodicals
694.2	TH2301-2311	Framing (Building)	700.79	NX700-750	Arts—Endowments
694.6	TH5640-5695	Finish carpentry	700.901	GN799.A	Art, Prehistoric
694.6	TH5662-5663	Joinery	700.9(4-9)	NX501-596.3	Arts—[By region or country]
696-697	TH6010-6013	Building fittings	700.94	NX542-571	Arts—Europe
696.1	TH6101-6729	Plumbing	700.941	NX543-547.6	Arts—Great Britain
696.10288	TH6681-6685	Plumbing—Repairing	700.943	NX550-.6	Arts—Germany
696.13	TH6571-6675	Drainage, House	700.9436	NX548	Arts—Austria
696.182	TH6498	Toilets	700.944	NX549	Arts—France
696.182	TH6493	Bathtubs	700.945	NX552	Arts—Italy
696.182	TH6485-6500	Bathrooms	700.946	NX562	Arts—Spain
696.182	TH6492	Showers (Plumbing fixtures)	700.9469	NX563	Arts—Portugal
696.2	TH6703-6729	Pipe fitting	700.947	NX556	Arts—Russia
696.2	TH6840	Gas-fitting	700.948	NX557-561	Arts—Scandinavia
696.2	TH6880	Gas-burners	700.9481	NX560	Arts—Norway
696.6	TH6561	Water heaters, Gas	700.9485	NX561	Arts—Sweden
696.6	TH6551-6568	Hot-water supply	700.9489	NX558	Arts—Denmark
697	TH7005-7699	Heating	700.94912	NX559	Arts—Iceland
697	TH6014-6085	Buildings—Environmental engineering	700.9492	NX554	Arts—Netherlands
			700.9493	NX555	Arts—Belgium
697.03	TH7461	Heating plants	700.9494	NX564	Arts—Switzerland
697.043	TH7453-7457	Gas—Heating and cooking	700.9495	NX551	Arts—Greece
697.043	TH7454-7457	Stoves, Gas	700.9496	NX566-569	Arts—Balkan Peninsula
697.044	TH7466.06	Oil burners	700.95	NX572-586	Arts—Asia
697.07	TH7400	Furnaces	700.951	NX583	Arts—China
697.07	TH7538	Boilers	700.9519	NX584.6-.7	Arts—Korea
697.07	TH7140	Fluidized-bed furnaces	700.952	NX584	Arts—Japan
697.1	TH7421-7434.7	Fireplaces	700.954	NX576	Arts—India
697.22	TH7443-7446	Stoves, Coal	700.95491	NX576.7	Arts—Pakistan
697.22	TH7437-7441	Stoves, Wood	700.95493	NX576.6	Arts—Sri Lanka
697.22	TH7435-7458	Stoves	700.955	NX574	Arts—Iran
697.24	TH7450.5	Kerosene heaters	700.956	NX573-.7	Arts—Middle East
697.3	TH7638	Heat pumps	700.9561	NX565	Arts—Turkey
697.3	TH7601-7635	Hot-air heating	700.95694	NX573.7	Arts—Israel
697.4	TH7511-7549	Hot-water heating	700.957	NX575.7	Arts—Asiatic Russia
697.5	TH7561-7599	Steam-heating	700.9581	NX575.6	Arts—Afghanistan
697.5	TH7570-7578	Steam-heating, Low pressure	700.9593	NX578.7	Arts—Thailand
697.507	TH7480-7495	Radiators	700.9594	NX578.6.L3	Arts—Laos
697.507	TH7588	Boilers	700.9595	NX579	Arts—Malaysia
697.78	TH7414	Solar houses	700.9596	NX578.6.C3	Arts—Cambodia
697.78	TH7413-7414	Solar heating	700.9597	NX578.6.V5-.V55	Arts—Vietnam
697.8	TH2281-2288	Flues	700.9598	NX580	Arts—Indonesia
697.92	TH7647-7699	Ventilation	700.9599	NX581	Arts—Philippines
697.93	TH7687-7688	Air conditioning	700.96	NX587-589.8	Arts—Afria
697.9354	TH7684.F2-.F3	Factories—Air conditioning	700.961	NX587.6-588.6	Arts—Africa, North
697.938	TH7688.H6	Dwellings—Air conditioning	700.962	NX588-.3	Arts—Egypt
698.1	TT320-324	House painting	700.963	NX588.7	Arts—Ethiopia
698.5	TH8251-8275	Glazing	700.966	NX589-.6	Arts—Africa, West
698.6	TH8441	Paperhanging	700.9676	NX588.8-.9	Arts—Africa, East
700	N	Art	700.968	NX589.7-.8	Arts—Africa, Southern

Dewey	LC	Subject Heading
700.971	NX513-.3	Arts—Canada
700.972	NX514	Arts—Mexico
700.9728	NX515-522	Arts—Central America
700.97281	NX518	Arts—Guatemala
700.97283	NX519	Arts—Honduras
700.97284	NX522	Arts—El Salvador
700.97285	NX520	Arts—Nicaragua
700.97286	NX517	Arts—Costa Rica
700.97287	NX521	Arts—Panama
700.9729	NX523-529	Arts—West Indies
700.97291	NX525	Arts—Cuba
700.97292	NX527	Arts—Jamaica
700.97294	NX526	Arts—Haiti
700.97295	NX528	Arts—Puerto Rico
700.97296	NX524	Arts—Bahamas
700.973	NX503-512.3	Arts—United States
700.98	NX530-541	Arts—South America
700.981	NX533	Arts—Brazil
700.982	NX531	Arts—Argentina
700.983	NX534	Arts—Chile
700.984	NX532	Arts—Bolivia
700.985	NX539	Arts—Peru
700.9861	NX535	Arts—Colombia
700.9866	NX536	Arts—Ecuador
700.987	NX541	Arts—Venezuela
700.9892	NX538	Arts—Paraguay
700.9895	NX540	Arts—Uruguay
700.993	NX593	Arts—New Zealand
700.994	NX590	Arts—Australia
700.99(5-6)	NX595-596	Arts—Oceania
701	N61-75	Art—Philosophy
701.15	N61-79	Imgination
701.17	N61-79	Aesthetics
701.170902	N61	Aesthetics, Medieval
701.1709031	N61	Aesthetics, Modern—16th century
701.1709032	N61	Aesthetics, Modern—17th Century
701.1709033	N61	Aesthetics, Modern—18th century
701.1709034	N61	Aesthetics, Modern—19th century
701.170904	N61	Aesthetics, Modern—20th century
701.18	N7475-7485	Art criticism
701.8	BH301.H3	Harmony (Aesthetics)
701.8	N7429.7-7433	Composition (Art)
702.5	N50-55	Art—Directories
702.8	N7429.7-7433	Art—Technique
702.8	N7574	Artists' models
702.84	N8543	Artists' tools
702.872	N8580	Pictures—Copying
702.874	NX636	Arts—Forgeries
702.88	N8554-8585	Art—Conservation and restoration
703	N33	Art—Dictionaries
704.942	N7616	Portrait miniatures
704.942	N7575-7649	Portraits
704.9421	N7572	Nude in art
704.9428	N8217.E6	Erotic art
704.9428	NX650.E7	Pornography
704.946	N7740-7745	Symbolism in art
704.947	N7760-7763	Art and mythology
704.9482	BV150-168	Christian art and symbolism
704.9482	N7810-8189.6	Christian art and symbolism
704.9482	N7832	Art, Early Christian
704.9489	NX688	Arts, Islamic
704.9497928	N8217.D3	Dance in art
705	N1-9.9	Art—Periodicals
706	N21	Art—Congresses
706	N10-17	Art—Societies, etc.
707.1	N81-390	Art—Study and teaching
707.1	N325-335	Art schools
707.104	N332	Art schools—Europe
707.1073	N328-330	Art schools—United States
707.4	N4390-5098	Art—Exhibitions
707.4	N8665	Sidewalk art exhibitions
708	N5198-5299	Art—Private collections
708	N400-3990	Art museums
708.1(3-9)	N5215-5220	Art—Private collections—United States
708.1(3-9)	N510-880	Art museums—United States
708.(2-8)	N5240-5280	Art—Private collections—Europe
708.(2-9)	N1010-3690	Art museums—Europe
708.2	N1020-1560	Art museums—Great Britain
708.3	N2210-2406	Art museums—Germany
708.4	N2010-2180	Art museums—France
708.5	N2510-3065	Art museums—Italy
708.6	N3410-3499	Art museums—Spain
708.7	N3310-3382	Art museums—Russia
708.92	N2450-2505	Art museums—Netherlands
708.93	N1750-1850	Art museums—Belgium
708.95	N2410-2430	Art museums—Greece
709	N5300-7418	Art—History
709.01	N5315-5899	Art, Ancient
709.011	N5310-5313	Art, Prehistoric
709.011	N5310-5313	Art, Primitive
709.02	N5940-6320	Art, Medieval
709.0216	N6280	Art, Romanesque
709.024	N6370-6375	Art, Renaissance
709.03	N6350-6494	Art, Modern
709.03(2-3)	N6410-6425	Art, Modern—17th-18th centuries
709.0332	N6410	Art, Rococo
709.034	N6450-6465	Art, Modern—19th century
709.0342	N70	Romanticism in art
709.0345	N6465.N44	Neo-impressionism (Art)
709.04	N6480-6494	Art, Modern—20th century
709.04012	N6494.A7	Art deco
709.04042	ND1265	Expressionism (Art)
709.04052	N6490	Art, Abstract
709.04062	N6494.D3	Dadaism
709.04062	NX600.S9	Surrealism
709.04062	NX600.D3	Dadaism
709.2	N40-43	Art—Biography
709.31	N5343-5345	Oriental antiquities
709.32	N5350-5351	Art, Egyptian
709.35	N5370	Art, Sumerian
709.37	N5760-5763	Art, Roman
709.38	N5603-5896.3	Art, Classical
709.38	N5630-5720	Art, Greek

Dewey	LC	Subject Heading	Dewey	LC	Subject Heading
709.392	N5480-5560	Art, Turkish	720.9437	NA1023-1034.5	Architecture—Czechoslovakia
709.394	N5470	Art, Arab	720.9438	NA1466.P6	Architecture—Poland
709.3943	N5460	Art, Syrian	720.9438	NA1466.P6	Architecture—Poland
709.436	N6805-6808.5	Art—Austria—History	720.9439	NA1012-1022	Architecture—Hungary
709.437	N6828-6831.5	Art—Czechoslovakia—	720.944	NA1041-1059	Architecture—France
		History	720.945	NA1111-1123.3	Architecture—Italy
709.439	N6819-6820.5	Art—Hungary—History	720.946	NA1301-1313.3	Architecture, Spanish
709.45	N6915-6923	Art—Italy—History	720.946	NA1301-1313.3	Architecture—Spain
709.46	N7105-7108.5	Art—Spain—History	720.9469	NA1321-1333.3	Architecture—Portugal
709.469	N7125-7128.5	Art—Portugal—History	720.947	NA1181-1199	Architecture—Russia
709.48	N7007-7088	Art—Scandinavia—History	720.948	NA1201-1293.3	Architecture—Scandinavia
709.493	N6967-6973	Art—Belgium—History	720.9481	NA1261-1273.3	Architecture—Norway
709.495	N6897-6898.5	Art—Greece—History	720.9485	NA1281-1293.3	Architecture—Sweden
709.5	N7260-7355.5	Art, Oriental	720.9489	NA1211-1223.3	Architecture—Denmark
709.71	N6540-6545.5	Art—Canada—History	720.94897	NA1455.F5	Architecture—Finland
709.72	N6555-.5	Art—Mexico—History	720.94897	NA1455.F5	Architecture—Finland
709.728	N6573.2-6582.5	Art—Central America—	720.94912	NA1241-1253.3	Architecture—Iceland
		History	720.9492	NA1141-1153.3	Architecture—Netherlands
709.8	N6635-6735.5	Art—South America—	720.9493	NA1161-1173.3	Architecture—Belgium
		History	720.9494	NA1341-1353.3	Architecture—Switzerland
711	NA9000-9284	City planning	720.9495	NA1091-1103	Architecture—Greece
711.09(4-9)	NA9101-9285	City planning—[By region	720.9497	NA1441-1453.3	Architecture—Yugoslavia
		or country]	720.9498	NA1421-1433.3	Architecture—Romania
711.3	NA9000-9428	Regional planning	720.9499	NA1381-1393.3	Architecture—Bulgaria
711.41	NA9053.B58	Blocks (City planning)	720.95	NA1460-1579	Architecture, Oriental
711.45	NA9053.N	New towns	720.95	NA1460-1570.3	Architecture, Oriental
711.55	NA9070-9072	Plazas	720.951	NA1540-1549.6	Architecture—China
712	SB472.45	Landscape design	720.951	NA1540-1547	Pagodas
712	SB469-476.4	Landscape architecture	720.9519	NA1560-1570.3	Architecture—Korea
714	NA9400-9425	Fountains	720.952	NA1550-1559.6	Architecture—Japan
714	SB475.8	Water in landscape	720.9538	NA1470-1472	Architecture—Saudi Arabia
		architecture	720.954	NA1501-1510.3	Architecture—India
719	SB439-.26	Natural landscaping	720.95491	NA1510.7-.73	Architecture—Pakistan
719.33	SB475.9.F67	Forest landscape design	720.95493	NA1510.6-.63	Architecture—Sri Lanka
720	NA	Architecture	720.955	NA1480-1489	Architecture—Iran
720.1	NA2500	Architecture—Aesthetics	720.9561	NA1361-1375	Architecture—Turkey
720.22	NA2790	Architectural models	720.9567	NA1467-1469	Architecture—Iraq
720.222	NA2700-2780	Architectural drawing	720.95691	NA1489.6-.8	Architecture—Syria
720.222	NA2600-2635	Architecture—Designs and	720.95692	NA1476.6-.8	Architecture—Lebanon
		plans	720.95694	NA1477-1479	Architecture—Israel
720.25	NA50-60	Architecture—Directories	720.95695	NA1479.6-.8	Architecture—Jordan
720.288	NA105-112	Architecture—Conservation	720.957	NA1492.6-1499	Architecture—Asiatic Russia
		and restoration	720.9581	NA1492-.3	Architecture—Afghanistan
720.3	NA31	Architecture—Encyclopedias	720.9591	NA1512-.3	Architecture—Burma
720.473	NA2542.7	Underground architecture	720.9593	NA1521-1523	Architecture—Thailand
720.483	NA6230-6234	Tall buildings	720.9594	NA1516-.3	Architecture—Laos
720.5	NA1-9	Architecture—Periodicals	720.9595	NA1525-.8	Architecture—Malaysia
720.6	NA10-17	Architecture—Societies, etc.	720.9596	NA1515-.3	Architecture—Cambodia
720.71	NA2000-2320	Architecture—Study and	720.9597	NA1514-.63	Architecture—Vietnam
		teaching	720.9598	NA1526-.8	Architecture—Indonesia
720.79	NA2335-2360	Architecture—Competitions	720.9599	NA1527-1529	Architecture—Philippines
720.87	NA2545	Architecture and the	720.96	NA1580-1599	Architecture—Africa
		handicapped	720.9611	NA1591-.3	Architecture—Tunisia
720.9154	NA2542.A73	Architecture—Arid regions	720.9612	NA1589-.3	Architecture—Libya
720.92	NA40	Architecture—Biography	720.962	NA1581-1585.3	Architecture, Egyptian
720.92	NA	Architects	720.963	NA1586-.3	Architecture—Ethiopia
720.94	NA950-1455	Architecture—Europe	720.964	NA1590-.3	Architecture—Morocco
720.941	NA961-981	Architecture—Great Britain	720.965	NA1588-.3	Architecture—Algeria
720.94209033	NA630	Architecture, Queen Anne	720.966	NA1598-1599	Architecture—Africa, West
720.943	NA1061-1089	Architecture—Germany	720.9676	NA1597-.6	Architecture—Africa, East
720.9436	NA1001-1011.6	Architecture—Austria	720.968	NA1591.7-1596.6	Architecture—Southern Africa

Dewey	LC	Subject Heading	Dewey	LC	Subject Heading
720.9(7-8)	NA702.5-939	Architecture, American	722	NA210-340	Architecture, Ancient
720.971	NA740-749.5	Architecture—Canada	722-724	NA190-1555.5	Architecture—History
720.972	NA750-759	Architecture—Mexico	722.2	NA215-216	Architecture, Egyptian
720.9728	NA760-790	Architecture—Central America	722.51	NA220-221	Architecture, Assyro-Babylonian
720.97281	NA776-778	Architecture—Guatemala	722.62	NA300-301	Architecture, Etruscan
720.97283	NA779-781	Architecture—Honduras	722.7	NA310-340	Architecture, Roman
720.97284	NA788-790	Architecture—El Salvador	722.70937	NA295-340	Architecture, Italian
720.97285	NA782-784	Architecture—Nicaragua	722.8	NA270-290	Architecture, Greek
720.97286	NA773-775	Architecture—Costa Rica	723	NA350-497	Architecture, Medieval
720.97287	NA785-787	Architecture—Panama	723.4	NA390-419	Architecture, Romanesque
720.9729	NA791-815	Architecture—West Indies	723.4	NA423-429	Architecture, Norman
720.97291	NA803-805	Architecture—Cuba	723.5	NA440-489	Architecture, Gothic
720.97292	NA809-811	Architecture—Jamaica	724	NA500-680	Architecture, Modern
720.97294	NA806-808	Architecture—Haiti	724.1	NA707	Architecture, Colonial
720.97295	NA812-814	Architecture—Puerto Rico	724.12	NA510-575	Architecture, Renaissance
720.97296	NA800-802	Architecture—Bahamas	724.16	NA590	Architecture, Baroque
720.973	NA705-738	Architecture—United States	724.19	NA640	Architecture, Georgian
720.98	NA820-939	Architecture—South America	724.19	NA627-640	Architecture, Modern—17th-18th centuries
720.981	NA850-859	Architecture—Brazil			
720.982	NA830-839	Architecture—Argentina	724.19	NA590	Architecture, Rococo
720.983	NA860-869	Architecture—Chile	724.2	NA600	Neoclassicism (Architecture)
720.984	NA840-849	Architecture—Bolivia	724.5	NA645-670	Architecture, Modern—19th century
720.985	NA910-919	Architecture—Peru			
720.9861	NA870-879	Architecture—Colombia	724.6	NA673-682	Architecture, Modern—20th century
720.9866	NA880-889	Architecture—Ecuador			
720.987	NA930-939	Architecture—Venezuela	725	NA4170-5095	Public buildings
720.9881	NA895	Architecture—Guyana	725	NA9050.5	Public architecture
720.9882	NA897	Architecture—French Guiana	725.087	NA2545.P5	Public buildings—Access for the physically handicapped
720.9883	NA896	Architecture—Surinam			
720.9892	NA900-909	Architecture—Paraguay	725.09(4-9)	NA4201-4385	Public buildings—[By region or country]
720.9895	NA920-929	Architecture—Uruguay			
720.993	NA1606-1608	Architecture—New Zealand	725.0973	NA4205-4228.3	Public buildings—United States
720.994	NA1600-1605.3	Architecture—Australia			
720.99(5-6)	NA1610-1613	Architecture—Oceania	725.11	NA4410-4417	Capitols
721	NA2835-3060	Architecture—Details	725.1109(4-9)	NA4415	[Other countries]—Capital and capitol
721	NA2750-2793	Architectural design			
721.0443	NA3705	Tiles	725.110973	NA4411-4413	United States—Capital and capitol
721.0445	NA4125	Concrete construction			
721.04496	NA4140	Glass construction	725.13	NA4430-4437	Municipal buildings
721.04497	NA8480	Buildings, Prefabricated	725.13	NA4430-4437	City halls
721.2	NA2940-2942	Walls	725.15	CD981-986.5	Archive buildings
721.3	NA2860	Columns, Ionic	725.15	NA4470-4477	Courthouses
721.3	NA2860-2875	Columns, Corinthian	725.16	NA4450-4457	Post office buildings
721.41	NA2880	Arches	725.17	NA4440-4447	Embassy buildings
721.46	NA2890	Domes	725.18	NA490-497	Military architecture
721.5	NA2930	Spires	725.18	NA4490-4497	Police stations
721.5	NA2920	Gables	725.2	NA6210-6280	Commercial buildings
721.5	NA2900	Roofs, Open-timbered	725.21	NA6225	Shop fronts
721.5	NA3040	Chimneys	725.23	NA6230-6234	Office buildings
721.5	NA2930	Towers	725.24	NA6240-6245	Bank buildings
721.6	NA2970	Floors	725.35	NA6340-6343	Warehouses
721.7	NA2950	Ceilings	725.38	NA8348	Garages
721.8	NA3050-3055	Fireplaces	725.39	NA6300-6307	Airport buildings
721.822	NA3010	Doorways	725.4	NA6400-6589	Architecture, Industrial
721.823	NA3000-3030	Windows	725.4	NA6598	Employees' buildings and facilities
721.832	NA3060	Stairs			
721.84	NA3070	Balconies	725.4	NA6400-6589	Factories
721.84	NA7125	Porches	725.4	NA6396-6589	Industrial buildings
722	GN414	Architecture, Primitive	725.822	NA6820-6846	Theater architecture
722	NA205-207	Architecture, Primitive	725.822	NA6820-6845	Theaters

Dewey	LC	Subject Heading	Dewey	LC	Subject Heading
725.823	NA6845-6846	Motion picture theaters	728.922	NA8230	Barns
725.827	NA6860-7010	Stadiums	728.922	NA8280	Dairy barns
725.83	NA6815	Auditoriums	728.93	NA8375	Patios
725.83	PN1585-1589	Centers for the performing arts	729	NA3310-4050	Decoration and ornament, Architectural
725.91	NA6880-.5	Convention facilities	729.1	NA2840-2841	Facades
725.91	NA6750-6751	Exhibition buildings	729.11	NA2760	Architecture—Composition, proportion, etc.
725.94	NA9325-9330	War memorials	729.2	TH1098	Modular construction
725.94	NA9335-9355	Monuments	729.24	NA2850-2856	Interior architecture
725.94	NA9325-9355	Soldiers' monuments	729.28	NA2794	Daylighting
725.96	NA9360-9380	Triumphal arches	729.28	TH7703	Lighting, Architectural and decorative
726.1	NA4610-4710	Temples			
726.2	NA4670	Mosques	729.29	NA2800	Architectural acoustics
726.3	NA4690	Synagogue architecture	729.7	NA3750-3860	Pavements, Mosaic
726.4	NA4910	Baptisteries	729.7	NA3750-3860	Mosaics
726.4	NA4870	Chapels	730	NB	Sculpture
726.5	NA4790-6113	Church architecture	730.11	NB1142.5	Sculpture—Appreciation
726.5	NA4790-5095	Church buildings	730.216	NB35	Sculpture—Catalogs
726.51	NA5000	Church decoration and ornament	730.5	NB1	Sculpture—Periodicals
			730.74	NB16-17	Sculpture—Exhibitions
726.5291	NA5070	Fonts	730.9	NB60-615	Sculpture—History
726.5291	NA5060	Altars	730.92	NB1115	Sculptors
726.58(1-9)	NA4828.5	Protestant church buildings	730.9(4-9)	NB201-1114	Sculpture—[By region or country]
726.6	NA4830	Cathedrals			
726.7	NA4850	Monasteries	730.94	NB450-955	Sculpture—Europe
726.7	NA4800-6113	Abbeys	730.941	NB461-481	Sculpture—Great Britain
726.8	NA6120-6199	Tombs	730.943	NB561-589	Sculpture—Germany
726.809	NA6149-6199	Tombs—[By region or country]	730.9436	NB501-511.6	Sculpture—Austria
			730.9437	NB523-534.5	Sculpture—Czechoslovakia
727.3	NA6600-6605	College buildings	730.9438	NB955.P6	Sculpture—Poland
728	NA7160	Concrete houses	730.9439	NB512-522.6	Sculpture—Hungary
728	NA7160	Stucco	730.944	NB541-553.3	Sculpture—France
728	NA7175	Half-timbered houses	730.945	NB611-623.3	Sculpture—Italy
728	NA7150	Brick houses	730.946	NB801-813.3	Sculpture—Spain
728	NA7127-7135	Architecture, Domestic—Designs and plans	730.9469	NB821-833.3	Sculpture—Portugal
			730.947	NB681-699	Sculpture—Russia
728	NA7100-7882	Dwellings	730.948	NB701-793.3	Sculpture—Scandinavia
728	NA7100-7884	Architecture, Domestic	730.9481	NB761-773.3	Sculpture—Norway
728	NA7180	Steel houses	730.9485	NB781-793.3	Sculpture—Sweden
728.0846	NA7195.A4	Aged—Dwellings	730.9489	NB711-723.3	Sculpture—Denmark
728.091733	NA7570-7572.5	Suburban homes	730.94897	NB955.F5	Sculpture—Finland
728.09(4-9)	NA7201-7333	Architecture, Domestic—[By region or country]	730.94912	NB741-753.3	Sculpture—Iceland
			730.9492	NB641-653.3	Sculpture—Netherlands
728.312	NA7520	Row houses	730.9493	NB661-673.3	Sculpture—Belgium
728.314	NA7860-7863	Apartment houses	730.9494	NB841-853.3	Sculpture—Switzerland
728.37	NA7551-7555	Cottages	730.9495	NB591-603	Sculpture—Greece
728.370473	NA7531	Earth sheltered houses	730.9497	NB941-953.3	Sculpture—Yugoslavia
728.4	HS1019-1021	Independent Order of Odd Fellows—Rituals	730.9498	NB921-933.3	Sculpture—Romania
			730.95	NB960-1070.3	Sculpture—Asia
728.4	NA7910-7977	Clubhouses	730.951	NB1040-1049.6	Sculpture, Chinese
728.5	NA7800-7853	Hotels	730.9519	NB1060-1070.6	Sculpture—Korea
728.6	NA8208-8210	Farmhouses	730.952	NB1050-1059.6	Sculpture, Japanese
728.7	NA7574-7579	Vacation homes	730.9538	NB970-972	Sculpture—Saudi Arabia
728.73	NA8470	Log cabins	730.954	NB1001-1010.3	Sculpture—India
728.78	VM335	Houseboats	730.95491	NB1010.7-.73	Sculpture—Pakistan
728.81	NA7710-7786	Castles	730.95493	NB1010.6-.63	Sculpture—Sri Lanka
728.82	NA7710-7786	Palaces	730.955	NB980-989	Sculpture—Iran
728.8209376	NA320	Palaces	730.9561	NB861-873.3	Sculpture—Turkey
728.820938	NA277	Palaces	730.9567	NB967-969	Sculpture—Iraq
728.92	NA8200-8260	Farm buildings	730.95691	NB989.6-.8	Sculpture—Syria
728.92	NA8240	Granaries			

Dewey	LC	Subject Heading	Dewey	LC	Subject Heading
730.95692	NB976.6-.8	Sculpture—Lebanon	731.2	NB1270.G5	Fiberglass craft
730.95694	NB977-979	Sculpture—Israel	731.2	NB1220	Metal sculpture
730.95695	NB979.6-.8	Sculpture—Jordan	731.2	NB1218	Marble sculpture
730.957	NB992.4-999	Sculpture—Asiatic Russia	731.2	NB1215	Concrete sculpture
730.9581	NB992-.3	Sculpture—Afghanistan	731.2	NB1270.P3	Paper sculpture
730.9591	NB1012-.3	Sculpture—Burma	731.2	NB1270.P5	Plastic sculpture
730.9593	NB1021-1023	Sculpture—Thailand	731.2	NB1270.G4	Glass sculpture
730.9594	NB1016-.3	Sculpture—Laos	731.42	NB1180-1185	Modeling
730.9595	NB1025-.8	Sculpture—Malaysia	731.452	NB1190	Plaster casts
730.9596	NB1015-.3	Sculpture—Cambodia	731.456	NB135-143	Bronze sculpture
730.9597	NB1014-.63	Sculpture—Vietnam	731.463	NB1208-1210	Stone carving
730.9598	NB1026-.8	Sculpture—Indonesia	731.48	NB1199	Sculpture—Conservation and restoration
730.9599	NB1027-1029	Sculpture—Philippines			
730.96	NB1080-1099	Sculpture—Africa	731.54	NB1280-1291	Bas-relief
730.9611	NB1091.6	Sculpture—Tunisia	731.55	NB1315	Mobiles (Sculpture)
730.9612	NB1089.3	Sculpture—Libya	731.7	NB	Statues
730.962	NB1081-1085.3	Sculpture—Egypt	731.74	NB1300	Busts
730.963	NB1086.3	Sculpture—Ethiopia	731.75	NB1310	Masks (Sculpture)
730.964	NB1090.3	Sculpture—Morocco	731.76	NB1330-1685	Monuments
730.965	NB1088.3	Sculpture—Algeria	731.7609(4-9)	NB1501-1685	Monuments—[By region or country]
730.966	NB1098-1099	Sculpture—Africa, West			
730.9676	NB1097-.6	Sculpture—Africa, East	731.81	NB1312-1313	Equestrian statues
730.968	NB1091.7-1096.6	Sculpture—Africa, Southern	731.82	NB1930-1936	Figure sculpture
730.971	NB240-249.5	Sculpture—Canada	731.82	NB1293-1310	Portrait sculpture
730.972	NB250-259	Sculpture—Mexico	731.832	NB1940-1942	Animal sculpture
730.9728	NB260-290	Sculpture—Central America	732	GN799.S4	Sculpture, Prehistoric
730.97281	NB276-278	Sculpture—Guatemala	732.2	NB62-64	Sculpture, Primitive
730.97283	NB279-281	Sculpture—Honduras	732.2	NB69-169	Sculpture, Ancient
730.97284	NB288-290	Sculpture—El Salvador	732.2	NB69-169	Marble sculpture, Ancient
730.97285	NB282-284	Sculpture—Nicaragua	733.3	NB144	Marble sculpture, Classical
730.97286	NB273-275	Sculpture—Costa Rica	733.3	NB90-105	Sculpture, Greek
730.97287	NB285-287	Sculpture—Panama	733.5	NB115-120	Sculpture, Roman
730.9729	NB291-315	Sculpture—West Indies	734	NB170-180	Sculpture, Medieval
730.97291	NB303-305	Sculpture—Cuba	734.224	NB172	Sculpture, Byzantine
730.97292	NB309-311	Sculpture—Jamaica	734.25	NB180	Sculpture, Gothic
730.97294	NB306-308	Sculpture—Haiti	735	NB185-198.5	Sculpture, Modern
730.97295	NB312-314	Sculpture—Puerto Rico	735.21	NB193	Sculpture, Rococo
730.97296	NB300-302	Sculpture—Bahamas	735.21	NB190	Sculpture, Renaissance
730.973	NB205-238	Sculpture—United States	736.20932	NK5561	Scarabs
730.98	NB320-439	Sculpture—South America	736.222	NK5720-5722	Cameos
730.981	NB350-359	Sculpture—Brazil	736.4	NK9700-9799	Wood-carving
730.982	NB330-339	Sculpture—Argentina	736.5	NB1800-1895	Sepulchral monuments
730.983	NB360-369	Sculpture—Chile	736.6	NK6020-6022	Bone carving
730.984	NB340-349	Sculpture—Bolivia	736.982	TT870	Origami
730.985	NB410-419	Sculpture—Peru	737	CJ	Numismatics
730.9861	NB370-379	Sculpture—Colombia	737.0971	CD5619	Seals (Numismatics)—Canada
730.9866	NB380-389	Sculpture—Ecuador			
730.987	NB430-439	Sculpture—Venezuela	737.0972	CD5620	Seals (Numismatics)—Mexico
730.9881	NB395	Sculpture—Guyana			
730.9882	NB397	Sculpture—French Guiana	737.09728	CD5621-5700	Seals (Numismatics)—Central America
730.9883	NB396	Sculpture—Surinam			
730.9892	NB400-409	Sculpture—Paraguay	737.22	CJ5501-6661	Medals
730.9895	NB420-429	Sculpture—Uruguay	737.2205	CJ5501	Medals—Periodicals
730.993	NB1106-1108	Sculpture—New Zealand	737.22071	CJ5525	Medals—Study and teaching
730.994	NB1100-1105.3	Sculpture—Australia	737.2209(4-9)	CJ5795-6661	Medals—[By Region or country]
730.99(5-6)	NB1110-1113	Sculpture—Oceania			
731.028	NB1170-1195	Sculpture—Technique	737.22093	CJ5581-5690	Medals, Ancient
731.2	NB1265	Terra-cotta sculpture	737.220937	CJ5641-5685	Medals, Roman
731.2	NB1250	Driftwood sculpture	737.220938	CJ5625	Medals, Greek
731.2	NB145-159	Terra-cotta sculpture	737.22094	CJ6091-6380	Medals—Europe
731.2	NB1240.I75	Iron sculpture	737.22095	CJ6381-6485	Medals—Asia

Dewey	LC	Subject Heading	Dewey	LC	Subject Heading
737.22096	CJ6491-6559	Medals—Africa	737.606	CD5005	Seals (Numismatics)—
737.2209728	CJ5841-5905	Medals—Central America			Societies, etc.
737.220973	CJ5801-5812	Medals—United States	737.6071	CD5045	Seals (Numismatics)—
737.220994	CJ6561-6569	Medals—Australia			Study and teaching
737.223	CJ5806	Campaign insignia	737.6074	CD5017-5018	Seals (Numismatics)—
737.224	CJ5793.R34	Religious medals			Exhibitions
737.3	CJ4801-5450	Tokens	737.609	CD5049	Seals (Numismatics)—
737.305	CJ4801	Tokens—Periodicals			History
737.3074	CJ4805-4808	Tokens—Exhibitions	737.6092	CD5051-5052	Seals (Numismatics)—
737.3074	CJ4805-4806	Tokens—Museums			Biography
737.309(4-9)	CJ4901-5336	Tokens—[By region or country]	737.609(4-9)	CD5592-6471	Seals (Numismatics)—[By region or country]
737.30973	CJ4901-4906	Tokens—United States	737.60973	CD5601-5617	Seals (Numismatics)—
737.4	CJ1-4625	Coins			United States
737.4	CJ125	Coins—Errors	737.60973	CD5610	United States—Seal
737.4	CJ161.F3	Facing heads (Numismatics)	738	NK3700-4695	Pottery
737.4	CJ101	Coins—Grading	738.075	NK4230	Pottery—Collectors and
737.401	CJ53	Coins—Philosophy			collecting
737.405	CJ1-9	Coins—Periodicals	738.0901	NK3800-3855	Pottery, Ancient
737.406	CJ27	Coins—Congresses	738.0902	NK3870-3885	Pottery, Medieval
737.406	CJ14-23	Coins—Societies, etc.	738.092	NK4200-4210	Potters
737.4074	CJ39-41	Coins—Exhibitions	738.09(4-9)	NK4001-4184	Pottery—[By region or country]
737.409	CJ59	Coins—History	738.2	NK4370-4584	Porcelain
737.40902	CJ1601-1715	Coins, Medieval	738.27	NK4277	Blue and white transfer ware
737.49(4-9)	CJ1021-1147	Coins, Ancient [By region or country]	738.3	NK4360-4367	Stoneware
737.493	CJ201-1397	Coins, Ancient	738.37	NK4295-.5	Delftware
737.4936	CJ1101-1147	Coins, Ancient—Europe	738.38	NK4695.T33	Ceramic tableware
737.4937	CJ937	AS (Coin)	738.4	NK4997-5024	Enamel and enameling
737.4937	CJ801-1147	Coins, Roman	738.5	NK8500	Mosaics
737.4937	CJ1021-1070	Coins, Ancient—Italy	738.8	NK4695.F6	Food warmers
737.4937	CJ517-542	Coins, Italian	738.82	NK4660	Hummel figurines
737.4938	CJ301-763	Coins, Greek	739	NK6400-8459	Art metal-work
737.4938	CJ359	Decadrachma	739	NK6400-8459	Metal-work
737.4938	CJ425-763	Coins, Greek	739.23	NK7100-7695	Silverwork
737.49396	CJ1087-1099	Coins, Ancient—Asian	739.2383	NK7234-7235	Silver flatware
737.49396	CJ1301-1397	Coins, Oriental	739.27	NK7300-7695	Jewelry
737.49398	CJ1201-1291	Coins, Byzantine	739.27	NK7650-7690	Precious stones
737.49398	CJ1101-1147	Coins, Ancient—Europe	739.27	TS747-770	Gems
737.49(4-9)	CJ1800-4625	Coins, Medieval—[By region or country]	739.27	TS740-770	Jewelry making
737.494	CJ2450-3369	Coins, European	739.2782	NK7440-7459	Rings
737.4941	CJ2484	Guinea (Coin)	739.2782	TS720-770	Rings
737.4946	CJ3189	Piece of eight	739.533	NK8400-8420	Pewter
737.4946	CJ3188	Doubloons	739.7	NK6600-6999	Weapons
737.495	CJ3370-3893	Coins, Oriental	739.70228	NK8475.A7	Miniature weapons
737.496	CJ3920-4389	Coins, African	739.722	NK6700-6799	Swords
737.496	CJ1071-1085	Coins, Ancient—Africa	739.752	NK6808	Shields
737.4968	CJ3948	Krugerrand (Coin)	741	NC	Drawing
737.4971	CJ1860-1879	Coins, Canadian	741.018	NC745	Proportion (Art)
737.4973	CJ1835	Half-dollar	741.0294	NC37-38.5	Drawing—Catalogs
737.4973	CJ1800-2449	Coins, American	741.05	NC1	Drawing—Periodicals
737.498	CJ1889-2449	Coins, Latin American	741.071	NC390-670	Drawing—Study and teaching
737.4994	CJ4400-4419	Coins, Australian	741.074	NC15-17	Drawing—Exhibitions
737.6	CD5001-6471	Seals (Numismatics)	741.074	NC30-33	Drawing—Private collections
737.6028	CD5085-5175	Seals (Numismatics)—	741.0902	NC70-75	Drawing, Medieval
		Techniques	741.090(24-31)	NC85	Drawing, Renaissance
737.605	CD5001	Seals (Numismatics)—	741.09032	NC86	Drawing—17th century
		Periodicals	741.09033	NC87-.5	Drawing—18th century
737.606	CD5009	Seals (Numismatics)—	741.09034	NC90-.5	Drawing—19th century
		Congresses	741.09(3-9)	NC101-377	Drawing—[By region or country]

| --- | --- | --- | --- | --- | --- |
741.09032	NC86	Drawing—17th century	741.097296	NC171-173	Drawing—Bahamas
741.09033	NC87-.5	Drawing—18th century	741.0973	NC105-139.3	Drawing—United States
741.09034	NC90-.5	Drawing—19th century	741.098	NC189-224	Drawing—South America
741.0904	NC95-.5	Drawing—20th century	741.0981	NC198-200	Drawing—Brazil
741.094	NC225-312	Drawing—Europe	741.0982	NC192-194	Drawing—Argentina
741.0941	NC228-242	Drawing—Great Britain	741.0984	NC195-197	Drawing—Bolivia
741.0943	NC249-251.6	Drawing—Germany	741.0985	NC216-218	Drawing—Peru
741.0944	NC246-248	Drawing—France	741.09861	NC204-206	Drawing—Colombia
741.0945	NC255-257	Drawing—Italy	741.09866	NC207-209	Drawing—Ecuador
741.0946	NC285	Drawing—Spain	741.0987	NC222-224	Drawing—Venezuela
741.09469	NC288-290	Drawing—Portugal	741.09892	NC213-215	Drawing—Paraguay
741.0947	NC267-269	Drawing—Russia	741.09895	NC219-221	Drawing—Uruguay
741.0948	NC270-284	Drawing—Scandinavia	741.0993	NC372-374	Drawing—New Zealand
741.09481	NC279-281	Drawing—Norway	741.0994	NC369-371	Drawing—Australia
741.09485	NC282-284	Drawing—Sweden	741.099(5-6)	NC375-376	Drawing—Oceania
741.09489	NC273-275	Drawing—Denmark	741.2	NC845-915	Drawing instruments
741.094912	NC276-278	Drawing—Iceland	741.2	NC730-758	Drawing—Technique
741.09494	NC291-293	Drawing—Switzerland	741.217	NC1920-1940	Drawing—Copying
741.09495	NC252-254	Drawing—Greece	741.22	NC850	Charcoal drawing
741.09496	NC297-308	Drawing—Balkan Peninsula	741.23	NC855-875	Crayon drawing
741.095	NC315-359	Drawing—Asia	741.235	NC880	Pastel drawing
741.0951	NC348-350	Drawing—China	741.24	NC890-895	Pencil drawing
741.09519	NC353.6-.7	Drawing—Korea	741.25	NC900-902	Silverpoint drawing
741.0952	NC351-353	Drawing—Japan	741.26	NC905	Pen drawing
741.0954	NC327-329	Drawing—India	741.26	ND2460	Brush drawing
741.095491	NC331	Drawing—Pakistan	741.5	NC1300-1766	Caricatures and cartoons
741.095493	NC330	Drawing—Sri Lanka	741.505	NC1300	Caricatures and cartoons—
741.0955	NC321-323	Drawing—Iran			Periodicals
741.0956	NC318-320	Drawing—Middle East	741.5074	NC1310-1312	Caricatures and cartoons—
741.09561	NC294-296	Drawing—Turkey			Exhibitions
741.095694	NC320	Drawing—Israel	741.58	NC1765-1766	Animated films
741.0957	NC325	Drawing—Asiatic Russia	741.58	PN1997.5	Animated films
741.09581	NC324.6	Drawing—Afghanistan	741.59(4-9)	NC1400-1762	Caricatures and cartoons—
741.09593	NC335	Drawing—Thailand			[By region or country]
741.09594	NC334.L3	Drawing—Laos	741.6	NC960-995.8	Illustration of books
741.09595	NC336-338	Drawing—Malaysia	741.6	NC965.85	Picture books
741.09596	NC334.C3	Drawing—Cambodia	741.6	NC997-1003	Commercial art
741.09597	NC334.V5-.V55	Drawing—Vietnam	741.605	NC997.A1	Commercial art—Periodicals
741.09598	NC339-341	Drawing—Indonesia	741.6071	NC1000	Commercial art—Study
741.09599	NC342-344	Drawing—Philippines			and teaching
741.096	NC360-368.6	Drawing—Africa	741.66	NC1882-1883.3	Sound recordings—Album
741.0961	NC361-365.6	Drawing—Africa, North			covers
741.0962	NC363-.3	Drawing—Egypt	741.672	TT509	Fashion drawing
741.0963	NC365.7	Drawing—Ethiopia	741.674	NC1800-1850	Posters
741.0966	NC367-.6	Drawing—Africa, West	741.674	NC1849.T68	Travel posters
741.09676	NC366-6	Drawing—Africa, East	741.683	NC1870-1879	Postcards
741.0968	NC368-.6	Drawing—Africa, Southern	741.685	NE965-.3	Business cards
741.0971	NC141-143.3	Drawing—Canada	741.7	NC910-.5	Silhouettes
741.0972	NC144-146	Drawing—Mexico	742	NC755	Shades and shadows
741.09728	NC147-167	Drawing—Central America	742	NC749-750	Perspective
741.097281	NC156-158	Drawing—Guatemala	743.4	NC765-778	Figure drawing
741.097283	NC159-161	Drawing—Honduras	743.42	NC770	Face
741.097284	NC167	Drawing—El Salvador	743.49	NC760-783.8	Anatomy, Artistic
741.097285	NC162-164	Drawing—Nicaragua	743.5	NC775	Drapery in art
741.097286	NC153-155	Drawing—Costa Rica	743.6	NC780-783.8	Animals in art
741.097287	NC165	Drawing—Panama	743.828	NC825.E76	Erotic drawing
741.09729	NC168-186	Drawing—West Indies	743.836	NC790-800	Landscape drawing
741.097291	NC174-176	Drawing—Cuba	745	N5312-5313	Folk art
741.097292	NC180-182	Drawing—Jamaica	745	NK1135-1149.5	Arts and crafts movement
741.097294	NC177-179	Drawing—Haiti	745	NK	Art objects
741.097295	NC183-185	Drawing—Puerto Rico	745.0228	NK8470-8475	Miniature objects

Dewey	LC	Subject Heading	Dewey	LC	Subject Heading
745.0294	NK1133-.26	Art objects—Catalogs	745.592	TL778	Paper airplanes
745.075	NK1125-1130	Art objects—Collectors and collecting	745.592	TT174-.5	Toys
			745.5922	TT175.7	Doll clothes—Patterns
745.08996073	NK839.3.A35	Afro-American decorative arts	745.59221	NK4891.3-4894.4	Dolls
745.0901	NK610-685	Art objects, Ancient	745.59221	TT175-.7	Dolls
745.09(4-9)	NK801-1094.5	Art objects—[By region or country]	745.5923	NK4891.3-4894.4	Dollhouses
			745.5923	TT175.3	Dollhouses
745.0938	NK665-680	Art objects, Classical	745.5923	TT175.5	Doll furniture
745.1	NK	Antiques	745.5928	NK492	Miniature objects
745.102872	NK1128	Antiques—Reproduction	745.5928	VM298.3	Ship models in bottles
745.103	NK30	Antiques—Dictionaries	745.5933	NK3685	Candlesticks
745.103	NK28	Antiques—Encyclopedias	745.5936	TT199.75	Decoys (Hunting)
745.105	NK1-9	Antiques—Periodicals	745.594	NK4870	Fans
745.1071	NK50-440	Antiques—Study and teaching	745.5941	TT900.E2	Easter decorations
			745.5941	TT900.P3	Party decorations
745.1074	NK512-520	Antiques—Exhibitions	745.5941	TT900.V34	Valentine decorations
745.1074	NK530-570	Antiques—Private collections	745.5943	TT890-894	Artificial flowers
745.4	NC703	Design	745.5944	TT896.7	Egg decoration
745.4	NK1160-1590	Decoration and ornament	745.61	NK3600-3640	Lettering
745.4	NK1160-1590	Design	745.61	Z43-45	Caligraphy
745.4071	NK1170	Design—Study and teaching	745.61	TT360	Lettering
745.40882943	NK1676	Decoration and ornament, Buddhist	745.67	ND2889-3416	Illumination of books and manuscripts
745.441	NK1177	Decoration and ornament, Primitive	745.67074	ND2893	Illumination of books and manuscripts—Exhibitions
745.442	NK1285	Decoration and ornament, Romanesque	745.670901	ND2910	Illumination of books and manuscripts, Ancient
745.442	NK1260-1295	Decoration and ornament, Medieval	745.670902	ND2920-2980	Illumination of books and manuscripts, Medieval
745.442	NK1180-1250	Decoration and ornament, Ancient	745.67090 (24-31)	ND2990	Illumination of books and manuscripts—Renaissance
745.442	NK1295	Decoration and ornament, Gothic	745.6709(4-9)	ND3001-3294.5	Illumination of books and manuscripts—[By region or country]
745.442	NK1652.25	Decoration and ornament, Byzantine	745.726	NK9900-.7	Lacquer and lacquering
745.442088297	NK1270-1275	Decoration and ornament, Islamic	745.73	TT270-273	Stencil work
			745.74	NK9510	Decalcomania
745.443	NK1345	Decoration and ornament, Baroque	745.8	N7436.5-.53	Panoramas
			745.92	SB449-450.87	Flower arrangement
745.443	NK1330	Decoration and ornament, Renaissance	745.926	SB449.5.W4	Wedding decorations
			746	NK8800-9505.5	Textile design
745.443	NK1355	Decoration and ornament, Rococo	746	TT699-854.5	Textile crafts
			746.12	TT847	Hand spinning
745.5	TT	Handicraft	746.14	TT848-849.2	Hand weaving
745.50288	TT151	Repairing	746.22	TT800-810	Lace and lace making
745.503	TT9	Handicraft—Encyclopedias	746.3	NK2910	Wall hangings
745.505	TT1	Handicraft—Periodicals	746.3	NK2975-3049	Tapestry
745.5074	TT6	Handicraft—Exhibitions	746.3	TT850.2	Wall hangings
745.509(4-9)	TT15-127	Handicraft—[By region or country]	746.4	NK8800-9505.5	Needlework
			746.4	TT740-897	Fancy work
745.51	NK9600-9955	Woodwork	746.4	TT700-845	Needlework
745.51	TT180-203.5	Woodwork	746.41	TT877.5	Palm frond weaving
745.531	NK6200-6210	Leatherwork	746.412	GN431	Basket making
745.531	TT290	Leatherwork	746.412	NK3649.5-.55	Basketwork
745.55	NK8643	Shellcraft	746.412	TT879.B3	Basket making
745.55	TT862	Shellcraft	746.432	TT819-829	Knitting
745.56	TT205-273	Metal-work	746.434	TT820-829	Crocheting
745.572	TT297-.5	Plastics craft	746.436	TT840.T38	Tatting
745.58	TT288	Bone carving	746.44	NK9206.4.H56	Embroidery, Hmong
745.582	NK3650-.5	Beadwork	746.44	TT840.S66	Smocking
745.582	TT860	Beadwork	746.442	TT778.C65	Counted thread embroidery

Dewey	LC	Subject Heading	Dewey	LC	Subject Heading
746.46	NK9100-9499	Patchwork	751.426	ND1535	Acrylic painting
746.46	TT835	Quilting	751.46	ND2480	Encaustic painting
746.46	TT835	Coverlets	751.6	ND1630-1662	Painting—Conservation and restoration
746.6	TT853-854.5	Dyes and dyeing			
746.662	TT852.5	Batik	751.73	ND2550-2877	Mural painting and decoration
746.70882971	NK2809.I8	Rugs, Islamic			
746.73	TT850	Rugs, Braided	751.7309(4-9)	ND2601-2877	Mural painting—[By region or country]
746.75095	NK2808-2810	Rugs, Oriental			
746.92092	HD6073.M7	Models (Persons)	751.74	ND2880-.5	Diorama
746.94	NK3175-3296.3	Drapery	751.74	ND2880-2881	Panoramas
747	NK1700-3505	Interior decoration	751.75	ND2885-2888	Scene painting
747.074	NK2210-2211	Furniture—Exhibitions	751.77	ND1159	Small painting
747.2(4-9)	NK2000-2096.3	Interior decoration—[By region or country]	754	ND1450-1452	Genre painting
			757	ND1290-1293	Figure painting
747.3	NK3375-3496.3	Wallpaper	757	ND1300-1337	Portrait painting
747.5	NK2775-2898	Rugs	757.090(24-31)	ND1308	Portrait painting—15th century
747.5	NK2115.5.D73	Drapery in interior decoration			
747.5	NK2775-2898	Carpets	757.09031	ND1308	Portrait painting—16th century
747.5074	NK2790	Rugs—Private collections			
747.75	NK2117.L5	Living room furniture	757.09032	ND1309.3	Portrait painting—17th century
747.76	NK2117.D5	Dining room furniture			
747.76	NK2117.D5	Dining rooms	757.09033	ND1309.4	Portrait painting—18th century
747.78	NK2117.B33	Bathrooms			
747.86	NK2190-2192	Church decoration and ornament	757.09034	ND1309.5	Portrait painting—19th century
			757.0904	ND1309.6	Portrait painting—20th century
748	NK5100-5440	Glass			
748.2	NK5100-5440	Glassware	757.0904	ND1313-1324	Portrait painting—Europe
748.50282	NK5300-5430	Glass painting and staining	757.0941	ND1314-.6	Portrait painting—Great Britain
748.50285	NK5430	Mosaics			
748.6	NK5200-5205	Cut glass	757.0943	ND1317-.7	Portrait painting—Germany
748.6	NK5439.E5	Enameled glass	757.0944	ND1316-.6	Portrait painting—France
748.62	NE2690	Glass engraving	757.0945	ND1318-.6	Portrait painting—Italy
748.8	NK8440-.2	Mirrors	757.0947	ND1320-.6	Portrait painting—Russia
748.8	NK5440.S49	Glass shoes	757.09492	ND1319-.6	Portrait painting—Netherlands
748.83	NK5440.D75	Drinking glasses			
748.83	NK5440.D85	Dwarf ale glasses	757.095	ND1325-1326.8	Portrait painting—Asia
748.84	NK5440.P3	Paperweights	757.0956	ND1322-.6	Portrait painting—Spain
749	NK2200-2750	Furniture	757.0973	ND1311-.9	Portrait painting—United States
749	NK2235	Furniture—Styles			
749.074	NK2220	Furniture—Private collections	757.7	ND1329.8-1337	Portrait miniatures
			758.1	ND1340-1367	Landscape painting
749.2(1-9)	NK2401-2694.5	Furniture—[By region or country]	758.1094	ND1353-1364	Landscape painting—Europe
749.3	NK2910	Screens	758.10941	ND1354-.6	Landscape painting—Great Britain
749.3	NK2740	Shelving (Furniture)			
750	ND	Painting	758.10943	ND1357-.6	Landscape painting—Germany
750	ND1142-1146	Pictures			
750.294	ND40-45	Painting—Catalogs	758.10944	ND1356-.6	Landscape painting—France
750.71	ND1115-1120	Painting—Study and teaching	758.10945	ND1358-.6	Landscape painting—Italy
			758.10946	ND1362-.6	Landscape painting—Spain
750.882971	ND146	Painting, Islamic	758.1095	ND1365-.96	Landscape painting—Asia
751.2	ND1510	Pigments	758.109(71-8)	ND1352	Landscape painting—[Other American countries]
751.4	ND1505	Brushwork			
751.422	ND1700-2495	Watercolor painting	758.10973	ND1351-.6	Landscape painting—United States
751.422071	ND2110-2115	Watercolor painting—Study and teaching			
			758.10973	ND1351-1367	Landscape painting—[By region or country]
751.42242	ND2200-2202	Portrait painting			
751.42242	ND2190-2192	Figure painting	758.2	ND1370-1375	Marine painting
751.422435	ND2290-2305	Still life painting	758.3	ND1380-1383	Animals in art
751.422436	ND2240-2243	Landscape painting	758.4	ND1390-1400	Still-life painting
751.422437	ND2270-2272	Marine painting			

177

Dewey	LC	Subject Heading	Dewey	LC	Subject Heading
759	ND34-38	Painting—Biography	759.96	ND1080-1099	Painting—Africa
759	ND49-813	Painting—History	759.9611	ND1091-.3	Painting—Tunisia
759	ND1328-1329	Portrait painting—Biography	759.9612	ND1089-.3	Painting—Libya
759.01	ND70-130	Painting, Ancient	759.962	ND1081-1085.3	Painting—Egypt
759.02	ND140-146	Painting, Medieval	759.963	ND1086-.3	Painting—Ethiopia
759.03	ND170-172	Painting, Renaissance	759.964	ND1090-.3	Painting—Morocco
759.04	ND177-188	Painting, Modern—17th-18th centuries	759.965	ND1088-.3	Painting—Algeria
			759.966	ND1098-1099	Painting—Africa, West
759.05	ND190-192	Painting, Modern—19th century	759.9676	ND1097-.6	Painting—Africa, East
			759.968	ND1091.7-1096.6	Painting—Africa, Southern
759.06	ND195-196	Painting, Modern—20th century	759.972	ND250-259	Painting—Mexico
			759.9728	ND260-290	Painting—Central America
759.06	ND160-196	Painting, Modern	759.97281	ND276-278	Painting—Guatemala
759.(1-9)	ND204-1113	Painting—[By region or country]	759.97283	ND279-281	Painting—Honduras
			759.97284	ND288-290	Painting—El Salvador
759.11	ND240-249.5	Painting—Canada	759.97285	ND282-284	Painting—Nicaragua
759.13	ND205-238	Painting—United States	759.97286	ND273-275	Painting—Costa Rica
759.(2-8)	ND450-955	Painting—Europe	759.97287	ND285-287	Painting—Panama
759.2	ND461-481	Painting—Great Britain	759.9729	ND291-315	Painting—West Indies
759.3	ND591-603.3	Painting—Greece	759.97291	ND303-305	Painting—Cuba
759.3	ND568-589	Painting—Germany	759.97292	ND309-311	Painting—Jamaica
759.36	ND501-511.6	Painting—Austria	759.97294	ND306-308	Painting—Haiti
759.38	ND999.P6	Painting—Poland	759.97295	ND312-314	Painting—Puerto Rico
759.39	ND512-522.6	Painting—Hungary	759.97296	ND300-302	Painting—Bahamas
759.4	ND541-553.3	Painting—France	759.98	ND320-439	Painting—South America
759.5	ND611-623.3	Painting—Italy	759.981	ND350-359	Painting—Brazil
759.6	ND801-813.3	Painting—Spain	759.982	ND330-339	Painting—Argentina
759.69	ND821-833.3	Painting—Portugal	759.983	ND360-369	Painting—Chile
759.7	ND681-699	Painting—Russia	759.984	ND340-349	Painting—Bolivia
759.8	ND701-793.3	Painting—Scandinavia	759.985	ND410-419	Painting—Peru
759.81	ND761-773.3	Painting—Norway	759.9861	ND370-379	Painting—Colombia
759.85	ND781-793.3	Painting—Sweden	759.9866	ND380-389	Painting—Ecuador
759.89	ND711-723.3	Painting—Denmark	759.987	ND430-439	Painting—Venezuela
759.897	ND955.F5	Painting—Finland	759.9881	ND395	Painting—Guyana
759.95	ND960-1070.3	Painting—Asia	759.9882	ND397	Painting—French Guiana
759.951	ND1040-1049.6	Painting—China	759.9883	ND396	Painting—Surinam
759.9519	ND1060-1070.3	Painting, Korean	759.9892	ND400-409	Painting—Paraguay
759.9519	ND1060-1070.3	Painting—Korea	759.9895	ND420-429	Painting—Uruguay
759.952	ND1050-1059.6	Painting, Japanese	759.993	ND1106-1108	Painting—New Zealand
759.952	ND1050-1059.6	Painting—Japan	759.994	ND1100-1105.3	Painting—Australia
759.9538	ND970-972	Painting—Saudi Arabia	759.99(5-6)	ND1110-1113	Painting—Oceania
759.954	ND1001-1010.3	Painting—India	760	NC915.R8	Rubbing
759.95491	ND1010.7-.73	Painting—Pakistan	760	NE	Engraving
759.95493	ND1010.6-.63	Painting—Sri Lanka	760	NE2800-2890	Engraving—Printing
759.955	ND980-989	Painting—Iran	760.04	NE886	Engraving—Themes, motives
759.9561	ND861-873.3	Painting—Turkey	760.074	NE1410-1412	Engraving—Exhibitions
759.9567	ND967-969	Painting, Iraqi	760.09023	NE1638	Engraving—14th century
759.95691	ND989.6-.8	Painting—Syria	760.09024	NE1655-1656	Engraving—15th century
759.95692	ND976.6-.8	Painting—Lebanon	760.09031	NE1665-1666	Engraving—16th century
759.95694	ND977-979	Painting—Israel	760.09032	NE1670-1690	Engraving—17th century
759.95695	ND979-.8	Painting—Jordan	760.09033	NE1710-1719	Engraving—18th century
759.957	ND992.4-999	Painting—Asiatic Russia	760.09034	NE1720.5-1739	Engraving—19th century
759.9581	ND992-.3	Painting—Afghanistan	760.0904	NE1740-1749	Engraving—20th century
759.9591	ND1012-.3	Painting—Burma	760.278	NE820	Engravers' marks
759.9593	ND1021-1023	Painting—Thailand	760.28	NE830-835	Prints—Technique
759.9594	ND1016-.3	Painting—Laos	761.2	NE1000-1325	Wood-engraving
759.9595	ND1025-.8	Painting—Malaysia	761.205	NE1000	Wood-engraving—Periodicals
759.9596	ND1015-.3	Painting—Cambodia	761.2074	NE1010-1012	Wood-engraving—Exhibitions
759.9597	ND1014-.63	Painting—Vietnam	761.209	NE1030-1196.3	Wood-engraving—History
759.9598	ND1026-.8	Painting—Indonesia	761.209024	NE1050-1075	Wood-engraving—15th century
759.9599	ND1027-1029	Painting—Philippines			

Dewey	LC	Subject Heading
761.209031	NE1050-1075	Wood-engraving—16th century
761.209032	NE1050-1075	Wood-engraving—17th century
761.209033	NE1085-1088	Wood-engraving—18th century
761.209034	NE1090-1093	Wood-engraving—19th century
761.20904	NE1095-1097	Wood-engraving—20th century
761.209(4-9)	NE1101-1196.3	Wood-engraving—[By region or country]
763	NE2250-2529	Lithography
763.0294	NE2280	Lithography—Catalogs
763.074	NE2272-2275	Lithography—Exhibitions
763.09	NE2295-2396.3	Lithography—History
763.09034	NE2297	Lithography—19th century
763.0904	NE2298	Lithography—20th century
763.092	NE2410	Lithographers
763.09(4-9)	NE2301-2396.3	Lithography—[By region or country]
764.2	NE2500-2529	Chromolithography
764.8	NE1843-1844	Serigraphy
765	NE2700-2710	Engraving (Metal-work)
766.2	NE1815-1816.5	Mezzotint engraving
766.3	NE2230	Aquatint
767.2	NE1940-2232.5	Etching
767.20294	NE1960	Etching—Catalogs
767.2074	NE1950-1955	Etching—Exhibitions
767.209	NE1980-2055.5	Etching—History
767.209033	NE1990-1992	Etching—18th century
767.209034	NE1994-1995	Etching—19th century
767.20904	NE1997-1998	Etching—20th century
767.2092	NE2110	Etchers
767.209(4-9)	NE2001-2096.3	Etching—[By region or country]
767.3	NE2220-2225	Dry-point
769	NE1850-1879	Color prints
769	NE	Prints
769.0288	NE380	Prints—Conservation and restoration
769.0294	NE63-75	Prints—Catalogs
769.03	NE20	Prints—Encyclopedias
769.05	NE1	Prints—Periodicals
769.08996073	NE539.3.A35	Afro-American prints
769.12	NE880-885	Prints—Collectors and collecting
769.12	NE57-59	Prints—Private collections
769.437	NE957-.3	Naval prints
769.49796	NE960-.3	Sporting prints
769.56	HE6184.D56	Disinfection markings (Philately)
769.56	HE6184.D4	Essays and proofs (Philately)
769.56	HE6184.F57	First day covers (Philately)
769.56	HE6187-6230	Stamp collecting
769.56075	HE6221	Postage-stamp albums
769.9	NE400-773	Prints—History
769.9(4-9)	NE501-794.5	Prints—[By region or country]
769.92	NE800	Engravers
770	N72.P5	Art and photography
770	TR183	Photography, Artistic
770	TR	Photography
770	TR269	Instant photography
770	TR640-688	Photography, Artistic
770.21	TR151	Photography—Tables
770.3	TR9	Photography—Encyclopedias
770.5	TR1	Photography—Periodicals
770.6	TR5	Photography—Congresses
770.71	TR161	Photography—Study and teaching
770.74	TR6	Photography—Exhibitions
770.9	TR15	Photography—History
770.92	TR139	Photographers
770.92	TR139-140	Photography—Biography
770.9(4-9)	TR21-127	Photography—[By region or country]
770.94	TR55-95	Photography—Europe
770.941	TR57-64	Photography—Great Britain
770.9415	TR59-60	Photography—Ireland
770.943	TR73-74.5	Photography—Germany
770.9436	TR65-.2	Photography—Austria
770.944	TR71-72.5	Photography—France
770.945	TR79-80	Photography—Italy
770.946	TR87-88	Photography—Spain
770.947	TR85-86	Photography—Russia
770.9481	TR81-82	Photography—Norway
770.9485	TR89-90	Photography—Sweden
770.9492	TR77-78	Photography—Netherlands
770.9494	TR91-92	Photography—Switzerland
770.9495	TR75-76	Photography—Greece
770.95	TR99-113	Photography—Asia
770.951	TR101-102	Photography—China
770.952	TR105-106	Photography—Japan
770.954	TR103-104	Photography—India
770.955	TR107-108	Photography—Iran
770.9561	TR111-112	Photography—Turkey
770.957	TR109-110	Photography—Asiatic Russia
770.96	TR115-119	Photography—Africa
770.962	TR117-118	Photography—Egypt
770.971	TR26-27	Photography—Canada
770.972	TR28-29	Photography—Mexico
770.9728	TR30-31	Photography—Central America
770.9729	TR32-33	Photography—West Indies
770.973	TR22-25	Photography—United States
770.981	TR41-42	Photography—Brazil
770.982	TR36-37	Photography—Argentina
770.983	TR43-44	Photography—Chile
770.984	TR38-39	Photography—Bolivia
770.985	TR52	Photography—Peru
770.9861	TR45-46	Photography—Colombia
770.9866	TR47	Photography—Ecuador
770.987	TR54	Photography—Venezuela
770.9892	TR51	Photography—Paraguay
770.9895	TR53	Photography—Uruguay
770.993	TR122.5-.6	Photography—New Zealand
770.994	TR121-122	Photography—Australia
770.99(5-6)	TR123-124	Photography—Oceania
771	TR268	Photography, Pinhole
771	TR196-199	Photography—Equipment and supplies

Dewey	LC	Subject Heading	Dewey	LC	Subject Heading
771.1	TR550-581	Photography—Studios and dark rooms	780.1	ML3800-3920	Music—Philosophy and aesthetics
771.3	TR250-265	Cameras	780.12	ML105-107	Music—Bio-bibliography
771.32	TR262	35mm cameras	780.14	ML108	Music—Terminology
771.352	TR270-271	Photographic lenses	780.14	MT35	Musical dictation
771.43	TR290-312	Photography—Negatives	780.1407	MT35	Musical shorthand
771.44	TR905	Photography—Enlarging	780.148	MT35	Musical notation
771.44	TR475	Photography—Enlarging	780.262	ML93-98	Musicians—Autographs
771.44	TR340	Photographs—Trimming, mounting, etc.	780.26609	ML1055	Phonograph
			780.3	ML100-110	Music—Dictionaries
771.47	TR225	Photography—Wastes, Recovery of	780.6	ML25-28	Music—Societies, etc.
			780.7	MT	Music—Instruction and study
771.49	TR295	Photography—Developing and developers	780.72	ML	Musicology
			780.76	MT9	Music—Examinations, questions, etc.
771.5	TR212	Photographic chemicals			
771.5	TR210-212	Photographic chemistry	780.7809	ML457	Music—Performance
771.5322	TR281	Photography—Plates	780.79	ML35-38	Music festivals
771.5324	TR283	Photography—Films	780.87107	MT38	Blind, Music for the
772.12	TR365	Daguerreotype	780.89	ML3797.7-3799	Ethnomusicology
772.16	TR400	Kallitype	780.9	ML159-3799	Music—History and criticism
772.774	TR330-333	Photography—Printing processes	780.9	ML3800	Music, Origin of
			780.9034	ML196	Romanticism in music
772.774	TR287-500	Photography—Processing	780.92	ML385-429	Music—Bio-bibliography
774.0153	QC449-.3	Holography	780.92	ML385-403	Musicians
778.2	TR504-508	Slides (Photography)	781	MT6-7	Music—Theory
778.34	TR755	Infrared photography	781.11	ML3830-3838	Music—Psychology
778.35	TR810	Aerial photography	781.17	MT90-145	Music appreciation
778.35	TR713	Space photography	781.2207	MT42	Tempo (Music)
778.36	TR661	Photography, Panoramic	781.224	ML3850	Musical Meter and rhythm
778.37	TR593	Photography, High-speed	781.226	ML3850	Musical Meter and rhythm
778.53	TR845-899.5	Cinematography	781.232	ML3807-3809	Musical pitch
778.53	TR855	Wide-screen processes (Cinematography)	781.24	ML3834	Melody
			781.24	ML3851	Melody
778.5345	TR858	Cinematography—Special effects	781.2407	MT47	Melody
			781.246	ML3809	Musical intervals and scales
778.5347	TR897.5-.75	Animation (Cinematography)	781.25	ML3815	Harmony
778.535	TR899-.5	Motion pictures—Editing	781.25	ML3836	Harmony
778.53859	TR893.5	Wildlife cinematography	781.25	ML3852	Harmony
778.6	TR510-545	Color photography	781.3	M1470	Chance compositions
778.71	TR659.5	Outdoor photography	781.307	MT40-67	Composition (Music)
778.719	TR610	Night photography	781.309	ML430-455	Composition (Music)
778.72	TR600	Photography—Aritifical light	781.42307	MT236	Sight-reading (Music)
778.72	TR590-620	Photography—Lighting	781.424	MT35	Ear training
778.73	TR800	Underwater photography	781.426	MT82	Music—Memorizing
778.8	TR148	Trick photography	781.4409	ML457	Performance practice (Music)
778.92	TR575-581	Portrait photography	781.4507	MT85	Conducting
778.92	TR680-681	Portrait photography	781.4707	MT68	Musical accompaniment
778.93	TR721-733	Nature photography	781.4707	MT68	Songs—Accompaniment
778.932	TR729.W54	Wildlife photography	781.542	M176	Silent film music
778.935	TR656.5	Still-life photography	781.54207	MT737	Silent films—Musical accompaniment
778.936	TR660-.5	Landscape photography			
778.937	TR670-.5	Marine photography	781.544	M176.5	Radio music
778.94	TR659	Architectural photography	781.552	ML3857-3862	Dramatic music
779.0288	TR465	Photographs—Conservation and restoration	781.55409	ML3400-3451	Dance music—History and criticism
			781.55609	ML3460	Ballet
779.074	N4000-4042	Photograph collections	781.56	ML3855	Program music
780	M	Music	781.5609	ML3300-3354	Program music
780	ML48-49	Librettos	781.592	M1977.P75	Protest songs
780	ML93-98	Music—Manuscripts	781.599	M1627-1844	National music
780.0365	ML3920	Music in prisons			
780.0398	ML3849	Music and mythology			

Dewey	LC	Subject Heading	Dewey	LC	Subject Heading
781.599	M1270	Military music	782.43	PR1195.M2	Madrigals
781.599	UH40-45	Trumpet-calls	782.47	M1621.4	Song cycles
781.599	UH40-45	Military calls	782.48	M1530-1546	Cantatas, Secular
781.599	UH40-45	Music in the army	782.5	M1547-1610	Choruses, Secular
781.599	VG30-35	Military music	782.5	M1609	Cantatas, Secular (Unison)
781.599	VG33	United States. Navy—Songs and music	782.507	MT875	Choral singing
			782.507	MT88	Choirs (Music)
781.59909	ML3545	National music—History and criticism	782.509	ML1500-1554	Choral music
			782.98	MT949.5	Whistling
781.63	M1627-1844	Popular music	783.1	M1578-1600	Part-songs
781.6309	ML3469-3541	Popular music	784	M5-1459	Instrumental music
781.645	M1366	Ragtime music	784	M1200-1268	Band music
781.65	M1366	Jazz	784.09	ML1300-1354	Bands (Music)
781.653	M1366	Dixieland music	784.117	MT125	Band music—Analysis, appreciation
781.71009	ML3000-3190	Church music			
781.71017	ML3869	Church music	784.16309	ML3469-3541	Popular instrumental music
781.76	M2114.3	Synagogue music	784.16409	ML3541	Western swing (Music)
781.76	M2186-2187	Synagogue music	784.164209	ML3519-3520	Bluegrass music
781.76	M2099.5	Synagogue music	784.164209	ML3523-3524	Country music
781.825	ML3845	Variation (Music)	784.164309	ML3521	Blues (Music)
782	M1495-2199	Vocal music	784.165309	ML3505.8-3509	Dixieland music
782.001	MT825-850	Singing—Methods	784.16609	ML3535	Rockabilly music
782.001	MT882	Singing—Methods	784.16609	ML3533.8-3534	Rock music
782.009	ML1400-3270	Vocal music—History and criticism	784.18307	MT62	Sonata
			784.184	M1001	Symphonies
782.042307	MT870	Sight-singing	784.18509	ML1158	Suite (Music)
782.0438	M1528-1529.5	Vocal ensembles	784.18509	ML1258	Suite (Music)
782.1	M1500-1508	Operas	784.18926	M1004	Overtures
782.1	M1500-1527.8	Dramatic music	784.1897	M1260	Marches (Band)
782.1	ML3858	Opera	784.1897	M1247	Marches (Band)
782.109	ML1699-2100	Dramatic music	784.1901	ML162-169	Musical instruments, Ancient
782.1209	ML1900	Operatta			
782.14	M1500-1508	Musicals	784.190294	ML155	Musical instruments—Catalogs, Manufacturers'
782.14	M1500-1508	Revues			
782.1409	ML1700-1751	Musicals—History and criticism	784.1907	MT170-805	Musical instruments
			784.1909	ML459-1093	Musical instruments
782.221438	M2018-2019.5	Sacred vocal ensembles	784.1928	ML3809	Musical temperament
782.23	M2000-2007	Oratorios	784.19(4-9)	ML475-1354	Musical instruments—[By region or country]
782.24	M2020-2036	Cantatas, Sacred			
782.253	M1670-1671	Spirituals (Songs)	784.194	ML489-522	Musical instruments—Europe
782.254	M2198-2199	Gospel music			
782.265	M2038-2099	Anthems	784.1941	ML501	Musical instruments—Great Britain
782.27	M2115-2145	Hymns			
782.3	M1999	Sacred vocal music	784.1943	ML499-500	Musical instruments—Germany
782.3209	ML3001	Music in churches			
782.32215009	ML3060	Church music—Catholic Church (Byzantine rite)	784.19436	ML491	Musical instruments—Austria
782.3222009	ML3002-3051	Church music—Catholic Church	784.19437	ML493	Musical instruments—Czechoslovakia
782.3223009	ML3166	Church music—Church of England	784.19439	ML494	Musical instruments—Hungary
782.3223009	ML3166	Church music—Episcopal Church	784.1944	ML497	Musical instruments—France
782.3224009	ML3100-3188	Church music—Protestant churches	784.1945	ML503	Musical instruments—Italy
			784.19469	ML519	Musical instruments—Portugal
782.3238	M2010-2014	Requiems			
782.42	M1977.C5	Songbooks	784.1948	ML513-516	Musical instruments—Scandinavia
782.4209	ML2500-2862	Songs—History and criticism			
782.421595	M1977.S2	Sea songs	784.19481	ML515	Musical instruments—Norway
782.42162	M1627	Folk songs			
782.43	M1627	Ballads			

181

Dewey	LC	Subject Heading	Dewey	LC	Subject Heading
784.19485	ML516	Musical instruments—Sweden	785.19	M900-986	Nonets
784.19489	ML514	Musical instruments—Denmark	785.43	M955-959	Wind ensembles
			785.8	M955-959	Woodwind ensembles
784.19492	ML505	Musical instruments—Netherlands	785.9	M955-959	Brass ensembles
			786.07	MT180-258	Keyboard instruments
784.19493	ML496	Musical instruments—Belgium	786.14707	MT190	Musical accompaniment
			786.2	M20-39	Piano music
784.19494	ML520	Musical instruments—Switzerland	786.207	MT220-255	Piano—Instruction and study
784.195	ML531	Musical instruments—China	786.209	ML649.8-747	Piano
784.195	ML525-541	Musical instruments—Asia	786.214707	MT239	Musical accompaniment
784.19519	ML537	Musical instruments—Korea	786.3	M20-39	Clavichord music
784.1952	ML535	Musical instruments—Japan	786.309	ML649.8-747	Clavichord
784.19538	ML527	Musical instruments—Saudia Arabia	786.4	M20-32	Electronic harpsichord music
			786.4	M20-39	Harpsichord music
784.1954	ML533	Musical instruments—India	786.5	M6-14	Organ music
784.1955	ML539	Musical instruments—Iran	786.507	MT180	Organ—Instruction and study
784.196	ML544	Musical instruments—Africa			
784.1971	ML478	Musical instruments—Canada	786.509	ML550-649	Organ
			786.509	ML597	Hammond organ
784.1972	ML482	Musical instruments—Mexico	786.55	M15-17	Reed-organ music
			786.5509	ML597	Reed-organ
784.19728	ML484	Musical instruments—Central America	786.59	M14.8	Electronic organ music
			786.607	MT700	Musical instruments (Mechanical)
784.19729	ML480	Musical instruments—West Indies	786.64	M172	Carillon music
			786.6509	ML1065-1066	Music box
784.1973	ML476	Musical instruments—United States	786.66	M20-32	Player-piano music
			786.6609	ML1058	Mechanical organs
784.198	ML486	Musical instruments—South America	786.707	MT724	Musical instruments, Electronic
784.199(3-6)	ML547	Musical instruments—[New Zealand/Australia/Oceania]	786.74	M1473	Synthesizer music
784.19946	ML518	Musical instruments—Spain	786.7409	ML1092	Electronic keyboard (Synthesizer)
784.2	M1000-1049	Orchestral music	786.8	M146	Percussion music
784.209	ML1200-1251	Orchestra	786.809	ML1030-1049	Percussion instruments
784.2117	MT125	Orchestral music—Analysis, appreciation	786.83	M175.C44	Celesta music
			786.843	M147	Glockenspiel music
784.4	M450-454	String quartets	786.843	M175.X6	Vibraphone music
784.4	M1350	Salon-orchestra music	786.843	M175.X6	Xylophone music
784.48	M1356	Dance-orchestra music	786.843	M175.X6	Marimba music
784.48	M1366	Big band music	786.848	M172	Chime music
784.4809	ML3518	Dance-orchestra music	786.873	M175.C35	Castanet music
784.7	M1100-1145	String-orchestra music	786.873	M146	Cymbal music
784.8307	MT733.4	Marching bands	786.8842	M175.T	Triangle music
784.84(0973)	VG33	United States. Navy—Songs and music	786.8848	CC200-255	Bells
			786.88485	M147	Handbell music
784.9	M1200-1269	Brass band music	786.8848507	MT710	Handbell ringing
785	M175.5	Solo instrument music	786.88709	ML1087	Jew's harp
785	M177-990	Chamber music	786.909	ML1035	Drum
785.009	ML1100-1165	Chamber music—History and criticism	786.93	M146	Tabla music
			786.93	M146	Timpani music
785.12	M177-298.5	Duets	786.94	M146	Snare drum music
785.13	M300-386	Trios	786.9409	ML1038.S	Snare drum
785.13	M349-353	String trios	786.95	M175.T	Tambourine music
785.14	M400-486	Quartets	787	M59.5	String instrument music
785.143807	MT728	Ensemble playing	787.07	MT259-338	Stringed instruments
785.15	M500-586	Quintets	787.09	ML749.5-927	Stringed instruments
785.17	M700-786	Septets	787.2	M40-44	Violin music
785.18	M800-886	Octets	787.209	ML800-897	Violin
			787.3	M45-49	Viola music

Dewey	LC	Subject Heading	Dewey	LC	Subject Heading
787.4	M50-54	Violoncello music	788.974	M110	Alto horn music
787.5	M55-58	Double-bass music	788.975	M90-94	Baritone music
787.5107	MT320-334	Double bass	788.975	M110.B33	Euphonium music
787.6	M59	Hardanger fiddle music	788.97509	ML990.E	Euphonium
787.6	M59	Baryton music	788.98	M95-99	Tuba music
787.6	M59.V53	Viol music	790.01	B105.P54	Play (Philosophy)
787.66	M59.V	Violetta d'amore music	790.0135	GV1-200	Leisure
787.69	M175.H9	Hurdy-gurdy music	790.068	GV182-.5	Recreation centers
787.7	M135-137	Zither music	790.068	HN41-46	Community centers
787.74	M142.D8	Dulcimer music	790.068(4-9)	HN43-46	Community centers—[By region or country]
787.7409	ML1015-1018	Dulcimer	790.06873	HN43-45	Community centers—United States
787.75	M142.A7	Appalachian dulcimer music			
787.75	M175.A8	Autoharp music	790.092	GV14.5	Recreation leadership
787.82	M142.S5	Sitar music	790.1	GV1199-1570	Games
787.83	M140-141	Lute music	790.102022	GV1201.42	Games—Rules
787.84	M130-134	Mandolin music	790.13	GV1201	Hobbies
787.87	M125-129	Bass guitar music	790.133	GV1220.7	Teddy bears
787.87	M125-129	Guitar music	790.133	GV1220	Dollhouses
787.8707	MT580-588	Guitar	790.133	GV1219	Dolls
787.875	M142.B2	Balalaika music	790.1330901	GN799.T75	Toys
787.88	M120-122	Banjo Music	790.134	GV1191-.75	Tournaments
787.8807	MT560-570	Banjo	790.138	GV1493	Literary recreations
787.89	M142.U5	Ukulele music	790.191	GV182.8	Family recreation
787.9	M115-119	Harp music	790.1926	GV184	Aged—Recreation
787.95	M142.C44	Celtic harp music	790.2	PN1560-1590	Performing arts
788	M111	Wind instrument music	790.209	PN1581	Performing arts—History
788.09	ML929-990	Wind instruments	791.068	GV1851-1860	Amusement parks
788.3	M60-64	Flute music	791.1	GV1835	Carnivals
788.307	MT340-348	Flute	791.1	GV1834.7-1835.56	Carnivals
788.33	M110.P5	Piccolo music			
788.33	M60-62	Fife music	791.12	M1365	Minstrel music
788.3307	MT356	Fife	791.3	GV1800-1831	Circus
788.3309	ML935-937	Piccolo	791.3	GV1838	Amateur circus
788.36	M110.R4	Recorder music	791.32	GV1829-1831	Animal training
788.3609	ML1055	Music recorder	791.33	GV1811	Clowns
788.49	M145	Bagpipe music	791.4092	PN1995.9.E77	Entertainers in motion pictures
788.4909	ML980	Gaita			
788.52	M65-69	Oboe music	791.43	PN1993-1999	Motion pictures
788.5207	MT360-378	Oboe	791.43	PN1995.9.F67	Foreign films
788.53	M110.E5	English-horn music	791.43028092	PN1995.9.S7	Stunt performers
788.58	M75-79	Bassoon music	791.4308996073	PN1995.9.N4	Blacks in motion pictures
788.5807	ML953	Bassoon	791.43655	PN1995.9.D78	Drugs in motion pictures
788.62	M70-74	Clarinet music	791.43657	PN1995.9.M86	Musical films
788.6207	MT380-388	Clarinet	791.43682	PN1995.5	Motion pictures—Religious aspects
788.65	M70-74	Bass clarinet music			
788.7	M105-109	Saxophone music	791.437	PN1996-1997	Motion picture plays
788.82	M175.M8	Harmonica music	791.4375	PN1995	Motion pictures—Reviews
788.8209	ML1088	Harmonica	791.44	PN1991-.9	Radio broadcasting
788.84	M175.B2	Bandonion music	791.446	PN1991.8.S4	Soap operas
788.84	M154	Concertina music	791.44617	PN1991.8.C65	Radio comedies
788.86	M175.A4	Accordion music	791.45	PN1992.95	Video recordings
788.8609	ML1083	Accordion	791.45028092	PN1992.4	Television actors and actresses
788.863	M175.M38	Melodeon music			
788.9	M111	Brass instrument music	791.456	PN1992.8.S4	Soap operas
788.907	MT418	Brass instruments	791.45617	PN1992.8.C66	Television comedies
788.92	M110	Alpenhorn music	791.53	PN1970-1979	Puppets
788.92	M85-89	Trumpet music	791.53	PN1979.S5	Shadow shows
788.92	M1270	Trumpet-calls	791.62	PN3202-3299	Pageants
788.93	M90-94	Trombone music	791.64	LB3635	Cheerleading
788.96	M85-89	Cornet music	791.82	GV1107-1108.6	Bullfights
788.9707	MT493	Fluegelhorn			

Dewey	LC	Subject Heading	Dewey	LC	Subject Heading
791.84	GV1834	Rodeos	793.38	GV1757	Balls (Parties)
791.84	GV1834.45.B35	Barrel racing	793.38	GV1746-1750	Balls (Parties)
792	PN2000-3299	Theater	793.73	GV1491-1507	Puzzles
792.022	PN2219.08	Theater, Open-air	793.73	PN6366-6377	Acrostics
792.0222	PN6119.9	Amateur plays	793.732	GV1507.C7	Crossword puzzles
792.0222	PN3151-3171	Amateur theater	793.734	GV1507.A5	Anagrams
792.02230973	PN2267	Little theater movement	793.8	GV1541-1561	Conjuring
792.023	PN2055	Acting—Vocational guidance	793.8	GV1541-1561	Tricks
792.025	PN2091.S8	Theaters—Stage-setting and scenery	793.8092	GV1545	Magicians
			793.85	GV1549	Card tricks
792.028	PN2061-2071	Acting	793.89	GV1557	Ventriloquism
792.028	PN2091.A	Theaters—Accidents	794	GV1312-1469	Board games
792.028	PN2071.I5	Improvisation (Acting)	794.1	GV1313-1457	Chess
792.028092	PN2205-2217	Actresses	794.2	GV1461-1463	Checkers
792.028092	PN2205-2217	Actors	794.3	GV1564-1565	Darts (Game)
792.08996073	PN2270.A35	Afro-American theater	794.6	GV910.5.D8	Duckpin bowling
792.09	PN2100-2193	Theater—History	794.6	GV901-909	Bowling
792.0901	PN2131-2145	Theater—History—To 500	794.73	GV891-899	Pool (Game)
792.0902	PN2152-2160	Theater—History—Medievel, 500-1500	794.8	GV1469.2	Electronic games
			794.8	GV1469.3	Video games
792.09033	PN2171-2179	Theater—History—18th century	794.8	GV1469.15-.25	Computer games
			795	GV1302	Gambling systems
792.09034	PN2181-2193	Theater—History—20th century	795	GV1301-1311	Gambling
			795.1	GV1303	Dice
792.09495	PN2660-2668	Theater—Greece	795.1	GV1303	Dice games
792.0951	PN2870-2878	Theater—China	795.23	GV1309	Roulette
792.0952	PN2920-2928	Theater—Japan	795.32	GV1467	Dominoes
792.0952	PN2924.5.K3	Kabuki	795.34	GV1299.M3	Mah jong
792.0973	PN2220-2298	Theater—United States	795.4	GV1232-1299	Card games
792.16	PN3203-3299	Passion-plays	795.412	GV1251-1255	Poker
792.3	PN2071.G4	Mime	795.413	GV1283	Duplicate whist
792.3	PN6120.P3-.P4	Pantomines	795.415	GV1282.8.D86	Duplicate contract bridge
792.319969	GV1796.H8	Hula (Dance)	795.416	GV1295.P6	Double pinochle
792.7	PN1960-1969	Music-halls (Variety-theaters, cabarets, etc.)	795.418	GV1295.R8	Rummy (Game)
			796	GV561-749.5	Athletics
792.7	PN1960-1969	Vaudeville	796	GV561-1198.995	Sports
792.7	PN6231.B84	Burlesques	796	GV1018	Racing
792.78	GV1794	Tap dancing	796.0284	GV749.M6	Mouth protectors
792.8	GV1783	Modern dance	796.0284	GV743-749	Athletics—Equipment and supplies
792.8	GV1580-1799.4	Dance			
792.8026	GV1789.2	Ballet—Costume	796.0284	GV743-749	Sporting goods
792.809	GV1600	Dance criticism	796.042	GV710	Intramural sports
792.8092	GV1785	Dance—Biography	796.042	GV346	School sports
792.84	GV1788	Ballet dancing	796.043	GV350.5	College athletes—Recruiting
792.84	GV1787	Ballet	796.043	GV346-350	College sports
793	GV1221-1229	Indoor games	796.06	GV713	Sports administration
793.083	GV1799	Dance for children	796.068	GV421-433	Playgrounds
793.0846	GV1799.3	Dance for the aged	796.068	GV411-416	Athletic fields
793.087	GV1799.2	Dance for the handicapped	796.068	GV403-405	Gymnasiums
793.2	GV1470-1521	Entertaining	796.068	GV401-433	Sports facilities
793.21	GV1205	Children's parties	796.068	GV415-416	Stadiums
793.24	PN6366-6377	Charades	796.068	GV563	Athletic clubs
793.3	GV1796.M5	Minuet	796.0680284	GV426-.5	Playgounds—Equipment and supplies
793.31	GV1580-1799	Folk dancing			
793.31	GV1796.P55	Polka (Dance)	796.0681	GV716	Sports—Economic aspects
793.33	GV1751	Ballroom dancing	796.07	GV201-555	Physical education and training
793.33	GV1796.L5	Lindy (Dance)			
793.33	GV1761	Waltz	796.077	GV711	Coaching (Athletics)
793.33	GV1796.D57	Disco dancing	796.087	GV709.3	Sports for the handicapped
793.33	GV1796.J6	Jitterbug (Dance)	796.092	GV697	Athletes
793.35	GV1796.S9	Sword-dance	796.154	GV761.5	Model airplane racing

Dewey	LC	Subject Heading	Dewey	LC	Subject Heading
796.156	GV1570	Model car racing	796.542087	GV197.H3	Camps for the handicapped
796.2	GV1099	Shuffleboard	796.5422	BV1650	Church camps
796.2	GV1213	Marbles (Game)	796.56	GV198.945-.975	Dude ranches
796.21	GV858.2-859.7	Roller-skating	796.58	GV200.4	Orienteering
796.3	GV861	Ball games	796.6	GV1029.7	Soap box derbies
796.30284	GV749.B34	Balls (Sporting goods)	796.6	GV1040-1059	Cycling
796.323	GV885	Basketball	796.6(2-4)	GV1040-1058	Bicycles
796.323092	GV884	Basketball players	796.6(2-4)	GV1040-1058	Tricycles
796.325	GV1015-.57	Volleyball	796.62	GV1049	Bicycle racing
796.325	GV1015.5.B43	Beach volleyball	796.63	GV1056	All terrain cycling
796.332	GV937-960	Football	796.64	GV1044-1046	Bicycle touring
796.33202022	GV955	Football—Rules	796.7	GV1021-1025	Automobile travel
796.332083	GV959.55.C45	Football for children	796.72	GV1029.3	Drag racing
796.332092	GV939	Football players	796.72	GV1029.9.D8	Dune buggy racing
796.3322	GV951.8	Football—Offense	796.72068	TE305	Racetracks (Automobile racing)
796.3322	GV951.25	End play (Football)			
796.3322	GV951.18	Football—Defense	796.72068759	GV1033.5.D	Daytona International Speedway Race
796.333	GV945	Rugby football			
796.334	GV943-944	Soccer	796.72092	GV1032	Automobile racing drivers
796.3343	GV942.7	Soccer referees	796.73	GV1029	Grand Prix racing
796.33464	GV943.45-.54	Soccer—Tournaments	796.73	GV1029.2	Automobile rallies
796.33466	GV943.5	Europa Cup (Soccer)	796.75	GV1060.14	Sidecar motocycle racing
796.34	GV1003.2	Paddleball	796.8092	GV35	Gladiators
796.342	GV990-1005	Tennis	796.8092	GV1113	Martial artists
796.346	GV1005	Table tennis	796.81	GV1111-1141	Hand-to-hand fighting
796.346	GV1006	Paddle tennis	796.812	GV1195	Wrestling
796.347	GV989	Lacrosse	796.812	GV1196.5	Arm wrestling
796.352	GV961-987	Golf	796.8152	GV1114	Judo
796.357	GV862-880.6	Baseball	796.8153	GV1114.3	Karate
796.357	GV877	Baseball—Records	796.8154	GV1114.35	Aikido
796.357075	GV875.3	Baseball cards	796.8159	GV1114.7	Kung fu
796.357083	GV880.5	Little League baseball	796.83	GV1115-1137	Boxing
796.357092	GV865	Baseball players	796.86	GV1143-1150.6	Swordplay
796.35724	GV870	Fielding (Baseball)	796.86	GV1143-1150.6	Fencing
796.3578	GV881-.4	Softball	796.86092	GV1144-.2	Fencers
796.3578	GV881	Slow pitch softball	796.9	GV841-857	Winter sports
796.3578	GV881.5	T-ball	796.91	GV848.9-852	Skating
796.42	GV1061-1069	Running	796.92	GV853	Snowshoes and showshoeing
796.42	GV1060.5-1098	Track-athletics			
796.4252	GV1065-.23	Marathon running	796.93	GV854	Skis and skiing
796.434	GV1079-1080	Vaulting	796.93068	GV854.35	Ski resorts
796.44	GV461-475	Gymnastics	796.932	GV855-.5	Cross-country skiing
796.47	GV551-553	Acrobatics	796.935	GV854-.87	Downhill skiing
796.48	GV721.8	Olympics—Records	796.935	GV854.9.R3	Downhill ski racing
796.5	GV191.2-200.56	Outdoor life	796.935	GV854.9.R3	Ski racing
796.5	GV200.5-.56	Wilderness survival	796.94	GV857.S6	Snowmobiling
796.51	GV199.6	Backpacking	796.95	GV856	Bobsledding
796.51	GV199-.5	Hiking	796.95	GV857.S57	Snowboarding
796.51	GV1071	Walking (Sports)	796.95	GV856	Tobogganing
796.52	GV200.3	Snow and ice climbing	796.962	GV847	Hockey
796.522	GV200.19.R34	Rappelling	796.97	GV843	Ice-boats
796.522	GV199.8-200.3	Mountaineering	797	GV771-840	Aquatic sports
796.5223	GV200.2	Rock climbing	797.1	GV771-836.15	Boats and boating
796.525	GV200.6-.66	Caving	797.122	GV781-785	Canoes and canoeing
796.53	GV454.B3	Beaches	797.1224	GV781-790.3	Kayaking
796.54	GV198.L3	Camp sites, facilities, etc.	797.1224	GV788.5	Sea kayaking
796.54	GV199.7	Packhorse camping	797.123	GV790.9-807.5	Rowing
796.54	GV198.95	Swamp camping	797.124	GV811	Sailing
796.54	GV191.68-198.9	Camping	797.124	GV811	Sailing, Single-handed
796.54	GV198.9	Snow camping	797.1246	GV811.8-833	Yachting
796.54	GV192-198	Camps	797.1246	GV811.57	Catamarans

185

Dewey	LC	Subject Heading	Dewey	LC	Subject Heading
797.1246	GV811.53-.58	Multihull sailboats	799.109	SH421	Fishing—History
797.125	GV833.5-835.9	Motorboats	799.1092	SH414-415	Fishers
797.125	GV835	Launches	799.1097	SH462	Fishing—North America
797.129	GV836	Houseboats	799.10971	SH571-572	Fishing—Canada
797.14	GV775	Regattas	799.10973	SH463-565	Fishing—United States
797.14	GV826.5-832	Yacht racing	799.12	SH457.5	Big game fishing
797.14091631	GV832	Fastnet Yacht Race	799.12	SH401-691	Fishing
797.21	GV838.53.L65	Long distance swimming	799.1205	SH401	Fishing—Periodicals
797.21	GV838.68-.76	Life-saving	799.1206	SH403	Hunting and fishing clubs
797.21	GV838.76	Survival swimming	799.1209729	SH577-578	Fishing—West Indies
797.21	GV838.5	Swimming—Records	799.122	SH455.6	Bottom fishing
797.21	GV838.52.C73	Swimming—Crawl stroke	799.122	SH455.4	Bait fishing
797.21	GV837	Swimming	799.124	SH454.2	Fly casting
797.23	GV840.S78	Deep diving	799.124	SH454-.9	Casting (Fishing)
797.23092	GV837.9-838	Skin divers	799.124	SH456-.2	Fly fishing
797.24	GV838.67.S65	Springboard diving	799.16	SH457-.5	Saltwater fishing
797.24	GV838.65.S84	Diving—Swan dive	799.1743	SH691.E4	Eel fishing
797.24	GV838.65.J32	Diving—Jackknife dive	799.1755	SH687-688	Trout fishing
797.24	GV837	Diving	799.1755	SH684-686.7	Salmon fishing
797.24081	GV838.62.M45	Diving for men	799.1758	SH681	Bass fishing
797.24082	GV838.62.W65	Diving for women	799.2	SK283-.6	Trapping
797.33	GV811.63.W56	Windsurfing	799.2	SK	Hunting
797.35	GV840.S5	Water skiing	799.2028	SK36.7	Poaching
797.5	GV750-770	Aeronautical sports	799.2028	SK273-275	Hunting—Equipment and supplies
797.5	GV770.27	Bungee jumping			
797.51	GV762-763	Ballooning	799.2028	SK335	Decoys (Hunting)
797.51	GV763	Balloon racing	799.20283	SK274	Hunting guns
797.55	GV764-766	Gliding and soaring	799.20283	SK274	Sporting guns
797.56	GV769.5-770	Skydiving	799.202832	SK274.2-.4	Rifles
797.56	GV769.5-770.2	Parachuting	799.202834	SK274.5	Shotguns
798	GV33	Chariot racing	799.205	SK7	Hunting—Periodicals
798	SF294.2-294.35	Horse sports	799.206	SK1	Hunting—Societies, etc.
798.2	SF309	Horsemanship	799.206	SK3	Hunting and fishing clubs
798.2028	SF296.R4	Reining (Horsemanship)	799.206	SK317	Shooting preserves
798.23	SF296.T75	Trick riding	799.2074	SK276	Hunting—Museums
798.23	SF309.48-.658	Dressage	799.209	SK21	Hunting—History
798.23	SF309.3	Western riding	799.2092	SK15-17	Hunters
798.23	SF309.28	Trail riding	799.21	SK37-39.5	Shooting
798.23	SF309.27	Sidesaddle riding	799.213	SK39.3	Handgun hunting
798.2306	SF310-.5	Riding clubs	799.215	SK36	Bowhunting
798.23071	SF310.4	Riding schools	799.23	SF295.65	Hunt riding
798.24	SF295.2	Show riding	799.23	SK293	Ferreting
798.25	SF296.V37	Vaulting (Horsemanship)	799.232	SK321	Falconry
798.4	SF321-359.7	Horse racing	799.24	SK36.2	Game and game-birds, Dressing of
798.40068	SF324-.4	Racetracks (Horse-racing)			
798.400976944	SF357.K4	Kentucky Derby, Louisville, Ky.	799.24	SK311-335	Fowling
			799.244	SK333.D8	Duck shooting
798.45	SF359-.7	Steeplechasing	799.244	SK331-335	Waterfowl
798.450942753	SF359.7.G7	Grand National Handicap Steeplechase	799.246	SK323-325	Upland game bird shooting
			799.246	SK325.P5	Pheasant shooting
798.46	SF338.7-345	Harness racing	799.24609(4-9)	SK324	Upland game bird shooting—[By region or country]
798.8	SF439.5-440.2	Dog racing			
798.83	SF440.15	Sled dog racing	799.258	SK319	Bird trapping
799.1028	SH452.9.K6	Fishing knots	799.259328	SK341.H3	Hare hunting
799.10284	SH447-453	Fishing—Equipment and supplies	799.2597	SK283-.6	Fur-bearing animals
			799.259775	SK284-287	Fox hunting
799.10284	SH448	Bait	799.26	SK295-305	Big game hunting
799.10284	SH451.3	Fish decoys	799.2765	SK301	Deer hunting
799.10284	SH447-453	Fishing tackle	799.27657	SK303	Elk hunting
799.10284	SH452-.2	Fishing rods	799.2767	SK305.E3	Elephant hunting
799.10284	SH452.9.H	Fishhooks	799.2798	SK305.A	Alligator hunting

Dewey	LC	Subject Heading	Dewey	LC	Subject Heading
799.292025	SK12	Hunters—Directories	808.801163	PN56.S87	Surrealism (Literature)
799.29(4-9)	SK40-267	Hunting—[By region or country]	808.8012	PN56.R3	Realism in literature
			808.8012	PN56.R3	Naturalism in literature
799.296	SK251-255	Hunting—Africa	808.8012	PN601	Naturalism in literature
799.297	SK40-157	Hunting—North America	808.80142	PN56.C6	Classicism
799.297(4-9)	SK47-145	Hunting—[United States, By state]	808.80145	PN750-759	Romanticism
			808.80145	PN603	Romanticism
799.2973	SK41-145	Hunting—United States	808.80145	PN56.R7	Romanticism
799.2975	SK43	Hunting—Southern States	808.80145	PN816	Romance fiction
799.2978	SK45	Hunting—West (U.S.)	808.8015	PN56.S9	Symbolism in literature
799.31	GV1151-1181.3	Shooting	808.8015	PN56.A5	Allegory
799.31	GV1167-1172	Shooting contests	808.8015	PN56.M94	Myth in literature
799.31	GV1175	Pistol shooting	808.8024	PN44	Literature—Stories, plots, etc.
799.31	GV1175.5	Fast draw pistol shooting			
799.31	GV1177	Rifle practice	808.8026	PN1551	Dialogue
799.3132	GV1181-.3	Trapshooting	808.803538	PN6071.E7	Erotic literature
799.3132	GV1181.3	Skeet shooting	808.8036	PN48	Nature in literature
799.32	GV1185-1189	Archery	808.8037	PN56.M95	Mythology in literature
801	PN45	Literature—Philosophy	808.8038291216	PN57.D4	Devil in literature
801.93	PN45	Literature—Aesthetics	808.804291	PN49	Mysticism in literature
801.959	P47	Criticism, Textual	808.81071	PN1101	Poetry—Study and teaching
805	PN1-9	Literature—Periodicals	808.813	PN6110.N17	Narrative poetry
806	PN20-29	Literature—Societies, etc.	808.8132	PN1301-1333	Epic poetry
807.1	PN59-72	Literature—Study and teaching	808.8132	PN6110.E6	Epic poetry
			808.814	PN691	Lyric poetry
808	PN6010-6078	Literature—Collections	808.8142	PN1514	Sonnet
808	PN171.4-229	Rhetoric	808.8143	PN6110.04	Odes
808	PN167-168	Plagiarism	808.8175	PN6231.L5	Limericks
808	PN203	Style, Literary	808.82	PN6110.5-6120	Drama—Collections
808	P301-.5	Rhetoric	808.82	PN688-691	Poetry, Medieval
808.02	PN101-249	Authorship	808.820512	PN6111-6120	Tragedy
808.027	PN162	Editing	808.8222	PN6120.R2	Radio plays
808.042	PE1402-1497	English language—Rhetoric	808.8245	PN1530	Monologue
808.0431	PF3410-3497	German language—Rhetoric	808.8245	PN4305.M6	Monologues
808.043931	PF410-497	Dutch language—Rhetoric	808.825232	PN1940-1949	Farce
808.0481	PA3265	Rhetoric, Ancient	808.825232	PN6120.F3	Farces
808.066	PN205	Exposition (Rhetoric)	808.82527	PN6120.M9	Detective and mystery plays
808.068	PZ5-90	Children's literature	808.82527	PN1910-1919	Melodrama
808.1	P311	Versification	808.8387	PN6120.95.A38	Adventure stories
808.1	PN1010-1525	Poetry	808.83872	PZ1-3	Detective and mystery stories
808.1	PN1031-1035	Versification	808.838762	PN3433-.8	Science fiction
808.1	PN1039-1049	Poetics	808.838762	P96.S34	Science fiction
808.108	PN6099-6110	Poetry—Collections	808.838762	PN6120.95.S33	Science fiction
808.14	PN1351-1389	Lyric poetry	808.84	PN6141-6145	Essays
808.2	PN1660-1692	Drama—Technique	808.85	PN6121-6129	Speeches, addresses, etc.
808.2	PN1600-1861	Drama	808.85	PN4001-4355	Oratory
808.20071	PN1701	Drama—Study and teaching	808.851	PN4121-4130	Public speaking
808.222	PN1991.73	Radio plays—Technique	808.851	PN6340-6348	Toasts
808.3	PN3311-3503	Fiction	808.86	PN6130-6140	Letters
808.3	PN3355-3383	Fiction—Technique	808.87	PN6149.P3	Parody
808.4	PN4500	Essay	808.87	PN6110.P3	Parodies
808.5	PN4142	Speechwriting	808.87	PN6231.S2	Satire
808.53	PN4177-4191	Debates and debating	808.87	PN6147-6231	Wit and humor
808.54	PN4199-4355	Recitations	808.87092	PN6147	Humorists
808.54	PN4145-4151	Oral interpretation	808.882	PN6279-6288	Epigrams
808.543	GR72.3	Storytelling	808.882	PN6366-6377	Riddles
808.54509	PN83	Reading	808.882	PN1441	Epigrams
808.8	PN6010-6065	Anthologies	808.882	PN6080-6095	Quotations
808.8002	PN665-694	Literature, Medieval	808.882	PN171.Q6	Quotation
808.800(24-32)	PN715-749	Renaissance	808.882	PN6259-6268	Anecdotes
808.800(3-4)	PN695-779	Literature, Modern	809	PN4096	Rhetorical criticism

Dewey	LC	Subject Heading	Dewey	LC	Subject Heading
809	PN441-595	Literature—History and criticism	811.509	PS324	American poetry—20th century
809	PN75-99	Literature—History and criticism	812.0071	PS335	American drama—Study and teaching
809.01	PN611-630	Literature, Ancient	812.008	PS623-635	American drama
809.1	PN1105-1279	Poetry—History and criticism	812.009	PS330-351	American drama
809.2	PN1707	Dramatic criticism	812.051209	PS336.T7	American drama (Tragedy)
809.2	PN1720-1861	Drama—History and criticism	812.052309	PS336.C7	American drama (Comedy)
809.2527	PN1761	Mysteries and miracle-plays	813	PZ1	American fiction
809.3	PN3329-3503	Fiction—History and criticism	813.009	PS371-379	American fiction
809.31	PN3373	Short story	814.008	PS680-688	American essays
809.381	PN3441	Historical fiction	814.009	PS420-428	American essays
809.387	PN3448.A3	Adventure stories	815.008	PS660-668	Speeches, address, etc., American
809.3872	PN3448.D4	Detective and mystery stories			
809.3872	PN3377.5.D4	Detective and mystery stories—Technique	815.009	PS400-408	Speeches, address, etc., American
809.5	PN4021-4055	Oratory—History	816.008	PS670-678	American letters
809.6	PN4400	Letters	816.009	PS410-418	American letters
809.91	PN597	Literary movements	817.008	PN6157-6162	American wit and humor
809.924	PN3378	Plots (Drama, novel, etc.)	817.009	PS430-438	American wit and humor
809.933538	HQ450-472	Erotic literature	818.03	PS409	American diaries
809.93522	BS535-537	Bible as literature	818.08	PS642-659.2	American prose literature
809.93592	CT21-22	Biography as a literary form	818.08	PS367-369	American prose literature—Revolutionary period, 1775-1783
810	PS	American literature			
810.80896073	PS508.N3	American literature—Afro-American authors			
810.809287	PS508.W7	American literature—Women authors	818.08	PS366	American prose literature—Colonial period, ca. 1600-1775
810.9	PS153-490	American literature—History and criticism	818.08	PS360-379	American prose literature
			818.3	PS669	American diaries
810.9001	PS185-191	American literature—Colonial period, ca. 1600-1775	820	PN849.G	British literature
			820	PR1-9680	English literature
			820	PR8631-8644	Scottish literature
810.9002	PS193	American literature—Revolutionary period, 1775-1783	820	PR9320-.9	Guyanese literature
			820	PR9600-9619.3	Australian literature
810.900(2-3)	PS208	American literature—1783-1850	820.0202	PR87	English literature—Outlines, syllabi, etc.
810.9003	PS201-214	American literature—19th century	820.3	PR19	English literature—Dictionaries
810.9005	PS221-228	American literature—20th century	820.71	PR31-55	English literature—Study and teaching
810.9896073	PS153.N5	Afro-American authors	820.8001	PR1119-1131	English literature—Middle English, 1100-1500
810.99287	PS147-151	American literature—Women authors	820.800(3-4)	PR1119-1131	English literature—Early modern, 1500-1700
811	PS	American poetry	820.8005	PR1134-1139	English literature—18th century
811.0080896073	PS591.N4	American poetry—Afro-American authors			
811.00809287	PS589	American poetry—Women authors	820.8008	PR1149	English literature—20th century
			820.8008	PR1301-1304	English literature—19th century
811.071	PS306-.5	American poetry—Study and teaching	820.8008	PR1143-1145	English literature—19th century
811.109	PS312	American poetry—Colonial period, ca 1600-1775	820.802	PN6081-6084	Quotations, English
811.209	PS314	American poetry—Revolutional period, 1775-1783	820.8022	PE1427	Description (Rhetoric)
			820.8022	PR1285	Description (Rhetoric)
			820.8023	PE1425	Narration (Rhetoric)
811.209	PS319	American poetry—1783-1850	820.809222	PR1110.C3	English literature—Catholic authors
811.309	PS316-321	American poetry—19th century	820.809287	PR1110.W6	English literature—Women authors

Dewey	LC	Subject Heading	Dewey	LC	Subject Heading
820.809411	PR8631-8693	English literature—Scottish authors	821.509	PR551-579	English poetry—18th century
820.809415	PR8831-8893	English literature—Irish authors	821.808	PR1221-1224	English poetry—19th century
820.809429	PR8900-8997	English literature—Welsh authors	821.809	PR581-599	English poetry—19th century
820.80952	PR9900.J	English literature—Japanese authors	821.908	PR1224-1227	English poetry—20th century
820.9	PR57-78	English literature—Criticism, Textual	821.909	PR601-609	English poetry—20th century
820.9	PR8510-8553	Scottish literature	822	PR9343	African drama (English)
820.9	PR1-978	English literature—History and criticism	822.008	PR1241-1273	English drama
			822.008	PR9347	African drama (English)
820.9	PR9340-9408	African literature (English)	822.009	PR621-739	English drama
820.900(1-2)	PR251-369	English literature—Middle English, 1100-1500	822.009	PR635.D45	Domestic drama, English
820.900(2-4)	PR401-439	English literature—Early modern, 1500-1700	822.051208	PR1257	English drama (Tragedy)
			822.051209	PR633	English drama (Tragedy)
820.9005	PR441-449	English literature—18th century	822.052308	PR1248	English drama (Comedy)
820.9008	PR451-469	English literature—19th century	822.052309	PR631	English drama (Comedy)
			822.(1-2)08	PR1260	English drama—To 1500
820.9009	PR471-479	English literature—20th century	822.(1-2)09	PR641-644	English drama—To 1500
			822.(2-3)08	PR1262-1263	English drama—Early modern and Elizabethan, 1500-1600
820.99287	PR111-119	English literature—Women authors	822.(2-3)09	PR646-658	English drama—Early modern and Elizabethan, 1500-1600
820.99411	PR8500-8621	English literature—Scottish authors	822.33	PR2750-3112	Shakespeare, William, 1564-1616
820.99415	PR8700-8821	English literature—Irish authors	822.408	PR1265.3-1266	English drama—17th century
821	PR1170-1227	English poetry	822.409	PR671-698	English drama—17th century
821.008	PR9346-.5	African poetry (English)			
821.00809287	PR1177	English poetry—Women authors	822.508	PR1269	English drama—18th century
821.00809411	PR8649-8663	English poetry—Scottish authors	822.509	PR701-719	English drama—18th century
821.00809415	PR8848-8863	English poetry—Irish authors	822.808	PR1271	English drama—19th century
821.00809429	PR8955-8969	English poetry—Welsh authors	822.809	PR721-734	English drama—19th century
821.0089411	PR8561-8581	English poetry—Scottish authors	822.908	PR1272	English drama—20th century
821.009	PR9342	African poetry (English)	822.909	PR736-739	English drama—20th century
821.009	PR500-611	English poetry			
821.009	PR500-609	English poetry—History and criticism	823	PR9344	African fiction (English)
821.00909429	PR8926-8932	English poetry—Welsh authors	823.008	PR1281-1309	English fiction
			823.00809287	PZ1	English fiction—Women authors
821.0099287	PR111-119	English poetry—Women authors	823.009	PR821-888	English fiction
821.03209	PR321-347	Epic poetry, English	823.009	PR9347.5	African fiction (English)
821.(1-2)08	PR1203	English poetry—Middle English, 1100-1500	823.909	PR881-888	English fiction—20th century
821.(1-2)09	PR311-369	English poetry, Middle English, 1100-1500	824.008	PR1361-1369	English essays
			824.009	PR921-927	English essays
821.(2-4)09	PR521-549	English poetry—Early modern, 1500-1700	825.008	PR1321-1329	Speeches, address, etc., English
821.(3-4)08	PR1204-1213	English poetry—Early modern, 1500-1700	825.009	PR901-907	Speeches, addresses, etc., English
821.508	PR1215-1219	English poetry—18th century	826.008	PR1341-1349	English letters
			826.009	PR911-917	English letters

Dewey	LC	Subject Heading	Dewey	LC	Subject Heading
827	PN931-937	English wit and humor	830.9002	PT175-230	German literature—Middle High German, 1050-1500
827.008	PN6173-6175	English wit and humor			
827.009	PR931-937	English wit and humor	830.900(3-5)	PT238-281	German literature—Early modern, 1500-1700
827.0222	NC1470-1479	English wit and humor, Pictorial			
			830.9006	PT285-321	German literature—18th century—History and criticism
828.03	PR1330	English diaries			
828.03	PR908	English diaries			
828.08	PR9637.25-.92	New Zealand prose literature	830.9007	PT341-395	German literature—19th century—History and criticism
828.08	PR8597-8607	English prose literature—Scottish authors			
			830.9009	PT401-403	German literature—20th century
828.08	PR8672-8687	English prose literature—Scottish authors	831.008	PT1151-1241	German poetry
828.08	PR1297	English prose literature—18th century	831.009	PT500-597	German poetry
			831.03208	PT1411-1418	Epic poetry, German
828.08	PR769	English prose literature—18th century	831.03208	PT1179-1181	Epic poetry, German
			831.(1-3)08	PT1391-1429	German poetry—Middle High German, 1050-1500
828.08	PR767-769	English prose literature—Early modern, 1500-1700			
828.08	PR750-888	English prose literature	831.209	PT175-227	German poetry—Middle High German, 1050-1500
828.08	PR1293-1295	English prose literature—Early modern, 1500-1700	831.(3-5)08	PT1163-1165	German poetry—Early modern, 1500-1700
828.08	PR1281-1300	English prose literature	831.(4-5)08	PT1163-1165	German poetry—Early modern, 1500-1700
829.009	PR171-236	English literature—Old English, ca 450-1100	831.(4-5)09	PT525-531	German poetry—Early modern, 1500-1700
829.1	PR1490-1508	English poetry—Old English, ca. 450-1100	831.608	PT1167-1169	German poetry—18th century
829.1009	PR201-217	English poetry—Old English, ca. 450-1100	831.609	PT533-535	German poetry—18th century
829.808	PR221-236	English prose literature—Old English, ca. 450-1100	831.708	PT1171-1173	German poetry—19th century
830	PT3830-3837.5	German literature—Czechoslovakia	831.709	PT541-547	German poetry—19th century
830	PT3900-3919	German American literature (German)	831.908	PT1174-1175	German poetry—20th century
830	PT3860-3878	Swiss literature (German)	831.909	PT551-553	German poetry—20th century
830	PT3840-3848	Hungarian literature (German)			
830	PT1-1021	German literature	832.008	PT1251-1299	German drama
830	PT3808-3809	German literature—Foreign countries	832.009	PT605-709	German drama
			832.051208	PT1271-1273	German drama (Tragedy)
830.3	PT41	German language dictionaries	832.052308	PT1275-1277	German drama (Comedy)
			833.008	PT1321-1340	German fiction
830.6	PT31	German literature—Congresses	833.009	PT741-772	German fiction
			833.0108	PT1337-1340	Short stories, German
830.71	PT51-65	German literature—Study and teaching	833.(3-5)09	PT753-756	German fiction—Early modern, 1500-1700
830.8	PT1100-1479	German literature			
830.8002	PT1375-1479	German literature—Middle High German, 1050-1700	833.608	PT1315	German fiction—18th century
			833.609	PT759	German fiction—18th century
830.800(3-5)	PT1121-1126	German literature—Early modern, 1500-1700	833.708	PT1332	German fiction—19th century
			833.709	PT763-771	German fiction—19th century
830.8006	PT1131	German literature—18th century	833.908	PT1334	German fiction—20th century
			833.909	PT772	German fiction—20th century
830.8007	PT1136	German literature—19th century	834.008	PT1354	German essays
			834.009	PT831	German essays
830.8009	PT1141	German literature—20th century	835.008	PT1344-1345	Speeches, address, etc., German
830.802	PN6090-6093	Quotations, German	835.009	PT801	Speeches, addresses, etc., German
830.9001	PT183	German literature—Old High German, 750-1050			
			836.008	PT1348-1352	German letters
			836.009	PT811	German letters

Dewey	LC	Subject Heading	Dewey	LC	Subject Heading
838.08	PT1301-1340	German prose literature	839.6071	PT7135-7139	Old Norse literature— Study and teaching
838.08	PT711-871	German prose literature			
839	PF3985-3991	German literature—Old High German, 750-1050	839.61008	PT7230-7252	Old Norse poetry
			839.61009	PT7170-7175	Old Norse Poetry
839.09	PJ5120-5192	Yiddish literature	839.6308	PT7261-7262	Sagas
839.2	PF1501-1541	Frisian literature	839.6309	PT7181-7193	Sagas
839.3009	PN836	Germanic fiction	839.6808	PT7177-7211	Old Norse prose literature
839.31	PT5001-5980	Dutch literature	839.6808	PT7255-7262	Old Norse prose literature
839.31	PT6000-6466.36	Flemish literature	839.69	PT7351-7550	Icelandic literature
839.31071	PT5040-5044	Dutch literature—Study and teaching	839.69071	PT7370-7373	Icelandic literature—Study and teaching
839.31071	PT6040	Flemish literature—Study and teaching	839.691008	PT7465-7467	Icelandic poetry
			839.692008	PT7470-7477	Icelandic drama
839.3109001	PT5121-5137	Dutch literature—To 1500	839.692009	PT7411	Icelandic drama
839.310900 (2-4)	PT5141-5165	Dutch literature— 1500-1800	839.693008	PT7485-7487	Icelandic fiction
			839.693009	PT7413	Icelandic fiction
839.3109005	PT5170-5175	Dutch literature—19th century	839.69808	PT412-418	Icelandic prose literature
			839.69808	PT7480-7495	Icelandic prose literature
839.3109006	PT5180-5185	Dutch literature—20th century	839.7	PT9201-9999	Swedish literature
			839.71008	PT9580-9599	Swedish poetry
839.311008	PT6330-6348	Flemish poetry	839.71009	PT9375-9405	Swedish poetry
839.311008	PT5470-5488	Dutch poetry	839.72008	PT9605-9625	Swedish drama
839.311009	PT5201-5245	Dutch poetry	839.72009	PT9415-9449	Swedish drama
839.311009	PT6140	Flemish poetry	839.73008	PT9627-9630	Swedish fiction
839.312008	PT5490-5515	Dutch drama	839.73009	PT9480-9492	Swedish fiction
839.312008	PT6350-6360	Flemish drama	839.7808	PT9460-9499	Swedish prose literature
839.312009	PT5250-5295	Dutch drama	839.7808	PT9626-9639	Swedish prose literature
839.313008	PT5520-5530	Dutch fiction	839.81	PT7601-8260	Danish literature
839.313009	PT5320-5336	Dutch fiction	839.81071	PT7640-7644	Danish literature—Study and teaching
839.314008	PT5539	Dutch essays			
839.317008	PN6222.N	Dutch wit and humor	839.8109001	PT7721-7737	Danish literature—To 1500
839.317008	PT5541	Dutch wit and humor	839.810900 (4-5)	PT7741-7747	Danish literature—18th century
839.317009	PT5346	Dutch wit and humor			
839.31808	PT5517-5547	Dutch prose literature	839.8109006	PT7751-7756	Danish literature—19th century
839.31808	PT5300-5336	Dutch prose literature			
839.31808	PT6365-6397	Flemish prose literature	839.8109007	PT7760	Danish literature—20th century
839.36	PT6500-6593.36	Afrikaans literature			
839.361008	PT6560	Afrikaans poetry	839.811008	PT7975-7994	Danish poetry
839.361008	PT6545	Afrikaans poetry	839.811009	PT7770-7795	Danish poetry
839.361009	PT6515	Afrikaans poetry	839.812008	PT7999-8020	Danish drama
839.362008	PT6570	Afrikaans drama	839.812009	PT7800-7832	Danish drama
839.362009	PT6520	Afrikaans drama	839.813008	PT8022-8024	Danish fiction
839.363008	PT6570	Afrikaans fiction	839.813009	PT7835-7862	Danish fiction
839.363009	PT6525	Afrikaans fiction	839.816008	PT8030	Danish letters
839.367	PN6222.S	Afrikaans wit and humor	839.816009	PT7866	Danish letters
839.36808	PT6570	Afrikaans prose literature	839.81808	PT8021-8024	Danish prose literature
839.36808	PT6525	Afrikaans prose literature	839.81808	PT7835-7862	Danish prose literature
839.36808	PT6590	Afrikaans prose literature	839.82	PT8301-9155	Norwegian literature
839.4	PT4801-4897	Low German literature	839.82071	PT8340-8344	Norwegian literature— Study and teaching
839.4071	PT4803	Low German literature— Study and teaching			
			839.821008	PT8675-8695	Norwegian poetry
839.409001	PT4813	Low German literature— To 1500	839.821009	PT8460-8490	Norwegian poetry
			839.822008	PT8699-8718	Norwegian drama
839.41008	PT4834-4836	Low German poetry	839.822009	PT8500-8534	Norwegian drama
839.41009	PT4817-4820	Low German poetry	839.823008	PT8720-8722	Norwegian fiction
839.42008	PT4837-4838	Low German drama	839.823009	PT8555-8567	Norwegian fiction
839.42009	PT4821	Low German drama	839.82808	PT8719-8722	Norwegian prose literature
839.5	PT7001-9999	Scandinavian literature	839.82808	PT8540-8567	Norwegian prose literature
839.5071	PT7035-7039	Scandinavian literature— Study and teaching	839.83	PT9000-9094	Norwegian literature (Nynorsk)
839.6	PT7101-7338	Old Norse literature			

Dewey	LC	Subject Heading	Dewey	LC	Subject Heading
840	PQ3960-3979	Vietnamese literature (French)	849.104	PC3304-3330	Troubadours
840	PQ1-3999	French literature	849.9	PC3900-3976	Catalan literature
840	PQ3900-3919.2	French-Canadian literature	850	PQ4001-5999	Italian literature
840	PQ3809	French literature—Foreign countries	850.71	PQ4013-4023	Italian literature—Study and teaching
840	PQ3810-3858	Belgian literature (French)	850.9	PQ4001-4199	Italian literature—History and criticism
840	PQ3998.5.N	New Caledonian literature (French)	850.9003	PQ4075	Italian literature—15th century
840	PQ3980-3989.2	African literature (French)	850.9004	PQ4079-4080	Italian literature—16th century
840	PQ3870-3888	Swiss literature (French)			
840	PQ3940-3949	West Indian literature (French)	850.9005	PQ4081-4082	Italian literature—17th century
840.71	PQ51-65	French literature—Study and teaching	850.9006	PQ4083-4084	Italian literature—18th century
840.800(1-2)	PQ1300-1595	French literature—To 1500	850.9007	PQ4085-4086	Italian literature—19th century
840.8003	PQ1121-1125	French literature—16th century	850.90091	PQ4087	Italian literature—20th century
840.8004	PQ1126-1130	French literature—17th century	851.009	PQ4091-4131	Italian poetry
840.8005	PQ1131-1135	French literature—18th century	852.009	PQ4133-4160	Italian drama
			854.009	PQ4183.E8	Italian essays
840.8007	PQ1136-1139	French literature—19th century	856.009	PQ4183.L4	Italian letters
			857.00222	PC1300-1766	Wit and humor, Pictorial
840.80091	PQ1141	French literature—20th century	858.08	PQ4161-4185	Italian prose literature
			859	PC800-872	Romanian literature
840.802	PN6086-6089	Quotations, French	859.9	PC951-986	Raeto-Romance literature
840.900(1-2)	PQ151-221	French literature—To 1500	860	PQ7900-8098.36	Chilean literature
840.9003	PQ230-239	French literature—16th century	860	PQ7801-7820	Bolivian literature
			860	PQ8160-8180.36	Colombian literature
840.9004	PQ241-251	French literature—17th century	860	PQ8200-8220.36	Ecuadorian literature
			860	PQ7500-7509.2	Honduran literature
840.9005	PQ261-276	French literature—18th century	860	PQ7420-7440	Puerto Rican literature
			860	PQ7600-7798.36	Argentine literature
840.9007	PQ281-299	French literature—19th century	860	PQ7480-7489.2	Costa Rican literature
			860	PQ7530-7539.2	Salvadoran literature
840.90091	PQ301-307	French literature—20th century	860	PQ7520-7529.2	Panamanian literature
			860	PQ7510-7519.2	Nicaraguan literature
841.008	PQ1160-1193	French poetry	860	PQ7020-8921	Spanish literature—Foreign countries
841.009	PQ400-491	French poetry			
841.03209	PQ201-205	Epic literature, French	860	PQ7100-7298.36	Mexican literature
841.(1-2)08	PQ1300-1391	French poetry—To 1500	860	PQ7370-7390	Cuban literature
841.309	PQ416-418	French poetry—16th century	860	PQ7490-7499.2	Guatemalan literature
841.409	PQ421-423	French poetry—17th century	860	PQ7400-7409.2	Dominican literature
841.509	PQ426-428	French poetry—18th century	860	PQ6001-8929	Spanish literature
841.709	PQ431-439	French poetry—19th century	860	PQ8250-8259	Paraguayan literature
841.9109	PQ441-443	French poetry—20th century	860	PQ8700-8899	Philippine literature
842.008	PQ1211-1241	French drama	860	PQ8530-8550.36	Venezuelan literature
842.(1-2)08	PQ1341-1385	French drama—To 1500	860	PQ8510-8519	Uruguayan literature
843.008	PQ1261-1279	French fiction	860	PQ8300-8498.36	Peruvian literature
843.009	PQ631-671	French fiction	860.009	PQ6022-6167	Spanish literature—History and criticism
843.909	PQ671	French fiction—20th century			
845.008	PQ1281-1283	Speeches, addresses, etc., French	860.71	PQ6013-6020	Spanish literature—Study and teaching
848.02	PN6282	Epigrams, French	860.900(1-2)	PQ6057-6060	Spanish literature—To 1500
848.08	PQ151-216	French prose literature—To 1500	860.900(2-3)	PQ6063-6072	Spanish literature—Classical period, 1500-1700
848.08	PQ601-657	French prose literature	861	PQ8210	Ecuadorian poetry
848.08	PQ1243-1279	French prose literature	861	PQ8214-.5	Ecuadorian poetry
849	PC3381-3420.5	Langue d'oc literature	861.008	PQ7406	Dominican poetry
849	PC3301-3359	Provencal literature	861.008	PQ6174.95-6215	Spanish poetry

Dewey	LC	Subject Heading	Dewey	LC	Subject Heading
861.009	PQ6075-6098	Spanish poetry	880.8002	PA5170-5198	Byzantine literature
861.009	PQ7402	Dominican poetry	880.9	PA3520-3564	Greek literature—Criticism, Textual
862.008	PQ6217-6241	Spanish drama			
862.009	PQ6099-6129	Spanish drama	880.9	PA47	Criticism, Textual
863	PQ8216.F5	Ecuadorian fiction	880.9	PA3527	Greek literature, Hellenistic—Criticism, Textual
863	PQ8212	Ecuadorian fiction			
863.008	PQ6251-6257	Spanish fiction	880.9002	PA5101-5167	Byzantine literature
863.009	PQ6138-6147	Spanish fiction	881.009	PA3092-3125	Greek poetry
868.08	PQ6247-6264	Spanish prose literature	881.009	PA3537-3543	Greek poetry, Hellenistic—Criticism, Textual
868.08	PQ6131-6153	Spanish prose literature			
869	PQ9900-9948	African literature (Portuguese)	881.009	PA3019-3022	Classical poetry
869	PQ9421	Portuguese literature—Foreign countries	881.03208	PA3437-3439	Epic poetry, Greek
			881.03209	PA3105-3107.5	Epic poetry, Greek
869	PQ9450-9469.2	Galician literature	881.208	PA5180-5189	Byzantine poetry
869	PQ9000-9999	Portuguese literature	881.209	PA5150-5155	Byzantine poetry
869	PQ9500-9699	Brazilian literature	882	PA3461-3468	Greek drama
869.071	PQ9008-9009.5	Portuguese literature—Study and teaching	882.008	PA3461-3466	Classical drama
			882.009	PA3131-3239	Greek drama
869.1008	PQ9149-9163	Portuguese poetry	882.009	PA3024-3029	Classical drama—History and criticism
869.1009	PQ9061-9081	Portuguese poetry			
869.2008	PQ9164-9170	Portuguese drama	882.051208	PA3461-3463	Greek drama (Tragedy)
869.2009	PQ9083-9095	Portuguese drama	882.051209	PA3131-3159	Greek drama (Tragedy)
869.808	PQ9172-9188	Portuguese prose literature	882.052308	PA3465-3466	Greek drama (Comedy)
869.808	PQ9097-9119	Portuguese prose literature	882.052309	PA3161-3199	Greek drama (Comedy)
870.8001	PA6101-6139	Latin literature	882.208	PA5190-5194	Byzantine drama
870.9001	PA6001-6098	Latin literature—History and criticism	882.209	PA5160-5163	Byzantine drama
			885.008	PA3482	Funeral orations
870.900(3-4)	PA8001-8595	Latin literature, Medieval and modern	885.108	PA3479-3842	Oratory, Ancient
			888.08	PA5165	Byzantine prose literature
871.032108	PA6125	Epic poetry, Latin	888.08	PA3473-3475	Greek prose literature
871.108	PA6121-6135	Latin poetry	888.08	PA5195-5196	Byzantine prose literature
871.109	PA6045-6063	Latin poetry	888.08	PA3473-3475	Greek prose literature
871.(3-4)08	PA8120-8133	Latin poetry, Medieval and modern	888.08	PA3255-3273	Greek prose literature
871.(3-4)09	PA8050-8065	Latin poetry, Medieval and modern—History and criticism	888.08	PA5265	Greek prose literature, Modern
			889	PA5201-5660	Greek literature, Modern
871.6	PA2329-2340	Latin language—Metrics and rhythmics	889.08001	PA5301-5395	Greek literature, Modern—1453-1800
			889.09	PA5230-5269	Greek literature, Modern—History and criticism
872.108	PA6137	Latin drama			
872.109	PA6067-6075	Latin drama—History and criticism	889.1008	PA5280-5289	Greek poetry, Modern
			889.1009	PA5259-5255	Greek poetry, Modern
872.(3-4)08	PA8135-8140	Latin drama, Medieval and modern	889.2008	PA5290-5294	Greek drama, Modern
			889.2009	PA5260-5263	Greek drama, Modern
872.(3-4)09	PA8073-8079	Latin drama, Medieval and modern	889.309	PA401-407	Greek language—Style
			889.808	PA5295	Greek prose literature, Modern
878.08	PA8145-8149	Latin prose literature, Medieval and modern			
878.08	PA8081-8096	Latin prose literature, Medieval and modern	891.0099415	PR8761-8781	English poetry—Irish authors
			891.1	PK80-85	Indo-Iranian literature
878.08	PA6138-6139	Latin prose literature	891.2	PK3591-4485	Sanskrit literature
878.08	PA6081-6095.5	Latin prose literature—History and criticism	891.29	PK2911	Vedic literature
			891.308	PK5003-5009	Prakrit literature
			891.309	PK4990-5001.8	Prakrit literature
880	PA3051-4505	Greek literature	891.37	PK4501-4681	Pali literature
880	PA3081-3084	Greek literature, Hellenistic	891.43	PK2030-2142	Hindustani literature
880.01	PA3013	Classical literature—Appreciation	891.439	PK2030-2058	Urdu literature
			891.47	PK1850-1888	Gujarati literature
880.09	PA3001-3045	Classical literature—History and criticism	891.499	PK7031-7037	Kashmiri literature
			891.55	PK6400-6599	Persian literature
880.8	PA3301-3671	Classical literature	891.551009	PK6416-6420	Persian poetry
880.8	PA3300-3516	Greek literature	891.552009	PK6421-6422	Persian drama

Dewey	LC	Subject Heading	Dewey	LC	Subject Heading
891.55808	PK6443	Persian prose literature	894.23	PL410-419	Mongolian literature
891.55808	PK6423	Persian prose literature	894.35	PL201-272	Turkish literature
891.62	PB1306-1449	Irish literature	894.352008	PL237-238	Turkish drama
891.6208001	PB1321	Irish literature—To 1100	894.352009	PL221	Turkish drama
891.6208002	PB1322	Irish literature—Middle Irish, 1100-1550	894.387	PL65.T35-.T39	Tatar literature
			894.511	PH3001-3445	Hungarian literature
891.621009	PB1321	Fili (Irish poets)	894.54109	PH300-405	Finnish literature
891.63	PB1605-1709	Gaelic literature	894.545	PH630-671	Estonian literature
891.64	PB1851-1867	Manx literature	894.55	PH731-735	Lapp literature
891.66	PB2206-2499	Welsh literature	894.56	PH781-785	Mordvin literature
891.67	PB2551-2621	Cornish literature	895	PJ306-489	Oriental literature
891.68	PB2856-2932	Breton literature	895	PL491-494	East Asian literature
891.7	PG2900-3580	Russian literature	895.1	PL2250-3207	Chinese literature
891.708004	PN849.R9-.R92	Soviet literature	895.10900 (2-3)	PL2283	Chinese literature—221 B.C.-960 A.D.
891.79	PG3900-3987	Ukrainian literature			
891.8	PG500-585	Slavic literature	895.109002	PL2285	Chinese literature—Three kingdoms, 220-265
891.81	PG700-716	Church Slavic literature			
891.8109	PG1000-1146	Bulgarian literature	895.109002	PL2284.5	Chinese literature—220-589
891.821008	PG1654-.5	Dalmatian poetry	895.109002	PL2287	Chinese literature—Liu Sung dynasty, 420-479
891.821009	PG1650-.5	Dalmatian poetry			
891.84	PG1900-1962	Slovenian literature	895.109002	PL2286	Chinese literature—Chin dynasty, 265-419
891.85	PG7001-7446	Polish literature			
891.86	PG5000-5146	Czech literature	895.1090024	PL2290	Chinese literature—Sui dynasty, 581-618
891.87	PG5400-5546	Slovak literature			
891.88	PG5661-5698	Sorbian literature	895.1090044	PL2294	Chinese literature—Yuan dynasty, 1260-1368
891.92	PG8701-8772	Lithuanian literature			
891.93	PG8998-9146	Latvian literature	895.1090046	PL2296	Chinese literature—Ming dynasty, 1368-1644
891.991	PG9601-9665	Albanian literature			
891.992	PK8501-8835	Armenian literature	895.1090048	PL2297	Chinese literature—Ch'ing dynasty, 1644-1912
891.992	PK8601-8661	Armenian literature—Europe			
			895.11008	PL2517-2565.8	Chinese poetry
891.992	PK8681-8689	Armenian literature—United States	895.11009	PL2306-2355.8	Chinese poetry
			895.1109	PL2280	Chinese literature—To 221 B.C.
892.009	PJ3097	Semitic literature			
892.1	PJ3601-3953	Assyro-Babylonian literature	895.12008	PL2566-2603	Chinese drama
892.3	PJ5601-5695	Syriac literature	895.12009	PL2356-2393	Chinese drama
892.4	PJ5001-5060	Hebrew literature	895.13008	PL2625-2653	Chinese fiction
892.4071	PJ5007	Hebrew literature—Study and teaching	895.13009	PL2415-2443	Chinese fiction
			895.14008	PL2606-2623	Chinese essays
892.408002	PJ5037	Hebrew literature, Medieval	895.14009	PL2395-2413	Chinese essays
892.408003	PJ5038	Hebrew literature, Modern	895.2008	PJ371	Oriental drama
892.409002	PJ5016	Hebrew literature, Medieval	895.4	PL3701-3775	Tibetan literature
892.409003	PJ5017-5021	Hebrew literature, Modern	895.408	PL772-.83	Japanese essays
892.7	PJ8500-8517	Arabic literature—America	895.6	PL700-889	Japanese literature
892.7	PJ8195-8390	Arabic literature—Africa	895.6009	PL742-.83	Japanese essays
892.7	PJ8030-8129	Arabic literature—Middle East	895.608	PL755.12	Japanese literature
			895.608002	PL790-792	Japanese literature—1185-1600
892.7	PJ8025-8190	Arabic literature—Asia			
892.7	PJ8395-8490	Arabic literature—Europe	895.608003	PL793-799	Japanese literature—Edo period, 1600-1868
892.7	PJ7501-8518	Arabic literature			
892.71008	PJ7631-7661	Arabic poetry	895.6080042	PL800-820	Japanese literature—Meiji period, 1868-1912
892.71009	PJ7541-7561	Arabic poetry			
892.72008	PJ7665	Arabic drama	895.60800 (44-5)	PL821-866	Japanese literature—Showa period, 1926-1989
892.72009	PJ7565	Arabic drama			
892.7808	PJ7671-7677	Arabic prose literature	895.609001	PL726.12	Japanese literature—To 794
892.7808	PJ7571-7577	Arabic prose literature	895.609001	PL726.1185-.1186	Japanese literature—To 1185
892.81	PJ9090-9101	Ethiopic literature			
893.1	PJ1481-1989	Egyptian literature	895.61008	PL757-763	Japanese poetry
893.12	PJ1571	Egyptian drama	895.61009	PL727-733	Japanese poetry
893.13	PJ1487	Egyptian fiction	895.6108001	PL787-789	Japanese literature—Heian period, 794-1185
893.2	PJ2190-2199	Coptic literature			

Dewey	LC	Subject Heading	Dewey	LC	Subject Heading
895.62008	PL764-769	Japanese drama	907.202	D14-15	Historians
895.62009	PL734-739	Japanese drama	909	D31-34	World politics
895.63008	PL770-777	Japanese fiction	909	CB	Civilization
895.63009	PL740-747	Japanese fiction	909	HM101	Civilization
895.7	PL950-998	Korean literature	909	D17-24.5	World history
895.71008	PL974-976.4	Korean poetry	909	CB481	War and civilization
895.71009	PL959-961.4	Korean poetry	909.04	CB195-281	Race
895.72008	PL977-979	Korean drama	909.0491497	DX	Gypsies
895.72009	PL962-964	Korean drama	909.0491497	DX135-145	Gypsies—History
895.73008	PL980-981.5	Korean fiction	909.04924	BS649.J5	Jews—Restoration
895.73009	PL965-967	Korean fiction	909.07	CB351-355	Civilization, Medieval
895.8	PL3970-3988	Burmese literature	909.07	CB351-355	Middle Ages
895.911	PL4200-4209	Thai literature	909.07	D111-203	Middle Ages—History
895.922	PL4378	Vietnamese literature	909.07	D151-173	Crusades
896	PL8010-8014	African literature	909.07	D161-.5	Crusades—First, 1096-1099
896.34	PL8123.5-.9	Dan literature			
899	PN849.026	Pacific Island literature	909.07	D162-.5	Crusades—Second, 1147-1149
899.21	PL5530-5547	Philippine literature			
899.211	PL6058	Tagalog literature	909.07	D163-.5	Crusades—Third, 1189-1192
899.222	PL5170-5179	Javanese literature			
899.92	PH5280-5490	Basque literature	909.07	D164-.5	Crusades—Fourth, 1202-1204
899.95	PJ4045-4083	Sumerian literature			
899.9623	PK9201.A35-.A39	Abkhaz literature	909.07	D165	Crusades—Fifth, 1218-1221
899.9624	PK9201.K35-.K39	Kabardian literature			
899.9625	PK9201.A45-.A49	Adygei literature	909.07	D166	Crusades—Sixth, 1228-1229
899.964	PK9201.D35-.D39	Dargwa literature			
899.964	PK9051.5-.8	Daghestan literature	909.07	D167	Crusades—Seventh, 1248-1250
899.969	PK9160-9169	Georgian literature			
900	D11-.5	Chronology, Historical	909.07	D168	Crusades—Eighth, 1270
900	C	Auxiliary sciences of history	909.07	D171-173	Crusades—Later, 13th, 14th, and 15th centuries
900	D	History			
901	CB19	Civilization—Philosophy	909.07	CB351-369	Renaissance
901	D16.9	Historicism	909.07072	D156.58	Crusades—Historiography
901	D16.7-.9	History—Philosophy	909.07092	D156-.5	Crusades—Biography
901	D16-.18	History—Methodology	909.07	CB351-369	Renaissance
901.9	D16.16	Psychohistory	909.08	D101-110.5	History, Modern
902.22	CB13	Civilization—Pictoral works	909.08	D839-850	History, Modern—1945-
902.28	D16	Historical models	909.08	CB357-430	Civilization, Modern
903	CB9	Civilization—Dictionaries	909.0803	D205	History, Modern—Dictionaries
903	D9	History—Dictionaries			
904	CT9970-9971	Adventure and adventurers	909.08072	D206	Historiography
904	G521-539	Adventure and adventurers	909.0971241	DA10-18.2	Commonwealth countries—History
904	PN4784.D57	Disasters in the press			
905	D1	History—Periodicals	909.09724	D880-888	Developing countries—History
905	C4	Auxiliary sciences of history—Periodicals			
			909.0974927	DS36-39.2	Arab countries
905	CB3	Civilization—Periodicals	909.0974927	DS36.77-.88	Civilization, Arab
906	D3	History—Congresses	909.0974927	DS37-39.2	Arab countries—History
906	C3	Auxiliary sciences of history—Congresses	909.0974927	DS36.77-.88	Arab countries—Civilization
			909.09749270 (5-821)	DS38.8	Arab countries—History—1517-1918
906	C2	Auxiliary sciences of history—Societies, etc.			
			909.097492708	DS38.9	Arab countries—History—1798-
907.1	C20	Auxiliary sciences of history—Study and teaching			
			909.0974927082	DS39	Arab countries—History—20th century
907.1	CB20	Civilization—Study and teaching			
			909.09749270821	DS39	Arab countries—History—Arab Revolt, 1916-1918
907.1	D16.2-.5	History—Study and teaching			
907.2	CB15-18	Civilization—Historiography	909.097645	DS423-425	Civilization, Hindu
907.2	D13-15	Historiography	909.097671	DS35.62	Civilization, Islamic
907.201822	DE8-9	Mediterranean Region—Historiography	909.09811	D890-893	Eastern Hemisphere—History

195

Dewey	LC	Subject Heading	Dewey	LC	Subject Heading
909.09812	CB245	Civilization, Western	912.1962	G1059-1061	Nautical charts
909.1	CB353	Twelfth century	912.1963	G2805-2839	Atlantic Ocean—Maps
909.5	D219-234	History, Modern—16th century	912.19632	G3055-3064	Arctic Ocean—Maps
			912.1964	G2860-2867	Pacific Ocean—Maps
909.5	CB367-401	Sixteenth century	912.19811	G1780-2799	Eastern Hemisphere—Maps
909.6	D242-283.5	History, Modern—17th century	912.19812	G1100-1779	Western Hemisphere—Maps
			912.19813	G1050	Northern Hemisphere—Maps
909.81	CB415-417	Nineteenth century			
909.82	CB425-430	Twentieth century	912.19813	G3210-3212	Northern Hemisphere—Maps
909.82	D410-893	History, Modern—20th century	912.19814	G1052	Southern Hemisphere—Maps
909.8(24-3)05	D839	History, Modern—1945- —Periodicals	912.19814	G3220-3222	Southern Hemisphere—Maps
910	G-GF	Geography	912.4	G5700-7153	Europe—Maps
910	GN476.4	Geography	912.41	G1805-1829.24	Great Britain—Maps
910	G149-922	Voyages and travels	912.41	G5740-5814	Great Britain—Maps
910	G149-180	Travel	912.411	G5770-5774	Scotland—Maps
910.01	G70-.4	Geography—Methodology	912.415	G5780-5784	Ireland—Maps
910.02	GB	Physical geography	912.416	G5790-5794	Northern Ireland—Maps
910.0211	G575-597	Polar regions	912.42	G5750-5754	England—Maps
910.0213	G905-910	Tropics	912.429	G5760-5764	Wales—Maps
910.0216327	G640-665	Northwest Passage	912.43	G1907-1924	Germany—Maps
910.021732	GF125	Urban geography	912.43	G6080-6428	Germany—Maps
910.021734	GF127	Rural geography	912.436	G1935-1939	Austria—Maps
910.021811	G680-700	Eastern Hemisphere	912.436	G6490-6494	Austria—Maps
910.021813	G912-916	Northern Hemisphere	912.43648	G6050-6054	Liechtenstein—Maps
910.021814	G918-922	Southern Hemisphere	912.437	G1945-1949	Czechoslovakia—Maps
910.202	G153	Travel—Guidebooks	912.437	G6510-6514	Czechoslovakia—Maps
910.21	G109-110	Distances—Tables	912.438	G1950-1954	Poland—Maps
910.41	G420-445	Voyages around the world	912.438	G6520-6524	Poland—Maps
910.41	G445	Flights around the world	912.439	G1940-1944	Hungary—Maps
910.45	G545	Whaling	912.439	G6500-6504	Hungary—Maps
910.45	G540-550	Ocean travel	912.44	G1837-1844.24	France—Maps
910.45	G540-550	Seafaring life	912.44	G5830-5834	France—Maps
910.45092	G535-537	Pirates	912.44949	G5980-5984	Monaco—Maps
910.45092	G535-537	Buccaneers	912.45	G1983-1989.53	Italy—Maps
910.45092	F2161	Buccaneers	912.45	G6710-6714	Italy—Maps
910.452	G521-539	Shipwrecks	912.458	G6760-6763	Sicily (Italy)—Maps
910.6	G2-55	Geography—Societies, etc.	912.46	G1965-1969	Spain—Maps
910.71	G72-76.5	Geography—Study and teaching	912.46	G6560-6564	Spain—Maps
910.83	G156.5.Y6	Youth—Travel	912.469	G1975-1979	Portugal—Maps
910.9	G200-336	Discoveries in geography	912.469	G6690-6694	Portugal—Maps
910.9	G80-99	Geography—History	912.4698	G9140-9144	Madeira Islands—Maps
910.92	G200-336	Travelers	912.4699	G9130-9134	Azores—Maps
910.92	G67-69	Geographers—Biography	912.47	G2110-2193	Russia—Maps
911	G141	Historical geography	912.47	G7060-7342	Russia—Maps
911.0902	G89-95	Geography, Medieval	912.4796	G7040-7043	Latvia—Maps
911.4	G1791-1799	Europe—Historical geography—Maps	912.4798	G7030-7033	Estonia—Maps
			912.48	G6910-6963	Scandinavia—Maps
911.41	G5741	Great Britain—Historical geography—Maps	912.481	G2065-2069	Norway—Maps
			912.481	G6940-6944	Norway—Maps
911.73	G3701	United States—Historical geography—Maps	912.485	G2070-2074	Sweden—Maps
			912.485	G6950-6954	Sweden—Maps
912	G1001-1046	World maps	912.489	G2055-2059	Denmark—Maps
912	G3200-9980	Maps	912.489	G6920-6924	Denmark—Maps
912	GA101-130	Outline maps	912.4897	G2075-2079	Finland—Maps
912.191	G1054-1055	Polar regions—Maps	912.4897	G6960-6964	Finland—Maps
912.191	G3260-3272	Polar regions—Maps	912.4912	G2060-2064	Iceland—Maps
912.193	G1053	Tropics—Maps	912.4912	G6930-6934	Iceland—Maps
912.193	G3240-3241	Tropics—Maps	912.492	G1850-1874	Benelux countries

Dewey	LC	Subject Heading	Dewey	LC	Subject Heading
912.492	G6000-6004	Netherlands—Maps	912.5691	G7460-7464	Syria—Maps
912.493	G6010-6014	Belgium—Maps	912.5692	G2225-2229	Lebanon—Maps
912.4935	G6020-6024	Luxemburg—Maps	912.5692	G7470-7474	Lebanon—Maps
912.494	G1895-1899	Switzerland—Maps	912.5693	G7450-7454	Cyprus—Maps
912.494	G6040-6044	Switzerland—Maps	912.5693	G2215-2219	Cyprus—Maps
912.4947	G6035-6036	Alps—Maps	912.5694	G7500-7504	Israel—Maps
912.495	G2000-2004	Greece—Maps	912.5694	G2235-2239	Israel—Maps
912.495	G6810-6814	Greece—Maps	912.5695	G7510-7514	Jordan—Maps
912.4965	G2005-2009	Albania—Maps	912.5695	G2240-2244	Jordan—Maps
912.497	G6840-6844	Yugoslavia—Maps	912.581	G7630-7634	Afghanistan—Maps
912.4971	G2015-2017	Serbia—Maps	912.581	G2265-2269	Afghanistan—Maps
912.4971	G6850-6853	Serbia—Maps	912.59	G8000-8198.54	Indochina—Maps
912.4972	G2030-2032	Croatia—Maps	912.591	G2285-2289	Burma—Maps
912.4972	G6870-6873	Croatia—Maps	912.591	G7720-7724	Burma—Maps
912.4972	G2025-2027	Dalmatia (Croatia)—Maps	912.593	G2375-2379	Thailand—Maps
912.4973	G6875-6878	Slovenia—Maps	912.593	G8025-8029	Thailand—Maps
912.49742	G6860-6863	Bosnia and Hercegovina—Maps	912.594	G2374.5-.54	Laos—Maps
			912.594	G8015-8019	Laos—Maps
912.49745	G2020-2022	Montenegro—Maps	912.595	G8030-8034	Malaysia—Maps
912.498	G2035-2039	Romania—Maps	912.5957	G8040-8044	Singapore—Maps
912.498	G6880-6884	Romania—Maps	912.596	G2374.3-.34	Cambodia—Maps
912.499	G2040-2044	Bulgaria—Maps	912.596	G8010-8014	Cambodia—Maps
912.499	G6890-6894	Bulgaria—Maps	912.597	G2370-2374	Vietnam—Maps
912.5	G7400-8198.54	Asia—Maps	912.597	G8020-8024	Vietnam—Maps
912.5	G2200-2444	Asia—Maps	912.598	G8070-8074	Indonesia—Maps
912.51	G2305-2321	China—Maps	912.599	G8060-8064	Philippines—Maps
912.51	G7820-7824	China—Maps	912.6	G2445-2739	Africa—Maps
912.51249	G2340-2344	Taiwan—Maps	912.6	G8200-8202	Africa—Maps
912.5125	G7940-7944	Hong Kong—Maps	912.61	G2455-2499	Africa, North—Maps
912.5126	G7945-7947	Macao—Maps	912.61	G8220-8222	Africa, North—Maps
912.517	G7895-7899	Mongolia—Maps	912.611	G8250-8254	Tunisia—Maps
912.519	G2330-2334.34	Korea—Maps	912.612	G8260-8264	Libya—Maps
912.52	G2355-2359	Japan—Maps	912.62	G8300-8304	Egypt—Maps
912.52	G7960-7964	Japan—Maps	912.63	G8330-8334	Ethiopia—Maps
912.533	G7550-7554	Yemen—Maps	912.64	G8230-8234	Morocco—Maps
912.5353	G7560-7564	Oman—Maps	912.649	G9150-9154	Canary Islands—Maps
912.5363	G7580-7584	Qatar—Maps	912.65	G8240-8244	Algeria—Maps
912.5365	G7590-7594	Bahrain—Maps	912.66	G2640-2714	Africa, West—Maps
912.5367	G7600-7604	Kuwait—Maps	912.661	G8820-8824	Mauritania—Maps
912.538	G2249.3-.34	Saudi Arabia—Maps	912.6623	G8800-8804	Mali—Maps
912.538	G7530-7534	Saudi Arabia—Maps	912.6625	G8805-8809	Burkina Faso—Maps
912.54	G7650-7654	India—Maps	912.6626	G8770-8774	Niger—Maps
912.54	G2280-2284	India—Maps	912.663	G8810-8814	Senegal—Maps
912.5491	G7640-7644	Pakistan—Maps	912.664	G8860-8864	Sierra Leone—Maps
912.5491	G2270-2274	Pakistan—Maps	912.6651	G8870-8874	Gambia—Maps
912.5492	G7645-7649	Bangladesh—Maps	912.6652	G8790-8794	Guinea—Maps
912.5492	G2275-2279	Bangladesh—Maps	912.6657	G8890-8894	Guinea-Bissau—Maps
912.5493	G2290-2294	Sri Lanka—Maps	912.6658	G9160-9164	Cape Verde—Maps
912.5493	G7750-7754	Sri Lanka—Maps	912.6662	G8880-8884	Liberia—Maps
912.5495	G9215-9219	Maldives—Maps	912.6668	G8780-8784	Cote d'Ivoire—Maps
912.5496	G7760-7764	Nepal—Maps	912.667	G8850-8854	Ghana—Maps
912.5496	G2295-2299	Nepal—Maps	912.6681	G8760-8764	Togo—Maps
912.5498	G7780-7784	Bhutan—Maps	912.6683	G8750-8754	Benin—Maps
912.55	G2255-2259	Iran—Maps	912.669	G8840-8844	Nigeria—Maps
912.55	G7620-7624	Iran—Maps	912.67	G2590-2639	Africa, Central—Maps
912.56	G7420-7624	Middle East—Maps	912.6711	G8730-8734	Cameroon—Maps
912.561	G2210-2214	Turkey—Maps	912.6715	G8675-8679	Sao Tome and Principe
912.561	G7430-7434	Turkey—Maps	912.6718	G8660-8664	Equatorial Guinea—Maps
912.567	G7610-7614	Iraq—Maps	912.6721	G8690-8694	Gabon—Maps
912.567	G2250-2254	Iraq—Maps	912.6724	G8700-8704	Congo (Brazzaville)—Maps
912.5691	G2220-2224	Syria—Maps	912.673	G8640-8644	Angola—Maps

Dewey	LC	Subject Heading	Dewey	LC	Subject Heading
912.6741	G8710-8714	Central African Republic—Maps	912.729	G4390-4392	Caribbean Area—Maps
			912.7291	G4920-4924	Cuba—Maps
912.6743	G8720-8724	Chad—Maps	912.7292	G4960-4964	Jamaica—Maps
912.6751	G8650-8654	Zaire—Maps	912.72921	G4965-4969	Cayman Islands—Maps
912.67571	G8430-8434	Rwanda—Maps	912.7293	G4950-4954	Dominican Republic—Maps
912.67572	G8435-8439	Burundi—Maps	912.7294	G4940-4944	Haiti—Maps
912.676	G2500-2559	Africa, East—Maps	912.7295	G4970-4974	Puerto Rico—Maps
912.6761	G8420-8424	Uganda—Maps	912.7296	G4980-4984	Bahamas—Maps
912.6762	G8410-8414	Kenya—Maps	912.7297	G5030-5059	Leeward Islands (West Indies)—Maps
912.6773	G8350-8354	Somalia—Maps			
912.678	G8440-8444	Tanzania—Maps	912.729722	G5010-5014	Virgin Islands of the United States—Maps
912.679	G8450-8454	Mozambique—Maps			
912.68	G8500-8504	South Africa—Maps	912.729725	G5020-5024	British Virgin Islands—Maps
912.682	G8540-8543	Transvaal—Maps	912.72973	G5040-5044	Saint Kitts (Island)—Maps
912.684	G8530-8533	Natal (South Africa)—Maps	912.72973	G5045-5049	Anguilla—Maps
912.6881	G8620-8624	Namibia—Maps	912.72974	G5050-5054	Antigua—Maps
912.6883	G8600-8604	Botswana—Maps	912.72975	G5055-5059	Montserrat—Maps
912.6885	G8580-8584	Lesotho—Maps	912.72976	G5070-5074	Guadeloupe—Maps
912.6887	G8590-8594	Swaziland—Maps	912.72981	G5140-5144	Barbados—Maps
912.6897	G8610-8614	Malawi—Maps	912.72982	G5080-5084	Martinique—Maps
912.691	G8460-8464	Madagascar—Maps	912.72983	G5150-5162	Trinidad and Tobago—Maps
912.694	G9210-9214	Comoro Islands—Maps	912.72984	G5090-5184	Windward Islands—Maps
912.696	G9200-9204	Seychelles—Maps	912.729841	G5100-5104	Dominica—Maps
912.6981	G9190-9194	Reunion—Maps	912.729843	G5110-5114	Saint Lucia—Maps
912.6982	G9185-9189	Mauritius—Maps	912.729844	G5120-5124	Saint Vincent—Maps
912.7	G1105-1692	North America—Maps	912.729845	G5130-5134	Granada—Maps
912.7	G3300-4884	North America—Maps	912.72986	G5170-5174	Aruba—Maps
912.7	G3290-5669	America—Maps	912.72986	G5175-5179	Bonaire—Maps
912.71	G1115-1193	Canada—Maps	912.72986	G5180-5184	Curacao—Maps
912.71	G3400-3612	Canada—Maps	912.73	G1200-1534.24	United States—Maps
912.711	G3510-3514	British Columbia—Maps	912.73	G3690-4383	United States—Maps
912.712	G3470-3504	Prairie Provinces—Maps	912.73	G3690-3691	United States—Territories and possessions—Maps
912.7123	G3500-3504	Alberta—Maps			
912.7124	G3490-3494	Saskatchewan—Maps	912.7(4-5)	G3709.3-3933	Atlantic States—Maps
912.7127	G3480-3484	Manitoba—Maps	912.74	G3720-3784	New England—Maps
912.713	G3460-3464	Ontario—Maps	912.74	G3790-3854	Middle Atlantic States—Maps
912.714	G3450-3454	Quebec (Province)—Maps			
912.715	G3410-3444	Maritime Provinces—Maps	912.741	G3730-3734	Maine—Maps
912.7151	G3430-3434	New Brunswick—Maps	912.742	G3740-3744	New Hampshire—Maps
912.716	G3420-3424	Nova Scotia—Maps	912.743	G3750-3754	Vermont—Maps
912.717	G3440-3444	Prince Edward Islands—Maps	912.744	G3760-3764	Massachusetts—Maps
			912.745	G3770-3774	Rhode Island—Maps
912.718	G3600-3604	Newfoundland—Maps	912.746	G3780-3784	Connecticut—Maps
912.7182	G3610-3612	Labrador (Nfld.)—Maps	912.747	G3800-3804	New York (State)—Maps
912.7191	G3520-3524	Yukon Territory—Maps	912.748	G3820-3824	Pennsylvania—Maps
912.7192	G3530-3564	Northwest Territories—Maps	912.749	G3810-3814	New Jersey—Maps
			912.75	G3870-3933	South Atlantic States—Maps
912.72	G1545-1549	Mexico—Maps			
912.72	G4410-4414	Mexico—Maps	912.751	G3830-3834	Delaware—Maps
912.728	G1550-1594	Central America—Maps	912.752	G3840-3844	Maryland—Maps
912.728	G4800-4884	Central America—Maps	912.753	G3850-3854	Washington (D.C.)—Maps
912.7281	G4810-4814	Guatemala—Maps	912.754	G3890-3894	West Virginia—Maps
912.7282	G4820-4824	Belize—Maps	912.755	G3880-3884	Virginia—Maps
912.7283	G4830-4834	Honduras—Maps	912.756	G3900-3904	North Carolina—Maps
912.7284	G4840-4844	El Salvador—Maps	912.757	G3910-3914	South Carolina—Maps
912.7285	G4850-4854	Nicaragua—Maps	912.758	G3920-3924	Georgia—Maps
912.7286	G4860-4864	Costa Rica—Maps	912.759	G3930-3934	Florida—Maps
912.7287	G4870-4874	Panama—Maps	912.761	G3970-3974	Alabama—Maps
912.729	G1600-1692	West Indies—Maps	912.762	G3980-3984	Mississippi—Maps
912.729	G4900-5184	West Indies—Maps	912.763	G4010-4014	Louisiana—Maps
912.729	G1535-1537	Caribbean Area—Maps	912.764	G4030-4034	Texas—Maps

Dewey	LC	Subject Heading	Dewey	LC	Subject Heading
912.766	G4020-4024	Oklahoma—Maps	912.9616	G9515-9517	Wallis and Futuna Islands—Maps
912.767	G4000-4004	Arkansas—Maps			
912.768	G3960-3964	Tennessee—Maps	912.9618	G9660-9664	Pitcairn Island—Maps
912.769	G3950-3954	Kentucky—Maps	912.9621	G9640-9644	Society Islands—Maps
912.771	G4080-4084	Ohio—Maps	912.9623	G9600-9604	Cook Islands—Maps
912.772	G4090-4094	Indiana—Maps	912.9631	G9620-9624	Marquesas Islands—Maps
912.773	G4100-4104	Illinois—Maps	912.964	G9530-9534	Line Islands—Maps
912.774	G4110-4114	Michigan—Maps	912.965	G2905-2934	Micronesia—Maps
912.775	G4120-4124	Wisconsin—Maps	912.965	G9400-9494	Micronesia—Maps
912.776	G4140-4144	Minnesota—Maps	912.966	G9420-9424	Caroline Islands—Maps
912.777	G4150-4154	Iowa—Maps	912.967	G9410-9414	Mariana Islands—Maps
912.778	G4160-4164	Missouri—Maps	912.9681	G9480-9484	Kiribati—Maps
912.78	G4050-4052	West (U.S.)—Maps	912.9683	G9460-9464	Marshall Islands—Maps
912.781	G4200-4204	Kansas—Maps	912.969	G4380-4384	Hawaii—Maps
912.782	G4190-4194	Nebraska—Maps	912.9711	G9175-9179	Falkland Islands—Maps
912.783	G4180-4184	South Dakota—Maps	912.973	G9170-9174	Saint Helena—Maps
912.784	G4170-4174	North Dakota—Maps	912.982	G1110-1114	Greenland—Maps
912.786	G4250-4254	Montana—Maps	912.982	G3380-3384	Greenland—Maps
912.787	G4260-4264	Wyoming—Maps	912.989	G9800-9804	Antarctica—Maps
912.788	G4310-4314	Colorado—Maps	912.989	G3100-3102	Antarctica—Maps
912.789	G4320-4324	New Mexico—Maps	912.991	G1000.3-.5	Moon—Maps
912.79	G4230-4232	Pacific States—Maps	912.991	G3195-3199	Moon—Maps
912.791	G4330-4334	Arizona—Maps	913	G83-88	Geography, Ancient
912.792	G4340-4344	Utah—Maps	913.104	DS707-712	China—Description and travel
912.793	G4350-4354	Nevada—Maps			
912.794	G4360-4364	California—Maps	913.104	DS799.15-.24	Taiwan—Description and travel
912.795	G4290-4294	Oregon—Maps			
912.796	G4270-4274	Idaho—Maps	913.2003	DT45	Egypt—Gazetteers
912.797	G4280-4284	Washington (State)—Maps	913.204	DT49.98-56	Egypt—Description and travel
912.798	G4370-4374	Alaska—Maps			
912.8	G1700-1779	South America—Maps	913.304	DS103-108.5	Israel—Description and travel
912.8	G5200-5668	South America—Maps			
912.81	G5400-5404	Brazil—Maps	913.304	DS153.2	Jordan—Description and travel
912.82	G5350-5354	Argentina—Maps			
912.83	G5330-5334	Chile—Maps	913.404	DS377	Pakistan—Description and travel
912.84	G5320-5324	Bolivia—Maps			
912.85	G5310-5314	Peru—Maps	913.5003	DS253	Iran—Gazetteers
912.861	G5290-5294	Colombia—Maps	913.5003	DS67.8	Iraq—Gazetteers
912.866	G5300-5304	Ecuador—Maps	913.504	DS255-259.2	Iran—Description and travel
912.87	G5280-5284	Venezuela—Maps	913.6104	DA969-988	Ireland—Description and travel
912.881	G5250-5254	Guyana—Maps			
912.882	G5270-5274	French Guiana—Maps	913.6204	DA600-632	England—Description and travel
912.883	G5260-5264	Surinam—Maps			
912.892	G5380-5384	Paraguay—Maps	913.63003	DD14	Germany—Gazetteers
912.895	G5370-5374	Uruguay—Maps	913.63003	DD308	Prussia (Germany)—Gazetteers
912.93	G9080-9084	New Zealand—Maps			
912.93	G2795-2799	New Zealand—Maps	913.63003	DB14	Austria—Gazetteers
912.94	G2750-2793	Australia—Maps	913.63003	DL4	Scandinavia—Gazetteers
912.94	G8960-8964	Australia—Maps	913.63003	DL405	Norway—Gazetteers
912.95	G8140-8142	New Guinea—Maps	913.63003	DL605	Sweden—Gazetteers
912.95	G2870-2894	Melanesia—Maps	913.63003	DL105	Denmark—Gazetteers
912.95	G9260-9262	Melanesia—Maps	913.63003	DJ14	Netherlands—Gazetteers
912.9593	G9280-9284	Solomon Islands—Maps	913.63003	DH14	Netherlands—Gazetteers
912.9595	G9295-9297	Vanuatu—Maps	913.6304	DD21.5-43	Germany—Description and travel
912.9597	G9340-9344	New Caledonia—Maps			
912.96	G9500-9652	Polynesia—Maps	913.6304	DD314-320	Prussia (Germany)—Description and travel
912.96	G2970-2984	Polynesia—Maps			
912.9611	G9380-9384	Fiji—Maps	913.6304	DB21-27.5	Austria—Description and travel
912.9612	G9570-9574	Tonga—Maps			
912.961(3-4)	G9555-9557	Samoan Islands—Maps	913.6304	DB888	Liechtenstein—Description and travel
912.9615	G9550-9554	Tokelau Islands—Maps			

Dewey	LC	Subject Heading	Dewey	LC	Subject Heading
913.6304	DL6.7-11.5	Scandinavia—Description and travel	913.973003	DT244	Tunisia—Gazetteers
913.6304	DL415-419.2	Norway—Description and travel	913.97304	DT248-250.2	Tunisia—Description and travel
913.6304	DL614.55-619.5	Sweden—Description and travel	913.97404	DT218-220.2	Libya—Description and travel
913.6304	DL115-120	Denmark—Description and travel	913.98003	DB904	Hungary—Gazetteers
913.6304	DJ33-41	Netherlands—Description and travel	913.98003	DR907	Albania—Gazetteers
			913.98003	DR1209	Yugoslavia—Gazetteers
			913.98003	DR204	Romania—Gazetteers
913.6304	DH31-40	Netherlands—Description and travel	913.98003	DR53	Bulgaria—Gazetteers
			913.9804	DB906.9-917.3	Hungary—Description and travel
913.64003	DC14	France—Gazetteers	913.9804	DR914-918	Albania—Description and travel
913.64003	DH414	Belgium—Gazetteers			
913.64003	DQ14	Switzerland—Gazetteers	913.9804	DR1218-1224	Yugoslavia—Description and travel
913.6404	DC21-29.3	France—Description and travel	913.9804	DR207-210	Romania—Description and travel
913.6404	DH431-435	Belgium—Description and travel	913.9804	DR57-61	Bulgaria—Description and travel
913.6404	DQ20-26	Switzerland—Description and travel	914	D901-980	Europe—Description and travel
913.66003	DP12	Spain—Gazetteers	914.1104	DA850-878	Scotland—Description and travel
913.66003	DP514	Portugal—Gazetteers			
913.6604	DP27-43.2	Spain—Description and travel	914.1504	DA969-988	Ireland—Description and travel
913.6604	DP520-526.5	Portugal—Description and travel	914.2003	DA640	Great Britain—Gazetteers
913.(7-8)	DE23-31	Classical geography	914.204	DA600-632	England—Description and travel
913.(7-8)	G87	Classical geography			
913.7	DG27-31	Rome—Geography	914.2904	DA725-731.2	Wales—Description and travel
913.7003	DG415	Italy—Gazetteers			
913.704	DG421.5-430.2	Italy—Description and travel	914.3003	DD308	Prussia (Germany)—Gazetteers
913.804	DF27-30	Greece—Description and travel	914.3003	DD14	Germany—Gazetteers
			914.304	DD314-320	Prussia (Germany)—Description and travel
913.9204	DR421-429.4	Turkey—Description and travel	914.304	DD21.5-43	Germany—Description and travel
913.93704	DS54.A4-Z	Cyprus—Description and travel	914.304	DAW1014-1015	Europe, Central—Description and travel
913.94003	DS43	Middle East—Gazetteers	914.36003	DB14	Austria—Gazetteers
913.9404	DS44.98-49.7	Middle East—Description and travel	914.3604	DB21-27.5	Austria—Description and travel
913.943003	DS92.6	Syria—Gazetteers			
913.94304	DS94	Syria—Description and travel	914.364804	DB888	Liechtenstein—Description and travel
913.944003	DS80.A5	Lebanon—Gazetteers	914.37003	DB2007	Czechoslovakia—Gazetteers
913.94404	DS80.2	Lebanon—Description and travel	914.3704	DB2018-2022	Czechoslovakia—Description and travel
913.94904	DS204.5-208	Saudi Arabia—Description and travel	914.373003	DB2707	Slovakia—Gazetteers
913.96003	DS351	Afghanistan—Gazetteers	914.37304	DB2718-2722	Slovakia—Description and travel
913.9604	DS352	Afghanistan—Description and travel	914.38003	DK4030	Poland—Gazetteers
913.9704	DT163-165.2	Africa, North—Description and travel	914.3804	DK4047-4081	Poland—Description and travel
913.971003	DT304	Morocco—Gazetteers	914.39003	DB904	Hungary—Gazetteers
913.971003	DT274	Algeria—Gazetteers	914.3904	DB906.9-917.3	Hungary—Description and travel
913.97104	DT307-310.2	Morocco—Description and travel			
			914.4003	DC14	France—Gazetteers
913.97104	DT277.8-280.2	Algeria—Description and travel	914.404	DC21-29.3	France—Description and travel

Dewey	LC	Subject Heading
914.4040904	DC29	France—Description and travel—1945-1974
914.5003	DG415	Italy—Gazetteers
914.504	DG421.5-430.2	Italy—Description and travel
914.6003	DP12	Spain—Gazetteers
914.604	DP27-43.2	Spain—Description and travel
914.69003	DP514	Portugal—Gazetteers
914.6904	DP520-526.5	Portugal—Description and travel
914.70003	DJK6	Europe, Eastern—Gazetteers
914.7003	DK14	Russia—Gazetteers
914.704	DK19-29	Russia—Description and travel
914.7004	DJK11-18	Europe, Eastern—Description and travel
914.75604	DS165	Armenia—Description and travel
914.78003	DK507.18	Belarus—Gazetteers
914.793003	DK505.18	Lithuania—Gazetteers
914.796003	DK504.18	Latvia—Gazetteers
914.798003	DK503.18	Estonia—Gazetteers
914.8003	DL4	Scandinavia—Gazetteers
914.804	DL6.7-11.5	Scandinavia—Description and travel
914.81003	DL405	Norway—Gazetteers
914.8104	DL415-419.2	Norway—Description and travel
914.843	G778-787	Arctic regions—Norwegian
914.85003	DL605	Sweden—Gazetteers
914.8504	DL614.55-619.5	Sweden—Description and travel
914.89003	DL105	Denmark—Gazetteers
914.8904	DL115-120	Denmark—Description and travel
914.897003	DL1007	Finland—Gazetteers
914.89704	DL1015-.4	Finland—Description and travel
914.912003	DL304	Iceland—Gazetteers
914.91204	DL309-315	Iceland—Description and travel
914.92003	DH14	Netherlands—Gazetteers
914.92003	DJ14	Netherlands—Gazetteers
914.9204	DJ33-41	Netherlands—Description and travel
914.9204	DH31-40	Netherlands—Description and travel
914.93003	DH414	Belgium—Gazetteers
914.9304	DH431-435	Belgium—Description and travel
914.935003	DH903	Luxembourg—Gazetteers
914.93504	DH906-907	Luxembourg—Description and travel
914.94003	DQ14	Switzerland—Gazetteers
914.9404	DQ20-26	Switzerland—Description and travel
914.95	DF518	Byzantine Empire—Geography
914.9504	DF721-728	Greece—Description and travel
914.9504	DF27-30	Greece—Description and travel
914.96003	DR5	Balkan Peninsula—Gazetteers
914.9604	DR11-16	Balkan Peninsula—Description and travel
914.965003	DR907	Albania—Gazetteers
914.96504	DR914-918	Albania—Description and travel
914.97003	DR1209	Yugoslavia—Gazetteers
914.9704	DR1218-1224	Yugoslavia—Description and travel
914.98003	DR204	Romania—Gazetteers
914.9804	DR207-210	Romania—Description and travel
914.99003	DR53	Bulgaria—Gazetteers
914.9904	DR57-61	Bulgaria—Description and travel
915.003	DS4	Asia—Gazetteers
915.04	DS5.95-10	Asia—Description and travel
915.1003	DS705	China—Gazetteers
915.104	DS707-712	China—Description and travel
915.1249003	DS798.96	Taiwan—Gazetteers
915.124904	DS799.15-.24	Taiwan—Description and travel
915.19003	DS901.8	Korea—Gazetteers
915.1904	DS902.2-.4	Korea—Description and travel
915.2003	DS805	Japan—Gazetteers
915.204	DS807-811	Japan—Description and travel
915.3804	DS204.5-208	Saudi Arabia—Description and travel
915.491003	DS376.8	Pakistan—Gazetteers
915.49104	DS377	Pakistan—Description and travel
915.492003	DS393.3	Bangladesh—Gazetteers
915.493003	DS488.9	Sri Lanka—Gazetteers
915.49304	DS489-.15	Sri Lanka—Description and travel
915.496003	DS493.3	Nepal—Gazetteers
915.49604	DS493.5-.53	Nepal—Description and travel
915.5003	DS253	Iran—Gazetteers
915.504	DS255-259.2	Iran—Description and travel
915.6003	DS43	Middle East—Gazetteers
915.604	DS44.98-49.7	Middle East—Description and travel
915.6104	DR421-429.4	Turkey—Description and travel
915.67003	DS67.8	Iraq—Gazetteers
915.691003	DS92.6	Syria—Gazetteers
915.69104	DS94	Syria—Description and travel
915.692003	DS80.A5	Lebanon—Gazetteers
915.69204	DS80.2	Lebanon—Description and travel

Dewey	LC	Subject Heading	Dewey	LC	Subject Heading
915.69304	DS54.A4-Z	Cyprus—Description and travel	916.504	DT277.8-280.2	Algeria—Description and travel
915.69404	DS103-108.5	Israel—Description and travel	916.61003	DT554.15	Mauritania—Gazetteers
915.69504	DS153.2	Jordan—Description and travel	916.6104	DT554.27	Mauritania—Description and travel
915.7	G820-839	Arctic regions—Siberian	916.623003	DT551.15	Mali—Gazetteers
915.81003	DS351	Afghanistan—Gazetteers	916.62304	DT551.27	Mali—Description and travel
915.8104	DS352	Afghanistan—Description and travel	916.625003	DT555.15	Burkina Faso—Gazetteers
915.9104	DS527.5-.7	Burma—Description and travel	916.62504	DT555.27	Burkina Faso—Description and travel
915.93003	DS563	Thailand—Gazetteers	916.62604	DT547.27	Niger—Description and travel
915.9304	DS564-566.2	Thailand—Description and travel	916.63003	DT549.15	Senegal—Gazetteers
915.94003	DS555.25	Laos—Gazetteers	916.6304	DT549.27	Senegal—Description and travel
915.9404	DS555.34-.382	Laos—Description and travel	916.64003	DT516.15	Sierra Leone—Gazetteers
915.95003	DS591.5	Malaysia—Gazetteers	916.6404	DT516.2	Sierra Leone—Description and travel
915.9504	DS592.4-.6	Malaysia—Description and travel	916.65104	DT509.27	Gambia—Description and travel
915.955003	DS650.2	Brunei—Gazetteers	916.65204	DT543.27	Guinea—Description and travel
915.95504	DS650.35	Brunei—Description and travel	916.65704	DT613.2	Guinea-Bissau—Description and travel
915.96003	DS554.25	Cambodia—Gazetteers	916.65804	DT671.C22	Cape Verde—Description and travel
915.9604	DS554.34-.382	Cambodia—Description and travel	916.662003	DT623	Liberia—Gazetteers
915.97003	DS556.25	Vietnam—Gazetteers	916.66204	DT625-627	Liberia—Description and travel
915.9704	DS556.34-.39	Vietnam—Description and travel	916.668003	DT545.15	Cote d'Ivoire—Gazetteers
915.98003	DS614	Indonesia—Gazetteers	916.66804	DT545.27	Cote d'Ivoire—Description and travel
915.9804	DS617-620	Indonesia—Description and travel	916.6704	DT510.2	Ghana—Description and travel
915.99003	DS654	Philippines—Gazetteers	916.681003	DT582.15	Togo—Gazetteers
915.9904	DS658-660	Philippines—Description and travel	916.68104	DT582.27	Togo—Description and travel
916.003	DT2	Africa—Gazetteers	916.68304	DT541.27	Benin—Description and travel
916.04	DT6.5-12.25	Africa—Description and travel	916.69003	DT515.15	Nigeria—Gazetteers
916.04	G516	Safaris	916.6904	DT515.27	Nigeria—Description and travel
916.104	DT163-165.2	Africa, North—Description and travel	916.711003	DT563	Cameroon—Gazetteers
916.11003	DT244	Tunisia—Gazetteers	916.71104	DT566-568	Cameroon—Description and travel
916.1104	DT248-250.2	Tunisia—Description and travel	916.71504	DT615.2	Sao Tome and Principe—Description and travel
916.1204	DT218-220.2	Libya—Description and travel	916.718003	DT620.15	Equatorial Guinea—Gazetteers
916.2003	DT45	Egypt—Gazetteers	916.721003	DT546.115	Gabon—Gazetteers
916.204	DT49.98-56	Egypt—Description and travel	916.72104	DT546.127-.128	Gabon—Description and travel
916.24003	DT154.4	Sudan—Gazetteers	916.724003	DT546.215	Congo (Brazzaville)—Gazetteers
916.2404	DT154.7-.75	Sudan—Description and travel	916.72404	DT546.227	Congo (Brazzaville)—Description and travel
916.3003	DT371.5	Ethiopia—Gazetteers	916.73003	DT1264	Angola—Gazetteers
916.304	DT375-378.3	Ethiopia—Description and travel	916.7304	DT1282-1286	Angola—Description and travel
916.4003	DT304	Morocco—Gazetteers			
916.404	DT307-310.2	Morocco—Description and travel			
916.5003	DT274	Algeria—Gazetteers			

Dewey	LC	Subject Heading	Dewey	LC	Subject Heading
916.741003	DT546.315	Central African Republic—Gazetteers	916.982003	DT469.M415	Mauritius—Gazetteers
			916.98204	DT469.M429	Mauritius—Description and travel
916.74104	DT546.327	Central African Republic—Description and travel			
			917.003	E35	North America—Gazetteers
916.74304	DT546.427	Chad—Description and travel	917.003	E14	America—Gazetteers
			917.04	E41	North America—Description and travel
916.75104	DT645-647.5	Zaire—Description and travel			
			917.1003	F1004	Canada—Gazetteers
916.7571003	DT450.115	Rwanda—Gazetteers	917.104	F1012-1017	Canada—Description and travel
916.757104	DT450.2	Rwanda—Description and travel			
			917.11003	F1086.4	British Columbia—Gazetteers
916.7572003	DT450.515	Burundi—Gazetteers			
916.757204	DT450.6	Burundi—Description and travel	917.123003	F1975.4	Alberta—Gazetteers
			917.124003	F1070.4	Saskatchewan—Gazetteers
916.761003	DT433.215	Uganda—Gazetteers	917.127003	F1061.4	Manitoba—Gazetteers
916.76104	DT433.227	Uganda—Description and travel	917.13003	F1056.4	Ontario—Gazetteers
			917.14003	F1051.4	Quebec (Province)—Gazetteers
916.762003	DT433.515	Kenya—Gazetteers			
916.76204	DT433.527	Kenya—Description and travel	917.151003	F1041.4	New Brunswick—Gazetteers
916.771003	DT411.15	Djibouti—Gazetteers	917.16003	F1036.4	Nova Scotia—Gazetteers
916.77104	DT411.27	Djibouti—Description and travel	917.18003	F1121.4	Newfoundland—Gazetteers
			917.182003	F1135.4	Labrador (Nfld.)—Gazetteers
916.773003	DT401.2	Somalia—Gazetteers			
916.77304	DT401.8	Somalia—Description and travel	917.191003	F1092	Yukon Territory—Gazetteers
			917.2003	F1204	Mexico—Gazetteers
916.78003	DT437	Tanzania—Gazetteers	917.204	F1211-1216.5	Mexico—Description and travel
916.7804	DT439-440.5	Tanzania—Description and travel			
			917.28003	F1424	Central America—Gazetteers
916.79003	DT3294	Mozambique—Gazetteers			
916.7904	DT3308-3312	Mozambique—Description and travel	917.2804	F1431-1433.2	Central America—Description and travel
916.8003	DT1714	South Africa—Gazetteers	917.281003	F1462	Guatemala—Gazetteers
916.804	DT1730-1738	South Africa—Description and travel	917.28104	F1464-.3	Guatemala—Description and travel
916.881003	DT1514	Namibia—Gazetteers	917.28204	F1444-.3	Belize—Description and travel
916.88104	DT1532-1536	Namibia—Description and travel			
			917.283003	F1502	Honduras—Gazetteers
916.883003	DT2434	Botswana—Gazetteers	917.28304	F1504	Honduras—Description and travel
916.885003	DT2554	Lesotho—Gazetteers			
916.88504	DT2572	Lesotho—Description and travel	917.284003	F1482	El Salvador—Gazetteers
			917.28404	F1484-.3	El Salvador—Description and travel
916.887003	DT2714	Swaziland—Gazetteers			
916.88704	DT2732	Swaziland—Description and travel	917.285003	F1522	Nicaragua—Gazetteers
			917.28504	F1524-.3	Nicaragua—Description and travel
916.891003	DT2884	Zimbabwe—Gazetteers			
916.89104	DT2900-2904	Zimbabwe—Description and travel	917.286003	F1542	Costa Rica—Gazetteers
			917.28604	F1544	Costa Rica—Description and travel
916.894003	DT3037	Zambia—Gazetteers			
916.89404	DT3050	Zambia—Description and travel	917.287003	F1562	Panama—Gazetteers
			917.28704	F1564-.3	Panama—Description and travel
916.897003	DT3169	Malawi—Gazetteers			
916.89704	DT3182	Malawi—Description and travel	917.29003	F1604	West Indies—Gazetteers
			917.2904	F1610-1613	West Indies—Description and travel
916.91003	DT469.M24	Madagascar—Gazetteers			
916.96003	DT469.S415	Seychelles—Gazetteers	917.291003	F1754	Cuba—Gazetteers
916.9604	DT469.S427	Seychelles—Description and travel	917.29104	F1761-1765.3	Cuba—Description and travel
916.981003	DT469.R32	Reunion—Gazetteers	917.292003	F1864	Jamaica—Gazetteers
916.98104	DT469.R35	Reunion—Description and travel	917.29204	F1870-1872.2	Jamaica—Description and travel

Dewey	LC	Subject Heading	Dewey	LC	Subject Heading
917.293003	F1932	Dominican Republic— Gazetteers	917.82003	F664	Nebraska—Gazetteers
917.29304	F1936-.3	Dominican Republic— Description and travel	917.83003	F649	South Dakota—Gazetteers
			917.84003	F634	North Dakota—Gazetteers
917.294003	F1913	Haiti—Gazetteers	917.86003	F729	Montana—Gazetteers
917.29404	F1917	Haiti—Description and travel	917.87003	F759	Wyoming—Gazetteers
			917.88003	F774	Colorado—Gazetteers
917.295003	F1954	Puerto Rico—Gazetteers	917.89003	F794	New Mexico—Gazetteers
917.29504	F1961-1965.3	Puerto Rico—Description and travel	917.91003	F809	Arizona—Gazetteers
			917.92003	F824	Utah—Gazetteers
917.296003	F1650.7	Bahamas—Gazetteers	917.93003	F839	Nevada—Gazetteers
917.29604	F1651	Bahamas—Description and travel	917.94003	F859	California—Gazetteers
			917.95003	F874	Oregon—Gazetteers
917.299003	F1630.7	Bermuda Islands— Gazetteers	917.96003	F744	Idaho—Gazetteers
			917.97003	F889	Washington (State)— Gazetteers
917.29904	F1631	Bermuda Islands— Description and travel	917.98003	F902	Alaska—Gazetteers
			917.98(6-7)	G725-770	Arctic regions—American
917.3003	E154	United States—Gazetteers	918.003	E14	America—Gazetteers
917.304	E161.5-169.04	United States— Description and travel	918.003	F1406	Latin America—Gazetteers
			918.04	F1409-.3	Latin America—Description and travel
917.4003	F2	New England—Gazetteers			
917.41003	F17	Maine—Gazetteers	918.1003	F2504	Brazil—Gazetteers
917.42003	F32	New Hampshire— Gazetteers	918.104	F2511-2517	Brazil—Description and travel
917.43003	F47	Vermont—Gazetteers	918.2003	F2804	Argentina—Gazetteers
917.44003	F62	Massachusetts— Gazetteers	918.204	F2811-2817	Argentina—Description and travel
917.45003	F77	Rhode Island—Gazetteers	918.3003	F3054	Chile—Gazetteers
917.46003	F92	Connecticut—Gazetteers	918.304	F3061-3065	Chile—Description and travel
917.47003	F117	New York (State)— Gazetteers	918.4003	F3304	Bolivia—Gazetteers
917.48003	F147	Pennsylvania—Gazetteers	918.404	F3311-3315	Bolivia—Description and travel
917.49003	F132	New Jersey—Gazetteers			
917.51003	F162	Delaware—Gazetteers	918.5003	F3404	Peru—Gazetteers
917.52003	F179	Maryland—Gazetteers	918.504	F3410.5-3425	Peru—Description and travel
917.53003	F192	Washington (D.C.)— Gazetteers	918.61003	F2254	Colombia—Gazetteers
917.54003	F239	West Virginia—Gazatteers	918.6104	F2261-2264.2	Colombia—Description and travel
917.55003	F224	Virginia—Gazetteers			
917.56003	F252	North Carolina—Gazetteers	918.66003	F3704	Ecuador—Gazetteers
917.57003	F267	South Carolina— Gazetteers	918.6604	F3711-3716	Ecuador—Description and travel
917.58003	F284	Georgia—Gazetteers	918.7003	F2304	Venezuela—Gazetteers
917.59003	F309	Florida—Gazetteers	918.704	F2311-2315	Venezuela—Description and travel
917.61003	F324	Alabama—Gazetteers			
917.62003	F339	Mississippi—Gazetteers	918.81003	F2364	Guyana—Gazetteers
917.63003	F367	Louisiana—Gazetteers	918.82003	F2444	French Guiana—Gazetteers
917.64003	F384	Texas—Gazetteers	918.8204	F2450-2452	French Guiana— Description and travel
917.66003	F692	Oklahoma—Gazetteers			
917.67003	F409	Arkansas—Gazetteers	918.83003	F2404	Surinam—Gazetteers
917.68003	F434	Tennessee—Gazetteers	918.8304	F2410-2413	Surinam—Description and travel
917.69003	F449	Kentucky—Gazetteers			
917.71003	F489	Ohio—Gazetteers	918.92003	F2664	Paraguay—Gazetteers
917.72003	F524	Indiana—Gazetteers	918.9204	F2671-2676	Paraguay—Description and travel
917.73003	F539	Illinois—Gazetteers			
917.74003	F564	Michigan—Gazetteers	918.95003	F2704	Uruguay—Gazetteers
917.75003	F579	Wisconsin—Gazetteers	918.9504	F2711-2715	Uruguay—Description and travel
917.76003	F604	Minnesota—Gazetteers			
917.77003	F619	Iowa—Gazetteers	919.3003	DU405	New Zealand—Gazetteers
917.78003	F464	Missouri—Gazetteers	919.304	DU409-413	New Zealand—Description and travel
917.81003	F679	Kansas—Gazetteers			

Dewey	LC	Subject Heading	Dewey	LC	Subject Heading
919.4003	DU90	Australia—Gazetteers	920.0493	DH513-516	Belgium—Biography
919.404	DU97-5-105.2	Australia—Description and travel	920.04935	DH904	Luxembourg—Biography
			920.0494	DQ52-.7	Switzerland—Biography
919.(5-6)04	DU19-23.5	Oceania—Description and travel	920.0495	DF506-.5	Byzantine Empire—Biography
919.69003	DU622	Hawaii—Gazetteers	920.0496	CT1399-1458	Balkan Peninsula—Biography
919.8	G600-839	Arctic regions			
919.89	G845-890	Antarctica	920.0496	DR33	Balkan Peninsula—Biography
919.890409034	G850	Expedition antarctique belge, 1897-1899	920.04965	DR928-934	Albania—Biography
920	CT25	Autobiography	920.0497	DR1233-1235	Yugoslavia—Biography
920	CT	Biography	920.0499	DR66	Bulgaria—Biography
920	CT101	Autobiographies	920.05	CT1498-1919	Asia—Biography
920.00901	D55	Biography—To 500	920.056	CT1870-1919	Middle East—Biography
920.00902	D115	Biography—Middle Ages, 500-1500	920.06	CT1920-2750	Africa—Biography
			920.07	E36	North America—Biography
920.00902	D107-110.5	Biography—Middle Ages, 500-1500	920.07	E17	America—Biography
			920.08	E17	America—Biography
920.00904	D1070-1075	Biography—20th century	920.071	CT280-310	Canada—Biography
920.009291497	DX125-127	Gypsies—Biography	920.072	CT550-558	Mexico—Biography
920.009296073	E185.96-.97	Afro-Americans—Biography	920.0728	CT570-638	Central America—Biography
920.0361	DA28-.9	Great Britain—Biography			
920.0363	DD85-.8	Germany—Biography	920.0729	CT329-448	West Indies—Biography
920.0363	DB36-.7	Austria—Biography	920.073	E176	United States—Biography
920.0363	DL444	Norway—Biography	920.08	CT640-758	South America—Biography
920.0363	DL644	Sweden—Biography	920.093(7/8)	DE7	Classical biography
920.0363	DJ103-106	Netherlands—Biography	920.0993	CT2880-2888	New Zealand—Biography
920.0363	DH103	Netherlands—Biography	920.0994	CT2800-2808	Australia—Biography
920.0364	DC36-.8	France—Biography	920.099(5-6)	CT2900-3090	Oceania—Biography
920.0364	DH513-516	Belgium—Biography	920.72	CT3200-3830	Women—Biography
920.0364	DQ52-.7	Switzerland—Biography	929.1	CS	Genealogy
920.0366	DP58	Spain—Biography	929.1025	CS5	Genealogy—Directories
920.0366	DP536	Portugal—Biography	929.103	CS6	Genealogy—Dictionaries
920.037	DG203-204	Rome—Biography	929.105	CS1	Genealogy—Periodicals
920.037	DG463-.8	Italy—Biography	929.106	CS2	Genealogy—Congresses
920.0398	DB922	Hungary—Biography	929.10720(4-9)	CS42-2209	[Region or country]—Genealogy
920.0398	DR928-934	Albania—Biography			
920.0398	DR1233-1235	Yugoslavia—Biography	929.107204	CS410-1059	Europe—Genealogy
920.0398	DR66	Bulgaria—Biography	929.1072041	CS410-479.5	Great Britain—Genealogy
920.04	CT759-1495	Europe—Biography	929.1072043	CS610-699	Germany—Genealogy
920.041	CT770-858	Great Britain—Biography	929.1072048	CS890-939	Scandinavia—Genealogy
920.041	DA28-.9	Great Britain—Biography	929.10720492	CS780-839	Benelux countries—Genealogy
920.0429	DA710	Wales—Biography			
920.043	CT1050-1099.8	Germany—Biography	929.107205	CS1080-1549.5	Asia—Genealogy
920.043	DD85-.8	Germany—Biography	929.107206	CS1550-1779	Africa—Genealogy
920.043	DD343-.8	Prussia (Germany)—Biography	929.1072071	CS80-90	Canada—Genealogy
			929.10720(72-8)	CS120-199	Central America—Genealogy
920.0436	DB36-.7	Austria—Biography			
920.0438	DK4130-4138.5	Poland—Biography	929.1072073	CS42-71	United States—Genealogy
920.0439	DB922	Hungary—Biography	929.1072094	CS2000-2009	Australia—Genealogy
920.044	DC36-.8	France—Biography	929.347	CS840-869	Russia—Genealogy
920.045	DG463-.8	Italy—Biography	929.372	CS100-110	Mexico—Genealogy
920.046	DP58	Spain—Biography	929.3729	CS200-261	West Indies—Genealogy
920.0469	DP536	Portugal—Biography	929.38	CS270-409	South America—Genealogy
920.047	DJK31	Europe, Eastern—Biography	929.393	CS2170-2179	New Zealand—Genealogy
920.048	CT1240-1328	Scandinavia—Biography	929.39(5-6)	CS2191-2209	Oceania—Genealogy
920.0481	DL444	Norway—Biography	929.4	CS2300-3090	Names, Personal
920.0485	DL644	Sweden—Biography	929.409(4-9)	CS2395-3090	Names, Personal—[By region or country]
920.04897	DL1024	Finland—Biography			
920.0492	DJ103-106	Netherlands—Biography	929.44	CT108	Nicknames
920.0492	DH103	Netherlands—Biography	929.50937	CN528.E6	Epitaphs

Dewey	LC	Subject Heading	Dewey	LC	Subject Heading
929.50938	CN375.E6	Epitaphs	930	CB311	Civilization, Ancient
929.6	CR	Heraldry	930	CB305	Protohistory
929.6	CR67-69	Badges	930	D51-95	History, Ancient
929.6	CR4553	Tournaments	930.03	D54	History, Ancient—
929.6	CR41.C5	Collars in heraldry			Dictionaries
929.6	CR41.F6	Flowers in heraldry	930.05	D51	History, Ancient—
929.6	CR55-57	Crests			Periodicals
929.6	CR29-69	Heraldry, Ornamental	930.072	D56-.52	History, Ancient—
929.6	CR67-69	Devices (Heraldry)			Historiography
929.6	CR73-75	Mottoes	930.1	CC	Archaeology
929.6	CR91-93	Shields	930.1	GN700-890	Archaeology
929.6	CR183-185	Heralds	930.1	T37	Industrial archaeology
929.601	CR14-16	Heraldry—Philosophy	930.1	GN783-784	Cave dwellings
929.6025	CR11	Heraldry—Directories	930.1	GN783-.5	Caves
929.603	CR13	Heraldry—Dictionaries	930.1	GN795-796	Mounds
929.605	CR1	Heraldry—Periodicals	930.101	CC72-81	Archaeology—Philosophy
929.606	CR2	Heraldry—Congresses	930.101	CC73-75	Archaeology—Methodology
929.6074	CR9	Heraldry—Exhibitions	930.1025	CC120-125	Archaeology—Directories
929.609	CR151-159	Heraldry—History	930.1028	CC77.5	Archaeological geology
929.7	CR4485.07	Orbs	930.1028	CC73-75	Archaeological surveying
929.7	CR4480.C7	Crowns	930.1028	GN789	Earthworks (Archaeology)
929.7	CR3575	Precedence	930.102804	CC77.U5	Underwater archaeology
929.7	CR3499-4420	Titles of honor and nobility	930.10283	CC75	Excavations (Archaeology)
929.71	CR	Knights and knighthood	930.10283	CC165	Excavations (Archaeology)
929.71	CR4501-6305	Orders of knighthood and chivalry	930.10288	CC135-137	Antiquities—Collection and preservation
929.7(2-3/094)	CR4801-6305	Orders of knighthood and chivalry—[By region or country]	930.103	CC70	Archaeology—Dictionaries
			930.105	CC1-15	Archaeology—Periodicals
			930.106	CC20-39	Archaeology—Societies, etc.
929.72	CR4801-4917	Orders of knighthood and chivalry—Great Britain	930.1092	CC110-115	Archaeologists
929.73	CR5100-5475	Orders of knighthood and chivalry—Germany	930.11	GN775-776	Eoliths
			930.1(2-4)	GN775-768	Stone age
929.736	CR4951-5005	Orders of knighthood and chivalry—Austria	930.12	GN771	Paleolithic period, Lower
			930.15	GN777-778	Copper age
929.738	CR5713-5737	Orders of knighthood and chivalry—Poland	930.15	GN777-778	Bronze age
			931	DS701-799.9	China
929.74	CR5025-5085	Orders of knighthood and chivalry—France	931	DS721-727	China—Civilization
			931	DS799.99-.833	Taiwan—History
929.75	CR5500-5580	Orders of knighthood and chivalry—Italy	931	DS799.4	Taiwan—Civilization
			931	DS799.64-.66	Taiwan—History—To 1895
929.76	CR5819-5889	Orders of knighthood and chivalry—Spain	931.003	DS705	China—Gazetteers
			931.003	DS798.96	Taiwan—Gazetteers
929.769	CR5900-5925	Orders of knighthood and chivalry—Portugal	931.004	DS730-731	Ethnology—China
			931.004	DS799.42-.43	Ethnology—Taiwan
929.77	CR5657-5703	Orders of knighthood and chivalry—Russia	931.0(1-3)	DS741-747.23	China—History—To 221 B.C.
929.78	CR5745-5809	Orders of knighthood and chivalry—Scandinavia	931.01	DS747.2	China—History—Warring States, 403-221 B.C.
929.795	CR5485-5489	Orders of knighthood and chivalry—Greece	931.01	DS747.15	China—History—Spring and Autumn period, 722-481 B.C.
929.81	CR4501-6305	Decorations of honor			
929.8143	CR5351	Iron Cross	931.04	DS747.28-749.76	China—History—221 B.C.-960 A.D.
929.8173	CR6253.Y	Young American Medal for Bravery	931.04	DS747.5-.9	China—History—Ch'in dynasty, 221-207 B.C.
929.82	JC345-347	Seals (Numismatics)	931.04	DS748-.164	China—History—Han dynasty, 202 B.C.-220 A.D.
929.88	Z41-42	Signatures (Writing)			
929.88	Z41-42.5	Autographs	931.04	DS748.17-.76	China—History—220-589
929.9	CR4480-4485	Insignia	931.04	DS748.2-.29	China—History—Three Kingdoms, 220-265
929.92	JC345-347	Seals (Numismatics)			
929.92	CR101-115	Flags			

Dewey	LC	Subject Heading
931.04	DS748.4-.44	China—History—Chin dynasty, 265-419
931.04	DS748.45-.48	China—History—Five Hu and the Sixteen kingdoms, 304-439
931.04	DS748.7-.76	China—History—Northern Wei dynasty, 386-534
932	DT83-93	Egypt—History—To 640 A.D.
932	DT70	Egypt—Civilization
932	DT43-154	Egypt—History
932.004	DT71-72	Ethnology—Egypt
932.0(1-2)	DT83-91	Egypt—History—To 332 B.C.
932.01	DT63-.5	Pyramids
932.014	DT87-.5	Egypt—History—Eighteenth dynasty, ca. 1570-1320
932.02	DT92-93	Egypt—History—Greco Roman period, 332 B.C.-640 A.D.
932.021	DT92-.7	Egypt—History—332-30 B.C.
932.021	DT92-.7	Alexandrine War, 48-47 B.C.
932.02(2-3)	DT93	Egypt—History—30 B.C.-640 A.D.
933	DS101-151	Jews
933	DS112-113	Jews—Civilization
933	DS101-151	Israel
933	DS114-128.19	Israel—History
933	DS109-.94	Jerusalem
933	DS109.85-.94	Jerusalem—History
933	DS153-154.9	Jordan
933	DS153.7-154.55	Jordan—History
933	DS153.4	Jordan—Civilization
933	DS110.S3	Samaria Region
933.004	DS113.2-.8	Ethnology—Israel
933.004	DS153.5-.55	Ethnology—Jordan
933.004926	DS121.4	Canaanites
933.02	DS121.6	Jews—History—953-586 B.C.
933.0(3-5)	DS109.912	Jews—History—586 B.C.-70 A.D.
933.03	DS109.912	Jews—History—Babylonian captivity, 598-515 B.C.
933.0(4-5)	DS121.7-.8	Jews—History—168 B.C.-135 A.D.
933.05	DS109.913	Jews—History—Rebellion, 66-73
934	DS421-486.8	India
934	DS421-428.2	India—Civilization
934	DS451-.9	India—History—324 B.C-1000 A.D.
934	DS381.7-388.2	Pakistan—History
934	DS379	Pakistan—Civilization
934	DS394.5-395.7	Bangladesh—History
934	DS393.8	Bangladesh—Civilization
934.004	DS430-432.5	Ethnology—India
934.004	DS380.A1-.A2	Ethnology—Pakistan
934.004	DS393.82-.83	Ethnology—Bangladesh

Dewey	LC	Subject Heading
934.02	DS425	Indo-Aryans
935	DS70.7	Civilization, Assyro-Babylonian
935	DS251-326	Iran
935	DS270-318.85	Iran—History
935	DS276	Iran—History—To 640
935	DS70.82-79.66	Iraq—History
935	DS70.7	Iraq—Civilization
935	DS69-70.5	Iraq—Antiquities
935.004	DS268-269	Ethnology—Iran
935.004	DS70.8	Ethnology—Iraq
935.01	DS72	Sumerians
935.05	DS281-284.7	Achaemenid dynasty, 559-330 B.C.
935.06	DS276	Iran—History—Macedonian Conquest, 334-325 B.C.
936	DA900-995	Ireland—History
936.1	DA930-932.6	Ireland—History—To 1172
936.1	DA750-890	Scotland
936.1	DA	Great Britain
936.1	DA28-690	Great Britain—History
936.1	DA134-162	Great Britain—History—To 1066
936.1	DA110-115	Great Britain—Civilization
936.1004	DA120-125	Ethnology—Great Britain
936.1005	DA750	Scotland—Periodicals
936.1005	DA900	Ireland—Periodicals
936.2	DA20-690	England
936.2005	DA20	England—Periodicals
936.3	DB1-879	Austria
936.3	DB46-99.2	Austria—History
936.3	DB51-57	Austria—History—To 1273
936.3	DB30	Austria—Civilization
936.3	DD	Germany
936.3	DD84-257.4	Germany—History
936.3	DD121-134.2	Germany—History—To 843
936.3	DD60-68	Germany—Civilization
936.3	DD301-491	Prussia (Germany)
936.3	DD341-454	Prussia (Germany)—History
936.3	DD331	Prussia (Germany)—Civilization
936.3	DB881-898	Liechtenstein
936.3	DB891-894	Liechtenstein—History
936.3	DH	Benelux countries
936.3	DJ	Netherlands
936.3	DH	Netherlands
936.3	DH95-207	Netherlands—History
936.3	DJ95-292	Netherlands—History
936.3	DH141-162	Netherlands—History—To 1384
936.3	DJ151-152	Netherlands—History—To 1384
936.3	DJ71	Netherlands—Civilization
936.3	DH71	Netherlands—Civilization
936.3	DL101-291	Denmark—History
936.3	DL131-133	Denmark—Civilization
936.3	DL	Scandinavia
936.3	DL43-87	Scandinavia—History
936.3	DL30-33	Scandinavia—Civilization

Dewey	LC	Subject Heading	Dewey	LC	Subject Heading
936.3	DL401-596	Norway—History	936.6004	DP52-53	Ethnology—Spain
936.3	DL460-478	Norway—History—To 1030	936.6004	DP533-534.5	Ethnology—Portugal
936.3	DL431-433	Norway—Civilization	936.6005	DP1	Spain—Periodicals
936.3	DL601-991	Sweden—History	936.6005	DP501	Portugal—Periodicals
936.3	DL660-700.9	Sweden—History—To 1397	936.6006	DP2	Spain—Congresses
936.3	DL631-635	Sweden—Civilization	936.60072	DP63-.83	Spain—Historiography
936.3004	DB33-34.5	Ethnology—Austria	936.60072	DP536.8-.96	Portugal—Historiography
936.3004	DL41-42	Ethnology—Scandinavia	936.603	DP94-95	Spain—History—Roman
936.3004	DL441-442	Ethnology—Norway			period, 218 B.C.-414 A.D.
936.3004	DL639-641	Ethnology—Sweden	937	DG	Classical antiquities
936.3004	DL141-142	Ethnology—Denmark	937	DE	Classical antiquities
936.3004	DH91-92	Ethnology—Netherlands	937	DE46-61	Civilization, Classical
936.3004	DJ91-92	Ethnology—Netherlands	937	DG11-365	Rome
936.3005	DD301	Prussia (Germany)—	937	DG61-365	Rome—History
		Periodicals	937	DG75-142	Rome—Civilization
936.3005	DB1	Austria—Periodicals	937	DG	Italy
936.3005	DB881	Liechtenstein—Periodicals	937	DG461-583	Italy—History
936.3005	DL1	Scandinavia—Periodicals	937	DG441-453	Italy—Civilization
936.3005	DL401-403	Norway—Periodicals	937.001	DG465.8	Italy—Study and teaching
936.3005	DL601	Sweden—Periodicals	937.004	DG455-457	Ethnology—Italy
936.3005	DL101	Denmark—Periodicals	937.005	DG11	Rome—Periodicals
936.3005	DH1	Netherlands—Periodicals	937.005	DG401	Italy—Periodicals
936.3005	DJ1	Netherlands—Periodicals	937.006	DG12.5	Rome—Congresses
936.3006	DL1.5	Scandinavia—Congresses	937.0071	DG206.5	Rome—Study and teaching
936.30072	DD345	Prussia (Germany)—	937.0072	DG205	Rome—Historiography
		Historiography	937.0072	DG465-.7	Italy—Historiography
936.30072	DD86-.7	Germany—Historiography	937.0099	DG124	Roman emperors
936.30072	DB36.8-.9	Austria—Historiography	937.0099	DG270-365	Emperors—Rome
936.30072	DL445	Norway—Historiography	937.0(1-2)	DG221-233.9	Rome—History—To
936.30072	DL645	Sweden—Historiography			510 B.C.
936.4	D70	Celts—History	937.0(2-5)	DG235-269	Rome—History—
936.4	DC62-63	Gaul—History			Republic, 510-30 B.C.
936.4	DC	France	937.04	DG243-244	Punic War, 1st, 264-
936.4	DC35-423	France—History			241 B.C.
936.4	DC33-.9	France—Civilization	937.04	DG247-249.4	Punic War, 2nd, 218-
936.4	DH401-811	Belgium			201 B.C.
936.4	DH571-584	Belgium—History—To 1555	937.04	DG252.6	Punic War, 3rd, 149-
936.4	DH471	Belgium—Civilization			146 B.C.
936.4	DQ	Switzerland—History	937.04	DG251	Macedonian War, 1st,
936.4	DQ79-84	Switzerland—History—			215-205 B.C.
		To 1648	937.04	DG251	Macedonian War, 2nd,
936.4	DQ85-87	Switzerland—History—			200-196 B.C.
		To 1032	937.04	DG251.6	Macedonian War, 3rd,
936.4	DQ36-39	Switzerland—Civilization			171-168 B.C.
936.4004	DC34-.5	Ethnology—France	937.05	DG252.9	Rome—History—Servile
936.4004	DH491-492	Ethnology—Belgium			Wars, 135-71 B.C.
936.4004	DQ48-49	Ethnology—Switzerland	937.05	DG263	Rome—History—First
936.4005	DC1	France—Periodicals			Triumvirate, 60-53 B.C.
936.4005	DH401	Belgium—Periodicals	937.05	DG264	Gaul—History—Gallic
936.4005	DQ1	Switzerland—Periodicals			Wars, 58-51 B.C.
936.4006	DQ2	Switzerland—Congresses	937.05	DG266	Durazzo, Battle of, 48 B.C.
936.40072	DQ52.8-.95	Switzerland—Historiography	937.05	DG268-269	Rome—History—Civil
936.402	DC62	Gaul—History—Gallic			War, 43-31 B.C.
		Wars, 58-51 B.C.	937.05	DG269	Actium, Battle of, 31 B.C.
936.402	DC62	Gergovie, Battle of, 52 B.C.	937.06	DG330-338	Rome—History—
936.6	DP1-402	Spain			Theodosians, 379-455
936.6	DP91-96	Spain—History—To 711	937.06	DG310-365	Rome—History—Empire,
936.6	DP48-.9	Spain—Civilization			284-476
936.6	DP501-900	Portugal—History	937.06	DG269.5-365	Rome—History—Empire,
936.6	DP558-618	Portugal—History—To 1385			30 B.C.-476 A.D.
936.6	DP532-.7	Portugal—Civilization			

Dewey	LC	Subject Heading	Dewey	LC	Subject Heading
937.06	DG279	Rome—History—Augustus, 30 B.C.-14 A.D.	938.01	DF222-224	Greece—History—Age of Tyrants, 7th-6th centuries, B.C.
937.07	DG282.5	Rome—History—Tiberius, 14-37	938.03	DF225-226	Greece—History—Persian Wars, 500-449 B.C.
937.07	DG283	Rome—History—Caligula, 37-41	938.03	DF225.3	Greece—History—Ionian Revolt, 499-494 B.C.
937.07	DG284	Rome—History—Claudius, 41-54	938.03	DF225.4	Marathon, Battle of, 490 B.C.
937.07	DG286	Rome—History—Civil War, 68-69	938.04	DF227-228	Greece—History—Athenian supremacy, 479-431 B.C.
937.07	DG288	Rome—History—Revolt of Civilis, 69-70	938.0(5-6)	DF231-232	Greece—History—Spartan and Theban Supremacies, 404-362 B.C.
937.07	DG289	Rome—History—Vitellius, 69	938.05	DF229-230	Greece—History—Peloponnesian War, 431-404 B.C.
937.07	DG290	Rome—History—Titus, 79-81			
937.07	DG291	Rome—History—Domitian, 81-96	938.05	DF231.32	Greece—History—Expedition of Cyrus, 401 B.C.
937.07	DG292-299	Rome—History—Antonines, 96-192	938.07	DF232.5-234.9	Greece—History—Macedonian Expansion, 359-323 B.C.
937.07	DG294	Rome—History—Trajan, 98-117			
937.07	DG59.D3	Dacian War, 1st, 101-102	938.07	DF233.4	Greece—History—Third Sacred War, 355-346 B.C.
937.07	DG59.D3	Dacian War, 2nd, 105-106			
937.07	DG294	Parthian War, 113-117	938.07	DF234.5	Gaugamela, Battle of, 331 B.C.
937.07	DG295	Rome—History—Hadrian, 117-138	938.08	DF235.3-.85	Greece—History—Macedonian Hegemony, 323-281 B.C.
937.07	DG300-304	Rome—History—Severans, 193-235	938.08	DF236-238.9	Greece—History—281-146 B.C.
937.07	DG306	Rome—History—Maximimus, 235-238			
937.07	DG307.5	Rome—History—Gallienus, 260-268	938.08	DF236.4	Greece—History—Galatian Invasion, 279-278 B.C.
937.08	DG314	Rome—History—Conference of Carnuntum, 308	938.08	DF236.5	Greece—History—Chremonidean War, 267-262 B.C.
937.08	DG315-317	Rome—History—Constantines, 306-363	938.09	DF239-241	Greece—History—146 B.C.-323 A.D.
937.08	DG315	Rome—History—Constantine I, the Great, 306-337	938.3	DF261.A2	Aetolia (Greece)
937.09	DG365	Rome—History—Romulus Augustulus, 475-476	938.8	DF261.05	Olympia (Greece : Ancient sanctuary)
938	DE	Greece	939.2	DR436-603	Turkey—History
938	DF	Greece	939.2	DR481	Turkey—History—To 1453
938	DF	Classical antiquities	939.2	DR432	Turkey—Civilization
938	DE	Classical antiquities	939.2003	DR414	Turkey—Gazetteers
938	DE46-61	Civilization, Classical	939.2004	DR434-435	Ethnology—Turkey
938.004	DF135	Ethnology—Greece	939.20072	DR438.8-.95	Turkey—Historiography
938.005	DF10	Greece—Periodicals	939.37	DS54.5-.9	Cyprus—History
938.0(1-8)	DF233-238	Macedonia—History—To 168 B.C.	939.37	DS54.35	Cyprus—Civilization
			939.37004	DS54.4-.44	Ethnology—Cyprus
938.0(1-8)	DF233.2	Corinthian League	939.4	DS41-66	Middle East
938.0(1-8)	DF218-238.9	Greece—History—To 146 B.C.	939.4	DS38	Middle East—History—To 622
938.01	DF221-.3	Greece—History—Dorian Invasions, ca. 1125-1025 B.C.	939.43	DS94.9-98.3	Syria—History
			939.43	DS94.6	Syria—Civilization
938.01	DF221.5	Greece—History—Geometric period, ca. 900-700 B.C.	939.43004	DS94.7-.8	Ethnology—Syria
			939.44	DS81-89	Phoenicians
			939.44	DS80.3	Phoenician antiquities

Dewey	LC	Subject Heading	Dewey	LC	Subject Heading
939.44	DS80.4	Lebanon—Civilization	939.8	DR1376-1450	Slovenia—History
939.44	DS80.7-87.53	Lebanon—History	939.8	DR1652-1785	Bosnia and Hercegovina
939.44	DS83	Lebanon—History—635-1516	939.8004	DB919-.2	Ethnology—Hungary
			939.8004	DR923-925	Ethnology—Albania
939.44004	DS80.5	Ethnology—Lebanon	939.8004	DR1229-1230	Ethnology—Yugoslavia
939.49	DS201-248	Saudi Arabia	939.8004	DR213-214	Ethnology—Romania
939.49	DS215	Saudi Arabia—Civilization	939.8004	DR64	Ethnology—Bulgaria
939.49	DS221-244.63	Saudi Arabia—History	939.8005	DR901	Albania—Periodicals
939.49004	DS218-219	Ethnology—Saudi Arabia	939.8005	DR1202	Yugoslavia—Periodicals
939.6	DS327-329.4	Asia, Central	939.8005	DR201	Romania—Periodicals
939.6	DS355-371.2	Afghanistan—History	939.8005	DR51	Bulgaria—Periodicals
939.6	DS354	Afghanistan—Civilization	939.8006	DR903.5	Albania—Congresses
939.6004	DS354.5-.6	Ethnology—Afghanistan	939.8006	DR1205	Yugoslavia—Congresses
939.7	DT160-177	Africa, North	939.80072	DR1239-1243	Yugoslavia—Historiography
939.7	DT160-176	Africa, North—History	939.80072	DR216.7-.92	Romania—Historiography
939.7	DT168-171	Africa, North—History—To 647	939.80072	DR66.7-.97	Bulgaria—Historiography
			940	D900-1075	Europe—History
939.71	DT179.2-.9	Africa, Northwest	940.182	D201.7-.8	Twelfth century
939.71	DT271-299	Algeria	940.2	D205-1075	History, Modern
939.71	DT283-299	Algeria—History	940.2(3-5)	D242-283.5	Seventeenth century
939.71	DT288	Algeria—History—To 647	940.24	D251-271	Thirty Years' War, 1618-1648
939.71	DT282	Algeria—Civilization			
939.71	DT301-330	Morocco	940.252	D274.5-.6	Anglo-French War, 1666-1667
939.71	DT313.7-325.92	Morocco—History			
939.71	DT318	Morocco—History—To 647	940.252	D277-278.5	Dutch War, 1672-1678
939.71	DT312	Morocco—Civilization	940.2525	D279-280.5	Grand Alliance, War of the, 1689-1697
939.71004	DT313-.6	Ethnology—Morocco			
939.71004	DT283-.6	Ethnology—Algeria	940.2(526-7)	CB411	Europe—Civilization—18th century
939.73	DT241-269	Tunisia			
939.73	DT253.4-264.49	Tunisia—History	940.2526	D281-283.5	Spanish Succession, War of, 1701-1714
939.73	DT258	Tunisia—History—To 647			
939.73	DT252	Tunisia—Civilization	940.2526	DP196	Spanish Succession, War of, 1701-1714
939.73004	DT253-.2	Ethnology—Tunisia			
939.74	DT211-239	Libya	940.253	D295	Neutrality, Armed
939.74	DT223.2-236	Libya—History	940.253	D283.5	Hague, Treaty of, 1717
939.74	DT228	Libya—History—To 642	940.253	D287.5	Quadruple Alliance, 1718
939.74	DT229	Libya—History—642-1551	940.2532	D291-294	Austrian Succession, War of, 1740-1748
939.74	DT222	Libya—Civilization			
939.8	DJK77	Pannonia Region	940.2532	DB72	Austrian Succession, War of, 1740-1748
939.8	DB901-999	Hungary			
939.8	DB920.5	Hungary—Civilization	940.2534	DD409-412.8	Seven Years' War, 1756-1763
939.8	DB927-928.9	Hungary—History—To 896			
939.8	DR51-98	Bulgaria	940.2(7-87)	CB204	Europe—Intellectual life—19th century
939.8	DR63	Bulgaria—Civilization			
939.8	DR65-93.34	Bulgaria—History	940.2(7-87)	CB204	Europe—Civilization—19th century
939.8	DR74.3	Bulgaria—History—To 681			
939.8	DR201-296	Romania	940.2(7-87)	D351-400	Nineteenth century
939.8	DR215-267.5	Romania—History	940.27	D301-309	Europe—History—1789-1815
939.8	DR238-241	Romania—History—To 1711			
			940.27	DC222.F6	Fleurus, Battle of, 1794
939.8	DR212	Romania—Civilization	940.27	DC226.N5	Nile, Battle of the, 1798
939.8	DR901-998	Albania	940.27	DC227.5.D8	Durnstein, Battle of, 1805
939.8	DR927-977.25	Albania—History	940.27	DC231-233.5	Peninsular War, 1807-1814
939.8	DR954-960.5	Albania—History—To 1501	940.27	DP204-208	Spain—History—Napoleonic Conquest, 1808-1813
939.8	DR922	Albania—Civilization			
939.8	DR1202-2285	Yugoslavia			
939.8	DR1232-1321	Yugoslavia—History	940.27	DC234.65	Graz (Austria), Battle of, 1809
939.8	DR1228	Yugoslavia—Civilization			
939.8	DR1502-1645	Croatia	940.27	DC236-238.5	Wars of Liberation, 1813-1814
939.8	DR1547-1598	Croatia—History			
939.8	DR1352-1485	Slovenia	940.27	DC236.7.D8	Dresden, Battle of, 1813

Dewey	LC	Subject Heading	Dewey	LC	Subject Heading
940.27	D383	Quadruple Alliance, 1815	940.45	D580-589	World War, 1914-1918—Naval operations
940.27	DC241-244.7	Waterloo, Battle of, 1815	940.45	D580	Freedom of the seas
940.284	DB83	Austria—History—Revolution, 1848-1849	940.467	D609	World War, 1914-1918—Registers of dead
940.284	DD424	Prussia (Germany)—History—Revolution, 1848-1849	940.5(1-2)	D652-659	Reconstruction (1914-1939)
			940.53	D731-838	World War, 1939-1945
940.284	DD207-209	Germany—History—Revolution, 1848-1849	940.5300222	D743.2	World War, 1939-1945—Pictorial works
940.284	DF823.65	Greece—History—Revolution, 1848	940.5308691	D808-809	World War, 1939-1945—Refugees
940.284	DR244	Romania—History—Revolution, 1848	940.53092	D736	World War, 1939-1945—Biography
940.(288-5)	D410-893	Twentieth century	940.531	D753.2	Lend-lease operations (1941-1945)
940.(288-559)	CB203-231	Europe—Intellectual life—20th century	940.5311	D741	World War, 1939-1945—Causes
940.288	D443	Triple Entente, 1907			
940.288	D511	Triple Entente, 1907	940.5312	D812	World War, 1939-1945—Armistice
940.3	D501-680	World War, 1914-1918			
940.3092	D507	World War, 1914-1918—Biography	940.531422	D818-819	World War, 1939-1945—Reparations
940.3092	D507	Generals	940.53144	D824-829	Reconstruction (1939-1951)
940.31426	D650.T4-651	Mandates	940.53170943	D805.P7	Auschwitz (Poland : Concentration camp)
940.4	D529-578	World War, 1914-1918—Campaigns	940.5317599	D805.P5	O'Donnell Camp (Philippines : Concentration camp)
940.405	D625-626	World War, 1914-1918—Atrocities			
940.414	D541-542	World War, 1914-1918—Campaigns—Belgium	940.5318	D810.J4	World War, 1939-1945—Jews
940.4143	D531-538.5	World War, 1914-1918—Campaigns—Germany	940.5318	D805.G3	Bergen-Belsen (Germany : Concentration camp)
940.4144	D530-549.5	World War, 1914-1918—Campaigns—Western front	940.5318	D805.G3	Buchenwald (Germany : Concentration camp)
940.4144	D544-545	World War, 1914-1918—Campaigns—France	940.5318	D805.G3	Neuengamme (Hamburg, Germany: Concentration camp)
940.4144	D548-549.5	World War, 1914-1918—Campaigns—France	940.5318	D805.G3	Flossenburg (Germany : Concentration camp)
940.4145	D569	World War, 1914-1918—Campaigns—Italy	940.5318	D805.G3	Dachau (Germany : Concentration camp)
940.4147	D550-569.5	World War, 1914-1918—Campaigns—Eastern front	940.532	D748-754	World War, 1939-1945—Diplomatic history
940.415	D566-568.9	World War, 1914-1918—Campaigns—Turkey	940.5336	D802	World War, 1939-1945—Underground movements
940.421	D545.L3	Le Cateau, Battle of, 1914	940.5336	D802.A2	World War, 1939-1945—Occupied territories
940.421	D545.V25	Verdun, Battle of, 1914			
940.422	D557.L5	Limanova, Battle of, 1914	940.54	D755-769.87	World War, 1939-1945—Campaigns
940.423	D582.F2	Falkland Islands, Battle of the, 1914	940.5400222	D745-.7	World War, 1939-1945—Caricatures and cartoons
940.424	D545.A6	Argonne, Battle of the, 1915	940.54021	D797	World War, 1939-1945—Casualties (Statistics, etc.)
940.4272	D545.V3	Verdun, Battle of, 1916	940.5405	D803-804.35	World War, 1939-1945—Atrocities
940.433	D568.7	Gaza, Battles of, 1917			
940.434	D545.A63	Argonne, Battle of the, 1918	940.5405	D804.S65	Katyn Forest Massacre, 1940
940.439	D613-614	World War, 1914-1918—Peace	940.541	D793	World War, 1939-1945—Tank warfare
940.439	D642-651	World War, 1914-1918—Peace			
940.44	D600-607	World War, 1914-1918—Aerial operations	940.541273	D769.346	United States. Army—Airborne troops

Dewey	LC	Subject Heading	Dewey	LC	Subject Heading
940.541273	D769.347	United States. Army—Parachute troops	940.5451	D780-784	World War, 1939-1945—Naval operations—Submarine
940.5421	D756-763	World War, 1939-1945—Campaigns—Western front	940.5452	D770-784	World War, 1939-1945—Blockades
940.54211	D759-760.8	World War, 1939-1945—Campaigns—Great Britain	940.5467	D797	World War, 1939-1945—Registers of dead
940.54213	D757-.9	World War, 1939-1945—Campaigns—Germany	940.5472	D805	World War, 1939-1945—Prisoners and prisons
940.542131	D756.5.A7	Ardennes, Battle of the, 1944-1945	940.5475	D806-807	World War, 1939-1945—Medical care
940.542138	D765-.2	World War, 1939-1945—Campaigns—Poland	940.5477	D808-809	World War, 1939-1945—Civilian relief
940.5421384	D765.2.W3	Warsaw, Battle of, 1945	940.548(1-2)	D811-.5	World War, 1939-1945—Personal narratives
940.54214	D761-762	World War, 1939-1945—Campaigns—France	940.5488	D810.P6-.P7	World War, 1939-1945—Propaganda
940.54214	D756.5.V3	Verdun, Battle of, 1940	940.(55-56)005	D1050	Europe—History—1945- —Periodicals
940.54214	D756.5.D5	Dieppe Raid, 1942	940.(55-56)0071	D1050.8-.82	Europe—History—1945- —Study and teaching
940.5421428	D756.5.D8	Dunkerque (France), Battle of, 1940	940.5(5-6)	D1050-1075	Europe—History—1945-
940.5421495	D766.3-.32	World War, 1939-1945—Campaigns—Greece	940.55004	D1056-.2	Ethnology—Europe
940.5421497	D766.6-.62	World War, 1939-1945—Campaigns—Yugoslavia	941.0042	CB216-220	Anglo-Saxon race
940.54217	D847-.2	Communist countries	941.01	DA134-162	Great Britain—History to 1066
940.5421721	D764.3.S7	Stalingrad, Battle of, 1942-1943	941.0(2-46)	DA170-260	Great Britain—History—To 1485
940.5421731	D764.3.M	Moscow, Battle of, 1941-1942	941.021	DA196	Hastings, Battle of, 1066
940.5421772	D764.3	Odessa (Ukraine), Battle of, 1941	941.0(5-6)	DS777.545-779.29	China—History—1949-
940.54219218	D763.N4	Arnhem, Battle of, 1944			
940.5423	D766.82	World War, 1939-1945—Campaigns—Africa, North	941.0(5-8)	DA300-591	Great Britain—History—Modern period, 1485-
940.5423	D766.9	El Alamein, Battle of, Egypt, 1942	941.05	DA310-360	Great Britain—History—Tudors, 1485-1603
940.5425	D767.2-.25	World War, 1939-1945—Campaigns—Japan	941.052	DA331-339	Great Britain—History—Henry VIII, 1509-1547
940.5425	D767.99.045	World War, 1939-1945—Campaigns—Japan—Okinawa Island	941.055	DA350-360	Great Britain—History—Elizabeth, 1558-1603
			941.055	DA86.22.D7	Lisbon Expedition, 1589
940.5425	D764-766.7	World War, 1939-1945—Campaigns—Eastern front	941.06	DA370-419.5	Great Britain—History—Early Stuarts, 1603-1649
940.5426	D767-.99	World War, 1939-1945—Campaigns—Pacific Ocean	941.061	DA392-.1	Gunpowder Plot, 1605
940.5426	D767.92	Pearl Harbor (Hawaii), Attack on, 1941	941.062	DA410-429	Great Britain—History—Civil War, 1642-1649
940.5426	D774.M5	Midway, Battle of, 1942	941.063	DA420-429	Fifth Monarchy Men
940.5426	D774.J	Java Sea, Battle of the, 1942	941.071	DA499	Great Britain—History—George I, 1714-1727
940.5426	D774.C	Coral Sea, Battle of the, 1942	941.072	DA500	Great Britain—History—George II, 1727-1760
940.5426	D767.917	Tarawa, Battle of, 1943	941.073	DA505-522	Great Britain—History—George III, 1760-1820
940.5426	D767.99.I9	Iwo Jima, Battle of, 1945	941.073	DA535	Luddites
940.5428	D772.G7	Rio de la Plata, Battle of the, 1939	941.073	DA87.5 1794	First of June, 1794, Battle of
940.544	D785-792	World War, 1939-1945—Aerial operations	941.074	DA537-538	Great Britain—History—George IV, 1820-1830
940.545	D770-784	World War, 1939-1945—Naval operations	941.075	DA539-542	Great Britain—History—William IV, 1830-1837
			941.081	DA550-565	Great Britain—History—Victoria, 1837-1901

Dewey	LC	Subject Heading	Dewey	LC	Subject Heading

940 - 943

Dewey	LC	Subject Heading	Dewey	LC	Subject Heading
941.082	DA566-592	Great Britain—History—20th century	943	CB213-214	Civilization, Germanic
941.0892	DA150-162	Anglo-Saxons	943.0005	DAW1001	Europe, Central—Periodicals
941.089916	DA140-143	Celts	943.0006	DAW1004	Europe, Central—Congresses
941.1	DA750-890	Scotland	943.0025	DD15.5	Germany—Directories
941.1005	DA750	Scotland—Periodicals	943.004	DAW1026-1028	Ethnology—Europe, Central
941.101	DA777-778.9	Scotland—History—To 1057	943.004	DD73-78	Ethnology—Germany
941.10(2-5)	DA779-790	Scotland—History—1057-1603	943.005	DD301	Prussia (Germany)—Periodicals
941.104	DA784.6	Flodden, Battle of, 1513	943.0072	DD86-.7	Germany—Historiography
941.1063	DA803.8	Scotland—History—1649-1660	943.0072	DD345	Prussia (Germany)—Historiography
941.10(69-72)	DA813-814	Jacobites	943.01(1-4)	DD121-134.2	Germany—History—To 843
941.10(69-73)	DA809-814.5	Scotland—History—18th century	943.013	DD128	Merovingians
			943.0(13-25)	DD126.5	Donation of Pepin
941.1081	DA815-818	Scotland—History—19th century	943.014	DD129-134.9	Carolingians
			943.02	DD125-198.7	Holy Roman Empire—History
941.1082	DA821-826	Scotland—History—20th century	943.021	DD134.3-135	Germany—History—843-918
941.5	DA900-995	Ireland—History	943.022	DD136-140.7	Germany—History—Saxon House, 919-1024
941.5005	DA900	Ireland—Periodicals			
941.50(1-2)	DA930-932.6	Ireland—History—To 1172	943.023	DD141-144	Germany—History—Franconian House, 1024-1125
941.50(3-5)	DA933-937.5	Ireland—History—1172-1603			
941.506	DA940-946	Ireland—History—17th century	943.024	DD145-155	Germany—History—Hohenstaufen, 1138-1254
941.507	DA947-949.5	Ireland—History—18th century	943.02(6-9)	DD156-174.6	Germany—History—1273-1517
941.5081	DA949.7-958	Ireland—History—19th century	943.03	D220-271	Counter-Reformation
			943.03	DD176-189	Counter-Reformation
941.5082	DA959-965	Ireland—History—20th century	943.0(41-52)	DD394-399.8	Prussia (Germany)—History—1640-1740
			943.041	DD188-.5	Germany—History—1618-1648
941.7081	DA954	Fenians	943.0(43-52)	DD190-.8	Germany—History—1648-1740
942	DA20-690	England			
942	DA28-690	Great Britain—History	943.044	DD394.3	Fehrbellin, Battle of, 1675
942	DA110-115	Great Britain—Civilization	943.05	DD191-199	Germany—History—18th century
942.004	DA120-125	Ethnology—Great Britain			
942.005	DA20	England—Periodicals	943.052	DD399-.8	Prussia (Germany)—History—Frederick William I, 1713-1740
942.017	DA150-162	Anglo-Saxons			
942.017	DA150-162	Saxons			
942.06(6-9)	DA430-463	Great Britain—History—1660-1714	943.053	DD401-413.2	Prussia (Germany)—History—Frederick II, 1740-1786
942.073	DA87.7 1797	Spithead Mutiny, 1797			
942.073	DA88.5 1805	Trafalgar, Battle of, 1805	943.054	DD407.5	Dresden, Peace of, 1745
942.1	DA675-689	London (England)—History	943.05(3-7)	DD406-413.2	Prussia (Germany)—History—1740-1789
942.9	DA700-745	Wales			
942.9	DA714-722.1	Wales—History	943.0(57-84)	DD197-231	Germany—History—1789-1900
942.9	DA711.5	Wales—Civilization			
942.9005	DA700	Wales—Periodicals	943.06	DD414-416	Prussia (Germany)—History—Frederick William II, 1786-1797
943	DAW	Europe, Central			
943	DAW1031-1051	Europe, Central—History			
943	DAW1024	Europe, Central—Civilization	943.07	DD206-214	Germany—History—1815-1866
943	DD301-491	Prussia (Germany)	943.07	DD424-.9	Prussia (Germany)—History—Frederick William IV, 1840-1861
943	DD341-454	Prussia (Germany)—History			
943	DD331	Prussia (Germany)—Civilization			
943	DD	Germany	943.0(76-83)	DD425-446	Prussia (Germany)—History—William I, 1861-1888
943	DD84-257.4	Germany—History			
943	DD60-68	Germany—Civilization			

Dewey	LC	Subject Heading	Dewey	LC	Subject Heading
943.081	DD214-216	Germany—History—1866-1871	943.7	DB2000-3150	Czechoslovakia
943.08(2-8)	DD446-454	Prussia (Germany)—History—1870-	943.7	DB2044-2232	Czechoslovakia—History
			943.7	DB2185-2232	Czechoslovakia—History
943.08(3-4)	DD217-231	Germany—History—1871-1918	943.7	DB2035	Czechoslovakia—Civilization
943.083	DD223-.9	Germany—History—William I, 1871-1888	943.70025	DB2009	Czechoslovakia—Directories
943.08(4-79)	DD232-257.4	Germany—History—20th century	943.7004	DB2040-2043	Ethnology—Czechoslovakia
			943.7005	DB2000	Czechoslovakia—Periodicals
943.084	DD228-231	Germany—History—William II, 1888-1918	943.7006	DB2003	Czechoslovakia—Congresses
943.084	DD224-226	Germany—History—Frederick III, 1888	943.7032	DB2195-2202	Czechoslovakia—History—1918-1939
943.085	DD650.M5	Germany—History—Allied occupation, 1918-1930	943.7033	DB2205-2211	Czechoslovakia—History—1938-1945
943.085	DD248	Germany—History—Revolution, 1918	943.704	DB2215-2232	Czechoslovakia—History—1945-1992
943.085	DD249	Germany—History—Kapp Putsch, 1920	943.7042	DB2222	Czechoslovakia—History—Coup d'etat, 1948
943.085	DD249	Germany—History—March Uprising, 1921	943.7042	DB2232	Czechoslovakia—History—Intervention, 1968
943.085	DD249	Germany—History—Beer Hall Putsch, 1923	943.7043	DB2225-2232	Czechoslovakia—History—1968-1989
943.086	DD253-256.5	National socialism	943.7102	DB2155-2162	Bohemia (Czech Republic)—History—1618-1848
943.086	DD253-256.5	Germany—History—1933-1945	943.71023	DB2080-2133	Bohemia (Czech Republic)—History—To 1526
943.086	DD256.3-.4	Anti-Nazi movement	943.710232	DB2135-2151	Bohemia (Czech Republic)—History—1526-1618
943.086	DD247.R56	Germany—History—Night of the Long Knives, 1934	943.71024	DB2165-2182	Bohemia (Czech Republic)—History—1848-1918
943.086	DD135.G3315	Germany—History—Kristallnacht, 1938	943.712	DB2600-2650	Prague (Czech Republic)
943.087	DD258-262	Germany (West)	943.72	DB2300-2421	Moravia
943.087(4-5)	DD257-.4	Germany—History—1945-1955	943.72	DK4600.S46	Silesia, Upper (Poland and Czech Republic)—History
943.0879	DD257-.4	Germany—History—Unification, 1990	943.72	DB2345-2421	Moravia (Czech Republic)—History
943.09(79-8)	DD257.4	Germany—History—1990-	943.72	DB2335	Moravia (Czech Republic)—Civilization
943.1087	DD280-289	Germany (East)			
943.155	DD851-900	Berlin (Germany)	943.72004	DB2340-2342	Moravia (Czech Republic)—Ethnography
943.21	DD801.S31-.S59	Saxony (Germany)—History			
943.3	DJK76.2-.8	Danube River Valley	943.72021	DB2385-2391	Moravia (Czech Republic)—History—To 906
943.6	DB1-879	Austria			
943.6	DB30	Austria—Civilization	943.73	DB2700-3150	Slovakia
943.6004	DB33-34.5	Ethnology—Austria	943.73	DB2744-3000	Slovakia—History
943.6005	DB1	Austria—Periodicals	943.73	DB2735	Slovakia—Civilization
943.60072	DB36.8-.9	Austria—Historiography	943.73004	DB2740-2743	Ethnology—Slovakia
943.60(25-3)	DB57-59	Austria—History—1273-1519	943.7302	DB2795-2791	Slovakia—History—To 1526
943.602	DB46-99.2	Austria—History			
943.603	DB65.2-77	Austria—History—1519-1740	943.73023	DB2795-2801	Slovakia—History—1526-1800
943.6051	DB96-99.2	Austria—History—1918-1938	943.7302(34-4)	DB2795-2801	Slovakia—History—1800-1918
943.6052	DB99	Austria—History—1938-1945	943.730(3-5)	DB2805-2841	Slovakia—History—1918-1993
943.6053	DB99.2	Austria—History—1955-	943.73033	DB2822	Slovakia—History—Uprising, 1944
943.613	DB841-860	Vienna (Austria)			
943.648	DB881-898	Liechtenstein	943.73042	DB2842	Slovakia—History—Intervention, 1968
943.648	DB891-894	Liechtenstein—History			
943.648005	DB881	Liechtenstein—Periodicals	943.8	DK4010-4800	Poland

Dewey	LC	Subject Heading	Dewey	LC	Subject Heading
943.8	DK4110-4115	Poland—Civilization	943.8056	DK4443	Poland—History—1980-1989
943.8004	DK4120-4122	Ethnology—Poland	943.8057	DK4442	Poland—History—1989-
943.8005	DK4010	Poland—Periodicals	943.82	DK4650-4685	Gdansk (Poland)
943.8006	DK4018	Poland—Congresses	943.84	DK4610-4645	Warsaw (Poland)
943.80072	DK4139-.25	Poland—Historiography	943.85	DK4600.S44	Silesia, Lower (Poland and Germany)
943.802	DK4186-4348	Poland—History—To 1795	943.85	DK4600.S46	Silesia, Upper (Poland and Czech Republic)—History
943.802(2-3)	DK4186-4289	Poland—History—To 1572			
943.8022	DK4210-.7	Poland—History—To 960 (ca.)	943.86	DK4700-4735	Krakow (Poland)
943.8022	DK4211-4249.5	Poland—History—Piast period, 960-1386	943.9	DB901-999	Hungary
			943.9	DB920.5	Hungary—Civilization
943.8022	DK4222	Poland—History—Mieszko II, 1025-1034	943.9004	DB919-.2	Ethnology—Hungary
			943.900494511	DB919	Magyars
943.8022	DK4223	Poland—History—Casimir I, 1040-1058	943.9005	DB901	Hungary—Periodicals
			943.901	DB927-928.9	Hungary—History—To 896
943.8022	DK4227-4246.5	Poland—History—1138-1305	943.902	DB929-.9	Hungary—History—896-1301
943.8022	DK4245.7	Poland—History—Mongol Invasion, 1241	943.903	DB930.2	Hungary—History—Charles Robert, 1308-1342
943.802(3-4)	DK4276	Poland—History—16th century	943.903	DB930.3	Hungary—History—Louis I, 1342-1382
943.8023	DK4249.7-4289	Poland—History—Jagellons, 1386-1572	943.903	DB930.4	Hungary—History—Sigismund, 1387-1437
943.802(4-5)	DK4289.5-4328	Poland—History—Elective monarchy, 1572-1763	943.9041	DB931.94-932.48	Hungary—History—Turkish occupation, 1529-1699
943.80(25-3)	DK4314.5	Poland—History—18th century	943.9042	DB940-953	Hungary—History—Francis Joseph, 1848-1916
943.8025	DK4328.9-4348	Poland—History—Parititon period, 1763-1796	943.90(43-54)	DB947-957	Hungary—History—20th century
943.8025	DK4330-4348	Poland—History—Stanislaus II Augustus, 1764-1795	943.9043	DB932.3-934	Hungary—History—1699-1848
			943.905(1-2)	DB955	Hungary—History—1918-1945
943.8025	DK4338-4345	Poland—History—Revolution of 1794	943.9052	DB957	Hungary—History—Revolution, 1956
943.8032	DK4359-4363	Poland—History—Revolution, 1830-1832	943.905(3-4)	DB956-957	Hungary—History—1945-
943.8032	DK4363.2	Poland—History—Partisan Campaign, 1833	943.912	DB981-999	Budapest (Hungary)
			944	DC	France
943.8032	DK4364	Poland—History—Revolution, 1846	944	DC35-423	France—History
			944	DC33-.9	France—Civilization
943.8033	DK4366-4378	Poland—History—Revolution, 1863-1864	944.0025	DC15	France—Directories
			944.004	DC34-.5	Ethnology—France
943.8033	DK4379.5-4395	Poland—History—1864-1918	944.005	DC1	France—Periodicals
			944.01	DC60-81.5	France—History—To 987
943.8033	DK4383-4389	Poland—History—Revolution, 1905-1907	944.02(4-6)	DC97.5-101.7	France—History—14th century
943.8033	DK4390-4395	Poland—History—German occupation, 1914-1918	944.025	DC96-105	Hundred Years War, 1339-1453
943.8033	DK4394-4395	Poland—History—Austrian occupation, 1915-1918	944.026	DC101-.7	France—History—Charles VI, 1380-1422
943.804	DK4404-4409	Poland—History—Wars of 1918-1921	944.026	DC101.5.C33	France—History—Cabochien Uprising, 1413
943.804	DK4409.4	Poland—History—Coup d'etat, 1926	944.026	DC101.5.A2	Agincourt, Battle of, 1415
943.804(4-53)	DK4397-4420	Poland—History—1918-1945	944.026	DC102-105.9	France—History—Charles VII, 1422-1461
943.8053	DK4410-4415	Poland—History—Occupation, 1939-1945	944.027	DC106-.9	France—History—Louis XI, 1461-1483
943.805(4-7)	DK4429-4442	Poland—History—1945-	944.027	DC107-.2	France—History—Charles VIII, 1483-1498

Dewey	LC	Subject Heading	Dewey	LC	Subject Heading
944.027	DC108-109	France—History—Louis XII, 1498-1515	944.083(7-8)	DC422	France—Politics and government—1974-1981
944.028	DC113-.5	France—History—Francis I, 1515-1547	944.0838	DC423	France—Politics and government—1981-
944.028	DC114-.5	France—History—Henry II, 1547-1559	944.36	DC701-790	Paris (France)
944.028	DC118	Saint Bartholomew's Day, Massacre of, France, 1572	944.9	DC608.1-.9	Riviera (France)
			944.945	DC611.C8-.C839	Corsica (France)—History
944.0(29-3)	DC116-118	France—History—War of the Huguenots, 1562-1598	944.949	DC941-947	Monaco
			945	DG	Italy
944.029	DC115	France—History—Francis II, 1559-1560	945	DG401-583	Italy
			945	DG461-583	Italy—History
944.029	DC116-118	France—History—Charles IX, 1560-1574	945.0025	DG413	Italy—Directories
			945.004	DG455-457	Ethnology—Italy
944.029	DC119-120	France—History—Henry III, 1574-1589	945.005	DG401	Italy—Periodicals
			945.0071	DG465.8	Italy—Study and teaching
944.03	DC120.8-138	France—History—Bourbons, 1589-1789	945.0072	DG465-.7	Italy—Historiography
			945.01	DG503-514.7	Italy—History—476-774
944.03(2-3)	DC124.45	Franco-Spanish War, 1635-1659	945.01	DG511-514.7	Lombards
			945.02	DG515-519	Franks
944.031	DC122-.9	France—History—Henry IV, 1589-1610	945.02	DG509	Italy—History—Gothic War, 535-555
944.032	DC123-.9	France—History—Louis XIII, 1610-1643	945.02	DG515-517	Italy—History—Carolingian rule, 774-887
944.033	DC124.5-130	France—History—Louis XIV, 1643-1715	945.02	DG517.5-518	Italy—History—Period of the Italian Kings, 887-962
944.033	DC124.45	Dunes, Battle of the, 1658	945.0(3-4)	DG520-529	Italy—History—Germanic rule, 962-1268
944.034	DC133-135	France—History—Louis XV, 1715-1774	945.0(4-5)	DG530-537.8	Italy—History—1268-1492
			945.0(5-84)	DG538-551.8	Italy—History—1492-1870
944.035	DC136-137.5	France—History—Louis XVI, 1774-1793	945.05	DG737.42	Medici, House of
			945.0(6-7)	DG539-541.8	Italy—History—16th century
944.04(1-2)	DC139-190.8	France—History—Revolution, 1789-1799	945.06	DG541	Fornovo, Battle of, 1495
			945.0(7-8)	DG550.5-551.8	Italy—History—1789-1870
944.0(46-5)	DC191.2-249	France—History—Consulate and First Empire, 1799-1815	945.0(7-83)	DG546-549	Italy—History—1789-1815
			945.08(3-4)	DG552-554.5	Italy—History—1849-1870
944.05	DC256-260	France—History—Louis XVIII, 1814-1824	945.083	DG551	Italy—History—Uprising, 1831
944.063	DC265-269	France—History—Louis Philip, 1830-1848	945.083	DG554.5	Italy—History—War of 1860-1861
944.063	DC261-262	France—History—July Revolution, 1830	945.083	DG554.5.E96	Expedition of the Thousand, Italy, 1860
			945.0(84-91)	DG555-569	Italy—History—1870-1915
944.07	DC271.5-274.5	France—History—Second Republic, 1848-1852	945.09(1-24)	DG572	Italy—History—Allied occupation, 1943-1947
944.07	DC274-.5	France—History—Coup d'etat, 1851	945.09(1-27)	DG577.5-579	Italy—History—1945-1976
			945.091	DG570-572	Italy—History—1914-1945
944.07	DC275-292	France—History—Second Empire, 1852-1870	945.091	DG571.75	Italy—History—March on Rome, 1922
944.081	DC342.8-396	France—History—Third Republic, 1870-1940	945.091	DG571	Fascism
944.0812	DC281-326.5	Franco-Prussian War, 1870-1871	945.091	DG572	Italy—History—German occupation, 1943-1945
944.0812	DC309.E8	Epinal (France), Battle of, 1870	945.091	DG572	Italy—History—Grand Council, 1943
944.0814	DC385	France—History—German occupation, 1914-1918	945.092(7-9)	DG581-583	Italy—History—1976-
			945.(1-3)	DG600-609	Italy, Northern
944.0816	DC397	France—History—German occupation, 1940-1945	945.18	DG975.R6	Riviera (Italy)
			945.182	DG631-645	Genoa (Italy)
944.08(2-4)	DC398-423	France—History—1945-	945.2	DG651-664.5	Lombardy (Italy)
944.083(6-7)	DC421	France—Politics and government—1969-1974	945.31	DG670-684.72	Venice (Italy)
			945.5	DG731-759.3	Tuscany (Italy)
			945.6	DG691-694	Italy, Central

Dewey	LC	Subject Heading
945.6	DG791-800	Papal States
945.6	DG796-800	Papal States—History
945.632	DG803-818	Rome (Italy)—History
945.7	DG819-831	Italy, Southern
945.73	DG845.8-851	Naples (Kingdom)—History
945.8	DG861-875	Sicily (Italy)—History
945.85	DG987-999	Malta
945.85	DG989.8-994.8	Malta—History
946	DP1-402	Spain
946	DP48-.9	Spain—Civilization
946.0025	DP11	Spain—Directories
946.004	DP52-53	Ethnology—Spain
946.005	DP1	Spain—Periodicals
946.006	DP2	Spain—Congresses
946.0072	DP63-.83	Spain—Historiography
946.01	DP91-96	Spain—History—To 711
946.0(2-3)	DP97.3-160.8	Spain—History—711-1516
946.03	DP161.5-166	Spain—History—Ferdinand and Isabella, 1479-1516
946.04	DP170-189	Spain—History—House of Austria, 1516-1700
946.042	DP172-175	Spain—History—Charles I, 1516-1556
946.043	DP176-181	Spain—History—Philip II, 1556-1598
946.051	DP182-183.9	Spain—History—Philip III, 1598-1621
946.052	DP184-185.9	Spain—History—Philip IV, 1621-1665
946.053	DP186-189	Spain—History—Charles II, 1665-1700
946.054	DP192-200.8	Spain—History—Bourbons, 1700-
946.054	DP194-200.8	Spain—History—18th century
946.055	DP195	Spain—History—Louis I, 1724
946.056	DP198-.7	Spain—History—Ferdinand VI, 1746-1759
946.057	DP199-.9	Spain—History—Charles III, 1759-1788
946.0(58-7)	DP201-232.6	Spain—History—19th century
946.058	DP200-.8	Spain—History—Charles IV, 1788-1808
946.07(3-4)	DP228-231.5	Spain—History—Carlist War, 1873-1876
946.072	DP214-215.9	Spain—History—Ferdinand VII, 1813-1833
946.072	DP212-220	Spain—History—Bourbon Restoration, 1814-1868
946.072	DP215	Spain—History—Revolution, 1820-1823
946.072	DP216-220	Spain—History—Isabella II, 1833-1868
946.072	DP219-.2	Spain—History—Carlist War, 1833-1840
946.072	DP217	Spain—History—Revolution, 1854
946.073	DP222-232.6	Spain—History—Revolutionary period, 1868-1875
946.073	DP230-231.5	Spain—History—Republic, 1873-1875
946.074	DP232-.6	Spain—History—Alfonso XII, 1875-1885
946.074	DP233-272.4	Spain—History—Alfonso XIII, 1886-1931
946.074	DP247	Spain—History—Dictatorship, 1923-1930
946.08	DP250	Spain—History—Revolution, 1931
946.081	DP250-269.9	Spain—History—Republic, 1931-1939
946.081	DP269.A1-.9	Spain—History—Civil War, 1936-1939
946.082	DP270-271	Spain—History—1939-1975
946.083	DP272-.4	Spain—History—1975-
946.083	DP272	Spain—History—Coup d'etat, 1981
946.41	DP350-374	Madrid (Spain)
946.79	DC921-930	Andorra
946.82	DP115-118	Granada (Kingdom)—History
946.9	DP501-900	Portugal—History
946.9	DP532-.7	Portugal—Civilization
946.9004	DP533-534.5	Ethnology—Portugal
946.9005	DP501	Portugal—Periodicals
946.90072	DP536.8-.96	Portugal—Historiography
946.901	DP558-618	Portugal—History—To 1385
946.90(1-2)	DP570	Portugal—History—Alfonso Henriques, 1139-1185
946.90(2-4)	DP620-682.2	Portugal—History—Modern, 1580-
946.902	DP571	Portugal—History—Sancho I, 1185-1211
946.902	DP572	Portugal—History—Alfonso II, 1211-1223
946.902	DP573	Portugal—History—Sancho II, 1223-1248
946.902	DP574	Portugal—History—Alfonso III, 1248-1279
946.902	DP575-.3	Portugal—History—Denis, 1279-1325
946.902	DP576	Portugal—History—Alfonso IV, 1325-1357
946.902	DP577	Portugal—History—Pedro I, 1357-1367
946.902	DP578	Portugal—History—Fernando, 1367-1383
946.902	DP580	Portugal—History—Interregnum, 1383-1385
946.902	DP582-618	Portugal—History—Period of discoveries, 1385-1580
946.902	DP585-590	Portugal—History—John I, 1385-1433

Dewey	LC	Subject Heading	Dewey	LC	Subject Heading
946.902	DP592-594	Portugal—History—Edward, 1433-1438	946.9044	DP681	Portugal—History—Revolution, 1974
946.902	DP596-598	Portugal—History—Alfonso V, 1438-1481	946.9044	DP681	Portugal—History—Coup d'etat, 1975
946.902	DP600-602	Portugal—History—John II, 1481-1495	946.9425	DP752-776	Lisbon (Portugal)
			947	DJK	Europe, Eastern
946.902	DP604-606	Portugal—History—Manual, 1495-1521	947	DJK24	Europe, Eastern—Civilization
946.902	DP608-610	Portugal—History—John III, 1521-1557	947	DK1-290.3	Russia
			947	DK510-651	Russia
946.902	DP612-616	Portugal—History—Sebastian, 1557-1578	947	DK65-290.3	Russia—History
			947	DK32-.7	Russia—Civilization
946.902	DP618	Portugal—History—Henry I, 1578-1580	947.0004	DJK26-28	Ethnology—Europe, Eastern
946.902	DP614	Kassr-el-Kebir, Battle of, 1578	947.0005	DJK1	Europe, Eastern—Periodicals
946.902	DP622-629	Portugal—History—Spanish dynasty, 1580-1640	947.0006	DJK1.5	Europe, Eastern—Congresses
946.902	DP628	Portugal—History—Revolution, 1640	947.00071	DJK35-36	Europe, Eastern—Study and teaching
946.903(3-4)	DP642-644.9	Portugal—History—Maria I, 1777-1816	947.00072	DJK32-34	Europe, Eastern—Historiography
946.903(4-5)	DP650-651	Portugal—History—John VI, 1816-1826	947.000904(1-4)	DJK49	Europe, Eastern—History—1918-1945
946.903(5-6)	DP653-660	Portugal—History—1826-1853	947.00090(44-5)	DJK50	Europe, Eastern—History—1945-
946.9032	DP634-.8	Portugal—History—John IV, 1640-1656	947.000904(4-8)	DJK50	Europe, Eastern—History—1945-1989
946.9032	DP635	Portugal—History—Alfonso VI, 1656-1683	947.00090(48-5)	DJK51	Europe, Eastern—History—1989-
946.9032	DP635	Elvas, Linhas de, Battle of, 1659	947.004	DK33-35	Ethnology—Russia (Federation)
946.9032	DP636-.8	Portugal—History—Peter II, 1683-1706	947.005	DK1	Russia—Periodicals
			947.006	DK2.5	Russia—Congresses
946.9032	DP638	Portugal—History—John V, 1706-1750	947.0(1-42)	DK70-104	Russia—History—To 1533
			947.02	DK511.G44	Didgora Mountain (Georgia), Battle of, 1121
946.9033	DP639-641.9	Portugal—History—Joseph I, 1750-1777	947.043	DK106-107	Russia—History—Ivan IV, 1533-1584
946.9034	DP650	Portugal—History—Conspiracy of 1817	947.045	DK111-112	Russia—History—Time of Troubles, 1598-1613
946.9035	DP650	Portugal—History—Revolution, 1820	947.04(6-9)	DK112.8-126	Russia—History—1613-1689
946.9035	DP659	Portugal—History—Civil War, 1846-1847	947.046	DK112.8-264.8	Russia—History—1613-1917
946.9035	DP659	Portugal—History—Uprising, 1846	947.0(47-83)	DK112.8-264.8	Russia—History—1613-1917
946.9036	DP665-.5	Portugal—History—Peter V, 1853-1861	947.048	DK116-122.5	Russia—History—Aleksei Mikhailovich, 1645-1676
946.9036	DP668-669	Portugal—History—Charles I, 1889-1908	947.048	DK118.5	Russia—History—Rebellion of Stenka Razin, 1667-1671
946.9036	DP662	Portugal—History—Revolution, 1891	947.049	DK125	Russia—History—Sofia Alekseevna, 1682-1689
946.904	DP670-682.2	Portugal—History—20th century	947.05	DK128-148	Russia—History—Peter I, 1689-1725
946.904(1-3)	DP675-680.5	Portugal—History—1910-1974	947.05	DK133	Russia—History—Streltsy Revolt, 1698
946.9041	DP674-682.2	Portugal—History—Revolution, 1910	947.05	DL733-743	Northern War, 1700-1721
946.9042	DP680	Portugal—History—Revolution, 1926	947.0(72-83)	DK188-264.8	Russia—History—1801-1917
946.9044	DP680	Portugal—History—1974-			

Dewey	LC	Subject Heading	Dewey	LC	Subject Heading
947.072	DK190-201	Russia—History—Alexander I, 1801-1825	947.560(7-83)	DS194-.5	Armenia—History—1801-1900
947.073	DK209-215.97	Russia—History—Nicholas I, 1825-1855	947.5608(3-6)	DS195-.3	Armenia—History—1901-
947.073	DK212	Russia—History—December Uprising, 1825	947.560 (83-841)	DS195.5	Armenian massacres, 1915-1923
947.0738	DK214-215	Crimean War, 1853-1856	947.560841	DS195.5	Armenia—History—Revolution, 1917-1920
947.081	DK219-223	Russia—History—Alexander II, 1855-1881	947.560841	DS195.5	Armenia (Republic)—History—Uprising, 1921
947.082	DK234-243	Russia—History—Alexander III, 1881-1894	947.58	DK670-679.5	Georgia (Republic)
947.083	DK251-264.8	Russia—History—Nicholas II, 1894-1917	947.(6-7)	DK509.1-.95	Bessarabia (Moldova and Ukraine)
947.083	DK263-264.7	Russia—History—Revolution, 1905-1907	947.7	DJK61-66	Black Sea Coast
947.0841	DK265-.95	Soviet Union—History—Revolution, 1917-1921	947.7	DK508-.95	Ukraine
947.0841	DK265.19	Russia—History—February Revolution, 1917	947.77	DK508.92-.939	Kiev (Ukraine)
947.0841	DK266-.5	Soviet Union—History—Allied interventon, 1918-1920	947.79	DJK71-76	Carpathian Mountains
			947.8	DK507-.95	Belarus
947.0841	DK265.42.F8	Black Sea Mutiny, 1919	947.8	DK507.37-.78	Belarus—History
947.0842	DK267-273	Soviet Union—History—1925-1953	947.9	DK502.3-.7	Baltic States
			947.9	DK502.7	Baltic States—History
947.0842	DK273	Soviet Union—History—1939-1945	947.93	DK505-.95	Lithuania
			947.93	DK505.37-.79	Lithuania—History
947.0842	DK273	Soviet Union—History—German occupation, 1941-1944	947.96	DK504-.95	Latvia
			947.96	DK504-.37-.79	Latvia—History
			947.98	DK503-.95	Estonia
947.085	DK274-282	Soviet Union—History—1953-1985	947.98	DK503.75-.77	Estonia—History—1944-1991
947.0854	DK285-290.3	Soviet Union—History—1985-1991	947.9808	DK503.8-.85	Estonia—History—1991-
			948	DL	Scandinavia
947.086	DK285-290.3	Soviet Union—History—Attempted coup, 1991	948	DL30-33	Scandinavia—Civilization
			948	DL43-87	Scandinavia—History
947.31	DK588-609	Moscow (Russia)	948.004	DL41-42	Ethnology—Scandinavia
947.48	DK34.K14	Kalmyks	948.005	DL1	Scandinavia—Periodicals
947.52004	DK34.K13	Kabardians	948.006	DL1.5	Scandinavia—Congresses
947.54	DK690-699.5	Azerbaijan	948.03	DL61-65	Scandinavia—History—15th century
947.56	DS161-195.5	Armenia	948.04	DL75-81	Scandinavia—History—The Count's War, 1534-1536
947.56	DS173-195.5	Armenia—History			
947.56	DS181-184	Armenia—History—To 428	948.08	DL83-87	Scandinavia—History—20th century
947.56	DS181-184	Armenia—History—Arsacid (Arshakuni) dynasty, 66-428	948.1	DL431-433	Norway—Civilization
			948.1	DL401-596	Norway—History
947.56	DS186-188	Armenia—History—428-1522	948.1004	DL441-442	Ethnology—Norway
			948.1005	DL401-403	Norway—Periodicals
947.56	DS186-188	Armenia—History—428-640	948.10072	DL445	Norway—Historiography
			948.101	DL460-478	Norway—History—To 1030
947.56	DS186-188	Armenia—History—Arab period, 640-885	948.101	DL480-502	Norway—History—1030-1397
947.56	DS186-188	Armenia—History—Turkic Mongol Domination, 1045-1522	948.10(2-3)	DL500-502	Norway—History—Christian Frederick, 1814
			948.102	DL485-502	Norway—History—1397-1814
947.56	DS171	Armenia—Civilization	948.102	DL490	Norway—History—Christian IV, 1588-1648
947.56	DK680-689.5	Armenia (Republic)			
947.56004	DS172	Ethnology—Armenia	948.102	DL490	Norway—History—Scottish Expedition, 1612
947.5607	DS191-193	Armenia—History—1522-1800	948.102	DL490	Norway—History—Hannibal's War, 1644-1645
			948.102	DL490	Norway—History—Frederick III, 1648-1670

Dewey	LC	Subject Heading	Dewey	LC	Subject Heading
948.102	DL495-.8	Norway—History—Christian V, 1670-1699	948.503	DL766	Sweden—History—Revolution, 1772
948.102	DL499	Norway—History—War of 1807-1814	948.505	DL860-879	Sweden—History—20th century
948.103	DL503-526	Norway—History—1814-1905	948.505(1-5)	DL867-870	Sweden—History—Gustavus V, 1907-1950
948.1041	DL530-532	Norway—History—1905-1940	948.5051	DL868	Sweden—History—Farmers' Demonstration, 1914
948.1041	DL525	Norway—History—Separation from Sweden, 1905	948.505(5-7)	DL872-876	Sweden—History—Gustavus VI Adolphus, 1950-1973
948.1041	DL532	Norway—History—German Occupation, 1940-1945	948.505(7-6)	DL877-879	Sweden—History—Carl XVI Gustav, 1973-
948.104(5-9)	DL533	Norway—History—1945-	948.73	DL976	Stockholm (Sweden)
948.5	DL631-635	Sweden—Civilization	948.9	DL101-291	Denmark—History
948.5	DL601-991	Sweden—History	948.9	DL131-133	Denmark—Civilization
948.5004	DL639-641	Ethnology—Sweden	948.9004	DL141-142	Ethnology—Denmark
948.5005	DL601	Sweden—Periodicals	948.9005	DL101	Denmark—Periodicals
948.50072	DL645	Sweden—Historiography	948.90(1-2)	DL174-183.9	Denmark—History—1241-1397
948.501	DL660-700.9	Sweden—History—To 1397			
948.501	DL689	Sweden—History—Magnus II Ericksson, 1319-1363	948.901	DL162-173.8	Denmark—History—To 1241
948.5014	DL65	Vikings	948.9015	DL176	Denmark—History—Waldemar IV, 1340-1375
948.5018	DL696-700.9	Sweden—History—1397-1523	948.90(2-3)	DL182-192.3	Denmark—History—1448-1660
948.5018	DL694	Kalmar, Union of, 1397	948.902	DL179-181.6	Denmark—History—1397-1448
948.50(2-3)	DL704.6-.7	Sweden—History—17th century	948.90(3-4)	DL201-249	Denmark—History—19th century
948.50(2-5)	DL701-879	Sweden—History—1523-1718	948.90(3-4)	DL205-208	Denmark—History—Frederick VI, 1808-1839
948.502	DL703	Sweden—History—Gustavus I Vasa, 1523-1560	948.903	DL185-192.8	Denmark—History—Frederick I, 1523-1533
948.502	DL703.8	Sweden—History—Eric XIV, 1560-1568	948.903	DL187	Denmark—History—Christian III, 1534-1559
948.502	DL704.8	Sweden—History—Charles IX, 1604-1611	948.903	DL187	Denmark—History—The Count's War, 1534-1536
948.502	DL705.A2-715	Sweden—History—Gustavus II, Adolphus, 1611-1632	948.903	DL187	Denmark—History—Coup d'etat, 1536
948.502	DL710	Kalmar War, 1611-1613	948.903	DL188-.8	Denmark—History—Frederick II, 1559-1588
948.50(3-4)	DL807-859	Sweden—History—1814-1905	948.903	DL189-.5	Denmark—History—Christian IV, 1588-1648
948.503	DL725.7	Sweden—History—Charles X Gustavus, 1654-1660	948.903	DL191.8	Denmark—History—Frederick III, 1648-1670
948.503	DL727-729	Sweden—History—Charles XI, 1660-1697	948.903	DL192.3	Denmark—History—Coup d'etat, 1660
948.503	DL730-743	Sweden—History—Charles XII, 1697-1718	948.903	DL195-.8	Denmark—History—Christian V, 1670-1699
948.503	DL747-805	Sweden—History—1718-1814	948.903	DL196-.8	Denmark—History—Fredrick IV, 1699-1730
948.503	DL753	Sweden—History—Ulrika Eleonora, 1718-1720	948.903	DL197-199	Denmark—History—18th century
948.503	DL755-759	Sweden—History—Frederick I, 1720-1751	948.903	DL199-.8	Denmark—History—Coup d'etat, 1784
948.503	DL757	Sweden—History—Insurrection, 1743	948.903	DL206	Denmark—History—War of 1807-1814
948.503	DL766-770	Sweden—History—Gustavus III, 1771-1792	948.90(4-7)	DL248-263	Denmark—History—1900-

Dewey	LC	Subject Heading
948.904	DL209-212	Denmark—History—Christian VIII, 1839-1848
948.904	DL213-228	Denmark—History—Frederick VII, 1848-1863
948.904	DL217-241	Denmark—History—1849-1866
948.904	DL234-249	Denmark—History—Christian IX, 1863-1906
948.905(1-5)	DL255-257	Denmark—History—Christian X, 1912-1947
948.9051	DL256.5-257	Denmark—History—German occupation, 1940-1945
948.913	DL276	Copenhagen (Denmark)
948.97	DL1002-1180	Finland
948.97	DL1017	Finland—Civilization
948.97004	DL1018-1020	Ethnology—Finland
948.97005	DL1002	Finland—Periodicals
948.97006	DL1004	Finland—Congresses
948.970072	DL1025	Finland—Historiography
948.9701	DL1050-1052.9	Finland—History—To 1523
948.9701	DL485	Kalmar, Union of, 1397
948.9701	DL179	Kalmar, Union of, 1397
948.9701	DL1055-1141.6	Finland—History—1523-1611
948.9701	DL1058-1063	Finland—History—Gustavus II Adolphus, 1611-1632
948.9701	DL190	Dano-Swedish War, 1643-1645
948.9701	DL190	Fehmarn, Battle of, 1644
948.9701	DL1060-.5	Finland—History—Charles X Gustavus, 1654-1660
948.9701	DL192	Dano-Swedish Wars, 1657-1660
948.9701	DL1063-.9	Finland—History—18th century
948.970(2-3)	DL1066-1141.6	Finland—History—20th century
948.9702	DL1065-.8	Finland—History—1809-1917
948.97031	DL1070-1075	Finland—History—Revolution, 1917-1918
948.97031	DL1084	Finland—History—1918-1939
948.9703(2-4)	DL1090-1105	Finland—History—1939-
948.97032	DL1095-1105	Russo-Finnish War, 1939-1940
948.971	DL1175-.95	Helsinki
949.12	DL301-398	Iceland
949.12	DL351-380	Iceland—History
949.12004	DL331-334	Ethnology—Iceland
949.12005	DL301	Iceland—Periodicals
949.1201	DL357-360	Iceland—History—To 1262
949.120(4-5)	DL375	Iceland—History—1918-1945
949.2	DJ	Netherlands
949.2	DH	Netherlands
949.2	DH	Benelux countries
949.2	DJ71	Netherlands—Civilization
949.2	DH71	Netherlands—Civilization
949.2	DH95-207	Netherlands—History
949.2	DJ95-292	Netherlands—History
949.2004	DH91-92	Ethnology—Netherlands
949.2004	DJ91-92	Ethnology—Netherlands
949.2005	DH1	Netherlands—Periodicals
949.2005	DJ1	Netherlands—Periodicals
949.201	DH141-162	Netherlands—History—To 1384
949.201	DJ151-152	Netherlands—History—To 1384
949.201	DH171-177	Netherlands—History—House of Burgundy, 1384-1477
949.20(2-3)	DH185-207	Netherlands—Wars of Independence, 1556-1648
949.202	DH179-184	Netherlands—History—House of Habsburg, 1477-1556
949.202	DJ151-152	Netherlands—History—House of Habsburg, 1477-1556
949.202	DH182	Netherlands—History—Charles V, 1506-1555
949.202	DJ151-152	Netherlands—History—Charles V, 1506-1555
949.203	DH199.D4	Deventer, Surrender of, 1587
949.203	DJ170	Netherlands—History—Twelve Years' Truce, 1609-1621
949.203	DH201	Netherlands—History—Twelve Years' Truce, 1609-1621
949.204	DJ180-209	Netherlands—History—1648-1795
949.204	DJ180-182	Anglo-Dutch War, 1664-1667
949.204	DJ190-191	Dutch War, 1672-1678
949.204	DJ205-206	Anglo-Dutch War, 1780-1784
949.205	DJ211	Netherlands—History—Batavian Republic, 1795-1806
949.205	DJ241	Netherlands—History—1815-1830
949.20(6-71)	DJ281-287	Netherlands—History—Wilhelmina, 1898-1948
949.206	DJ241-251	Netherlands—History—1830-1849
949.206	DJ251	Netherlands—History—William II, 1840-1849
949.206	DJ261	Netherlands—History—William III, 1849-1890
949.207(1-3)	DJ288-292	Netherlands—History—1945-
949.2071	DJ287	Netherlands—History—German occupation, 1940-1945
949.2072	DJ288-289	Netherlands—History—Juliana, 1948-1980

Dewey	LC	Subject Heading	Dewey	LC	Subject Heading
949.2073	DJ290-292	Netherlands—History—Beatrix, 1980-	949.405	DQ131-151	Switzerland—History—Helvetic Republic, 1798-1803
949.213	DJ401.F5-.F59	Frisians	949.40(6-74)	DQ154-191	Switzerland—History—1815-
949.2352	DJ411.A5-59	Amsterdam (Netherlands)			
949.3	DH401-811	Belgium	949.4062	DQ154	Switzerland—History—1815-1830
949.3	DH471	Belgium—Civilization			
949.30(1-2)	DH571-584	Belgium—History—To 1555	949.4062	DQ156	Switzerland—History—1830-1848
949.3004	DH491-492	Ethnology—Belgium			
949.3005	DH401	Belgium—Periodicals	949.4062	DQ158-161	Switzerland—History—Sonderbund, 1845-1847
949.302	DH584	Belgium—History—Charles V, 1506-1555	949.40(63-74)	DQ171-210	Switzerland—History—1848-
949.302	DH585-606	Belgium—History—1555-1648	949.407	DQ201-210	Switzerland—History—20th century
949.302	DH607-619	Belgium—History—1648-1794	949.451	DQ458	Geneva (Switzerland)—History—1536-1603
949.302	DH616-618.5	Belgium—History—Revolution, 1789-1790	949.47	DQ820-829	Alps
949.302	DH620-631	Belgium—History—1794-1814	949.5	DF	Greece
			949.5004	DF135	Ethnology—Greece
949.303	DH650-665	Belgium—History—Revolution, 1830-1839	949.5005	DF10	Greece—Periodicals
			949.501	DF559	Adrianople, Battle of, 378
949.303	DH671-676	Belgium—History—Leopold II, 1865-1909	949.50(13-3)	DF501-649	Byzantine Empire
			949.50(13-3)	DF550-649	Byzantine Empire—History
949.3041	DH681-685	Belgium—History—Albert I, 1909-1934	949.50(13-3) 004	DF542-.4	Ethnology—Byzantine Empire
949.3041	DH682	Belgium—History—German occupation, 1914-1918	949.50(13-3) 005	DF501	Byzantine Empire—Periodicals
949.3042	DH687	Belgium—History—German occupation, 1940-1945	949.50(13-3) 006	DF501.5	Byzantine Empire—Congresses
949.304(3-4)	DH690-692	Belgium—History—Baudoin I, 1951-	949.50(13-3) 0071	DF505.8-.82	Byzantine Empire—Study and teaching
949.332	DH802-809.95	Brussels (Belgium)	949.50(13-3) 0072	DF505-.7	Byzantine Empire—Historiography
949.35	DH901-925	Luxembourg			
949.35	DH908-918.5	Luxembourg—History	949.50(13-3) 0099	DF506-.5	Emperors—Byzantine Empire
949.3502	DH913	Luxembourg (Luxembourg)—History—Siege, 1684	949.5013	DF553.5-568	Byzantine Empire—History—To 527
949.4	DQ	Switzerland—History	949.5013	DF561	Byzantine Empire—History—Arcadius, 395-408
949.4	DQ36-39	Switzerland—Civilization			
949.4004	DQ48-49	Ethnology—Switzerland	949.5013	DF562	Byzantine Empire—History—Theodosius II, 408-450
949.4005	DQ1	Switzerland—Periodicals			
949.4006	DQ2	Switzerland—Congresses	949.5013	DF564	Byzantine Empire—History—Leo I, 457-474
949.40072	DQ52.8-.95	Switzerland—Historiography			
949.40(1-3)	DQ79-84	Switzerland—History—To 1648	949.5013	DF566	Byzantine Empire—History—Zeno, 474-491
949.40(1-2)	DQ88-110	Switzerland—History—1032-1499	949.5013	DF565	Byzantine Empire—History—Leo II, 474
949.401	DQ85-87	Switzerland—History—To 1032	949.5013	DF572-.8	Byzantine Empire—History—Justinian I, 527-565
949.401	DQ85-87	Carolingians			
949.402	DQ90-91	Switzerland—History—Perpetual League, 1291	949.5013	DF573	Byzantine Empire—History—Justine II, 565-578
949.403	DQ104-118	Switzerland—History—1499-1648	949.5013	DF573.2	Byzantine Empire—History—Tiberius II, 578-582
949.403	DQ107.S8	Dornach, Battle of, 1499			
949.40(4-5)	DQ131-151	Switzerland—History—1789-1815	949.5013	DF573.5	Byzantine Empire—History—Maurice, 582-602
949.404	DQ111-123	Switzerland—History—1648-1798			
949.40(5-6)	DQ124	Switzerland—History—19th century			

Dewey	LC	Subject Heading	Dewey	LC	Subject Heading
949.5013	DF574	Byzantine Empire—History—Heraclius, 610-641	949.5075	DF853	Greece—History—Coup d'etat, 1967 (December 13)
949.5013	DF575.3	Byzantine Empire—History—Constans II, 641-668	949.5075	DF853	Greece—History—Coup d'etat, 1967 (April 21)
949.502	DF582	Byzantine Empire—History—Leo III the Isaurian, 717-741	949.5075	DF853	Greece—History—Coup d'etat, 1973 (May 22-23)
			949.5076	DF854-.32	Greece—History—1974-
949.502	DF583	Byzantine Empire—History—Constantine V Copronymus, 741-775	949.512	DF915-936	Athens (Greece)
			949.53	DF261.E65	Epirus (Greece and Albania)
949.502	DF586	Byzantine Empire—History—Irene, 797-802	949.5(4-9)005	DF701	Greece—Periodicals
			949.55	DF901.I57-.I69	Ionian Islands (Greece)
949.502	DF589	Byzantine Empire—History—Basil I, 867-886	949.59	DF901.C78-.C89	Crete (Greece)—History
			949.6	DR	Balkan Peninsula
949.502	DF592	Byzantine Empire—History—Leo VI, 886-911	949.6	DR22-23	Balkan Peninsula—Civilization
949.502	DF594	Byzantine Empire—History—Romanus II, 959-963	949.6	DR32-48.5	Balkan Peninsula—History
			949.65	DR901-998	Albania
949.50(3-4)	DF604-649	Byzantine Empire—History—1081-1453	949.65	DR927-977.25	Albania—History
			949.65	DR922	Albania—Civilization
949.503	DF605	Byzantine Empire—History—Alexius I Comnenus, 1081-1118	949.65004	DR923-925	Ethnology—Albania
			949.65005	DR901	Albania—Periodicals
949.503	DF606	Byzantine Empire—History—John II Comnenus, 1118-1143	949.65006	DR903.5	Albania—Congresses
			949.6501	DR954-960.5	Albania—History—To 1501
949.503	DF607	Byzantine Empire—History—Manuel I Comnenus, 1143-1180	949.6501	DR959-960.5	Albania—History—Turkish War, 15th century
949.50(4-9)	DF701-854.32	Greece	949.6501	DR961-969	Albania—History—1501-1912
949.50(4-9)	DF750-854.32	Greece—History			
949.50(4-9)004	DF745-747	Ethnology—Greece	949.6501	DR965.9-969	Albania—History—1840-1912
949.504	DF610-629	Latin Empire, 1204-1261	949.6501	DR966	Albania—History—1878-1912
949.504	DF625	Byzantine Empire—History—Lascarid dynasty, 1208-1259	949.6502	DR970-975	Albania—History—1912-1944
			949.6502	DR969	Albania—History—Uprising, 1912
949.504	DF638	Byzantine Empire—History—John V Palaeologus, 1341-1391	949.6502	DR972	Albania—History—Peasant Uprising, 1914-1915
			949.6502	DR973	Albania—History—June Revolution, 1924
949.505	DF801-.9	Greece—History—1453-1821	949.6502	DR975	Albania—History—Axis occupation, 1939-1944
949.50(6-76)	DF802-854.32	Greece—History—1821-	949.650(2-3)	DR976-977.25	Albania—History—1944-1990
949.5072	DF823-.7	Greece—History—Otho I, 1832-1862	949.650(3-4)	DR976-977.25	Albania—History—1990-
949.5072	DF823.6	Greece—History—Acarnanian Revolt, 1836	949.7	DR1202-2285	Yugoslavia
			949.7	DR1228	Yugoslavia—Civilization
949.5072	DF823.68	Greece—History—Arta Revolt, 1854	949.7	DR1232-1321	Yugoslavia—History
			949.7004	DR1229-1230	Ethnology—Yugoslavia
949.5072	DF825-832	Greece—History—George I, 1863-1913	949.7005	DR1202	Yugoslavia—Periodicals
			949.7006	DR1205	Yugoslavia—Congresses
949.5072	DF831.5	Greece—History—Coup d'etat, 1909	949.70072	DR1239-1243	Yugoslavia—Historiography
			949.70(2-3)	DR1281-1312	Yugoslavia—History—1918-1945
949.5072	DF837-841	Greece—History—Constantine I, 1913-1917	949.7022	D802.Y8	Yugoslavia—History—Axis occupation, 1941-1945
949.5074	DF849.5-.58	Greece—History—Civil War, 1944-1949	949.7022	DR1297-1298	Yugoslavia—History—Coup d'etat, 1941
949.5075	DF853-.5	Greece—History—1967-1974	949.7023	DR1300	Yugoslavia—History—1945-1980
			949.70(24-3)	DR1306-1313.8	Yugoslavia—History—1980-1992

Dewey	LC	Subject Heading
949.71	DR1932-2125	Serbia
949.71	DR343	Serbia—History
949.71013	DR1977-1999.5	Serbia—History—To 1456
949.71013	DR2000-2005	Serbia—History—1456-1804
949.71013	DR2004.8	Serbia—History—Great Emigration, 1690
949.71013	DR2005	Serbia—History—Insurrection, 1788
949.7101(4-5)	DR2006-2032	Serbia—History—1804-1918
949.71014	DR343	Serbia—History—Insurrection, 1804-1813
949.71014	DR2016	Serbia—History—Milos Obrenovic, 1814-1839
949.71015	DR2026.8	Serbia—History—Revolt, 1883
949.710(2-3)	DR2033-2047	Serbia—History—1918-
949.710(2-3)	DR2041-2047	Serbia—History—1945-1992
949.7102	DR20 33-2040	Serbia—History—1918-1945
949.7103	DR2047	Serbia—History—1992-
949.7103	DR1306-1312	Yugoslavia—History—1992-
949.72	DR1502-1645	Croatia
949.72	DR1547-1598	Croatia—History
949.73	DR1352-1485	Slovenia
949.73	DR1376-1450	Slovenia—History
949.730(2-3)	DR1452-1457.5	Slovenia—History—1990-
949.7302	DR1444-1450	Slovenia—History—1945-1990
949.742	DR1652-1785	Bosnia and Hercegovina
949.742	DR1697-1785	Bosnia and Hercegovina—History
949.745	DR1802-1928	Montenegro
949.745	DR1827-1928	Montenegro—History
949.76	DR2152-2285	Macedonia
949.76	DR701.M13-.M14	Macedonia—History
949.8016	DR242-250	Romania—History—1821-1859
949.8016	DR241	Romania—History—Revolution, 1821
949.80(2-31)	DR267	Romania—History—1944-1989
949.802	DR250-266	Romania—History—Charles I, 1866-1914
949.802	DR248	Romania—History—War of Independence, 1876-1878
949.802	DR256	Romania—History—Peasants' Uprising, 1888
949.802	DR252-258	Romania—History—Peasants' Uprising, 1907
949.802	DR263	Romania—History—1914-1918
949.802	DR264-266	Romania—History—Uprising, 1941
949.8031	DR267-.5	Romania—History—1989-
949.8032	DR269.5-.6	Romania—History—Revolution, 1989
949.84	DR279-280.74	Transylvania (Romania)
949.84	DR2	Transylvania (Romania)—History
949.9	DR51-98	Bulgaria
949.9	DR65-93.34	Bulgaria—History
949.9	DR63	Bulgaria—Civilization
949.90025	DR53.7	Bulgaria—Directories
949.9004	DR64	Ethnology—Bulgaria
949.9005	DR51	Bulgaria—Periodicals
949.90072	DR66.7-.97	Bulgaria—Historiography
949.901	DR74.3	Bulgaria—History—To 681
949.9013	DR74.5	Bulgaria—History—681-1018
949.9014	DR79	Bulgaria—History—1018-1185
949.9015	DR82-.5	Bulgaria—History—1393-1878
949.90(2-3)	DR89.9-93.34	Bulgaria—History—1944-
949.902	DR84.9-.8	Bulgaria—History—1878-1944
949.98	DR2211	Macedonia—History—Karpos Uprising, 1689
949.99	DR97	Sofia (Bulgaria)
950	DS	Asia
950	DS31-35.2	Asia—History
950	DS501-519	East Asia
950	CB253-256	Civilization, Oriental
950	DS11	Oriental antiquities
950.04	DS13-28	Ethnology—Asia
950.04	DS25	Hsiung-nu
950.04942	DS19-23	Mongols
950.04942	DS22.7	Golden Horde
950.0494387	DS25	Tatars
950.05	DS1	Asia—Periodicals
950.(3-41)	DS740.6-.63	Eastern question (Far East)
950.4	DS35-.2	Asia—History—20th century
950.4(2-3)	DS35.2	Asia—History—1945-
950.4(2-3)	DS518.1	East Asia—History—1945-
951	DS701-799.9	China
951	DS721-727	China—Civilization
951.01	DS747.28-749.76	China—History—221 B.C.-960 A.D.
951.01	DS748.5-.76	China—History—Northern and Southern dynasties, 386-589
951.01(5-6)	DS748.7-.76	China—History—Ch'en dynasty, 557-589
951.015	DS748.7-.76	China—History—Northern Wei dynasty, 386-534
951.015	DS748.6-.66	China—History—Liu Sung dynasty, 420-479
951.015	DS748.6-.66	China—History—Ch'i dynasty, 479-502
951.015	DS748.6-.66	China—History—Liang dynasty, 502-557
951.015	DS748.7-.76	China—History—Northern Ch'i dynasty, 550-577
951.015	DS748.7-.76	China—History—Northern Chou dynasty, 557-581
951.017	DS749.46	China—History—An Lu shan Rebellion, 755-763

Dewey	LC	Subject Heading	Dewey	LC	Subject Heading
951.017	DS749.47	China—History—Huang Ch'ao Rebellion, 874-884	951.041	DS777.43	China—History—May Fourth movement, 1919
951.0(18-24)	DS749.5-.76	China—History—Five dynasties and the Ten kingdoms, 907-979	951.041	DS777.45	China—History—May Thirtieth movement, 1925
951.0(18-24)	DS749.7-.76	China—History—Southern Han kingdom, 917-971	951.042	DS777.47-.514	China—History—1928-1937
951.0(18-24)	DS749.7-.76	China—History—Later Shu kingdom, 934-965	951.042	DS777.462	China—History—Tsinan Incident, 1928
951.0(18-24)	DS749.7-.76	China—History—Southern T'ang kingdom, 937-975	951.042	DS777.5132-.5139	China—History—Long March, 1934-1935
951.0(18-24)	DS751.72.-.78	China—History—Liao dynasty, 947-1125	951.042	DS775	China—History—December Ninth Movement, 1935
951.018	DS749.7-.76	China—History—Earlier Shu kingdom, 907-925	951.042	DS777.51393	China—History—December Ninth Movement, 1935
951.024	DS751.82-.88	China—History—Hsi Hsia dynasty, 1038-1227	951.042	DS777.514	China—History—Sian Incident, 1936
951.024	DS751.92-.98	China—History—Chin dynasty, 1115-1234	951.042	DS777.518-.5316	China—History—1937-1945
951.026	DS753.65	China—History—Li Tzu ch'eng Rebellion, 1628-1645	951.042	DS777.534	China—History—Southern Anhui Incident, 1941
951.03	DS753.82-773.6	Manchus	951.042	DS777.535-.544	China—History—Civil War, 1945-1949
951.033	DS756.3-.37	China—History—White Lotus Rebellion, 1796-1804	951.05(5-7)	DS777.55	China—History—1949-1976
951.033	DS757.4-.7	China—History—Opium War, 1840-1842	951.055	DS778.4	China—History—Hundred Flowers Campaign, 1956
951.03(4-5)	DS759.5	China—History—Nien Rebellion, 1853-1868	951.055	DS778.5	China—History—Antirightist Campaign, 1957-1958
951.03(4-5)	DS763.65	China—History—Self-strengthening movement, 1861-1895	951.056	DS778.7	China—History—Cultural Revolution, 1966-1969
951.03(4-6)	DS763.5-773.6	China—History—1861-1912	951.058	DS779.32	China—History—Tiananmen Square Incident, 1989
951.034	DS758.7-759.4	China—History—Taiping Rebellion, 1850-1864	951.2490(3/4)	DS799.69-.72	Taiwan—History—1895-1945
951.03(5-6)	DS773-.6	China—History—Hsuan t'ung, 1908-1912	951.24904	DS799.69	Taiwan—History—Insurrection, 1895
951.0(35-59)	DS774	China—History—20th century	951.24905	DS799.77-.833	Taiwan—History—1945-
951.035	DS764.4-767.6	Chinese-Japanese War, 1894-1895	951.24905	DS799.823	Taiwan—History—February Twenty Eighth Incident, 1947
951.035	DS770-772.3	China—History—Boxer Rebellion, 1899-1901	951.24905	DS799.83-.833	Taiwan—History—1975-
951.035	DS771.5	German Expedition to China, 1900-1901	951.24905	DS799.834	Taiwan—History—Kaohsiung Incident, 1979
951.036	DS773.32-.6	China—History—Revolution, 1911-1912	951.8	DS781-784.2	Manchuria (China)
951.04	DS773.83-777.544	China—History—Republic, 1912-1949	951.8	DS781-784.2	Manchus
951.04(1-2)	DS776.4-777.46	China—History—1912-1928	951.9	DS904	Korea—Civilization
951.04(1-2)	DS777.36	China—History—Warlord period, 1916-1928	951.9004	DS904.5-.7	Ethnology—Korea
951.041	DS777.2	China—History—Revolution, 1913	951.901	DS911-.78	Korea—History—To 935
951.041	DS777.25	China—History—Revolution, 1915-1916	951.901	DS912-.43	Korea—History—Koryo period, 935-1392
951.041	DS777.38	China—History—Ch'ing Dynasty Restoration Attempt, 1917	951.901	DS912.4-.43	Korea—History—Mongolian Invasions, 1231-1270
			951.90(2-3)	DS915.56-922.42	Korea—History—20th century
			951.902	DS913-915.5	Korea—History—Yi dynasty, 1392-1910
			951.902	DS913-.45	Korea—History—Japanese Invasions, 1592-1598
			951.902	DS913.615-.675	Korea—History—Manchu Invasions, 1627-1637
			951.902	DS915-.5	Korea—History—1864-1910

Dewey	LC	Subject Heading	Dewey	LC	Subject Heading
951.903	DS916.525-.58	Korea—History—Japanese occupation, 1910-1945	952.02(3-4)	DS868-869.6	Japan—History—Period of civil wars, 1480-1603
951.904	DS916.6-922.42	Korea—History—1945-	952.02(4-5)	DS870-881.84	Japan—History—Tokugawa period, 1600-1868
951.9041	DS917.5-.55	Korea—History—Allied occupation, 1945-1948	952.0(25-3)	DS881.2-.84	Japan—History—Restoration, 1853-1870
951.9042	DS918-921.8	Korean War, 1950-1953	952.0(25-31)	DS881-.84	Japan—History—19th century
951.90422	DS921.7	Korean War, 1950-1953—Armistices	952.025	DS871.5	Japan—History—Keicho Peasant Uprising, 1614-1615
951.90422	DS921.7	Korean Demilitarized Zone (Korea)	952.025	DS871.5	Japan—History—Ako Vendetta, 1703
951.904242	DS918.2	Korean War, 1950-1953—Campaigns	952.025	DS881.83-.84	Japan—History—Civil War, 1868
951.904242	DS918.2	Naktong River (Korea), Battle of, 1950	952.025	DS881.4	Japan—History—Sakai Incident, 1868
951.904248	DS920.2	Korean War, 1950-1953—Aerial operations	952.0(3-5)	DS881.85-890.3	Japan—History—1868-
951.90427	DS921-.2	Korean War, 1950-1953—Prisoners and prisons	952.031	DS881.98-884	Japan—History—Meiji period, 1868-1912
951.90428	DS920.8-.9	Korean War, 1950-1953—Atrocities	952.031	DS881.4	Japan—History—Kobe Incident, 1868
951.93	DS930-937	Korea (North)	952.031	DS882.5	Japan—History—Takehashi Incident, 1878
951.95	DS922-.42	Korea (South)—History—April Revolution, 1960	952.031	DS882.5	Japan—History—Kioizaka Incident, 1878
951.95	DS922.44	Korea (South)—May Revolution, 1961	952.031	DS516-517.9	Russo-Japanese War, 1904-1905
951.95	DS922.445	Kwangju Uprising, Kwangju-si, Korea, 1980	952.032	DS885.8-888	Japan—History—Taisho period, 1912-1926
952	DS801-897	Japan	952.0(33-5)	DS888.84-890.3	Japan—History—1945-
952	DS820.8-827	Japan—Civilization	952.033	DS888.15-890.3	Japan—History—Showa period, 1926-1989
952.004	DS830-832	Ethnology—Japan	952.033	DS888.4-.5	Japan—History—1926-1945
952.004946	DS832	Ainu	952.033	DS888.5	Japan—History—March and October Incidents, 1931
952.01	DS855-.73	Japan—History—To 794			
952.01	DS855.6	Japan—History—Taika Reform, 645-710	952.033	DS888.5	Japan—History—May Incident, 1932 (May 15)
952.01	DS855.7-.73	Japan—History—Nara period, 710-794	952.033	DS888.4-.5	Japan—History—February Incident, 1936 (February 26)
952.01	DS855.87-856.72	Japan—History—Heian period, 794-1185	952.04(4-5)	DS889.16	Japan—History—Allied occupation, 1945-1952
952.01	DS850-856.72	Japan—History—To 1185	952.29	DS895.R97	Ryukyu Islands—History
952.01	DS854	Japan—History—Earlier Nine Years' War, 1051-1062	953.8	DS201-248	Saudi Arabia
			953.8	DS215	Saudi Arabia—Civilization
952.01	DS856.3	Japan—History—Later Three Years' War, 1083-1087	953.8	DS221-244.63	Saudi Arabia—History
			953.8	DS232	Ditch, Battle of the, 627
952.02(1-2)	DS863	Japan—History—Kenmu Restoration, 1333-1336	953.8004	DS218-219	Ethnology—Saudi Arabia
952.02(1-4)	DS856.75-869.6	Japan—History—1185-1600	953.80099	DS234-238	Abbasids
			953.80099	DS234-238	Caliphs
952.021	DS858-861	Japan—History—Kamakura period, 1185-1333	954	DS421-486.8	India
			954	DS421-428.2	India—Civilization
952.021	DS861	Japan—History—Jokyu Revolt, 1221	954.004	DS430-432.5	Ethnology—India
			954.0049144	DS432.B4	Bengali (South Asian people)
952.021	DS861	Japan—History—Attempted Mongol Invasions, 1274-1281	954.0(2-223)	DS451-.9	India—History—324 B.C-1000 A.D.
952.021	DS861	Japan—History—Genko Incident, 1331-1333	954.02	DS451.8	Gurjara-Pratihara dynasty
952.02(2-3)	DS863.75-869.6	Japan—History—Muromachi period, 1336-1573			

Dewey	LC	Subject Heading	Dewey	LC	Subject Heading
954.02(23-25)	DS457-460	India—History—1000-1526	955.0(4-51)	DS313	Iran—History—1905-1911
954.02(23-96)	DS452-462.8	India—History—1000-1765	955.04	DS298-316	Iran—History—Qajar dynasty, 1794-1925
954.0234	DS459.2	Khilji dynasty			
954.025	DS461-.9	Mogul Empire	955.04	DS307.5	Iran—History—War with Great Britain, 1856-1857
954.0(296-4)	DS463-480.83	India—History—British occupation, 1765-1947	955.05(2-3)	DS316.2-318.7	Iran—History—Paklavi dynasty, 1925-1979
954.029	DS473	Maratha War, 1775-1782			
954.0311	DS474.1	India—History—Mysore War, 1790-1792	955.053	DS318-.7	Iran—History—Mohammed Reza Pahlavi, 1941-1979
954.0312	DS475.3	India—History—Mysore War, 1799	955.054	DS318.72-.85	Iran—History—1979-
			955.054	DS318.72-.85	Iran—History—Revolution, 1979
954.0313	DS475.5	India—History—Mutiny, 1809	955.0542	DS318.85	Iran-Iraq War, 1980-1988
954.0313	DS485.N4	Nepalese War, 1814-1816	956	DS41-66	Middle East
954.0313	DS475.6	Maratha War, 1816-1818	956.004926	DS121.4	Canaanites
954.0317	DS478-.3	India—History—Sepoy Rebellion, 1857-1858	956.01(3-4)	DS38.6	Islamic Empire—History—750-1258
954.0357	DS480.5	Massacres—India—Amritsar	956.01(4-5)	DS38.7	Islamic Empire—History—1258-1517
954.0359	DS480.82	India—History—Quit India movement, 1942	956.013	DS38.1	Dhat al-Sawari, Battle of, 655
954.0(4-5)	DS480.832-481	India—History—1947-	956.013	DS38.5	Islamic Empire—History—661-750
954.042	DS480.85	Sino-Indian Border Dispute, 1957-			
954.904	DS385.9	India-Pakistan Conflict, 1947-1949	956.042	DS126.9-.99	Israel-Arab War, 1948-1949
			956.046	DS127-.9	Israel-Arab War, 1967
954.91	DS381.7-388.2	Pakistan—History	956.048	DS128.1-.19	Israel-Arab War, 1973
954.91	DS379	Pakistan—Civilization	956.1	DR436-603	Turkey—History
954.91004	DS380.A1-.A2	Ethnology—Pakistan	956.1	DR432	Turkey—Civilization
954.92	DS394.5-395.7	Bangladesh—History	956.1003	DR414	Turkey—Gazetteers
954.92	DS393.8	Bangladesh—Civilization	956.1004	DR434-435	Ethnology—Turkey
954.92004	DS393.82-.83	Ethnology—Bangladesh	956.10072	DR438.8-.95	Turkey—Historiography
954.92051	DS395.5	Bangladesh—History—Revolution, 1971	956.101(3-5)	DR481	Turkey—History—To 1453
			956.101(4-5)	DR485-486	Turkey—History—Ottoman Empire, 1288-1918
954.93	DS488-490	Sri Lanka			
954.93	DS489.5-490	Sri Lanka—History	956.101(4-5)	DR493-502	Turkey—History—1288-1453
954.93004	DS489.2-.25	Ethnology—Sri Lanka			
954.930(1-2)	DS489.7-.73	Sri Lanka—History—1505-1948	956.1015	DR496	Turkey—History—Bayezid I, 1389-1403
954.9301	DS489.6-.63	Sri Lanka—History—To 1505	956.1015	DR496	Turkey—History—Invasion of Timur, 1402
954.9302	DS489.7	Sri Lanka—History—Rebellion, 1818	956.1015	DR501-.7	Turkey—History—Mehmed II, 1451-1481
954.9302	DS489.7	Sri Lanka—History—Rebellion, 1848	956.1015	DR502-536	Turkey—History—1453-1683
954.9303	DS489.8-.86	Sri Lanka—History—1948-	956.1015	DR503	Turkey—History—Bayezid II, 1481-1512
954.93031	DS489.8	Sri Lanka—History—Rebellion, 1971	956.1015	DR505-506	Turkey—History—Suleyman I, 1520-1566
954.96	DS493.7	Nepal—Civilization			
954.96	DS494.4-495.592	Nepal—History	956.1015	DR523	Turkey—History—Wars with Persia, 1576-1639
954.96	DS495	Nepal—History—To 1768	956.1015	DR525	Turkey—History—Mehmed III, 1595-1603
954.96	DS495.3	Nepal—History—1768-1951			
954.96004	DS493.8-.9	Ethnology—Nepal	956.1015	DR529	Turkey—History—Murad IV, 1623-1640
955	DS251-326	Iran			
955	DS270-318.85	Iran—History	956.1015	DR534-536.5	Turkey—History—Mehmed IV, 1648-1687
955.004	DS268-269	Ethnology—Iran			
955.02	DS288-290	Iran—History—640-1500	956.1015	DR534.5.D3	Dardanelles, Battle of the, 1656
955.02	DS287.8-288.9	Iran—History—640-1256			
955.02	DS288.95-289.8	Iran—History—1256-1500	956.1015	DR536-562	Turkey—History—1683-1829
955.03	DS292-297	Iran—History—16th-18th centuries			

Dewey	LC	Subject Heading	Dewey	LC	Subject Heading
956.1015	DR537	Turkey—History—Suleyman II, 1687-1691	956.93	DS54.35	Cyprus—Civilization
956.1015	DR541.3	Turkey—History—Mustafa II, 1695-1703	956.93004	DS54.4-.44	Ethnology—Cyprus
			956.94	DS101-151	Israel
956.1015	DR542-545	Turkey—History—Ahmed III, 1703-1730	956.94	DS114-128.19	Israel—History
			956.94	DS101-151	Jews
956.1015	DR542	Turkey—History—Rebellion, 1703	956.94	DS112-113	Jews—Civilization
			956.94004	DS113.2-.8	Ethnology—Israel
956.1015	DR547-548	Turkey—History—Mahmud I, 1730-1754	956.9402	DS121.7-.8	Jews—History—168 B.C.-135 A.D.
956.1015	DR551-553	Turkey—History—Mustafa III, 1757-1773	956.9402	DS109.913	Jews—History—Rebellion, 66-73
956.1015	DR555	Turkey—History—Abdul Hamid I, 1774-1789	956.9402	DS123.5	Jews—History—70-638
			956.9402	DS109.913	Palestine—History—70-638
956.1015	DR559-.5	Turkey—History—Selim III, 1789-1807	956.9402	DS122.8	Jerusalem—History—Siege, 70 A.D.
956.1015	DR562-564	Turkey—History—Mahmud II, 1808-1839	956.9402	DS122.9	Jews—History—Bar Kokhba Rebellion, 132-135
956.1015	DR564-573.7	Turkey—History—1829-1878	956.940(3-4)	DS109.92-.93	Jews—History—1789-1945
956.1015	DR565	Turkey—History—Tanzimat, 1839-1876	956.9403	DS109.916-.925	Palestine—History—638-1917
956.1015	DR567	Crimean War, 1853-1856	956.9403	DS125	Palestine—History—1799-1917
956.1015	DR573.7-584.5	Turkey—History—1878-1909	956.9404	DS125.5-126.4	Palestine—History—1917-1948
956.1015	DR583-588	Turkey—History—Mehmed V, 1909-1918	956.9404	DS109.93	Palestine—History—Arab riots, 1920
956.1015	DR583	Turkey—History—Revolution, 1909	956.9404	DS126-.4	Palestine—History—1929-1948
956.10(23-36)	DR589-590	Turkey—History—1918-1960	956.9404	DS126	Palestine—History—Arab riots, 1929
956.1023	DR589	Turkey—History—Revolution, 1918-1923	956.9404	DS126	Palestine—History—Arab rebellion, 1936-1939
956.1023	DR589	Turkey—History—Mehmed VI, 1918-1922	956.9404	DS109.93	Palestine—History—Proposed partition, 1937
956.10(36-4)	DR593-603	Turkey—History—1960-	956.9404	DS109.93	Palestine—History—Partition, 1947
956.1036	DR593	Turkey—History—Revolution, 1960	956.9405	DS126.5	Israel—History—Declaration of Independence, 1948
956.1037	DR600	Turkey—History—Coup d'etat, 1971	956.94052	DS126.5-126.99	Israel—History—1948-1949
956.1038	DR601	Turkey—History—Coup d'etat, 1980	956.94054	DS119.7	Entebbe Airport Raid, 1976
956.7	DS70.82-79.66	Iraq—History	956.9442	DS109-.94	Jerusalem
956.7	DS70.7	Iraq—Civilization	956.9442	DS109.85-.94	Jerusalem—History
956.7004	DS70.8	Ethnology—Iraq	956.944203	D175-195	Jerusalem—History—Latin Kingdom, 1099-1244
956.70442	DS79.72	Persian Gulf War, 1991	956.95	DS153-154.9	Jordan
956.91	DS94.6	Syria—Civilization	956.95	DS153.7-154.55	Jordan—History
956.91	DS94.9-98.3	Syria—History	956.95	DS153.4	Jordan—Civilization
956.91004	DS94.7-.8	Ethnology—Syria	956.95004	DS153.5-.55	Ethnology—Jordan
956.92	DS80.7-87.53	Lebanon—History	956.950(3-44)	DS154.5-.55	Jordan—History—20th century
956.92	DS80.4	Lebanon—Civilization			
956.92004	DS80.5	Ethnology—Lebanon	956.95043	DS154.55	Jordan—History—Intervention, 1958
956.9203(2-4)	DS84	Lebanon—History—1516-1918			
			956.953	DS110.S3	Samaria Region
956.92044	DS87.5	Lebanon—History—Civil War, 1975-	957	DK751-781	Siberia (Russia)
			958	DK845-860	Asia, Central
956.92044	DS87.53	Lebanon—History—Israeli intervention, 1982-1984	958	DS327-329.4	Asia, Central
			958.1	DS354	Afghanistan—Civilization
956.9232	DS83	Lebanon—History—635-1516	958.1	DS355-371.2	Afghanistan—History
			958.1004	DS354.5-.6	Ethnology—Afghanistan
956.93	DS54.5-.9	Cyprus—History			

Dewey	LC	Subject Heading	Dewey	LC	Subject Heading
958.104(5-6)	DS371.3	Afghanistan—History—1989-	959.70(3-4)	DS556.8-.83	Vietnam—History—19th century
958.1045	DS371.2	Afghanistan—History—Soviet occupation, 1979-1989	959.703	DS556.6-.63	Vietnam—History—To 939
			959.703	DS556.7-.73	Vietnam—History—Later Le dynasty, 1428-1787
958.43	DK911-919.5	Kyrgyzstan	959.703	DS556.815	Vietnam—History—August Revolution, 1945
958.45	DK901-909.5	Kazakhstan			
958.5	DK931-939.5	Turkmenistan	959.704342	DS557.8.I	Ia Drang Valley (Vietnam), Battle of, 1965
958.6	DK921-929.5	Tajikistan			
958.7	DK941-949.5	Uzbekistan	959.704342	DS557.8.K5	Khe Sanh, Battle of, 1968
959	DS524-526.7	Asia, Southeastern—History	959.704342	DS557.8.S6	Sontay Raid, 1970
			959.704342	DS557.8.E23	Easter Offensive, 1972
959.1	DS527.9	Burma—Civilization	959.704342	DS557.8.I	Ia Drang Valley (Vietnam), Battle of, 1965
959.1004	DS538-539	Ethnology—Burma			
959.1004	DS528-.2	Ethnology—Burma	959.704342	DS557.8.E23	Easter Offensive, 1972
959.10(2-4)	DS529.7-530.32	Burma—History—1824-1948	959.704342	DS557.8.S6	Sontay Raid, 1970
			959.704342	DS557.8.K5	Khe Sanh, Battle of, 1968
959.102	DS527.2-.3	Burma—History—To 1824	959.8	DS625	Indonesia—Civilization
959.104	DS530	Burma—History—Peasant Uprising, 1931	959.8	DS633-644.4	Indonesia—History
			959.8004	DS631-632	Ethnology—Indonesia
959.104	DS530	Burma—History—Japanese occupation, 1942-1945	959.8012	DS641	Indonesia—History—To 1478
959.105	DS530.4	Burma—History—1948-	959.80(15-21)	DS641.5-642.22	Indonesia—History—1478-1798
959.3	DS570.95-586	Thailand—History			
959.3	DS568	Thailand—Civilization	959.8022	DS643-.22	Indonesia—History—1798-1942
959.3004	DS569-570	Ethnology—Thailand			
959.4	DS555.5-86	Laos—History	959.8022	DS643	Indonesia—History—British occupation, 1811-1816
959.4	DS555.42	Laos—Civilization			
959.4004	DS555.44-.45	Ethnology—Laos	959.8022	DS643	Indonesia—History—Java War, 1825-1830
959.4042	DS555.84-.86	Laos—History—1975-			
959.5	DS594	Malaysia—Civilization	959.8022	DS643	Indonesia—History—Achinese War, 1873-1904
959.5	DS595.8-597.215	Malaya—History			
			959.8022	DS643.5	Indonesia—History—Japanese occupation, 1942-1945
959.5004	DS595-.2	Ethnology—Malaysia			
959.503	DS596.6	Malaya—History—Japanese occupation, 1942-1945	959.803(5-6)	DS644-.1	Indonesia—History—1950-1966
959.504	DS597	Malaya—History—Malayan Emergency, 1948-1960	959.8035	DS644	Indonesia—History—Revolution, 1945-1949
959.5074	DF850-852.5	Greece—History—1950-1967	959.8036	DS644.4	Indonesia—History—1966-
			959.8036	DS644.32	Indonesia—History—Coup d'etat, 1965
959.55	DS650.4	Brunei—Civilization			
959.55	DS650.44-.83	Brunei—History	959.9	DS651-689	Philippines
959.55004	DS650.42-.43	Ethnology—Brunei	959.9	DS663-664	Philippines—Civilization
959.6	DS554.5-.842	Cambodia—History	959.90(1-2)	DS674	Philippines—History—1521-1812
959.6	DS554.42	Cambodia—Civilization			
959.6004	DS554.44-.46	Ethnology—Cambodia	959.90(1-27)	DS674-.9	Philippines—History—1521-1898
959.60(3-41)	DS554.7-.73	Cambodia—History—1863-1953	959.901	DS673.8	Philippines—History—To 1521
959.603	DS554.6-.64	Cambodia—History—To 800			
959.603	DS554.6-.64	Cambodia—History—800-1444	959.902	DS675	Philippines—History—1812-1898
959.603	DS554.6-.64	Cambodia—History—1444-1863	959.902	DS675.5	Philippines—History—Cavite Mutiny, 1872
959.604	DS554.8-.83	Cambodia—History—1953-1975	959.9027	DS676	Philippines—History—Insurrection, 1896-1898
959.6042	DS554.84	Cambodia—History—Civil War, 1970-1975	959.9031	DS679	Philippines—History—Insurrection, 1899-1901
959.6042	DS554.84-.842	Cambodia—History—1975-	959.9032	DS685	Dajo, Mount, Battle of, 1906
959.7	DS556-559.916	Vietnam			
959.7	DS556.42	Vietnam—Civilization			
959.7004	DS556.44-.45	Ethnology—Vietnam			

229

Dewey	LC	Subject Heading	Dewey	LC	Subject Heading
959.9035	DS686.4	Philippines—History—Japanese occupation, 1942-1945	962.0(2-3)	DT95-107.4	Egypt—History—640-1882
			962.02	DT95-.88	Egypt—History—640-1250
			962.02	DT95.8-.88	Egypt—History—Saladin, 1171-1193
959.904(1-6)	DS686.5-.6	Philippines—History—1946-1986			
			962.02	DT95.8	Egypt—History—Invasion of Saint Louis, 1249
959.904(7-8)	DS686.614	Philippines—History—1986-			
959.9047	DS686.62	Philippines—History—Revolution, 1986	962.02	DT96-.7	Egypt—History—1250-1517
			962.0(3-4)	DT107-.4	Egypt—History—Tewfik, 1879-1892
959.9047	DS686.6	Philippines—History—Attempted coup, 1987	962.0(3-55)	DT100-107.87	Egypt—History—1798-
			962.03	DT97-107.4	Egypt—History—1517-1882
959.9047	DS686.6	Philippines—History—Coup d'etat, 1989	962.03	DT103	Egypt—French occupation, 1798-1801
960	DT	Africa	962.03	DT104	Egypt—History—Mohammed Ali, 1805-1849
960	DT14	Africa—Civilization			
960	DT17-39	Africa—History	962.03	DT106	Egypt—History—Ismail, 1863-1879
960.04	DT15-16	Ethnology—Africa			
960.(1-21)	DT25	Africa—History—To 1498	962.0(4-51)	DT107.3-.8	Egypt—History—British occupation, 1882-1936
960.(1-23)	DT24-28	Africa—History—To 1884			
960.(23-314)	DT29	Africa—History—1884-1918	962.0(4-51)	DT107.8	Egypt—History—Fuad, 1917-1936
960.(23-326)	DT29-30.2	Africa—History—1884-1960			
960.3(26-3)	DT30.5	Africa—History—1960-	962.0(4-55)	DT107.8-.87	Egypt—History—1919-
961	DT160-177	Africa, North	962.04	DT107.8	Egypt—History—Insurrection, 1919
961	DT160-176	Africa, North—History			
961.0(22-45)	DT172	Africa, North—History—647-1517	962.052	DT107.82	Egypt—History—Revolution, 1952
			962.05(3-5)	DT107.821-.87	Egypt—History—1952-
961.0(3-5)	DT176	Africa, North—History—1882-	962.053	DT107.83	Egypt—History—Intervention, 1956
961.1	DT241-269	Tunisia			
961.1	DT252	Tunisia—Civilization	962.4	DT154.1-159.9	Sudan
961.1	DT253.4-264.49	Tunisia—History	962.4	DT154.9	Sudan—Civilization
961.1004	DT253-.2	Ethnology—Tunisia	962.4	DT155.3-157.67	Sudan—History
961.102	DT259	Tunisia—History—647-1516	962.4004	DT155-.2	Ethnology—Sudan
961.103	DT261-263.76	Tunisia—History—1516-1881	962.40(1-2)	DT156-.3	Sudan—History—To 1820
			962.40(3-4)	DT156.4-157.67	Sudan—History—1820-
961.103	DT262	Tunisia—History—Expedition of Charles V, 1535	962.40(3-4)	DT157.67	Sudan—History—Civil War, 1955-1972
			962.403	DT156.6	Sudan—History—1862-1899
961.103	DT262	Tunisia—History—Conquest, 1573			
			962.403	DT156.6	Fashoda Crisis, 1898
961.104	DT263.9-264.3	Tunisia—History—French occupation, 1881-1956	962.403	DT156.7-157.67	Sudan—History—1899-1956
961.105	DT264.35-.49	Tunisia—History—1956-	962.404	DT156.7	Sudan—History—Coup d'etat, 1985
961.2	DT211-239	Libya			
961.2	DT222	Libya—Civilization	963	DT371-398	Ethiopia
961.2	DT223.2-236	Libya—History	963	DT380.5-387.954	Ethiopia—History
961.2004	DT223-.2	Ethnology—Libya			
961.202	DT229	Libya—History—642-1551	963	DT379.5	Ethiopia—Civilization
961.202	DT231	Libya—History—1551-1912	963.004	DT380-.4	Ethnology—Ethiopia
961.20(3-41)	DT235.5	Libya—History—1951-1969	963.0(1-2)	DT383	Ethiopia—History—To 1490
961.203	DT235	Libya—History—1912-1951	963.0(2-4)	DT384-386.73	Ethiopia—History—1490-1889
961.2042	DT236	Libya—History—1969-			
961.2042	DT236	Libya—History—Coup d'etat, 1969	963.0(43-6)	DT387-.92	Ethiopia—History—1889-1974
			963.054	DT387.7-.8	Ethiopia—History—Rebellion, 1928-1930
961.2042	DT236	Libya—History—Bombardment, 1986			
			963.06	DT387.9	Ethiopia—History—Coup d'etat, 1960
961.22	DT168-171	Africa, North—History—To 647			
			964	DT179.2-.9	Africa, Northwest
962	DT43-154	Egypt—History	964	DT301-330	Morocco
962	DT70	Egypt—Civilization			
962.004	DT71-72	Ethnology—Egypt			

Dewey	LC	Subject Heading	Dewey	LC	Subject Heading
964	DT313.7-325.92	Morocco—History	966.3	DT532.23	Niumi (Kingdom)
964	DT312	Morocco—Civilization	966.3	DT532.128	Fuladu (Kingdom)
964.004	DT313-.6	Ethnology—Morocco	966.3004	DT549.42-.45	Ethnology—Senegal
964.0(2-3)	DT324	Morocco—History—19th century	966.30(1-3)	DT549.7-.73	Senegal—History—To 1960
			966.305	DT549.8-.83	Senegal—History—1960-
964.02	DT319	Morocco—History—647-1516	966.305	DT549.8	Senegal—History—Coup d'etat, 1962
964.02	DT321-323.5	Morocco—History—1516-1830	966.4	DT516.5-.82	Sierra Leone—History
			966.4	DT516.4	Sierra Leone—Civilization
964.02	DT322	Kassr-el-Kabir, Battle of, 1578	966.4004	DT516.42-.45	Ethnology—Sierra Leone
			966.40(1-2)	DT516.65-.72	Sierra Leone—History—To 1896
965.02	DT289	Algeria—History—647-1516			
965.02	DT291-292	Algeria—History—1516-1830	966.51	DT509.4	Gambia—Civilization
			966.51	DT509.5-.83	Gambia—History
965.02	DT292	Algeria—History—Expedition of Charles V, 1541	966.51	DT532.23	Niumi (Kingdom)
			966.51	DT532.128	Fuladu (Kingdom)
			966.51004	DT509.42-.45	Ethnology—Gambia
965.02	DT291	Algeria—History—English expedition, 1620-1621	966.51031	DT509.8	Gambia—History—Coup d'etat, 1981
965.02	DT291	Algeria—History—Spanish Expedition, 1775	966.52	DT543.5-.827	Guinea—History
			966.52	DT543.4	Guinea—Civilization
965.02	DT291	Algeria—History—English Expedition, 1816	966.52004	DT543.42-.45	Ethnology—Guinea
			966.5205	DT543.8	Guinea—History—Portuguese Invasion, 1970
965.03	DT294-295.3	Algeria—History—1830-1962	966.5205	DT543.822	Guinea—History—Coup d'etat, 1984
965.03	DT294	Algeria—History—French Expedition, 1830	966.57	DT613.5-.83	Guinea-Bissau—History
965.03	DT295-.3	Algeria—History—1945-1962	966.57	DT613.4	Guinea-Bissau—Civilization
			966.57004	DT613.42-.45	Ethnology—Guinea-Bissau
965.046	DT295	Algeria—History—Revolution, 1954-1962	966.5702	DT613.78	Guinea-Bissau—History—Revolution, 1963-1974
965.05	DT295.5-.55	Algeria—History—1962-	966.5703	DT613.8	Guinea-Bissau—History—Coup d'etat, 1980
966	DT470-671	Africa, West			
966	DT331-346	Sahara	966.58	DT671.C25-.C28	Cape Verde—History
966.0(1-2)	DT476	Africa, West—History—To 1884	966.58	DT671.C23	Cape Verde—Civilization
			966.58004	DT671.C242-.C245	Ethnology—Cape Verde
966.0(23-326)	DT476.2-.23	Africa, West—History—1884-1960	966.580(1-2)	DT671.C265	Cape Verde—History—To 1975
966.03(26-3)	DT476.5-.523	Africa, West—History—1960-	966.5803	DT671.C28	Cape Verde—History—1975-
966.1	DT554.4	Mauritania—Civilization			
966.1	DT554.52-.83	Mauritania—History	966.62	DT629	Liberia—Civilization
966.1004	DT554.42-.45	Ethnology—Mauritania	966.62	DT630.8-636.53	Liberia—History
966.105	DT554.8-.83	Mauritania—History—1960-	966.62004	DT630-.5	Ethnology—Liberia
966.23	DT551.4	Mali—Civilization	966.6201	DT633-.3	Liberia—History—To 1847
966.23	DT551.5-.82	Mali—History	966.620(2-3)	DT635-636	Liberia—History—1944-1971
966.23	DT551.45.S	Songhai Empire			
966.23004	DT551.42-.45	Ethnology—Mali	966.6202	DT634-.3	Liberia—History—1847-1944
966.23051	DT551.8	Mali—History—Coup d'etat, 1968	966.6203	DT636.2-.4	Liberia—History—1971-1980
966.25	DT555.52-.83	Burkina Faso—History	966.6203	DT636.5-.53	Liberia—History—1980-
966.25	DT555.4	Burkina Faso—Civilization	966.6203	DT636.5	Liberia—History—Coup d'etat, 1980
966.25004	DT555.42-.45	Ethnology—Burkina Faso			
966.2505	DT555.8	Burkina Faso—History—Coup d'etat, 1987	966.6203	DT636.5	Liberia—History—Civil War, 1989-
966.26	DT547.4	Niger—Civilization			
966.26	DT547.5-.83	Niger—History	966.68	DT545.4	Cote d'Ivoire—Civilization
966.260(1-3)	DT547.65-.75	Niger—History—To 1960	966.68	DT545.52-.83	Cote d'Ivoire—History
966.26004	DT547.42-.45	Ethnology—Niger	966.68	DT532.12	Denkyira (Kingdom)
966.3	DT549.4	Senegal—Civilization	966.68004	DT545.42-.45	Ethnology—Cote d'Ivoire
966.3	DT549.47-.83	Senegal—History	966.7	DT510.4	Ghana—Civilization

Dewey	LC	Subject Heading	Dewey	LC	Subject Heading
966.7	DT510.5-512.34	Ghana—History	967.18	DT620.4	Equatorial Guinea—Civilization
966.7004	DT510.42-.43	Ethnology—Ghana			
966.70(1-3)	DT511-.3	Ghana—History—To 1957	967.18004	DT620.42-.45	Ethnology—Equatorial Guinea
966.701(6-8)	DT511	Ghana—History—Danish Settlements, 1659-1850			
			967.1804	DT620.27	Equatorial Guinea—Description and travel
966.7016	DT511	Ghana—History—Portuguese rule, 1469-1637	967.21	DT546.14	Gabon—Civilization
			967.21	DT546.15-.183	Gabon—History
966.705	DT512-.34	Ghana—History—1957-	967.21004	DT546.142-.145	Ethnology—Gabon
966.705	DT512	Ghana—History—Coup d'etat, 1966	967.2101	DT546.165	Gabon—History—To 1839
			967.2102	DT546.165-.175	Gabon—History—1839-1960
966.705	DT512	Ghana—History—Coup d'etat, 1972	967.2104	DT546.18-.183	Gabon—History—1960-
966.705	DT512.32	Ghana—History—Coup d'etat, 1979	967.24	DT546.24	Congo (Brazzaville)—Civilization
966.705	DT512.32	Ghana—History—Coup d'etat, 1981	967.24	DT546.25-.283	Congo (Brazzaville)—History
966.81	DT582.5-.82	Togo—History	967.24004	DT546.242-.245	Ethnology—Congo (Brazzaville)
966.81	DT582.4	Togo—Civilization			
966.81004	DT582.42-.45	Ethnology—Togo	967.240(1-3)	DT546.265-.275	Congo (Brazzaville)—History—To 1960
966.8103	DT582.75	Togo—History—1922-1960			
966.83	DT541.4	Benin—Civilization	967.3	DT1314-1436	Angola—History
966.83	DT541.5-.845	Benin—History	967.3	DT1302	Angola—Civilization
966.83004	DT541.42-.45	Ethnology—Benin	967.3004	DT1304-1308	Ethnology—Angola
966.8301	DT541.65-.67	Benin—History—To 1894	967.301	DT1357	Angola—History—To 1482
966.83051	DT541.845	Benin—History—Coup d'etat, 1977	967.301	DT1357-1369	Angola—History—1482-1648
966.9	DT515.4	Nigeria—Civilization	967.30(2-3)	DT1385-1396	Angola—History—1885-1961
966.9	DT515.53-.84	Nigeria—History			
966.9004	DT515.42-.45	Ethnology—Nigeria	967.302	DT1373-1382	Angola—History—1648-1885
966.90(1-3)	DT515.7-.72	Nigeria—History—1851-1899			
			967.303	DT1398-1417	Angola—History—Revolution, 1961-1975
966.901	DT515.65-.67	Nigeria—History—To 1851			
966.903	DT515.7-.77	Nigeria—History—1900-1960	967.304	DT1428	Angola—History—Civil War, 1975-
966.905	DT515.8-.84	Nigeria—History—1960-	967.41	DT546.34	Central African Republic—Civilization
966.9051	DT515.832	Nigeria—History—Coup d'etat, 1966 (July 29)			
			967.41	DT546.348-.384	Central African Republic—History
966.9051	DT515.832	Nigeria—History—Coup d'etat, 1966 (January 15)	967.41004	DT546.342-.345	Ethnology—Central African Republic
966.9052	DT515.836	Nigeria—History—Civil War, 1967-1970	967.410(1-3)	DT546.365-.37	Central African Republic—History—To 1960
966.9053	DT515.84	Nigeria—History—Coup d'etat, 1983	967.4103	DT546.37	Kongo Wars, 1928-1931
967.0(1-2)	DT352.65	Africa, Central—History—To 1884	967.4105	DT546.375-.384	Central African Republic—History—1960-
967.03(1-25)	DT352.7	Africa, Central—History—1884-1960	967.4105	DT546.38	Central African Republic—History—Coup d'etat, 1979
967.0312	DT363	Emin Pasha Relief Expedition, 1887-1889	967.43	DT546.44	Chad—Civilization
			967.43	DT546.457-.483	Chad—History
967.11	DT569.5	Cameroon—Civilization	967.43004	DT546.422-.445	Ethnology—Chad
967.11	DT572-578.4	Cameroon—History	967.4304	DT546.48-.483	Chad—History—1960-
967.11004	DT570-571	Ethnology—Cameroon	967.4304(1-4)	DT546.48	Chad—History—Civil War, 1965-
967.1104	DT578	Cameroon—History—Coup d'etat, 1984			
967.15	DT615.5-.8	Sao Tome and Principe—History	967.51	DT649	Zaire—Civilization
			967.51	DT650.2-663	Zaire—History
			967.51004	DT649.5-650	Ethonology—Zaire
967.15004	DT615.42-.45	Ethnology—Sao Tome and Principe	967.510(1-22)	DT654-655.2	Zaire—History—To 1908
			967.51024	DT657-.2	Zaire—History—1908-1960
967.18	DT620.46-.83	Equatorial Guinea—History	967.5103	DT658-.25	Zaire—History—1960-

Dewey	LC	Subject Heading	Dewey	LC	Subject Heading
967.51031	DT658	Zaire—History—Civil War, 1960-1965	967.902	DT3361-3374	Mozambique—History—1698-1891
967.51033	DT658.25	Zaire—History—Shaba Invasion, 1977	967.903	DT463-.3	Mozambique—History—Revolution, 1964-1975
967.51033	DT658.25	Zaire—History—Shaba Uprising, 1978	967.905	DT3389-3398	Mozambique—History—1975-
967.571	DT450.22	Rwanda—Civilization	968	DT1772-1969	South Africa—History
967.571	DT450.26-.437	Rwanda—History	968	DT1752	South Africa—Civilization
967.571004	DT450.24-.25	Ethnology—Rwanda	968.0009034	DT1123	Africa, Southern—History—Mfecane period, 1816-ca. 1840
967.57104	DT450.435	Rwanda—History—Civil War, 1994			
967.572	DT450.66-.855	Burundi—History	968.004	DT1754-1770	Ethnology—South Africa
967.572	DT450.63	Burundi—Civilization	968.0(2-42)	DT1807-1845	South Africa—History—To 1836
967.572004	DT450.64-.65	Ethnology—Burundi	968.0(3-45)	DT1837	South Africa—History—Frontier Wars, 1811-1878
967.6	DT365-469	Africa, East			
967.6	DT365.5-.8	Africa, East—History	968.044	DT1853	South Africa—History—Great Trek, 1836-1840
967.601	DT365.65	Africa, East—History—To 1886	968.045	DT1875-1882	Zulu War, 1879
967.61	DT433.252-.287	Uganda—History	968.045	DT1888	South Africa—History—Usutu Uprising, 1888
967.61	DT433.24	Uganda—Civilization	968.045	DT1889	Jameson's Raid, 1895-1896
967.61004	DT433.242-.245	Ethnology—Uganda			
967.610(1-3)	DT433.27-.273	Uganda—History—1890-1962	968.04(2-9)	DT1848-1922	South Africa—History—1836-1909
967.6101	DT433.265-.267	Uganda—History—To 1890	968.0(49-5)	DT1924-1941	South Africa—History—1906-1961
967.6104(2-4)	DT433.284-.286	Uganda—History—1979-			
967.61042	DT433.282	Uganda—History—1971-1979	968.052	DT1933	South Africa—History—Rebellion, 1914-1915
967.62	DT433.54	Kenya—Civilization	968.06	DT1945-1970	South Africa—History—1961-
967.62	DT433.552-.584	Kenya—History			
967.62004	DT433.542-.545	Ethnology—Kenya	968.0627	DT1959	South Africa—History—Soweto Uprising, 1976
967.620(1-3)	DT433.565-.577	Kenya—History—To 1963	968.29	DT1760	Homelands (South Africa)
967.6201	DT433.565-.567	Kenya—History—To 1895	968.81	DT1552	Namibia—Civilization
967.6203	DT433.57-.577	Kenya—History—1895-1963	968.81	DT1564-1648	Namibia—History
967.6204	DT433.58-.584	Kenya—History—1963-	968.81004	DT1554-1558	Ethnology—Namibia
967.71	DT411-.9	Djibout	968.8101	DT1587-1601	Namibia—History—To 1884
967.71	DT411.4	Djibouti—Civilization	968.8102	DT1603-1622	Namibia—History—1884-1915
967.71	DT411.5-.83	Djibouti—History			
967.71004	DT411.42-.45	Ethnology—Djibouti	968.8103	DT1618	Namibia—History—Herero Revolt, 1904-1907
967.73	DT401-409	Somalia	968.8103	DT1625-1636	Namibia—History—1915-1946
967.73	DT402.2	Somalia—Civilization			
967.73	DT402.5-407.3	Somalia—History	968.8103	DT1638-1648	Namibia—History—1946-1990
967.73004	DT402.3-.45	Ethnology—Somalia			
967.7305	DT407-.3	Somalia—History—1960-1991	968.8104	DT1648	Namibia—History—1990-
967.73053	DT407	Somalia—History—1991-	968.83	DT2452	Botswana—Civilization
967.8	DT443.5-448.25	Tanzania—History	968.83	DT2464-2502	Botswana—History
967.8	DT443.5-448.25	Tanzania—History—To 1964	968.83004	DT2454-2458	Ethnology—Botswana
967.8	DT442.5	Tanzania—Civilization	968.830(1-2)	DT2483-2493	Botswana—History—To 1966
967.8004	DT443-.3	Ethnology—Tanzania			
967.9	DT3320	Mozambique—Civilization	968.8303	DT2496-2502	Botswana—History—1966-
967.9	DT3330-3398	Mozambique—History	968.8304	DT2448	Botswana—Description and travel
967.9004	DT3324-3328	Ethnology—Mozambique			
967.90(1-2)	DT3350-3359	Mozambique—History—1505-1698	968.85	DT2582	Lesotho—Civilization
			968.85	DT2604-2660	Lesotho—History
967.901	DT3345-3348	Mozambique—History—To 1505	968.85004	DT2592-2596	Ethnology—Lesotho
			968.850(1-2)	DT2630-2648	Lesotho—History—To 1966
967.90(2-3)	DT3376-3387	Mozambique—History—1891-1975	968.8503	DT2652-2660	Lesotho—History—1966-
967.902	DT3381	Mozambique—History—War of 1894-1895	968.87	DT2742	Swaziland—Civilization

996 - 968

233

Dewey	LC	Subject Heading	Dewey	LC	Subject Heading
968.87	DT2754-2806	Swaziland—History	969.6	DT469.S48	Seychelles—History—
968.87004	DT2744-2746	Ethnology—Swaziland			Coup d'etat, 1981
968.91	DT2908	Zimbabwe—Civilization	969.6	DT469.S44	Seychelles—Civilization
968.91	DT2914-3000	Zimbabwe—History	969.6004	DT469.S442-	Ethnology—Seychelles
968.91004	DT2910-2913	Ethnology—Zimbabwe		.S443	
968.910(2-4)	DT2959-2979	Zimbabwe—History—	969.8	DT469.M39	Mascarene Islands
		1890-1965	969.81	DT469.R37	Reunion—Civilization
968.9102	DT2970	Zimbabwe—History—Shona	969.81	DT469.R42-	Reunion—History
		Insurrection, 1896-1897		.R458	
968.9102	DT2968	Zimbabwe—History—	969.81004	DT469.R38-.R39	Ethnology—Reunion
		Ndebele Insurrection, 1896	969.8102	DT469.R44-	Reunion—History—
968.9104	DT2981-2994	Zimbabwe—History—		.R443	To 1764
		1965-1980	969.8102	DT469.R45-	Reunion—History—
968.9104	DT2988	Zimbabwe—History—		.R453	1764-1946
		Chimurenga War,	969.8102	DT469.R45	Reunion—History—British
		1966-1980			occupation, 1810-1815
968.9105	DT2996-3000	Zimbabwe—History—1980-	969.8104	DT469.R455-	Reunion—History—1946-
968.94	DT3064-3119	Zambia—History		.R458	
968.94	DT3052	Zambia—Civilization	969.82	DT469.M45-	Mauritius—History
968.94004	DT3054-3058	Ethnology—Zambia		.M497	
968.9401	DT3079-3089	Zambia—History—To 1890	969.82	DT469.M44	Mauritius—Civilization
968.9402	DT3091-3101	Zambia—History—1890-	969.82004	DT469.M442-	Ethnology—Mauritius
		1924		.M445	
968.9402	DT3103-3106	Zambia—History—1924-	969.8201	DT469.M465-	Mauritius—History—
		1953		.M467	To 1810
968.940(3-4)	DT3108-3111	Zambia—History—1953-	970	E31-45	North America
		1964	970	E40	North America—Civilization
968.9404	DT3113-3119	Zambia—History—1964-	970	E45-46	North America—History
968.97	DT3187	Malawi—Civilization	970	E	America
968.97	DT3194-3237	Malawi—History	970	E16-18.85	America—History
968.97004	DT3189-3192	Ethnology—Malawi	970-989	F	America—History
968.9701	DT3211-3214	Malawi—History—To 1891	970.00497	E51-73	Indians
968.9702	DT3216-3225	Malawi—History—1891-	970.00497	E58	Indians—History
		1953	970.005	E31	North America—Periodicals
968.9702	DT3225	Malawi—History—	970.01	E101-135	America—Discovery and
		Chilembwe Rebellion, 1915			exploration
968.970(3-4)	DT3227-3230	Malawi—History—1953-	971	F1001-1040	Canada
		1964	971	F1021-.2	Canada—Civilization
968.9704	DT3232-3240	Malawi—History—1964-	971.004114	F1027	French-Canadians
969.1	DT469.M274	Madagascar—Civilization	971.005	F1001	Canada—Periodicals
969.1	DT469.M282-	Madagascar—History	971.01	F1030-.9	Canada—History—To
	.M345				1763 (New France)
969.1004	DT469.M276-	Ethnology—Madagascar	971.018	F1030	Lake of the Woods
	.M277				Massacre, 1736
969.10(1-3)	DT469.M34-	Madagascar—History—	971.0188	F1030.9	Canada—History—1755-
	.M342	1885-1960			1763
969.101	DT469.M31-	Madagascar—History—	971.02	F1031	Canada—History—1763-
	.M313	To 1810			1791
969.101	DT469.M32-	Madagascar—History—	971.02(2-49)	F1032	Canada—History—1763-
	.M335	Hova rule, 1810-1885			1867
969.103	DT469.M34	Madagascar—History—	971.024	F1032	Canada—History—1775-
		Menalamba Rebellion,			1783
		1895-1899	971.03	F1032	Canada—History—1791-
969.103	DT469.M34	Madagascar—History—			1841
		French Invasion, 1895	971.038	F1032	Canada—History—
969.103	DT469.M34	Madagascar—History—			Rebellion, 1837-1838
		Revolution, 1947	971.04	F1032	Canada—History—1841-
969.6	DT469.S452-	Seychelles—History			1867
	.S483		971.048	F1033	Canada—History—Fenian
969.6	DT469.S48	Seychelles—History—			Invasions, 1866-1870
		Coup d'etat, 1977			

Dewey	LC	Subject Heading	Dewey	LC	Subject Heading
971.05	F1033	Canada—History—Confederation, 1867	972.0816	F1234	Mexico—History—Decena Tragica, 1913
971.06(12-32)	F1034	Canada—History—1914-1945	972.0816	F1234	El Ebano, Battle of, 1915
971.063(2-48)	F1034.2-.3	Canada—History—1945-	972.0822	F1234	Mexico—History—Revolution, 1923-1924
971.1	F1086-1089.7	British Columbia—History	972.08(27-31)	F1235-.5	Mexico—History—1946-1970
971.1005	F1086	British Columbia—Periodicals	972.083(2-4)	F1236	Mexico—History—1970-1988
971.23	F1075-1080	Alberta—History			
971.23005	F1075	Alberta—Periodicals	972.083(5-6)	F1236	Mexico—History—1988-
971.24	F1070-1074.7	Saskatchewan—History	972.8	F1421-1577	Central America
971.24005	F1070	Saskatchewan—Periodicals	972.8	F1430	Central America—Civilization
971.27	F1061-1065	Manitoba—History	972.8	F1435.4-1439.5	Central America—History
971.27005	F1061	Manitoba—Periodicals	972.800497	F1434-1435.3	Indians of Central America
971.3	F1056-1059.7	Ontario—History	972.8005	F1421	Central America—Periodicals
971.3005	F1056	Ontario—Periodicals	972.81	F1461-1477	Guatemala
971.4	F1051-1055	Quebec (Province)—History	972.81	F1465-1466.7	Guatemala—History
971.4005	F1051	Quebec (Province)—Periodicals	972.81	F1463.5	Guatemala—Civilization
			972.81005	F1461	Guatemala—Periodicals
971.5	F1035.8	Maritime Provinces—History	972.810(1-3)	F1466.4	Guatemala—History—To 1821
971.51005	F1041	New Brunswick—Periodicals			
971.6	F1036-1040	Nova Scotia—History	972.810(4-52)	F1466.45	Guatemala—History—1821-1945
971.6005	F1036	Nova Scotia—Periodicals			
971.7	F1046-1049.7	Prince Edward Islands—History	972.8105(2-3)	F1466.7	Guatemala—History—1985-
			972.81052	F1466.5	Guatemala—History—1945-1985
971.7005	F1046	Prince Edward Islands—Periodicals	972.82	F1441-1457	Belize
971.8	F1121-1124	Newfoundland—History	972.82	F1443.8	Belize—Civilization
971.8005	F1121	Newfoundland—Periodicals	972.82	F1445.5-1448	Belize—History
971.82	F1135-1139	Labrador (Nfld.)—History	972.82005	F1441	Belize—Periodicals
971.82005	F1135	Labrador (Nfld.)—Periodicals	972.83	F1501-1517	Honduras
971.91	F1091-1095.5	Yukon Territory—History	972.83	F1505.5-1508.33	Honduras—History
971.91005	F1091.A1	Yukon Territory—Periodicals			
971.92	F1060-.97	Northwest, Canadian	972.83	F1503.8	Honduras—Civilization
971.94	F1106-1110.5	Keewatin—History	972.83005	F1501	Honduras—Periodicals
971.94005	F1106.A1	Keewatin—Periodicals	972.830(1-4)	F1507	Honduras—History—To 1838
972	F1201-1392	Mexico			
972	F1210	Mexico—Civilization	972.8305(1-2)	F1507.5	Honduras—History—1838-1933
972.00497	F1219-1221	Indians of Mexico			
972.00497452	F1219.73-.75	Aztecs	972.83051	F1507.5	Honduras—History—Coup d'etat, 1904
972.00497452	F1219.73-.75	Nahuas			
972.005	F1201	Mexico—Periodicals	972.83051	F1507.5	Honduras—History—Revolution, 1919
972.0(1-2)	F1229-1231	Mexico—History—To 1810			
972.01	F1228.98	Mexico—History—To 1519	972.8305(2-3)	F1508-.22	Honduras—History—1933-1982
972.02	F1230	Mexico—History—Conquest, 1519-1540	972.83053	F1508.3-.33	Honduras—History—1982-
972.02	F1231	Mexico—History—Spanish colony, 1540-1810	972.84	F1481-1497	El Salvador
			972.84	F1485.5-1488.53	El Salvador—History
972.0(3-6)	F1232-.5	Mexico—History—1821-1861			
972.0(3-83)	F1231.5-1236.6	Mexico—History—1810-	972.84	F1483.8	El Salvador—Civilization
972.07	F1233	Mexico—History—European intervention, 1861-1867	972.84005	F1481	El Salvador—Periodicals
			972.840(1-42)	F1487	El Salvador—History—To 1838
972.081(2-4)	F1233.5	Mexico—History—1867-1910	972.840(4-52)	F1487.5	El Salvador—History—1838-1944
972.08(16-21)	F1234	Mexico—History—Revolution, 1910-1920	972.84052	F1488	El Salvador—History—1944-1979
972.08(16-26)	F1234	Mexico—History—1910-1946	972.84052	F1487.5	El Salvador—History—Revolution, 1944
			972.84052	F1488	El Salvador—History—Revolution of 1948

Dewey	LC	Subject Heading	Dewey	LC	Subject Heading
972.84052	F1488	El Salvador-Honduras Conflict, 1969	972.87051	F1566.5	Panama—History—Revolution, 1903
972.84053	F1488.3-.53	El Salvador—History—1979-	972.87051	F1566.5	Panama—History—Coup d'etat, 1968
972.84053	F1488.3	El Salvador—History—1979-1992	972.87053	F1567	Panama—History—1981-
972.84053	F1488.5-.53	El Salvador—History—1992-	972.87053	F1567	Panama—History—American Invasion, 1989
972.85	F1521-1537	Nicaragua	972.9	F1601-1629	West Indies
972.85	F1525.5-1528.22	Nicaragua—History	972.9	F1609.5	West Indies—Civilization
			972.9	F1620-1623	West Indies—History
972.85	F1523.8	Nicaragua—Civilization	972.9	F2155-2191	Caribbean Area
972.85005	F1521	Nicaragua—Periodicals	972.9	F2173-2191	Caribbean Area—History
972.850(1-42)	F1526.25	Nicaragua—History—To 1838	972.900497	F1619	Indians of the West Indies
			972.9005	F1601	West Indies—Periodicals
972.8503	F1526.25	Nicaragua—History—English Invasion, 1780-1781	972.903	F1621	English West Indian Expedition, 1654-1655
972.850(44-51)	F1526.27	Nicaragua—History—1838-1909	972.903	F1621	English West Indian Expedition, 1695
972.85044	F1526.27	Nicaragua—History—Filibuster War, 1855-1860	972.903	F2151	English West Indian Expedition, 1759
972.8505(1-2)	F1526.3	Nicaragua—History—1909-1937	972.903	F1621	English West Indian Expedition, 1793-1794
972.85051	F1526.3	Nicaragua—History—Revolution, 1909-1910	972.903	F1621	English West Indian Expedition, 1795-1796
972.85051	F1526.3	Nicaragua—History—Revolution of 1912	972.910(1-4)	F1779	Cuba—History—To 1810
			972.9103	F1781	Cuba—History—British occupation, 1762-1763
972.85051	F1526.3	Nicaragua—History—Revolution, 1926-1929	972.910(5-6)	F1786-1788.22	Cuba—History—1895-
972.85052	F1527	Nicaragua—History—1937-1979	972.9105	F1783	Cuba—History—1810-1899
			972.9105	F1783	Cuba—History—Black Eagle Conspiracy, 1830
972.85052	F1527	Nicaragua—History—San Carlos Barracks Attack, 1977	972.9105	F1783	Cuba—History—Negro Conspiracy, 1844
972.85052	F1527	Nicaragua—History—Uprising, 1978	972.9105	F1783	Cuba—History—Insurrection, 1849-1851
972.85052	F1528	Nicaragua—History—Revolution, 1979	972.9105	F1785	Cuba—History—Insurrection, 1868-1878
972.85053	F1528	Nicaragua—History—1979-1990	972.9105	F1785	Cuba—History—1878-1895
			972.9105	F1785	Cuba—History—Revolution, 1879-1880
972.85054	F1528	Nicaragua—History—1990-			
972.86	F1541-1557	Costa Rica	972.9105	F1786	Cuba—History—Revolution, 1895-1898
972.86	F1543.8	Costa Rica—Civilization			
972.86005	F1541	Costa Rica—Periodicals	972.9106(1-2)	F1787	Cuba—History—1899-1906
972.860(1-3)	F1547	Costa Rica—History—To 1821	972.91062	F1787	Cuba—History—1909-1933
			972.91062	F1787	Cuba—History—American occupation, 1906-1909
972.8604	F1547.5	Costa Rica—History—1821-1948	972.91063	F1787.5	Cuba—History—Revolution, 1933
972.86044	F1547.5	Costa Rica—History—Uprising, 1932	972.91063	F1787.5	Cuba—History—Moncada Barracks Attack, 1953
972.8605	F1548	Costa Rica—History—1948-1986	972.91063	F1787.5	El Jigue (Cuba), Battle of, 1958
972.8605	F1548.2-.23	Costa Rica—History—1986-	972.91064	F1788	Cuba—History—Revolution, 1959
972.87	F1561-1577	Panama			
972.87	F1563.8	Panama—Civilization	972.91064	F1788	Cuba—History—Invasion, 1961
972.87	F1565.5-1567	Panama—History			
972.87005	F1561	Panama—Periodicals	972.92	F1861-1896	Jamaica
972.870(1-3)	F1566.45	Panama—History—To 1903	972.92	F1874	Jamaica—Civilization
972.8705(1-3)	F1566.5-1567	Panama—History—1946-1981	972.92	F1878-1887	Jamaica—History
			972.92005	F1861-1896	Jamaica—Periodicals
972.87051	F1566.5	Panama—History—1903-1946	972.920(1-5)	F1884-1886	Jamaica—History—To 1962

Dewey	LC	Subject Heading	Dewey	LC	Subject Heading
972.92034	F1884	Jamaica—History—Maroon War, 1795-1796	972.950(1-4)	F1973	Puerto Rico—History—To 1898
972.92034	F1886	Jamaica—History—Slave Insurrection, 1831	972.950(4-52)	F1975	Puerto Rico—History—1898-1952
972.9204	F1886	Jamaica—History—Insurrection, 1865	972.9504	F1973	Puerto Rico—History—Insurrection, 1868
972.9206	F1887	Jamaica—History—1962-	972.95052	F1975	Puerto Rico—History—Nationalist Insurrection, 1950
972.921	F2048.5	Cayman Islands			
972.93	F1931-1941	Dominican Republic	972.95053	F1976-.3	Puerto Rico—History—1952-
972.93	F1935	Dominican Republic—Civilization	972.96	F1650-1660	Bahamas
			972.96	F1655.3-1657.2	Bahamas—History
972.93	F1937-1938.58	Dominican Republic—History	972.96	F1654	Bahamas—Civilization
			972.96005	F1650	Bahamas—Periodicals
972.93005	F1931	Dominican Republic—Periodicals	972.9(7-8)	F2001-2151	Antilles, Lesser
972.930(1-4)	F1938.3	Dominican Republic—History—To 1844	972.97	F2006	Leeward Islands (West Indies)
972.930(4-52)	F1938.4	Dominican Republic—History—1844-1930	972.9722	F2136	Virgin Islands of the United States
972.93052	F1938.45	Dominican Republic—History—American occupation, 1916-1924	972.9722	E263.W5	Virgin Islands of the United States—History—1775-1783
972.9305(3-4)	F1938.5-.58	Dominican Republic—History—1930-	972.9722	E263.W5	Virgin Islands of the United States—History—1775-1793
972.93053	F1938.5	Dominican Republic—History—1930-1961	972.9722	F2105	Saint Thomas (V.I.)
972.93053	F1938.5	Dominican-Haitian Conflict, 1937	972.9722	F2098	Saint John (V.I.)
			972.9722	F2096	Saint Croix (V.I.)
972.93053	F1938.5	Dominican Republic—History—Invasion, 1959	972.9725	F2129	British Virgin Islands
			972.973	F2091	Saint Kitts and Nevis
972.93054	F1938.55-.58	Dominican Republic—History—1961-	972.973	F2033	Anguilla
			972.974	F2035	Antigua
972.93054	F1938.55	Dominican Republic—History—Coup d'etat, 1963	972.975	F2082	Montserrat
			972.976	F2066	Guadeloupe
972.93054	F1938.55	Dominican Republic—History—Revolution, 1965	972.976	F2070	Saintes Islands (Guadeloupe)
972.93054	F1938.55	Dominican Republic—History—Revolution, 1973	972.976	F2050	Desirade (Guadeloupe)
			972.976	F2076	Marie Galante
972.93054	F1938.55	Dominican Republic—History—Uprising, 1984	972.976	F2103	Saint Martin
			972.977	F2088	Saba (Netherlands Antilles)
972.94	F1900-1930	Haiti	972.977	F2097	Saint Eustatius (Netherlands Antilles)
972.94	F1918-1939	Haiti—History			
972.94	F1916	Haiti—Civilization	972.98	F2011	Windward Islands
972.94005	F1900	Haiti—Periodicals	972.981	F2041	Barbados
972.940(1-3)	F1923	Haiti—History—To 1791	972.982	F2081	Martinique
972.9403	F1923	Haiti—History—Revolution, 1791-1804	972.983	F2116-2123	Trinidad and Tobago
			972.9841	F2051	Dominica
972.9404	F1924	Haiti—History—1804-1844	972.9843	F2100	Saint Lucia
972.9404	F1938.3	Haiti—History—Revolution, 1843	972.9844	F2061	The Grenadines
			972.9845	F2056	Grenada
972.9404	F1926	Haiti—History—1844-1915	972.986	F2049	Curacao
972.9405	F1927	Haiti—History—American occupation, 1915-1934	972.986	F2048	Bonaire
			972.99	F1630-1640	Bermuda Islands
972.940(6-72)	F1927-1928	Haiti—History—1934-1986	972.99	F1635-1637	Bermuda Islands—History
972.94073	F1928.2-.23	Haiti—History—1986-	972.99	F1633	Bermuda Islands—Civilization
972.94073	F1928.2	Haiti—History—Coup d'etat, 1991	972.99005	F1630	Bermuda Islands—Periodicals
972.95	F1951-1983	Puerto Rico			
972.95	F1960	Puerto Rico—Civilization	973	E151-887	United States
972.95	F1970-1976.3	Puerto Rico—History	973	E169.1-.12	United States—Civilization
972.95005	F1951	Puerto Rico—Periodicals	973	E162-168	United States—Civilization

Dewey	LC	Subject Heading
973	E171-183.9	United States—History
973	E179.5	United States—Territorial expansion
973	HN51-90	United States—Social conditions
973.0071075	V438	Naval education—Confederate States of America
973.025	E154.5-.7	United States—Directories
973.04	E184-185.98	Ethnology—United States
973.04(2-8)073	E184.E95	European Americans
973.043931073	E184.D9	Dutch Americans
973.043981073	E184.S19	Danish Americans
973.0468073	E184.S75	Hispanic Americans
973.046872073	E184.M5	Mexican Americans
973.04687293073	E184.D6	Dominican Americans
973.04914073	E184.E2	East Indian Americans
973.04917073	E184.E17	East European Americans
973.0494541073	E184.F5	Finnish Americans
973.0496073	E185.18-.98	Afro-Americans—History
973.0496073	E185.86	Afro-Americans—Social conditions
973.0496073	E185.86	Afro-Americans—Social life and customs
973.0497	E75-99	Indians of North America
973.0497	E98.S7	Indians of North America—Social life and customs
973.04971	E99.E7	Yupik Eskimos
973.04971	E99.A12	Abitibi Indians
973.04971	E99.E7	Eskimos
973.04971	E99.E7	Nunamiut Eskimos
973.04971	E99.E7	Koniagmiut Eskimos
973.04972	E99.A6	Apache Indians
973.04972	E99.N3	Navajo Indians
973.04973	E78.045	Five Civilized Tribes
973.04973	E78.I5	Five Civilized Tribes
973.04973	E99.S28	Seminole Indians
973.04973	E99.S35	Shawnee Indians
973.04973	E99.M12	Mahican Indians
973.04973	E99.A349	Algonquin Indians
973.04973	E99.A7	Arapaho Indians
973.04973	E99.C53	Cheyenne Indians
973.04973	E99.M83	Mohegan Indians
973.04973	E99.M44	Menominee Indians
973.04973	E99.M95	Muskogean Indians
973.04973	E99.A35	Algonquian Indians
973.04973	E99.C6	Ojibwa Indians
973.04973	E99.A13	Abnaki Indians
973.04974	E99.P9	Pueblos
973.04974	E99.P9	Pueblo Indians
973.04974	E99.P9	Cliff-dwellers
973.04974	E78	Pueblo Indians—Antiquities
973.049741	E99.N5	Nez Perce Indians
973.049745	E99.U8	Ute Indians
973.049745	E99.C85	Comanche Indians
973.049745	E99.S4	Shoshoni Indians
973.049745	E99.H7	Hopi Indians
973.049745	E99.P6	Pima Indians
973.049745	E99.S39	Shoshonean Indians
973.049749	E99.T2	Taos Indians
973.049752	E99.C92	Crow Indians
973.049752	E99.D1	Dakota Indians
973.049752	E99.08	Osage Indians
973.049752	E99.03	Oglala Indians
973.049752	E99.T34	Teton Indians
973.049755	E78.045	Five Civilized Tribes
973.049755	E78.I5	Five Civilized Tribes
973.049755	E99.M8	Mohawk Indians
973.049755	E99.I69	Iroquoian Indians
973.049755	E99.C5	Cherokee Indians
973.049757	E99.D5	Diegueno Indians
973.049757	E99.M77	Mohave Indians
973.04979	E99.P3	Pawnee Indians
973.04979	E99.Z9	Zuni Indians
973.049921073	E184.F4	Filipino Americans
973.05	E151	United States—Periodicals
973.072	E175-.7	United States—Historiography
973.(1-2)	E186-199	United States—History—Colonial period, ca. 1600-1775
973.(1-26)	E82	Indians of North America—Wars—1600-1750
973.(1-7)0496073	E185.18	Afro-Americans—History—To 1863
973.(1-8)	E81-83.895	Indians of North America—Wars
973.1	E159.5	United States—Antiquities
973.1	E75-99	United States—Antiquities
973.23	E83.655	Esopus Indians—Wars, 1655-1660
973.23	E83.663	Esopus Indians—Wars, 1663-1664
973.24	E83.67	Falls Fight, 1676
973.25	E196	United States—History—King William's War, 1689-1697
973.25	E197	United States—History—Queen Anne's War, 1702-1713
973.(26-53)	E81	Indians of North America—Wars—1750-1815
973.26	E198	United States—History—King George's War, 1744-1748
973.26	E199	Necessity, Fort, Battle of, 1754
973.26	E199	United States—History—French and Indian War, 1755-1763
973.26	E199	Fort Oswego (Oswego, N.Y.)—Capture, 1756
973.26	E199	Fort William Henry (N.Y.)—Capture, 1757
973.26	E199	Forbes Expedition against Fort Duquesne, 1758
973.26	E199	Ticonderoga, Battle of, 1758
973.3	E83.775	Indians of North America—Wars—1775-1783
973.3	E201-298	United States—History—Revolution, 1775-1783

Dewey	LC	Subject Heading	Dewey	LC	Subject Heading
973.3	E301-655	United States—History—1783-1865	973.57	E83.835	Seminole War, 2nd, 1835-1842
973.3112	E215.3	Non-importation agreements, 1768-1769	973.62	E401-415.2	Mexican War, 1846-1848
973.3113	E215.4	Boston Massacre, 1770	973.623	E405.2	Doniphan's Expedition, 1846-1847
973.3115	E215.7	Boston Tea Party, 1773	973.623	E406.M7	Monterrey (Mexico), Battle of, 1846
973.3115	E215.7	Tea tax (American colonies)	973.623	E405.2	Kearny's Expedition, 1846
973.318	E303-309	United States—History—Confederation, 1783-1789	973.(63-82)	E671-680	United States—History—1849-1877
973.33	E230-241	United States—History—Revolution, 1775-1783—Campaigns	973.(63-82)	E415.6-680	United States—History—1849-1877
973.33(1-2)	E231	Canadian Invasion, 1775-1776	973.(64/7113)	E423	Compromise of 1850
			973.(7-82) 0496073	E185.2	Afro-Americans—History—1863-1877
973.3311	E241.L6	Lexington, Battle of, 1775			
973.3311	E241.C7	Concord, Battle of, 1775	973.7	E456-459	Lincoln, Abraham, 1809-1865
973.3312	E241.B9	Bunker Hill, Battle of, 1775	973.7	E456-655	United States—History—Civil War, 1861-1865
973.333	E241.P2	Paoli Massacre, 1777			
973.334	E241.M7	Monmouth, Battle of, 1778	973.7	E83.863	Indians of North America—Wars—1862-1865
973.335	E241.K48	Kettle Creek (Ga.), Battle of, 1779	973.7	E83.863	Shoshoni Indians—Wars, 1863-1865
973.335	E235	Sullivan's Indian Campaign, 1779	973.711	E415.7	Squatter sovereignty
			973.711	E441-453	Slavery
973.337	E241.G9	Guilford Court House, Battle of 1781	973.7113	E373	Missouri compromise
			973.7115	E450	Underground railroad
973.337	E241.E	Eutaw Springs, Battle of, 1781	973.713	E482-489	Confederate States of America
973.338	E271	Dominica, Battle of, 1782	973.713	E487-488	Confederate States of America—History
973.339	E239	Evacuation Day, Nov. 25, 1783	973.713	E458-459	Secession—Southern States
973.343	E277	American loyalists			
973.34(4-5)	E259	United States. Continental Army—History	973.731	E472.18	Bull Run, 1st Battle of, Va., 1861
973.4	E310-337	United States—History—Constitutional period, 1789-1809	973.731	E473.54	Shiloh, Battle of, 1862
			973.731	E472.96	Fort Henry (Tenn.), Battle of, 1862
973.41	E83.79	Indians of North America—Wars—1790-1794	973.73(1-2)	E473.6-.68	Peninsular Campaign, 1862
973.43	E315	Whiskey Rebellion, Pa., 1794	973.73(2-3)	E474.65	Antietam, Battle of, Md., 1862
973.44	E326	Fries Rebellion, 1798-1799	973.732	E473.68	Seven Days' Battles, 1862
973.523	E356.D4	Detroit (Mich.)—Surrender to the British, 1812	973.732	E473.7	Shenandoah Valley Campaign, 1862
973.523	E356.D8	Dudley's Defeat, 1813	973.732	E473.77	Bull Run, 2nd Battle of, Va., 1862
973.523	E356.B2	Baltimore, Battle of, 1814			
973.523	E356.B5	Bladensburg, Battle of, 1814	973.733	E474.85	Fredericksburg (Va.), Battle of, 1862
973.5239	E356.N5	New Orleans (La.), Battle of, 1815	973.733	E475.35	Chancellorsville (Va.), Battle of, 1863
973.525	E357.2-.3	Impressment	973.7336	E474.61	Maryland Campaign, 1862
973.5254	E356.E6	Erie, Lake, Battle of, 1813	973.734	E475.3	Kelly's Ford (Va.), Battle of, 1863
973.(53-82)	E81	Indians of North America—Wars—1815-1875	973.7349	E475.53	Gettysburg (Pa.), Battle of, 1863
973.53	E365	United States—History—War with Algeria, 1815	973.73(6-7)	E476.66	Shenandoah Valley Campaign, 1864 (May-August)
973.54	E371-375	United States—History—1817-1825			
973.55	E376-380	United States—History—1825-1829	973.736	E476.52	Spotsylvania Court House, Battle of, Va., 1864
973.56	E83.83	Black Hawk War, 1832			
973.561	E384.3	Nullification			

239

Dewey	LC	Subject Heading	Dewey	LC	Subject Heading
973.736	E476.65	Lynchburg (Va.), Battle of, 1864	973.92(3-9) 0496073	E185.615	Afro-Americans—History—1964-
973.736	E476.66	Maryland Campaign, 1864	973.924	E860	Watergate Affair, 1972-1974
973.737	E477.21	Fort Harrison (Va.), Battle of, 1864	973.925	E865	Mayaguez Incident, 1975
973.737	E477.33	Shenandoah Valley Campaign, 1864 (August-November)	974	F1-15	New England—History
			974	F106	Middle Atlantic States
			974-975 + .02	E83.72	Eastern Indians, Wars with, 1722-1726
973.7371	E476.7	Atlanta Campaign, 1864	974.005	F1	New England—Periodicals
973.7378	E476.69	Sherman's March to the Sea	974.0(1-2)	F7-.75	New England—History—Colonial period, ca. 1600-1775
973.738	E477.65	Shenandoah Valley Campaign, 1865	974.0(2-3)	F8	New England—History—1775-1865
973.738	E477.67	Appomattox Campaign, 1865	974.0(2-3)	F8	New England—History—Revolution, 1775-1783
973.738	E477.67	Dinwiddie Court House, Battle of, Dinwiddie, Va., 1865	974.02	E199	New England—History—French and Indian War, 1755-1763
973.742	E545	Confederate States of America—History, Military	974.02008825	F7	Puritans
973.742	E470.2	Confederate States of America—History, Military	974.03	E357-359	New England—History—War of 1812
973.75	E476.85	Mobile Bay (Ala.), Battle of, 1864	974.1	F16-30	Maine—History
			974.1005	F16	Maine—Periodicals
973.752	E473.2	Hampton Roads (Va.), Battle of, 1862	974.10(1-2)	F23	Maine—History—Colonial period, ca. 1600-1775
973.771	E611-612	Confederate States of America. Army—Prisons	974.10(1-3)	F24	Maine—History—1775-1865
973.(8-9)	E660-887	United States—History—1865-	974.102	F23	Maine—History—King William's War, 1689-1697
973.(8-913)	E660-783	United States—History—1865-1921	974.102	F23	Maine—History—King George's War, 1744-1748
973.8(1-7)	E83.866	Indians of North America—Wars—1866-1895	974.103	F24	Maine—History—War of 1812
973.8(1-8)	E660-735	United States—History—1865-1898	974.2	F31-45	New Hampshire—History
973.81	E83.866	Indians of North America—Wars—1868-1869	974.2005	F31	New Hampshire—Periodicals
973.(83-923) 0496073	E185.6	Afro-Americans—History—1877-1964	974.20(1-2)	F37	New Hampshire—History—Colonial period, ca. 1600-1775
973.893	E717.1	El Caney, Battle of, 1898	974.20(2-3)	E263.N4	New Hampshire—History—Revolution, 1775-1783
973.895	E717.7	Manila Bay, Battle of, 1898	974.202	E198	New Hampshire—History—King George's War, 1744-1748
973.91	E740-887	United States—History—20th century			
973.911	E740-760	United States—History—1901-1909	974.203	F38	New Hampshire—History—1775-1865
973.912	E761-765	United States—History—1909-1913	974.203	E520	New Hampshire—History—Civil War, 1861-1865
973.91(3-6)	E784-805	United States—History—1919-1933	974.2043	F40	New Hampshire—History—1951-
973.913	E766-783	United States—History—1913-1921	974.3	F46-60	Vermont—History
			974.3005	F46	Vermont—Periodicals
973.917	E806-812	United States—History—1933-1945	974.30(2-3)	E263.V5	Vermont—History—Revolution, 1775-1783
973.918	E813-816	United States—History—1945-1953	974.303	F52	Vermont—History—To 1791
973.921	E835-837.7	United States—History—1953-1961	974.303	E359.5.V3	Vermont—History—War of 1812
973.92(2-3)	E838-851	United States—History—1961-1969	974.303	E533	Vermont—History—Civil War, 1861-1865

Dewey	LC	Subject Heading	Dewey	LC	Subject Heading
974.4	F61-75	Massachusetts—History	974.70(2-3)	E263.N6	New York (State)—History—Revolution, 1775-1783
974.4005	F61	Massachusetts—Periodicals			
974.40(1-2)	F67	Massachusetts—History—Colonial period, ca. 1600-1775	974.702	E196	New York (State)—History—King William's War, 1689-1697
974.40(2-3)	E263.M4	Massachusetts—History—Revolution, 1775-1783	974.702	E197	New York (State)—History—Queen Anne's War, 1702-1713
974.40(2-3)	F69	Massachusetts—History—1775-1865	974.702	F123	New York (State)—History—French and Indian War, 1755-1763
974.402	F68	Massachusetts—History—New Plymouth, 1620-1691			
974.402	E198	Massachusetts—History—King George's War, 1744-1748	974.703	E359.5.N6	New York (State)—History—War of 1812
			974.703	F128.44	Draft Riot, New York, N.Y., 1863
974.402	E199	Massachusetts—History—French and Indian War, 1755-1763	974.71	F128-.9	New York (N.Y.)
			974.74	F124-125	New York (State)—History—1865-
974.402008825	F68	Pilgrims (New Plymouth Colony)	974.8	F146-160	Pennsylvania—History
974.403	E197	Massachusetts—History—Queen Anne's War, 1702-1713	974.8004310748	F160.G3	Pennsylvania Dutch
			974.8005	F146	Pennsylvania—Periodicals
			974.80(1-2)	F152-.2	Pennsylvania—History—Colonial period, ca. 1600-1775
974.403	E359.5.M3	Massachusetts—History—War of 1812	974.803	F153	Buckshot War, Harrisburg, Pa., 1838
974.403	E513	Massachusetts—History—Civil War, 1861-1865	974.804	F154-155.3	Pennsylvania—History—1865-
974.404	F70-71	Massachusetts—History—1865-	974.811	F158.1-.9	Philadelphia (Pa.)
974.461	F73-.9	Boston (Mass.)	974.9	F131-145	New Jersey—History
974.5	F76-90	Rhode Island—History	974.9005	F131	New Jersey—Periodicals
974.5005	F76	Rhode Island—Periodicals	974.90(1-2)	F137	New Jersey—History—Colonial period, ca. 1600-1775
974.50(1-2)	F82	Rhode Island—History—Colonial period, ca. 1600-1775	974.90(2-3)	F138	New Jersey—History—1775-1865
974.50(2-3)	E263.R4	Rhode Island—History—Revolution, 1775-1783	974.90(2-3)	E263.N5	New Jersey—History—Revolution, 1775-1783
974.502	E198	Rhode Island—History—King George's War, 1744-1748	974.903	E521	New Jersey—History—Civil War, 1861-1865
974.503	F83.4	Dorr Rebellion, 1842	974.903	F138	New Jersey—History—War of 1812
974.503	E528	Rhode Island—History—Civil War, 1861-1865	974.904	F139-140.22	New Jersey—History—1865-
974.6	F91-105	Connecticut—History	975	F206-220	Southern States—History
974.6005	F91	Connecticut—Periodicals	975	E482-489	Confederate States of America
974.60(1-2)	F97	Connecticut—History—Colonial period, ca. 1600-1775	975	E487	Confederate States of America—Social conditions
974.60(2-3)	F99	Connecticut—History—1775-1865	975	E487-488	Confederate States of America—History
974.604(1-3)	F100	Connecticut—History—1865-1950	975.03	E83.817	Seminole War, 1st, 1817-1818
974.604(3-4)	F101	Connecticut—History—1951-	975.1	F161-175	Delaware—History
974.7	F116-130	New York (State)—History	975.1005	F161	Delaware—Periodicals
974.7005	F116	New York (State)—Periodicals	975.10(2-3)	E263.D3	Delaware—History—Revolution, 1775-1783
974.70(1-2)	F122-.1	New York (State)—History—Colonial period, ca. 1660-1775	975.103	E359.5.D3	Delaware—History—War of 1812
974.70(2-3)	F123	New York (State)—History—1775-1865	975.103	E500	Delaware—History—Civil War, 1861-1865

Dewey	LC	Subject Heading	Dewey	LC	Subject Heading
975.104(3-4)	F170	Delaware—History—1951-	975.603	E573	North Carolina—History—Civil War, 1861-1865
975.14(1-3)	F169	Delaware—History—1865-1950	975.604	F259-260.42	North Carolina—History—1865-
975.2	F176-190	Maryland—History	975.7	F266-280	South Carolina—History
975.2005	F176	Maryland—Periodicals	975.7005	F266	South Carolina—Periodicals
975.20(1-2)	F184	Maryland—History—Colonial period, ca. 1600-1775	975.70(1-2)	F272	South Carolina—History—Colonial period, ca. 1600-1775
975.20(2-3)	E263.M3	Maryland—History—Revolution, 1775-1783	975.70(2-3)	F273	South Carolina—History—1775-1865
975.203	E359.5.M2	Maryland—History—War of 1812	975.70(2-3)	E263.N8	North Carolina—History—Revolution, 1775-1783
975.210(2-3)	E263.D3	Delmarva Peninsula—History—Revolution, 1775-1783	975.70(2-3)	E263.S7	South Carolina—History—Revolution, 1775-1783
975.256	F189.A6	Annapolis (Md.)	975.702	E197	South Carolina—History—Queen Anne's War, 1702-1713
975.26	F189.B1	Baltimore (Md.)			
975.3	F191-205	Washington (D.C.)	975.703	E577	South Carolina—History—Civil War, 1861-1865
975.3005	F191	Washington (D.C.)—Periodicals	975.703	E471.1	South Carolina—History—Civil War, 1861-1865
975.302	E356.W3	Washington (D.C.)—History—Capture by the British, 1814	975.703	E529	South Carolina—History—Civil War, 1861-1865
975.4	F236-250	West Virginia	975.704	F274-275.42	South Carolina—History—1865-
975.4005	F236	West Virginia—Periodicals	975.8	F281-295	Georgia
975.403	E536	West Virginia—History—Civil War, 1861-1865	975.8005	F281	Georgia—Periodicals
975.403	E582	West Virginia—History—Civil War, 1861-1865	975.80(2-3)	F290	Georgia—History—1775-1865
975.404(3-4)	F245-.42	West Virginia—History—1951-	975.80(2-3)	E263.G3	Georgia—History—Revolution, 1775-1783
975.5	F221-235	Virginia—History	975.803	E359.5.G4	Georgia—History—War of 1812
975.5005	F221	Virginia—Periodicals			
975.50(1-2)	F229	Virginia—History—Colonial period, ca. 1600-1775	975.803	E559	Georgia—History—Civil War, 1861-1865
975.50(2-3)	F230	Virginia—History—1775-1865	975.803	E503	Georgia—History—Civil War, 1861-1865
975.50(2-3)	E263.V8	Virginia—History—Revolution, 1775-1783	975.804	F291-.3	Georgia—History—1865-
975.502	F229	Bacon's Rebellion, 1676	975.8231	F294.A8	Atlanta (Ga.)
975.502	E83.77	Dunmore's Expedition, 1774	975.9	F306-320	Florida—History
			975.9005	F306	Florida—Periodicals
975.503	E359.5.V8	Virginia—History—War of 1812	975.90(1-3)	F314	Florida—History—To 1821
975.503	E534	Virginia—History—Civil War, 1861-1865	975.901	F314	Florida—History—To 1565
975.503	F234.E	Emporia (Va.)—History—Civil War, 1861-1865	975.901	F314	Florida—History—Huguenot colony, 1562-1565
975.503	E581	Virginia—History—Civil War, 1861-1865	975.901	F314	Florida—History—Spanish colony, 1565-1763
975.6	F251-265	North Carolina	975.90(2-3)	F314	Florida—History—English colony, 1763-1784
975.6005	F251	North Carolina—Periodicals	975.903	F314	Florida—History—Spanish colony, 1784-1821
975.60(1-2)	F257	North Carolina—History—Colonial period, ca. 1600-1775	975.903	E83.813	Creek War, 1813-1814
975.60(2-3)	F258	North Carolina—History—1775-1865	975.903	F314	Florida—History—Cession to the United States, 1819
975.602	F257	North Carolina—History—Regulator Insurrection, 1766-1771	975.90(4-5)	F315	Florida—History—1821-1865
			975.905	E558.1-.9	Florida—History—Civil War, 1861-1865
975.603	E524	North Carolina—History—Civil War, 1861-1865	975.906	F316-.23	Florida—History—1865-
			975.906(3-4)	F316.2-.23	Florida—History—1951-

Dewey	LC	Subject Heading	Dewey	LC	Subject Heading
976	F296	Gulf States—History	976.8005	F431	Tennessee—Periodicals
976	F396	Southwest, Old	976.804	E531	Tennessee—History—Civil War, 1861-1865
976.1	F321-355	Alabama			
976.1005	F321	Alabama—Periodicals	976.804	E579	Tennessee—History—Civil War, 1861-1865
976.10(5-63)	F326	Alabama—History—1819-1950			
			976.9	F446-460	Kentucky—History
976.105	F326	Alabama—History—To 1819	976.9005	F446	Kentucky—Periodicals
976.106(3-4)	F330-.3	Alabama—History—1951-	976.90(1-2)	F454	Kentucky—History—To 1792
976.2	F336-350	Mississippi			
976.2005	F336	Mississippi—Periodicals	976.902	F454	Estill's Defeat, 1782
976.20(1-4)	F341	Mississippi—History—To 1803	976.903	F455	Kentucky—History—1792-1865
			976.904	F456-.26	Kentucky—History—1865-
976.202	F347.A25	Ackia, Battle of, 1736	976.9041	F456	Black Patch War, 1906-1909
976.204	F351-353	Louisiana Purchase			
976.205	E568	Mississippi—History—Civil War, 1861-1865	977	F516-520	Ohio River Valley
			977	F551	Northern boundry of the United States
976.205	E516	Mississippi—History—Civil War, 1861-1865			
			977	F476-485	Northwest, Old
976.3	F366-380	Louisiana	977	F350.5-358.2	Mississippi River Valley
976.3005	F366	Louisiana—Periodicals	977.1	F486-500	Ohio
976.30(1-3)	F372-373	Louisiana—History—To 1803	977.1005	F486	Ohio—Periodicals
976.30(2-3)	E263.L	Louisiana—History—Revolution, 1775-1783	977.10(1-2)	F495	Ohio—History—To 1787
			977.102	E263.0	Ohio—History—Revolution, 1775-1783
976.30(4-5)	F374	Louisiana—History—1803-1865			
			977.103	F495	Ohio—History—1787-1865
976.304	E359.5.L8	Louisiana—History—War of 1812	977.103	E359.5.02	Ohio—History—War of 1812
976.305	E565	Louisiana—History—Civil War, 1861-1865	977.103	E525	Ohio—History—Civil War, 1861-1865
976.305	E510	Louisiana—History—Civil War, 1861-1865	977.104	F496-.2	Ohio—History—1865-
			977.2	F521-535	Indiana
976.306(1-3)	F375	Louisiana—History—1865-1950	977.2005	F521	Indiana—Periodicals
			977.20(1-2)	F526	Indiana—History—To 1787
976.306(3-4)	F376-.3	Louisiana—History—1951-	977.204(3-4)	F530-.22	Indiana—History—1951-
976.335	F379.N5	New Orleans (La.)	977.252	F534.I3	Indianapolis (Ind.)
976.357068	GV879.5	Baseball fields	977.3	F536-550	Illinois
976.4	F381-395	Texas	977.3005	F536	Illinois—Periodicals
976.4005	F381	Texas—Periodicals	977.30(1-2)	F544	Illinois—History—To 1778
976.40(1-4)	F389-390	Texas—History—To 1846	977.30(2-3)	F545	Illinois—History—1778-1865
976.402	F389	Texas—History—1810-1821			
976.403	F390	Texas—History—Revolution, 1835-1836	977.304	F546-.4	Illinois—History—1865-
			977.304(3-4)	F546.2-.4	Illinois—History—1951-
976.404	F390	Texas—History—Republic, 1836-1846	977.311	F548-.9	Chicago (Ill.)
			977.4	F561-575	Michigan
976.40(5-63)	F391	Texas—History—1846-1950	977.4005	F561	Michigan—Periodicals
976.405	E532	Texas—History—Civil War, 1861-1865	977.40(1-3)	F566	Michigan—History—To 1837
			977.40(3-4)	F566	Michigan—History—1837-
976.406(3-4)	F391.2-.4	Texas—History—1951-	977.404(3-4)	F570-.2	Michigan—History—1951-
976.41411	F394.H8	Houston (Tex.)	977.434	F574.D4	Detroit (Mich.)
976.42812	F394.D21	Dallas (Tx.)	977.5	F576-590	Wisconsin
976.481	E99.P244	Panhandle culture	977.5005	F576	Wisconsin—Periodicals
976.6	F691-705	Oklahoma	977.50(1-3)	F584	Wisconsin—History—To 1848
976.6005	F691	Oklahoma—Periodicals			
976.604	F699	Oklahoma—History—Land Rush, 1889	977.50(3-4)	F586-.42	Wisconsin—History—1848-
			977.503	E537	Wisconsin—History—Civil War, 1861-1865
976.604	F699	Oklahoma—History—Land Rush, 1893			
			977.595	F589.M6	Milwaukee (Wi.)
976.7	F406-420	Arkansas	977.6	F601-615	Minnesota
976.7005	F406	Arkansas—Periodicals	977.6005	F601	Minnesota—Periodicals
976.8	F431-445	Tennessee			

Dewey	LC	Subject Heading	Dewey	LC	Subject Heading
977.60(1-4)	F606	Minnesota—History—To 1858	978.752	F722	Yellowstone National Park
			978.8	F771-785	Colorado
977.60(4-5)	F606	Minnesota—History—1858-	978.8005	F771	Colorado—Periodicals
977.6579	F614.M5	Minneapolis (Minn.)	978.80(1-2)	F780	Colorado—History—To 1876
977.7	F616-630	Iowa			
977.7005	F616	Iowa—Periodicals	978.802	E83.863	Sand Creek Massacre, Colo., 1864
977.702	E507	Iowa—History—Civil War, 1861-1865			
			978.803(1-3)	F781	Colorado—History—1876-1950
977.703(3-4)	F625-.42	Iowa—History—1951-			
977.8	F461-475	Missouri	978.803(3-4)	F781.2-.3	Colorado—History—1951-
977.8005	F461	Missouri—Periodicals	978.883	F784.D4	Denver (Colo.)
977.803	E517	Missouri—History—Civil War, 1861-1865	978.9	F791-805	New Mexico
			978.9005	F791	New Mexico—Periodicals
977.803	E569	Missouri—History—Civil War, 1861-1865	978.90(1-3)	F799-800	New Mexico—History—To 1848
977.866	F474.S2	Saint Louis (Mo.)	978.90(4-5)	F801-.2	New Mexico—History—1848-
978	F590.3-596.3	West (U.S.)—History			
978	E470.9	West (U.S.)—History—Civil War, 1861-1865	978.904	E571	New Mexico—History—Civil War, 1861-1865
978	F721-722	Rocky Mountains	978.904	E522	New Mexico—History—Civil War, 1861-1865
978	F598	Missouri River			
978.0(1-2)	F592-.7	West (U.S.)—History—To 1848	979	F786-790	Southwest, New
			979.02	E83.84	Pacific Coast Indians, Wars with, 1847-1865
978.0(2-32)	F595	West (U.S.)—History—1890-1945			
			979.1	F806-820	Arizona
978.02	F593	West (U.S.)—History—1848-1860	979.1005	F806	Arizona—Periodicals
			979.10(1-4)	F811	Arizona—History—To 1912
978.02	F594	West (U.S.)—History—1860-1890	979.105(2-3)	F811	Arizona—History—1912-1950
978.02	E83.86	Dakota Indians—Wars, 1862-1865	979.105(3-4)	F815-.3	Arizona—History—1951-
			979.173	F819.P57	Phoenix (Ariz.)
978.02	E83.876	Dakota Indians—Wars, 1876	979.2	F821-835	Utah
			979.2005	F821	Utah—Periodicals
978.02	E83.89	Dakota Indians—Wars, 1890-1891	979.202	E532.95	Utah—History—Civil War, 1861-1865
978.033	F595-.3	West (U.S.)—History—1945-	979.202	F826	Morrisite War, 1862
			979.3	F836-850	Nevada
978.1	F676-690	Kansas—History	979.3005	F836	Nevada—Periodicals
978.1005	F676	Kansas—Periodicals	979.4	F856-870	California
978.102	F685	Kansas—History—1854-1861	979.4005	F856	California—Periodicals
			979.40(1-3)	F864	California—History—To 1846
978.1031	E508	Kansas—History—Civil War, 1861-1865	979.40(3-4)	F865	California—History—1846-1850
978.2	F661-675	Nebraska—History			
978.2005	F661	Nebraska—Periodicals	979.40(4-53)	F866	California—History—1850-1950
978.3	F646-660	South Dakota			
978.3005	F646	South Dakota—Periodicals	979.405(3-4)	F866.2-.4	California—History—1950-
978.303	E99.D1	Wounded Knee Massacre, S.D., 1890	979.461	F869.S3	San Francisco (Calif.)
			979.49	F867	California, Southern
978.3031	E83.89	Wounded Knee Massacre, S.D., 1890	979.494	F869.L8	Los Angeles (Calif.)
			979.5	F851.7	Cascade Range
978.4	F631-645	North Dakota	979.5	F871-885	Oregon
978.4005	F631	North Dakota—Periodicals	979.5005	F871	Oregon—Periodicals
978.6	F726-740	Montana	979.50(1-3)	F879-880	Oregon—History—To 1859
978.6005	F726	Montana—Periodicals	979.503	F880	Oregon Trail
978.602	E83.876	Little Bighorn, Battle of the, Mont., 1876	979.504	F881-.35	Oregon—History—1859-
			979.504(3-4)	F881.2-.35	Oregon—History—1951-
978.603(3-4)	F735-.2	Montana—History—1951-	979.6	F741-755	Idaho
978.7	F756-770	Wyoming	979.6005	F741	Idaho—Periodicals
978.7005	F756	Wyoming—Periodicals	979.603(3-4)	F750-.22	Idaho—History—1951-
978.701	F761	Fetterman Fight, Wyo., 1866	979.7	F886-900	Washington (State)

Dewey	LC	Subject Heading	Dewey	LC	Subject Heading
979.7	F853	Columbia River Valley	981.05	F2537	Brazil—History—Revolution, 1922
979.7005	F886	Washington (State)—Periodicals	981.05	F2537	Brazil—History—Revolution, 1924-1925
979.70(1-3)	F891	Washington (State)—History—To 1889	981.05	F2538	Brazil—History—Revolution, 1930
979.704	F891	Washington (State)—History—1889-	981.061	F2538	Brazil—History—1930-1945
979.7772	F899.S4	Seattle (Wash.)	981.061	F2538	Brazil—History—Uprising, 1935
979.8	F901-951	Alaska	981.061	F2538	Brazil—History—Revolution, 1938
979.8005	F901	Alaska—Periodicals	981.061	F2538	Brazil—History—1945-1954
979.80(1-2)	F907	Alaska—History—To 1867	981.062	F2538.2-.22	Brazil—History—1954-1964
979.80(3-4)	F908-909	Alaska—History—1867-1959	981.063	F2538.25-.27	Brazil—History—1964-1985
979.805	F910-.7	Alaska—History—1959-	981.064	F2538.3-.5	Brazil—History—1985-
979.84	F951	Aleutian Islands (Alaska)	982	F2801-3021	Argentina
980	E	America	982	F2827-2849.22	Argentina—History
980	E16-18.85	America—History	982	F2810	Argentina—Civilization
980	F2201-3799	South America	982.005	F2801	Argentina—Periodicals
980	F2201-2239	South America—History	982.0(1-22)	F2841	Argentina—History—1515-1535
980	F1408.3-.4	Latin America—Civilization	982.0(1-24)	F2841	Argentina—History—To 1810
980.00498	F2229-2290	Indians of South America	982.023	F2841	Argentina—History—1535-1617
980.005	F1401	Latin America—Periodicals	982.023	F2841	Argentina—History—1617-1776
980.0099	F2217	Gauchos	982.023	F2841	Argentina—History—1776-1810
980.01	E101-135	America—Discovery and exploration	982.0(24-5)	F2843	Argentina—History—19th century
981	F2501-2656	Brazil	982.024	F2845	Argentina—History—English Invasions, 1806-1807
981	F2520.3-2538.5	Brazil—History	982.0(3-4)	F2846	Argentina—History—1817-1860
981	F2510	Brazil—Civilization	982.0(3-6)	F2843	Argentina—History—1810-
981.005	F2501	Brazil—Periodicals	982.03	F2845	Argentina—History—War of Independence, 1810-1817
981.0(1-33)	F2526-2534	Brazil—History—To 1822	982.0(4-5)	F2847	Argentina—History—1860-1910
981.03(1-2)	F2526	Brazil—History—1500-1548	982.04	F2846	Argentina—History—Revolution, 1833
981.032	F2528	Brazil—History—1548-1580			
981.032	F2528	Brazil—History—1549-1762	982.05	F2847	Argentina—History—Revolution, 1890
981.032	F2529	Brazil—History—French colony, 1555-1567	982.061	F2848	Argentina—History—1910-1943
981.032	F2530	Brazil—History—1580-1640	982.061	F2848	Argentina—History—Revolution, 1930
981.032	F2532	Brazil—History—Dutch Conquest, 1624-1654	982.06(1-2)	F2849	Argentina—History—1943-1955
981.032	F2528	Brazil—History—War of the Emboabas, 1707-1709	982.06(1-4)	F2849-.22	Argentina—History—1943-
981.033	F2534	Brazil—History—1763-1822	982.06(3-4)	F2849.2	Argentina—History—1955-1983
981.033	F2534	Brazil—History—United Kingdom, 1815-1822	982.063	F2849.2	Argentina—History—Revolution, 1955
981.033	F2536	Brazil—History—Declaration of Independence, 1822	982.063	F2849.2	Argentina—History—Peronist Revolt, 1956
981.0(4-6)	F2535-2538.5	Brazil—History—1822-	982.063	F2849.2	Argentina—History—Coup d'etat, 1966
981.04	F2536	Brazil—History—Empire, 1822-1889	982.064	F2849.2	Argentina—History—1983-
981.04	F2536	Brazil—History—Revolution, 1842	983	F3051-3285	Chile
981.04	F2536	Brazil—History—Quebra Quilos' Revolt, 1874			
981.05	F2537	Brazil—History—1889-1930			
981.05	F2537	Brazil—History—Canudos Campaign, 1893-1897			
981.05	F2537	Brazil—History—Naval Revolt, 1893-1894			
981.05	F2537	Brazil—History—Naval Revolt, 1910			
981.05	F2537	Brazil—History—Contestado Insurrection, 1912-1916			

Dewey	LC	Subject Heading	Dewey	LC	Subject Heading
983	F3081-3098	Chile—History	985.005	F3401	Peru—Periodicals
983	F3060	Chile—Civilization	985.0(1-2)	F3442	Peru—History—To 1548
983.005	F3051	Chile—Periodicals	985.0(1-4)	F3442-3444	Peru—History—To 1820
983.0(1-3)	F3091	Chile—History—To 1565	985.0(2-4)	F3444	Peru—History—1548-1820
983.0(1-3)	F3091	Chile—History—To 1810	985.02	F3442	Peru—History—Conquest, 1522-1548
983.03	F3091	Chile—History—1565-1810			
983.0(4-6)	F3093	Chile—History—1810-	985.03	F3444	Peru—History—Insurrection of Tupac Amaru, 1780-1781
983.0(4-63)	F3095	Chile—History—1824-1920			
983.04	F3094	Chile—History—War of Independence, 1810-1824	985.0(4-5)	F3446	Peru—History—War of Independence, 1820-1829
983.05	F3095	Chile—History—Insurrection, 1851	985.0(5-631)	F3447	Peru—History—1829-1919
983.05	F3095	Chile—History—Insurrection, 1859	985.05	F3447	Peru—History—Spanish question, 1864
983.061	F3095	Chile—History—War with Spain, 1865-1866	985.061	F3447	Peru—History—Revolution of 1872
983.062	F3098	Chile—History—Revolution, 1891	985.063(1-2)	F3448	Peru—History—1919-1968
983.06(3-45)	F3099	Chile—History—1920-1970	985.0631	F3448	Peru—History—Revolution, 1930
983.06(3-6)	F3099	Chile—History—20th century	985.0633	F3448.2	Peru—History—1968-1980
983.0641	F3099	Chile—History—Naval Revolt, 1931	985.0633	F3448.2	Peru—History—Coup d'etat, 1968
983.0642	F3099	Chile—History—Uprising, 1938	985.0633	F3448.2	Peru—History—1980-
983.0646	F3100	Chile—History—1970-1973	986.1	F2251-2299	Colombia
983.065	F3100	Chile—History—1973-1988	986.1	F2270.3-2279.22	Colombia—History
983.065	F3100	Chile—History—Coup d'etat, 1973	986.1	F2260	Colombia—Civilization
984	F3301-3359	Bolivia	986.1005	F2251	Colombia—Periodicals
984	F3320.3-3327	Bolivia—History	986.10(1-2)	F2272	Colombia—History—To 1810
984	F3310	Bolivia—Civilization	986.102	F2272.5	English West Indian Expedition, 1739-1742
984.005	F3301	Bolivia—Periodicals			
984.0(1-3)	F3322	Bolivia—History—To 1809	986.102	F2272	Colombia—History—Insurrection of the Comuneros, 1781
984.041	F3323	Bolivia—History—Wars of Independence, 1809-1825			
984.04(2-5)	F3324	Bolivia—History—1825-1879	986.10(3-4)	F2274	Colombia—History—War of Independence, 1810-1822
984.0(45-51)	F3324-3325	Bolivia—History—1879-1938	986.10(3-6)	F2273	Colombia—History—1810-
984.05(1-2)	F3326	Bolivia—History—1938-1982	986.104	F2275	Colombia—History—1822-1832
984.05(1-2)	F3326-3327	Bolivia—History—1938-	986.105(2-61)	F2276	Colombia—History—1832-1886
984.051	F3326	Bolivia—History—Coup d'etat, 1943	986.1053	F2276	Colombia—History—Civil War, 1860-1862
984.051	F3326	Bolivia—History—Revolution, 1946	986.106(2-31)	F2277	Colombia—History—1903-1946
984.052	F3326	Bolivia—History—Revolution, 1952	986.1062	F2276.5	Colombia—History—1886-1903
984.052	F3326	Bolivia—History—Revolution, 1964	986.1062	F2276.5	Colombia—History—Revolution, 1899-1903
984.052	F3326	Bolivia—History—Coup d'etat, 1979	986.1063(2-3)	F2278	Colombia—History—1946-1974
984.052	F3326	Bolivia—History—Coup d'etat, 1980	986.10632	F2278	Colombia—History—Coup d'etat, 1953
984.052	F3327	Bolivia—History—1982-	986.1063(4-5)	F2279-.22	Colombia—History—1974-
984.06(5-6)	F3100	Chile—History—1988-	986.1(2-62)	F2273	Colombia—History—19th century
985	F3401-3619	Peru	986.6	F3701-3799	Ecuador
985	F3430.3-3448.4	Peru—History	986.6	F3710	Ecuador—Civilization
			986.6	F3723.3-3738.4	Ecuador—History
985	F3410	Peru—Civilization	986.6005	F3701	Ecuador—Periodicals

Dewey	LC	Subject Heading	Dewey	LC	Subject Heading
986.60(1-2)	F3733	Ecuador—History—To 1809	988.1	F2361-2391	Guyana
986.60(2-4)	F3734	Ecuador—History—Wars of Independence, 1809-1830	988.1	F2369.8	Guyana—Civilization
			988.1	F2380.3-2391	Guyana—History
986.60(5-6)	F3736	Ecuador—History—1830-1895	988.1005	F2361	Guyana—Periodicals
			988.10(1-31)	F2384	Guyana—History—1803-1966
986.60(6-72)	F3737	Ecuador—History—1895-1944	988.101	F2383	Guyana—History—To 1803
986.606	F3736	Ecuador—History—Revolution, 1895	988.1032	F2385	Guyana—History—1966-
			988.2	F2441-2471	French Guiana
986.607	F3737	Ecuador—History—20th century	988.2	F2460.3-2464	French Guiana—History
			988.2	F2449.8	French Guiana—Civilization
986.607(2-4)	F3738	Ecuador—History—1944-	988.2005	F2441	French Guiana—Periodicals
986.6072	F3737	Ecuador—History—Coup d'etat, 1925	988.3	F2401-2431	Surinam
			988.3	F2409.8	Surinam—Civilization
986.6072	F3737	Ecuador-Peru Conflict, 1941	988.3	F2420.3-2425.23	Surinam—History
986.6072	F3738	Ecuador—History—Coup d'etat, 1944			
			988.3005	F2401	Surinam—Periodicals
986.6074	F3738	Ecuador-Peru Conflict, 1981	988.30(1-31)	F2424	Surinam—History—1814-1950
987	F2301-2349	Venezuela			
987	F2310	Venezuela—Civilization	988.301	F2423	Surinam—History—To 1814
987	F2319.5-2328.52	Venezuela—History	988.303(1-2)	F2425-.23	Surinam—History—1950-
			988.3032	F2425	Surinam—History—Coup d'etat, 1980
987.005	F2301	Venezuela—Periodicals			
987.0(1-3)	F2322	Venezuela—History—To 1810	988.3032	F2425	Surinam—History—Coup d'etat, 1982
987.0(1-3)	F2322	Venezuela—History—To 1556	989.2	F2661-2699	Paraguay
			989.2	F2670	Paraguay—Civilization
987.03	F2322	Venezuela—History—1556-1810	989.2	F2679.35-2689.23	Paraguay—History
987.03	F2322	Venezuela—History—Insurrection of the Comuneros, 1781	989.2005	F2661	Paraguay—Periodicals
			989.20(1-3)	F2683-2684	Paraguay—History—To 1811
987.03	F2322	Venezuela—History—Miranda's Expedition, 1806	989.203	F2683	Paraguay—History—Revolution of the Comuneros, 1721-1735
987.0(4-5)	F2324	Venezuela—History—War of Independence, 1810-1823	989.203	F2683	Paraguay—History—War of Independence, 1810-1811
987.0(4-5)	F2324	Venezuela—History—1810-1830	989.20(4-5)	F2686-2687	Paraguay—History—1811-1870
987.0(4-6)	F2322.8	Venezuela—History—1810-	989.20(6-7)	F2688	Paraguay—History—20th century
987.061	F2325	Venezuela—History—1830-1935	989.20(6-71)	F2688-.5	Paraguay—History—1870-1938
987.061	F2325	Venezuela—History—Federal Wars, 1858-1863	989.207(1-3)	F2689	Paraguay—History—1938-1989
987.063(2-3)	F2326-2327	Venezuela—History—1935-1974	989.2071	F2688	Paraguay—History—Revolution, 1904
987.0632	F2326	Venezuela—History—1935-1958	989.2071	F2688	Paraguay—History—Revolution, 1922-1923
987.0632	F2326	Venezuela—History—Revolution, 1945	989.2071	F2688	Paraguay—History—Revolution, 1936
987.0632	F2326	Venezuela—History—Coup d'etat, 1948	989.2072	F2689	Paraguay—History—Revolution, 1947
987.0632	F2326	Venezuela—History—Revolution, 1958	989.2073	F2689.2-.23	Paraguay—History—1989-
987.0633	F2328-.52	Venezuela—History—1974-	989.2073	F2689.2	Paraguay—History—Coup d'etat, 1989
987.0633	F2328	Venezuela—History—Attempted coup, 1992 (February 4)	989.5	F2701-2799	Uruguay
			989.5	F2720-2729.52	Uruguay—History
			989.5	F2710	Uruguay—Civilization
987.0633	F2328	Venezuela—History—Attempted coup, 1992 (November 27)	989.5005	F2701	Uruguay—Periodicals
			989.50(1-3)	F2723	Uruguay—History—To 1810

247

Dewey	LC	Subject Heading	Dewey	LC	Subject Heading
989.50(1-4)	F2725	Uruguay—History—1810-1830	994.0(2-3)	DU114-115.2	Australia—History—1788-1900
989.50(5-61)	F2726	Uruguay—History—1875-1904	994.02	DU115	Australia—History—1788-1851
989.505	F2726	Uruguay—History—1830-1875	994.0(4-65)	DU116-117.2	Australia—History—20th century
989.505	F2726	Uruguay—History—Great War, 1843-1852	995-996	DU28.11-66	Oceania—History
989.506(1-5)	F2728	Uruguay—History—1904-1973	995	DU739-747	New Guinea
			995	DU490	Melanesia
989.5061	F2726	Uruguay—History—Revolution, 1886	995	DU	Oceania
			995.3	DU740	Papua New Guinea
989.5061	F2726	Uruguay—History—Revolution, 1897	995.93	DU850	Solomon Islands
			995.95	DU760	Vanuatu
989.5063	F2728	Uruguay—History—Revolution, 1935	995.97	DU720	New Caledonia
			996	DU	Oceania
989.5066	F2729	Uruguay—History—1973-1985	996	DU510	Polynesia
			996.003	DU10	Oceania—Gazetteers
989.5066	F2729	Uruguay—History—Coup d'etat, 1973	996.11	DU600	Fiji
			996.12	DU880	Tonga
989.5067	F2729	Uruguay—History—1985-	996.1(3-4)	DU817	Samoan question
993	DU419-422	New Zealand—History	996.1(3-4)	DU810-819	Samoan Islands
993	DU418	New Zealand—Civilization	996.13	DU819.A1	American Samoa
993.004	DU422.5-424.5	Ethnology—New Zealand	996.14	DU819.A2	Western Samoa
993.01	DU420.12-.14	New Zealand—History—To 1840	996.15	DU910	Tokelau
			996.16	DU920	Wallis and Futuna Islands
993.02(1-2)	DU420.16-.18	New Zealand—History—1840-1876	996.18	DU800	Pitcairn Island
			996.18	F3169	Easter Island
993.021	DU420.16	New Zealand—History—Maori War, 1845-1847	996.21	DU870	Society Islands
			996.211	DU870	Tahiti
993.022	DU420.22-.34	New Zealand—History—Taranaki War, 1860-1861	996.31	DU700-701	Marquesas Islands
			996.4	DU650	Line Islands
993.0(23-31)	DU420.22-.24	New Zealand—History—1876-1918	996.5	DU500	Micronesia
			996.6	DU560-568	Caroline Islands
993.032	DU420.26-.28	New Zealand—History—1918-1945	996.6	DU565-567	Caroline Islands—History
			996.7	DU640-648	Mariana Islands
993.03(5-7)	DU420.32-.34	New Zealand—History—1945-	996.81	DU615	Kiribati
			996.81	DU790	Phoenix Islands (Kiribati)
994	DU108-117.2	Australia—History	996.83	DU710	Marshall Islands
994.004	DU120-125	Ethnology—Australia	996.9	DU625-629	Hawaii—History
994.01	DU98.1	Australia—History—To 1788	996.9	DU624.5	Hawaii—Civilization
			996.9004	DU624.6-.7	Ethnology—Hawaii
994.01	GN871-875	Australian aborigines—Antiquities	999	QB54	Life on other planets